INTERNATIONAL LAW STUDIES

Volume 86

The War in Iraq: A Legal Analysis

Raul A. "Pete" Pedrozo
Editor

Naval War College
Newport, Rhode Island
2010

EDITORIAL OFFICE
International Law Studies
International Law Department
Naval War College (36)
686 Cushing Road
Newport, RI 02841-1207
Telephone: +1-401-841-4949
Fax: +1-401-841-3989
DSN: 841-4949
E-mail: ILD@usnwc.edu
Website: http://www.usnwc.edu/ild

USNWC ONLINE
Facebook
www.facebook.com/NavalWarCollege
Twitter
www.twitter.com/NavalWarCollege
Online Discussions
www.usnwc.edu/OnlineDiscussion

Proper Citation

The International Law Studies should be cited according to the following examples:

– For citing a Blue Book with an editor: Title (editor, year) (Vol. __, US Naval War College International Law Studies);
– For citing a Blue Book with an author: Author, Title (year) (Vol. __, US Naval War College International Law Studies);
– For citing a chapter: Author, Title of Chapter, pages, finish citation with one of the two previous samples, as appropriate.

INTERNATIONAL LAW STUDIES

Volume 86

Table of Contents

The War in Iraq: A Legal Analysis

BLUE BOOKS
International Law
Studies/Documents/Situations/Decisions/Topics/Discussions

VOL 85

THE WAR IN AFGHANISTAN: A LEGAL ANALYSIS (Michael N. Schmitt ed., 2009) (Vol. 85, US Naval War College International Law Studies).

VOL 84

INTERNATIONAL LAW AND MILITARY OPERATIONS (Michael D. Carsten ed., 2008) (Vol. 84, US Naval War College International Law Studies).

VOL 83

GLOBAL LEGAL CHALLENGES: COMMAND OF THE COMMONS, STRATEGIC COMMUNICATIONS AND NATURAL DISASTERS (Michael D. Carsten ed., 2007) (Vol. 83, US Naval War College International Law Studies).

VOL 82

THE LAW OF WAR IN THE 21ST CENTURY: WEAPONRY AND THE USE OF FORCE (Anthony M. Helm ed., 2006) (Vol. 82, US Naval War College International Law Studies).

VOL 81

INTERNATIONAL LAW CHALLENGES: HOMELAND SECURITY AND COMBATING TERRORISM (Thomas McK. Sparks & Glenn M. Sulmasy eds., 2006) (Vol. 81, US Naval War College International Law Studies).

VOL 80

ISSUES IN INTERNATIONAL LAW AND MILITARY OPERATIONS (Richard B. Jaques ed., 2006) (Vol. 80, US Naval War College International Law Studies).

VOL 79

INTERNATIONAL LAW AND THE WAR ON TERROR (Fred L. Borch & Paul S. Wilson eds., 2003) (Vol. 79, US Naval War College International Law Studies).

VOL 78

LEGAL AND ETHICAL LESSONS OF NATO'S KOSOVO CAMPAIGN (Andru E. Wall ed., 2002) (Vol. 78, US Naval War College International Law Studies).

VOL 77

LILLICH ON THE FORCIBLE PROTECTION OF NATIONALS ABROAD (Thomas C. Wingfield & James E. Meyen eds., 2002) (Vol. 77, US Naval War College International Law Studies).

VOL 76

COMPUTER NETWORK ATTACK AND INTERNATIONAL LAW (Michael N. Schmitt & Brian T. O'Donnell eds., 2002) (Vol. 76, US Naval War College International Law Studies).

VOL 75

INTERNATIONAL LAW ACROSS THE SPECTRUM OF CONFLICT: ESSAYS IN HONOUR OF PROFESSOR L.C. GREEN ON THE OCCASION OF HIS EIGHTIETH BIRTHDAY (Michael N. Schmitt ed., 2000) (Vol. 75, US Naval War College International Law Studies).

VOL 74

GEORGE K. WALKER, THE TANKER WAR, 1980–88: LAW AND POLICY (2000) (Vol. 74, US Naval War College International Law Studies).

VOL 73

ANNOTATED SUPPLEMENT TO THE COMMANDER'S HANDBOOK ON THE LAW OF NAVAL OPERATIONS (A.R. Thomas & James C. Duncan eds., 1999) (Vol. 73, US Naval War College International Law Studies).

VOL 72

THE LAW OF MILITARY OPERATIONS: LIBER AMICORUM PROFESSOR JACK GRUNAWALT (Michael N. Schmitt ed., 1998) (Vol. 72, US Naval War College International Law Studies).

VOL 71

THE LAW OF ARMED CONFLICT: INTO THE NEXT MILLENNIUM (Michael N. Schmitt & Leslie C. Green eds., 1998) (Vol. 71, US Naval War College International Law Studies).

VOL 70

LEVIE ON THE LAW OF WAR (Michael N. Schmitt & Leslie C. Green eds., 1998) (Vol. 70, US Naval War College International Law Studies).

VOL 69

PROTECTION OF THE ENVIRONMENT DURING ARMED CONFLICT (Richard J. Grunawalt, John E. King & Ronald S. McClain eds., 1996) (Vol. 69, US Naval War College International Law Studies).

VOL 68

READINGS ON INTERNATIONAL LAW FROM THE NAVAL WAR COLLEGE REVIEW 1978–1994 (John Norton Moore & Robert F. Turner eds., 1995) (Vol. 68, US Naval War College International Law Studies).

VOL 67

LEGAL AND MORAL CONSTRAINTS ON LOW-INTENSITY CONFLICT (Alberto R. Coll, James S. Ord & Stephen A. Rose eds., 1995) (Vol. 67, US Naval War College International Law Studies).

VOL 66

J. ASHLEY ROACH & ROBERT W. SMITH, EXCESSIVE MARITIME CLAIMS (1994) (Vol. 66, US Naval War College International Law Studies).

VOL 65

TARGETING ENEMY MERCHANT SHIPPING (Richard J. Grunawalt ed., 1993) (Vol. 65, US Naval War College International Law Studies).

VOL 64

THE LAW OF NAVAL OPERATIONS (Horace B. Robertson ed., 1991) (Vol. 64, US Naval War College International Law Studies).

VOL 63

ALFRED P. RUBIN, THE LAW OF PIRACY (1988) (Vol. 63, US Naval War College International Law Studies).

VOL 62

READINGS IN INTERNATIONAL LAW FROM THE NAVAL WAR COLLEGE REVIEW 1947–1977, II *The Use of Force, Human Rights and General International Legal Issues* (Richard B. Lillich & John Norton Moore eds., 1980) (Vol. 62, US Naval War College International Law Studies).

VOL 61

READINGS IN INTERNATIONAL LAW FROM THE NAVAL WAR COLLEGE REVIEW 1947–1977, I *Role of International Law and an Evolving Ocean Law* (Richard B. Lillich & John Norton Moore eds., 1980) (Vol. 61, US Naval War College International Law Studies).

VOL 60

DOCUMENTS ON PRISONERS OF WAR (Howard S. Levie ed., 1979) (Vol. 60, US Naval War College International Law Studies).

VOL 59

HOWARD S. LEVIE, PRISONERS OF WAR IN INTERNATIONAL ARMED CONFLICT (1977) (Vol. 59, US Naval War College International Law Studies).

VOL 58

WILLIAM T. MALLISON JR., STUDIES IN THE LAW OF NAVAL WARFARE: SUBMARINES IN GENERAL AND LIMITED WARS (1966) (Vol. 58, US Naval War College International Law Studies).

VOL 57

(Not Published)

VOL 56

NEILL H. ALFORD JR., MODERN ECONOMIC WARFARE: LAW AND THE NAVAL PARTICIPANT (1963) (Vol. 56, US Naval War College International Law Studies).

VOL 55

CARL Q. CHRISTOL, THE INTERNATIONAL LAW OF OUTER SPACE (1962) (Vol. 55, US Naval War College International Law Studies).

VOL 54

NATO AGREEMENTS ON STATUS: TRAVAUX PRÉPARATOIRES (Joseph M. Snee ed., 1961) (Vol. 54, US Naval War College International Law Studies).

VOL 53

CARL M. FRANKLIN, THE LAW OF THE SEA: SOME RECENT DEVELOPMENTS (WITH PARTICULAR REFERENCE TO THE UNITED NATIONS CONFERENCE OF 1958) (1959–60) (Vol. 53, US Naval War College International Law Studies).

VOL 52

ROLAND J. STANGER, CRIMINAL JURISDICTION OVER VISITING ARMED FORCES (1957–58) (Vol. 52, US Naval War College International Law Studies).

VOL 51

BRUNSON MACCHESNEY, SITUATION, DOCUMENTS AND COMMENTARY ON RECENT DEVELOPMENTS IN THE INTERNATIONAL LAW OF THE SEA (1956) (Vol. 51, US Naval War College International Law Situation and Documents).

VOL 50

ROBERT W. TUCKER, THE LAW OF WAR AND NEUTRALITY AT SEA (1955) (Vol. 50, US Naval War College International Law Studies).

VOL 49

HANS KELSEN, COLLECTIVE SECURITY UNDER INTERNATIONAL LAW (1954) (Vol. 49, US Naval War College International Law Studies).

VOL 48

INTERNATIONAL LAW DOCUMENTS 1952–53: *Peace Treaties; Defense Agreements; European Unions* (Manley O. Hudson ed., 1954) (Vol. 48, US Naval War College International Law Documents).

VOL 47

INTERNATIONAL LAW DOCUMENTS 1950–51: *The Protection of Victims of War* (*Part I: Conventions before 1949; Part II: Geneva Conventions of 1949*) (Manley O. Hudson ed., 1952) (Vol. 47, US Naval War College International Law Documents).

VOL 46

INTERNATIONAL LAW DOCUMENTS 1948–49: *International Organization; Trials of War Criminals; Rights Claimed by Littoral States in Adjacent Seas; et al.* (Manley O. Hudson ed., 1950) (Vol. 46, US Naval War College International Law Documents).

VOL 45

INTERNATIONAL LAW DOCUMENTS 1946–47: *The Treaties of Peace of 1947; Instrument of Japanese Surrender; et al.* (Manley O. Hudson ed., 1948) (Vol. 45, US Naval War College International Law Documents).

VOL 44

INTERNATIONAL LAW DOCUMENTS 1944–45: *Contraband of War; The Crimea Conference; Act of Chapultepec; et al.* (Payson S. Wild Jr. ed., 1946) (Vol. 44, US Naval War College International Law Documents).

VOL 43

INTERNATIONAL LAW DOCUMENTS 1943: *Visit and Search; Destruction of Prizes; War Zones; Defense Zones; et al.* (Payson S. Wild Jr. ed., 1945) (Vol. 43, US Naval War College International Law Documents).

VOL 42

INTERNATIONAL LAW DOCUMENTS 1942: *Orders to American Military Forces in India; Crimes against Civilian Populations in Occupied Countries; et al.* (Payson S. Wild Jr. ed., 1943) (Vol. 42, US Naval War College International Law Documents).

VOL 41

INTERNATIONAL LAW DOCUMENTS 1941: *Freezing of Japanese and Chinese Assets in the United States; The Atlantic Charter; et al.* (Payson S. Wild Jr. ed., 1943) (Vol. 41, US Naval War College International Law Documents).

VOL 40

INTERNATIONAL LAW DOCUMENTS 1940: *Proclamations and Regulations Concerning Neutrality of the United States in the War between Germany and Norway; et al.* (Payson S. Wild Jr. ed., 1942) (Vol. 40, US Naval War College International Law Documents).

VOL 39

INTERNATIONAL LAW SITUATIONS 1939: *Neutral Duties and State Control of Enterprise; Neutrality Problems; Contiguous Zones; et al.* (Payson S. Wild Jr. ed., 1940) (Vol. 39, US Naval War College International Law Situations).

VOL 38

INTERNATIONAL LAW SITUATIONS 1938: *Belligerent and Neutral Rights in Regard to Aircraft; Force Short of War; et al.* (Payson S. Wild Jr. ed., 1940) (Vol. 38, US Naval War College International Law Situations).

VOL 37

INTERNATIONAL LAW SITUATIONS 1937: *Protection by Vessels of War; Naval Protection during Strained Relations; et al.* (George G. Wilson ed., 1939) (Vol. 37, US Naval War College International Law Situations).

VOL 36

INTERNATIONAL LAW SITUATIONS 1936: *Insurrection, Belligerency, Statehood; Visit by and Internment of Aircraft; et al.* (George G. Wilson ed., 1937) (Vol. 36, US Naval War College International Law Situations).

VOL 35

INTERNATIONAL LAW SITUATIONS 1935: *Vessels and Neutral Ports; Action during Civil Strife; et al.* (George G. Wilson ed., 1936) (Vol. 35, US Naval War College International Law Situations).

VOL 34

INTERNATIONAL LAW SITUATIONS 1934: *Transfer and Capture; Interference with Ships; et al.* (George G. Wilson ed., 1936) (Vol. 34, US Naval War College International Law Situations).

VOL 33

INTERNATIONAL LAW SITUATIONS 1933: *Contraband and Blockade; Independent Philippine Islands; et al.* (George G. Wilson ed., 1934) (Vol. 33, US Naval War College International Law Situations).

VOL 32

INTERNATIONAL LAW SITUATIONS 1932: *Belligerents in Neutral Waters; Artificial Structures and Maritime Jurisdiction; et al.* (George G. Wilson ed., 1934) (Vol. 32, US Naval War College International Law Situations).

VOL 31

INTERNATIONAL LAW SITUATIONS 1931: *Neutrality and Aircraft; Neutrality and Territorial Waters; Belligerency and Maritime Jurisdiction* (George G. Wilson ed., 1932) (Vol. 31, US Naval War College International Law Situations).

VOL 30

INTERNATIONAL LAW SITUATIONS 1930: *London Naval Treaty; Absence of Local Authority; Belligerent Aircraft; et al.* (George G. Wilson ed., 1931) (Vol. 30, US Naval War College International Law Situations).

VOL 29

INTERNATIONAL LAW SITUATIONS 1929: *Neutrality and Vessels; Status of Islands in Pacific Ocean; Neutral Obligations* (George G. Wilson ed., 1931) (Vol. 29, US Naval War College International Law Situations).

VOL 28

INTERNATIONAL LAW SITUATIONS 1928: *Maritime Jurisdiction; Carriage of Mail in Time of War; Enemy Persons on Neutral Vessels* (George G. Wilson ed., 1929) (Vol. 28, US Naval War College International Law Situations).

VOL 27

INTERNATIONAL LAW SITUATIONS 1927: *Goods on Neutral Merchant Vessels; Visit and Search; Armed Merchant Vessels* (George G. Wilson ed., 1929) (Vol. 27, US Naval War College International Law Situations).

VOL 26

INTERNATIONAL LAW SITUATIONS 1926: *Continuous Voyage; Submarines; Angary; Aircraft in Neutral Ports* (George G. Wilson ed., 1928) (Vol. 26, US Naval War College International Law Situations).

VOL 25

INTERNATIONAL LAW DOCUMENTS 1925: REGULATION OF MARITIME WARFARE (George G. Wilson ed., 1926) (Vol. 25, US Naval War College International Law Documents).

VOL 24

INTERNATIONAL LAW DOCUMENTS 1924: INTERNATIONAL AGREEMENTS (*Five Power Limitation of Naval Armament; Nicaraguan Canal Route; Danish West Indies; et al.*) (George G. Wilson ed., 1926) (Vol. 24, US Naval War College International Law Documents).

VOL 23

INTERNATIONAL LAW DECISIONS 1923: *Vessels (The Haelen, etc.); Armed Vessels (Submarine E14, etc.); Search in Port (The Bernisse, etc.); et al.* (George G. Wilson ed., 1925) (Vol. 23, US Naval War College International Law Decisions).

VOL 22

INTERNATIONAL LAW DECISIONS 1922: *The Berlin; The Miramichi; The Maria; et al.* (George G. Wilson ed., 1924) (Vol. 22, US Naval War College International Law Decisions).

VOL 21

INTERNATIONAL LAW DOCUMENTS 1921: CONFERENCE ON THE LIMITATION OF ARMAMENT (George G. Wilson ed., 1923) (Vol. 21, US Naval War College International Law Documents).

VOL 20

INTERNATIONAL LAW DOCUMENTS 1920: THE TREATIES OF PEACE WITH AUSTRIA AND WITH HUNGARY AND PROTOCOLS AND DECLARATIONS ANNEXED THERETO (George G. Wilson ed., 1922) (Vol. 20, US Naval War College International Law Documents).

VOL 19

INTERNATIONAL LAW DOCUMENTS 1919: THE TREATY OF PEACE WITH GERMANY (George G. Wilson ed., 1920) (Vol. 19, US Naval War College International Law Documents).

VOL 18

INTERNATIONAL LAW DOCUMENTS 1918: NEUTRALITY, CONDUCT AND CONCLUSION OF HOSTILITIES (George G. Wilson ed., 1919) (Vol. 18, US Naval War College International Law Documents).

VOL 17

INTERNATIONAL LAW DOCUMENTS 1917: NEUTRALITY; BREAKING OF DIPLOMATIC RELATIONS; WAR (George G. Wilson ed., 1918) (Vol. 17, US Naval War College International Law Documents).

VOL 16

INTERNATIONAL LAW TOPICS 1916: NEUTRALITY PROCLAMATIONS AND REGULATIONS (George G. Wilson ed., 1917) (Vol. 16, US Naval War College International Law Topics).

VOL 15

INTERNATIONAL LAW TOPICS 1915: DOCUMENTS ON NEUTRALITY AND WAR (George G. Wilson ed., 1916) (Vol. 15, US Naval War College International Law Topics).

VOL 14

INTERNATIONAL LAW TOPICS AND DISCUSSIONS 1914: *Classification of Public Vessels; Regulations Relating to Foreign Ships of War in Waters under the Jurisdiction of the United States; et al.* (George G. Wilson ed., 1915) (Vol. 14, US Naval War College International Law Topics and Discussions).

VOL 13

INTERNATIONAL LAW TOPICS AND DISCUSSIONS 1913: *Marginal Sea and Other Waters; Commencement of Hostilities; Limitation of Armaments; et al.* (George G. Wilson ed., 1914) (Vol. 13, US Naval War College International Law Topics and Discussions).

VOL 12

INTERNATIONAL LAW SITUATIONS 1912: *Merchant Vessels and Insurgents; Air Craft in War; Cuba Neutral; et al.* (George G. Wilson ed., 1912) (Vol. 12, US Naval War College International Law Situations).

VOL 11

INTERNATIONAL LAW SITUATIONS 1911: *Asylum in Neutral Port; Protection to Neutral Vessels; Destruction of Neutral Vessels; et al.* (George G. Wilson ed., 1911) (Vol. 11, US Naval War College International Law Situations).

VOL 10

INTERNATIONAL LAW SITUATIONS 1910: *Coaling within Neutral Jurisdiction; Declaration of War; Days of Grace; et al.* (George G. Wilson ed., 1911) (Vol. 10, US Naval War College International Law Situations).

VOL 9

INTERNATIONAL LAW TOPICS 1909: THE DECLARATION OF LONDON OF FEBRUARY 26, 1909 (George G. Wilson ed., 1910) (Vol. 9, US Naval War College International Law Topics).

VOL 8

INTERNATIONAL LAW SITUATIONS 1908: *Termination of Liability for Breach of Blockade; The Twenty-Four Hour Rule; Sequestration of Prize; et al.* (George G. Wilson ed., 1909) (Vol. 8, US Naval War College International Law Situations).

VOL 7

INTERNATIONAL LAW SITUATIONS 1907: *Fugitive from Cuban Justice at Guantanamo; Status of United States Auxiliary Collier in Foreign Harbor; et al.* (George G. Wilson ed., 1908) (Vol. 7, US Naval War College International Law Situations).

VOL 6

INTERNATIONAL LAW TOPICS AND DISCUSSIONS 1906: *Use of False Colors; Transfer of Flag of Merchant Vessels during or in Anticipation of War; et al.* (George G. Wilson ed., 1907) (Vol. 6, US Naval War College International Law Topics and Discussions).

VOL 5

INTERNATIONAL LAW TOPICS AND DISCUSSIONS 1905: *Inviolability of Private Property at Sea; Contraband of War; Restriction of Visit and Search; et al.* (George G. Wilson ed., 1906) (Vol. 5, US Naval War College International Law Topics and Discussions).

VOL 4

INTERNATIONAL LAW SITUATIONS 1904: *Merchant Vessels Adapted for Conversion into Auxiliary Cruisers; Rights of Foreigner under Martial Law; Asylum for Insurgent Troops on War Vessel; et al.* (George G. Wilson ed., 1905) (Vol. 4, US Naval War College International Law Situations).

VOL 3

INTERNATIONAL LAW DISCUSSIONS 1903: THE UNITED STATES NAVAL WAR CODE OF 1900 (George G. Wilson ed., 1904) (Vol. 3, US Naval War College International Law Discussions).

VOL 2

INTERNATIONAL LAW SITUATIONS 1902: *Submarine Telegraphic Cables in Time of War; Asylum on Ships of War; Waters of Leased Territory; et al.* (George G. Wilson ed., 1903) (Vol. 2, US Naval War College International Law Situations).

VOL 1

INTERNATIONAL LAW SITUATIONS 1901: *Coast Warfare; Contraband; Transportation of Military Persons; et al.* (John B. Moore ed., 1901) (Vol. 1, US Naval War College International Law Situations).

Foreword

The International Law Studies ("Blue Book") series was initiated by the Naval War College in 1901 to publish essays, treaties and articles that contribute to the broader understanding of international law. This, the eighty-sixth volume of the "Blue Book" series, is a compilation of scholarly papers and remarks derived from the proceedings of a conference hosted here at the Naval War College on June 23–25, 2009 and entitled "The War in Iraq: A Legal Analysis."

The June 2009 "War in Iraq" conference served as a second and "companion" proceeding to the Experts Workshop "The War in Afghanistan: A Legal Analysis," hosted by the Naval War College in June 2008 and the resulting scholarly works of which appear in Volume 85 of the "Blue Book" series. The purpose of the conference, similar to the previous year's Afghanistan workshop, was to provide a comprehensive legal examination of the armed conflict in Iraq during the second Gulf War that began in 2003. The issues were examined by five panels of experts, addressing topics that spanned the entire spectrum of the conflict and the re-establishment of Iraqi sovereignty. Panelists discussed legal issues associated with the initial decision to use armed force, the manner in which force was employed, the legal framework and evolution of military activities from invasion to occupation, detention and counterinsurgency operations, as well as policy and legal issues associated with the establishment of the rule of law and return of governance to the people of Iraq.

Renowned international academics and legal advisers, both military and civilian, representing military, diplomatic, non-governmental and academic institutions from the international community contributed to the conference and this "Blue Book." Readers and researchers will find within this volume a detailed study of the Iraq conflict, as well as its profound implications on the ongoing development of international law, the law of armed conflict and military operations.

The conference and the "Blue Book" were made possible with generous support from the Naval War College Foundation, the Center for National Security Law, University of Virginia School of Law and the *Israel Yearbook on Human Rights*. The International Law Department of the Center for Naval Warfare Studies, Naval War College hosted the event.

On behalf of the Secretary of the Navy, the Chief of Naval Operations and the Commandant of the Marine Corps, I extend our thanks and gratitude to all the participants, contributing authors and editors for their invaluable contributions to this project and to the future understanding of the laws of war.

JAMES WISECUP
Rear Admiral, U.S. Navy
President, Naval War College

Introduction

On March 20, 2003, after a year of very dramatic public discourse concerning the appropriate response to Iraq's continuing violation of its international obligations under numerous UN Security Council resolutions, the United States, together with the United Kingdom and a coalition of "willing" partners, including Australia, Denmark and Poland, launched Operation Iraqi Freedom (OIF). OIF commenced the military operations intended to eliminate Saddam Hussein's regime and the specter of his use of weapons of mass destruction. From OIF's inception, and continuing through the next six years of military operations spanning invasion, occupation and restoration of Iraqi sovereignty, the meaning, application and viability of the law of armed conflict were repeatedly tested.

Following its tradition of the in-depth study and teaching on the manner in which the law impacts military operations, the Naval War College hosted a conference entitled "The War in Iraq: A Legal Analysis." The conference was envisioned as a companion colloquium to the Experts Workshop hosted by the Naval War College the previous June entitled "The War in Afghanistan: A Legal Analysis." By the time of the June 2009 conference, events in Iraq had sufficiently progressed to begin developing an objective assessment of what had transpired. The conference brought together distinguished international law scholars and practitioners to examine international and operational law issues that arose throughout the various phases of the Iraq conflict.

Judge Raid Juhi al-Saedi, the former chief investigative judge for the Iraqi High Tribunal, opened the conference by sharing his experiences with the trial of Saddam Hussein, as well as the current status of the Iraqi judiciary. The speakers presented their material over the next two and a half days in five thematic panels. On the first day, attendees were privileged to attend a luncheon address delivered by Major General Michael Oates, US Army, on the "commander's perspective" of military operations in Iraq. Professor Yoram Dinstein provided conference-concluding remarks in which he reflected on the influence the conflict in Iraq would have on the future development of the international law of armed conflict. The presenters remained in Newport for an additional day after the general conference to attend an experts' working group to clarify the overall conference themes and focus in on their respective scholarly contributions.

This edition of the International Law Studies ("Blue Book") series encapsulates the incredibly thoughtful insights and lessons learned that each presenter brought to the conference, including many gained from personal experience while serving in the conflict zone. The product of their scholarship and roundtable discussions is found within this volume.

The conference was organized by Major Michael D. Carsten, US Marine Corps, of the International Law Department (ILD) with the invaluable assistance of Mrs. Jayne Van Petten and other ILD faculty and staff. The conference was made possible through the support of the Naval War College Foundation, the Center for National Security Law, University of Virginia School of Law and the *Israel Yearbook on Human Rights*. Without the dedicated efforts and support of these individuals and organizations, the conference would not have been the exceptional success that it was.

I would like to thank Professor Raul (Pete) A. Pedrozo and Commander Sandra K. Selman, US Coast Guard, for serving as the editor and managing editor, respectively, for this volume and to thank Professor Ralph Thomas, Captain, US Navy (Ret.), for his meticulous work during the editing process along with the staff of the College's Desktop Publishing department, particularly Susan Meyer, Ken DeRouin, Albert Fassbender and Shannon Cole. I also extend thanks to Captain Charles "Chuck" Passaglia, JAGC, US Navy, and Captain Rymn Parsons, JAGC, US Navy, the former and current Commanding Officer of Navy Reserve, Naval War College (Law), the reserve unit that directly supports the International Law Department. Their willingness to assist with the project and make personnel available to facilitate timely publication of the "Blue Book" was essential. I am grateful to all of the reserve officers who participated in making this volume happen, but specifically appreciate the exceptional work of Commander Todd Richards, JAGC, US Navy, for his comprehensive and painstaking work on the index. This publication is the culmination of the tireless effort of each of the previously named individuals, as well as numerous others, and is a tribute to their devotion to the Naval War College and the International Law Series.

Special thanks go to Rear Admiral James P. "Phil" Wisecup, the President of the Naval War College, and Professor Robert "Barney" Rubel, Dean of the Center for Naval Warfare Studies, for their leadership and support in the planning and conduct of the conference, and publication of this 86th volume of the "Blue Book" series.

The International Law Studies series is published by the Naval War College and distributed worldwide to US and international military organizations, academic institutions and libraries. A catalogue of all previous "Blue Books" appears after the table of contents. Volumes 59–86 of the International Law Studies series are available electronically at http://www.usnwc.edu/ild. This "Blue Book" continues the Naval War College's long tradition of compiling the highest quality of scholarly inquiry into the most contemporary and challenging legal issues arising from the entire hierarchy of military operations.

DENNIS MANDSAGER
Professor of Law & Chairman
International Law Department

Preface

From June 23 to 25, 2009 the Naval War College hosted over one hundred renowned international scholars and practitioners, military and civilian, and students representing government and academic institutions at a conference that examined a number of legal issues pertaining to the war in Iraq. The conference featured opening, luncheon and closing addresses, as well as five panel discussions addressing specific legal issues encountered during the conflict. Panelist comments were summarized by a commentator, followed by questions from attendees. These discussions resulted in a detailed analysis of the key issues.

The following conference summary was prepared by Commander Eric Hunt, JAGC, US Navy, a member of NR Naval War College (Law), the reserve unit that supports the International Law Department. The summary expertly recaps the highlights of each of the conference speakers' presentations. As editor, I am deeply indebted to Commander Hunt for his attention to detail and assistance in facilitating the publication of this "Blue Book." I would also be remiss if I did not thank Captain Ralph Thomas, JAGC, US Navy (Ret.), Commander Sandra Selman, US Coast Guard, and Major Michael Carsten, US Marine Corps, for their outstanding support and dedication in preparing this work.

I also extend my sincere appreciation to Susan Meyer and Ken DeRouin of the Naval War College's Desktop Publishing office, who were responsible for expertly preparing the page proofs. Additionally, I would like to thank Albert Fassbender and Shannon Cole for their excellent work in proofreading the conference papers. The quality of this volume is a reflection of their professionalism and outstanding expertise.

Tribute to Professor Howard S. Levie

With the passing of former Charles H. Stockton Professor of International Law Howard S. Levie on April 19, 2009, this year's conference was dedicated to his memory. Professor Jack Grunawalt, the current Stockton professor, opened the conference with a tribute to Professor Levie.

> Soldier and scholar, Professor Levie leaves a legacy of scholarly excellence in the development and study of the law of war. One of the nation's foremost legal experts on the law of war and the key draftsman of the Korean War Armistice Agreement,

Professor Levie authored ten books (several of them multi-volume works) and over eighty articles. He was internationally recognized as an authority on matters ranging from the treatment of prisoners of war to the legality of conventional and nuclear/chemical/biological weapons; from war crimes and terrorism to the protection of the victims of armed conflict. Among the books he authored are *Prisoners of War in International Armed Conflict, The Code of International Armed Conflict,* and *Terrorism in War: The Law of War Crimes.* He also served as the editor of six volumes of the series *Terrorism: Documents of International and Local Control.* The last volume was published in 1997 when he was 88.

In 1998, the U.S. Naval War College in Newport, Rhode Island published *Levie on the Law of War* to honor Professor Levie and to recognize the enormous impact of his writings on the law applicable during armed conflict. In the book's Foreword, it was observed:

> Once in a great while, someone comes along who makes a significant and lasting contribution to his or her chosen profession, a contribution that comes to define the paradigm of that calling. With respect to the development and articulation of the law of war, Professor Howard Levie is just such an individual.

A veteran of World War II and the Korean Conflict, Professor Levie served in New Guinea and the Philippines, in post-war Japan, and in Korea. He provided legal reviews of Japanese war crime trials for General Douglas MacArthur. He was assigned to the Staff of the United Nations Command Armistice Delegation when he drafted the Korean Armistice Agreement. A member of the US Army Judge Advocate General's Corps, Professor Levie was the first Chief of the Army JAG Corps' International Affairs Division at the Pentagon. Other assignments included postings in Italy, France, Fort Leavenworth, Kansas and the Presidio of San Francisco. He retired in 1963 in the rank of Colonel.

In September of 1963 he joined the faculty of Saint Louis University School of Law. While there, Professor Levie authored over 20 articles on a broad spectrum of law of war topics. It was also during this tenure that he spent a sabbatical year at the Naval War College as the Charles H. Stockton Professor of International Law. He retired from Saint Louis University in 1977 having attained Professor Emeritus of Law status, and returned to Rhode Island where he resumed his association with the Naval War College as a lecturer on the 1949 Geneva Conventions and the laws of war. In October 1994, his enormous contribution to the College was formally recognized with the establishment of the Howard S. Levie Military Chair of Operational Law.

On the occasion of his 100th birthday, Professor Levie was awarded the prestigious Morris I. Leibman Award by the American Bar Association's Standing Committee on National Security Law. The award citation noted that his career as a soldier and a scholar spanned more than six decades and was marked by distinction throughout. It concluded, "The impact of [his] enormous body of work on the thinking of domestic and international policy makers, military commanders and scholars cannot be overstated."

Howard S. Levie was born on December 19, 1907 in Wolverine, Michigan and grew up in Baltimore and New York City. He earned Bachelor of Arts and Juris Doctor degrees from Cornell University and a Master of Laws degree from George Washington University. He also studied at the Sorbonne in Paris and the Academy of International Law at The Hague.

Professor Levie was married to the late Blanche Krim Levie, an artist and WAC during WWII. Together in their 90s, they worked on writing an autobiography[,] *Memories of an Ordinary Couple*. Professor Levie died on April 19, 2009 at his home in Portsmouth, Rhode Island. He was 101.

Opening Address

Judge Raid Juhi al-Saedi, formerly the Chief Investigative Judge of the Iraqi High Tribunal, provided the keynote address on the restoration of the rule of law in Iraq. Judge Juhi outlined the history of modern Iraq and explored how the rule of law had eroded into virtual non-existence during the Saddam Hussein era. He stated that, since 2003, Iraq has been on the road to restoring the rule of law. One step in this long and difficult process was the fair trial received by Saddam Hussein, where he enjoyed the right to confront witnesses. Judge Juhi indicated, however, that, while the restoration of the rule of law in Iraq is progressing, there are still many challenges ahead that will require the assistance of the international community.

Panel I: Legal Bases for Military Operations in Iraq

Panel I explored the "legal bases for military operations in Iraq." The panel opened with Andru Wall laying out the legal bases of the United States for using force against Iraq in 2003. These were, for the most part, grounded in UN Security Council resolutions dating back to 1991's first Gulf War, including finding Iraq in grave breach of the ceasefire agreement. With these resolutions in hand, the United States viewed itself as legally justified in resuming military action against Iraq. Ms. Alexandra Perina argued that regardless of the bases for invading Iraq, once in Iraq the United States took on the role of occupier with all of the attendant responsibilities, responsibilities made more difficult by a rising insurgency. Professor David Turns sought to address the nature of the conflict in Iraq in terms of whether it should, at any particular time, be classified as an international armed conflict or non-international armed conflict. He observed that "armed conflict" is not defined in international law, making it difficult to properly categorize the conflict in Iraq. This categorization is vital in determining what laws apply to situations such as detainee treatment. Finally, the issue of a new category of conflict, "transnational armed conflict," was touched upon as a possible way to describe conflicts with non-State actors. The attendees posed a number of questions, dealing mainly with the rationale for the invasion of Iraq and the issue of anticipatory self-defense.

Luncheon Address

Major General Michael Oates, US Army, Commanding General of the 10th Mountain Division, gave the luncheon address, the "Commander's Perspective in Iraq." His remarks and opinions were based on his personal experiences in Iraq during various periods of the conflict. General Oates indicated that the major lesson learned during the initial phase of the war can be summed up by the age-old military maxim: "you fight like you train." The US military forces were tremendously successful during the opening phase of the war because they fought like they trained. What was not known then is that the forces were not well trained, well resourced or well prepared for the post-combat phase.

In turning to counterinsurgency (COIN) operations, General Oates observed that it is important to look at the situation that gave rise to the insurgency in the first place. He observed that the insurgency was split along religious, cultural and ethnic lines. In addition to their desire for power and control, most of these groups shared an intense hatred of the coalition forces, which they saw as occupiers. How to defeat the insurgency in Iraq was something of a "chicken and egg" dilemma: do you concentrate on solving the problems of the Iraqi people, most notably things like "essential services first," or do you focus on killing and capturing the bad guys, and, once things are secure, concentrate on improving the daily lives of the Iraqi people?

He indicated that the United States and the other coalition forces traveled along the "essential services first" school of thought for the first few years, but eventually it was determined that the successes were not widespread or sustainable. Too often raw numbers were relied on, instead of an analysis of what those numbers really meant. What was learned over time was that counterinsurgency is about people, not about data. As a military force, the United States became much more successful against the insurgency when, under the leadership of General Petraeus and others who had taken a hard look at counterinsurgency, it was realized that this fight was about people. He observed that people and relationships are the center of gravity in a COIN fight. Under General Petraeus and General Odierno, the United States transitioned to the alternate view of improving daily lives and began to secure the population.

General Oates concluded his remarks with a discussion of stability operations. He indicated the development of Iraqi security forces was the key to stability. By letting the Iraqi forces take the lead, the Iraqi people began to see them as a force that could be trusted.

Rule of law was one of the major lines of effort. Two things combined to jump-start rule of law efforts during the last year. The first was the improved security situation. The second was the implementation of the US-Iraq security agreement. One of the major keys to stability in any country is having a legal system the citizens can trust and depend on. Without a system for the peaceful resolution of disputes, order breaks down and people take the law into their own hands. He observed that the work in the rule of law arena had been a significant force in promoting stability, especially in central and southern Iraq.

Panel II: The Law of Armed Conflict and the War in Iraq

Panel II focused on the application of the law of armed conflict to the war in Iraq. Major General Charles Dunlap, US Air Force, opened the panel presentation with a discussion of the impact of technology and advanced information systems on the calculus of the war in Iraq. The combination of real-time, detailed intelligence from the battlefront and the predominant use of precision-guided weapons has resulted in a heightened threshold of error for bombing missions. This heightened threshold is not necessarily consistent with the standards imposed by the law of armed conflict. As the enemy puts forth the concept that 100 percent accuracy is required, it is engaged in a sort of "lawfare" that creates an unrealistic expectation that little or no collateral damage can result. General Dunlap argued that "lawfare" must be countered through effective strategic communications.

Mr. Marc Warren then returned to the always-present issue of detainees in Iraq. While the nature of the conflict might have changed over time and the determination of which portion of the law was applicable was often unclear, detainees were always treated as though Common Article 3 of the 1949 Geneva Conventions applied. This treatment was important, as the detainee pool contained a mixture of criminals, prisoners of war and insurgents. As the number of detainees grew to overwhelming size, the detainee policy continued to require compliance with the Geneva Conventions; any deviations were isolated and non-sanctioned.

Commodore Neil Brown, Royal Navy, addressed the application of the laws of armed conflict to the sea campaign in the war in Iraq. Spatially, this area was limited since Iraq's navy had been virtually destroyed during the first Gulf War. Establishment and enforcement of regulations applying to the various maritime zones during naval operations in the region involved visit and search, stop and inspection, and diversion of ships. Commodore Brown discussed the application of rules of engagement by coalition naval forces during combat operations, as well as during post-hostilities maritime zone enforcement activities.

Before opening the panel to questions, Professor Wolff Heintschel von Heinegg observed that misinterpretations of the requirements imposed by the laws of war need to be quickly countered and that countering information operations must be proactive. A failure to confront false perceptions allows the enemy to control the information war and win the battle for public support. Questioners explored the issues of the enemy's use of the law to attempt to negate the advantages of technology. Professor Heintschel von Heinegg stressed that the canard that 100 percent weapon accuracy is required ignores that the law of armed conflict recognizes that there will be civilian casualties.

Panel III: Occupation in Iraq

Panel III began the second day of the conference by shifting focus to the "occupation of Iraq." Professor Eyal Benvenisti delved into the issue of when an occupation begins. The Hague Conventions speak in terms of control over territory, while the Geneva Conventions address control of the population. Whether a State can exercise control, and the nature of its ability to establish control, may establish occupation as a matter of law regardless of the formal declarations of the parties. Professor Benvenisti argued that the occupying power has the ability to alter the occupied State's domestic laws. In fact, it would be almost impossible to maintain the status quo, since the original regime has been overthrown. But the ability to alter the law left unanswered the question of what Iraqi laws the occupiers were required to observe. Another question was whether the occupiers' own national human rights laws applied to their actions as an occupying power.

Brigadier General Clyde Tate, US Army, spoke from the perspective of the military forces as implementers of an occupation. He emphasized that for occupiers it is imperative that the rule of law be observed in all situations. This meant investigating soldiers for all misconduct involving the occupied population. Brigadier General Tate stressed that following the return of governance to Iraqi authorities, the focus of US forces shifted to respecting Iraqi law, but not to the detriment of safety or operational requirements.

The panel was questioned concerning the Hague and Geneva Conventions and their application to the occupation of Iraq. The sense was that the Hague

Conventions were concerned with preserving the status quo of an occupied territory, while the Fourth Geneva Convention was focused on the protection of the occupied population. A question was also raised as to whether the applicable UN Security Council resolutions concerning Iraq provided more protections for Iraqi sovereignty than did the traditional law of occupation.

Panel IV: Stability Operations in Iraq

Panel IV turned its attention to the issue of stability operations in Iraq and the dynamic nature of these operations given the changing legal status and environment in Iraq. Although the Iraqi government requested a continued US presence in Iraq after December 31, 2008, this created its own set of problems. Ms. Shelley Young observed that in negotiating a security agreement to address the post-2008 US presence in Iraq, many issues needed to be resolved. Ms. Young noted the final agreement established exclusive US jurisdiction over US military personnel and civilians, provided for the withdrawal of US forces and established a termination date for the agreement of December 31, 2011.

Colonel Richard Pregent provided the military view on stability operations. He stressed the need to appreciate three truths: security drives everything, nothing in Iraq is simple and the rule of law is Iraqi—not American—justice. The change in the US status from occupying power to an invited presence created challenges. Foremost among these was the treatment of detainees. Under Iraqi law there is no provision for internment; detainees must be charged or released. This and the continued re-establishment of the rule of law are but two of the challenges going forward in the conduct of stability operations.

Mr. Laurent Colassis outlined the role of the International Committee of the Red Cross (ICRC) in stability operations. With the decrease in violence, the activities of the ICRC have increased. Mr. Colassis noted that Iraq is now the third-largest mission of the ICRC, behind Darfur and Somalia, with a focus on detainee operations. Despite the requirement to charge or release, releasing detainees is not always simple. Where and to whom detainees are released is an issue with legal implications. Ultimately, a balance must be found between security and possible mistreatment by the State to whom the detainee is released.

The questions for the panel covered a broad gamut of issues, including whether the US military is proficient at nation building and whether nation building should even be a military mission. There was general agreement that military forces are not particularly adept at nation building, but that they possess capabilities and resources to complete non-traditional missions. It was observed that many nation-building tasks should be handled by civilian agencies but these agencies were often not effectively resourced. A question was also raised about the status of individuals covered as protected persons and who should receive those protections during an insurgency, illustrating again that the issue of detainees was of prime concern—and importance.

Panel V: Issues Spanning the War in Iraq

Panel V looked at "legal issues spanning the war in Iraq." Captain Brian Bill, JAGC, US Navy, addressed the issue of detainees. At the height of operations in Iraq there were twenty-six thousand detainees in US custody. Task Force 134 was created to oversee all detainee operations. Detentions under the authority of UN Security Council resolutions were driven by a determination as to whether the detainee posed an imperative threat. Captain Bill pointed out that the determination of this status involved giving the detainee a certain level of due process. In fact, the due process afforded detainees was above and beyond that required by Article 78 of the Fourth Geneva Convention. Task Force 134 directives went so far as to provide women, children and those who needed assistance in understanding the proceedings with special representatives to aid them in their detention hearings.

Mr. Robert Boorda noted the difficulties that arise when there are multiple agencies involved in stability and reconstruction efforts. In Iraq there was, and continues to be, little coordination or communication between civil and military agencies. This creates a chaotic environment on the ground and hampers reconstruction efforts. Mr. Boorda explained that Iraqis are often targeted by insurgents for cooperating with US efforts to rebuild the country, making local involvement difficult to obtain. These problems, combined with the inability to determine the needs of Iraqi civil society, make the restoration of Iraq an ongoing challenge.

Ms. Naz Modirzadeh posed the question as to what human rights law applied during an armed conflict, during an occupation and during the post-occupation period while coalition forces remained in Iraq. While the United States does not recognize the extraterritorial application of human rights law, other countries have been moving in that direction. Ms. Modirzadeh argued that, while on its face it would appear to benefit civilians by creating new levels of legal protections, extraterritorial application of human rights law may not bring the positive results that its proponents seek. As human rights laws are applied extraterritorially, a corollary question arises as to which rights should be recognized and applied.

Many questions were addressed to the panel, with a focus on the impact of the application of human rights law to armed conflicts. Comments of both panelists and conference attendees suggested that while it would not "mean the end of the world," it would certainly create a new layer of "fog of war" in the legal context.

Closing Address

The conference ended with Professor Yoram Dinstein assessing the highlights of the conference. He indicated that the concept of "lawfare" cannot be ignored, that it must be dealt with proactively and with a focus on educating societies on the true legal requirements in an armed conflict. He argued that the conflict in Iraq began as an international armed conflict and, in his opinion, continues to be an international armed conflict because hostilities have not concluded. Additionally, international armed conflict is a prerequisite to belligerent occupation of the type that occurred in Iraq. He stated that military forces must adapt to the circumstances in using high technology to fight an enemy using very low technology. Precision in striking the wrong target can lead to defeat in the war of information.

Professor Dinstein noted that in deciding who is entitled to protection as a civilian, the concept of direct participation in hostilities comes to the fore. An individual who is an insurgent during the day cannot come home at night and expect to have the protections accorded to a civilian. The concept of direct participation has interesting applications to private military contractors. Their role must be strictly defined if contractors are to be employed in the conflict. One of the main goals of belligerent occupation is to ensure security. Occupation begins when control is exercised, but when does occupation end? Finally, the application of human rights law in the context of armed conflict may not be a positive development. The law of armed conflict is a well-understood body of law that is designed to protect civilians and military members alike. To interject an array of other laws into the arena would not be beneficial for those in harm's way.

Conclusion

In closing, I trust that you will find the articles from the preeminent scholars and practitioners that contributed to this volume to be thought provoking and useful in shaping the debate on the conflict in Iraq for future generations.

RAUL "PETE" PEDROZO
Associate Professor
International Law Department

PART I

OPENING ADDRESS

I

Regime Change and the Restoration of the Rule of Law in Iraq

Raid Juhi al-Saedi*

Introduction

After Allied forces overthrew Hitler's regime at the end of World War II, the US blueprint for running Germany included dismantling the Nazi Party, dismissing Nazis from government employment, prosecuting Hitler and his officials as war criminals, dissolving all German courts and forbidding any political activity without permission from US military authorities.

Following the overthrow of Saddam Hussein's regime in 2003, the United States tried to use the same strategy in Iraq, albeit using a new formula. Coalition Provisional Authority (CPA) Order No. 1[1] was issued to de-Baathificate[2] Iraqi society. CPA Order No. 2[3] dissolved the Iraqi intelligence and security agencies, and the armed forces, as well as dismissed the Baathist employees and members of those organizations. Subsequently, CPA Order No. 15 was issued with the stated purpose of reforming the "Iraqi justice system [which] has been subjected to political interference and corruption over the years of Iraqi Baath Party rule."[4] This order established the Judicial Review Committee, which dismissed a large number of judges and prosecutors.

* Clarke Middle East Fellow, Cornell University Law School. Former Chief Investigative Judge, Iraqi High Tribunal. Portions of this article are derived from Raid Juhi al-Saedi, *Glance into the Criminal Procedures under the Iraqi Judiciary*, 41 CREIGHTON LAW REVIEW 713 (2008).

On September 13, 2003 the CPA issued Order No. 35,[5] which re-established the Council of Judges that had existed prior to the Hussein regime, and charged it with the supervision of Iraq's judicial and prosecutorial systems. Order No. 35 gave the Council of Judges independence from the Ministry of Justice in terms of its budget and authority. At the end of 2003, the CPA issued Order No. 48,[6] which gave the Governing Council[7] the authority to establish an Iraqi Special Tribunal.[8] These were important steps in the transitional justice process. Even though the strategy used in Iraq was modeled after the successful US policy in post–World War II Germany, policies in Iraq failed to take into consideration the history of the country following the assassination of the Iraqi royal family in 1958.

Iraq's modern history is full of stories that illustrate the lack of the rule of law. In 1958 General Abdul Kareem Qassim ended the royal regime, which had been in power since 1921. He executed the king and his family without trial, as well as Prime Minister Nori Al-Saed, who is today considered one of the most respected politicians of that period. Qassim changed Iraq from a monarchy to a republic. The royal family's executions were illegal and based on a desire for revenge, a trait that many believe is deeply entrenched in Iraqi culture. History repeated itself five years later when a group of Baath Party members and military officers headed by General Abdul Salam Arif overthrew the regime. Qassim and his officials were executed. Qassim's body was thrown in the Tigris River and never found.

The Baath Party conducted another coup in 1968, when General Ahmed Hassan Al-Baker took power. Then in July 1979, Saddam Hussein became president when he overthrew General Al-Baker. Hussein's reign was bloody from the start: on his first day in office he held a meeting with high-level Baath Party leaders and accused certain members of attempting a coup. He asked them to leave the room. They were never seen again; rumors circulated that they had been executed.

During Hussein's presidency, Iraqis suffered tremendously. One of the hardships was the deportation of Iraqis of Iranian origin. Numerous families were sent back to Iran under difficult and dangerous circumstances. These families were left on the border during the Iran-Iraq war; that was the first step to dividing Iraqis based on race. Older Iraqis of Iranian origins were sent back to Iran, while younger men, aged eighteen to forty, were arrested and executed.[9] The government seized and sold all their property and belongings.

In 1988 the regime used chemical weapons against Kurdish villages because they had allegedly supported Iran in its war with Iraq; those allegations were later proven wrong. The Al-Anfal attack on the Kurds began in February 1988 and ended in mid-September despite the fact that a ceasefire was announced on August 8, 1988. The fact that the attacks continued even after the ceasefire was announced made it clear that the operation was intended to annihilate the Kurds.[10]

The cruelest page in Iraq's history was written on a single day in March 1991, when Hussein quelled an uprising in the south by killing, it is estimated, over two thousand men, women and children, and burying them in mass graves.[11] These killings led to suppressed anger and a desire for revenge in the hearts of the Shiites and the Kurds.

After the fall of Hussein's regime in 2003, it was important to find a salve for the wounds the Hussein era had wrought.

The Judicial System in Iraq

Reliable judicial institutions are critical to developing stable nations, and establishing and expanding the rule of law. In Iraq, however, the role of judicial institutions is sometimes confusing to the public because before 2003 many courts were not part of the judiciary or because the Ministry of Justice circumvented the judicial system entirely in applying its own concepts of justice. Outside the judicial system, courts could be found in the Ministry of Interior, the General Security Agency and the intelligence agencies. These courts often answered to the president's office alone.

Because the Iraqi legal system is so complex, it is useful to review the judicial system as it existed prior to 2003, and then address the changes that have occurred since Saddam's overthrow.

The Judicial System before 2003

Iraq's temporary constitution of 1970[12] referred to the judicial system in only two simple, vague articles in chapter 4. Article 60 addressed the types of courts and procedures for appointing judges and for their retirement, and Article 61 addressed the General Prosecutor Department.

Civil Procedures and Action Law No. 83 of 1969[13] categorized the types of courts in Articles 31 through 35 as the Courts of First Instance, including the Courts of Personal Status (for Muslims) and Courts of Personal Issues (for non-Muslims); the Courts of Appeal; and the Courts of Cassation, the highest courts in Iraq.

According to Article 137 of Criminal Procedures Code Law No. 23 of 1971,[14] the criminal courts included the Courts of Misdemeanor, Courts of Felony and Courts of Cassation (the appellate courts). Articles 1 through 136 explained the authority of investigative judges and the procedures to be followed. Juvenile court procedures were covered in Articles 233 through 242.

It was not until enactment of Judicial Organization Law No. 160 in 1979[15] that courts were categorized through Article 11 into ten civil and criminal courts, including Juvenile Courts, Investigative Courts and Labor Courts. At the same time, the law clarified that the Courts of Appeal (also called Courts of Cassation) are the highest courts of Iraq. In addition to these courts, there were "special courts" that were independent from the Council of Justice[16] and the Ministry of Justice. Most of these courts were established to serve for a temporary purpose, such as the court established in 1970 to prosecute Mohammed Al-Madhlum and other defendants for allegedly conducting a coup attempt. Other special courts, such as those associated with the Ministry of Interior and the General Security Agency, were permanent. Their decisions were usually sent to the president's office, not to the Court of Cassation.

The procedures for the Council of Justice's courts included investigation, trial and appeal for criminal cases; and first-degree court session, Supreme, and cassation for civil cases. The special courts, which were all criminal courts connected to the Revolutionary Command Council,[17] handled political cases, and their decisions were final. However, a copy of the decision would be sent to the president's office for approval if the verdict was the death penalty. In all other cases the decision was sent for review only.

The system continued to function in this manner until the regime was overthrown in April 2003.

The Judicial System after 2003

After the fall of the Hussein regime and the establishment of the CPA, US Ambassador Paul Bremer, the CPA Administrator, issued CPA Order No. 35,[18] which gave the Council of Judges independence from the Ministry of Justice in terms of budget and authority. The Council expanded the number of courts to one in each province and two in Baghdad, giving the country a total of sixteen. Kurdistan[19] is the only region where courts do not fall under the Council of Judges. Following the first Gulf War, the three provinces in Kurdistan came under the protection of the international community and were semi-independent from the central government in terms of its judicial system. Kurdistan has its own separate Cassation Court and Courts of Appeal.

The requirements to be a judge in the Iraqi judicial system differ not only from those of the United States, but from those of most other judicial systems as well. Some nations elect their judges; others like Jordan, Egypt and Italy appoint them; while still others, like the United States, use both election and appointment. In order for an individual to be a judge in Iraq, he must fulfill the requirements found in Article 36(1) of the Iraq Judicial Organization Law. These requirements are to have graduated from law school with a bachelor of laws degree, have three years' experience in the legal field, be no younger than twenty-eight or older than forty-five, be born of Iraqi parents, be married and have no criminal record.

An individual becomes a judge by applying to the Judicial Institute and being accepted into its internship program. That program consists of two years of working for and with judges in the morning and taking classes in the evening. To graduate the student must demonstrate his mastery of the legal and judicial sciences, and pass the required exams and tests.

There is an exception in Article 36(3) that allows a lawyer, who must be younger than forty-five, to be appointed as a judge by presidential order without the Judicial Institute degree with ten years of legal experience.

The Judicial Authority in Iraq

According to Article 89 of the Iraqi Constitution of 2005, "The federal juridical power is comprised of the Higher Juridical Council, the Federal Supreme Court, the Federal Court of Cassation, the Public Prosecution Department, the Judiciary Oversight Commission, and other federal courts that are regulated in accordance with the law."[20]

The Higher Juridical Council

The Higher Juridical Council oversees the affairs of the judicial committees.[21] It is comprised of the following:

- The Court of Cassation: There are two Courts of Cassation now in Iraq; one is federal for all of Iraq except the northern region of Iraq, Kurdistan, where there is another just for that region.
- The Supreme Court: There are sixteen Supreme Courts all over Iraq except in Kurdistan.
- The Board of the Supreme Judicial Council: The Council is comprised of the following:
    - The President: He is the Chief Justice of the Judicial Authority in Iraq; therefore he is the Chief Justice of the Court of Cassation, the Federal Supreme Court and the Supreme Judicial Council.
    - The Chief Justice Deputies of the Federal Court of Cassation. There are five justices.
    - The sixteen Chief Judges of the Supreme Courts
    - The Director of the Public Prosecution Department
    - The Director of the Judiciary Oversight Commission
    - The Director of the State Council.

According to Article 91 of the Iraqi Constitution, the Higher Juridical Council exercises the following authorities:

First: To manage the affairs of the judiciary and supervise the federal judiciary.

Second: To nominate the Chief Justice and members of the Federal Court of Cassation, the Chief Public Prosecutor, and the Chief Justice of the Judiciary Oversight Commission, and to present them to the Council of Representatives [the Parliament of Iraq] to approve their appointment.

Third: To propose the draft of the annual budget of the federal judiciary authority, and present it to the Council of Representatives for approval.

Federal Supreme Court

Article 93 provides that the Federal Supreme Court shall have jurisdiction over the following:

First: Overseeing the constitutionality of laws and regulations in effect.

Second: Interpreting the provisions of the Constitution.

Third: Settling matters that arise from the application of the federal laws, decisions, regulations, instructions, and procedures issued by the federal authority. The law shall guarantee the right of direct appeal to the Court to the Council of Ministers, those concerned individuals, and others.

Fourth: Settling disputes that arise between the federal government and the governments of the regions and governorates, municipalities, and local administrations.

Fifth: Settling disputes that arise between the governments of the regions and governments of the governorates.

Sixth: Settling accusations directed against the President, the Prime Minister and the Ministers, and this shall be regulated by law.

Seventh: Ratifying the final results of the general elections for membership in the Council of Representatives.

Eight[h]: A. Settling competency disputes between the federal judiciary and the judicial institutions of the regions and governorates that are not organized in a region.

B. Settling competency disputes between judicial institutions of the regions or governorates that are not organized in a region.

Decisions of the Federal Supreme Court are final and binding for all authorities.[22]

Court of Cassation

According to Article 12 of Judicial Organization Law No. 160 of 1979,[23] the Court of Cassation is considered the highest federal court in Iraq. There was only one Court of Cassation in Iraq before the establishment of the Court of Cassation in Kurdistan. The Court of Cassation supervises all the courts of Iraq. There are no trials at the Court of Cassation; it reviews other courts' judgments.

The Court of Cassation has the following committees:

- The General Committee, which is comprised of the thirty judges of the Court of Cassation. These consist of the chief justice, five justice deputies and all justices in the Court of Cassation.
- The High Committee: It has seven justices—a chief and six justices.
- The Civil Committee: It has five justices—a chief and four justices.
- The Criminal Cases Committee: It has five justices—a chief and four justices.
- The Committee of Personal Status: It has three justices—a chief and two justices.

Public Prosecution Department

The Public Prosecution Department is regulated by Public Prosecution Law No. 159 of 1979.

The goals of the Public Prosecution Department are as follows:

- protect the State's order;
- participate in revealing crimes;
- supervise the exercise of the law, the regulations and the penalties;
- evaluate current regulations;
- monitor the criminal phenomena and recommend solutions to reduce them; and
- work on protecting the family, the cell of the society.

The Public Prosecution Department is comprised of a director and two deputies, at least one prosecutor in each felony court, and two prosecutors and their deputies on the board of the Department.

The tasks of the Public Prosecutor are

- asking for public rights in front of the judiciary;
- supervising the collection of information and the detection of crimes;

- attending investigation sessions conducted by the investigative judge;
- visiting detention centers and prisons;
- attending trials at the Felony and Misdemeanor Courts, but not at sessions of the Court of Cassation; and
- appealing the decisions and/or the procedures of the investigative and/or the trial judges.

Judiciary Oversight Commission
The Commission has a director, a deputy director and judicial supervisors. The Judiciary Oversight Commission supervises the judiciary and the decisions of the courts. It also follows up on the rank of the judiciary personnel and the judiciary records.

Other Courts
There are two types of courts under the judiciary authority in Iraq: civil courts and criminal courts.

Civil Courts. Civil courts are divided into the Courts of First Instance, the Courts of Appeal or Supreme Courts, the Courts of Personal Status, the Courts of Civil Matters and the Labor Courts.

The Courts of First Instance have one judge each. The courts handle cases of debt, real estate, contracts and compensation for illegal work. The decisions of the courts are usually considered primary and are reviewed by the Courts of Appeal, which consist of panels of three judges.

The Courts of Personal Status have one judge apiece and handle marriage, divorce, wills and estates for Muslims.

The Courts of Civil Matters each have one judge and handle marriage, divorce, wills and estates for non-Muslims.

The Labor Courts have one judge each and handle labor cases.

Criminal Courts. There are two different kinds of criminal courts, depending on the age of the defendant: Criminal Courts for Adults and Juvenile Courts.

Defendants in the Criminal Courts for Adults are adults who are over the age of eighteen at the time the alleged crime was committed. There are three courts that handle criminal cases. The Investigation Courts, each consisting of one judge, conduct the investigation from the time the crime is committed until the case is referred to a trial court. There is one Investigation Court or more in each location that has a Court of First Instance.[24]

The trial courts are the Felony and Misdemeanor Courts. The Felony Courts are equivalent to the civil Supreme Courts. They are established in the centers of the provinces. The cases are referred to the Felony Courts by the investigative judges. The court has the right to either conduct the trial[25] or hear an appeal of the investigative judge's decision. The Felony Courts consist of three-judge panels, and the courts' decisions are usually based on the majority of opinions. The Misdemeanor Courts are usually established wherever there is a Court of First Instance. Cases of misdemeanor violations are referred to the courts by the investigative judges.

The Juvenile Courts handle those cases in which the defendant is younger than eighteen but older than nine.[26] The Juvenile Courts are divided into the investigation chamber and the trial court. The chamber in the trial court is comprised of a chief judge, a right member who is a specialist in sociology and a left member who should have a law degree with experience as investigator or legal assistant.

The Iraqi High Tribunal

After US and coalition forces entered Iraq and the discussion turned to promoting the rule of law in Iraq, concerned parties began to wonder how Saddam Hussein would be prosecuted—whether he would be tried by Iraqi courts or whether he would be prosecuted by an international court similar to the International Criminal Tribunal for the former Yugoslavia (ICTY).

Given the political disagreements among the five permanent members of the Security Council concerning the war in Iraq, obtaining Security Council approval for the establishment of an ICTY-type international court was not an available option. Moreover, history shows that such international courts take years to conduct trials and reach decisions; therefore, it was logical to try Hussein in Iraq.

In December 2003, the CPA issued Order No. 48,[27] which gave Iraq's Governing Council the authority to establish an Iraqi Special Tribunal "to try Iraqi nationals or residents of Iraq accused of genocide, crimes against humanity, war crimes or violations of certain Iraqi laws."[28] This Tribunal was established as an independent entity of the judicial system by Statute Number 1 of 2003 of the Iraqi Governing Council. That statute was replaced by Law No. 10 of 2005,[29] which also renamed the Tribunal as the Iraqi High Tribunal (IHT).

The Iraqi Constitution considers the IHT to be a transitional court in a transitional period with the duty to examine "the crimes of the defunct dictatorial regime and its symbols."[30] The IHT has jurisdiction over Iraqi nationals or residents of Iraq accused of war crimes, genocides and crimes against humanity committed between July 17, 1968 and May 1, 2003 in Iraq or elsewhere.[31] The Council of Representatives has the right to dissolve the Tribunal after the completion of its work.[32]

The IHT is independent, both financially and administratively, from the Higher Juridical Council of Iraq.

The IHT contains two entities: the judicial and prosecution committees. The Judicial Committee consists of the Appeal Chamber, the Trial Chamber, the Investigative Judges and the Prosecution. The Appeal Chamber has a chief judge and eight judges. It is equivalent to the Court of Cassation. The Trial Chamber has a chief judge and four judges. It is equivalent to the Felony Courts. The investigative judges are a chief judge and twenty-four investigative judges. They are each the equivalent of the Investigative Courts. The prosecution has a chief and sixteen prosecutors. It is equivalent to the Public Prosecution Department under the Higher Juridical Council. There is a separate Administrative Department to support the IHT.

The New Rule of Law in Iraq

The Iraqi High Tribunal began its mission in 2004. By the end of 2006, it had made substantial headway in addressing the claims presented to it, and processing the documents and other evidence that supported those claims. As the number of complainants increased from different parts of the country, however, it became important to open additional offices, to reduce the amount of work in the Baghdad headquarters. Offices were opened in Sulaymaniyah and Erbil to cover the northern region of Iraq, in Najaf to cover the central region and in Basra to cover the southern region. All four offices were supplied with the necessary personnel, investigative resources and equipment to facilitate their tasks. These offices and the headquarters in Baghdad interviewed thousands of witnesses, victims and complainants.

Additionally, they dealt with a huge number of documents. In addition to the official Iraqi government records, the IHT received approximately eighteen tons of documents during the first six months of its existence. It was impossible to read and authenticate each document manually; therefore it was important to find a process to organize and categorize them. The documents were moved to a special building and more than one hundred individuals specialized in analyzing documents were hired. The documents were categorized, scanned and entered into an electronic database.

The investigative judges, along with their staff of investigators and paralegals, went through the documents they needed in the cases to which they were assigned. At the same time, prosecutors and defense attorneys were provided access to the documents used in the investigation. The electronic database proved to be an effective way to save time and effort. Millions of important documents were categorized in that database.

A huge issue in Iraq was the mass graves in which the victims of the Hussein regime's atrocities were buried. Two sources were used in locating the burial sites. The first source was witnesses who helped not just in locating them and establishing the year they were buried, but also in identifying the victims.[33] The second source was non-governmental human rights organizations, working in coordination with US military forces, who used modern technology in locating the graves. More than 250 mass grave sites were found; each contained more than eighty skeletal remains.

Because the grave sites were often found in isolated locations, the concerned Iraq government ministries (Ministry of Human Rights, Ministry of Health and the Archaeology Department) didn't possess the resources to investigate each site. The IHT, with the support from the Regime Crimes Liaison Office based in the US embassy in Iraq, was able to hire international experts and purchased a mobile laboratory to assist in the investigation of the grave sites. Taken together, the testimony of the witnesses, the documentary evidence and the mass graves starkly illustrated the policy of the former regime toward each group of victims.

Conclusion

Many experts have questioned the work of the Iraqi High Tribunal. In doing so, however, the critics neglected to analyze its work in the context of Iraq's modern judicial history. The IHT achieved justice and helped keep peace in Iraq in the period immediately following the fall of the former regime in 2003. It represented the hopes of Iraqis for the rule of law, and contributed to the process of restoring faith and confidence in the Iraqi judicial system.

Notes

1. CPA Order No. 1, De-Ba`athification of Iraqi Society (May 16, 2003). All CPA orders and regulations are available at http://www.cpa-iraq.org/regulations/ (then hyperlink by name of order or regulation). The CPA was established as a transitional government following the invasion of Iraq by the United States, United Kingdom and the other members of the coalition of the willing which was formed to oust the government of Saddam Hussein. The CPA's authority was set forth in CPA Regulation No. 1 and was based on "relevant U.N. Security Council resolutions, and the laws and usages of war." *Id.*, pmbl.

2. "De-Baathification" is a term the CPA used to describe ridding the country of Baathism by dismissing high-ranking Baath Party members from government employment.

3. CPA Order No. 2, Dissolution of Entities (May 23, 2003).

4. CPA Order No. 15, Establishment of the Judicial Review Committee, pmbl. (June 23, 2003).

5. CPA Order No. 35, Re-Establishment of the Council of Judges (Sept. 13, 2003).

6. CPA Order No. 48, Delegation of Authority Regarding Establishment of an Iraqi Special Tribunal (Dec. 9, 2003).

7. The Governing Council was formed on July 13, 2003. It included twenty-five members chosen by the US-led coalition: thirteen Shiite Muslims, five Sunni Muslims, five Kurds, one Christian and one Turk. The Council's priorities were to achieve stability and security, revive the economy and deliver public services. *See* Iraq Governing Council, GLOBALSECURITY.ORG, http://www.globalsecurity.org/military/world/iraq/igc.htm (last visited June 23, 2009).

8. The name of the court was later changed from Iraqi Special Tribunal (IST) to Iraqi High Tribunal (IHT) in 2005. *See infra* p. 11 and note 29.

9. It was not known until 2003 that they were executed.

10. For more information about the Al-Anfal genocide, see HUMAN RIGHTS WATCH, GENOCIDE IN IRAQ (1993), *available at* http://www.hrw.org/reports/1993/iraqanfal/. According to the chief prosecutor at the trial of those responsible for the campaign against the Kurds, up to 182,000 civilians were killed.

11. Hussein's regime killed more than half a million Iraqis. This number does not include the victims of the wars in Iraq between 1980 and 2003. *See, e.g.*, Secondary Wars and Atrocities of the Twentieth Century, http://users.erols.com/mwhite28/warstat3.htm#sadhus (last visited June 19, 2009).

12. Interim Constitution of Iraq (1970), *available at* http://www.gjpi.org/library/primary/iraqi-constitution/ (then 1970 Interim Constitution hyperlink).

13. Unofficial translation available at http://www.gjpi.org/library/primary/statutes/ (then Civil Procedure and Actions Law No. 83 of 1969 hyperlink).

14. Criminal Procedures Code (Law No. 23), Feb. 14, 1971. An unofficial version of the code is available at http://www.gjpi.org/library/primary/statutes/ (then Criminal Procedure Code 23 of 1971 hyperlink) [hereinafter Law No. 23].

15. Judicial Organization Law (Law No. 160), Dec. 10, 1979, *available at* http://www.gjpi.org/wp-content/uploads/judicial-organization.pdf [hereinafter Law No. 160].

16. This was the organization that replaced the Council of Judges during the Hussein regime and was itself replaced by the re-established Council of Judges in 2003. In turn, the Council of Judges was itself replaced in 2004 by the Higher Juridical Counsel. CPA Order No. 100, Transition of Laws, Regulations, Orders, and Directives Issued by the Coalition Provisional Authority § 3 (June 28, 2004).

17. For information on the role of the Revolutionary Command Council, see IRAQ: A COUNTRY STUDY (Helen Chapin Metz ed., 1988), *available at* http://countrystudies.us/iraq/.

18. *Supra* note 5.

19. Kurdistan Iraq is the northern region of the country. It contains three provinces: Erbil, Sulaymaniyah and Duhok. For more information on Kurdistan Iraq, see the Kurdistan Regional Government website at http://www.krg.org/.

20. Const. (2005) (Iraq). The UN, UK and US agreed-on English translation of the Constitution is available at http://www.gjpi.org/library/primary/iraqi-constitution/ (then 2005 Constitution – English hyperlink).

21. *Id.*, art. 90.

22. *Id.*, art. 94.

23. Law No. 160, *supra* note 15.

24. *Id.*, art. 35

25. Law No. 23, *supra* note 14, art. 265.

26. Article 233, *id.,* established a minimum age of seven to be prosecuted in Juvenile Court. The Juveniles Welfare Law (Law No. 76) art. 3, July 20, 1983, *available at* http://www.gjpi.org/wp-content/uploads/juvenile-welfare-law-76-of-1983.pdf, increased the minimum age to ten for prosecution.

27. *Supra* note 6.

28. *Id.*, § 1, ¶ 1.

29. Law of the Supreme Iraqi Criminal Tribunal (Law No. 10), Oct. 18, 2005, *available at* http://www.cpa-iraq.org/human_rights/Statute.htm [hereinafter Law No. 10].

30. Const. (2005) (Iraq), *supra* note 20, art. 134.

31. Law No. 10, *supra* note 29, art. 10.

32. Const. (2005) (Iraq), *supra* note 20, art. 134.

33. Genocide against Kurds stopped in 1988, while that against Arabs continued after 1991.

PART II

OVERVIEW OF THE CONFLICT IN IRAQ

II

Iraq and the "Fog of Law"

John F. Murphy*

The conference "The War in Iraq: A Legal Analysis," from which this volume derives, covered a variety of topics and a plethora of legal issues. It was followed by a workshop consisting of moderators of the various panels, panelists and commentators with a view to continuing the dialogue begun at the conference. As a commentator at the conference,[1] this author was struck not only by the large number of controversial issues arising out of the conflict in Iraq, but also by the absence of clear resolution of many of these issues, both at the conference and in the wider world outside of the conference, hence my choice of the "fog of law" as part of the title of this article.[2]

By the "fog of law," I mean not only the debate over the law as it was interpreted and applied in Iraq; but also the issue of what law applied—national law, especially the law of Iraq; the law of armed conflict (or, as preferred by some, "international humanitarian law"); the law of the United Nations Charter, including Security Council resolutions adopted under Chapter VII; or no law at all.[3]

Although the first panel of the conference was titled "Legal Bases for Military Operations in Iraq," and Andru Wall presented a defense of the legality of the March 2003 invasion of Iraq and the removal of the Saddam Hussein regime from power,[4] this topic was not a primary focus of the conference. Perhaps this was just as well, since the legality of the war in Iraq under the *jus ad bellum*, the law of resort

* Professor of Law, Villanova University School of Law.

to the use of armed force, has been debated extensively in various other forums. Moreover, with the passage of time and a rash of developments in Iraq that have raised a host of other issues, the legality of the 2003 invasion has arguably become a matter of academic interest only. It may be appropriate, however, to make two brief observations before leaving the topic. The first is that there was general agreement in the Security Council debates concerning Iraq on a "strict constructionist" approach to the *jus ad bellum.* That is, the strict limits on the use of force set forth in Article 2(4) of the UN Charter[5] are subject to only two exceptions: (1) self-defense in response to an armed attack and (2) military action taken or authorized by the Security Council.

In the Security Council debates prior to and after the invasion, there was no invocation of Article 51[6] as a basis for the invasion. Rather, the debate focused on whether the particular Security Council resolutions on Iraq, including especially, but not limited to, Resolution 1441,[7] authorized the March 2003 invasion of Iraq without the need for a further resolution explicitly authorizing such an action. The "fog of law" in this case may have been Resolution 1441 itself, which this author has described elsewhere as "a masterpiece of diplomatic ambiguity that masked real differences of view between the United States and the United Kingdom, on the one hand, and France, Germany, and Russia, on the other, in how Iraq's failure to fulfill its obligations under Resolution 687 should be handled."[8] In a similar vein, Michael Glennon has suggested that Resolution 1441 "can accurately be said to lend support to both claims. This is not the hallmark of great legislation."[9]

The second observation concerns whether, assuming *arguendo* that none of the applicable Security Council resolutions authorized the March 2003 invasion of Iraq, this was a "failure of the Security Council," as suggested by Glennon, or whether the Security Council should have accepted the US and UK proposal that it adopt a resolution explicitly authorizing the use of force if Iraq failed to carry out its obligation to disarm. There has been considerable debate over whether it was necessary or desirable *as a matter of policy* to remove the Saddam regime to maintain international peace and security, but a discussion of the arguments for and against this proposition are beyond the scope of this article. For present purposes, it suffices to note that there was little or no prospect that the Security Council would adopt a resolution authorizing such action, however compelling the reasons for doing so. There is considerable evidence that, far from helping to enforce Resolution 687, France, Russia and China engaged in deals with the Saddam Hussein government that undermined the resolution's enforcement.[10] In short, the Saddam regime was one favored by three permanent members of the Security Council, and it is reasonable to conclude that they had no interest in its removal and would have exercised their veto power to block any Security Council resolution that sought to authorize such removal.[11]

Parenthetically, it may be noted that Michael Reisman has argued that Article 2(4) of the UN Charter should be construed in such a way as to enhance "the ongoing right of peoples to determine their own political destinies" and "to maintain the political independence of territorial communities so that they can continue to express their desire for political community in a form appropriate to them."[12] Hence, in his view, some interventions are permissible under Article 2(4) if they "serve, in terms of aggregate consequences, to increase the probability of the free choice of peoples about their government and political structure."[13] Since the Saddam Hussein regime was a brutal dictatorship on a local level and had twice invaded its neighbors to deny them the right of self-determination, it could be argued that the March 2003 invasion of Iraq was not a violation of Article 2(4) and that there was therefore no need for a Security Council resolution authorizing it.

To be sure, this kind of argument has been effectively, in my opinion, refuted by Oscar Schachter. In a direct response to Reisman,[14] Schachter stated:

> The difficulty with Reisman's argument is not merely that it lacks support in the text of the Charter or in the interpretation that states have given Article 2(4) in the past decades. It would introduce a new normative basis for recourse to war that would give powerful states an almost unlimited right to overthrow governments alleged to be unresponsive to the popular will or to the goal of self-determination.[15]

Assuming *arguendo* that, as a policy matter, the Saddam Hussein regime *should* have been removed from power, but the lack of Security Council authorization stood in the way of such removal, what are the implications for appropriate action should such a situation arise again in the future? If one agrees with Michael Glennon's argument that, because they have been so often flouted in the past, Article 2(4) and other limitations on resort to force in the UN Charter are no longer in effect, it necessarily follows that one would agree with Glennon that "[b]y 2003 the main question facing countries considering whether to use force was not whether it was lawful. Instead, as in the nineteenth century, they simply questioned whether it was wise."[16] But for reasons I have set forth elsewhere, Glennon's premise that limitations on the use of force in the UN Charter are no longer in effect is not valid.[17]

Shortly after the March 2003 invasion of Iraq, Lee Feinstein, then Acting Director of the Washington Program of the Council on Foreign Relations, and Anne-Marie Slaughter, then Dean of the Woodrow Wilson School of Public and International Affairs at Princeton University and President of the American Society of International Law, proposed a new doctrine, a "collective 'duty to prevent' nations run by rulers without internal checks on their power from acquiring or using WMD [weapons of mass destruction]."[18] With specific reference to Iraq, the authors suggested:

> Consider, for instance, how recognizing a duty to prevent could have changed the debate over the war in Iraq. Under existing law, the Bush administration could justify intervention only by arguing that Iraq held WMD in violation of Security Council resolutions. . . . Now suppose that last March, the United States and the United Kingdom had accepted a proposal by France, Germany, and Russia to blanket Iraq with inspectors instead of attacking it. Presumably those inspectors would have found what U.S. forces seem to be finding today—evidence of Iraq's intention and capacity to build WMD, but no existing stocks. Would the appropriate response then have been to send the inspectors home and leave Saddam's regime intact? The better answer would have been to recognize from the beginning the combined threat posed by the nature of his regime and his determination to acquire and use WMD. Invoking the duty to prevent, the Security Council could have identified Iraq as a subject of special concern and, as it was blanketing the country with inspectors, sought to prosecute Saddam for crimes against humanity committed back in the 1980s.[19]

There are a number of problems with this proposed alternative approach to Saddam's Iraq. First, it should be noted that Security Council Resolution 687 had established a Special Commission (UNSCOM) consisting of inspectors who were to inspect and verify that Iraq had destroyed all capability for weapons of mass destruction, but Iraq had consistently refused to allow UNSCOM to carry out its mandate, and in 1998 had forced it to leave Iraq and refused it or a successor team to resume this function. Only in 1999 was the Security Council able to establish the United Nations Monitoring, Verification and Inspection Commission (UNMOVIC)[20] as a successor to UNSCOM. This result is largely attributable to heavy bombing by the United States and the United Kingdom as part of Operation Desert Fox, which occurred in response to the withdrawal by Iraq of cooperation with the UN weapons inspectors.[21] In mid-September 2002, Iraq finally acceded to the Council's demand that it allow UN inspectors back into its territory, and Resolution 1441 decided that

> the Government of Iraq shall provide to UNMOVIC, the IAEA [International Atomic Energy Agency], and the Council, not later than 30 days from the date of this resolution, a currently accurate, full, and complete declaration of all aspects of its programmes to develop chemical, biological, and nuclear weapons, ballistic missiles, and other delivery systems . . . .[22]

In Resolution 1441, the Council also decided that

> false statements or omissions to the declarations submitted by Iraq pursuant to this resolution and failure by Iraq at any time to comply with, and cooperate fully in the implementation of, this resolution shall constitute a further material breach of Iraq's obligations and will be reported to the Council for assessment in accordance with paragraphs 11 and 12 below.[23]

On December 7, 2002, Iraq's declaration of its weapons fell far short of the full disclosure demanded by Resolution 1441. Nonetheless, Hans Blix, the chief UN inspector for chemical and biological weapons, in a clash with the view of US Secretary of State Colin Powell, maintained that the inspection process was working and should be given more time and requested four more months.[24]

In light of Saddam's refusal to cooperate with UN inspectors, it is highly unlikely that he would have accepted "blanketing the country with inspectors," especially if this was part of an effort to prosecute him for crimes against humanity committed in the 1980s. Carrying out this policy would have required the use of armed force. Support of Saddam by the Russian, French, German and Chinese governments would have precluded any Security Council authorization of such use of force.

More generally, Feinstein and Slaughter, in support of their proposal for a doctrine of a duty to prevent weapons of mass destruction falling into the hands of regimes like North Korea or Iran, recognize that the "contentious issue is who decides when and how to use force." They further recognize that the Security Council "remains the preferred enforcer of collective measures."[25] At the same time they state:

> Given the Security Council's propensity for paralysis, alternative means of enforcement must be considered. The second most legitimate enforcer is the regional organization that is most likely to be affected by the emerging threat. After that, the next best option would be another regional organization, such as NATO, with a less direct connection to the targeted state but with a sufficiently broad membership to permit serious deliberation over the exercise of a collective duty. It is only after these options are tried in good faith that unilateral action or coalitions of the willing should be considered.
>
> In any event, the resort to force is subject to certain "precautionary principles." All nonmilitary alternatives that could achieve the same ends must be tried before force may be used, unless they can reasonably be said to be futile. Force must be exerted on the smallest scale, for the shortest time, and at the lowest intensity necessary to achieve its objective; the objective itself must be reasonably attainable when measured against the likelihood of making matters worse. Finally, force should be governed by fundamental principles of the laws of war: it must be a measure of last resort, used in

> proportion to the harm or the threat of the harm it targets, and with due care to spare civilians.[26]

From a strict legal perspective, it must be noted that the Security Council is not only the "preferred enforcer of collective measures"; it is the only enforcer of collective measures under the UN Charter paradigm qualified to use or to authorize the use of force as a collective measure. Regional organizations, including NATO, require Security Council approval to use force unless they are acting in collective self-defense. But in the case of Security Council paralysis, as suggested by Feinstein and Slaughter, they may well be the most legitimate alternative to the Security Council to engage in armed force, subject to certain "precautionary principles" and "fundamental principles of the laws of war."

At this point it is time to turn to the "fog of law" topics that will be the primary focus of the rest of this article: the occupation in Iraq and the relationship between the law of armed conflict and international human rights law.

The Occupation in Iraq

It is generally recognized that the 1907 Hague Regulations on land warfare[27] and the Fourth Geneva Convention of 1949[28] constitute the primary legal documents governing the traditional law of belligerent occupation.[29] According to Eyal Benvenisti, however, in the case of the 2003 occupation of Iraq by the United States, Great Britain and the "coalition of the willing," the occupants "were initially reluctant to use the term *occupation.*"[30] They also did not "explicitly acknowledge their status as occupying powers nor did they invoke the Hague Regulations of 1907 or the Fourth Geneva Convention as applicable to their actions in Iraq."[31]

Approximately seven months after the coalition invaded Iraq on March 20, 2003, David J. Scheffer published an article that demonstrates why the United States and Great Britain were reluctant to use the term occupation.[32] For example, as stated by Scheffer, "[t]he occupation clauses of the Fourth Geneva Convention are far more relevant to a belligerent occupation than to an occupation designed to liberate a society from its repressive governance and transform it as a nation guided by international norms and the self-determination of its liberated populace."[33] Elaborating on this thesis, Scheffer states:

> In recent years, multilateral or humanitarian occupation, particularly that aimed at enforcing international human rights law and atrocity law, has become the more relevant factor in occupation practice. Occupation law was never designed for such transforming exercises. While the humanitarian condition of the occupied society is a paramount concern of the Hague Regulations of 1907, [under] the Fourth Geneva

> Convention, and Geneva Protocol I, a society in political, judicial, and economic collapse or a society that has overthrown a repressive leader and seeks radical transformation requires far more latitude for transformational development than would be anticipated under these instruments. The society may require revolutionary changes in its economy (including a leap into robust capitalism), rigorous implementation of international human rights standards, a new constitution and judiciary, and a new political structure (most likely consistent with principles of democracy) never contemplated by occupation law or the domestic law of the occupied territory. As just one example, the penal law requirements set forth in Article 64 of the Fourth Geneva Convention serve little, if any, purpose in areas such as Kosovo or Iraq or, had it been in force at the time, in Germany after World War II where the Nazi-era national penal system failed to protect individual and collective rights.[34]

Despite the reluctance of the United States and the United Kingdom to use the term "occupation," and despite their clear intention to transform Iraqi society, they acknowledged their respective obligations to act in accordance with the Hague Regulations of 1907 and the Fourth Geneva Convention.[35] This was followed by the Security Council issuing Resolution 1483,[36] which "[*c*]*alls upon* all concerned to comply fully with their obligations under international law including in particular the Geneva Conventions of 1949 and the Hague Regulations of 1907."[37]

Scheffer criticizes Resolution 1483 and suggests that

> [t]he methodology that should have been invoked . . . was a UN Security Council mandate establishing the transformational tasks of a military deployment and civilian administration of a liberated society that explicitly or implicitly implemented only the provisions of occupation law relevant to the particular situation. That methodology was rejected by the United States immediately following the intervention.[38]

Instead of supporting a Security Council resolution along the lines suggested by Scheffer, the United States and the United Kingdom established the "Coalition Provisional Authority" (CPA), which "replaced the domestic system of governance with a temporary command structure that ruled the country based on the authority of the 'relevant U.N. Security resolutions, and the laws and usages of war.'"[39] The Security Council formally recognized the CPA in Resolution 1511 of October 16, 2003.[40]

These developments created a major "fog of law" in Iraq because, as noted by Yoram Dinstein, "[w]ithin a brief stretch of time, the Coalition Provisional Authority carried a whole string of legislative and other measures designed to bring about large-scale reforms."[41] As Scheffer notes, however, by enacting Resolution 1483, the Council "specified additional obligations not required by occupation law, but in doing so invited the Authority to act beyond some of the barriers that occupation law otherwise would impose on occupying powers."[42] He suggests further that

> [i]n each of these areas of responsibility, a strict reading of occupation law likely would prohibit such bold and transformational control of Iraqi society and economy, unless one views the Security Council decisions as legitimately overriding conflicting norms of occupation law.[[43]] If such is the case, then the Council's insistence elsewhere in Resolution 1483 on compliance with occupation law breeds confusion.[44]

Interestingly, Scheffer sets forth a lengthy list of acts or omissions of the occupying powers in Iraq that "[i]f proven true . . . may invite varying degrees of civil liability or criminal culpability under occupation law . . . ."[45] Later, Scheffer admits that

> this rather anemic body of international law remains difficult to enforce against either governments or individuals. This is not surprising given the paucity of enforceable penalties under international treaties and national criminal codes and the reluctance of national courts to second guess the public policy decisions that dominate occupation practice. For example, a private right of action against the U.S. government for its conduct during an occupation of foreign territory would be problematic.[46]

Gregory Fox has extensively examined the issue of the extent to which the CPA's actions were compatible with the traditional law of occupation.[47] As an "alternative source" of legitimacy of CPA reforms, he also evaluates the argument that, by adopting Resolution 1483, the Security Council "ratified the [CPA] reforms by effectively legislating a set of goals for the occupation that superseded the limitations of Hague and Geneva law."[48] He concludes, correctly in this author's view, that many of the CPA's reforms were incompatible with the traditional law of occupation and that the Security Council had not ratified these reforms.[49]

Eyal Benvenisti has a somewhat different view from Fox's concerning the effect of Resolution 1483 on the law of occupation applicable to the CPA:

> Resolution 1483 can be seen as the latest and most authoritative restatement of several basic principles of the contemporary law of occupation. It endorses several theses developed in this book. First, it revives the neutral connotation of the doctrine. Occupation is a temporary measure for reestablishing order and civil life after the end of active hostilities, benefiting also, if not primarily, the civilian population. As such, occupation does not amount to unlawful alien domination that entitles the local population to struggle against it. Second, sovereignty inheres in the people, and consequently regime collapse does not extinguish sovereignty. Thus, the Resolution implicitly confirms the demise of the doctrine of *debellatio,* which would have passed sovereign title to the occupant in case of total defeat and disintegration of the governing regime. Instead, and notwithstanding the requirement of Article 43 of the

> Hague Regulations to "respect . . . , unless absolutely prevented, the laws in force in the country," Resolution 1483 grants a mandate to the occupants to transform the previous legal system to enable the Iraqi people "freely to determine their own political future and control their own natural resources . . . to form a representative government based on the rule of law that affords equal rights and justice to all Iraqi citizens without regard to ethnicity, religion, or gender." Hence, the law of occupation, according to Resolution 1483, connotes respect to popular sovereignty, not to the demised regime. Third, the Resolution recognizes in principle the continued applicability of international human rights law in occupied territories in tandem with the law of occupation. Human rights law may thus complement the law of occupation on specific matters. Fourth, Resolution 1483 envisions the role of the modern occupant as the role of the heavily involved regulator, when it calls upon the occupants to pursue an "effective administration" of Iraq. This call stands in contrast to the initial orientation of the Hague Regulations, which envisioned a disinterested occupant who does not intervene in the lives of the occupied population. In the years since, such an "inactive custodian" approach has been rejected as unacceptable. The call to administer the occupied area "effectively" acknowledges the several duties that the occupants must perform to protect the occupied population. It precludes the occupant from hiding behind the limits imposed on its powers as a pretext for inaction.[50]

Elsewhere, Benvenisti acknowledges that Resolution 1483 "did not address a number of key questions concerning the further adaptation of the law of occupation to contemporary governance."[51] Nonetheless, it is clear that he considers the contemporary law of occupation more adequate for governing an occupation like that in Iraq, where the goal is regime change and radical changes in law and policy of the occupied territory, than do Scheffer and Fox. In such situations, the latter two commentators appear to favor "the establishment of a United Nations legal framework to govern the foreign military deployment and civilian administration."[52]

This author tends to favor the Scheffer/Fox approach because a United Nations legal framework would have the potential to bring greater clarity to a murky area and thus lift, at least in part, the "fog of law." It is unclear, however, the extent to which future occupations will have goals similar to those of the occupation in Iraq. If UN member States were to take seriously the so-called "responsibility to protect," there would be a considerable likelihood of occupations along the Iraq model. At this writing, however, the "responsibility to protect" is under attack in the United Nations and its future is uncertain.[53]

The Law of International Armed Conflict and International Human Rights

By way of transition from the previous section, it should be noted, as Yoram Dinstein has helpfully pointed out, that, despite the reluctance of the occupying powers in Iraq to apply the ordinary norms of belligerent occupation because of their being ill-suited to the transformative objectives they had in mind, "[i]n the event, the status of belligerent occupation in Iraq remained legally valid for just a little over a year . . . ."[54] By adopting Resolution 1546,[55] the Security Council set in train the process whereby the belligerent occupation came to an end. Specifically, the Council declared that "by 30 June 2004, the occupation will end and the Coalition Provisional Authority will cease to exist, and . . . Iraq will reassert its full sovereignty."[56] Two days earlier than the deadline CPA Administrator Paul Bremer formally transferred political authority to the Iraqi interim government and left the country.[57]

The practical effect of Resolution 1546, however, is unclear. Yoram Dinstein has suggested:

> In theory, since the end of June 2004, the continued presence of coalition forces in Iraq is by invitation of the new Iraqi government. In practice, there was little change on the ground following the decreed termination of the occupation. As long as coalition forces are engaged in combat in order to extinguish pockets of resistance of the *ancien regime* (or its putative supporters)—exercising at least some administrative authority in certain areas of Iraq—the occupation has come to a close only "notionally."[58]

As we shall see later in this article, the situation has changed radically recently with the adoption of two international agreements between the United States and the Iraq government.

As to the applicability of human rights law to the period of belligerent occupation of Iraq, this has been a question of some controversy. The United States, for example, takes the position that the International Covenant on Civil and Political Rights (ICCPR)[59] does not apply outside of the United States or its special maritime and territorial jurisdiction and that it does not apply to operations of the military during an international armed conflict.[60] The US position that the ICCPR does not apply outside of the territory of the United States has been rejected by the United Nations Human Rights Committee[61] and the International Court of Justice (ICJ) in an advisory opinion.[62] It is worth noting, however, that neither the views of the Human Rights Committee nor the ICJ's advisory opinion has any binding effect, and the United States and other countries have maintained their position.

The United States has also maintained that the Convention against Torture and Other Cruel, Inhuman or Degrading Treatment or Punishment applies only within US territory, although the territorial scope clause that appears in several articles of this convention contains the phrase "in any territory under its jurisdiction."[63] Leading authorities on the drafting history of the Convention have concluded that this phrase extends the treaty to "territories under military occupation, to colonial territories and to any other territories over which a State has factual control."[64] For its part, the UN Committee against Torture, which is the Convention's counterpart to the UN Human Rights Committee, has endorsed an "effective control" standard and concluded that "this includes all areas under the de facto effective control of the State party, by whichever military or civil authorities such control is exercised. The Committee considers [the US] view that those provisions are geographically limited to its own de jure territory to be regrettable."[65] Again, the United States is not bound by the views of the Committee against Torture and has maintained its position to the contrary. As is so often his practice, however, Dinstein adds another consideration to the mix:

> As treaty laws, the Covenant and the European Convention (whatever the correct interpretations of their texts) are, of course, limited in application to Contracting Parties. But it is necessary to pay heed to the customary law of human rights, which is frequently reflected in the substantive clauses of these instruments. Customary human rights are conferred on human beings wherever they are. Irrefutably, the inhabitants of occupied territories are in principle entitled to benefit from the customary *corpus* of human rights that coexists with the law of belligerent occupation. The International Court of Justice observed, in the *Armed Activities* case, that "both branches of international law, namely, international human rights law and international humanitarian law, would have to be taken into consideration" in occupied territories.[66]

The US view that the ICCPR does not apply to operations of the military during international armed conflict is contrary to the view expressed in two advisory opinions of the International Court of Justice: *Legality of the Threat or Use of Nuclear Weapons*[67] and *Legal Consequences of the Construction of a Wall in the Occupied Palestinian Territory*.[68] In its *Nuclear Weapons* opinion, the Court stated that "the protection of the International Covenant of Civil and Political Rights does not cease in times of war, except by operation of Article 4 of the Covenant whereby certain provisions may be derogated from in a time of emergency."[69] Similarly, the Court opined in *Wall* that "the Court considers that the protection offered by human rights conventions does not cease in case of armed conflict, save through the effect of provisions for derogation of the kind found in Article 4 of the International Covenant on Civil and Political Rights."[70]

Dinstein has provided a concise rationale to support the ICJ view: "The very fact derogation is required to suspend the operation of given stipulations of the Covenant in wartime attests that—when no permissible derogation is in effect—human rights continue to be in force."[71]

To be sure, as Dinstein notes, Article 4(1) of the ICCPR[72] does not contain any explicit reference to war or even armed conflict.[73] Dinstein, however, quotes Thomas Buergenthal, now a judge on the International Court of Justice and an eminent authority on human rights, to deny any legal significance to this omission: "the omission of specific reference to war was surely not intended to deny the right of derogation in wartime; war is the most dramatic example of a public emergency which might 'threaten the life of the nation.'"[74] It is noteworthy that neither the United States nor the United Kingdom has invoked Article 4 of the Covenant with respect to Iraq.

Elsewhere in his treatise *The International Law of Belligerent Occupation*, Dinstein discusses in detail Article 4(1), as well as the general subject of derogations from obligations to respect human rights.[75] In a section on non-derogable human rights,[76] Dinstein compares the non-derogable provisions of the ICCPR, the European Convention on Human Rights and Fundamental Freedoms, and the American Convention on Human Rights.[77] He concludes that "[t]he lists of non-derogable human rights appearing in the three instruments coincide in part but they are not conterminous"[78] and illustrates this fact in some detail.[79] Perhaps the most interesting observation Dinstein makes in this exercise is set forth below:

> It is surprising that the human right to judicial guarantees of fair trial—enshrined in all the instruments—is not included in the list of non-derogable rights. Only the American Convention enumerates as non-derogable those judicial guarantees that are essential to the protection of other non-derogable rights. This loose end was deftly used by the Inter-American Court of Human Rights—in two Advisory Opinions delivered on the subject in 1987—to extrapolate that judicial remedies like the writs of habeas corpus and *amparo* can never be derogated, and they can therefore be used to exercise control also over the suspension of derogable rights.[80] More radically, the Human Rights Committee expressed the non-binding view—in General Comment No. 29 of 2001—that the list of non-derogable rights (as it appears in Article 4(2) of the Covenant) is not exhaustive, and there can be no derogation (in particular) from judicial guarantees.[81]

In subsequent sections of his treatise, Dinstein, in a *tour de force*, explores the many nuances of the following topics: "Built-in limitations of human rights," including "Explicit limitations" and "Implicit limitations";[82] "Balance between competing human rights";[83] and "The Interaction between the law of belligerent occupation and the law of human rights," including "Convergence and divergence," "The advantages of the law of belligerent occupation," "The advantages of human rights law" and "The *lex specialis* rule."[84] Time and space limitations preclude exploring Dinstein's treatment of these important topics in any depth. It is fair to say, however, that it helps to lift the "fog of law" covering some very important issues. In particular, it effectively refutes the thesis that the law of international armed conflict and international human rights are mutually exclusive;

illustrates how, "[f]or the most part, in occupied territories, there is enough room for a symbiotic relationship between the two [branches of international law]";[85] suggests that

> [w]hen both alternative paths of human rights law and the law of belligerent occupation are open to a protected person whose rights have been infringed in an occupied territory, there may be a practical advantage in exploring the former, since an international mechanism may be readily available, enabling the injured party to seek and obtain effective redress . . . [86]

and points out that, in the event of an irreconcilable conflict between the two fields of law, "the special law of belligerent occupation trumps the general law of human rights on the ground of *lex specialis derogat lex generali.*"[87]

As noted earlier, on June 28, 2004, CPA Administrator Paul Bremer formally transferred political authority to the Iraqi interim government,[88] two days prior to the date decreed by the Security Council in Resolution 1546.[89] At that time, pursuant to Resolution 1546, the occupation came to an end and Iraq asserted its full sovereignty.[90] To be sure, as reported earlier, Dinstein, quoting and citing Adam Roberts, has suggested that the occupation came to a close only "notionally" because there was little change on the ground following the decreed termination of the occupation.[91]

At present, however, the occupation has come to a close more than notionally. Exercising its sovereign powers, the government of Iraq has entered into two international agreements with the United States that have radically changed the power balance in Iraq.

The Strategic Framework Agreement and the Security Agreement

In Resolution 1511,[92] the Security Council authorized the multinational force in Iraq. This resolution was followed by Resolution 1546,[93] which, in addition to bringing the occupation of Iraq to an end, reaffirmed the authorization for the multinational force.[94] Resolution 1546 was in turn followed by a series of other resolutions that reaffirmed and extended the authorization for the multinational force. The last of these was Resolution 1790,[95] which provided that the authorization of the multinational force would expire on January 1, 2009. Prior to the expiration of the authorization of the multinational force, on November 17, 2008 the United States and Iraq entered into two bilateral agreements that took the authorization's place.

The two agreements are (1) the Strategic Framework Agreement for a Relationship of Friendship and Cooperation between the United States of America and the Republic of Iraq (SFA)[96] and (2) the Agreement Between the United States of America and the Republic of Iraq on the Withdrawal of United States Forces from Iraq and the Organization of Their Activities during Their Temporary Presence in Iraq (SA).[97] Interestingly, the executive branch initially intended that the SFA would be a non-binding political commitment in order that it would be free from the US constitutional constraints that apply to international legal agreements;[98] however, the United States and Iraq decided to recast the SFA as a legally binding treaty commitment, like the SA.[99]

It is noteworthy that neither agreement uses the term "status of forces agreement" or SOFA.[100] Commander Trevor A. Rush has explained the reason for the absence of the term SOFA:

> First, in a technical sense, it is not accurate to use the term SOFA for either of the two agreements. The SFA is an agreement that defines the long-term strategic relationship between the U.S. Government and the [government of Iraq]. It contains none of the typical provisions one might expect to find in a SOFA and, with regard to "Defense and Security Cooperation," the SFA contains no actual substance. Instead, it specifically refers to the U.S.-Iraq SA, for the nature of that cooperation. On the other hand, the SA goes far beyond a regular SOFA, to include authorizing combat missions and detentions, discussing the deterrence of "security threats" and the termination of U.N. Security Council measures, as well as U.S. efforts to safeguard Iraqi economic assets and obtain Iraq debt forgiveness.[[101]]
>
> Second, and more importantly, the reason not to use the term SOFA for these two agreements is related to the significant political sensitivities surrounding the presence of foreign forces in the Middle East. The coalition campaigns in Iraq and Afghanistan have added new twenty-first century images to those deep-seated regional concerns. History has witnessed various western powers seek to control Middle Eastern territories, but these attempts at colonization and foreign domination have ultimately, always, been rejected. In this context, a "SOFA" can give the impression of a willing consent to *permanent* foreign military occupation. Skeptics need only look to such places as Europe, Korea, and Japan and see more than half a century of U.S. military presence operating under SOFAs.[102]

Rush gives an extensive and excellent overview of both the SFA and the SA. No attempt will be made in this article to match Rush's efforts. It is significant, however, that Rush is of the view that "these U.S.-Iraq agreements should be heralded as a major step forward in Iraq's assumption of responsibility for its own security and governance."[103] At the same time, Rush recognizes that application of the agreements can give rise to disputes between the United States and Iraq. He notes that, at the time of writing, the United States had already been accused of violating the SA through a military raid that left two people dead,[104] and suggests that "the first true test of public perception could come in 2009 if an Iraqi referendum on the agreements is held as planned."[105] At this writing, however, it is uncertain whether such a referendum will take place. Although Sunni lawmakers insisted that a referendum on the SA be held as a condition for their support, and a referendum was originally scheduled for July of 2009, it was delayed. In August, Iraq's cabinet officially set a new date of January 16, 2010 for the referendum, a date coinciding with nationwide parliamentary polls.[106]

The SA calls for all American troops to be out of Iraq by the end of 2011.[107] If Iraqi voters reject the SA in a referendum held on January 16, 2010, this would force an accelerated US withdrawal, resulting in a full American troop withdrawal almost a year ahead of schedule. Recent reports, however, indicate that worry over Iraq's ability to take over security from the United States faster—should the referendum force an early American withdrawal—"appears to have cooled some Sunnis' insistence on the referendum," and some Sunni politicians have reportedly said that a referendum was no longer necessary because the US military had so far abided by the SA.[108]

Even if no referendum is held on the SA, Article 30, paragraphs 1 and 3, of the SA allows either party to terminate the agreement one year after written notice is given to the other party.[109] As noted by Rush in his article, there are a number of provisions in the SA that may prove to be significant friction points between the United States and Iraq.[110] As to ways to minimize the chances of a breakdown in US-Iraqi relations leading to termination of the SA, Rush sets forth the following poignant suggestions in the concluding paragraph of his article:

> There are two clear ways to help ensure the SA is viewed positively by the Iraqis. First, U.S. leaders must make every effort to adhere to the terms. This article has identified various gray areas where friction may occur. These areas must be handled delicately and in cooperation with Iraqi counter-parts [sic]. Although the United States must protect its interests, it must not do so in a way that sacrifices the greater objective of maintaining good relations with Iraq. The United States cannot be seen as exploiting its position or strong-arming Iraq. To do so risks public condemnation and loss of public support. The second way to help ensure the SA is viewed positively falls on the shoulders of every Soldier, Sailor, Airman, Marine, Coast Guardsman, and Civilian of the U.S. Forces serving in Iraq. There is no room for any misconduct toward Iraqi citizens, nor can individuals afford to act beyond the scope of their missions. A single failure in this area is potentially catastrophic to the U.S.-Iraq Security Agreement. The U.S. chain of command must continue to impress upon all members of the U.S. Forces in Iraq that mission success can only be achieved through their individual good

> conduct and their good relations with the Iraqis that they are in Iraq to support and protect.[111]

A Few Concluding Observations

At this writing, the SA appears to be functioning effectively. In accordance with Article 24 of the SA,[112] all US combat forces have been withdrawn from Iraqi cities, villages and localities and have been stationed in agreed facilities and areas outside these cities, villages and localities. Although this is not entirely clear from published reports, it appears that the primary function of US troops in their new locations is to train and advise Iraqi forces, rather than carry a major burden in combat.

To be sure, areas of instability still remain, especially in the city of Mosul and northern Iraq, where unresolved Kurdish-Arab tensions over oil and political control of the area remain. Nonetheless, the top US commander in Iraq, General Raymond Odierno, has reportedly said he is

> increasingly confident Iraq's recent security gains are irreversible despite high-profile attacks like the string of bombings in Baghdad last month [August] that killed roughly 100 people. "We'll have bad days in Iraq," he said. "But the bad days are becoming fewer. The numbers of deaths are becoming fewer. We're making slow, deliberate progress."[113]

Perhaps the most encouraging development at this juncture is reports of the decline of the religious and sectarian parties that have fractured Iraq since 2003 and of a movement emphasizing national unity that seeks to reach across ethnic or sectarian lines.[114] If this movement continues, the chances of the national elections scheduled for January 2010 going well will greatly improve.

Last year the United States and Iraq agreed that American combat forces would be out of Iraq by August 2010, leaving fifty thousand troops to advise and support the Iraqis.[115] General Odierno, however, has reportedly stated that he could reduce American forces to that level even before the summer of 2010 if the expected January elections in Iraq go well.[116] This could ease the current strain on US forces and free up extra combat troops for duty in the Afghanistan war, especially if the Obama administration decides to accede to the military's request for more combat troops in Afghanistan.

There is, of course, no guarantee of success in Iraq. But it is clear that ultimate success or failure is now largely in the hands of a sovereign Iraq government. If success in Iraq is ultimately achieved, the implications for greater stability in the Middle East will be enormous. Not a bad denouement for a "war of choice."

Notes

1. The author was the commentator on the panel "Issues Spanning the War in Iraq," which was the closing panel of the conference.

2. The concept of the "fog of law" is not, of course, original with me, especially as it applies to armed conflict. *See, e.g.,* Michael J. Glennon, *The Fog of Law: Self-Defense, Inherence, and Incoherence in Article 51 of the United Nations Charter*, 25 HARVARD JOURNAL OF LAW & PUBLIC POLICY 539 (2002). *See also* Yoram Dinstein, *Concluding Remarks on Terrorism and Afghanistan,* 39 ISRAEL YEARBOOK ON HUMAN RIGHTS 315, 330 (2009) ("the fog of the law of war").

3. Michael J. Glennon has famously and controversially contended that "international 'rules'" concerning use of force are no longer considered obligatory by States. *See* Glennon, *supra* note 2, at 540, 541. For a more elaborate development of this thesis, see MICHAEL J. GLENNON, LIMITS OF LAW, PREROGATIVES OF POWER: INTERVENTIONISM AFTER KOSOVO (2001).

4. *See* Andru E. Wall, *Was the 2003 Invasion of Iraq Legal?*, which is Chapter IV in this volume, at 69.

5. Article 2(4) provides: "All Members shall refrain in their international relations from the threat or use of force against the territorial integrity or political independence of any state, or in any other manner inconsistent with the Purposes of the United Nations."

6. Article 51 of the UN Charter provides:

> Nothing in the present Charter shall impair the inherent right of individual or collective self-defence if an armed attack occurs against a Member of the United Nations, until the Security Council has taken measures necessary to maintain international peace and security. Measures taken by Members in the exercise of this right of self-defence shall be immediately reported to the Security Council and shall not in any way affect the authority and responsibility of the Security Council under the present Charter to take at any time such action as it deems necessary in order to maintain or restore international peace and security.

7. S.C. Res. 1441, U.N. Doc. S/RES/1441(Nov. 8, 2002).

8. JOHN F. MURPHY, THE UNITED STATES AND THE RULE OF LAW IN INTERNATIONAL AFFAIRS 169 (2004).

9. Michael J. Glennon, *Why the Security Council Failed*, FOREIGN AFFAIRS, May–June 2003, at 16, 27.

10. *Id.* at 16.

11. For a detailed discussion of the extent of the dealings between the Saddam government and France, Russia and China, see JOHN F. MURPHY, THE EVOLVING DIMENSIONS OF INTERNATIONAL LAW: HARD CHOICES FOR THE WORLD COMMUNITY 127–32 (2010).

12. Michael Reisman, *Coercion and Self-Determination: Construing Charter Article 2(4)*, 78 AMERICAN JOURNAL OF INTERNATIONAL LAW 642, 643 (1984).

13. *Id.*

14. Oscar Schachter, *The Legality of Pro-Democratic Invasion*, 78 AMERICAN JOURNAL OF INTERNATIONAL LAW 645 (1984).

15. *Id.* at 649.

16. Glennon, *supra* note 9, at 16.

17. *See* MURPHY, *supra* note 8, at 177–81.

18. Lee Feinstein & Anne-Marie Slaughter, *A Duty to Prevent*, FOREIGN AFFAIRS, Jan.–Feb. 2004, at 136, 137.

19. *Id.* at 138–39.

20. *See* S.C. Res. 1284, U.N. Doc. S/RES/1284 (Dec. 17, 1999).

21. For discussion, see MURPHY, *supra* note 8, at 152–54.

22. *See* operative para. 3, S.C. Res. 1441, *supra* note 7.

23. *Id.*, operative para. 4. In operative paragraph 11, the Council "[*d*]*irects* the Executive Chairman of UNMOVIC and the Director General of IAEA to report immediately to the Council any interference by Iraq with inspection activities, as well as any failure by Iraq to comply with its disarmament obligations, including its obligations regarding inspections under this resolution." In operative paragraph 12, the Council "[*d*]*ecides* to convene immediately upon receipt of a report in accordance with paragraphs 4 or 11 above, in order to consider the situation and the need for full compliance with the relevant Council resolutions in order to secure international peace and security." Lastly, operative paragraph 13 "[*r*]*ecalls*, in that context, that the Council has repeatedly warned Iraq that it will face serious consequences as a result of its continued violations of its obligations."

24. *See* MURPHY, *supra* note 8, at 170.

25. Feinstein & Slaughter, *supra* note 18, at 148.

26. *Id.* at 148–149.

27. Convention No. IV Respecting the Laws and Customs of War on Land, Regulations Respecting the Laws and Customs of War on Land, Annex, Oct. 18, 1907, 36 Stat. 2227, *reprinted in* DOCUMENTS ON THE LAWS OF WAR 69 (Adam Roberts & Richard Guelff eds., 3d ed. 2000).

28. Convention Relative to the Protection of Civilian Persons in Time of War, Aug. 12, 1949, 6 U.S.T. 3516, 75 U.N.T.S. 287, *reprinted in* DOCUMENTS ON THE LAWS OF WAR, *supra* note 27, at 301.

29. *See, e.g.,* Gregory H. Fox, *The Occupation of Iraq*, 36 GEORGETOWN JOURNAL OF INTERNATIONAL LAW 195, 229–32 (2005).

30. *See Preface to the Paperback Edition, in* EYAL BENVENISTI, THE INTERNATIONAL LAW OF OCCUPATION ix (2004).

31. *Id.*

32. David J. Scheffer, *Beyond Occupation Law*, 97 AMERICAN JOURNAL OF INTERNATIONAL LAW 842 (2003).

33. *Id.* at 849.

34. *Id.*

35. *Id.* at 850, citing, *inter alia*, the Letter of 8 May 2003 from the Permanent Representatives of the United States of America and the United Kingdom of Great Britain and Northern Ireland to the President of the Security Council, U.N. Doc. S/2003/538 (2003).

36. S.C. Res. 1483, U.N. Doc. S/RES/1483 (May 22, 2003).

37. *Id.*, operative para. 5.

38. *See* Scheffer, *supra* note 32, at 850, citing Roger Hardy, *Struggle for Power in Iraq*, BBC NEWS, Apr. 13, 2003, http://news.bbc.co.uk/2/hi/middle_east/2944915.stm; Jane Perlez, *U.S. Team Arrives in Iraq to Establish Postwar Base*, NEW YORK TIMES, Apr. 9, 2003, at B10; Richard W. Stevenson, *Bush Sees Aid Role of U.N. as Limited in Rebuilding Iraq*, NEW YORK TIMES, Apr. 9, 2003, at A1.

39. See Benvenisti, supra note 30, at ix, citing the preamble to the Coalition Provisional Order No. 1 (De-Baathification of Iraqi Society), May 16, 2003, *available at* http:// www.iraqcoalition .org/regulations/20030603_CPAMEMO_1_Implementation_of_De-Ba _athification.pdf.

40. S.C. Res. 1511, U.N. Doc. S/RES/1511 (Oct. 16, 2003).

41. YORAM DINSTEIN, THE INTERNATIONAL LAW OF BELLIGERENT OCCUPATION 12 (2009).

42. Scheffer, *supra* note 32, at 846 n.18 (citing as examples "the Security Council's decisions regarding the Development Fund for Iraq, the management of petroleum, petroleum products,

and natural gas, and the formation of an Iraqi interim administration as a transitional administration run by Iraqis").

43. Article 103 of the UN Charter provides that "[i]n the event of a conflict between the obligations of the Members of the United Nations under the present Charter and their obligations under any other international agreement, their obligations under the present Charter shall prevail."

44. Scheffer, *supra* note 32, at 846 n.18.

45. *Id.* at 855–56.

46. *Id.* at 857.

47. Fox, *supra* note 29, at 229–97.

48. *Id.* at 246, 255–62.

49. *Id.* at 295–97.

50. BENVENISTI, *supra* note 30, at xi.

51. *Id.* at xii. As one example, Benvenisti mentions "the question of whether an occupant can undertake international obligations as part of its temporary administration of the occupied territory." *Id.*

52. Scheffer, *supra* note 32, at 843.

53. *See, e.g.*, Neil MacFarquhar, *When to Step In to Stop War Crimes Causes Fissures*, NEW YORK TIMES, July 23, 2009, at A10; *An idea whose time has come–and gone?*, ECONOMIST, July 25, 2009, at 58.

54. *See* DINSTEIN, *supra* note 41, at 12.

55. S.C. Res. 1546, U.N. Doc. S/RES/1546 (June 8, 2004).

56. *Id.*, operative para. 2.

57. *See* Fox, *supra* note 29, at 227.

58. *See* DINSTEIN, *supra* note 41, at 273. In using the term "notionally," Dinstein cites and quotes Adam Roberts, *Transformative Military Occupation: Applying the Laws of War and Human Rights*, *in* INTERNATIONAL LAW AND ARMED CONFLICT: EXPLORING THE FAULTLINES, ESSAYS IN HONOUR OF YORAM DINSTEIN 448 (Michael Schmitt & Jelena Pelic eds., 2007).

59. International Covenant on Civil and Political Rights, G.A. Res. 2200A (XXI), U.N. Doc. A/6316 (Dec. 16, 1966) [hereinafter ICCPR].

60. *See, e.g.*, Ralph Wilde, *The Applicability of International Human Rights Law to the Coalition Provisional Authority (CPA) and Foreign Military Presence in Iraq*, 11 ILSA JOURNAL OF INTERNATIONAL & COMPARATIVE LAW 485, 487 (2005), citing US Department of Defense, Working Group Report on Detainee Interrogations in the Global War on Terrorism: Assessment of Legal, Historical, Policy, and Operational Considerations (Apr. 4, 2003), *available at* http://www.defenselink.mil/news/Jun2004/d20040622doc8.pdf; U.N. Human Rights Committee, *Third Periodic Report of the United States of America*, U.N. Doc. CCPR/C/USA/Q/3/Annex (Oct. 21, 2005); *United States Responses to Selected Recommendations of the Human Rights Committee*, U.N. Doc. CCPR/C/USA/CO/3/Rev.1/Add.1 (2007).

61. *See* U.N. Human Rights Committee, *Concluding Observations of the Human Rights Committee: United States of America*, U.N. Doc. CCPR/C/USA/CO/3/Rev.1 (Dec. 18, 2006).

62. Legal Consequences of the Construction of a Wall in the Occupied Palestinian Territory, Advisory Opinion, 2004 I.C.J. 136, paras. 108–9, 111 (July 9) [hereinafter Legal Consequences of the Construction of a Wall].

63. Convention against Torture and Other Cruel, Inhuman or Degrading Treatment or Punishment arts. 3(1), 5(1), 6(1), 7(1), 11(1), 12, 13, 16(1), 20, Dec. 10, 1984, 1465 U.N.T.S. 85.

64. J. HERMAN BURGERS & HANS DANELIUS, THE UNITED NATIONS CONVENTION AGAINST TORTURE: A HANDBOOK ON THE CONVENTION AGAINST TORTURE AND OTHER

CRUEL, INHUMAN OR DEGRADING TREATMENT OR PUNISHMENT 131 (1988), *cited* and *quoted in* LOUIS HENKIN ET AL., HUMAN RIGHTS 22 (2d ed. 2009).

65. U.N. Committee against Torture, *Conclusions and Recommendations on the United States' Second Periodic Report*, para. 15, CAT/C/USA/CO/2 (July 25, 2006), *cited* and *quoted in* LOUIS HENKIN ET AL., *supra* note 64, at 22–23.

66. DINSTEIN, *supra* note 41, citing Case Concerning Armed Activities on the Territory of the Congo (Dem. Rep. Congo v. Uganda), 2005 I.C.J. 1 (Dec. 19).

67. Legality of the Threat or Use of Nuclear Weapons, Advisory Opinion, 1996 I.C.J. 226 (July 8) [hereinafter Nuclear Weapons].

68. Legal Consequences of the Construction of a Wall, *supra* note 62, at 136.

69. Nuclear Weapons, *supra* note 67, at 240.

70. Legal Consequences of the Construction of a Wall, *supra* note 62, at 1038.

71. DINSTEIN, *supra* note 41, at 70.

72. Article 4(1) of the Covenant provides:

> In time of public emergency which threatens the life of the nation and the existence of which is officially proclaimed, the States Parties to the present Covenant may take measures derogating from their obligations under the present Covenant to the extent strictly required by the exigencies of the situation, provided that such measures are not inconsistent with their other obligations under international law and do not involve discrimination solely on the ground of race, colour, sex, language, religion or social origin.

73. DINSTEIN, *supra* note 41, at 72.

74. Thomas Buergenthal, *To Respect and to Ensure State Obligations and Permissible Derogations, in* THE INTERNATIONAL BILL OF RIGHTS: THE COVENANT ON CIVIL AND POLITICAL RIGHTS 72, 79 n.375 (Louis Henkin ed., 1981). *Cited in* DINSTEIN, *supra* note 41, at 72.

75. DINSTEIN, *supra* note 41, at 71–74.

76. *Id.* at 74–77.

77. ICCPR, *supra* note 59, art. 4(1); European Convention for the Protection of Human Rights and Fundamental Freedoms art. 25(2), Nov. 4, 1950, Europ. T.S. No. 5, 213 U.N.T.S. 222; American Convention on Human Rights art. 27(2), Nov. 22, 1969, O.A.S.T.S. No. 36, 1144 U.N.T.S. 123.

78. DINSTEIN, *supra* note 41, at 75.

79. *Id.* at 75–77.

80. The two advisory opinions referred to are Habeas Corpus in Emergency Situations (Arts. 27(2) and 7(6) of the American Convention on Human Rights), Advisory Opinion OC-8/87, Inter-Am. Ct. H.R. (ser. A) No. 8 (Jan. 30, 1987) and Judicial Guarantees in States of Emergency (Arts. 27(2), 25 and 8 American Convention on Human Rights), Advisory Opinion OC-9/87, 1987 Inter-Am. Ct. H.R. (ser. A) No. 9 (Oct. 8, 1987).

81. DINSTEIN, *supra* note 41, at 76–77, citing U.N. Human Rights Committee, *General Comment 29: States of Emergency (Article 4)*, paras. 13–15, U.N. Doc. CCPR/C/21/Rev.1/Add.11 (Aug. 31, 2001).

82. DINSTEIN, *supra* note 41, at 77–79.

83. *Id.* at 80–81.

84. *Id.* at 81–88.

85. *Id.* at 81.

86. *Id.* at 85.

87. *Id.* To illustrate an application of the *lex specialis* rule, Dinstein quotes from the International Court of Justice's *Nuclear Weapons* advisory opinion. The issue facing the Court in these proceedings was the relationship between the law of international armed conflict and Article 6(1) of the ICCPR, which provides that "[n]o one shall be arbitrarily deprived of his life." The Court stated:

> In principle, the right not arbitrarily to be deprived of one's life applies also in hostilities. The test of what is an arbitrary deprivation of life, however, then falls to be determined by the applicable *lex specialis*, namely, the law applicable in armed conflict which is designed to regulate the conduct of hostilities. Thus whether a particular loss of life, through the use of a certain weapon in warfare, is to be considered an arbitrary deprivation of life contrary to Article 6 of the Covenant, can only be decided by reference to the law applicable in armed conflict and not deduced from the terms of the Covenant itself.

Nuclear Weapons, *supra* note 67, at 240.

88. *See supra* text accompanying note 57.

89. *See* S.C. Res. 1546, *supra* note 55.

90. *See id.*, operative para. 2, quoted *supra* in text accompanying note 56.

91. *See* Dinstein analysis, *supra* note 58, and accompanying text.

92. S.C. Res. 1511, *supra* note 40.

93. *See* S.C. Res. 1546, *supra* note 55.

94. *Id.*, operative para. 9.

95. S.C. Res. 1790, U.N. Doc. S/RES/1790 (Dec. 18, 2007).

96. Strategic Framework Agreement for a Relationship of Friendship and Cooperation between the United States of America and the Republic of Iraq, U.S.-Iraq, Nov. 17, 2008, *available at* http://www.mnf-iraq.com/images/CGs_Messages/strategic_framework_agreement.pdf.

97. Agreement Between the United States of America and the Republic of Iraq on the Withdrawal of United States Forces from Iraq and the Organization of Their Activities during Their Temporary Presence in Iraq, U.S.-Iraq, Nov. 17, 2008, *available at* http://www.mnf-iraq.com/images/CGs_Messages/security_agreement.pdf [hereinafter SA].

98. *See* Duncan B. Hollis & Joshua J. Newcomber, *"Political" Commitments and the Constitution*, 49 VIRGINIA JOURNAL OF INTERNATIONAL LAW 507, 510 (2009).

99. *Id.* at 510.

100. *See* Trevor A. Rush, *Don't Call It a SOFA! An Overview of the U.S. Security Agreement*, ARMY LAWYER, May 2009, at 34.

101. Rush cites the following provisions of the SA: Article 4 (missions), Article 22 (detention), Article 25 (measures to terminate the application of Chapter VII to Iraq), Article 26 (Iraqi assets) and Article 27 (deterrence of security threats).

102. Rush, *supra* note 100, at 34–35.

103. *Id.* at 35.

104. *Id.*

105. *Id.*

106. Gina Chon, *Iraq Vote on Pullout Put on Back Burner*, WSJ.COM, Oct. 5, 2009, http://online.wsj.com/article/SB125470311713563191.html.

107. *See* SA, *supra* note 97, art. 30, para. 1.

108. Chon, *supra* note 106.

109. Article 30, paragraph 1, of the SA provides: "This Agreement shall be effective for a period of three years, unless terminated sooner by either Party pursuant to paragraph 3 of

this Article." Paragraph 3 provides: "This Agreement shall terminate one year after a Party provides written notification to the other Party to that effect."

110. For example, Rush highlights Article 4 of the SA, which covers "missions" or military operations. As to Article 4, Rush states:

> Article 4 of the SA covers "missions" or military operations and is one of the articles which make the agreement fundamentally different from all other U.S. SOFAs. Article 4 begins with a request from the GOI [government of Iraq] for "the temporary assistance of the United States Forces for the purposes of supporting Iraq in its efforts to maintain security and stability in Iraq, including cooperation in the conduct of operations against al-Qaeda and other terrorist groups, outlaw groups, and remnants of the former regime." Standard SOFAs do not discuss engaging in combat operations, whereas this SA provision invites U.S. Forces to participate in Iraq's internal armed conflict. It also provides internationally accepted legal authority for U.S. Forces to conduct combat operations in Iraq. This was necessary to fill the legal vacuum created by the expiration of [UN Security Council Resolution] 1790.
>
> The SA's grant of authority for military operations is based upon Iraq's sovereignty, which includes the right to consent to the presence of the U.S. military and to allow the United States to conduct military operations that comply with international and domestic Iraqi law. This differs from the U.N. Security Council's Chapter VII authorization to the multinational force to "take all necessary measures to contribute to the maintenance of security and stability in Iraq." Now, instead of U.S. Forces operating unilaterally, subject only to multinational force regulations and rules, their operations must be . . . "conducted with the agreement of the Government of Iraq" and, in fact, must "be fully coordinated with Iraqi authorities." This coordination "shall be overseen by a Joint Military Operations Coordination Committee [hereinafter JMOCC] to be established pursuant to" the SA. Lastly, military operations "shall not infringe upon the sovereignty of Iraq and its national interests, as defined by the Government of Iraq."
>
> The practical reality of these limitations is that U.S. commanders must work "by, with, and through" the Iraqis and develop processes for obtaining the appropriate Iraqi operating authorities. Preferably this cooperation and coordination is occurring at the lowest levels through U.S. commanders' relationships with the GOI and Iraqi Security Forces (ISF) leadership. However, the exact level of mission coordination required by Article 4 may prove to be a significant friction point between the United States and Iraq. For instance, in April 2009, U.S. Forces conducted a raid in Wasit province that left two Iraqis dead and resulted in the detention of six men. The raid "set off public protests and drew a pointed complaint from Prime Minister Nuri Kamal al-Maliki that the operation violated [the SA]." U.S. Forces issued a statement that "the raid had been 'fully coordinated and approved' by the Iraqi government." At the same time, "the Iraqi Defense Ministry announced it had detained two top Iraqi military officials in Wasit province for authorizing the American raid without obtaining approval from their commanders." This incident illustrates the difficulties of coordination, but despite the inherent challenges in such processes, the transition of security responsibilities to the ISF is a necessary part of creating a stable Iraq in which the ISF assumes the major role for defending the nation.

Rush, *supra* note 100, at 38–40.

111. *Id.* at 60.

112. Article 24 of the SA, *supra* note 97, reads as follows:

Article 24
Withdrawal of the United States Forces from Iraq

Recognizing the performance and increasing capacity of the Iraqi Security Forces, the assumption of full security responsibility by those Forces, and based upon the strong relationship between the Parties, an agreement on the following has been reached:

1. All the United States Forces shall withdraw from all Iraqi territory no later than December 31, 2011.

2. All United States combat forces shall withdraw from Iraqi cities, villages, and localities no later than the time at which Iraqi Security Forces assume full responsibility for security in an Iraqi province, provided that such withdrawal is completed no later than June 30, 2009.

3. United States combat forces withdrawn pursuant to paragraph 2 above shall be stationed in the agreed facilities and areas outside cities, villages, and localities to be designated by the JMOCC [Joint Military Operations Coordination Committee] before the date established in paragraph 2 above.

4. The United States recognizes the sovereign right of the Government of Iraq to request the departure of the United States Forces from Iraq at any time. The Government of Iraq recognizes the sovereign right of the United States to withdraw the United States Forces from Iraq at any time.

5. The Parties agree to establish mechanisms and arrangements to reduce the number of the United States Forces during the periods of time that have been determined, and they shall agree on the locations where the United States Forces will be present.

113. *See* Youchi J. Dreazen, *U.S. General Says Iraq Exit Is on Track*, WSJ.COM, Sept. 30, 2009, http://online.wsj.com/article/SB125426788854050939.html.

114. *See* Steven Lee Myers, *National Unity is Rallying Cry in Iraq Elections*, NEW YORK TIMES, Oct. 1, 2009, at A1.

115. *See* Thom Shanker, *U.S. General Says Iraq Troop Reductions May Quicken if Elections Go Well*, NEW YORK TIMES, Sept. 30, 2009, at A5.

116. *Id.*

PART III

THE LEGAL BASES FOR MILITARY OPERATIONS

III

Legal Bases for Military Operations in Iraq

Raul A. "Pete" Pedrozo*

Introduction

On March 23, 2003 coalition forces invaded Iraq after it was found to be in material breach of its obligations under numerous UN Security Council resolutions. Less than two months later, on May 1, 2003, President Bush made his historic "mission accomplished" speech from the flight deck of the *USS Abraham Lincoln*, declaring that "major combat operations in Iraq have ended [and that] in the battle of Iraq, the United States and our allies have prevailed."[1] Six years later, US combat troops remain in Iraq fighting a violent insurgency. Although the situation has improved over the past year, President Obama has vowed to end US combat operations no later than August 31, 2010.[2] Even if the President does not live up to his campaign promise, all US forces must withdraw from Iraq no later than December 31, 2011, unless otherwise authorized by the Iraqi government.[3] This article will briefly discuss the legal bases for the invasion of Iraq in March 2003, the legal bases for follow-on operations after May 1, 2003 and the characterization of the conflict across the spectrum of operations.

Legal Bases for Launch of Operations

Justifications for Going to War

On March 23, 2003 US, British and other coalition forces invaded Iraq. The military intervention was justified primarily along two lines: repeated Iraqi violations

---

* Associate Professor, International Law Department, US Naval War College.

of a number of United Nations Security Council resolutions and the right of self-defense, and, to a lesser extent, humanitarian intervention.[4] While I tend to agree with the UK Attorney General that the right of self-defense and the principle of humanitarian intervention did not provide a sound legal basis for the invasion,[5] I do believe there was sufficient justification to attack Iraq based on its continuous and flagrant disregard of its disarmament and other obligations under numerous Security Council resolutions. It is true that weapons inspectors failed to find large quantities of chemical and biological weapons following the invasion and that evidence relied on by the United States and the United Kingdom to justify the invasion—e.g., Iraqi ties to al-Qaeda, Iraq's pursuit of biological, chemical and nuclear weapons programs, etc.—was subsequently shown to be based on fraudulent documents or unsubstantiated assertions of Iraqi defectors.[6] However, the fact remains that, at the time of the invasion, Iraq was in breach of all fourteen of its weapons of mass destruction (WMD) obligations set out in numerous Security Council resolutions, as well as its obligations under Resolution 687 (1991)[7] to renounce terrorism; under Resolution 688 (1991)[8] to cease internal oppression of its civilian population; under Resolutions 686 (1991),[9] 687 and 1284 (1999)[10] to account for Kuwaiti and third-country nationals wrongfully detained by Iraq; and Resolutions 686 and 687 to return all Kuwaiti property it had seized.[11]

Iraq's Violations of Its Obligations under UN Security Council Resolutions

No one disagrees with the fact that Iraq flagrantly and repeatedly violated countless Security Council resolutions,[12] as well as its obligations under various international instruments,[13] and that it failed to cooperate with United Nations and International Atomic Energy Agency (IAEA) weapons inspectors for more than two decades. Four months after agreeing to the ceasefire terms in Resolution 687 that ended the first Gulf War, Iraq commenced its pattern of noncompliance with the ceasefire agreement and failure to fully cooperate with UN and IAEA weapons inspectors.[14] This pattern continued throughout the remainder of the decade,[15] culminating in US and UK airstrikes against military targets in Iraq in December 1998 after the UN Special Commission (UNSCOM) submitted a report to the Security Council indicating that Iraq had failed to cooperate fully with its inspectors.[16] Iraqi officials did not allow weapons inspectors to return to Iraq until 2002.[17]

Adoption of UN Security Council Resolution 1441 (2002)

In September 2002, Iraqi officials met with UN Monitoring, Verification and Inspection Commission (UNMOVIC)[18] and IAEA officials to discuss the resumption of weapons inspections in Iraq. During that meeting, Iraqi officials agreed to accept "all the rights of inspection provided for in all of the relevant Security Council resolutions . . . [and that this] acceptance was stated to be without any conditions attached."[19] Specifically, Iraq agreed that UNMOVIC and the IAEA would be "granted immediate, unconditional and unrestricted access to sites" in Iraq.[20] On October 8, 2002, UNMOVIC and the IAEA sent a letter to the government of Iraq requesting that it confirm the terms of the inspection arrangements agreed to in September. Concerned by the continued failure by Iraq to provide the requested confirmation, the Security Council adopted Resolution 1441 on November 2, 2002 in order to afford Iraq "a final opportunity to comply with its disarmament obligations under relevant resolutions of the Council."[21] Two months later, in its Twelfth Quarterly Report to the Security Council, UNMOVIC reported that Iraq had yet to comply as required with its disarmament obligations.[22]

The Need for Further Security Council Action?

In Resolution 1441 the Security Council decided, *inter alia*,

- That Iraq was in "material breach of its obligations under relevant resolutions," including Resolution 687 (operative paragraph 1);
- To afford Iraq a "final opportunity to comply with its disarmament obligations" under previous resolutions and establish an enhanced inspection regime (operative paragraph 2);
- That "false statements or omissions in the declarations submitted by Iraq pursuant to this resolution and failure by Iraq at any time to comply with and cooperate fully in the implementation of this resolution shall constitute a further material breach of Iraq's obligations and will be reported to the Council for assessment in accordance with paragraphs 11 and 12" (operative paragraph 4);
- That "UNMOVIC and . . . IAEA . . . report immediately to the Council any interference by Iraq with inspection activities, as well as any failure by Iraq to comply with its disarmament obligations, including its obligations regarding inspections under this resolution" (operative paragraph 11);
- To "convene immediately upon receipt of a report in accordance with paragraph 4 or 11 . . ., in order to consider the situation and the need for full compliance with all of the relevant Council resolutions in order to secure international peace and security" (operative paragraph 12).

It is clear from the foregoing that even though Iraq was found to be in "material breach" of its obligations under Resolution 687 and other relevant resolutions, the Security Council did not intend that the use of force authorization in Resolution 678 should revive immediately, since Resolution 1441 afforded Iraq a "final opportunity to comply with its disarmament obligations."[23] What is less clear is whether paragraph 12 of 1441 required the Council to adopt a second resolution before States could use force against Iraq. The US[24] and UK[25] ambassadors clearly believed that a second resolution was not necessary. France, Russia, China, Ireland, Mexico, Bulgaria, Colombia, Cameroon and Syria indicated that the use of force had to be authorized by the Security Council.[26] A close analysis of the language in the resolution, as well as that of previous resolutions, supports the US and British position.

Resolution 687 "suspended, but did not terminate," the authority to use force in Resolution 678.[27] Moreover, the ceasefire was conditioned on Iraqi compliance with the obligations imposed by 687 and subsequent relevant resolutions.[28] In this regard, the Security Council decided in Resolution 1441 that Iraq "has been and remains in material breach of its obligations under relevant resolutions," including 687, and indicated that Iraq had "been warned repeatedly that 'serious consequences'" would result from continued violations of its obligations.[29] Resolution 1441 also makes clear that compliance with its terms was Iraq's last chance before the ceasefire resolution would be enforced should Iraq fail to comply with the enhanced inspection regime established by paragraphs 3 and 4.[30]

Pursuant to paragraph 11 of 1441, UNMOVIC reported to the Security Council in its Twelfth Quarterly Report in January 2003 that Iraq was not in compliance with the disarmament obligations established in paragraphs 3 and 4 and other relevant resolutions.[31] The Council then convened "in order to consider the situation and the need for full compliance with all of the relevant Council resolutions in order to secure international peace and security."[32] But does paragraph 12 require a further Security Council resolution authorizing the use of force? I would suggest that the answer to that question is "no."

Resolution 1441 does not indicate that the Security Council must "decide" what action to take based on a report from UNMOVIC that Iraq is not in compliance with its disarmament obligations. It simply requires that the Council "consider the situation." There is a clear distinction between the meaning of "consider" and "decide" in resolutions.[33] Note, for example, the language used in paragraph 33 of Resolution 1874 (2009), condemning North Korea's nuclear test of May 25, 2009, in which the Council specifically states "that further decisions will be required, should additional measures be necessary."[34] Moreover, during the drafting of 1441 France and Russia proposed language that would have required the Security Council to "decide" that subsequent Iraqi conduct amounted to a "material breach"; however, the proposal was rejected by the US and UK representatives precisely to avoid the need for a second resolution.[35] The US delegation clearly indicated throughout the debate "that they would not accept a text which subjected the use of force to a further Council decision," arguing that the determination of "material breach" in paragraphs 1 and 4 of 1441 remained valid regardless of further Security Council action.[36] Therefore, the French and other members of the Council knew what they were voting for when they chose to use the word "consider" rather than "decide" in paragraph 12. Additionally, the Security Council determination in Resolution 1137 (1997) that the situation in Iraq "continues to constitute a threat to international peace and security" remained in effect.[37] Under these circumstances, Iraq's failure to comply with the enhanced inspection regime established in 1441, as reported by UNMOVIC, revived the use of force authorization contained in Resolution 678.[38]

Operation Desert Fox (1998)

It is also important to note that the United States and United Kingdom had taken a similar position in 1998, when US and British forces conducted a series of airstrikes against Iraqi military targets after an UNSCOM report clearly indicated that Iraq had failed to keep its promises to cooperate fully with UNSCOM.[39] They justified their action on Iraq's failure to cooperate fully with UNSCOM, arguing that Resolution 687 (or any subsequent resolution) did not terminate the authority to use force in Resolution 678, but, rather, only suspended that authority.[40] It was further argued that a serious violation of Iraq's obligations under 687 that undermined the basis of the ceasefire would revive the use of force authorization in 678.[41] Portugal[42] and Japan[43] supported the US and UK position. Russia, China, France, Brazil, Costa Rica, Kenya and Sweden disagreed, however, indicating that Security Council action was necessary before military strikes could be conducted to enforce Resolution 687.[44] Slovenia, Gambia and Gabon voiced neither opposition to nor support for the operation.[45] Under these circumstances, it should have come as no surprise that the United States and United Kingdom would take military action independent of further Security Council action if Iraq did not comply with the terms of Resolution 1441.

Effect of Ceasefire Violations?

One additional point regarding whether a second resolution was required to authorize the use of force against Iraq to implement Resolution 1441 also merits discussion. The ceasefire agreement established in Resolution 687 was between the coalition forces and Iraq, not the United Nations and Iraq. In accordance with the agreement and long-standing principles of international law reflected in the 1907 Hague Regulations,[46] the coalition agreed to suspend offensive military operations against Iraq in exchange for Iraq's full compliance with the terms of the ceasefire and its disarmament obligations under previous Security Council resolutions. Once Iraq was found to be in material breach of the conditions of the ceasefire, beginning with Resolution 707 in 1991 and culminating with Resolution 1441 in 2002, the coalition partners were free to nullify the ceasefire and rely on the use of force authorization in Resolution 678 to resume hostilities against Iraq to enforce Resolution 687 and restore international peace and security to the area.[47]

Legal Bases for Follow-On Operations

Occupation and the Coalition Provisional Authority

President Bush declared an end to major combat operations on May 1, 2003.[48] One week later, while avoiding the use of the term "occupying power," the member States of the coalition created the Coalition Provisional Authority (CPA) on May 8, 2003 "to exercise powers of government temporarily, and, as necessary, . . . to provide security, to allow the delivery of humanitarian aid, and to eliminate weapons of mass destruction."[49] Specifically, the coalition partners, working through the CPA, were to provide for security in Iraq, eliminate Iraq's WMD program, facilitate the return of refugees and displaced persons, maintain civil law and order, eliminate all terrorist infrastructure and resources within Iraq and work to ensure terrorists were denied safe haven, coordinate demining operations, promote accountability for crimes and atrocities committed by the previous regime and assume control of the institutions responsible for military and security matters.[50] The statuses of CPA, Multi-National Forces (MNF), foreign liaison missions, diplomatic and consular missions and contractor personnel were governed by CPA Order No. 17 (Revised).[51] Specifically, section 2 of the Order provided that the MNF, CPA and foreign liaison mission personnel, as well as international consultants, were "immune from Iraqi legal process" and were "subject to the exclusive jurisdiction of their Sending State." Similarly, section 3 granted contractors immunity, albeit more limited, for acts performed pursuant to the terms and conditions of their contracts. Additionally, section 14 authorized the MNF and private security company personnel to "possess and carry arms while on official duty in accordance with their orders or under the terms and conditions of their contracts." Similarly, diplomatic and consular personnel could carry arms while on official duty if authorized by the ambassador or chargé d'affaires of a sending State.

Consistent with the 1907 Hague Regulations,[52] 1949 Geneva Convention Relative to the Protection of Civilian Persons[53] and 1977 Geneva Protocol I,[54] CPA Regulation No. 1 provided that the CPA would "exercise powers of government temporarily in order to provide for the effective administration of Iraq . . ., to restore conditions of security and stability, [and] to create conditions in which the Iraqi people can freely determine their own political future . . . ." Regulation 1 also vested the CPA "with all executive, legislative and judicial authority necessary to achieve its objectives" and provided that Commander, US Central Command, as the commander of coalition forces, would "directly support the CPA by deterring hostilities; maintaining Iraq's territorial integrity and security; . . . destroying weapons of mass destruction; and assisting in carrying out Coalition policy. . . ."[55]

Security Council Resolution 1483 recognized the "special authorities, responsibilities, and obligations under applicable international law of these states [the United States and United Kingdom] as occupying powers" and called on the CPA "to promote the welfare of the Iraqi people through the effective administration of the territory, including in particular working towards the restoration of conditions of security and stability and the creation of conditions in which the Iraqi people can freely determine their own political future."[56] Resolution 1483 also supported "the formation . . . of an Iraqi interim administration as a transitional administration run by Iraqis, until an internationally recognized, representative government is established by the people of Iraq and assumes the responsibilities of the Authority."

On July 13, 2003, consistent with Resolution 1483, the CPA "recognized the formation of the Governing Council as the principal body of the Iraqi interim administration, pending the establishment of an internationally recognized, representative government by the people of Iraq."[57] Section 2 of CPA Regulation No. 6 provided that "the Governing Council and the CPA shall consult and coordinate on all matters involving the temporary governance of Iraq . . . ." The Security Council welcomed the establishment of the Governing Council on August 14, 2003.[58] On June 1, 2004, the Governing Council was dissolved following the establishment of a sovereign Interim Government of Iraq.[59] The CPA officially ceased to exist, and the occupation phase ended on June 30, 2004 when the Interim Government of Iraq assumed full responsibility and authority for governing Iraq until an elected transitional government of Iraq could assume office.[60]

United Nations Mandate

In view of the increasingly unstable security conditions in Iraq, the Security Council authorized a multinational force "to take all necessary measures to contribute to the maintenance of security and stability in Iraq" and urged "Member States to contribute . . . military forces to the multinational force . . . ."[61] This mandate was reaffirmed by the Security Council on June 8, 2004 at the request of the Interim Government of Iraq.[62] However, the Iraqi request did impose some conditions on the MNF, to include

- The MNF and Iraqi security forces (ISF) would coordinate "on all security policy and operations issues in order to achieve unity of command of military operations" in which the ISF were engaged with the MNF.

- The MNF and Iraqi government leaders would "keep each other informed of their activities, consult regularly to ensure effective allocation and use of personnel, resources and facilities, [would] share intelligence, and [would] refer issues up the respective chains of command where necessary."
- The ISF would progressively assume greater responsibility.
- The MNF would work with the Ministerial Committee for National Security to "reach agreement on the full range of fundamental security and policy issues, including policy on sensitive offensive operations, and . . . ensure full partnership between MNF and Iraqi forces, through close coordination and consultation."[63]

Operative paragraph 13 of Resolution 1546 also established a new mission for the MNF, the establishment of a separate organization under unified command of the MNF with a dedicated mission to provide security for the United Nations Assistance Mission for Iraq, and paragraph 14 recognized that the MNF would also assist in building the capacity of the ISF and institutions through a program of "recruitment, training, equipping, mentoring and monitoring."

The Transitional National Assembly was elected on January 30, 2005 and the draft constitution was approved by the Iraqi people on October 15, 2005.[64] Notwithstanding these positive political developments, the Iraqi government recognized that the ISF was not prepared to assume full responsibility for the security of Iraq and requested that the UN extend the MNF mandate for another year in accordance with the tasks and arrangements outlined in Resolution 1546 (2004).[65] Accordingly, on November 8, 2005, the Security Council extended the mandate (including participation in the provision of humanitarian and reconstruction assistance) of the MNF until December 31, 2006.[66]

The following month elections for a new Iraqi National Assembly were held under the 2005 constitution and a new national unity government was formed in May 2006.[67] Again, despite progress on the political front and the turnover of security responsibilities to the ISF in Muthanna and Dhi Qar provinces, the Iraqi government renewed its request for military assistance on June 9, 2006[68] and November 11, 2006,[69] and the Security Council extended the MNF's mandate for another year.[70]

UNMOVIC and IAEA mandates were terminated in June 2007 following a Security Council determination that Iraq was in compliance with its disarmament obligations under relevant resolutions.[71] Five months later, on November 26, 2007, the United States and Iraq issued a Declaration of Principles for a Long-Term Relationship of Cooperation and Friendship Between the Republic of Iraq and the United States of America.[72] The United States agreed to provide "security assurances and commitments to . . . Iraq to deter foreign aggression against Iraq" and support Iraq "in its efforts to combat all terrorist groups."[73] Iraq agreed to request an extension of the MNF mandate "for a final time"[74] and on December 7, 2007 submitted a letter to the Security Council requesting an extension of the mandate "one last time," subject to the following conditions:

- "The functions of recruiting, training, arming and equipping of the Iraqi Army and . . . [ISF] are the responsibility of the Government of Iraq."
- "The Government of Iraq will assume responsibility for command and control of all Iraqi forces, and MNF, in coordination with the Government of Iraq, will provide support and backing to those forces."
- "The Government of Iraq will be responsible for arrest, detention and imprisonment tasks. When those tasks are carried out by MNF-I, there will be maximum levels of coordination, cooperation and understanding with the Government of Iraq."
- "The Government of Iraq considers this to be its final request" for the extension of the MNF mandate.[75]

Following the signing of the Agreement Between the United States of America and the Republic of Iraq on the Withdrawal of United States Forces from Iraq (hereinafter US-Iraq security agreement),[76] the Prime Minister of Iraq informed the Security Council on December 7, 2008 that the MNF mandate would terminate on December 31, 2008.[77]

US-Iraq Security Agreement

The US military presence and activities in Iraq are currently authorized by the US-Iraq security agreement, which entered into force on January 1, 2009. Pursuant to Article 24, all US forces shall be withdrawn from Iraq no later than December 31, 2011. Article 24 also provides that all US combat forces were to be withdrawn from Iraqi cities and villages when the ISF assumed full responsibility for security in an Iraqi province or by June 30, 2009, whichever occurred first, and would be stationed in agreed facilities and areas designated by the Joint Military Operations Coordination Committee (JMOCC). In addition, the government of Iraq will assume full responsibility for the Green Zone, although it may request "limited and temporary support" from the US forces to secure the zone.[78]

While US forces may continue to engage in offensive military operations within Iraq, their freedom to do so is limited by the security agreement. Article 4 authorizes US forces to support Iraq "in its efforts to maintain security and stability in Iraq, including cooperation in the conduct of operations against al-Qaeda and other terrorist groups, outlaw groups, and remnants of the former regime." Article 4 further specifies that all "military operations that are carried out pursuant to this Agreement shall be conducted with the agreement of the Government of Iraq" and "shall be fully coordinated with Iraqi authorities." Any disagreement regarding a proposed military operation that cannot be resolved by the JMOCC shall be forwarded to the Joint Ministerial Committee for resolution.[79] US forces are also prohibited from conducting a detention or arrest unless authorized or requested by Iraqi officials, provided that any person detained or arrested by US forces must be handed over to competent Iraqi authorities within twenty-four hours of the arrest or detention.[80] Additionally, Article 22 prohibits US forces from searching a house or other property "except by order of an Iraqi judicial warrant and in full coordination with the Government of Iraq," except in the case of combat operations authorized by Article 4 of the security agreement.

Notwithstanding these provisions, US forces retain the right of self-defense[81] and are authorized to carry weapons owned by the United States "according to the authority granted to them under orders and according to their requirements and duties."[82] The United States retains the primary right to exercise criminal jurisdiction over US forces, including the civilian component, for "matters arising inside agreed facilities and areas; during duty status outside agreed facilities and areas." Iraq has primary jurisdiction over "grave premeditated felonies . . . when such crimes are committed outside agreed facilities and areas outside duty status."[83] With that exception, the United States has primary jurisdiction over members of the force even for crimes committed outside agreed facilities and areas and even if the member is not in a duty status. Iraq does have the primary right to exercise jurisdiction over US contractors and their employees.[84]

In addition to authorizing US military operations in Iraq, the US-Iraq security agreement provides for more traditional security assistance activities. In this regard, Article 4 provides that US forces shall continue to "cooperate to strengthen Iraq's security capabilities including, as may be mutually agreed, on training, equipping, supporting, supplying, and establishing and upgrading logistical systems, including transportation, housing and supplies" for the ISF. Similarly, Article 27 provides that the parties "agree to continue close cooperation in strengthening and maintaining military and security institutions . . . in Iraq, including, as may be mutually agreed, cooperation in training, equipping, and arming . . ." the ISF upon the request by the Iraqi government. Article 27 also provides that, in the event of an external or internal threat or aggression against Iraq and upon the request of the Iraqi government, the "Parties shall immediately initiate strategic deliberations and, as may be mutually agreed, the United States shall take appropriate measures, including diplomatic, economic, or military measures, or any other measure, to deter such a threat."

It has been argued by some that the US-Iraq security agreement is invalid because the domestic legal authority to engage in military operations in Iraq expired on December 31, 2008.[85] Section 3 of Congress's 2002 Joint Resolution to Authorize the Use of Military Force Against Iraq[86] authorizes the President to use the US armed forces to (1) defend US national security against the continuing threat posed by Iraq and (2) enforce all relevant Security Council resolutions regarding Iraq. However, in November 2008 the United States agreed that Iraq's designation as a threat to international peace and security would end on December 31, 2008,[87] contemporaneously with the expiration of the MNF mandate. Consequently, the authority to use force under the 2002 Joint Resolution has expired. Of course, this argument has merit only if you subscribe to the position that the President does not have the constitutional authority to deploy US forces abroad without the concurrence of Congress.

It should also be noted that a bill was introduced in the US House of Representatives on January 8, 2009 that would invalidate the US-Iraq security agreement.[88] H.R. 335, which is currently in committee, provides in section 3 that any agreement that sets out broad parameters for the overall bilateral relationship between the United States and Iraq should "involve a joint decision by the executive and legislative branches." Section 6 goes on to prohibit the entry into force of any agreement between the United States and Iraq that contains a security commitment or security arrangement, as well as the obligation or expenditure of funds to implement such an agreement, unless the agreement has been authorized by a subsequent law or has the advice and consent of the Senate. The proposed legislation is based on a faulty premise that the President cannot enter into a bilateral agreement without the advice and consent of the Senate. Clearly, executive agreements have the same legal effect under US law as a treaty that has received Senate advice and consent.[89] However, should such a law be enacted in conjunction with legislation that restricts the expenditure of Department of Defense appropriations to fund military activities under the security agreement, the status of US personnel in Iraq would be in question.

Characterization of the Conflict

Without question, the invasion of Iraq by coalition forces in March 2003 was an international armed conflict, which quickly transitioned into a period of belligerent occupation in May 2003.[90] With the disestablishment of the CPA in June 2004, the occupation period ended; however, a violent insurgency quickly evolved. As a result, coalition forces remained in Iraq at the request of the Iraqi government to help suppress the insurgency and restore international peace and security.[91] During this period was the coalition engaged in a non-international armed conflict or an international armed conflict? There was significant international involvement in the insurgency, but coalition forces were not fighting against the government of Iraq. From a US perspective, does it really matter? US policy applies the laws of war to all armed conflicts, regardless of how they are characterized, and to all other military operations.[92] From a practicable point of view, the real question is: does human rights law applicable during a non-international armed conflict provide greater protection to combatants and noncombatants than is afforded to these individuals under international humanitarian law applicable during an international armed conflict? I would suggest that the answer to that question is "no." The protections afforded to combatants and noncombatants under both bodies of law are qualitatively and quantitatively alike.

Conclusion

The invasion of Iraq on March 20, 2003 clearly constituted a short-lived international armed conflict between the States of the Multi-National Forces and Iraq. Whether the United States can justify the military intervention on the grounds of self-defense and/or humanitarian intervention is questionable; however, there is no doubt that Iraq failed to fully cooperate with the United Nations and International Atomic Energy Agency, and was in material breach of its obligations under at least twenty-five Security Council resolutions covering two decades. Although Resolution 1441 could have been clearer, it did not specifically indicate that a further decision would be required should additional measures be necessary if Iraq failed to comply with its terms. In fact, efforts by France and Russia to include such a requirement failed in the Security Council. Additionally, traditional armistice law would support the resumption of hostilities by coalition forces. Under these circumstances, Iraq's violation of its obligations under Resolution 1441 and the Resolution 687 ceasefire agreement revived the use of force authorization contained in Resolution 678 and provided a sufficient legal basis for coalition forces to conduct offensive military operations against Iraq.

The international armed conflict quickly transformed into a period of belligerent occupation that began on May 8, 2003 with the establishment of the CPA. Although the occupation phase ended on June 30, 2004 when the CPA was disestablished and the Interim Government of Iraq assumed full authority for governing Iraq, coalition forces and the ISF remained engaged in an armed conflict with the insurgents. Whether that conflict should be characterized as non-international or international is a matter of academic debate, but has little practical effect on the way US forces conduct themselves on the battlefield.

The continued presence of the MNF during this phase of the conflict was at the request of the government of Iraq and was authorized by Security Council Resolutions 1511, 1546, 1637, 1723 and 1790. Each of these resolutions incrementally reduced the authority of the MNF to engage in offensive military operations without coordination with the government of Iraq. With the expiration of the UN mandate on December 31, 2008 and the entry into force of the US-Iraq security agreement on January 1, 2009, US military activities have been further limited. It will be interesting to see if the security agreement stands the test of time and survives US congressional scrutiny, and whether the President vetoes any legislation that would purport to invalidate it.

Notes

1. David Sanger, *Bush calls military phase over; He says defeat of Saddam has removed "ally of Al Qaeda,"* INTERNATIONAL HERALD TRIBUNE, May 3, 2003, at 3.

2. Christina Bellantoni, *Obama outlines withdrawal from Iraq: Most troops will be out by August 2010*, WASHINGTON TIMES, Feb. 28, 2009, at A01, *available at* http://www.washingtontimes.com/news/2009/feb/28/obama-outlines-withdrawal-from-iraq/.

3. Agreement Between the United States of America and the Republic of Iraq on the Withdrawal of United States Forces from Iraq and the Organization of Their Activities during Their Temporary Presence in Iraq art. 24(1), Nov. 17, 2008, *available at* http://graphics8.nytimes.com/packages/pdf/world/20081119_SOFA_FINAL_AGREED_TEXT.pdf [hereinafter US-Iraq Security Agreement].

4. The legal justification for the invasion is discussed in recently released documents from the US Department of Justice, including two opinions from the Office of Legal Counsel. *See* Jay S. Bybee, Memorandum Opinion for the Counsel to the President, Authority of the President Under Domestic and International Law to Use Military Force Against Iraq (Oct. 23, 2002), http://www.usdoj.gov/olc/2002/iraq-opinion-final.pdf [hereinafter Authority of the President]; John C. Yoo, Memorandum Opinion for the Counsel to the President, Effect of a Recent United Nations Security Council Resolution on the Authority of the President Under International Law to Use Military Force Against Iraq (Nov. 8, 2002), http://www.usdoj.gov/olc/2002/iraq-unscr-final.pdf. *See also* Letter dated March 20, 2003 from the Permanent Representative of the United States of America to the President of the United Nations Security Council, U.N. SCOR, 58th Sess., U.N. Doc. S/2003/351 (2003).

Reasons enumerated by Congress in the legislation that authorized the use of force against Iraq can be found in Authorization for Use of Military Force Against Iraq Resolution of 2002, Pub. L. No. 107-243, 116 Stat. 1498 (2002), *reprinted in* 41 INTERNATIONAL LEGAL MATERIALS 1440 (2002) [hereinafter Authorization for Use of Military Force], and include

- Iraq posed a continuing threat to the national security of the United States and international peace and security in the Persian Gulf region.
- Iraq remained in material breach and unacceptable breach of its international obligations by continuing to possess and develop a WMD capability, actively seeking a nuclear weapons capability, and supporting and harboring terrorist organizations.

- Iraq persisted in violating Security Council resolutions by continuing to engage in brutal repression of its civilian population; by refusing to release, repatriate or account for non-Iraqi citizens wrongfully detained by Iraq; and by failing to return property wrongfully seized by Iraq from Kuwait.
- The Iraqi regime had demonstrated its capability and willingness to use WMD against other nations and its own people.
- The Iraqi regime had demonstrated its continuing hostility toward, and willingness to attack, the United States, including by attempting in 1993 to assassinate former President Bush and by firing on thousands of occasions on US and coalition forces engaged in enforcing Security Council resolutions.
- Members of al-Qaeda were known to be in Iraq.
- Iraq continued to aid and harbor other international terrorist organizations, including organizations that threaten the lives and safety of US citizens.
- The September 11, 2001 attacks on the United States underscored the gravity of the threat posed by the acquisition of WMD by international terrorist organizations.
- Iraq had demonstrated the capability and willingness to use WMD and there was a risk Iraq would either employ those weapons against the United States or its armed forces, or provide them to international terrorists who would do so.
- Security Council Resolution 678 authorized the use of all necessary means to enforce Resolution 660 and subsequent relevant resolutions and to compel Iraq to cease certain activities that threatened international peace and security, including the development of WMD, refusal or obstruction of UN weapons inspections in violation of Resolution 687, repression of its civilian population in violation of Resolution 688, and threatening its neighbors or UN operations in Iraq in violation of Resolution 949.

Reasons articulated by the UK government can be found at Foreign and Commonwealth Office, Iraq, http://collections.europarchive.org/tna/20080205132101/www.fco.gov.uk/servlet/Front%3Fpagename=OpenMarket/Xcelerate/ShowPage&c=Page&cid=1068716801627 (last visited Aug. 3, 2009) [hereinafter Iraq Military Action]. These include

- During the four months following the adoption of Resolution 1441, Iraq "failed to answer a single outstanding question about its WMD programmes, or resolve any outstanding issues as requested by the UN."
- Iraq failed to account for thousands of tons of chemical and biological weapons materials left unaccounted for when UN weapons inspectors were forced to leave in 1998.
- Iraq's refusal to cooperate with the UN left the United Kingdom no option but "to take military action to enforce Iraq's disarmament obligations" pursuant to the relevant Security Council resolutions.
- "Authority to use force against Iraq derived from the combined effect of" Resolutions 678, 687 and 1441 without the need for another resolution.

5. Attorney General Note to the Prime Minister (Mar. 7, 2003), http://collections.europarchive.org/tna/20080205132101/number-10.gov.uk/output/Page7445.asp.

6. *See, e.g.*, Select Committee on Intelligence, Postwar Findings about Iraq's WMD Programs and Links to Terrorism and How They Compare with Prewar Assessments, S. Rep. No. 109-331 (2006); INSTITUTE FOR DEFENSE ANALYSES, IRAQI PERSPECTIVES PROJECT, SADDAM AND TERRORISM: EMERGING INSIGHTS FROM CAPTURED IRAQI DOCUMENTS (2007), *available at* http://www.fas.org/irp/eprint/iraqi/index.html; CHARLES DUELFER, COMPREHENSIVE REPORT

OF THE SPECIAL ADVISOR TO THE DIRECTOR OF CENTRAL INTELLIGENCE ON IRAQ'S WMD (2004), *available at* https://www.cia.gov/library/reports/general-reports-1/iraq_wmd_2004/index.html.

7. S.C. Res. 687, U.N. Doc. S/RES/687 (Apr. 3, 1991).
8. S.C. Res. 688, U.N. Doc. S/RES/688 (Apr. 5, 1991).
9. S.C. Res. 686, U.N. Doc. S/RES/686 (Mar. 2, 1991).
10. S.C. Res. 1284, U.N. Doc. S/RES/1284 (Dec. 17, 1999).
11. *See, e.g.*, Iraq Military Action, *supra* note 4; S.C. Res. 1284, *supra* note 10, paras. 7 & 8; S.C. Res. 1441, para. 8, U.N. Doc. S/RES/1441 (Nov. 8, 2002).
12. Iraqi violations included:
    - Security Council Resolution 660 (Aug. 2, 1990) demands Iraq's withdrawal from Kuwait.
    - Security Council Resolution 661 (Aug. 6, 1990) imposes economic sanctions on Iraq for its failure to comply with Resolution 660.
    - Security Council Resolution 662 (Aug. 9, 1990) demands once again that Iraq withdraw from Kuwait.
    - Security Council Resolution 664 (Aug. 18, 1990) demands Iraq take no action to harm third-State nationals in Kuwait.
    - Security Council Resolution 665 (Aug. 25, 1990) imposes a maritime blockade of Iraq for its failure to comply with Resolutions 660, 661, 662 and 664.
    - Security Council Resolution 666 (Sept. 13, 1990) reaffirms Iraq's obligations under Resolution 664 with regard to third-State nationals.
    - Security Council Resolution 667 (Sept. 16, 1990) condemns aggressive acts perpetrated by Iraq against diplomatic premises and personnel in Kuwait, including the abduction of foreign nationals, and demands their immediate release.
    - Security Council Resolution 670 (Sept. 25, 1990) condemns Iraq for its continued violation of Resolutions 660, 662, 664 and 667 and the treatment of Kuwaiti nationals by Iraqi forces, and enhances economic sanctions imposed by Resolution 661.
    - Security Council Resolution 674 (Oct. 29, 1990) demands Iraq cease and desist from taking third-State nationals hostage, and mistreating and oppressing Kuwaiti and third-State nationals, and comply with its obligations under various international agreements regarding third-State nationals and diplomatic and consular missions.
    - Security Council Resolution 677 (Nov. 28, 1990) condemns attempts by Iraq to alter the demographic composition of Kuwait and to destroy civil records maintained by the government.
    - Security Council Resolution 678 (Nov. 29, 1990) affords Iraq one last opportunity to comply fully with Security Council Resolution 660 and all subsequent relevant resolutions, and authorizes member States to use all necessary means to uphold and implement Resolution 660 and all subsequent relevant resolutions and to restore international peace and security in the area.
    - Security Council Resolution 687 (Apr. 3, 1991) suspends Resolution 678 by declaring a formal ceasefire between Iraq and Kuwait and the member States cooperating with Kuwait; decides that Iraq shall unconditionally accept the destruction, removal or rendering harmless, under international supervision, of all chemical and biological weapons and all stocks of agents and related

subsystems and components and all research, development, support and manufacturing facilities, and all ballistic missiles with a range greater than 150 kilometers and related major parts and repair and production facilities; decides that Iraq shall unconditionally agree not to acquire or develop nuclear weapons or nuclear-weapons-usable material or any subsystems or components of any research, development, support or manufacturing facilities; and requires Iraq to inform the Security Council that it will not commit or support any act of international terrorism or allow any terrorist organization to operate within its territory.

- Security Council Resolution 688 (Apr. 5, 1991) condemns, and demands that Iraq end, the repression of the Iraqi civilian population, including the Kurds.
- Security Council Resolution 707 (Aug. 15, 1991) affirms Iraq is in material breach of Resolution 687; condemns Iraq for failing to comply with the terms of the ceasefire agreement and cooperate with the UN Special Commission and IAEA inspectors; and requires Iraq to comply fully and without delay with all its obligations, including Resolution 687.
- Security Council Resolution 715 (Oct. 11, 1991) demands that Iraq meet unconditionally all its obligations under the plans approved in the resolution and cooperate fully with the UN Special Commission and the IAEA.
- Security Council Resolution 949 (Oct. 15, 1994) condemns Iraq's military deployment in the direction of the border with Kuwait, and demands the immediate withdrawal of all forces and that Iraq not take any other action to enhance its military capacity in southern Iraq.
- Security Council Resolution 1060 (June 12, 1996) deplores the refusal by Iraq to allow access to sites designated by the UN Special Commission and in violation of Resolutions 687, 707 and 715, and demands Iraq cooperate fully with the UN Special Commission and allow inspection teams immediate, unconditional and unrestricted access to anything they wish to inspect.
- Security Council Resolution 1115 (June 21, 1997) condemns the repeated refusal of Iraq to allow access to sites designated by the UN Special Commission, in violation of Resolutions 687, 707, 715 and 1060, and demands that Iraq cooperate fully with the UN Special Commission and allow inspection teams immediate, unconditional and unrestricted access to anything they wish to inspect.
- Security Council Resolution 1134 (Oct. 23, 1997) condemns the repeated refusal of Iraq to allow access to sites designated by the UN Special Commission, actions by Iraq endangering the safety, and interfering with the freedom of movement, of UN Special Commission personnel and the removal and destruction of documents of interest to the UN Special Commission; decides Iraq is in flagrant violation of Resolutions 687, 707, 715 and 1060; and demands that Iraq fully cooperate with the UN Special Commission and allow the inspection teams immediate, unconditional and unrestricted access to anything they wish to inspect and personnel they wish to interview.
- Statement by the President of the Security Council (Oct. 29, 1997) condemns the October 29 decision of Iraq to try to dictate the terms of its compliance with its obligations to cooperate with the UN Special Commission, demands that Iraq cooperate fully without conditions or restrictions with the UN Special

Commission, and reminds Iraq of its responsibility for the safety and security of the personnel of the UN Special Commission.

• Security Council Resolution 1137 (Nov. 12, 1997) determines that the situation continues to constitute a threat to international peace and stability; condemns the continued violations by Iraq of its obligations to cooperate fully and unconditionally with the UN Special Commission, including Iraq's October 29 decision to seek to impose conditions on cooperation with the UN Special Commission, its refusal on October 30 and November 2 to allow entry to two officials of the UN Special Commission, its denial of entry to inspectors on November 3–7 to sites designated by the UN Special Commission for inspection, its implicit threat to the safety of surveillance aircraft operating on behalf of the UN Special Commission, its removal of significant pieces of dual-use equipment from their previous sites, and its tampering with monitoring cameras of the UN Special Commission; demands that Iraq rescind immediately its October 29 decision; demands that Iraq cooperate fully and immediately and without condition or restrictions with the UN Special Commission; imposes travel restrictions on Iraqi officials responsible for these violations; and reaffirms Iraq's responsibility to ensure the safety and security of the personnel and equipment of the UN Special Commission.

• Statement of the President of the Security Council (Nov. 13, 1997) condemns the unacceptable decision of Iraq to expel personnel of the UN Special Commission, demands the immediate and unequivocal revocation of this action and demands that Iraq comply immediately and fully with its obligations under the relevant resolutions.

• Statement of the President of the Security Council (Jan. 14, 1998) deplores Iraq's statement of January 12 and its subsequent failure to fulfill its obligations to provide the UN Special Commission full, unconditional and immediate access to all sites, which is a clear violation of relevant resolutions, and reiterates the demand that Iraq cooperate fully and immediately and without conditions or restrictions with the UN Special Commission.

• Security Council Resolution 1154 (Mar. 2, 1998) endorses the February 23, 1998 memorandum of understanding between the Deputy Prime Minister of Iraq and the Secretary-General and looks forward to its early and full implementation.

• Security Council Resolution 1194 (Sept. 9, 1998) condemns the decision of Iraq of August 5, 1998 to suspend cooperation with the UN Special Commission and the IAEA, which constitutes a totally unacceptable contravention of its obligations under Resolutions 687, 707, 715, 1060, 1115 and 1154 and the Memorandum of Understanding signed by the Deputy Prime Minister of Iraq and the Secretary-General on February 23, 1998.

• Security Council Resolution 1205 (Nov. 5, 1998) condemns the decision by Iraq of October 31, 1998 to cease cooperation with the UN Special Commission as a flagrant violation of Resolution 687 and other relevant resolutions; demands that Iraq rescind immediately and unconditionally the decision of October 31, as well as the decision of August 5, 1998, to suspend cooperation with the UN Special Commission and to maintain restrictions on the work of the IAEA; and demands that Iraq provide immediate, complete and unconditional cooperation with the UN Special Commission and the IAEA.

- Security Council Resolution 1284 (Dec. 17, 1999) recalls that Iraq has not yet complied with its obligations under Resolutions 686 and 687 to return all Kuwaiti and third-country nationals present in Iraq and to return all Kuwaiti property it had seized, and established the United Nations Monitoring, Verification and Inspection Commission (UNMOVIC) to replace the UN Special Commission.
- Security Council Resolution 1441 (Nov. 8, 2002) deplores that Iraq failed to cooperate fully with UNSCOM and the IAEA; deplores that Iraq failed to comply with its commitments in Resolution 687 with regard to terrorism, Resolution 688 to end repression of its civilian population, and Resolutions 686, 687 and 1284 to account for Kuwaiti and third-country nationals; decides that Iraq remains in material breach of its obligations under relevant resolutions through its failure to cooperate with UNSCOM and IAEA inspectors and to complete actions required by Resolution 687; decides to afford Iraq, by this resolution, a final opportunity to comply with its disarmament obligations under relevant resolutions; decides that Iraq shall provide UNMOVIC, the IAEA and the Security Council within thirty days a currently accurate, full and complete declaration of all aspects of its WMD and ballistic missile programs; decides that false statements or omissions in the declarations submitted by Iraq and failure by Iraq at any time to comply with and cooperate fully in the implementation of this resolution shall constitute a further material breach of Iraq's obligations; decides that Iraq will provide UNMOVIC and the IAEA immediate, unimpeded, unconditional and unrestricted access to anything they wish to inspect or any persons they wish to interview; directs UNMOVIC and the IAEA to report immediately to the Council any interference with inspection activities or Iraq's failure to comply with its disarmament obligations; and decides to convene immediately upon receipt of a report of noncompliance in order to consider the situation.

13. *E.g.*, U.N. Charter; Convention Relative to the Protection of Civilian Persons in Time of War, Aug. 12, 1949, 6 U.S.T. 3516, 75 U.N.T.S. 287, *reprinted in* DOCUMENTS ON THE LAWS OF WAR 301 (Adam Roberts & Richard Guelff eds., 3d ed. 2000) (treatment of Kuwaiti nationals by Iraqi forces during its occupation in 1990) [hereinafter Geneva Convention IV]; Vienna Convention on Diplomatic Relations, Apr. 18, 1961, 23 U.S.T. 3227, 500 U.N.T.S. 95 (Iraqi acts against diplomatic premises and personnel in Kuwait); Vienna Convention on Consular Relations, Apr. 24, 1963, 21 U.S.T. 77, 596 U.N.T.S. 261 (Iraqi acts against diplomatic and consular missions in Kuwait); Protocol for the Prohibition of the Use in War of Asphyxiating, Poisonous or Other Gases, and of Bacteriological Methods of Warfare, June 17, 1925, 26 U.S.T. 571, T.I.A.S. 8061, *reprinted in* DOCUMENTS ON THE LAWS OF WAR, *supra*, at 158 (Iraq made statements threatening to use chemical and biological weapons and used chemical weapons on prior occasions); Treaty on the Non-Proliferation of Nuclear Weapons, July 1, 1968, 21 U.S.T. 483, 729 U.N.T.S. 161 (Iraq made attempts to acquire materials for a nuclear weapons program).

14. S.C. Res. 707, U.N. Doc. S/RES/707 (Aug. 15, 1991).

15. Joint Resolution, Iraq Compliance with International Obligations, Pub. L. No. 105-235, 112 Stat. 1538 (1998); Iraq Liberation Act of 1998, Pub. L. No. 105-338, 112 Stat. 3178 (1998); Authorization for Use of Military Force, *supra* note 4. Examples of Iraq's continuing material breach of its obligations under relevant Security Council resolutions include:

- August 1991—Iraq failed to comply with the terms of the ceasefire agreement and cooperate fully with UN and IAEA inspectors.
- January/February 1992—Iraq rejected plans to install long-term monitoring equipment and cameras called for in Security Council resolutions.

- February 1992—Iraq continued to obstruct the installation of monitoring equipment and failed to comply with UNSCOM orders to allow destruction of missiles and other proscribed weapons.
- July 1992—Iraq denied UNSCOM inspectors access to the Iraqi Ministry of Agriculture.
- December 1992—Iraq violated the southern no-fly zone, raided a weapons depot in Kuwait and denied landing rights to a plane carrying UN weapons inspectors.
- April 1993—Iraq orchestrated a failed plot to assassinate former President George Bush during his visit to Kuwait.
- June 1993—Iraq prevented UNSCOM's installation of cameras and monitoring equipment.
- October 1994—Iraq threatened to end cooperation with weapons inspectors if sanctions were not ended and massed ten thousand troops along the border with Kuwait.
- April 1995—UNSCOM reported that Iraq had concealed its biological weapons program and had failed to account for seventeen tons of biological weapons material.
- April 1995—Iraq continued repression of its civilian population, including the Kurds.
- July 1995—Iraq threatened to end cooperation with UNSCOM.
- March 1996—Iraq barred UNSCOM inspectors from sites containing documents and weapons on four separate days.
- June 1996—Iraq repeatedly barred UNSCOM inspectors from military sites.
- August 1996—Iraqi troops overran Irbil in Iraqi Kurdistan.
- December 1996—Iraq prevented UNSCOM from removing 130 Scud missile engines from Iraq for analysis.
- April 1997—Iraq violated the southern no-fly zone.
- June 1997—Iraqi officials on board UNSCOM aircraft interfered with the controls and inspections, endangering inspectors and obstructing the UNSCOM mission.
- September 1997—an Iraqi official attacked UNSCOM officials engaged in photographing illegal Iraqi activities.
- October 1997—Iraq announced that it would no longer allow US inspectors working with UNSCOM to conduct inspections in Iraq, blocked UNSCOM teams containing US inspectors from conducting inspections and threatened to shoot down US U-2 surveillance flights in support of UNSCOM.
- November 1997—Iraq expelled US inspectors from Iraq, leading to UNSCOM's decision to pull out its remaining inspectors.
- January 1998—an UNSCOM team led by an American was barred from conducting inspections.
- June 1998—the UNSCOM director presented information to the Security Council indicating clearly that Iraq, in direct contradiction to information provided to UNSCOM, had a weaponized nerve agent.
- August 1998—Iraq ceased all cooperation with UNSCOM and threatened to end long-term monitoring activities by the IAEA and UNSCOM.
- October 1998—UN weapons inspectors were withdrawn from Iraq.

• December 1998—Iraq ceased all cooperation with UNSCOM and IAEA inspectors, and did not agree to allow inspectors to return until 2002.
• November 2002—Iraq failed to provide complete disclosure of its WMD programs and to cooperate fully with weapons inspectors.

16. S.C. Res. 1441, *supra* note 11.

17. *Id.*

18. UNMOVIC was the successor organization to UNSCOM and was established pursuant to Security Council Resolution 1284 (1999).

19. S.C. Res. 1441, *supra* note 11, Annex.

20. *Id.*

21. *Id.*, operative para. 2.

22. Letter and enclosure from the Secretary of State for Foreign and Commonwealth Affairs to Donald Anderson MP, Chair, Foreign Affairs Committee: Iraq: Legal Position Concerning the Use of Force (Mar. 17, 2003), *available at* http://collections.europarchive.org/tna/20080205132101/fco.gov.uk/Files/kfile/Iraq%20-%20use%20of%20force.pdf [hereinafter Secretary of State letter].

23. S.C. Res. 1441, *supra* note 11, operative paras. 1 & 2.

24. The US ambassador to the United Nations indicated that

> if there is a further Iraqi breach, reported to the council by UNMOVIC, the IAEA, or a Member State, the matter will return to the council for discussion. . . . But if the Security Council fails to act decisively in the event of further Iraqi violations, this resolution does not constrain any member state from acting to defend itself against the threat posed by Iraq or to enforce the relevant United Nations resolutions and protect world peace and security.

WorldPress.org, The United Nations, International Law, and the War in Iraq, http://www.worldpress.org/specials/iraq/ (last visited Aug. 3, 2009).

25. The UK government was of the opinion that, although a second resolution would have been desirable, it was not a legal prerequisite ("all that was required was reporting to and discussion by the Security Council of Iraq's failures, but not an express further decision to authorize force"). Iraq Military Action, *supra* note 4.

26. The French ambassador indicated that "a two-stage approach would ensure that the Security Council would maintain control of the process at each stage." The Russian representative "made clear that the resolution just adopted contains no provisions for the automatic use of force. . . ." The Chinese delegate agreed with the French, indicating that "China supports the two-stage approach." The Irish delegate stated that "it is for the Council to decide on any ensuring action." The Mexican ambassador agreed, saying "that the use of force is valid only . . . with prior explicit authorization required from the Security Council." The Bulgarian delegate said that the "resolution is not a pretext for automatic recourse to the use of force." The Colombian representative agreed, indicating that the "resolution is not . . . a resolution to authorize the use of force." The Cameroonian ambassador stated that the "resolution does not contain traps or automaticity." The Syrian ambassador said that "the resolution should not be interpreted . . . as authorizing any State to use force . . . [and that] it reaffirms the central role of the Security Council." The United Nations, International Law, and the War in Iraq, *supra* note 24.

27. Attorney General Note to the Prime Minister, *supra* note 5, para. 7.

28. S.C. Res. 1441, *supra* note 11, para. 12.

29. According to the Attorney General:

> The previous practice of the Council and statements made by Council members during the negotiation of resolution 1441 demonstrate that the phrase "material

> breach" signifies a finding by the Council of a sufficiently serious breach of the cease-fire conditions to revive the authorisation in resolution 678 and that "serious consequences" is accepted as indicating the use of force.

Attorney General Note to the Prime Minister, *supra* note 5, para. 10.

30. *Id.*, para. 12.
31. Secretary of State letter, *supra* note 22, para. 12.
32. Attorney General Note to the Prime Minister, *supra* note 5, para. 13.
33. *Id.*, para. 15.
34. S.C. Res. 1874, U.N. Doc. S/RES/1874 (June 12, 2009).
35. Attorney General Note to the Prime Minister, *supra* note 5, para. 20.
36. *Id.*, para. 22.
37. S.C. Res. 1137, para. 11, U.N. Doc. S/RES/1137 (Nov. 12, 1997).
38. If the United States and Great Britain made any diplomatic mistakes in the months leading up to the invasion, it was in introducing a draft resolution with Spain in February 2003 that proposed realizable "tests and a timetable for completion of those tests." The draft also "sought an understanding that, if Iraq failed those tests, it would not have taken the final opportunity" that had been afforded to it under Resolution 1441. The Security Council was unable, however, to reach consensus on the draft resolution, so it was tabled on February 24, 2003, with the United States, the United Kingdom and Spain reserving "the right to take their own steps to secure the disarmament of Iraq." Iraq Military Action, *supra* note 4.

In my opinion, these efforts weakened the US and UK position and bolstered the opposition's argument that a second resolution was necessary to authorize the use of force against Iraq for its failure to comply with Resolution 1441. The US and UK efforts beg the question: if they really felt that they had sufficient legal authority to conduct military operations against Iraq under 1441, why did they seek a second resolution?

39. Press Release SC/6611, UN Security Council, Security Council Meets to Discuss Military Strikes Against Iraq; Some Members Challenge Use of Force without Council Consent (Dec. 16, 1998), *available at* http://www.un.org/News/Press/docs/1998/19981216.sc6611.html.
40. The US representative stated that US and British forces "were acting under the authority provided by Council resolutions" and that the airstrikes were "undertaken only when it was evident that diplomacy had been exhausted." He further indicated that Iraq was aware of the Council's conditions requiring "full, final and complete disclosure of all aspects of Iraq's programmes to develop weapons of mass destruction," but that Iraq was repeatedly in flagrant material breach of Council resolutions. Specifically, "by refusing to make available documents and information requested by UNSCOM . . ., by imposing new restrictions on the weapons inspectors and by repeatedly denying access to facilities which UNSCOM wished to inspect, Iraq had acted in flagrant material breach of resolution 687 (1991)." *Id.*

The UK representative indicated that Resolution 687 "had made it a condition of ceasefire both that Iraq destroy its weapons of mass destruction and agree to the monitoring of its obligation to destroy such weapons." He further reiterated that Iraq had never cooperated with UNSCOM and had "concealed evidence, blocked inspections and failed to produce documents relevant to its programmes of mass destruction weapons which were known to exist." *Id.*

41. Attorney General Note to the Prime Minister, *supra* note 5.
42. The Portuguese representative supported the US and the UK position, arguing that the United States and the United Kingdom had made it clear in November that "in the absence of full cooperation by Iraq, they would act without returning to the Council." He also emphasized that the "main cause of the current crisis was the obstinate policy of Iraq's rulers in refusing to comply

with Council resolutions," highlighting that the latest UNSCOM report stated that Iraq had "not lived up to its commitments." Press Release SC/6611, *supra* note 39.

43. The Japanese representative also supported the use of force by the United States and the United Kingdom, emphasizing that "Iraq had failed to provide its full cooperation to UNSCOM" and that had led to the airstrikes. He also strongly urged Iraq "to comply immediately and unconditionally with all its obligations under Council resolutions." *Id.*

44. The Russian representative, on the other hand, argued that the airstrikes "violated the principles of international law and the principle of the Charter," arguing that "no one could act independently on behalf of the United Nations . . . ." The Chinese representative agreed, indicating that the airstrikes were "completely groundless," and the French representative "deplored the situation that had led to the airstrike." Costa Rica supported the Russian Federation's position indicating that the use of force "was the sole and exclusive faculty of the Council . . . [and that] only the United Nations could authorize such actions." The Brazilian representative agreed, emphasizing that "the Council remained the sole body with legal authority to mandate actions aimed at reinforcing compliance with its own resolutions." Kenya also supported the Russian position, indicating that "Kenya had repeatedly said any decision to take further action against Iraq remained the sole responsibility of the Security Council." The Swedish representative, while recognizing that "Iraq had again and again refused to abide by the clear obligations decided by a unanimous Security Council, and it was clear Iraq had not fulfilled the promise given to the Secretary-General only a month ago that it would cooperate fully and without conditions with United Nations weapons inspectors," indicated that he regretted that the attacks had occurred before the Council had "a chance to conclude its evaluation of the latest developments . . . ." *Id.*

45. *Id.*

46. Hague Convention No. IV Respecting the Laws and Customs of War on Land, Oct. 18, 1907, 36 Stat. 2227, *reprinted in* DOCUMENTS ON THE LAWS OF WAR, *supra* note 13, at 69 [hereinafter Hague IV].

47. Authority of the President, *supra* note 4; YORAM DINSTEIN, WAR, AGGRESSION AND SELF-DEFENCE 57–59, 298–299 (4th ed. 2005). *See also* Hague IV, *supra* note 46, arts. 36 & 40.

48. Sanger, *supra* note 1.

49. Letter from the Permanent Representatives of the United States of America and the United Kingdom of Great Britain and Northern Ireland to the President of the UN Security Council, U.N. Doc. S/2003/538 (May 8, 2003) [hereinafter United States/United Kingdom letter].

50. *Id.*

51. CPA Order No. 17 (Revised) (June 27, 2004), *available at* http://www.cpa-iraq.org/regulations/20040627_CPAORD_17_Status_of_Coalition__Rev__with_Annex_A.pdf.

52. *See* Hague IV, *supra* note 46, arts. 42–56.

53. Geneva Convention IV, *supra* note 13, arts. 47–78.

54. Protocol Additional to the Geneva Conventions of 12 August 1949, and Relating to the Protection of Victims of International Armed Conflicts, June 8, 1977, 1125 U.N.T.S. 3, *reprinted in* DOCUMENTS ON THE LAWS OF WAR, *supra* note 13, at 422.

55. CPA Regulation No. 1, sec. 1 (May 16, 2003), *available at* http://www.cpa-iraq.org/regulations/20030516_CPAREG_1_The_Coalition_Provisional_Authority_.pdf.

56. S.C. Res. 1483, para. 13 & operative para. 4, U.N. Doc. S/RES/1483 (May 22, 2003).

57. CPA Regulation No. 6, sec. 1 (July 13, 2003), *available at* http://www.cpa-iraq.org/regulations/20030713_CPAREG_6_Governing_Council_of_Iraq_.pdf.

58. S.C. Res. 1500, U.N. Doc. S/RES/1500 (Aug. 14, 2003).

59. S.C. Res. 1546, para. 7 & operative para. 1, U.N. Doc. S/RES/1546 (June 8, 2004).

60. *Id.*, operative paras. 1 & 2.

61. S.C. Res. 1511, operative paras. 13 & 14, U.N. Doc. S/RES/1511 (Oct. 16, 2003).
62. S.C. Res. 1546, *supra* note 59, operative paras. 9–11 & 14–15.
63. *Id.*, Annex.
64. S.C. Res. 1637, U.N. Doc. S/RES/1637 (Nov. 8, 2005).
65. *Id.*, Annex I.
66. *Id.*, para. 12 & operative para. 1.
67. S.C. Res. 1723, Annex, U.N. Doc. S/RES/1723 (Nov. 28, 2006).
68. Letter from the Minister of Foreign Affairs of the Republic of Iraq to the United Nations, U.N. Doc. S/2006/377 (June 9, 2006).
69. S.C. Res. 1723, *supra* note 67, Annex I.
70. *Id.*, paras. 1–2 & operative para. 1.
71. S.C. Res. 1762, para. 6 & operative para. 1, U.N. Doc. S/RES/1762 (June 29, 2007).
72. Declaration of Principles for a Long-Term Relationship of Cooperation and Friendship Between the Republic of Iraq and the United States of America, Nov. 26, 2007, *available at* http://georgewbush-whitehouse.archives.gov/news/releases/2007/11/20071126-11.html.
73. *Id.*, Security Sphere, para. 1.
74. *Id.*, Security Sphere, para. 2.
75. S.C. Res. 1790, paras. 13, 14 & 16, operative para. 1 & Annex I (Dec. 18, 2007).
76. US-Iraq Security Agreement, *supra* note 3.
77. S.C. Res. 1859, Annex, U.N. Doc. S/RES/1859 (Dec. 22, 2008).
78. US-Iraq Security Agreement, *supra* note 3, art. 28.
79. *Id.*, art. 4.
80. *Id.*, art. 22.
81. *Id.*, art. 4.
82. *Id.*, art. 13.
83. *Id.*, art. 12.
84. *Id.*
85. *Renewing the United Nations Mandate for Iraq: Plans and Prospects: Hearing Before Subcomm. on International Organizations, Human Rights, and Oversight of the H. Comm. on Foreign Affairs*, 110th Cong. 16 (2008) (statement of Professor Oona A. Hathaway, University of California, Berkeley, School of Law, available at http://foreignaffairs.house.gov/110/hat111908 .pdf).
86. Authorization for Use of Military Force, *supra* note 4.
87. Strategic Framework Agreement for a Relationship of Friendship and Cooperation between the United States of America and the Republic of Iraq, Nov. 17, 2008, *available at* http://www.globalsecurity.org/military/library/policy/national/iraq-strategic-framework-agreement.htm.
88. Iraq Security Agreement Act of 2009, H.R. 335, 111th Cong. (2009).
89. *See, e.g.*, American Insurance Association v. Garamendi, 539 U.S. 396 (2003). In that case the Court stated, "[O]ur cases have recognized that the President has authority to make 'executive agreements' with other countries, requiring no ratification by the Senate or approval by Congress, this power having been exercised since the early years of the Republic." *Id.* at 415.
90. United States/United Kingdom letter, *supra* note 49; CPA Regulation No. 1, *supra* note 55; S.C. Res. 1483, *supra* note 56.
91. S.C. Res. 1511, *supra* note 61; S.C. Res. 1546, *supra* note 59; S.C. Res. 1637, *supra* note 64; S.C. Res. 1723, *supra* note 67; S.C. Res. 1790, *supra* note 75.
92. Department of Defense, DoD Directive 2311.01E, DoD Law of War Program (2006), *available at* http://www.dtic.mil/whs/directives/corres/pdf/231101p.pdf.

IV

Was the 2003 Invasion of Iraq Legal?

Andru E. Wall*

I. Introduction

Discussion of the *jus ad bellum* and the Iraq war is anything but simple and uncontroversial. There is certainly no shortage of opinions on the subject. One of the author's favorite quotes is from General Wesley Clark, who said the 2003 invasion was legal, but illegitimate.[1] You will appreciate the irony if you remember that the Independent International Commission on Kosovo established by the United Nations called General Clark's 1999 Kosovo campaign illegal, but legitimate.[2]

When several leading international law professors were asked by a British newspaper, "Was the 2003 Iraq war legal?" their responses were illustrative.[3] Professor Malcom Shaw replied: "[O]n the basis of the intelligence we had at the time and the publicly available knowledge, there was a credible and reasonable argument in favor of the legality of the war." Professor Christine Chinkin answered "no" because she believed UN Security Council Resolution 1441 preserved for the Security Council the decision on enforcement action. Professor Sir Adam Roberts replied: "There was in principle a possible case for the lawfulness of resort to war by the US and its small coalition." Professor James Crawford answered simply: "It comes down to a political judgment."

Unfortunately this author thinks Professor Crawford's statement is quite accurate, as it reflects the truism that law and policy are mutually affecting; nowhere is

---

*Lieutenant Commander, JAGC, US Navy. This article is derived in part from Andru E. Wall, *The Legal Case for Invading Iraq*, 32 ISRAEL YEARBOOK OF HUMAN RIGHTS 165 (2002).

the interrelationship between law and policy more evident than in the *jus ad bellum*. Nevertheless, let us briefly examine the legality of the recourse to force in 2003. First, the legal argument articulated by the coalition will be summarized; then three criticisms of the coalition's legal basis will be examined.

II. The Legal Justification for the 2003 Invasion

On March 20, 2003 as the invasion of Iraq began, the United States, United Kingdom and Australia delivered letters to the President of the Security Council providing notice that coalition forces had commenced military operations in Iraq. The letters stated the use of force was necessary in response to Iraq's material breach of the ceasefire agreement reached at the end of hostilities in 1991 and the disarmament obligations contained in Security Council Resolution 687. The US letter succinctly stated: "In view of Iraq's material breaches, the basis for the ceasefire has been removed and use of force is authorized under resolution 678 (1990)."[4]

The legal justifications are explained more fully in a memorandum from the British Attorney General, Lord Goldsmith, to Prime Minister Tony Blair on March 7, 2003 and three US Department of Justice, Office of Legal Counsel opinions written in October, November and December of 2002.[5] As there are no significant differences among the US, UK and Australian legal justifications, they will be considered as the singular coalition case.

For the coalition, the war with Iraq began on August 2, 1990 when Iraq invaded Kuwait—not with the recommencement of hostilities in March 2003. Iraq justified its invasion of Kuwait on the basis of long-standing claims of sovereignty over Kuwait, and claims that Kuwait engaged in various forms of economic warfare against Iraq.[6] However, there was little question that Iraq's actions violated the requirement contained in Article 2(3) of the UN Charter that States resolve their disputes by pacific means and Article 2(4)'s prohibition on the use of force against the territorial integrity and political independence of another State. As a result, within a few hours of the Iraqi invasion of Kuwait the Security Council declared the Iraqi action a breach of the peace in Resolution 660. Four days later the Security Council explicitly recognized the right of Kuwait and its coalition partners to use force in collective self-defense in Resolution 661. Throughout the fall of 1990 the Security Council passed eleven resolutions that collectively denounced Iraq's invasion, declared it a breach of the peace, demanded Iraq's immediate, unconditional withdrawal from Kuwait, recognized the right of individual or collective self-defense, imposed an arms embargo and economic sanctions, and recognized Iraq's obligation to pay reparations.[7]

Even as a US-led coalition commenced maritime interdiction operations and began massing military forces, US diplomats aggressively pursued a Security Council resolution explicitly authorizing the use of military force against Iraq. Finally, on November 27, 1990, the Security Council passed Resolution 678, which authorized "all necessary means" to eject Iraq from Kuwait and "to uphold and implement . . . all subsequent relevant resolutions and to restore international peace and security to the area."[8] The resolution provided Iraq with "one final opportunity" to comply with the Security Council's previous Chapter VII resolutions by January 15, 1991.

Iraq failed to avail itself of this final opportunity, and so on the evening of January 16, 1991 a twenty-eight-nation, US-led coalition commenced Operation Desert Storm. It is worth noting here that the Security Council did not make a further determination regarding whether Iraq had complied with its January 15 deadline. Member States made that determination themselves and relied upon the Security Council's November 1990 decision as authority to use force.

After six weeks of bombing and an astonishingly successful 100-hour ground campaign Kuwait was liberated and the Iraqi army was in full retreat. As the Iraqi army fled north, coalition aircraft continued to bomb Iraqi military targets. The four-lane highway from Kuwait to Basra began to clog with the charred hulks of hundreds of military vehicles and reporters began referring to it as the "Highway of Death." While the laws of war permitted the continued destruction of the Iraqi army, at least until surrender, the coalition did not want to be seen as engaging in "slaughter for the sake of slaughter."[9] And so, at 5 a.m. on February 28, 1991, Operation Desert Storm was unilaterally halted. Three days later General H. Norman Schwarzkopf, the commander of coalition forces, and his Iraqi counterpart negotiated a ceasefire agreement that established a demarcation line and contained provisions for the repatriation of Kuwaitis and prisoners of war held in Iraq.[10]

The ceasefire agreement was put into writing by the United States, vetted by the Security Council and codified in Resolution 687 on April 3, 1991.[11] It was the longest resolution and most detailed ceasefire agreement in modern time and included extensive disarmament provisions. The Resolution stated its provisions established the "conditions essential to the restoration of peace and security." The Security Council predicated activation of the ceasefire upon Iraq's unconditional acceptance, which reluctantly came in a letter delivered to the Security Council on April 6, 1991.[12]

Even before accepting the ceasefire, Iraq began violently suppressing uprisings by the Shia in the south and the Kurds in the north. The Security Council responded by passing Resolution 688, which called on Iraq to cease such repression "as a contribution to removing the threat to international peace and security in the region."[13] The Security Council believed Iraq's suppression of its citizens, which was causing a destabilizing flow of refugees into neighboring countries, was a threat to international peace and security. The United States and United Kingdom used Resolution 688's linkage between Iraq's internal unrest and international peace and security as the basis for invoking Resolution 678's authorization of the use of force as the enforcement authority.[14] In other words, from the outset of the ceasefire, the coalition believed Resolution 678's authorization to use force to restore international peace and security in the region survived the ceasefire of Resolution 687.

On several occasions between 1991 and 2003, the coalition used force in response to what it deemed to be Iraq's material breaches of the disarmament provisions of Resolution 687 and justified its actions under the authority of Resolution 678.[15] The Security Council never condemned these actions, nor questioned the reliance on the continuing validity of 678. In fact, in Resolution 949 on October 4, 1994, the Security Council explicitly reaffirmed Resolution 678.

In the fall and winter of 2002 as Saddam Hussein again impeded the work of UN weapons inspectors, the Security Council adopted Resolution 1441, which after recounting and deploring Iraq's various violations of Resolution 687 at some length, found Iraq to be in material breach of the ceasefire and afforded Iraq a "final opportunity" to comply.

In accordance with the customary international law governing armistices, the United States properly provided notice on March 17, 2003 that it considered the ceasefire agreement to be denounced by Iraq: just as a right of self-defense may be exercised unilaterally without resort to the Security Council, so too may any party to a ceasefire agreement, even one endorsed by the Security Council, determine that the ceasefire has been materially breached and announce that it is resuming hostilities with the breaching party. As a final opportunity to avoid the resumption of offensive hostilities, the United States gave Saddam Hussein and his sons 48 hours to leave Iraq. They failed to seize this final reprieve and the invasion of Iraq commenced, leading ultimately to Hussein's capture and the fall of his government.

III. Criticism of the Legal Basis for the 2003 Invasion

The legal basis put forth by the coalition to justify the 2003 invasion of Iraq was hardly without criticism. The Security Council does not conduct straw polls, but France made no effort to hide the fact it would veto the so-called second or eighteenth resolution—a resolution finding Iraq in violation of Resolution 1441 and explicitly authorizing the use of force to compel compliance.[16] Any attempt to prognosticate the level of support in the Security Council, or in the international community writ large, was complicated by the fact that France was quite public in its insistence that the Security Council would not explicitly authorize force, and the United States was equally public in its insistence that such authorization was not legally required.

Over the intervening six years, many international law scholars have critiqued the *jus ad bellum* basis for the 2003 invasion.[17] Their criticism of the coalition's legal case generally revolves around three concerns: 1) Resolution 678 only authorized the use of force to expel Iraq from Kuwait, 2) Resolution 687 does not permit unilateral enforcement and 3) Resolution 1441 required further authorization or findings by the Security Council before force could be used.

Resolution 678 Only Authorized Expelling Iraq from Kuwait

The coalition's legal basis was grounded on the belief that Resolution 678 authorized not just the expulsion of Iraq from Kuwait, but more broadly the use of force to restore international peace and security to the region and that Iraq's material breaches of Resolution 687 constituted a continuing threat to such peace and security. The plain language of Resolution 678 authorized "all necessary means to uphold and implement resolution 660 (1990) *and* all subsequent relevant resolutions *and* to restore international peace and security in the area" (emphasis added). Resolution 687 recalled the thirteen previous resolutions on the Iraq-Kuwait conflict, reiterated its objective of restoring international peace and security in the area, and affirmed all thirteen previously referenced resolutions, including 678. Read as such, Resolution 687 arguably sets the terms for what would be required to restore international peace and security to the region.

At least two objections can be raised against this position. First, the United States in 1991 did not believe Resolution 678 authorized anything more than expelling Iraq from Kuwait. In explaining the decision to implement a ceasefire rather than pursue Hussein to surrender, several members of the US administration indicated they believed the coalition's mandate was limited to freeing Kuwait.[18] However, Brent Scowcroft, the National Security Advisor at the time, couched the rationale in political rather than legal terms in a book he wrote with President George H.W. Bush: "Going in and occupying Iraq, thus unilaterally exceeding the United Nations' mandate, would have destroyed the precedent of international response to aggression that we hoped to establish.... Unilaterally going significantly beyond that mandate, we might have undermined the confidence of the United Nations to make future grants of authority."[19] Remember the context of 1991: the fall of the Soviet Union, the Security Council's first authorization of the use of force since Korea, and the hope that a new world order would be ushered in, a world order that would see the Security Council finally take its place as the primary guarantor of international peace and security. Nevertheless, even if the United States initially viewed its mandate as limited, that view quickly evaporated with the establishment of the no-fly zones and the legal rationale put forth to justify the no-fly zones, a rationale grounded in 678's authority to restore international peace and security in the region.

A second objection to the relevance of Resolution 678 in 2003 is that Resolution 678 only authorized those member States "co-operating with the Government of Kuwait" to use force. In 1991, Kuwait communicated to the Security Council that it requested assistance from the coalition in expelling Iraq from Kuwait. In 2003, however, Kuwait made this statement to the Security Council: "Kuwait reaffirms that it has not participated and will not participate in any military operation against Iraq and that all measures we are undertaking are aimed at protecting our security, safety and territorial integrity."[20] Admittedly, it is a bit of a stretch to argue that the 2003 coalition was "cooperating" with the government of Kuwait.

This argument weakens, however, in light of the operational reality of the intervening twelve years. During that period, the coalition repeatedly took action against Iraq, especially the establishment and enforcement of the no-fly zones that extended beyond strict protection of and cooperation with Kuwait. Those uses of force were consistently justified as authorized by Resolution 678 and the Security Council never formally objected or ruled otherwise. Thus, the argument that 678 had a very limited purpose weakens in light of subsequent State practice and the at-least-tacit acceptance of such practice by the Security Council.

Resolution 687 Does Not Authorize Unilateral Enforcement

A second general criticism of the coalition's legal basis for the 2003 invasion is that once the ceasefire was encapsulated in a Security Council resolution it became an agreement between Iraq and the Security Council and only the Security Council could redress violations. The belief is that once the Security Council directs the parties to a conflict to comply with a ceasefire agreement, as it did here in Resolution 687, the Security Council's ceasefire directive has the force of law under Article 24 of the UN Charter and the parties may not resume hostilities without the express permission of the Security Council. In essence, a Security Council–approved ceasefire agreement, such as Resolution 687, extinguishes the right of self-defense and any prior Security Council authorization to use force and revives the controlling norm of Article 2(4).

This argument makes the fundamental error of confusing the suspension of hostilities with their termination and it confuses a Security Council order to "cease hostilities" with an order to "cease hostilities so long as the following ceasefire terms are complied with." A ceasefire, which is synonymous with what was historically termed an armistice, is a suspension of arms that does not end the hostile relations between the two sides—the state of war remains both de jure and de facto.[21]

The customary international law governing armistices was codified in the Fourth Hague Convention of 1907. It states an armistice only "suspends" military operations and the parties may resume hostilities after providing proper notice, and any "serious violation" of the armistice gives the other party the right to denounce the ceasefire and resume hostilities.[22] A "serious violation" under Hague IV is consistent with the "material breach" phrase that appears in Article 60(1) of the 1969 Vienna Convention on the Law of Treaties.[23]

As the continuing nature of the Iraq conflict seems to often be forgotten, the following briefly summarizes the ongoing nature of the conflict between 1991 and 2003.[24]

- Between April 1991 and early 2003 over 250,000 sorties were flown by coalition combat and reconnaissance aircraft over Iraq in enforcement of the ceasefire agreement and no-fly zones. Those aircraft were fired upon by Iraqi forces thousands of times and returned fire thousands of times, dropping bombs, firing missiles and launching hundreds of cruise missiles into Iraq.[25]

- Within two days of Iraq's acceptance of the formal ceasefire agreement, the coalition (led by the United States, United Kingdom and France) established a no-fly zone in northern Iraq in response to Iraq's repression of its Kurdish population. The coalition established a second no-fly zone a few months later in southern Iraq after Shiite dissidents were brutally attacked by Iraqi helicopter gunships.[26]

- On December 27, 1992, US aircraft shot down an Iraqi fighter plane flying in the no-fly zone.

- In January 1993 the President of the Security Council twice issued statements declaring Iraq to be in material breach of Resolution 687. US, British and French aircraft attacked several air defense targets in southern Iraq and forty-five Tomahawk cruise missiles were launched at a nuclear fabrication facility.

- On June 26, 1993 the United States launched twenty-four Tomahawk cruise missiles against the Iraqi intelligence headquarters in Baghdad in response to an Iraqi assassination plot against former President George H.W. Bush.

- On September 3, 1996 the United States launched forty-four cruise missiles at fifteen air defense sites located in the newly extended portion of the no-fly zone. Fighter aircraft followed up these attacks the next day by bombing air defense sites that had survived the cruise-missile attacks.

- After another broken promise by Iraq in November 1998 to permit resumption of inspections, President Clinton declared Iraq to be in material breach of the ceasefire and ordered the execution of Operation Desert Fox, which lasted four days, and involved 29,900 troops, thirty-seven ships and 348 aircraft from the United States and additional forces from the United Kingdom. Those forces launched nearly four hundred cruise missiles and over six hundred other bombs and missiles at Iraqi military and weapons of mass destruction targets.[27]
- Between 1999 and 2002 Iraqi forces shot missiles and anti-aircraft fire at coalition aircraft on over one thousand separate occasions. In the majority of those incidents the coalition responded by bombing the offending Iraqi site and in the process damaged or destroyed over four hundred targets. On other occasions US and British aircraft attacked anti-ship missile sites, command-and-control sites, military communications sites, and fuel and ammunition dumps.[28]
- In February 2001 two dozen coalition aircraft attacked five Iraqi targets located just outside of the southern no-fly zone.
- Coalition aircraft dropped 606 bombs or missiles on 391 targets in 2002 alone.[29]

This may be low-intensity conflict, but only a lawyer could argue it was not an ongoing armed conflict. This State practice strengthens the argument that the determination of material breach of a ceasefire agreement, even one endorsed by the Security Council, can be unilaterally made by parties to the agreement. The United States and other members of the coalition determined on numerous occasions that Iraq materially breached the 1991 ceasefire agreement and unilaterally responded to those violations with the use of force. Not only were those unilateral determinations of material breach not condemned by the Security Council, but the Council itself recognized in 1994 in Resolution 949 the continuing validity of Resolution 678 and at least tacitly accepted the unilateral enforcement.

To argue that the coalition needed Security Council authorization before resuming offensive combat operations against Iraq in 2003 is to argue that the right of self-defense and the use of force authorized by the Security Council in Resolution 678 were extinguished upon acceptance of the ceasefire agreement. Simply put, such a contention is without basis in State practice and contrary to an international public policy that should encourage utilization of the Security Council—not punish resort to it. If the right to use force were extinguished and the norm set forth in Article 2(4) again became controlling upon acceptance of a ceasefire agreement, the law would create a perverse disincentive to enter into such agreements. The State prevailing in a conflict would be disinclined to agree to a ceasefire at any time prior to unconditional surrender. Such a law would leave no room for magnanimous efforts to limit the horrors of war through potentially life-saving reprieves.

Resolution 1441 Required Additional Action by the Security Council

A final criticism of the coalition's legal justification for the 2003 invasion relates to the failure to secure a second or eighteenth (depending on your perspective) resolution explicitly authorizing the use of force in response to Iraq's continued material breach of Resolution 687. Resolution 1441 recounted and deplored Iraq's history of violating Resolution 687 at some length, then found Iraq to be in material breach of the ceasefire and afforded Iraq a "final opportunity" to comply. While France and Russia stated publicly they did not believe the finding of "material breach" automatically authorized the use of force against Iraq, the United States and United Kingdom argued that "the resolution established that Iraq's violations of its obligations had crossed the threshold that earlier practice had established for coalition forces to use force consistently with resolution 678."[30]

No permanent member of the Security Council believed Iraq had complied with Resolution 1441. While the Security Council held several sessions on this issue, the United States and United Kingdom believed nothing in Resolution 1441 required the Security Council to adopt another resolution to establish the continuing existence of a material breach, nor did they believe the use of force was predicated on any other "triggering" mechanism.

The US State Department Legal Advisor noted there are important similarities between Resolution 1441 and Resolution 678: "Using the same terminology that it later adopted in Resolution 1441, the Council in Resolution 678 decided to allow Iraq a 'final opportunity' to comply with the obligations that the Council had established in previous resolutions."[31] There was no requirement that coalition members return to the Security Council for a determination that Iraq had failed to comply, nor did they do so before commencing operations. "The language of Resolution 1441 tracked the language of Resolution 678, and the resolution operated in the same way to authorize coalition forces to bring Iraq into compliance with its obligations."[32]

Resolution 1441 is a classic example of diplomatic finesse: it provided the coalition with a clear finding of "material breach," while also requiring that Iraqi noncompliance be reported to the Security Council for "assessment." In other words, Resolution 1441 can be fairly read as an agreement to disagree—or simply as tacit acceptance of the operational code that existed for more than twelve years. Specifically, political differences prevented positive action by the Security Council, which meant that member States acting of their own volition would step into the void and take the action they believed was necessary to restore international peace and security; those actions, based on the belief they were authorized by Resolution 678, were never condemned by the Security Council.

IV. Conclusion

Today we see a vast disparity between the sophisticated institutions established to regulate international trade and the relatively primitive system in place to regulate the international use of force. To the extent its Chapter VII resolutions are legally binding on all member States, the Security Council exercises very limited quasi-legislative and -judicial powers, yet has no real enforcement powers. While the UN Charter envisions a standing UN military force available to enforce the Security Council's Chapter VII authorities, member States declined in practice to cede such enforcement authority to the Security Council, preferring instead to keep those powers to themselves.

The modalities of enforcement of Security Council resolutions will continue to be debated, yet the normative foundation of the Charter survives the 2003 invasion of Iraq. Remember the lengths to which the United States, United Kingdom and Australia went to couch their legal rationale in terms of the Charter's framework and the relevant Security Council Chapter VII resolutions. The Charter lives on, even when the Security Council is unable or unwilling to act, and even when that inaction forces member States to take enforcement action themselves.

Notes

1. Wesley K. Clark, Address at the UCLA School of Law: Iraq War Legal, Not Legitimate (Jan. 22, 2007), summary *available at* http://www.international.ucla.edu/article.asp?parentid=61882.

2. INDEPENDENT INTERNATIONAL COMMISSION ON KOSOVO, THE KOSOVO REPORT: CONFLICT, INTERNATIONAL RESPONSE, LESSONS LEARNED 4 (2000), *available at* http://www.reliefweb.int/library/documents/thekosovoreport.htm.

3. Owen Bowcot, *Was the War Legal? Leading Lawyers Give Their Verdict*, GUARDIAN.CO.UK, Mar. 2004, http://www.guardian.co.uk/politics/2004/mar/02/uk.internationaleducationnews.

4. Letter Dated 20 March 2003 from the Permanent Representative of the United States of America to the United Nations Addressed to the President of the Security Council, U.N. Doc. S/2003/351 (2003). *See also* Letter Dated 20 March 2003 from the Permanent Representative of the United Kingdom of Great Britain and Northern Ireland to the United Nations Addressed to the President of the Security Council, U.N. Doc. S/2003/350 (2003); Letter Dated 20 March 2003 from the Permanent Representative of Australia to the United Nations Addressed to the President of the Security Council, U.N. Doc. S/2003/352 (2003).

5. *See* Memorandum from Peter H. Goldsmith, Attorney General, to Anthony Blair, Prime Minister, Iraq: Resolution 1441 (Mar. 7, 2003), *available at* http://news.bbc.co.uk/2/shared/bsp/hi/pdfs/28_04_05_attorney_general.pdf; Memorandum from Jay S. Bybee, Assistant Attorney

General, Office of Legal Counsel, to Alberto R. Gonzales, Counsel to the President, Authority of the President Under Domestic and International Law to Use Military Force Against Iraq (Oct. 23, 2002) [hereinafter OLC Memorandum Opinion]; Memorandum from John C. Yoo, Deputy Assistant Attorney General, Office of Legal Counsel, to Alberto R. Gonzales, Counsel to the President, Effect of a Recent United Nations Security Council Resolution on the Authority of the President Under International Law to Use Military Force Against Iraq (Nov. 8, 2002); Memorandum from John C. Yoo, Deputy Assistant Attorney General, Office of Legal Counsel, to Alberto R. Gonzales, Counsel to the President, Whether False Statements or Omissions in Iraq's Weapons of Mass Destruction Declaration Would Constitute a "Further Material Breach" Under U.N. Security Council Resolution 1441 (Dec. 7, 2002). The US memoranda are available at http://www.justice.gov/olc/2002opinions.htm.

6. *See* Andru E. Wall, *The Legal Case for Invading Iraq*, 32 ISRAEL YEARBOOK OF HUMAN RIGHTS 165, 174 (2002).

7. S.C. Res. 660, U.N. Doc. S/RES/660 (Aug. 2, 1990), declared the Iraqi invasion of Kuwait a "breach of the peace," condemned it, and demanded an immediate and unconditional withdrawal; S.C. Res. 661, U.N. Doc. S/RES/661 (Aug. 6, 1990), affirmed the "inherent right of individual or collective self-defence" and imposed arms and economic sanctions; S.C. Res. 662, U.N. Doc. S/RES/662 (Aug. 9, 1990), declared Iraq's annexation of Kuwait "null and void"; S.C. Res. 664, U.N. Doc. S/RES/664 (Aug. 18, 1990), demanded the protection and release of third-country nationals; S.C. Res. 665, U.N. Doc. S/RES/665 (Aug. 25, 1990), authorized the use of force in maritime interdiction operations to enforce the sanctions; S.C. Res. 666, U.N. Doc. S/RES/666 (Sept. 13, 1990), again demanded the immediate release of third-country nationals; S.C. Res. 667, U.N. Doc. S/RES/667 (Sept. 16, 1990), condemned Iraq's "aggressive acts" and violations of international law; S.C. Res. 669, U.N. Doc. S/RES/669 (Sept. 24, 1990), addressed the issue of assisting countries harmed by the sanctions regime; S.C. Res. 670, U.N. Doc. S/RES/670 (Sept. 25, 1990), condemned Iraq's "flagrant violation . . . of international humanitarian law" and strengthened the sanctions regime; S.C. Res. 674, U.N. Doc. S/RES/674 (Oct. 29, 1990), condemned Iraq's treatment of third-country nations and reminded Iraq of its obligation under international law to pay reparations for the "invasion and illegal occupation of Kuwait"; and S.C. Res. 677, U.N. Doc. S/RES/677 (Nov. 28, 1990), condemned Iraqi treatment of the Kuwaiti population.

8. See Security Council Resolution 678, which authorized the use of force against Iraq; Resolution 687, which affirmed the continuing validity of 678; and Resolution 949, which again affirmed the continuing validity of Resolution 678. S.C. Res. 678, U.N. Doc. S/RES/678 (Nov. 29, 1990); S.C. Res. 687, U.N. Doc. S/RES/687 (Apr. 3, 1991); and S.C. Res. 949, U.N. Doc. S/RES/949 (Oct. 15, 1994).

9. COLIN POWELL, AN AMERICAN JOURNEY 521 (1995).

10. *See* H. NORMAN SCHWARZKOPF, IT DOESN'T TAKE A HERO 485–90 (1992). Schwarzkopf's account should dispel the notion that the ceasefire was dictated by the Security Council and that Schwarzkopf merely conveyed its terms to the Iraqis. Rather, the terms of the ceasefire were dictated by the coalition to Iraq, which then accepted the terms in the field after gaining the concession regarding the presence of helicopters in the ceasefire zone established in southern Iraq.

11. S.C. Res. 687, *supra* note 8.

12. *See* Identical Letters Dated 6 April 1991 from the Permanent Representative of Iraq to the United Nations Addressed Respectively to the Secretary-General and the President of the Security Council, U.N. Doc. S/22456 (Apr. 6, 1991).

13. S.C. Res. 688, U.N. Doc. S/RES/688 (Apr. 5, 1991); S.C. Res. 687, *supra* note 8.

14. *See* Michael N. Schmitt, *Clipped Wings: Effective and Legal No-Fly Zone Rules of Engagement*, 20 LOYOLA OF LOS ANGELES INTERNATIONAL AND COMPARATIVE LAW JOURNAL 727, 732–37 (Dec. 1998).

15. *See* OLC Memorandum Opinion, *supra* note 5, at 4–6.

16. *See* Speech by Mr. Dominique de Villepin, Minister of Foreign Affairs, before the Security Council (Feb. 14, 2003), http://www.ambafrance-uk.org/Speech-by-M-Dominique-de-Villepin ,4954.html.

17. An excellent summary of the arguments critiquing the legality of the recourse to force against Iraq in 2003 is contained in Sean D. Murphy, *Assessing the Legality of Invading Iraq*, 92 GEORGETOWN LAW JOURNAL 173 (2004). For a more balanced presentation of views on this subject, see *Agora: Future Implications of the Iraq Conflict*, 97 AMERICAN JOURNAL OF INTERNATIONAL LAW 553–642 (2003) for articles by Lori Fisler Damrosh & Bernard H. Oxman, William Howard Taft IV & Todd Buchwald, John Yoo, Ruth Wedgwood, Richard N. Gardner, Richard M. Falk, Miriam Sapiro, Thomas M. Franck, Tom Farer and Jane Stromseth.

18. POWELL, *supra* note 9, at 521.

19. GEORGE H.W. BUSH & BRENT SCOWCROFT, A WORLD TRANSFORMED 489 (1998).

20. Letter to the President of the Security Council, U.N. SCOR, 58th Sess., 4726th mtg. at 14, U.N. Doc. S/PV.4726 (2003).

21. > [W]hether the armistice convention is to contain provisions purely and simply for regulating the suspension of hostilities, or it is to include articles of surrender, or the vital conditions on which peace proposals will be entertained, are matters also for the determination of the combatants—or depend, rather, on the will and dictation of the victorious belligerent.

COLEMAN PHILLIPSON, TERMINATION OF WAR AND TREATIES OF PEACE 64 (1916).

22. Regulations Respecting the Laws and Customs of War on Land, annexed to Convention No. IV Respecting the Laws and Customs of War on Land art. 40, Oct. 18, 1907, 36 Stat. 2227, *reprinted in* DOCUMENTS ON THE LAWS OF WAR 69 (Adam Roberts & Richard Guelff eds., 3d ed. 2000).

23. YORAM DINSTEIN, WAR, AGGRESSION AND SELF-DEFENCE 57 (4th ed. 2005). Dinstein clarifies, however, that "[t]he *lex specialis* of Article 36 of the Hague Regulations clearly overrides the *lex generalis* of Article 56(2) of the Vienna Convention on the Law of Treaties, which requires a twelve months' minimum notice of intention to denounce a treaty." *Id.*

24. *See* White House Background Paper: A Decade of Deception and Defiance (Sept. 12, 2002), *available at* http://georgewbush-whitehouse.archives.gov/infocus/iraq/decade/book.html.

25. *See* Randall Richard, *Iraq—A Decade of War*, PROVIDENCE JOURNAL, Nov. 7, 2001, at A1.

26. For more on the establishment and enforcement of the no-fly zones, see Michael N. Schmitt, *Clipped Wings: Effective and Legal No-fly Zone Rules of Engagement*, 20 LOYOLA OF LOS ANGELES INTERNATIONAL & COMPARATIVE LAW JOURNAL 727 (1998).

27. Department of Defense News Briefing, Secretary of Defense William S. Cohen & General Anthony C. Zinni, Operation Desert Fox, DEFENSE.GOV, Dec. 21, 1998, http://www.defense.gov/transcripts/transcript.aspx?transcriptid=1792.

28. DoD News Briefing, Lieutenant Colonel S. Campbell (Aug. 10, 2002).

29. MICHAEL R. GORDON & BERNARD E. TRAINOR, COBRA II: THE INSIDE STORY OF THE INVASION AND OCCUPATION OF IRAQ 79 (2007).

30. Taft & Buchwald, *supra* note 17, at 557, 561.

31. *Id.* at 562.

32. *Id.* at 563.

V

Legal Bases for Coalition Combat Operations in Iraq, May 2003–Present

Alexandra Perina*

I. Introduction

US combat operations in Iraq in 2003 began with airstrikes on March 19 and swiftly overwhelmed the Iraqi armed forces. Within six weeks, US and coalition forces were in control of almost all major cities in Iraq, and Saddam Hussein's army was considered defeated. On May 1, 2003, from the deck of the *USS Abraham Lincoln*, President Bush famously declared that major combat operations in Iraq had ended.[1] His observation that "Americans, following a battle, want nothing more than to return home [a]nd that is your direction tonight" proved, however, to be premature. Six-and-a-half years later, 120,000 US troops remain in Iraq.[2] This article examines the legal underpinnings for US-led military operations in Iraq following the defeat of regular Iraqi military forces.

International law reflects a number of legal bases on which a State may undertake military operations in foreign territory. The most common legal grounds include a State's exercise of self-defense, the authorization of the United Nations Security Council and the consent of the foreign State. A further ground, though it may at first glance appear to conflate issues of *jus ad bellum* and *jus in bello,* is found in the obligations of an occupying State under the laws of war. Each of these legal

* Attorney Adviser in the Office of the Legal Adviser, US Department of State. The views presented in this paper are not necessarily representative of those of the State Department or the US government.

grounds has formed a basis—often in overlapping and interdependent ways—for the US military operations in Iraq during the past six-and-a-half years.

For purposes of this paper, the US presence in Iraq will be examined in three phases: first, during the occupation of Iraq, which formally ended on June 28, 2004; second, the period following the end of formal occupation until December 31, 2008; and finally, the current period, which began on January 1, 2009, and continues today.

II. Belligerent Occupation of Iraq (May 2003 to June 28, 2004)

Whether a territory is occupied is a question of fact, namely, whether "it is actually placed under the authority of the hostile army."[3] This requirement includes both a physical and an administrative component: an occupying power must both have firm physical possession of enemy territory and substitute its authority for that of the local government in that area. Occupation "extends only to the territory where such authority has been established and can be exercised."[4]

While it may be difficult to establish from public records specific dates on which particular areas of Iraq became occupied by US and coalition forces, contemporaneous documents indicate that the occupation of Iraq more or less in its entirety was established by mid-May 2003. In a letter to the President of the UN Security Council on May 8, 2003, the US and UK Permanent Representatives to the United Nations announced the establishment of the Coalition Provisional Authority (CPA) "to exercise power of government temporarily."[5] While the word "occupation" appears nowhere in the letter, it nonetheless made clear that the United States and the United Kingdom, through the CPA, undertook the role and responsibilities of powers belligerently occupying Iraq under the laws of war. Subsequently, on May 22, 2003, the UN Security Council, noting the May 8 letter, "recogniz[ed] the specific authorities, responsibilities, and obligations under applicable international law of [the United States and the United Kingdom] as occupying powers under unified command."[6]

The insurgency emerged soon afterward, with attacks directed not only against US and coalition forces, but against Iraqis perceived to be "collaborating" with the coalition, emerging Iraqi political leaders, and Iraqi police and military forces. Insurgent targets included the UN headquarters, the Jordanian Embassy, the Al Rasheed hotel, power stations, foreign companies and oil installations. The insurgents themselves were composed of various groups, including Shia militants, foreign fighters with anti-coalition motives, Al Qaeda in Iraq and Iraqi nationalists (most of whom were Baath Party members). With the exception of the Baathists, none of the insurgent groups represented or was loyal to the government of

Saddam Hussein. Their tactics included the use of car bombs, improvised explosive devices, suicide bombs, hostage taking and indiscriminate rocket attacks. Insurgents often intentionally targeted Iraqi and foreign civilians and evidenced little regard for civilian casualties when targeting military objects.[7]

Throughout the time they were present in Iraq, US and coalition forces retained the right of individual self-defense, that is, the right to use force to defend themselves against attacks by hostile forces. US and coalition forces also, however, undertook offensive military operations to combat the insurgency. During the period of occupation, the basis under international law for these operations derived from two sources. The first ground stems from the rights and obligations of the occupying power under laws of war to provide for public order. A second and supplemental ground was conveyed in the October 16, 2003 UN Security Council authorization for coalition forces "to take all necessary measures to contribute to the maintenance of security and stability in Iraq."[8]

Law of War

While the lawfulness of the US invasion of Iraq remains a matter of debate,[9] it has no bearing on the rights and obligations of the occupying US and coalition forces and the occupied population once that relationship is established. The *Hostages Trial* at the International Military Tribunal at Nuremberg[10] affirmed that whether or not an initial act of invasion was lawful is a *jus ad bellum* question separate and legally distinct from the *jus in bello* rules concerning an occupant's (and occupied population's) rights and obligations.[11]

Upon recognizing the United States and United Kingdom as occupying powers, the UN Security Council, in Resolution 1483 of May 22, 2003, "call[ed] upon all concerned to comply fully with their obligations under international law including in particular the Geneva Conventions of 1949 and the Hague Regulations of 1907." Of the many rights and responsibilities of an occupying power, one of the most fundamental is the obligation reflected in Article 43 of the Hague Regulations, which reads in its common English translation:

> The authority of the legitimate power having in fact passed into the hands of the occupant, the latter shall take all the measures in his power to restore, and ensure, as far as possible, public order and safety, while respecting, unless absolutely prevented, the laws in force in the country.

It has been noted that the authoritative French text of the Regulations refers to "*l'ordre et la vie publics*," i.e., public order and life, whereas the accepted English translation inexplicably substitutes "safety" for "life."[12] This peculiarity of translation not only creates a redundancy, insofar as it is not clear what "public safety" encompasses beyond "public order," but, more importantly, omits the social and commercial aspects related to the broader concept of "public life." Consistent with the authoritative text, this paper focuses on the obligation relating to "public order."

The duty on the occupying power to "take all the measures in his power to restore, and ensure, as far as possible" public order reflects both an authorization for the occupying power and important limitations on its obligation. The duty is to take affirmative measures to provide order for the population under its control—it is not permitted to ignore chaos and unrest affecting the public even if occupying forces themselves can avoid these risks—and this obligation necessarily implies a corresponding authority to take such measures. That duty is qualified in two important regards. First, the obligation on the occupying power stops short of requiring a result; the caveat that measures be taken to ensure order "as far as possible" reflects the recognition that the occupying power may not be able to achieve public order, even upon dutifully taking all measures in its power.[13] Second, measures taken by the occupying power to these ends must respect local law "unless absolutely prevented." The duty to respect local law would include domestic provisions relating to human rights, unless such provisions are displaced by specific rules of the law of occupation, as the *lex specialis*, or the occupying power is "absolutely prevented" from implementing them.[14]

The Fourth Geneva Convention also addresses an occupying power's duty and authority to take measures to address security in occupied territories. As a general matter, Article 27 states that parties to a conflict, whether in their own territories or in occupied territory, "may take such measures of control and security in regard to protected persons as may be necessary as a result of the war."[15] More specifically, Article 78 of the Fourth Convention provides that in occupied territory, if an occupying power "considers it necessary, for imperative reasons of security, to take safety measures concerning protected persons, it may, at the most, subject them to assigned residence or to internment."

Article 78 acknowledges the potential threat posed by civilians in occupied territory to the occupying power; the purpose of internment pursuant to Article 78, much like detention of prisoners of war under the Third Geneva Convention, is preventative.[16] The Fourth Convention leaves broad discretion to the occupying power to determine whether internment is "necessary for imperative reasons of security"; its official commentary notes only that such internment should be "exceptional" and that internment must be based on individualized threat determinations, not collective measures.[17] In practice, "imperative reasons" in this context have been understood to be distinct from criminal justice standards that require, for example, probable cause of past criminal activity or indictment for criminal prosecution. Article 78 also requires that internees have a right of appeal of the decision to detain them, and periodic review of that decision at least every six months. As discussed further below, detention operations, undertaken in reliance on Article 78, formed a crucial part of coalition forces' counterinsurgency strategy.

In the May 8 letter to the Security Council, the United States and the United Kingdom affirmed their commitment to provide for public order and security, noting that they, with coalition partners and through the CPA,

> shall inter alia, provide for security in and for the provisional administration of Iraq, including by: deterring hostilities; maintaining the territorial integrity of Iraq and securing Iraq's borders; . . . maintaining civil law and order, including through encouraging international efforts to rebuild the capacity of the Iraqi civilian police force; eliminating all terrorist infrastructure and resources within Iraq and working to ensure that terrorists and terrorist groups are denied safe haven. . . .[18]

The reference in the May 8 letter to "deterring hostilities"—drafted before the major onslaught of the insurgency—recognizes that hostilities can re-emerge in occupied territory. Armed opposition to occupation has not been viewed as negating the ongoing status of occupation so long, at least, as the opposition does not actually wrest effective control of an occupied area.[19]

Renewed combat during an occupation requires the occupying power to apply concurrently two branches of the law of war: the law on the conduct of hostilities will apply with regard to combatants and civilians taking direct part in hostilities, and the law of occupation will continue to apply concerning civilians not taking direct part in hostilities.[20] Combatants who met the criteria for prisoners of war established in the Third Geneva Convention continued to receive the protections and treatment due to prisoners of war under the laws of war. More prevalent in the Iraqi insurgency, however, were guerillas or saboteurs who did not qualify as prisoners of war and were not entitled to combatants' privileges.[21] Such insurgents could be detained as civilians under Article 78 of the Fourth Convention and prosecuted for their hostile acts pursuant to existing local law or laws promulgated by the occupying power.

UN Security Council Authorization

By the fall of 2003, insurgent attacks had become frequent and widespread. In Resolution 1511 in October 2003, the Security Council expressly noted the terrorist bombings of the Jordanian and Turkish Embassies, the United Nations headquarters and the Imam Ali Mosque, and the murders of a Spanish diplomat and a member of the Iraqi Governing Council, Dr. Akila al-Hashimi, all of which had occurred in the preceding 10 weeks.[22] Resolution 1511 also acknowledged the Iraqi Governing Council's intent to convene a conference to prepare a new constitution, and called for the CPA to cooperate with the Governing Council and "to return governing responsibilities and authority to the people of Iraq as soon as practicable."[23] Finding that security and stability would be essential to accomplishing the political goals outlined in the Resolution, the Security Council, acting under Chapter VII of the UN Charter, which allows it to take actions necessary to maintain or restore international peace and security, went on to "[authorize] a multinational force under unified command to take all necessary measures to contribute to the maintenance of security and stability in Iraq."[24] Coalition forces, effectively already under the unified command of the United States, became known as the Multinational Force–Iraq (MNF-I).

The broad UN mandate for the MNF-I provided a legal basis for counterinsurgency and counterterrorism operations independent of the authorities in the law of war. This authorization from the Security Council was not strictly speaking necessary, as a matter of international law, for coalition forces at the time it was conveyed, because the coalition had pre-existing and robust bases upon which to provide for security. Nevertheless, it established the legal framework that would become of primary importance at the end of occupation the following year.

III. Authorization for MNF-I under UN Security Council Resolutions 1546 et seq. (June 28, 2004 to December 31, 2008)

On June 28, 2004, the belligerent occupation of Iraq by the United States and United Kingdom ended as a matter of international law, with the formal transfer of administrative authority and responsibility from the CPA to the interim government of Iraq. While in popular parlance the transfer of authority was heralded as the "transfer of sovereignty" back to Iraq, under the law of occupation, Iraqi sovereignty always remained vested in Iraq—occupying powers are simply administrators of the State until the period of occupation terminates.[25]

The presence and activities of the MNF-I in Iraq remained sizable and significant. During this middle period, the legal bases for US military operations were the continued authorization of the UN Security Council, acting under Chapter VII of the UN Charter, and the consent of the government of Iraq, upon which the UN authorization was predicated.

UN Security Council Authorization

In anticipation of the transfer of authority to the interim government of Iraq and the end of belligerent occupation, the Security Council passed Resolution 1546 on

June 8, 2004. Acting again under Chapter VII of the UN Charter, the Security Council reiterated the authorization and mandate of the MNF-I, stating that it

> shall have the authority to take all necessary measures to contribute to the maintenance of security and stability in Iraq in accordance with the letters annexed to this resolution expressing, inter alia, the Iraqi request for the continued presence of the [MNF-I] and setting out its tasks, including by preventing and deterring terrorism.[26]

One of the annexed letters, from US Secretary of State Colin Powell, explicitly notes that the agreed tasks of the MNF-I would entail combat operations, including detention operations, to address insurgent and other violent forces threatening Iraq's internal security.

> The MNF stands ready to continue to undertake a broad range of tasks . . . . These include activities necessary to counter ongoing security threats posed by forces seeking to influence Iraq's political future through violence. This will include combat operations against members of these groups, internment when necessary for imperative reasons of security, and the continued search for and securing of weapons that threaten Iraq's security.[27]

Consent of the Government of Iraq

Unlike the original Security Council authorization for the MNF-I in Resolution 1511, the extension of the authorization in Resolution 1546 was premised upon the consent of the government of Iraq. Resolution 1546 noted "the Iraqi request for the continued presence of the multinational force" in the annexed letter from the Prime Minister of the Iraqi interim government, Ayad Allawi, which stated:

> There continue . . . to be forces in Iraq, including foreign elements, that are opposed to our transition to peace, democracy, and security. . . . Until we are able to provide security for ourselves . . . we ask for the support of the Security Council and the international community in this endeavor. We seek a new resolution on the Multinational Force (MNF) mandate to contribute to maintaining security in Iraq, including through the tasks and arrangements set out in the letter from Secretary of State Colin Powell.[28]

Resolution 1546 further established that the mandate for MNF-I would be reviewed "at the request of the Government of Iraq" or in twelve months, and declared that the Security Council "will terminate this mandate earlier if requested by the Government of Iraq."[29] Secretary of State Colin Powell separately affirmed that US forces would leave Iraq if the interim Iraqi government so requested.[30]

The authorization of the Security Council acting under Chapter VII of the Charter and the consent of the government of Iraq would each suffice independently to provide a basis in international law for the US and coalition military presence and counterinsurgency activities in Iraq. As a political matter, however, the two grounds were mutually dependent. It is doubtful that the Security Council would have continued to authorize the MNF-I without the consent of the government of Iraq. Conversely, given the nascent state of the interim Iraqi government, it is questionable whether its consent alone would have been perceived to be fully independent and legitimate without the imprimatur of the international community for the MNF-I and its actions. As it was, the Security Council mandate for the MNF-I was annually reviewed and renewed, at the request of the government of Iraq, through December 31, 2008.[31]

Consequences of the End of Belligerent Occupation

While in popular and sometimes cynical terminology, the US and coalition presence in Iraq continued to be referred to as an "occupation" long after June 2004, as a matter of law the consent of the Iraqi government and the decision of the Security Council were each independently sufficient to terminate the occupation. First, the Security Council decision welcoming the end of occupation in Resolution 1546 could itself effect the end of belligerent occupation, given the effect of Security Council decisions under Chapter VII. Because member States of the United Nations agree to accept decisions of the Security Council, even where such decisions may conflict with otherwise applicable international law,[32] the decision of the Security Council that an occupation will terminate is sufficient to make it so as a matter of international law.[33]

Second, the consent of the Iraqi government also terminated belligerent occupation, and with it, the authorities and responsibilities that accrue to a belligerently occupying power under the law of war. Yoram Dinstein has noted examples of "consensual occupation," such as the Allied powers' presence in and administration of France, Belgium and the Netherlands at the end of World War II with the consent of the sovereign governments in exile. In such "consensual" circumstances, the established law of occupation, including Article 43 of the Hague Regulations, was not applied.[34]

While there have been circumstances in which the military forces of a formerly occupying power remained in a country after the occupation terminated, such as in Germany and Japan in the 1950s, in those cases, the purpose of the continued foreign military presence was primarily to defend the host nation against external threats.[35] The end of an occupation typically presupposes that internal military operations have ceased and, under the law of war, prisoners of war and civilian internees must be released. In the post-occupation period in Iraq, however, MNF-I military operations continued in significant force, and security detentions not only continued but increased dramatically in volume.

Which legal rules, then, applied to the post-occupation military operations in Iraq? Secretary of State Powell's letter annexed to Resolution 1546 affirmed that the "forces that make up MNF are and will remain committed at all times to act consistently with their obligations under the law of armed conflict, including the Geneva Conventions."[36] This commitment to the continued application of the law of war failed to clarify, however, which branches of humanitarian law were appropriate—namely, whether the situation continued to qualify as an international armed conflict subject to the full array of provisions under the Third and Fourth Geneva Conventions, or whether, given the absence of any conflict between the United States and coalition countries and the government of Iraq, it had become a non-international armed conflict, to which Common Article 3 alone among the provisions of the Geneva Conventions and other customary laws of war applied. On this question there was no consensus. The International Committee of the Red Cross (ICRC) took the view that the residual conflict between insurgent forces, on the one hand, and the United States, coalition forces and the government of Iraq, on the other, constituted a non-international armed conflict.[37] Others, including Adam Roberts, suggested that given the non-Iraqi character of the MNF-I and foreign insurgent fighters, and the language of Resolution 1546, the more robust provisions of the Geneva Conventions should continue to apply.[38]

While the United States did not formally revisit its 2003 determination that the conflict was of an international character, it generally avoided characterizing the status of the conflict by pointing to the authorization in the Security Council resolution. This response can be fairly criticized for conflating *jus ad bellum* issues—the basis for the use of force, i.e., the authorization of the Security Council and the consent of the Iraqi government—with *jus in bello* questions of which rules of the law of armed conflict applied to the conduct of the MNF-I.

In practice, the MNF-I generally continued to apply the more robust rules applicable to international armed conflicts to its operations in Iraq. During this period, however, MNF-I's operations also began to shift from a purely war paradigm to a law-enforcement paradigm, which fostered cooperation with the government of Iraq and paved the way for Iraqi assumption of security responsibility. Detention operations, in particular, incorporated law-enforcement elements within the purview of the Iraqi government alongside the security detentions authorized under Resolution 1546.

The standards and procedures of MNF-I internment operations evolved over time, and increasingly worked in coordination with Iraqi law and the criminal justice system. The day before the occupation ended, the CPA promulgated a revision to CPA Memorandum Number 3, which outlined the types of detentions MNF-I would undertake and the procedures applicable to each type.[39] Reflective of the US reluctance to pin down the applicability of the Geneva Conventions to post-occupation activities, the revised memorandum was careful to avoid any implication that the Fourth Convention terms on security internees continued to apply as a matter of law. Language that appeared in the original memorandum, issued in June 2003, stating that certain provisions were undertaken "in accordance with" the Fourth Geneva Convention was omitted. Indeed, the chapeau of the Revised CPA Memorandum Number 3 stated, "Determining, that the relevant and appropriate provisions of the [Fourth Convention] constitute an appropriate framework consistent with its mandate in continuance of measures previously adopted."[40]

CPA Memorandum Number 3 as revised established a review process that would satisfy the right of appeal provided in Article 78. In addition, juvenile detainees were to be held for no longer than 12 months from the date of internment, and adult internees held for 18 months were to receive review before a Joint Detention Committee, which included Iraqi participation, to authorize further internment. The revised memorandum also gave MNF-I the right to apprehend individuals who were not considered security internees but who were suspected of violating Iraqi law. Criminal detainees were to be "handed over to Iraqi authorities as soon as reasonably practicable," though they could be kept in MNF-I custody upon Iraqi request, based on security or capacity considerations. The revised memorandum affirmed that the ICRC would continue to have access to both categories of detainees, and extended similar access to the Iraqi ombudsman for prisons and detainees.[41]

The procedures applicable to both security internees and criminal detainees continued to develop over the course of MNF-I's operations in Iraq during this period. For example, the review procedures for security internees were revised to allow detainees to be present at their review board hearings.[42] Cooperation with Iraqi authorities also increased, in particular in terms of sharing evidence to facilitate criminal prosecutions, and MNF-I and the interim Iraqi government signed a separate memorandum of understanding concerning arrangements for high-value detainees held pending prosecution for war crimes or other atrocities.

IV. January 1, 2009 to the Present

In the fall of 2007, Iraq's political leaders announced that they sought to normalize the status of Iraq in the international community and bilaterally with the United States. This entailed foremost seeking an end to the Security Council actions under

Chapter VII that relied on a finding that the situation in Iraq constituted a "threat to international peace and security." In November 2007, President George W. Bush and Prime Minister Nouri al-Maliki outlined their approach to these ends: Iraq requested a renewal of the MNF-I mandate from the Security Council for a final year, during which time Iraq and the United States would negotiate the details of a bilateral relationship addressing security, economic, diplomatic, political and cultural matters.[43] The results of these negotiations were two international agreements that entered into force on January 1, 2009: the Agreement Between the United States of America and the Republic of Iraq on the Withdrawal of United States Forces from Iraq and the Organization of Their Activities during Their Temporary Presence in Iraq (the "Security Agreement")[44] and the Strategic Framework Agreement for a Relationship of Friendship and Cooperation between the United States of America and the Republic of Iraq (the "Strategic Framework Agreement").[45]

The Security Agreement addresses a variety of security and military issues, including authorization from the Iraqi government for US combat and detentions operations, and status provisions for US forces, while the Strategic Framework Agreement covers political, economic, and cultural cooperation.[46] Since the expiration of the UN mandate for the MNF-I and the entry into force of the Security Agreement on January 1, 2009, the legal basis for the US military presence and operations in Iraq has been the consent of the Iraqi government.

Iraqi authorization for the US military presence and operations in Iraq need not have been conveyed in a legally binding document—or even in writing—to be valid as a matter of law. There were advantages, however, to memorializing Iraqi authorization in a public, binding instrument. First, reducing the terms of the arrangement into such a document ensured transparency as to the terms under which US forces remain in Iraq. Second, placing the authorization in a legally binding international agreement rendered it, under Iraqi domestic law, subject to the approval of the Iraqi Council of Representatives, which enhanced the legitimacy of the arrangement within Iraq.

Consent of the Government of Iraq

Acknowledging ongoing insurgent and terrorist acts, Article 4 of the Security Agreement reflects Iraqi consent for US forces' presence in Iraq and defines the purpose of their mission: "The Government of Iraq requests the temporary assistance of the United States Forces for the purposes of supporting Iraq in its efforts to maintain security and stability in Iraq, including cooperation in the conduct of operations against al-Qaeda and other terrorist groups, outlaw groups, and remnants of the former regime."[47]

This authorization departs significantly in a number of respects from the broad UN mandate for the MNF-I to take "all necessary measures" to provide for security and stability in Iraq. The Security Agreement reflects the Iraqi assumption of primary responsibility for security in Iraq; consequently, the US mission is framed in terms of "supporting Iraq in its efforts." Consistent with this approach, the agreement requires that all such military operations are subject to the agreement of the government of Iraq and must be coordinated with Iraqi authorities.[48]

Detention operations under the Security Agreement also reflect a significant departure from the law of war detentions the coalition undertook under the Article 78 framework in the earlier phases of its activities. Under a law of war framework, detentions are conceived of as incident to military combat authorities; under the Security Agreement, detentions are addressed separately from the authorization to conduct military operations and are integrated into Iraqi law-enforcement operations. Article 22 of the Security Agreement addresses two categories of detainees: the so-called "legacy security detainees," individuals in US custody at the time the agreement came into force who had been taken into custody by the MNF-I under UN authorization, and new captures who would come into US forces' custody after the entry into force of the agreement.[49]

Signaling the end of law of war security internment, the agreement outlines the three general disposition options for legacy security detainees. Under the agreement, the government of Iraq is to review the cases of all of the approximately 15,800 legacy security detainees to determine whom it could criminally prosecute.[50] Detainees for whom Iraqi authorities issued a valid criminal arrest warrant and detention order are to be transferred to Iraqi authorities for prosecution. Detainees against whom a criminal case cannot or was not brought must be released by US forces "in a safe and orderly manner, unless otherwise requested by the Government of Iraq and in accordance with Article 4 of this Agreement."[51] Such a request by the government of Iraq for another disposition might include repatriation to a third country. Iraqi authorities may also request that a detainee remain in US custody pending prosecution if Iraqi authorities determine that they do not have the capacity to detain certain criminal suspects safely and humanely in custody.

Resolving the cases of the thousands of security detainees in US custody has proved time-consuming and politically delicate. By December 2009, 1,441 legacy security detainees had been transferred to Iraqi authorities for prosecution, 7,499 legacy security detainees had been released and approximately 4,600 detainees remained in US custody. US forces estimated that disposition of all detainees would not be complete until August 2010.[52] The Security Agreement does not specify a timetable for the completion of this process, and the requirement that releases occur in "safe and orderly manner" reflects an understanding that releases will be implemented with care to facilitate the safety of the individual and the stability of Iraqi society. To mitigate security risks, US forces release detainees whom Iraqi authorities determined would not be prosecuted in order of least to greatest security threat. While many welcomed the end of "indefinite" MNF-I detentions, the release of these detainees was also criticized as contributing to an uptick in violence.[53]

Under the Security Agreement, new captures are processed in accordance with the domestic judicial system. The agreement precludes US forces from arresting or detaining individuals "except through an Iraqi decision issued in accordance with Iraqi law and pursuant to Article 4" of the Security Agreement, which authorizes US military operations and requires US forces to respect Iraqi law.[54] The preference is to arrest individuals pursuant to an Iraqi-issued arrest warrant. If a warrant is not feasible, individuals may be taken into US forces' custody and must be turned over to a competent Iraqi authority within 24 hours, at which point Iraqi authorities determine whether continued detention is warranted.

As during the second phase of the conflict, questions remain about how to characterize the nature of US engagement in Iraq. Given the normalized bilateral relationship between the two countries, there is little basis for the position that the conflict remains of an international character. The ICRC continues to view the situation in Iraq as constituting a non-international armed conflict.[55] However, the government of Iraq has not publicly characterized the state of affairs as an armed conflict or invoked the state of emergency provisions in its constitution. Moreover, in its handling of detention operations, it strictly follows a law-enforcement model. While the United States also has declined to publicly characterize the status of its activities, US forces remain at all times bound by the rules of Common Article 3 of the Geneva Conventions and other customary rules of the law of war.

Finally, although the United States has not asserted this ground, the possibility exists—at least in theory—that during any of these phases the United States could have asserted a self-defense basis for conducting counterterrorism operations in Iraq against Al Qaeda and its affiliates, even if the government of Iraq requested that US forces depart. Such an argument would likely require the United States to determine that the host nation was itself unable or unwilling to address the threat posed by Al Qaeda as a prerequisite to asserting that intervention without host-nation consent would be warranted. While the United States has not relied on this theory, and any such assertion during the duration of the Security Agreement would provoke difficult questions about compliance with international legal obligations incurred under the Security Agreement, the self-defense basis remains a theoretical, if highly speculative, option.

Notes

1. Address to the Nation on Iraq from the USS Abraham Lincoln, 1 PUBLIC PAPERS 410 (May 1, 2003), full text *available at* WASHINGTONPOST.COM, May 1, 2003, http://www.washingtonpost.com/ac2/wp-dyn/A2627-2003May1.

2. *See, e.g.*, DoD News Briefing with Gen. Raymond Odierno from Iraq, DEFENSE.GOV, Oct. 1, 2009, http://www.defenselink.mil/transcripts/transcript.aspx?transcriptid=4490.

3. Regulations Respecting the Laws and Customs of War on Land, annexed to Hague Convention No. IV Respecting the Laws and Customs of War on Land art. 42, Oct. 18, 1907, 36 Stat. 2227, *reprinted in* DOCUMENTS ON THE LAWS OF WAR 69 (Adam Roberts & Richard Guelff eds., 3d ed. 2000).

4. *Id.*

5. Letter of 8 May 2003 from the Permanent Representatives of the United States of America and the United Kingdom of Great Britain and Northern Ireland to the President of the Security Council, U.N. Doc. S/2003/538 (2003) [hereinafter US/UK Letter].

6. S.C. Res. 1483, U.N. Doc. S/RES/1483 (May 22, 2003).

7. On the insurgency generally, see, e.g., AHMED S. HASHIM, INSURGENCY AND COUNTER-INSURGENCY IN IRAQ (2006); Kenneth Katzman, *Iraq: U.S. Regime Change Efforts and Post-Saddam Governance*, CRS REPORT FOR CONGRESS 29–31 (Jan. 7, 2004), *available at* http://fpc.state.gov/documents/organization/28648.pdf; Lionel Beehner, *Iraq: Status of Iraq's Insurgency*, Council on Foreign Relations Backgrounder (Sept. 13, 2005), http://www.cfr.org/publication/8853/iraq.html.

8. S.C. Res. 1511, U.N. Doc. S/RES/1511 (Oct. 16, 2003).

9. *See, e.g.*, Andru E. Wall, *Was the 2003 Invasion of Iraq Legal?*, which is Chapter IV in this volume, at 69.

10. *In re* List (Hostages Trial, 1948), 8 LAW REPORTS OF TRIALS OF WAR CRIMINALS 34 (1949).

11. YORAM DINSTEIN, THE INTERNATIONAL LAW OF BELLIGERENT OCCUPATION 3 (2009).

12. *Id.* at 89; EYAL BENVENISTI, THE INTERNATIONAL LAW OF OCCUPATION 7 n.1 (2d ed. 2004).

13. DINSTEIN, *supra* note 11, at 92–93.

14. The relation between international humanitarian law and international human rights law in circumstances of armed conflict remains much debated and generally unsettled. For discussion of the interaction between the law of war and human rights law in the context of maintaining order in occupied territory, see Kenneth Watkins, *Maintaining Law and Order During Occupation: Breaking the Normative Chain*, 41 ISRAEL LAW REVIEW 175, 189 (2008).

15. Convention Relative to the Protection of Civilian Persons in Time of War, Aug. 12, 1949, 6 U.S.T. 3516, 75 U.N.T.S. 287, *reprinted in* DOCUMENTS ON THE LAWS OF WAR, *supra* note 3, at 301.

16. COMMENTARY ON THE FOURTH GENEVA CONVENTION OF 12 AUGUST 1949, at 368 (Jean S. Pictet ed., 1952) ("Article 78 relates to people who have not been guilty of any infringement of the penal provisions enacted by the Occupying Power, but that Power may, for reasons of its own, consider them dangerous to its security and is consequently entitled to restrict their freedom of action").

17. *Id.*

18. US/UK Letter, *supra* note 5.

19. Adam Roberts, *The End of Occupation: Iraq 2004*, 54 INTERNATIONAL & COMPARATIVE LAW QUARTERLY 27, 34 (2005) (noting that "in practice the status of occupation has not been viewed as being negated by the existence of violent opposition, especially when that opposition has not had full control of a portion of the state's territory").

20. *See* DINSTEIN, *supra* note 11, at 100.

21. *Id.* at 94–95. Von Glahn notes the view that insurgents who pledged allegiance to the government in exile, aimed to drive out the occupying forces and followed the laws of war (excepting the requirements to openly carry arms and display identifying insignia) should be treated as lawful combatants. GERHARD VON GLAHN, THE OCCUPATION OF ENEMY TERRITORY 52 (1957). The modern view has rejected this position, and in any event, most insurgents in Iraq would fail to meet even von Glahn's more permissive criteria, as most did not act on behalf of the Baathists and failed to abide by the law of war.

22. S.C. Res. 1511, *supra* note 8.

23. *Id.*, paras. 6, 10.

24. *Id.*, para. 13.

25. Roberts, *supra* note 19, at 41; DINSTEIN, *supra* note 11, at 49, citing L. Oppenheim, *The Legal Relations between an Occupying Power and the Inhabitants,* 33 LAW QUARTERLY REVIEW 363, 364 (1917) ("[t]here is not an atom of sovereignty in the authority of the Occupying Power"); VON GLAHN, *supra* note 21, at 31. Accordingly, Security Council Resolutions S.C. Res. 1483, *supra* note 6; S.C. Res. 1511, *supra* note 8; and S.C. Res. 1546, U.N. Doc. S/RES/1546 (June 8, 2004), all relating to Iraq during the period of belligerent occupation, recognized Iraq's continuing "sovereignty."

26. S.C. Res. 1546, *supra* note 25, para. 10.

27. *Id.* at 10 (Annexed letter from United States Secretary of State Colin Powell to Lauro L. Baja, Jr., President of the Security Council, dated June 5, 2004) [hereinafter Powell Letter].

28. *Id.* at 8 (Annexed letter from Prime Minister of the Interim Government of Iraq Dr. Ayad Allawi to Lauro L. Baja, Jr., President of the Security Council, dated June 5, 2004).

29. *Id.*, para. 12.

30. Glenn Kessler, *Powell Says Troops Would Leave Iraq if New Leaders Asked,* WASHINGTON POST, May 15, 2004, at A01, *available at* http://www.washingtonpost.com/wp-dyn/articles/A27950-2004May14.html.

31. S.C. Res. 1637, U.N. Doc. S/RES/1637 (Nov. 8, 2005); S.C. Res. 1723, U.N. Doc. S/RES/1723 (Nov. 28, 2006); S.C. Res. 1790, U.N. Doc. S/RES/1790 (Dec. 18, 2007).

32. U.N. Charter arts. 25, 103.

33. *See* DINSTEIN, *supra* note 11, at 273. This power of the Security Council is widely recognized, though in tension with the general principle that whether an occupation exists depends on the facts on the ground rather than the statements or characterizations of the parties.

34. *Id.* at 37. Dinstein further notes that when status of consent changes, occupation may take on belligerent character. He cites the case of German forces in Italy in the Second World War, which initially established a presence with the consent of Mussolini, but acquired the status of belligerent occupiers after the Mussolini government fell and the royal government declared war on Germany.

35. Roberts, *supra* note 19, at 29–30.

36. Powell Letter, *supra* note 27.

37. *See, e.g.*, Posting of the International Committee of the Red Cross, Iraq post 28 June 2004: protecting persons deprived of freedom remains a priority, http://www.icrc.org/Web/Eng/siteeng0.nsf/iwpList322/89060107D77D7299C1256EE7005200E8.

38. Roberts, *supra* note 19, at 47. For further discussion of the characterization of the conflict over time, see David Turns, *The International Humanitarian Law Classification of Armed Conflicts in Iraq since 2003,* which is Chapter VI in this volume, at 97.

39. CPA Memorandum Number 3 (Revised), Criminal Procedures (Revised) (June 27, 2004), *available at* http://www.iraqcoalition.org/regulations/#Orders (then the Criminal Procedures (Revised) hyperlink). *Compare* CPA Memorandum Number 3, Criminal Procedures

(June 18, 2003), *available at* www.gjpi.org/wp-content/uploads/cpa-memo-3-og.pdf. At the end of occupation, all CPA orders and memoranda became incorporated into Iraqi domestic law until rescinded or amended, under Article 26(c) of the Law of Administration for the State of Iraq During the Transitional Period, Mar. 8, 2004, *available at* http://www.cpa-iraq.org/government/TAL.html.

40. CPA Memorandum Number 3 (Revised), *supra* note 39; CPA Memorandum Number 3, *supra* note 39.

41. CPA Memorandum Number 3 (Revised), *supra* note 39.

42. See Brian J. Bill, *Detention Operations in Iraq: A View from the Ground*, which is Chapter XVII in this volume, at 411, for a discussion of the revised review procedures.

43. Declaration of Principles for a Long-Term Relationship of Cooperation and Friendship Between the Republic of Iraq and the United States of America, Nov. 27, 2007, *available at* http://merln.ndu.edu/archivepdf/iraq/WH/20081204-6.pdf.

44. Agreement Between the United States of America and the Republic of Iraq on the Withdrawal of United States Forces from Iraq and the Organization of Their Activities during Their Temporary Presence in Iraq, U.S.-Iraq, Nov. 17, 2008, *available at* http://www.mnf-iraq.com/images/CGs_Messages/security_agreement.pdf [hereinafter Security Agreement].

45. Strategic Framework Agreement for a Relationship of Friendship and Cooperation between the United States of America and the Republic of Iraq, U.S.-Iraq, Nov. 17, 2008, *available at* https://www.mnf-iraq.com/images/CGs_Messages/strategic_framework_agreement.pdf.

46. The security agreement is often referred to as a SOFA, or status of forces agreement. While it addresses typical status provisions, such as jurisdiction over US forces, taxation, import and export, and entry and exit of forces, it includes additional provisions, such as authorization for military operations and a timetable for the withdrawal of forces, unusual in SOFAs because SOFAs generally govern the status of forces in foreign territory during peacetime. Status provisions for the MNF-I had been addressed in an order promulgated by the CPA prior to the end of occupation, the effective period of which by its terms was tied to the UN mandate of the MNF-I and its presence in Iraq. CPA Order Number 17 (Revised), Status of the Coalition Provisional Authority, MNF-Iraq, Certain Missions and Personnel in Iraq, sec. 20 (June 27, 2004), *available at* http://www.iraqcoalition.org/regulations/#Orders (then the Status of the CPA, MNF-I, Certain Missions and Personnel in Iraq hyperlink).

47. Security Agreement, *supra* note 44, art. 4(1).

48. *Id.*, art. 4(2).

49. *Id.*, art. 22.

50. Blackanthem Military News, Inaugural Meeting of Detention Committee – GOI and MNF-I (Dec. 11, 2008), http://www.blackanthem.com/News/iraqi-freedom/Inaugural-Meeting-of-Detention-Committee---GoI-and-MNF-I19014.shtml.

51. Security Agreement, *supra* note 44, art. 22(4).

52. *U.S. Timetable for Handing Over Iraq Detainees Slips*, REUTERS.COM, Dec. 7, 2009, http://www.reuters.com/article/idUSTRE5B629P20091207.

53. Interview by Jim Muir, BBC News, with Prime Minister Maliki, in Baghdad, Iraq (Apr. 27, 2009), http://news.bbc.co.uk/2/hi/middle_east/8020815.stm.

54. Security Agreement, *supra* note 44, arts. 22(1), 4(1)–(5).

55. *See* Philip Spoerri, Director of International Law, International Committee of the Red Cross, Official Statement at the Ceremony to Celebrate the 60th Anniversary of the 1949 Geneva Conventions: The Geneva Conventions of 1949: Origins and Current Significance (Aug. 12, 2009), http://www.icrc.org/web/eng/siteeng0.nsf/htmlall/geneva-conventions-statement-120809?opendocument.

VI

The International Humanitarian Law Classification of Armed Conflicts in Iraq since 2003

David Turns*

Introduction: Review of the Timeline of Events in Iraq

An armed conflict, within the meaning of international humanitarian law (IHL), began in Iraq when that country was invaded by military forces of the coalition composed primarily of the United States, the United Kingdom and Australia in March 2003. It continues to this day, notwithstanding a certain decline in intensity since the British withdrawal in July 2009 and the reorganization of US forces under a new security agreement with the Iraqi government in December of the same year. Over the course of its duration, the Iraq conflict has undergone three definite mutations in terms of its participants, mutations which have had the effect of altering its characterization under IHL. The four phases of the conflict have been as follows:

1. the initial invasion, which saw hostilities between the coalition forces and those of the Iraqi government of President Saddam Hussein (March to April 2003);

* Senior Lecturer in International Laws of Armed Conflict, Defence Academy of the United Kingdom (Cranfield University). All opinions expressed herein are entirely personal to the author and in no way represent any official view of the British government or Ministry of Defence.

2. the *debellatio* of Iraq and its belligerent occupation by the victors, represented by the Coalition Provisional Authority (CPA), confronted by an increasingly violent insurgency (April 2003 to June 2004);

3. the transformation of the coalition occupying forces, with broader international participation and a United Nations mandate, but still opposed by the insurgency, into the Multinational Force–Iraq (MNF-I) (June 2004 to December 2008); and

4. the continuing presence of US forces (all others having withdrawn) to help confront the insurgency, without a UN mandate but with a security agreement negotiated between the United States and the Iraqi government (since January 2009).

The question of the nature of the armed conflict in Iraq is not of merely academic interest, nor can it be dismissed as an exercise in sterile semantics of no practical importance to the troops on the ground. On the contrary, the determination of the nature of an armed conflict in the sense of IHL has a very real significance for the military forces engaged in the conflict, for it impacts directly such practical military activities as the status of the participants, their consequent classification and treatment after capture by an opposing party, the conduct of hostilities and the use of weaponry. Above all, it determines the international law framework and rules applicable to the situation.

IHL recognizes two basic types of armed conflict: international (IAC) and non-international (NIAC). Although, broadly speaking, many of the same principles of customary international law are now considered applicable in both types of conflict,[1] the fact remains that the detailed legal regulation of conduct in armed conflicts is still contained primarily in the various treaties that have accumulated over the last one hundred fifty years—principally the Hague Regulations of 1907, the Geneva Conventions of 1949 and their Additional Protocols of 1977. The scope of application of each of these instruments is precisely defined, but they were designed for conflicts that were comparatively clear in nature: one State against another State or a State against insurgents, that is, its own nationals in its own territory. A salient feature of the hostilities in Iraq from an Anglo-American perspective, after the CPA was wound down in June 2004 and the coalition occupying forces became a multinational force present with a mandate from the UN Security Council and the consent of the new Iraqi government, has been the fact of State forces being engaged in foreign territory against foreign non-State actors. This situation, not having been expressly envisaged in 1907, 1949 or 1977, is not covered as such in the relevant treaties and its legal characterization remains a matter of some uncertainty.[2] The United States and the United Kingdom, the two principal MNF-I partners in Iraq, did not agree on the legal characterization of the conflict in that country: the United Kingdom considered it to be de facto non-international, while the United States, intellectually hobbled by the Bush administration's insistence on viewing the use of force through the prism of the so-called Global War on Terror,[3] vacillated between the two paradigms of armed conflict. They cannot both have been correct, at least not simultaneously. The controversy surrounding the classification of the armed conflict in Iraq after the belligerent occupation phase was over, and the tendency of governments to rely on their own assessments of such classification—which are usually determined on the basis of the government's own concerns, e.g., its unwillingness to contemplate questions surrounding the status of captured "terrorists" under IHL—rather than on the basis of objective legal considerations, is understandable but unfortunate: firstly from the perspective of the troops in theater, and secondly from the judicial perspective. As to the latter, a British asylum and immigration tribunal has stated (in a case concerning the existence of an armed conflict in Iraq for the purposes of determining whether an Iraqi refugee qualified for admission to the United Kingdom as an asylum seeker):

> [T]he reasons [the immigration judge at first instance] gave for finding that Iraq was not in a state of internal armed conflict were misconceived. It was wrong to view it as a matter settled by the (assumed) fact that the United Kingdom government has not accepted Iraq is in such a state. *It is a matter to be judicially determined by applying legal criteria to the factual situation in that country.*[4]

Therefore, this article considers the characterization of the armed conflict in Iraq under IHL in each of the four stages enumerated above. While the characterization of the conflict as an IAC in its early stages (invasion through occupation) was clear enough, after the end of occupation it could not have been an IAC on a plain reading of the scope of application provisions of the Geneva Conventions, but nor could it have been a NIAC by the same terms or by any application of logic. The British determination, however reticent in its expression, that it was a NIAC was a policy decision based on a mixture of expediency and a literalist interpretation of the Geneva Conventions, but its accuracy as a matter of legal doctrine—to say nothing of its desirability—is in this author's opinion highly questionable in light of the aims and objectives of the humanitarian treaties that form the kernel of the contemporary law of armed conflict (LOAC). Since the law applicable in situations of NIAC is minimalist, vague and general in nature by comparison with that applicable in IAC, and the humanitarian aims and objectives of the law indicate that the greatest possible protection should be afforded to victims in armed conflicts, it is suggested that it would have been better to have treated the conflict in Iraq post-2004 as de facto international in nature; such an approach would also arguably have been better for the MNF-I soldiers on the ground, as it would simultaneously have provided them with greater explicit freedom of action and legal protection under the LOAC. As a preliminary to this discussion, however, it is necessary first to recall the typology of armed conflicts in international humanitarian law, for it is the law's scope of application—the determination of the existence of different types of conflict—that determines its substantive content.

Review of the Scope of Application of IHL

Armed Conflicts

The spectrum of conflict in international law is classically said to comprise several stages of increasing intensity, from the violent (but legally non-conflict) stage of riots, disturbances and tensions through to full-blown international armed conflict, but it would be helpful first to consider as a starting question: what is an armed conflict, generically, in international law? Strangely enough for such a detailed specialist area of the law, there is no answer to this question in the treaty texts that dominate the *lex lata*. Of the principal treaty instruments that comprise the majority of contemporary IHL, the Hague Regulations do not specify a notion of armed conflict in the modern sense, referring merely to their applicability to "war" and "belligerents [who] are parties to the Convention";[5] the Geneva Conventions and their Additional Protocols do specify the types of conflicts to which they apply, but without actually defining those types of conflict generically. The authoritative International Committee of the Red Cross (ICRC) *Commentary* to the Geneva Conventions attempted to cast the net as wide as possible, asserting that "[a]ny difference arising between two States and leading to the intervention of armed forces is an armed conflict,"[6] but this position is not supported by State practice[7] and, in any event, in its State-centric approach, is of relatively limited use for contemporary conflicts, the vast majority of which are not between States. The conflict in Iraq after the defeat of Saddam's regime in April 2003 is a case in point.

It has thus been left to customary international law, through the mechanism of a judicial decision, to come up with a definition. In the *Tadic* case before the International Criminal Tribunal for the former Yugoslavia (ICTY), the defendant argued, *inter alia*, that there had been no armed conflict in Bosnia and Herzegovina at the time when he had committed the acts with which he was charged, and that therefore they could not have constituted criminal violations of IHL, because, absent an armed conflict, that body of law was not applicable to the situation. The ICTY Appeals Chamber held that

> an armed conflict exists whenever there is a resort to armed force between States or protracted armed violence between governmental authorities and organized armed groups or between such groups within a State. International humanitarian law applies from the initiation of such armed conflicts and extends beyond the cessation of hostilities until a general conclusion of peace is reached; or, in the case of internal conflicts, a peaceful settlement is achieved. Until that moment, international humanitarian law continues to apply in the whole territory of the warring States or, in the case of internal conflicts, the whole territory under the control of a party, whether or not actual combat takes place there.[8]

Despite its generic wording, the formula suggested in *Tadic*—which has since been reaffirmed in international[9] and national[10] jurisprudence and has come to be regarded as expressing customary international law—plainly refers to criteria specific to international ("between States") and non-international ("between governmental authorities and organized armed groups or between such groups within a State") armed conflicts. The emphasis of the formula is also on the territorial extent of the armed conflict; with the exception of the single term "*protracted* armed violence," there is no reference to other factors affecting the determination of the existence of a conflict, such as intensity, escalation, etc. However, the requirement of a degree of organization on the parts of the actors in a conflict—whether as States in international armed conflicts or "governmental authorities and organized armed groups" in non-international conflicts—is made clear, and this has been reaffirmed in subsequent case law as the "first element" of the *Tadic* test.[11] The "second element" of the test, which has been developed by subsequent jurisprudence,[12] relates to the intensity of the conflict and includes such indicia as the protracted nature of the fighting and seriousness or increase in armed clashes,[13] spread of clashes over the territory,[14] increase in the number of governmental forces deployed to deal with the violence[15] and the type of weaponry used by both parties to the conflict.[16] If a situation does not satisfy these customary law criteria for the existence of an armed conflict, then, however unpleasant it may be and notwithstanding the deployment of armed forces to assist in the maintenance of law and order, it will not qualify as an armed conflict under international law; instead, it will fall into the looser category of "banditry, criminal activity, riots, or sporadic outbreaks of violence and acts of terrorism,"[17] which are normally dealt with under national criminal law but to which the LOAC does not apply.

International Armed Conflicts

Once it is accepted that an armed conflict within the meaning of IHL is taking place, it is necessary to determine what type of armed conflict it is, so that the applicable rules of IHL can be identified. Classically the main type of armed conflict—indeed, the only type of armed conflict regulated by international law until 1949—was one which took place between two or more States: international armed conflict. This was never comprehensively defined by the LOAC prior to the adoption of the Geneva Conventions,[18] since (a) it was obvious to one and all when two States were at war with each other, a condition which usually—though not invariably—resulted from mutual declarations of war; and (b) in the absence of any other type of war regulated by international law, an international legal definition of international conflicts was never thought necessary. Even at the time of the adoption of the Geneva Conventions in 1949, it was still fondly believed that the main frame of reference for armed conflicts in the modern world would continue to be international conflicts; hence the Conventions' strong bias in favor of their detailed regulation.

The traditional certainty surrounding the scope and ambit of international armed conflicts is reflected in the fact that, to this day, the definition of such conflicts is essentially the scope of application provisions of the Geneva Conventions and their first Additional Protocol. Common Article 2 of the Geneva Conventions provides that they "shall apply to all cases of declared war or of any other armed conflict which may arise between two or more of the High Contracting Parties, even if the state of war is not recognized by one of them." The scope of application of the Conventions under Common Article 2 expressly includes situations of belligerent occupation of territory, whether violently opposed or not, which is significant for the situation in Iraq during the period of the CPA in 2003–4. Since only States can be high contracting parties to the Geneva Conventions,[19] the interpretation of the scope of application is clear enough. Additional Protocol I of 1977, however, added to the definition of an international armed conflict by extending its scope to cover "armed conflicts in which people are fighting against colonial domination and alien occupation and against racist regimes in the exercise of their right of self-determination."[20] Although this would seem to be a very substantial widening of the definition of international armed conflicts, it is additionally necessary for an authority representing a "people" engaged in a conflict of the kind referred to, to make a unilateral declaration undertaking to apply the Protocol and the Conventions in its struggle.[21] To date, no such unilateral declarations have been successfully registered, and certain States have entered reservations to the Protocol asserting their right not to accept any such declaration unless the State is satisfied that the authority genuinely represents the "people" concerned.[22] In relation to these provisions of Protocol I, the United Kingdom entered a statement on ratification to the effect that "the term 'armed conflict' of itself and in its context denotes a situation of a kind which is not constituted by the commission of ordinary crimes including acts of terrorism whether concerted or in isolation."[23] Although made specifically in relation to Articles 1(4) and 96(3) of Protocol I, the point is of equal relevance to Article 1(2) of Protocol II.

In the event that an international armed conflict is taking place, States participating as belligerents in such a conflict will be bound by the entire corpus of customary international humanitarian law[24] (including the Hague Regulations of 1907) and the four Geneva Conventions of 1949, along with any specifically applicable treaties regulating the use of weaponry. States that are also parties to the 1977 Additional Protocol I will be bound by that instrument also; even certain States that have not accepted the Protocol as a whole accept that substantial parts of it reflect customary international law and apply its terms as such.[25]

Non-international Armed Conflicts

The other main type of conflict recognized in international law, at least since 1949, is that of non-international armed conflict. In that year, Common Article 3 of the Geneva Conventions introduced, for the first time, legal regulation of the protection of victims in "armed conflict[s] not of an international character occurring in the territory of one of the High Contracting Parties." Beyond the phrase "armed conflict not of an international character," the article does not explain its scope of application. The authoritative ICRC *Commentary* provides a list of "convenient criteria" to assist in the differentiation of an "armed conflict not of an international character" from "any act committed by force of arms [not amounting to armed conflict]—any form of anarchy, rebellion, or even plain banditry":

> (1) That the Party in revolt against the de jure Government possesses an organized military force, an authority responsible for its acts, acting within a determinate territory and having the means of respecting and ensuring respect for the Convention.
>
> (2) That the legal Government is obliged to have recourse to the regular military forces against insurgents organized as military and in possession of a part of the national territory.
>
> (3) (a) That the de jure Government has recognized the insurgents as belligerents; or
>
> (b) that it has claimed for itself the rights of a belligerent; or
>
> (c) that it has accorded the insurgents recognition as belligerents for the purposes only of the present Convention; or

(d) that the dispute has been admitted to the agenda of the Security Council or the General Assembly of the United Nations as being a threat to international peace, a breach of the peace, or an act of aggression.

(4) (a) That the insurgents have an organisation purporting to have the characteristics of a State.

(b) That the insurgent civil authority exercises de facto authority over persons within a determinate territory.

(c) That the armed forces act under the direction of the organized civil authority and are prepared to observe the ordinary laws of war.

(d) That the insurgent civil authority agrees to be bound by the provisions of the Convention.[26]

These indicia are both non-exhaustive and non-mandatory, thereby supporting the ICRC's desire that Common Article 3 should be applied "as widely as possible."[27] Arguably the logical *ne plus ultra* of this approach was achieved in 2006, when a plurality of the US Supreme Court held that the "Global War on Terror" being prosecuted in various locations around the world by the Bush administration after the terrorist attacks of September 11, 2001 was an "armed conflict not of an international character" to which Common Article 3 applied because the conflict was not directed against any other State.[28] Minimalist and very general though its protections are, Common Article 3 has indeed come to be accepted, as the International Court of Justice (ICJ) stated in the 1980s, as "a minimum yardstick" of humanitarian protection in all armed conflicts, whatever their characterization.[29]

The very minimalism of Common Article 3 and its perceived ineffectiveness in protecting the victims of non-international armed conflicts led to the adoption of a second Additional Protocol in 1977, which is exclusively concerned with the regulation of such conflicts. At the opposite extreme from Common Article 3's all-encompassing scope of application, however, Protocol II was given a scope of application so restricted as to render it all but unworkable in practice. Article 1(1) of Protocol II states that the Protocol applies to

> all armed conflicts which are not covered by [the Geneva Conventions and Additional Protocol I] and which take place in the territory of a High Contracting Party between its armed forces and dissident armed forces or other organized armed groups which, under responsible command, exercise such control over a part of its territory as to enable them to carry out sustained and concerted military operations and to implement this Protocol.

Article 1(2) goes on to specify that the Protocol does not apply to "situations of internal disturbances and tensions, such as riots, isolated and sporadic acts of violence and other acts of a similar nature, as not being armed conflicts." In practice, this is the real fault line when considering the spectrum of conflict for the purposes of the scope of application of IHL: once a situation in a State escalates beyond "internal disturbances and tensions," it will be considered (absent the involvement of any other State) to be a non-international armed conflict. Whether it is such a conflict within the terms of Common Article 3 of the Geneva Conventions or Article 1(1) of Additional Protocol II will then be a question of degree depending on the facts on the ground.

If an armed conflict is deemed non-international in nature, the question remains as to what provisions of the LOAC would have to be applied in such a conflict apart from the basic rules in Common Article 3 and, if applicable, Additional Protocol II. In particular, these treaty law provisions applicable in NIAC are considerably less detailed and developed than those that are applicable in IAC and they focus overwhelmingly on the protection of victims, while saying nothing at all about the methods and means of warfare. It is true, however, that some of the other treaties that comprise the LOAC, including treaties regulating the use of specific weapons, have been extended to cover situations of NIAC[30] or, indeed, apply in all circumstances and therefore in all types of armed conflict.[31] In its seminal decision in *Tadic*, the ICTY Appeals Chamber confirmed the generalities of this trend in customary international law, stating that

> elementary considerations of humanity and common sense make it preposterous that the use by States of weapons prohibited in armed conflicts between themselves be allowed when States try to put down rebellion by their own nationals on their own territory. What is inhumane, and consequently proscribed, in international wars, cannot but be inhumane and inadmissible in civil strife.[32]

Although the ICTY's comments in *Tadic* in respect to this trend were rather too general to clarify much of the *lex lata* with regard to the regulation of methods and means of warfare in NIAC,[33] the ICRC's study, *Customary International Humanitarian Law*, published in 2005, extends most of its 161 identified rules to NIAC;[34] however, its methodology and the evidence supporting its approach have not been free from criticism.[35]

"Other" Armed Conflicts

Although the essential dichotomy of international versus non-international armed conflicts remains securely in place as regards the basic typologies of armed conflict explicitly recognized in international humanitarian law, it represents what might be termed a very classical approach to the nature of war. As the history of modern warfare reveals, the last two decades of the twentieth century and the first decade of the twenty-first century have seen the increasing prevalence of—if not exactly new *types* of conflict—new *methodologies* of conflict.[36] These may be referred to by a variety of terms indicating their unorthodox nature according to traditional military thinking: the most widely used such terms are "asymmetrical," "low-intensity," "hybrid" and "unconventional" conflicts. These notions, along with the concepts of counterinsurgency and stability operations, belong to the realms of military and strategic doctrine, not to that of international law. In the contemporary legal discourse their counterparts are the potentially confusing and ambiguous terms "internationalized" and "transnational" conflicts. Like all armed conflicts, these must be subject to the LOAC, but because the Geneva Conventions and Additional Protocols do not *prima facie* take account of them in their scope of application provisions, the question has arisen with increasing urgency: for the purposes of determining the applicability of IHL, what types of conflict are these under the law, and which provisions of the LOAC apply to them?[37] What comparatively little legal authority there is on point derives from either decided case law or scholarly commentary.

The concept of internationalized armed conflict first arose in the jurisprudence of the ICTY as a result of the 1992–95 Bosnian war, which was essentially a conflict internal to Bosnia and Herzegovina, but in which forces of the Federal Republic of Yugoslavia and the Republic of Croatia intervened. An internationalized conflict has been held to be one that is *prima facie* internal, but has been rendered international in nature if

1. it exceeds the boundaries of the State within which it was initially taking place;[38] or

2. another State intervenes directly in the conflict with its own forces, particularly if in doing so it occupies territory within the meaning of Article 42 of the Hague Regulations and Geneva Convention IV;[39] or

3. another State intervenes indirectly in the conflict by virtue of some of the participants in the internal conflict acting on behalf of that other State.[40]

The third of these possibilities has been the most problematic in practice, but current international jurisprudence confirms that the correct test for determining the internationalization of an internal conflict by the indirect intervention of a foreign

State is a test of "overall control" under the doctrine of State responsibility in general public international law, whereby

> it is by no means necessary that the controlling authorities should plan all the operations of the units dependent on them, choose their targets, or give specific instructions concerning the conduct of military operations and any alleged violations of international humanitarian law. The control required by international law may be deemed to exist when a State (or, in the context of an armed conflict, the Party to the conflict) *has a role in organizing, coordinating or planning the military actions* of the military group, in addition to financing, training and equipping or providing operational support to that group. Acts performed by the group or members thereof may be regarded as acts of *de facto* State organs regardless of any specific instruction by the controlling State concerning the commission of each of those acts.[41]

Once it has been determined that a particular armed conflict has been internationalized, the entire range of the LOAC applicable in international armed conflicts comes into play because the status of the conflict effectively becomes just that: an internationalized internal armed conflict becomes neither less nor more than an international armed conflict. The entire corpus of the customary law of IAC, together with the Hague Regulations, Geneva Conventions, and any other treaties that the relevant State has ratified, will then govern the conduct of its armed forces.

The term "transnational conflict," as has been suggested by some commentators, "represents an evolution of the law, more properly characterized as *lex ferenda* than *lex lata*."[42] It has been used in the contemporary international security context to refer principally to the US conflict against Al-Qaeda since September 2001 as a conflict that technically satisfies the scope of application requirements of neither IAC nor NIAC but undeniably involves military combat operations and displays features of both types of conflict—namely, the extraterritorial location of the fighting coupled with the absence of a State-actor adversary. A concept of such conflicts as a new typology of armed conflict has been "in the air" since the displacement of the Taliban regime in Afghanistan in December 2001. The end of belligerent occupation in Iraq in June 2004 transformed both those conflicts—which continued unabated and, indeed, even intensified—from ones that had been clearly international in nature into something else.

The premise of the theory is that an armed conflict that is not IAC is governed, in default, by Common Article 3; but the latter is deficient inasmuch as it only provides for the general protection of victims, while saying nothing at all about the methods and means of warfare and the conduct of hostilities. In itself, this is not a new point: it has been made before, by the present author among others.[43] Corn and Jensen suggest that

> while the term "transnational" armed conflict . . . may be new, the substantive impact of this concept is . . . a very old paradigm—that armed forces carry norms of conduct with them during all combat operations. In other words, a State cannot invoke the authorities of armed conflict and not concurrently accept the obligations. Accordingly, the use of the term "transnational" is really just semantic; what . . . is significant is that armed conflict must be understood as triggering the normative framework of the LOAC. And that is a proposition that . . . is really as old as organized warfare itself.[44]

As such, the suggested concept of transnational armed conflicts is a functional one that finds no direct support in the letter of the law, but rather in its spirit. It proposes that once the "trigger" of armed conflict—any armed conflict—has been generated, in respect to conflicts that are neither clearly IAC nor NIAC, such as the conflict with Al-Qaeda,[45] then "fundamental principles" of the LOAC apply. Such principles may be derived from customary international law, as evidenced by State practice. For example, one oft-cited current military manual lists "military necessity, humanity, distinction, and proportionality."[46] Corn and Jensen refer to "targeting principles" as part of their suggested "fundamental principles of the LOAC,"[47] a suggestion which subsumes distinction and proportionality and is certainly supported by some State practice.[48] By logical extension most of the customary international humanitarian law rules identified by the ICRC would also be applicable in transnational armed conflicts since its study explicitly specifies in most cases that they apply in both international and non-international armed conflicts;[49] the proof of this, however, would have to be conclusively determined by future State practice.

Application of the Typology of Armed Conflicts to Iraq since 2003

The Initial Invasion Phase

The conflict in Iraq, in its first or main invasion phase, commenced with an unsuccessful attempt to "decapitate" the Ba'athist regime by killing President Saddam Hussein on March 19, 2003; waves of airstrikes by British and American aircraft then went in on March 20, followed by a ground invasion conducted by coalition forces contributed by the United States, the United Kingdom, Australia and Poland, subsequently supported also by Spain, Denmark and a number of other countries. Saddam's regime was effectively removed from power as US forces progressively penetrated Baghdad during the first week of April, leading to the city's complete occupation and the end of organized resistance by regular Iraqi government forces on April 9. Large-scale looting and communal violence then erupted, however, and fighting with irregular armed elements did not cease. On May 1, 2003, US President George W. Bush formally declared an end to major combat operations.[50]

The period from March 19 to April 30, 2003 "clearly constituted an international armed conflict between the coalition States and Iraq."[51] Shortly before the start of invasion, the ICRC sent a "Memorandum on the Rules of International Humanitarian Law to Be Respected by the States Involved in Military Hostilities" to the anticipated belligerents, in which it emphasized the need to respect the detailed provisions of the four Geneva Conventions.[52] Iraq, the United States, the United Kingdom and Australia were all at the material time party to the Geneva Conventions; the latter two States were also party to Additional Protocol I and therefore were equally bound by that instrument's provisions. Although the United States was not technically so bound, certain provisions of the Protocol which the United States believes reflect customary international law were applied by US forces as a matter of policy.[53] Finally, all belligerents were bound by the entire corpus of customary international humanitarian law, including notably the Hague Regulations of 1907 (to which Iraq, for example, was not a party).[54]

The Belligerent Occupation Phase

The technical details of the law of belligerent occupation are considered elsewhere in this volume,[55] but at the outset of this section the main point to note is that belligerent occupation of territory is considered to be effectively an extension of international armed conflict for the purposes of IHL because it is generally the territory of another State that is being occupied consequent upon an armed conflict with that other State. Occupation is governed specifically by 1949 Geneva Convention IV, relative to the protection of civilian persons, and by certain provisions of the Hague Regulations. Although there is some doctrinal controversy as to the precise moment during hostilities when an occupation legally begins,[56] the application of Geneva Convention IV ceases one year after the general close of military operations[57] (which in the case of Iraq would suggest an end date of April 30, 2004 if President Bush's announcement of the end of major combat operations[58] is to be taken at face value). The CPA was in fact established to represent the occupying powers' administration of Iraq on May 16, 2003,[59] ten days after President Bush had appointed Ambassador L. Paul Bremer III to head the Authority[60] and more than two weeks after the announcement of the end of major combat operations. A transfer of power from the CPA to a transitional Iraqi administration took place on June 28, 2004,[61] at which point the MNF-I had already been established and the law of belligerent occupation technically ceased to be formally applicable in Iraq.

After some initial reluctance to use the international law terminology of belligerent occupation,[62] the United States and United Kingdom recognized themselves as occupiers when they voted in favor of Security Council Resolution 1483 on May 22, 2003.[63] The Resolution refers to the United States and United Kingdom as "occupying powers" in its preamble[64] and also refers expressly, in its substantive paragraph 5, to obligations relating to belligerent occupation arising under the Hague Regulations and Geneva Convention IV. Even had the United States and United Kingdom formally declined to recognize themselves as occupying powers, the Geneva Convention would have been applicable automatically as the United States, United Kingdom and Iraq are all high contracting parties and the Convention specifies its scope of application as extending to

> all cases of declared war or of any other armed conflict which may arise between two or more of the High Contracting Parties . . . [and] . . . all cases of partial or total occupation of the territory of a High Contracting Party, even if the said occupation meets with no armed resistance.[65]

The Hague Regulations contain no such statement concerning their scope of application, but Article 42 states that "[t]erritory is considered occupied when it is actually placed under the authority of the hostile army." In his briefing to the Security Council on May 22, 2003 regarding the provision of humanitarian assistance in Iraq, Jakob Kellenberger, the President of the International Committee of the Red Cross, noted:

> As far as the legal framework is concerned, we are, in terms of humanitarian law . . . in a situation of occupation. The applicability of the relevant provisions of the Geneva Conventions, in particular the Fourth Geneva Convention, and of the Hague Regulation is accepted by the occupying Power [*sic*].[66]

However—at least as far as the United Kingdom is concerned—significant developments in the UK domestic courts following reported abuses of Iraqi civilians by British troops have resulted in a major expansion of human rights law. These courts have held that where British troops have physical custody of local civilians in certain circumstances during an occupation, the latter's rights are protected not only by the law of armed conflict but also by the UK Human Rights Act 1998 (implementing the 1950 European Convention on Human Rights and Fundamental Freedoms into domestic law in the United Kingdom).[67]

The Post-occupation Phase

The phase of operations in Iraq which followed the termination of the CPA occupation regime in June 2004, and which has persisted, with varying degrees of intensity, to the present time, is usually characterized simply as an "insurgency" in lay language; but in terms of the scope of application of the LOAC, it is by far the most difficult to pin down. The insurgent forces have comprised a mixture of renegade

Ba'athist supporters of the late Saddam regime, Iraqi nationalists, Sunni Islamists, Shi'a Islamists, diverse foreign fighters and alleged Al-Qaeda operatives, who between them constitute at least a dozen major organizations and probably several dozen discrete smaller groups. Many of these groups have fought against the coalition, while others have fought against each other for local control. The hostilities have been at varying stages of intensity, from set-piece urban operations like the battles of Fallujah and Najaf in 2004 to isolated individual shootings and bomb attacks on coalition troops. The coalition forces officially became the MNF-I in June 2004[68] when the UN Security Council passed Resolution 1546.[69] Eventually a total of thirty-seven States (excluding the United States, United Kingdom and Australia, the original members of the coalition at the time of the invasion) contributed military forces to the MNF-I under the Security Council mandate. All of these other States progressively withdrew their forces from Iraq until July 2009, when the United Kingdom and Australia also withdrew. The Security Council mandate expired in December 2008, leaving the remaining foreign forces present in Iraq with the permission of the Iraqi government but without an international mandate. US forces have since been re-designated United States Forces–Iraq, effective January 2010, and their presence in Iraq is now governed by the security agreement, under which their complete withdrawal from Iraqi territory is provisionally required by December 2011.[70]

It is easy enough to provide a factual description of counterinsurgency operations—which are evidently what coalition forces were engaged in from 2004 onward—but how do they fit into the typology of armed conflicts under IHL, and (crucially) what law is applicable in such military operations? In the specific case of Iraq, the complications arose from the following factors:

- the fact that the occupation was officially no longer in place but coalition troops remained in Iraq, undertaking military operations under Security Council authority and with the permission of a government those forces had themselves installed;
- the fact that coalition States had deployed forces to undertake military operations in a foreign State and against foreign nationals; and
- the fact that any armed conflict was no longer directed against any other State.

These salient features gave rise to the fundamental question of how to characterize the situation in Iraq, for IHL purposes, after the end of occupation in June 2004. Was it an international armed conflict, a non-international armed conflict or something else? The question would not have arisen but for the Iraq situation's failure to fit neatly into any of the categories of armed conflict that are recognized in IHL:

- once the state of occupation officially ended, the detailed technical provisions of the law of belligerent occupation were no longer applicable;
- the situation did not constitute an international armed conflict on a plain reading of the Geneva Conventions, since (from the point of view of the MNF-I) it was not directed against any other State and, indeed, the MNF-I was present on the territory with host-State consent;
- neither of the 1977 Additional Protocols could have been formally applicable as neither Iraq nor the United States (as the main contributor to and leader of the MNF-I) was a party to either instrument—although they could have been applicable to British and Australian forces; and
- the situation logically could not have been said to be "not of an international character," since both semantically and logically there is nothing non-international about the use of troops to fight against foreign nationals abroad.

The consequent difficulty would be the lack of any readily apparent legal framework within which the military operations of the MNF-I could be situated. As one highly respected commentator neatly put it more than two decades before the conflict in Iraq:

> A . . . relationship, between the insurgents and a foreign state that has been invited by the established government to help it overcome the rebellion, gives rise to great difficulties in determining what law is applicable. The traditional answer, which makes the situation subject to the rules of non-international armed conflict, clashes with *the undeniably international character of this type of relationship.*[71]

The "received opinion" concerning the nature of the conflict in Iraq after the end of the occupation phase has been that the conflict ceased to be international, and became non-international, in nature. This was the consistent and unambiguous position of the ICRC,[72] as noted by the UN High Commissioner for Refugees.[73] The British government for years after 2004 assiduously resisted making any public statement as to the classification of the conflict in Iraq; instead, it kept repeating the mantra that British forces were present in Iraq as part of MNF-I with the consent of the Iraqi government and under a mandate from the UN Security Council. This unsatisfactory obfuscation—it purported to answer a *jus in bello* question with a *jus ad bellum* rejoinder and placed undue emphasis on strictly political factors, as discussed below—ceased to be necessary when the British government conceded, in the course of litigation about an asylum applicant's entitlement to humanitarian protection, that "Iraq as a whole is in a state of internal armed conflict for the purposes of IHL and [the government of Iraq] is one of the parties to the conflict."[74]

This position is broadly consistent with the approach adopted by a plurality of the US Supreme Court in *Hamdan v. Rumsfeld*,[75] in which it was suggested that the conflict between the United States and Al-Qaeda should be treated as an "armed conflict not of an international character" within the terms of Common Article 3 of the Geneva Conventions. It should be noted, however, that this finding was not an essential part of the decision (i.e., it was an *obiter dictum*), and was concerned with the relevance of IHL exclusively for the relatively narrow purpose of ascertaining the correct standard of treatment for detainees held in Guantánamo Bay and whether the military commissions created to try them were lawfully established. The interest of the scope of application question in Iraq, on the other hand, is not confined to the legality of a particular type of domestic tribunal established for the trial of criminal offenses. The view that the Iraqi conflict after the end of occupation became non-international in nature is based, legally, on a literalist reading of Common Article 2 of the Geneva Conventions and, strictly speaking, is technically correct on the law as far as the application of the Conventions is concerned. The main difficulty with the British government's approach, in fact, is that it gives undue prominence to aspects that are entirely political in nature, namely the fact of an "invitation" from the new Iraqi government at the end of the occupation phase and the executive mandate from the Security Council (of which the United States and the United Kingdom are conveniently permanent members). It also, in this author's submission, takes an unduly restrictive and minimalist approach to IHL, which is fundamentally inappropriate in light of the law's humanitarian aims and objectives.

As regards the former point, the authority of the Security Council is clearly open to abuse if certain permanent members who are the prime movers behind a decision then claim that such authority trumps all objections. The legal counterpart of this approach was given judicial expression in the United Kingdom by the House of Lords when, in a legal challenge to the detention without charge of a civilian by British forces in Iraq since October 2004, it was held that the Security Council's authority for the MNF-I to maintain law, order and security in Iraq by (*inter alia*) "internment where this is necessary for imperative reasons of security,"[76] trumped any inconsistent provisions of IHL or human rights law by virtue of Articles 25 and 103 of the UN Charter.[77] At the very least, such a position is politically self-serving, given that the United Kingdom (along with the United States) was the principal instigator of Resolution 1546. As to the "invitation," no allowance is made either for the fact that the government doing the inviting was installed by those same States (which is again a politically self-serving position) or for the linked fact that that government may not have been truly empowered to issue such an invitation to foreign forces because it lacked either domestic or international legitimacy. For example, during the Hungarian, Czechoslovak and Afghan crises of 1956, 1968 and 1979, respectively, the Soviet Union in each case claimed to have been invited to intervene militarily; however, it was far from clear that the "governments" which had issued those invitations were legitimately installed in power and legally competent to issue them. Although the position of the interim Iraqi government in 2004 was different to some extent, in that it was installed with the imprimatur of the Security Council (albeit without a democratic mandate), does that necessarily make the coalition action any more legitimate than that of the USSR in the earlier instances? Arguably it does not, since the change of regime was effected as a result of a foreign armed intervention of dubious legality under international law, something as true in the case of Iraq as in the cases of Hungary, Czechoslovakia and Afghanistan. It was inevitable that the Iraqi government in 2004 would "consent" to the continuing presence and actions of the MNF-I on its territory, since it was in essence the MNF-I that put the government in place. In these circumstances, the issue of host-State consent is arguably meaningless.

The characterization of the situation in Iraq post-2004 as a non-international armed conflict is not inaccurate on a literalist interpretation of Common Article 2 of the Geneva Conventions, and is arguably supported by the US Supreme Court's decision in *Hamdan*. Neither Iraq nor the United States is a party to Additional Protocol II and the United Kingdom (which is a party to that instrument) has never conceded that the Iraqi insurgents satisfy its scope of application under Article 1(1), so the only clearly applicable IHL—if this characterization of the situation is accepted—would be Common Article 3 and customary international humanitarian law. Common Articles 2 and 3 are, of course, concerned exclusively with the scope of application of the Geneva Conventions—and there is more to IHL than just those Conventions. There is the large corpus of customary international humanitarian law, much of which is now believed to be of general applicability in all armed conflicts.[78] Which precise rules of that body of law would be applicable would depend on the extent to which the coalition States agree with the ICRC study's conclusions as to what are the rules.[79]

It should also be noted that the jurisprudence of the ICTY has extensively discussed the possibility of a non-international armed conflict becoming internationalized through the participation of another State in the (otherwise internal) hostilities.[80] In such cases, the normal range of IAC law becomes applicable to the conflict, as in any "normal" international armed conflict. Although *prima facie* this might be of direct relevance to the situation in Iraq, actually it is of somewhat limited utility, since the cases all concerned instances of intervention by foreign States (principally the Republic of Croatia and the Federal Republic of Yugoslavia in the Bosnian conflict) on the side of the insurgents, rather than that of the government. In that situation, it is clear that the conflict effectively became one between "two or more of the High Contracting Parties" to the Geneva Conventions, within the terms of Common Article 2 thereof. In Iraq, on the other hand, the foreign States were fighting on the side of the government rather than that of the insurgents. Only if another State—Iran, for example—had openly intervened on the side of any insurgent groups in Iraq to the extent that it could be said to have overall control over them would the conflict vis-à-vis such groups have become internationalized within the terms of the ICTY jurisprudence.

There is a viable alternative approach to the characterization of the situation in Iraq post-occupation as non-international armed conflict, and that is to treat it—at least on a de facto basis—as *international* in nature. One rationale for this approach, made elsewhere in this volume,[81] is the argument that the conflict retains its original characterization throughout its duration, and that a government installed in Iraq as a result of the invasion cannot "magically" convert the conflict from an international to a non-international one by purporting to "invite" the coalition forces to be present in the territory which they had already invaded and occupied as a hostile act. It has further been asserted as a matter of doctrine that "a government established by the occupying power cannot in law give its agreement to the presence of the occupying troops in its territory and thereby transmute occupation by the armed forces of an outside state into the friendly presence of [the same] state."[82] Although this author is greatly in sympathy with these views, as far as the scope of application provisions of the Geneva Conventions are concerned, they appear to be contradicted by a plain reading of Common Article 2, as discussed above.

On the other hand, the US Secretary of State in 2004 seemed at least implicitly to consider that coalition forces in Iraq after the occupation would continue to apply the law of international armed conflict when he wrote that "the forces that make up the MNF are and will remain committed at all times to act consistently with their obligations under the law of armed conflict, *including the Geneva Conventions*."[83] Why would the last phrase be expressed in the plural if it were not intended that the obligations of *IAC* law were to be applied, thereby arguably implying a presumption that the conflict in Iraq continued to be international in nature?

A less dogmatic and semantic approach is to be found in the reasoning of the Supreme Court of Israel in *Public Committee against Torture in Israel v. Government of Israel*,[84] where the Court held that the conflict between Israel and non-State actors in the Palestinian Territories should be treated as international in nature, partly because of their transnational nature as evidenced by the deployment of Israeli forces outside the borders of the State of Israel, and partly because of the advanced military capabilities of many contemporary non-State armed organizations, which mean that the scale and intensity of the hostilities effectively rise to the level of an international armed conflict. The former proposition, in particular, has received some support in the literature since.[85]

Finally, a case—arguably the most powerful case—for the de facto internationalization of the conflict against Iraqi insurgents could also be made based on a teleological interpretation of IHL in light of its aims and purposes. In relation to international armed conflicts, the LOAC is much more detailed and developed, with a far higher degree of internationally recognized regulation of both the conduct of hostilities and the protection of victims, than in relation to non-international armed conflicts. To put it crudely, there is more law in relation to international armed conflicts; this implies not only more precise protection for "victims," but also a more regulated approach to the actions of soldiers on the ground, with greater consequent protections for them in the event of any accusations of wrongdoing. Writing a dozen years ago, one of America's most respected experts on IHL stated that "[i]n interpreting the law, our goal should be to avoid paralyzing the legal process as much as possible and, in the case of humanitarian conventions, to enable them to serve their protective goals."[86] In relation to the Soviet intervention in Afghanistan, the interest of the State in having the conflict considered as international in nature was summarized as follows:

> [T]he Soviet Union's interests would impel it to apply the whole of international humanitarian law to the conflict [in Afghanistan]. The Soviet Union would be especially concerned with having its troops benefit from the greatest possible measure of protection. The law on non-international armed conflicts does not provide any special status for the combatants, even when captured. Only the law that is applicable to international conflicts, specifically the Third Geneva Convention of 1949, protects the combatant and guarantees him favored status as a prisoner of war. Thus, the Soviet Union should seek to have international [armed conflict] law applied if the Soviet authorities are concerned with the fate of their soldiers who fall into the insurgent's [*sic*] hands. Considerations of this kind might tempt an intervening power to opt for the extensive protection of the rules governing international armed conflicts, even if this would require that power to abide by the same rules.[87]

The fundamental reason for the insistence on characterizing the conflict in Iraq post-occupation as non-international, of course, is the unwillingness of coalition States to put themselves in a position where they would have to apply the rules of Geneva Convention III to captured insurgents by according them the status of POWs. This is partly because of the long-held view that to accord such status would confer on the insurgents a legitimacy to which they should not strictly speaking be entitled, and partly because of all the other technical provisions concerning POWs that would then also have to be applied, with certain negative implications for the coalition States.[88] There is also the undeniable fact that the notion of reciprocity in observing the law, relied upon by Gasser, simply does not obtain in Iraq: the insurgents have consistently shown no regard whatsoever for the observance of IHL rules in their fight against foreign forces. Indeed, the same author's statement of the insurgents' interest in having the conflict considered international clearly demonstrates a compelling reason for *not* considering it as such:

> The intervention of an outside state would provide [insurgents] with proof of the international nature of the struggle. The insurgents would argue that the intervention of foreign armed forces alongside government troops makes the conflict an international one. The insurgents would have an interest in capturing members of the [foreign] armed forces, calling them "prisoners of war," and demanding that the adversaries adhere to the same rules.[89]

The insurgents in Iraq would do no such thing. Moreover, their struggle would be to some extent "legitimated" in the eyes of the international community—at least in terms of the application of IHL—and that is precisely the effect the multinational forces (and, latterly, the US forces) in Iraq seek to avoid.

Conclusions

The classification of armed conflicts in Iraq during and after the second Gulf War in 2003 presents certain specific problems. The initial invasion phase, in March and April 2003, and the belligerent occupation phase, from May 2003 to June 2004, are uncontroversial in that they clearly constituted an international armed conflict under the scope of application provisions of the Geneva Conventions. The international law applicable in those phases consisted of the corpus of customary international humanitarian law, specifically including the Hague Regulations, plus the Geneva Conventions. As far as the United Kingdom and Australia—but not the United States and Iraq—were concerned, Additional Protocol I would have been applicable too. During the occupation phase, only certain specific provisions of the Hague Regulations, plus Geneva Convention IV, applied as the *lex specialis* of occupation. After the end of occupation in June 2004, the position became substantially less clear.

Although the United States refrained from conclusively classifying the conflict and the United Kingdom considered it to be non-international in nature because of the absence of a State adversary, decided case law and academic commentary are more ambivalent. If the option of creating a "new" typology of armed conflicts, which might be known variously as "transnational" or "mixed" conflicts, is dismissed, we are left with the standard two possibilities: international or non-international armed conflict. While the latter is supported by the practice of certain coalition States—principally the United Kingdom—it is a policy determination based on expediency, rather than a legal classification based on a proper analysis of the facts and the law. As such it is undesirable. This author takes the view that the conflict would have been better treated as a de facto international armed conflict, notwithstanding its failure to comply strictly with the wording of Common Article 2 of the Geneva Conventions. This would not necessarily have required slavish adherence to every dot and comma of every article of the Conventions: coalition forces could have announced that they would treat captured insurgents as POWs, without actually according them such formal status. In light of the detainee abuse scandals at Abu Ghraib, Camp Breadbasket and other such places of ill repute, public adherence to the higher legal standards derived from the law of international armed conflict would have sent a powerful, and positive, message to the world about the coalition's values and behavior. The IAC law of targeting was applied in any event, so no change in practice would have been required there. The policy reasons for adopting this approach were at least as compelling, in this author's view, as the policy reasons against. Nevertheless, it is recognized that governments are often likely to take the easier option. Applying the law of non-international armed conflict—which in Iraq basically meant just Common Article 3 of the Geneva Conventions since neither the United States nor Iraq is a party to Additional Protocol II—means much less law to worry about, especially in relation to detainees.

However, the emergence of human rights law as a body of regulation applicable (at least for certain States) in certain post-conflict situations analogous to occupations means that the advocates of increased humanitarian protection and oversight of military forces' behavior may yet have the last laugh over those who would prefer unfettered executive discretion. As Gasser has written:

> [I]t would be wishful thinking to postulate the application of the whole body of international humanitarian law to the relations between the intervening power and the insurgents. Nevertheless, humanitarian policy demands that some agreement be made to give better protection for all actual and potential victims of the conflict. Among the top priorities must be achieving greater respect for the civilian population, treating captured combatants similarly to prisoners of war, and guaranteeing respect for the protective emblem.[90]

Notes

1. *See* Prosecutor v. Tadic, Case No. IT-94-1-AR72, Interlocutory Appeal on Jurisdiction, paras. 96–127 (Oct. 2, 1995); CUSTOMARY INTERNATIONAL HUMANITARIAN LAW (2 volumes: Vol. I, Rules; Vol. II, Practice (2 Parts)) (Jean-Marie Henckaerts & Louise Doswald-Beck eds., 2005).

2. This has *a fortiori* been the case in relation to Afghanistan since the Taliban were ousted as the de facto government in December 2001. *See* David Turns, Jus ad Pacem in Bello? *Afghanistan, Stability Operations and the International Laws Relating to Armed Conflict, in* THE WAR IN AFGHANISTAN: A LEGAL ANALYSIS 387 (Michael N. Schmitt ed., 2009) (Vol. 85, US Naval War College International Law Studies).

3. *See* David Turns, *The "War on Terror" through British and International Humanitarian Law Eyes: Comparative Perspectives on Selected Legal Issues*, 10 NEW YORK CITY LAW REVIEW 435 (2007).

4. KH (Article 15(c) Qualification Directive) Iraq CG [2008] UKAIT 00023, para. 11 (emphasis added) [hereinafter KH].

5. Convention No. IV Respecting the Laws and Customs of War on Land art. 2, Oct. 18, 1907, 36 Stat. 2227, *reprinted in* DOCUMENTS ON THE LAWS OF WAR 69 (Adam Roberts & Richard Guelff eds., 3d ed. 2000) [hereinafter Hague Convention No. IV].

6. COMMENTARY I GENEVA CONVENTION FOR THE AMELIORATION OF THE CONDITION OF THE WOUNDED AND SICK IN ARMED FORCES IN THE FIELD 32 (Jean S. Pictet ed., 1960) [hereinafter ICRC Commentary].

7. *Cf.* UNITED KINGDOM MINISTRY OF DEFENCE, THE MANUAL OF THE LAW OF ARMED CONFLICT para. 3.3.1 (2004) [hereinafter UK Manual].

8. Tadic, *supra* note 1, para. 70.

9. *See, e.g.*, Prosecutor v. Kunarac, Case No. IT-96-23/1-A, Judgment, paras. 56–57 (June 12, 2002); Prosecutor v. Slobodan Milosevic, Case No. IT-02-54-T, Decision on Motion for Judgment of Acquittal, paras. 15–17 (June 16, 2004).

10. *See, e.g.*, HH & others (Mogadishu: armed conflict: risk) Somalia CG [2008] UKAIT 00022, para. 257.

11. Milosevic, *supra* note 9, paras. 23–25.

12. For a useful summary of the case law, see Prosecutor v. Haradinaj, Case No. IT-04-84-T, Judgment, paras. 39–49 (Apr. 3, 2008).

13. Milosevic, *supra* note 9, para. 28.

14. *Id.*, para. 29.

15. *Id.*, para. 30.

16. *Id.*, para. 31.

17. UK Manual, *supra* note 7, para. 3.5.1.

18. *See* ICRC Commentary, *supra* note 6, at 28.

19. In 1989 Switzerland, as the depositary of the Geneva Conventions, declined to transmit to the high contracting parties a "letter of adherence" concerning the Conventions and Additional Protocols from the "State of Palestine" on the grounds of "uncertainty within the international community as to the existence or the non-existence" of such a State. *See* DOCUMENTS ON THE LAWS OF WAR, *supra* note 5, at 362.

20. Protocol Additional to the Geneva Conventions of 12 August 1949, and Relating to the Protection of Victims of International Armed Conflicts art. 1(4), June 8, 1977, 1125 U.N.T.S. 3, *reprinted in* DOCUMENTS ON THE LAWS OF WAR, *supra* note 5, at 422.

21. *Id.*, art. 96(3).

22. *E.g.*, the United Kingdom. *See* DOCUMENTS ON THE LAWS OF WAR, *supra* note 5, at 510.
23. *Id.*
24. The ICRC has identified 161 rules of customary international humanitarian law, all of which are applicable in international armed conflicts. *See* CUSTOMARY INTERNATIONAL HUMANITARIAN LAW, *supra* note 1, vol. I.
25. *E.g.*, the United States. For detailed commentary on the US position, see Michael J. Matheson, *The United States Position on the Relation of Customary International Law to the 1977 Protocols Additional to the 1949 Geneva Conventions*, 2 AMERICAN UNIVERSITY JOURNAL OF INTERNATIONAL LAW & POLICY 419, 423–29. *See also* Ronald Reagan, Message to the Senate Transmitting a Protocol to the 1949 Geneva Conventions, 1 PUBLIC PAPERS 88, 91 (Jan. 29, 1987), *reprinted in* 26 INTERNATIONAL LEGAL MATERIALS 561 (1987); George H. Aldrich, *Prospects for United States Ratification of Additional Protocol I to the 1949 Geneva Conventions*, 85 AMERICAN JOURNAL OF INTERNATIONAL LAW 1, 19 (1991).
26. ICRC Commentary, *supra* note 6, at 49–50.
27. *Id.* at 49.
28. Hamdan v. Rumsfeld, 548 U.S. 557 (2006).
29. Military and Paramilitary Activities (Nicar. v. U.S.), 1986 I.C.J. 14, para. 218 (June 27).
30. *See, e.g.*, Convention on Prohibitions or Restrictions on the Use of Certain Conventional Weapons Which May Be Deemed to Be Excessively Injurious or to Have Indiscriminate Effects amended art. 1, Oct. 10, 1980, 1342 U.N.T.S. 137, *reprinted in* 19 INTERNATIONAL LEGAL MATERIALS 1523 (1980).
31. *See, e.g.*, Ottawa Convention on the Prohibition of the Use, Stockpiling, Production and Transfer of Anti-Personnel Mines and on Their Destruction, Sept. 18, 1997, 2056 U.N.T.S. 211.
32. Tadic, *supra* note 1, at 119.
33. *See* David Turns, *At the "Vanishing Point" of International Humanitarian Law: Methods and Means of Warfare in Non-international Armed Conflicts*, 45 GERMAN YEARBOOK OF INTERNATIONAL LAW 115 (2002).
34. *See* CUSTOMARY INTERNATIONAL HUMANITARIAN LAW, *supra* note 1, vol. I.
35. *See* PERSPECTIVES ON THE ICRC STUDY ON CUSTOMARY INTERNATIONAL HUMANITARIAN LAW (Elizabeth Wilmshurst & Susan Breau eds., 2007).
36. *See* MARTIN VAN CREVELD, THE CHANGING FACE OF WAR: LESSONS OF COMBAT FROM THE MARNE TO IRAQ (2007).
37. Among the first conflicts to give rise to such legal questions was the Soviet intervention in Afghanistan (1979–89). *See* W. Michael Reisman & James Silk, *Which Law Applies to the Afghan Conflict?*, 82 AMERICAN JOURNAL OF INTERNATIONAL LAW (1988).
38. This point, which is mentioned but not elaborated upon in the jurisprudence, will probably depend more on the status of the parties to the conflict, rather than the territory in which the conflict takes place. Arguably it is of more relevance to the concept of a transnational than an internationalized armed conflict *stricto sensu*.
39. Armed Activities on the Territory of the Congo (Dem. Rep. Congo v. Uganda), 2005 I.C.J. 116, paras. 172–80 (Dec. 19).
40. Prosecutor v. Tadic, Case No. IT-94-1-A, Appeals Judgment (July 15, 1999), *reprinted in* 38 INTERNATIONAL LEGAL MATERIALS 1518 (1999).
41. *Id.*, para. 137 (original emphasis); confirmed in Prosecutor v. Dyilo, Doc. No. ICC-01/04-01/06, Decision on Confirmation of Charges, paras. 210–11 (Jan. 29, 2007).
42. Geoffrey Corn & Eric Talbot Jensen, *Transnational Armed Conflict: A "Principled" Approach to the Regulation of Counter-Terror Combat Operations*, 42 ISRAEL LAW REVIEW 46, 50 (2009).

43. *See* Turns, *supra* note 33.
44. Corn & Jensen, *supra* note 42.
45. While the plurality of the US Supreme Court in *Hamdan v. Rumsfeld, supra* note 28, characterized the "War on Terror" as an "armed conflict not of an international character" within the terms of Common Article 3, the Bush administration tended—where it said anything at all on point—to describe the struggle more in terms of international armed conflict. *See* Turns, *supra* note 3, at 468.
46. UK Manual, *supra* note 7, para. 2.1.
47. Corn & Jensen, *supra* note 42, at 60–67.
48. The United Kingdom applies the specific targeting rules contained in Additional Protocol I, which are clearly based on humanity, distinction and proportionality, to all armed conflicts, irrespective of their formal characterizations.
49. *See* CUSTOMARY INTERNATIONAL HUMANITARIAN LAW, *supra* note 1, vol. I.
50. Address to the Nation on Iraq from the *USS Abraham Lincoln*, 1 PUBLIC PAPERS 410 (May 1, 2003), full text *available at* WASHINGTONPOST.COM, May 1, 2003, http://www.washingtonpost.com/ac2/wp-dyn/A2627-2003May1 [hereinafter Bush Address].
51. Knut Dörmann & Laurent Colassis, *International Humanitarian Law in the Iraq Conflict*, 47 GERMAN YEARBOOK OF INTERNATIONAL LAW 293, 295 (2004).
52. International Committee of the Red Cross, *Conflict in Iraq: Memorandum to the Belligerents*, 85 INTERNATIONAL REVIEW OF THE RED CROSS 423 (2003), *available at* http://www.icrc.org/Web/eng/siteeng0.nsf/htmlall/5PXGBD/$File/irrc_850_memorandum.pdf.
53. On their application in the first Gulf War, see US Department of Defense, Final Report to Congress on the Conduct of the Persian Gulf War, Appendix O: The Role of the Law of War (1992), *reprinted in* 31 INTERNATIONAL LEGAL MATERIALS 615 (1992).
54. *See* Dörmann & Colassis, *supra* note 51, at 295–96.
55. *See* Eyal Benvenisti & Guy Keinan, *The Occupation of Iraq: A Reassessment*, which is Chapter XIII in this volume, at 263.
56. That is, whether it can begin already during the invasion phase while advancing troops take physical possession of territory, or whether there is a hiatus until the formal inauguration of a stable occupation regime after the invasion phase has been completed. *See* Dörmann & Colassis, *supra* note 51, at 299–301. Although a strict interpretation of the wording of Article 42 of the Hague Regulations, annexed to Hague Convention No. IV, *supra* note 5 ("Territory is considered occupied when it is actually placed under the authority of the hostile army. The occupation extends only to the territory where such authority has been established and can be exercised."), would suggest that the latter interpretation may be technically correct, the present author agrees with Dörmann and Colassis that it cannot have been intended that there should be an intermediate period between invasion and occupation, when notionally no IHL at all would be technically applicable.
57. Convention Relative to the Protection of Civilian Persons in Time of War art. 6, Aug. 12, 1949, 6 U.S.T. 3516, 75 U.N.T.S. 287, *reprinted in* DOCUMENTS ON THE LAWS OF WAR, *supra* note 5, at 301 [hereinafter Geneva Convention IV].
58. Bush Address, *supra* note 50.
59. CPA Order Number 1, De-Ba'athification of Iraqi Society and Government, CPA/ORD/16 May 2003/01 (May 16, 2003), *available at* http://www.cpa-iraq.org/regulations/ (then De-Ba'athification of Iraqi Society and Government hyperlink).
60. Remarks on the Appointment of L. Paul Bremer III as Presidential Envoy to Iraq and an Exchange with Reporters, 1 PUBLIC PAPERS 440 (May 6, 2003). Note that the terms "CPA,"

"occupation" and "Administrator" (the latter being Bremer's eventual title in Iraq) are not mentioned.

61. Provisions for the transfer of power from the CPA to the Iraqi interim government were made by CPA Order Number 100, Transition of Laws, Orders, Regulations, and Directives Issued by the Coalition Provisional Authority, CPA/ORD/28 June 2004/100 (June 28, 2004), *available at* http://www.cpa-iraq.org/regulations/ (then Transition of Laws, Orders, Regulations, and Directives Issued by the Coalition Provisional Authority hyperlink). The Order cited the advertised date of June 30, 2004 for the transfer of power; in fact, the CPA ceased to exist two days earlier, on the date that the Order itself was promulgated.

62. *See* Letter of 8 May 2003 from the Permanent Representatives of the United States of America and the United Kingdom of Great Britain and Northern Ireland to the President of the Security Council, U.N. Doc. S/2003/538 (2003) [hereinafter US/UK Letter]. This neither mentions the term "occupation" or "occupying powers" nor makes any reference to the 1907 Hague Regulations, *supra* note 56, or 1949 Geneva Convention IV, *supra* note 57. Instead, it speaks only of ill-specified "obligations under international law" for the coalition and refers to the then–newly created Coalition Provisional Authority as an institution which would "exercise powers of government temporarily."

63. S.C. Res. 1483, U.N. Doc. S/RES/1483 (May 22, 2003).

64. Although the Security Council in *id.* noted the US/UK Letter, *supra* note 62, it recognized in the same paragraph of the preamble "the specific authorities, responsibilities, and obligations under applicable international law of [the United States and the United Kingdom] as occupying powers under unified command (the 'Authority')." The next paragraph further emphasized this identification of the United States and the United Kingdom by distinguishing them from "other States that are not occupying powers [that] are working now or in the future may work under the Authority."

65. Geneva Convention IV, *supra* note 57, art. 2. *See also* Paul Bowers, Iraq: Law of Occupation, Research Paper 03/51, House of Commons Library 11 (June 2, 2003) ("[a]s they took control of Iraqi territory the coalition entered the legal condition [*sic*] of being occupying powers"); Jordan Paust, *The U.S. as Occupying Power over Portions of Iraq and Relevant Responsibilities under the Laws of War*, ASIL Insights, Apr. 2003, http://www.asil.org/insights/insigh102.htm ("the duties of an occupying power are coextensive with its *de facto* control of territory").

66. U.N. SCOR, 58th Sess., 4762d mtg. at 11, U.N. Doc. S/PV.4762 (May 22, 2003).

67. R (Al-Skeini and others) v. Secretary of State for Defence [2008] 1 AC 153.

68. The multinational force that was to become known as MNF-I was first authorized by the Security Council on October 16, 2003. S.C. Res. 1511, U.N. Doc. S/RES/1511 (Oct. 16, 2003).

69. S.C. Res. 1546, U.N. Doc. S/RES/1546 (June 8, 2004).

70. Agreement Between the United States of America and the Republic of Iraq on the Withdrawal of United States Forces from Iraq and the Organization of Their Activities during Their Temporary Presence in Iraq art. 24(1), U.S.-Iraq, Nov. 17, 2008, *available at* http://www.mnf-iraq.com/images/CGs_Messages/security_agreement.pdf.

71. Hans-Peter Gasser, *International Non-International Armed Conflicts: Case Studies of Afghanistan, Kampuchea, and Lebanon*, 31 AMERICAN UNIVERSITY LAW REVIEW 911, 913 (1982) (emphasis added).

72. International Committee of the Red Cross, Iraq post June 28, 2004: Protecting persons deprived of freedom remains a priority, http://www.icrc.org/Web/Eng/siteeng0.nsf/iwpList322/89060107D77D7299C1256EE7005200E8.

73. United Nations High Commissioner for Refugees, *UNHCR Eligibility Guidelines for Assessing the International Protection Needs of Iraqi Asylum-Seekers* 19 n.23 (2009).

74. KH, *supra* note 4, para. 75.

75. Hamdan v. Rumsfeld, *supra* note 28.

76. S.C. Res 1546, *supra* note 69, at 8 (text of letter from the Prime Minister of the Interim Government of Iraq Dr. Iyad Allawi to the President of the Council), 10 (text of letter from the United States Secretary of State Colin L. Powell to the President of the Council).

77. R (Al-Jedda) v. Secretary of State for Defence [2008] 1 AC 332. Article 25 of the Charter requires all member States of the UN to comply with legally binding resolutions of the Security Council passed under Chapter VII of the Charter (which Resolution 1546 was); Article 103 provides that legal obligations deriving from the Charter override all inconsistent legal obligations deriving from any other rule of public international law.

78. E.g., the United Kingdom applies the targeting rules from IAC (which are contained in Additional Protocol I), as customary international law, in all armed conflicts in which British forces are engaged, irrespective of their formal characterizations. So does the United States, despite not being a party to the Protocol. This is also true for both countries with respect to the "fundamental guarantees" of humane treatment contained in Article 75 of Protocol I.

79. The United Kingdom has not recorded a formal position on the ICRC study, although the matter will doubtless be addressed in the forthcoming second edition of the *Manual of the Law of Armed Conflict*. The provisional US response to the study is contained in Letter from John Bellinger III, Legal Advisor, U.S. Deptartment of State, and William J. Haynes, General Counsel, U.S. Department of Defense, to Dr. Jakob Kellenberger, President, International Committee of the Red Cross, Regarding Customary International Law Study, 46 INTERNATIONAL LEGAL MATERIALS 514 (2007).

80. For a summary of the relevant case law, see Christine Byron, *Armed Conflicts: International or Non-International?*, 6 JOURNAL OF CONFLICT & SECURITY LAW 63 (2001).

81. *See* Yoram Dinstein, *Concluding Observations: The Influence of the Conflict in Iraq on International Law*, which is Chapter XIX in this volume, at 479.

82. Gasser, *supra* note 71, at 920.

83. S.C. Res. 1546, *supra* note 69, at 11 (emphasis added).

84. Public Committee against Torture in Israel v. Government of Israel, HCJ 769/02, Judgment (Dec. 13, 2006), 46 INTERNATIONAL LEGAL MATERIALS 373 (2007), *available at* http://elyon1.court.gov.il/files_eng/02/690/007/a34/02007690.a34.pdf.

85. *See, e.g.*, Andreas Paulus & Mindia Vashakmadze, *Asymmetrical War and the Notion of Armed Conflict—A Tentative Conceptualization*, 91 INTERNATIONAL REVIEW OF THE RED CROSS 95, 112 (2009). See also the discussion of the 2006 conflict between Israel and Hezbollah in Lebanon in Sylvain Vité, *Typology of Armed Conflicts in International Humanitarian Law: Legal Concepts and Actual Situations*, *id.* at 69, 90–92.

86. Theodor Meron, *Classification of Armed Conflict in the Former Yugoslavia: Nicaragua's Fallout*, 92 AMERICAN JOURNAL OF INTERNATIONAL LAW 236, 239 (1998).

87. Gasser, *supra* note 71, at 914–15.

88. E.g., under Article 12 of Geneva Convention III, the continuing international legal responsibility of the detaining power for POWs transferred to another authority where the latter fails to respect the Convention; under Articles 118–19, release and repatriation of POWs "after the cessation of active hostilities." Convention Relative to the Treatment of Prisoners of War, Aug. 12, 1949, 6 U.S.T. 3316, 75 U.N.T.S. 135, *reprinted in* DOCUMENTS ON THE LAWS OF WAR, *supra* note 5, at 244.

89. Gasser, *supra* note 71, at 915.

90. *Id.* at 917–18.

PART IV

THE LAW OF ARMED CONFLICT IN IRAQ

VII

Legal Considerations in Relation to Maritime Operations against Iraq

Neil Brown*

It is twenty years since I first visited the headquarters of US Naval Forces Central Command (USNAVCENT) in Bahrain. I have been there on many occasions since, whether on board visiting ships or on headquarters staffs. On my last visit, in May 2009, to call on the UK's Maritime Component Commander—who is also the Deputy Commander of the Combined Maritime Forces (CMF) under the operational command of the Commander, Naval Forces United States Central Command—I was struck not only by the enormous physical development of the US and CMF headquarters footprint in Bahrain, but by the pace and character of the maritime security operations that stretch from the northern Arabian Gulf to the Horn of Africa, the developed legal underpinning of those missions, and by the unprecedented levels of genuine international cooperation, particularly between the US-led CMF and the task groups of NATO, the European Union and the many other nations conducting counter-piracy operations. In examining the conduct of maritime operations by coalition forces in Iraq since 2003, and the reasons for them, it is first necessary to consider what is a highly complex background.

---

* Commodore, Royal Navy. The views expressed in this article are those of the author and do not represent those of the Royal Navy, the United Kingdom Ministry of Defence or Her Majesty's Government.

Background

A simple list of the major maritime operations conducted in the USNAVCENT area of responsibility during the last twenty years—from the protection of merchant shipping during the Iran-Iraq war, the first Gulf War following the Iraqi invasion of Kuwait, the use of maritime interdiction operations to enforce UN sanctions against Iraq, the use of maritime aviation in policing the southern Iraqi no-fly zones, and maritime security operations in relation to international terrorism and weapons of mass destruction (WMD) proliferation after the 9/11 attacks on the United States to the mission in Iraq since 2003—demonstrates how this area has been at the cutting edge of maritime operations, many of which generated novel and complex legal issues. It is striking, therefore, to observe at the outset that notwithstanding their scale and complexity, they have not generated the development in the case of the law of armed conflict at sea that has been seen in other areas of the law of armed conflict (LOAC) over the same period.[1]

There are a number of reasons for this. The simplest, of course, is that with only two exceptions, namely the Gulf wars in 1991 and 2003, maritime operations were not a part of an international armed conflict at sea. Whether conducted under the explicit authority of the UN Security Council (e.g., Security Council Resolution 665,[2] authorizing maritime interdiction to enforce the sanctions against Iraq established under Resolution 661[3]), or amid the confusion that prevailed after 9/11 concerning international terrorism or in the face of the increasing dangers of the proliferation of WMD, the laws that regulated the conduct of maritime operations were generally not found in the LOAC but in other areas of existing international law and the use of force was generally consistent with domestic law enforcement.

It is also appears that much legal debate during the Cold War and in its immediate aftermath was complicated by a reticence on the parts of some States to claim for themselves—or even to recognize in others—certain belligerent rights or use even the language of the law of armed conflict at sea.[4] When asked in 1990 whether coalition naval forces had established a blockade, US Secretary of State James Baker replied accurately, but in a manner that set the tone for a considerable period subsequently: "Let's not call it a blockade. Let's say we now have the legal basis for interdicting those kinds of shipments."[5]

Against this background, the focus of debate in 1990 was thus centered on whether boarding operations were conducted under Article 41 or 42 of the UN Charter, the relationship between those UN Security Council authorizations and the right of national self-defense under Article 51 of the Charter, and, of course, the great question that became prevalent again in 2003, that of Iranian neutrality.

Iranian Neutrality

While the mechanism in the 1990–91 Security Council resolutions restricting the legal authorization to conduct operations against Iraq to "those states cooperating with the Government of Kuwait" provided an effective and helpful legal limitation on membership of the 1991 coalition, the general duty on other States to cooperate was not so restricted and so the notion of Iranian or any other neutrality (as opposed to support) was the cause of some legal debate. If coalition forces were acting under Article 51, the thinking went, Iranian territorial seas would be neutral waters to be respected by all belligerents. If, however, operations were carried out under the direct authority of Resolution 678[6] and those participating were able to use all necessary means, how could Iran, requested like all States to provide appropriate support, claim to be neutral?

Why was this significant in 2003? Three issues stand out; each influenced consideration of maritime operations in 2003. First, one reading of the US position on the *jus ad bellum* in 2003 suggested the 1991 Security Council authority had been resuscitated[7] and the 1991 debate on the impact of UN authority on neutrality therefore revived, although many commentators have suggested that this would only have been a real issue had there been a so-called "second resolution" in 2003 authorizing the immediate use of force to disarm Iraq. Second, certain resolutions, not least Resolution 665, which authorized maritime interdiction operations against all vessels entering and leaving Iraq in order to enforce the UN sanctions, were still in place in 2003. And finally, while the coalition operations in 1991 to remove Iraqi forces from Kuwait were most likely welcomed by Iran and were conducted without encroaching near Iranian territory or disputed maritime zones, the same could not be said for operations after the invasion in 2003.

Although considerations of the law of neutrality and the question of Iran neutrality are important, their practical significance was initially limited. The international armed conflicts involving coalition forces in 1991 and 2003 presented, in relation to Iraq, Iran and Kuwait, particular operational and tactical complexities that considerably affected both the conduct of maritime operations and the application of the law that underpinned them. The foremost was geography: set at the head of the northern Arabian Gulf, Iraq has a coastline of only thirty-five miles and a very small territorial sea. Iraqi territorial seas are significantly bounded by those of Kuwait and Iran, and the history of all three States during the rule of Saddam Hussein was not only one of strikingly different positions in relation to the West, but of sustained animosity toward each other due in no small part to historical disputes over their territories and over the maritime borders that subdivided a small and heavily congested sea area through which were accessed the great waterways of the Khor Al-Abdullah and, in particular, the Shatt Al-Arab.[8]

In 1991, Iran had made its intention to "refrain from engagement in the present armed conflict" clear in statements to the United Nations,[9] and subsequently warned belligerents that their aircraft and vessels should not enter Iranian airspace and territorial seas, and threatened to impound aircraft from either side. In the politico-legal circumstances that preceded the 2003 invasion of Iraq, Iran did not make formal statements at the United Nations but there is evidence that in 2003 it was determined to be cast again as a neutral and was widely reported in the press as expecting this to be respected. Indeed, it appears that in the early stages of offensive operations, the Iranian government set up field hospitals near the Kurdish border to treat victims of the war in Iraq, but then refused admission to injured fighters of Ansar al-Islam.[10] It could, of course, be speculated that this was an Iranian attempt to be seen to be neutral in relation to Operation Enduring Freedom, as well as Operation Iraqi Freedom.

While coalition forces involved in the invasion of Iraq in 2003 took steps to avoid encroaching upon Iranian territory, the nature of the invasion and occupation inevitably brought them close to Iran in a way that had not occurred in 1991. While during offensive operations in 2003 there was no Iranian interference with coalition forces—quite possibly due in part to the decision of coalition commanders not to conduct a full-scale amphibious assault—the disputes in relation to the maritime border and the status of the Treaty of Algiers created ambiguity that, along with Iran's questionable "neutrality" from 2004, became problematic during the occupation and thereafter while coalition forces remained in Iraq under the authority of Security Council Resolution 1483[11] and subsequent resolutions. With the regime changes in Baghdad and Tehran in the intervening period, the contradictory statements emanating from each capital and the small matter of the 1980–88 war, the status of the Treaty of Algiers[12] is a matter of much debate. As a minimum, the treaty agreed that the riverine border would follow the thalweg (which it identified), and established a detailed process for the parties acting together to track the natural movement of the thalweg and verify the border on a regular basis. Relations between the countries ensured that after the signing of the treaty none of these events ever occurred and this, and the shifting river delta, was later to create a toxic situation, notably for UK forces in command of Multi-National Division South East based in Basrah, which saw Royal Navy and Royal Marines personnel in small boats on the Shatt Al-Arab waterway captured and in due course held for short periods by the Iranian authorities in two separate incidents in 2004 and 2007.[13] On each occasion, UK personnel were demonstrably on the Iraqi "side" of the waterway. In both cases, which occurred after the conclusion of the international armed conflict with Iraq, Iran was not entitled to seize the UK personnel and under international law would only have had the authority to request (and if necessary require) them to leave Iranian territorial seas immediately. An interesting legal issue, although not tested at the time, may have been whether, either during the belligerent occupation or subsequently when present in Iraq under explicit UN Security Council authority (and charged with preserving the sovereignty and territorial integrity of Iraq), the coalition forces may have been able to represent themselves as agents of the new Iraqi government and rely on Article 7 of the Treaty of Algiers, which provides warships and State vessels of Iran and Iraq access to the whole of the Shatt Al-Arab waterway and the navigable channels to the territorial sea, irrespective of the line delimiting the territorial seas of each of the two countries.

Other Aspects of Maritime Operations from 2003

Given the profile of the tortuous process of international diplomacy, including that at the Security Council, and the added dimension of UN weapons inspections in Iraq, much press speculation has surrounded the political and legal controversy of the decision to commence coalition operations against Iraq in 2003. It was clear to those involved in military contingency planning during that period that any operation to disarm Iraq would require the removal of the regime of Saddam Hussein and would precipitate an international armed conflict between sovereign States that comprised conventional hostilities and belligerent occupation as regulated by the LOAC.[14]

Press speculation as to possible land operations launched from Turkey (from where the northern no-fly zone had been policed by US and UK aircraft) is well documented. The subsequent refusal of Turkey to approve the northern option meant that Operation Iraqi Freedom would require a massive sealift to the northern Arabian Gulf, the presence there of maritime aviation and amphibious capability and of maritime-launched missiles, and, of course, the presence of maritime forces to counter the limited naval-mine and land-launched-missile threat and to protect the oil terminals crucial to Iraq's future economic viability.

Sealift

Notwithstanding prepositioning, the requirement to move naval units and massive volumes of military equipment from the United States and the United Kingdom in particular to the northern Arabian Gulf saw extensive use of the Strait of Gibraltar, the Suez Canal, the Strait of Bab al-Mandeb and the Strait of Hormuz. Although predominantly conducted prior to the invasion, this movement through international straits and the Suez Canal continued during the operation and, notwithstanding the lack of international support, no real threat was made to the transits nor were there protests against the nonsuspendable right of straits passage applicable in peace and war.[15] While it may be stretching the point to say that every littoral State was consciously discharging its obligations as a neutral under international law, it is probably safe to assert that each acted consistently with the obligations in international law set out in the *San Remo Manual*.[16] Indeed, the only documented attempts to interfere with coalition shipping occurred at Marchwood Military Port in the United Kingdom where anti-war protesters attempted to prevent Royal Fleet Auxiliary and other supply ships from sailing. The protestors were subsequently tried and convicted of trespass and criminal damage offenses, the defense that their action was permitted under UK domestic law as necessary to avert the crime of aggression having failed.[17]

Maritime Aviation

While significant air assets were based on land in the Gulf region, the presence of US and UK aircraft carriers, operating both fixed-wing aircraft and helicopters, was critical to the coalition in providing fighter and strike capability, airborne early warning and helicopter lift for the invasion force. Although easily taken for granted, the freedom of maneuver afforded by the 1982 UN Convention on the Law of the Sea[18] to move maritime forces to the territorial sea limits of any State and to operate there with direct access to Iraq from the high seas and international airspace provided a unique operating capability for maritime forces free from the risk of outright refusal to operate from or over territories, or from restrictions and conditions in relation to aircraft numbers and missions, by any host State. Airstrikes by carrier-borne aircraft were integrated into the combined and joint coalition targeting process and the air tasking order (ATO) cycle, which enabled a coherent approach to deliberate targeting to be conducted under the direct command of the coalition targeting coordination board that sat daily (and at which the senior US and UK legal advisers were Navy lawyers). In contrast to the first Gulf War, where the air campaign generated much debate about the application of Additional Protocol I, it is probably fair to say that, although it still did not apply as a matter of law (because Iraq had not signed and the United States had not ratified), the principles codified in Article 57 in particular were followed in practice. This was made possible by increased technology, better coalition interoperability and the fact that, in reality, high-intensity offensive operations were conducted only for a short period and were successful.

Naval Fires

While much air targeting was deliberate and subject to the ATO process, even expedited processes could not keep pace with the pace of the land maneuvers, and in the same manner close air support and artillery were provided, warships were also used to provide crucial indirect fires. In these circumstances the role of legal advisers in theater was to ensure that those authorizing the fires (ground commanders, forward controllers or ship's commanding officers based on the tactical situation) fully understood their legal obligations in relation to precautions in attack.

Maritime Offensive Operations

With the Iraqi navy largely destroyed in 1991, conventional naval operations against belligerent naval units were largely restricted to dealing with what was a very limited naval mining capability. Coalition forces having quickly established sea control, the remaining threat was essentially an asymmetric one and the potential threat carried in vessels entering and, in particular, leaving Iraq.

Maritime Interdiction Operations

Although permitted under the law of armed conflict, for geographical and operational reasons there was no realistic prospect of establishing an effective blockade of Iraq in accordance with the rules set out in the *San Remo Manual*.[19] During the international armed conflict in 2003, while it was determined by coalition partners that their naval forces could as a matter of law have exercised belligerent rights of visit and search against enemy and (in certain circumstances) neutral vessels, this never occurred. Indeed, on this issue there was greater legal divergence in coalition positions than in any other area, even if in practice the units themselves performed identical missions. While the law of armed conflict at sea permits belligerent warships to board enemy merchant vessels and those neutral vessels suspected of carrying contraband to enemy territory, these powers were narrower than those available under Resolution 665. Faced with this reality, and mindful of the requirement to prevent key personnel, weaponry and WMD or related materials from leaving Iraq (given that the UK legal basis was Iraqi disarmament), the United Kingdom decided to rely solely upon the UN Security Council resolutions that permitted the use of all necessary means to stop and search all inward and outward shipping, and to seize any goods breaking the comprehensive sanctions against Iraq. US naval forces, on the other hand, sought in addition to establish the necessary mechanisms to be able to exercise the belligerent rights of visit and search. A contraband list was produced, US courts to conduct prize court hearings and special commissioners were identified, and a concept of operations developed. Neither the United Kingdom nor Australia established similar processes, both noting the unique circumstances of the Resolution 665 authority. Neither country issued a disavowal of the right of visit and search.

Prisoners of War

The Third Geneva Convention states that prisoners of war (PWs) may be interned only in premises located on land.[20] While adequate provision was made for both UK and US prisoner of war camps in Iraq with sufficient capacity for the expected numbers, it was clear that the invasion, and in particular the helicopter assault of the Al Faw Peninsula by 3 Commando Brigade Royal Marines, would generate PWs and casualties in the earliest stages of the operation and before the first PW camps were in place. In these circumstances, arrangements were made by senior UK commanders for PWs and casualties to be transported to and temporarily held in Royal Navy warships until PW facilities were available ashore. While not an ideal scenario for naval commanders, and not a measure to be taken lightly in view of the existing law, this was deemed a prudent contingency to provide a realistic and reasonably safe temporary option in view of the relatively low risk to the warships in the northern Arabian Gulf.

Casualties

Whereas the Royal Navy during the Falklands war had participated in the establishment of a "Red Cross Box" along with Argentina and the International Committee of the Red Cross,[21] no such provisions had been adopted in 1991 when, among other factors, there were extensive facilities available ashore. Commentators have speculated as to why similar shore-based facilities were not available in 2003, notably in neighboring States. In their absence a similar problem to that encountered with prisoners of war presented itself to the coalition. The Royal Navy, for its part, while mindful that it was not protected against attack under the law, used the Royal Fleet Auxiliary *RFA Argus*, an aviation training ship with troop accommodation that had been extensively equipped as a primary casualty reception ship, for the treatment of both coalition and Iraqi casualties alike, strictly according to their medical need.[22] Iraqi casualties were transferred to medical facilities or the United Kingdom's PW camp at Umm Qasr at the earliest opportunity. While *Argus* is capable of being used as an "other medical ship" within the definition of Article 23 of Additional Protocol I, any protection afforded to it would have ceased in 2003 (in accordance with Art 23.3) given that its wider operational tasking brought it within Article 34 of the Second Geneva Convention.

Protection of Iraq's Oil Terminals

While Iraqi oil was not a coalition war aim, it was well understood that Iraq's future economic viability and its ability to recover after years of neglect under the regime of Saddam Hussein would require Iraq to gain early access to oil revenue. While Iraqi oil facilities and pipelines ashore came under sporadic attack, the key facilities were the Al Basrah and Khawr Al Amaya oil terminals in Iraqi territorial seas where almost all Iraqi oil was loaded into oil tankers. Protection of those facilities was therefore accommodated within wider operational planning (they were seized by US and Polish forces during the opening hours of the invasion) and on completion of the high-intensity operations became perhaps the most significant maritime task. When on April 24, 2004 a suicide attack by a vessel-borne improvised explosive device killed two US Navy sailors and one Coast Guardsman, the two-nautical-mile security zone around each terminal was replaced with a three-thousand-meter warning zone and a two-thousand-meter exclusion zone. The greatest legal significance of this step was what the zones did not do. Neither zone, even the exclusion zone, created a trigger or "line of death." Instead, the zones complemented a system of layered defense that permitted combat indicators of threats to be detected and warnings given, and so inform commanders as to whether and what force was necessary to protect the terminals and the people on them (both military and oil workers). This took into account the density of merchant shipping in what is a confined area, the proximity of international waters and both Iranian and Kuwaiti territorial seas. It left judgment with commanders who were clear as to their mission, who could choose not to use lethal force against fishing vessels inadvertently drifting close to the terminal, but who at the same time could be confident that if they detected an imminent threat at a distance even beyond the outermost warning zone, they could act decisively. In the aftermath of the April 24 attack, these proposals, made by the USNAVCENT Staff Judge Advocate, were staffed by UK legal advisers and commanders, and received UK approval in a day.

Conclusion

The establishment in 2009 of Combined Task Force Iraqi Maritime, under alternate US and UK command, with a mission to train the Iraq navy to take responsibility for the policing of Iraqi territorial seas and protection of the oil terminals brought within sight the end of a mission commenced in 2003, and perhaps engagement in the northern Arabian Gulf—an engagement that can be traced to the naval patrols that began to protect shipping during the Iran-Iraq war.

While maritime forces conducting operations in the armed conflicts of 1991 and 2003 did operate within the parameters of the law of armed conflict, it is clear that, due to a unique combination of geographical, geopolitical, historical and operational factors at play, elements of the law of armed conflict at sea were not utilized in full or at all. That does not mean that those parts are necessarily less relevant or that they are somehow discredited; maritime powers must be slow to see them removed from national manuals, doctrine and training. As recent activity in the USNAVCENT area of responsibility, and not least off the Horn of Africa, continues to demonstrate, maritime operations have a key role to play in global security, particularly where the maritime powers are called upon to deal with threats to security caused or exacerbated by failed or failing States. Dealing with these within the existing international law framework, and understanding the implications for maritime operations of the growing impact of human rights legislation on operations generally, is an essential element in preserving freedom of maneuver for maritime commanders. Careful consideration of high-intensity maritime operations and those parts of the law of armed conflict that will regulate them is a critical element in future-proofing that process. In operations in the northern Arabian Gulf since 2003 some important modern lessons have been learned.

Notes

1. Reflected in such studies as CUSTOMARY INTERNATIONAL HUMANITARIAN LAW (2 volumes: Vol. I, Rules; Vol. II, Practice (2 Parts)) (Jean-Marie Henckaerts & Louise Doswald-Beck eds., 2005) and in the categorization of combatants. *See* NILS MELZER, INTERPRETIVE GUIDANCE ON THE NOTION OF DIRECT PARTICIPATION IN HOSTILITIES UNDER INTERNATIONAL HUMANITARIAN LAW (2009), *available at* http://www.icrc.org/Web/eng/siteeng0.nsf/htmlall/review-872-p991/$File/irrc-872-reports-documents.pdf.

2. S.C. Res. 665, U.N. Doc. S/RES/665 (Aug. 25, 1990).

3. S.C. Res. 661, U.N. Doc. S/RES/661 (Aug. 6, 1990).

4. The example often cited involves the UK statements following the torpedoing by *HMS Conqueror* of the Argentine cruiser *ARA General Belgrano* during the 1982 Falklands conflict, but a more pertinent example here might be the differing positions taken by the United States and the United Kingdom on ship boardings by Iranian forces during the Iran-Iraq war of 1980–88. Whereas the United States characterized the boarding operations as an exercise of belligerent rights, the United Kingdom, in relation to the boarding of a UK-flagged vessel, referred to the Iranian right to rely on the UN Charter Article 51 right of self-defense, which would appear to limit the belligerent right to exercise visit and search of neutral shipping. 90 Hansard, House of Commons, col 426, Jan. 28, 1986.

5. Simon Tisdall, *Crisis in the Gulf: West seeks total naval blockade*, GUARDIAN (London), Aug. 13, 1990.

6. S.C. Res. 678, ¶ 3, U.N. Doc. S/RES/678 (Nov. 29, 1990) ("Requests all States to provide appropriate support for the actions undertaken in pursuance of paragraph 2," which authorized all necessary means).

7. Letter Dated 20 March 2003 from the Permanent Representative of the United States of America to the United Nations Addressed to the President of the Security Council, U.N. Doc. S/2003/351 (Mar. 21, 2003).

8. Although there is no formal agreement between Iraq and Kuwait over their shared border, the UK commander of Combined Task Force 158 in 2006 brokered an agreement between the Iraqi and Kuwaiti navies and coast guards to coordinate access to maritime zones.

9. Letter Dated 23 January 1991 from the Permanent Representative of the Islamic Republic of Iran to the United Nations Addressed to the Secretary-General, U.N. Doc. S/22141 (Jan. 23, 1991).

10. Ansar al-Islam (Supporters of Islam) is a militant Islamic Kurdish separatist movement with ties to Iraq that seeks to transform Iraq into an Islamic state. *See* Background Q&A: Ansar al-Islam (Iraq, Islamists/Kurdish Separatists), http://www.cfr.org/publication/9237/ (last updated Nov. 5, 2008).

11. S.C. Res. 1483, U.N. Doc. S/RES/1483 (May 22, 2003).

12. Treaty Concerning the State Frontier and Neighbourly Relations between Iran and Iraq, Iraq-Iran, June 13, 1975, 1017 U.N.T.S. 136.

13. On June 21, 2004 eight Royal Navy/Royal Marines personnel were captured while conducting a riverine patrol in the Shatt Al-Arab and held for three days before being released. On March 23, 2007 fifteen Royal Navy/Royal Marines personnel were captured in the approaches to the Shatt Al-Arab in the vicinity of a vessel they were about to conduct a routine boarding of; they were held for twelve days before being released.

14. Convention Relative to the Treatment of Prisoners of War, Aug. 12, 1949, 6 U.S.T. 3316, 75 U.N.T.S. 135 [hereinafter GPW]; Convention Relative to the Protection of Civilian Persons in Time of War, Aug. 12, 1949, 6 U.S.T. 3516, 75 U.N.T.S. 287; Protocol Additional to the Geneva Conventions of 12 August 1949, and Relating to the Protection of Victims of International Armed Conflicts, June 8, 1977, 1125 U.N.T.S. 3; all *reprinted in* DOCUMENTS ON THE LAWS OF WAR (Adam Roberts & Richard Guelff eds., 3d ed. 2000) at 244, 301 and 422, respectively.

15. United Nations Convention on the Law of the Sea art. 38, Dec. 10, 1982, 1833 U.N.T.S. 3, *reprinted in* 21 INTERNATIONAL LEGAL MATERIALS 1261.

16. INTERNATIONAL INSTITUTE OF HUMANITARIAN LAW, SAN REMO MANUAL ON INTERNATIONAL LAW APPLICABLE TO ARMED CONFLICTS AT SEA 105, para. 29 (1995) [hereinafter San Remo Manual].

17. R v. Jones and others [2006 UKHL 16]. The House of Lords ruled that customary international law was, without the need for any domestic statute or judicial decision, part of the domestic law of England and Wales, but that the appellants had no defense in arguing that they were trying to prevent what they referred to as a war of aggression.

18. *Supra* note 15.

19. San Remo Manual, *supra* note 16, 176–80.

20. GPW, *supra* note 14, art. 22.

21. *See* SYLVIE-STOYANKA JUNOD, PROTECTION OF THE VICTIMS OF ARMED CONFLICT FALKLAND-MALVINAS ISLANDS, 1982: INTERNATIONAL HUMANITARIAN LAW AND HUMANITARIAN ACTION ch. 3 (1984).

22. GPW, *supra* note 14, art. 30 ("Prisoners of war . . . whose condition necessitates special treatment . . . or . . . care . . . must be admitted to any military or civilian medical unit where such treatment can be given . . .").

VIII

Come the Revolution: A Legal Perspective on Air Operations in Iraq since 2003

Charles J. Dunlap, Jr.*

Introduction

Has the early part of the twenty-first century shown the most dramatic revolution in the role of law in armed conflict in history?[1] Evidence suggests that it has. Today, for example, allegations about civilian casualties often dominate our discussions about strategy in irregular war, itself a phenomenon that, according to the *National Defense Strategy*, will preoccupy our military services for years to come.[2]

Indeed, as will be discussed below in more detail, adherence to law in armed conflict fact *and perception* is increasingly a central, if not defining, concern of field commanders, as well as military and civilian leaders at every level. It is appropriate then to pause for a moment and discuss our experiences in Iraq since 2003, and to see what lessons we should—and should not—draw from them. Of course, there are many aspects of the role of law—and lawyers—but this paper will confine itself to some of the issues that arose from the use of airpower.

Combat Operations

Perhaps the most dramatic change during the major combat operations (MCO) phase of Operation Iraqi Freedom (OIF)[3] that impacted adherence to the law of

* Major General, United States Air Force. The views and opinions expressed are those of the author alone and not necessarily those of the Department of Defense or any of its components.

armed conflict (LOAC) was the vast increase in precision-guided munitions (PGMs)[4] employed by coalition air forces (even though their employment is not, per se, required by LOAC).[5] During 1991's Operation Desert Storm, just 8 percent of the air-delivered bombs and missiles were PGMs.[6] By contrast, during the MCO phase of OIF that percentage rose to nearly 68 percent.[7] Today, virtually all are PGMs.

PGMs provided unique opportunities to minimize the risk to civilians and their property, a central aim of LOAC. Consider this 2003 report from *Time* magazine about the early phases of OIF:

> Judging from the look of the [OIF] battlefields today, the bombing was largely surgical. In the open market in Mahmudiyah, five tanks were hit from the air while they were parked in alleyways so narrow that their gun turrets could not be turned. The storefront windows a few feet away were blown out, but otherwise the surrounding buildings are intact.[8]

Besides PGMs, something of a more strategic mindset was at play during OIF. In short, simply because a particular target might lawfully be struck, that did *not* mean that it *would* be attacked. In fact, "hundreds of bridges, rail lines, power stations and other facilities" as well as "communication nodes and a few leadership sites" were spared.[9]

The targeting restraint demonstrated not only a better understanding of legal and moral imperatives, but also the practicalities of twenty-first-century operations. For example, one aviator observed that "[a] lot of care was put into selecting only those valid military targets that were absolutely essential to assist in taking Baghdad and securing the country" because planners knew that "anything destroyed from the air, like Iraqi roads, bridges, and power-generating stations, would have to be rebuilt during the post-war period."[10]

It appears that this pragmatic mindset, along with the revolutionary new munitions technologies, helped OIF air operations adhere to LOAC. Even Human Rights Watch (HRW), in its December 2003 report entitled *Off Target: The Conduct of the War and Civilian Casualties in Iraq*, gave a largely favorable assessment to the air campaign.[11] Although highly critical of leadership targeting and the use of cluster munitions, HRW nevertheless acknowledged that coalition forces "took significant steps to protect civilians during the air war."[12] In particular, HRW concluded that "air strikes on preplanned fixed targets apparently caused few civilian casualties, and . . . air forces generally avoided civilian infrastructure."[13]

Despite an initially slower pace of kinetic air operations after 2003,[14] the Air Force continued to develop technologies to enhance the ability to apply force with great discretion. While the MCO phase did feature a "far greater use of overhead imagery" than in previous conflicts,[15] the truly revolutionary improvement in intelligence, surveillance and reconnaissance (ISR)[16] capabilities did not come to fruition until unmanned aerial vehicles (UAVs) became widely available.[17]

The growth in the number of drones—many of which are now armed—has been mind-boggling. From a mere 167 in the military's inventory in 2001, there are now over 5,500.[18] These assets have been especially important during the insurgency or "irregular war" phase of operations in Iraq because they can provide what some are calling an "unblinking eye" on enemy activities without risk to friendly troops.[19] Consider this 2008 report from journalist Mark Benjamin:

> The Air Force recently watched one man in Iraq for more than five weeks, carefully recording his habits—where he lives, works and worships, and whom he meets. . . . The military may decide to have such a man arrested, or to do nothing at all. Or, at any moment they could decide to blow him to smithereens.[20]

The new technologies are transforming the way twenty-first-century conflicts are fought. According to retired Army General Barry McCaffrey the marriage of unmanned ISR platforms like the MQ-1 Predator,[21] the MQ-9 Reaper[22] and the RQ-4 Global Hawk,[23] with PGMs such as the various Joint Direct Attack Munitions[24] constitutes a "100 year war-fighting leap-ahead" that has, McCaffrey insists, "fundamentally changed the nature of warfare."[25]

The synergistic effect of *persistent* ISR with *precision* strike in irregular warfare was exemplified by the 2006 airstrike in Iraq that killed the notorious Al Qaeda leader Abu Musab al-Zarqawi. In a recent CBS *60 Minutes*' interview, General Norton Schwartz, the Air Force Chief of Staff, explained:

> Here's the way it goes. You had 600 hours of Predator time over a lengthy period . . . following Zarqawi. And then you had maybe six minutes of F-16 time to finish the target. It reflects again the power of the unmanned systems to produce the kind of intelligence that leads you to a guy like Zarqawi, who was very good at maintaining his anonymity.[26]

When ISR capabilities are available, the task of the legal advisor is greatly facilitated because the deliberateness they allow also permits steps to be taken to limit civilian casualties, especially with respect to *preplanned* targets. The senior Air Force judge advocate currently forward deployed notes the revolutionary impact of ISR on LOAC compliance relative to previous conflicts:

> It's airborne ISR that gives us the ability to actually apply [LOAC] principles (with almost mathematical precision) that were originally just concepts. In WWII, for

> example, we could merely speculate about where a bomb or an artillery round would land. Frequently, we were guessing about the target at which we were aiming. Now, we most often have photos of the target and often have FMV [full motion video] of the target area before, during and after the strike, so we can know with near certainty what collateral casualties or damage we are likely to cause.[27]

Without question, the key to such "near certainty" is, again, the availability of *both* accurate ISR *and* the time to digest the data it produces. The proverbial "fog"[28] of war still applies, and command decisions may have to be made on the basis of "incomplete" data, as was especially the case early in OIF.[29] Nevertheless, airpower has rather unexpectedly proved vital to the counterinsurgency success the United States has enjoyed in Iraq in recent years.

Ironically, even the relatively recently published counterinsurgency doctrine does not fully reflect the full potential of contemporary airpower. In fact, the Army and Marine Corps counterinsurgency manual,[30] unveiled in December of 2006, sought to discourage the use of airstrikes,[31] largely because, it appears, the drafters relied heavily upon case studies from the 1950s, '60s, and '70s, long before today's ISR and precision-strike capabilities became available. Regardless, it is extremely noteworthy that, despite the doctrine, real success in suppressing insurgent activity in Iraq did not come until 2007, a year that saw airstrikes skyrocket by fivefold.[32]

New technologies have served to significantly reduce—albeit not eliminate—the risk to innocent civilians. To the surprise of some observers, airstrikes have *not* been a leading cause of civilian casualties in Iraq.[33] Specifically, although critical of air attacks in civilian areas, a just-published *New England Journal of Medicine* study of civilian casualties in Iraq from 2003 to 2008 found that aerial bombs and missiles accounted for only 5 percent of the civilian casualties (as opposed to, for example, 20 percent attributed to small arms fire).[34]

That said, it is a mistake to conceive of the LOAC revolution strictly in terms of new technologies; it also involves fresh approaches to organizing, training and employing judge advocates (JAGs).

The Legal Architecture

Although Air Force JAGs had been forward deployed for operations virtually since the service's inception,[35] they were not typically found[36] in what we would now call air and space operations centers (AOCs).[37] However, a 1988 Joint Chiefs of Staff directive required legal review of operations' planning, and that provided a basis to regularize the JAG presence in AOCs beginning with 1989's Operation Just Cause in Panama.[38] That presence continued through various operations, including Operation Desert Storm as well as the enforcement of the no-fly zone over Iraq during the 1990s.[39]

The air-oriented operations in Afghanistan during Operation Enduring Freedom in 2001–2 had "heavy" JAG involvement.[40] Thus, prior to the start of MCO in Iraq in 2003, it was expected that JAGs would serve in the AOC. Preparation for that service was facilitated by the participation of several Judge Advocate General's Corps members in Internal Look, an exercise that took place in late November and early December of 2002. According to one participant, the "rigorous exercise enabled JAs to gain experience . . . while [also] learning the computer software applications that would be utilized during the conflicts."[41]

Mastering the computer systems used in AOCs is an essential skill for JAG advisors. Because many of these systems are unique to that environment, all Air Force JAGs who serve in AOCs must attend the Air Force Air Operations Center Initial Qualification Training Offensive Course conducted at Hurlburt Field, Florida.[42] This five-week course is standard for all AOC personnel, regardless of career field, and covers doctrine, AOC organization and processes, air battle plan development, air tasking order[43] production and execution, operational assessment and more.[44]

While the course is much concerned with developing a common understanding of the concepts applicable to the command and control of the air component, it also provides "hands on" instruction on the Theater Battle Management Core Systems and the Automated Deep Operations Coordination System. Those systems, along with the Information Work Space communications process, as well as the "mIRC" system (an Internet Relay Chat network), are critical tools for anyone working in the AOC, to include legal personnel. Beyond mastering these technologies, JAGs must also learn the applicable collateral damage estimation methodology.[45]

Writing in a 2006 article for *Foreign Affairs*, Dr. Colin Kahl, now Deputy Assistant Secretary of Defense for the Middle East,[46] describes this process as one that "uses computer software and human analysis to estimate possible civilian casualties for every target studied."[47] In essence, Dr. Kahl says, it requires commanders and their legal advisors to ask themselves five questions which he phrases this way:

> Can they positively identify the person or the site according to the current ROE [rules of engagement[48]]? Is there a protected civilian facility or significant environmental concern within the range of the weapon to be used? Can damage to that concern be avoided by attacking the target with a different weapon or a different method? If not, how many people are likely to be injured or killed in the attack? Must a higher commander be called for permission?[49]

Although advanced computer and communications systems help answer such questions and indeed have revolutionized how JAG personnel do their jobs, there is no substitute for physical presence in the AOC. At its height, there were twelve JAG personnel assigned to the AOC during OIF.[50] Some of these focused on Air Force support issues, but most were used to directly advise commanders and others on the conduct of operations. What was particularly revolutionary about JAG utilization was how they were distributed.

The complexity of preplanned air operations is such that legal advice must be integrated long before the plan is ready for final approval. Accordingly, JAGs had a constant presence in the AOC's Strategy Division, as well as its Plans Division.[51] This is a lesson, incidentally, that the Air Force learned prior to OIF. General Ronald E. Keys, who had served as the commander of NATO's AIRSOUTH, Stabilization Forces Air Component and Kosovo Forces Air Component, insisted in a 2002 interview that "[t]he important thing is that the legal advisor has got to be integrated into the operational team. He can't be an afterthought. He has to be there when the plan is being made."[52]

This early involvement by JAGs in operational planning is now *de rigueur* in AOCs. In fact, in July of 2008 the *New York Times* noted that "Air Force lawyers vet all the airstrikes approved by the operational air commanders."[53] In this way they can provide input at the very early stages of an air tasking order's development so that today there rarely are legal issues associated with preplanned targets. As a result, the Air Force has, according to Human Rights Watch's Marc Garlasco, "all but eliminated civilian casualties in Afghanistan" in strikes that are a product of the deliberate planning process. This is true even though more stringent ROE for Afghanistan require "a significantly lower risk of civilian casualties than was acceptable in Iraq."[54]

Of course not all airstrikes are a product of preplanning. Dynamic targeting,[55] such as airstrikes in response to urgent requests for close air support[56] coming from friendly troops in contact with enemy forces, presents the most difficult challenge. To the extent such targets can be vetted by JAGs, the responsibility falls to the JAG assigned to the Combat Operations Division. During the critical, early phases of OIF this JAG "sat at a console in the elevated platform in the center of the [AOC] floor" next to the chief of combat operations.[57] Among other things the proximity to senior leaders allowed "face to face" conversations that significantly enhanced the assigned JAG's situational awareness.[58]

Still, challenges existed then—and persist today—with respect to dynamic targeting. The same *New York Times* article that noted the contribution of JAGs and the near absence of civilian casualties in *preplanned* strikes also observed that most civilian casualties occur during strikes conducted at the request of ground commanders.[59] Likewise, a September 2008 report by Human Rights Watch about operations in Afghanistan concluded that civilian casualties "rarely occur during planned airstrikes on suspected Taliban targets" but rather "almost always occurred during the fluid, rapid-response strikes, *often carried out in support of ground troops*."[60]

Providing timely legal advice in these difficult situations re-emphasizes the importance of physical presence and proximity. In the effort to address the civilian casualty dilemma journalist Anna Mulrine points out that "the JAG officer [in the AOC] sits through the shift next to the Afghanistan duty officer, where they can consult easily."[61] Keeping a JAG close to decisionmakers is but one example of the several lessons to be learned from air operations in Iraq since 2003.

Lessons Learned

Though this article does not purport to be an exhaustive listing of "lessons learned," such an endeavor would surely begin with the importance of the institutionalization of JAGs as essential players in the command and control process of combat air operations.[62] Dr. Peter Singer comments in his new book, *Wired for War*, that given "advancing technology and thorny legal questions, many advise that [commanders] had better get used to the growing presence of lawyers inside military operations."[63] Because of the importance of legal legitimacy of military operations not just to the US electorate, but also to the publics of America's warfighting allies, Dr. Rebecca Grant bluntly insists that in "modern coalition warfare, attention to the law of war is a strategic necessity."[64]

Importantly, Dr. Singer also notes that the "other side knows the [legal] limits, and will do everything possible to take advantage."[65] We live in an age where adversaries increasingly seek to employ the fact or perception of illegalities, to especially include allegations of excessive civilian casualties, as a means of offsetting not just US airpower, but America's overall military prowess. Law professor and veteran William Eckhardt points out that that today "our enemies carefully attack our military plans as illegal and immoral and our execution of those plans as contrary to the 'law of war' making law, in essence, a 'center of gravity' in modern conflicts."[66]

This phenomenon—which may be called lawfare[67]—is more than simply exploiting incidents of collateral damage; it extends to actually *orchestrating* events designed to put civilians at unnecessary risk. As Anthony Cordesman puts it in his 2007 report about airpower in Iraq and Afghanistan, "both the Taliban and Iraqi insurgents often located hostile forces in civilian areas and compounds, and steadily increased their efforts to use them as human shields."[68]

This deliberate use of human shields has hardly diminished, especially in Afghanistan. At a June 2009 news conference, Secretary of Defense Robert Gates told reporters that "we know the Taliban target innocent civilian Afghans, use them as shields, mingle with them and lie abut their actions."[69] He recognizes that "a principal strategic tactic of the Taliban . . . is either provoking or exploiting civilian casualties."[70]

Addressing such challenges starts with what might be called "legal preparation of the battlespace" (LPB).[71] There are many facets to LPB. Quite obviously, the immediate access[72] to expert legal advice can help avoid LOAC incidents that an adversary can exploit. However, advising commanders in operations that involve the complex weaponry and the sophisticated ISR capabilities available today requires specialized knowledge. JAG advisors must be thoroughly familiar not only with the applicable law, but also with a myriad of technical specifics related to weapons, platforms, strategies and other aspects of the military art.

It is an axiom of the practice of law that a lawyer must understand the facts of the client's business in order to apply the law properly to issues that arise from it. This is particularly important with respect to the complexities of air warfare. For example, seemingly slight adjustments in munitions' delivery can make real differences in terms of limiting collateral damage.

Specifically, "[d]elaying an explosion by just a few milliseconds can mean that a bomb gets buried deeper into the ground before exploding."[73] Thus, a JAG must understand how fusing and other technicalities of weaponeering can affect blast patterns and, in turn, the lives of innocent civilians. Wherever possible, JAGs must try to help to offer alternatives that fulfill the commanders' intent, while also limiting collateral damage. To reiterate, competence to do so requires an intimate understanding of the client's "business," so to speak, of war making.

Several other dimensions of LPB exist. It necessarily includes ensuring that forces are fully trained in the requirements of LOAC, as well as the additional limitations imposed by policy and incorporated in the ROE. Beyond the basic LOAC training all members of the US military receive, the Air Force also has developed an advanced LOAC presentation which has been integrated into the Joint Force Air Component Commander Course mandated for all senior officers destined to command AOCs.[74] This training addresses difficult topics such as targeting dual-use facilities, human shields, the use of cluster munitions and much more.

Today, for example, commanders must be concerned about the investigation of complaints about airstrikes. While this is currently being effectively accomplished via ad hoc teams assembled for specific cases,[75] it may be better to establish a standing investigatory capability explicitly designed for such purposes. The teams should be interdisciplinary, to include JAGs, intelligence officers, operations experts, public affairs professionals and other specialties that would enable a timely explanation of incidents that carry the potential for enemy exploitation.

Interestingly, the Israelis seem very conscious of the possibility that lawfare might be waged against them. Accordingly, combat units in the 2008–9 Gaza operation were accompanied by operational verification teams equipped with cameras, tape recorders and other equipment to document the facts as operations were conducted.[76] Apparently this was done in anticipation of receiving various allegations of LOAC violations.[77] Clearly, this approach to preserving evidence is worthy of further study and possible emulation.

LPB also should involve preparing the media[78] and the public generally with a proper understanding of LOAC.[79] In this way misunderstandings and unrealistic expectations can be avoided. For example, LOAC recognizes that the tragedy of civilian deaths inevitably occurs in war. Thus, LOAC does not prohibit attacks even when such losses can be anticipated;[80] rather, attacks are forbidden where the civilian casualties would be "excessive in relation to the concrete and direct military advantage anticipated."[81]

Unfortunately, today the enemy is trying to exploit LOAC to deter attacks not just by intermingling with civilians, but also—as already indicated—by affirmatively forcing civilians to remain in targeted buildings.[82] If the wrong perception about LOAC requirements in such circumstances becomes accepted wisdom, that is, that the mere presence of *any* civilians is interpreted as creating a de facto safe haven for adversaries,[83] it could result in commanders' hands being needlessly tied with respect to the air weapon.[84] In essence, the enemy would be "rewarded" for a grotesque LOAC violation of deliberately putting innocent civilians at risk.

Finally, it is worth re-emphasizing that the fundamental responsibility of JAGs to provide candid advice[85]—even when it may be unwelcome—is especially important in combat operations. Lieutenant General Michael Short, who commanded the air component during the successful Kosovo campaign, counsels operational lawyers to be thoroughly familiar with the mission, its challenges and the rules that will govern it. He further observes that if necessary

> do not be afraid to tell [the commander] what he really does not want to hear—that he has put together this exquisite plan, but his targets indeed are not valid ones or his targets may in fact violate the law of armed conflict. . . . It will take enormous courage to do that in particular circumstances because you're always going to be junior to your boss. . . . But you have got to be able to do that.[86]

While military lawyers can get support from their JAG superiors,[87] they still must demonstrate *valor* in war.[88] True, JAGs are not often called upon to demonstrate the physical courage so central to close combat situations; however, they more often are required to demonstrate *moral* courage. It is a rather melancholy observation of some experts that the former type of courage is common in armed forces while the latter—moral courage—can often be in short supply.[89] Yet if there is a lesson for the military lawyer that has emerged in the years since 9/11, it is the vital importance of moral courage.

It is clear that the fact or perception of illegalities, whether from the mistreatment of detainees captured in ground operations[90] or from the infliction of excessive civilian casualties in an airstrike, are among the greatest threats to mission success in twenty-first-century operations.[91] Ensuring adherence to the rule of law must involve many more actors than JAGs, but JAGs must be ready to provide leadership.

As this article seeks to demonstrate, preparing to exercise such leadership is a complex and demanding task that requires real dedication and discipline. But prepare we must; the stakes are just too great. Listen to these words attributed to Winston Churchill:

> To every person, there comes in their lifetime that special moment when they are tapped on the shoulder and offered that chance to do a very special thing, unique to them and fitted to their talents. What a tragedy if that moment finds them unprepared and unqualified for the work that would be their finest hour.[92]

Fortunately, it is conferences like the one that brought us together in Newport that help us—and those who look to us for leadership—to get ready for that inevitable Churchillian moment in this era of revolutionary change in the roles of law and lawyers in armed conflict.

Notes

1. The author previously discussed this subject. *See generally* Charles J. Dunlap, Jr., *The Revolution in Military Legal Affairs: Air Force Legal Professionals in 21st Century Conflicts*, 51 AIR FORCE LAW REVIEW 293 (2001).

2. "For the foreseeable future, winning the Long War against violent extremist movements will be the central objective of the U.S." *See* Department of Defense, National Defense Strategy 7 (June 2008), *available at* http://www.defenselink.mil/pubs/2008NationalDefenseStrategy.pdf.

3. For a summary of the purposes of OIF, see Catherine Dale, Congressional Research Service, *Operation Iraqi Freedom: Strategies, Approaches, Results, and Issues for Congress*, No. RL34387 (Apr. 2, 2009), *available at* http://fas.org/sgp/crs/natsec/RL34387.pdf. Dr. Dale describes the mission of OIF as follows:

> Operation Iraqi Freedom (OIF), the U.S.-led coalition military operation in Iraq, was launched on March 20, 2003, with the immediate stated goal of removing Saddam Hussein's regime and destroying its ability to use weapons of mass destruction or to make them available to terrorists. Over time, the focus of OIF shifted from regime

removal to the more open-ended mission of helping the Government of Iraq (GoI) improve security, establish a system of governance, and foster economic development.

Id. at Summary.

4. A precision-guided munition is defined as a "weapon that uses a seeker to detect electromagnetic energy reflected from a target or reference point and, through processing, provides guidance commands to a control system that guides the weapon to the target. Also called PGM." *See* "precision-guided munitions," Joint Chiefs of Staff, Joint Publication 1-02, Department of Defense Dictionary of Military and Associated Terms (as amended through Oct. 17, 2008), *available at* http://www.dtic.mil/doctrine/jel/doddict/data/p/877.html [hereinafter DoD Dictionary].

5. *See, e.g.*, Danielle L. Infeld, Note, *Precision-Guided Munitions Demonstrated Their Pinpoint Accuracy in Desert Storm; But Is a Country Obligated to Use Precision Technology to Minimize Collateral Civilian Injury and Damage?*, 26 GEORGE WASHINGTON JOURNAL OF INTERNATIONAL LAW AND ECONOMICS 109 (1992).

6. THOMAS G. MAHNKEN, TECHNOLOGY AND THE AMERICAN WAY OF WAR SINCE 1945, at 223 (2008).

7. *Id.*

8. Terry McCarthy, *Whatever Happened to the Republican Guard?*, TIME, May 4, 2003, at 38, *available at* http://www.time.com/time/magazine/article/0,9171,1101030512-449441,00.html.

9. Bradley Graham & Vernon Loeb, *An Air War of Might, Coordination and Risks*, WASHINGTON POST, Apr. 27, 2003, at A01, *available at* http://www.iraqwararchive.org/data/apr27/US/wp10.pdf.

10. Gerry J. Gilmore, *Air Strategy Preserved Iraqi Infrastructure, Lives*, DEFENSELINK, Apr. 10, 2006, http://www.defenselink.mil/news/newsarticle.aspx?id=15498 (*quoting* Major Michael Norton, Air National Guard).

11. HUMAN RIGHTS WATCH, OFF TARGET: THE CONDUCT OF THE WAR AND CIVILIAN CASUALTIES IN IRAQ (2003), *available at* http://www.hrw.org/en/reports/2003/12/11/target.

12. *Id.* at 17.

13. *Id.* at 6.

14. *See, e.g.*, ANTHONY H. CORDESMAN, US AIRPOWER IN IRAQ AND AFGHANISTAN: 2004–2007 (2007), *available at* http://www.csis.org/media/csis/pubs/071213_oif-oef_airpower.pdf.

15. Graham & Loeb, *supra* note 9.

16. DoD defines ISR as "[a]n activity that synchronizes and integrates the planning and operation of sensors, assets, and processing, exploitation, and dissemination systems in direct support of current and future operations. This is an integrated intelligence and operations function." *See* "intelligence, surveillance, and reconnaissance," DoD Dictionary, *supra* note 4, *available at* http://www.dtic.mil/doctrine/jel/doddict/data/i/11775.html.

17. DoD defines a UAV as a "powered, aerial vehicle that does not carry a human operator, uses aerodynamic forces to provide vehicle lift, can fly autonomously or be piloted remotely, can be expendable or recoverable, and can carry a lethal or nonlethal payload. Ballistic or semiballistic vehicles, cruise missiles, and artillery projectiles are not considered unmanned aerial vehicles." *See* "unmanned aerial vehicle," DoD Dictionary, *supra* note 4, *available at* http://www.dtic.mil/doctrine/jel/doddict/data/u/94.html.

18. Christopher Drew, *Drones Are Weapons of Choice in Fighting Qaeda*, NEW YORK TIMES, Mar. 17, 2009, at A1, *available at* http://www.nytimes.com/2009/03/17/business/17uav.html.

19. John Barry & Evan Thomas, *Up in the Sky, An Unblinking Eye*, NEWSWEEK, June 9, 2008, at 2, *available at* http://www.newsweek.com/id/139432.

20. Mark Benjamin, *Killing "Bubba" from the Skies*, SALON.COM, Feb. 15, 2008, http://www.salon.com/news/feature/2008/02/15/air_war/.

21. MQ-1 Predator Unmanned Aircraft System (Factsheet), AF.MIL, Sept. 2008, http://www.af.mil/information/factsheets/factsheet.asp?id=122.

22. MQ-9 Reaper Unmanned Aircraft System (Factsheet), AF.MIL, Sept. 2008, http://www.af.mil/information/factsheets/factsheet.asp?fsID=6405.

23. RQ-4 Global Hawk Unmanned Aircraft System (Factsheet), AF.MIL, Oct. 2008, http://www.af.mil/information/factsheets/factsheet.asp?fsID=13225.

24. Joint Direct Attack Munition GBU 31/32/38 (Factsheet), AF.MIL, Nov. 2007, http://www.af.mil/information/factsheets/factsheet.asp?id=108.

25. Memorandum from General Barry R. McCaffrey to Colonel Mike Meese, United States Military Academy, Subject: After Action Report 5 (Oct. 15, 2007), *available at* http://www.mccaffreyassociates.com/pages/documents/AirForceAAR-101207.pdf.

26. Lara Logan, *Drones—America's New Air Force*, CBSNEWS.COM, May 10, 2009, updated Aug. 14, 2009, http://www.cbsnews.com/stories/2009/05/08/60minutes/main5001439.shtml.

27. E-mail from Gary Brown, CAOC Input – 2009 International Law Conference (Apr. 23, 2009) (on file with author).

28. *See* CARL VON CLAUSEWITZ, ON WAR 140 (Michael Howard & Peter Paret eds. & trans., Princeton University Press 1989) (1832) (discussing the uncertainty of all information in war).

29. *See* William C. Smith, *Lawyers at War*, ABA JOURNAL, Feb. 2003, at 14–15.

30. Headquarters, Department of the Army & Headquarters, Marine Corps Combat Development Command, FM 3-24/MCWP 3-33.5, Counterinsurgency (2006), *available via* Jim Garamone, *Army, Marines Release New Counterinsurgency Manual*, AMERICAN FORCES INFORMATION SERVICE, Dec. 15, 2006, http://www.fas.org/irp/doddir/army/fm3-24 .pdf [hereinafter FM 3-24].

31. For example, FM 3-24 admonishes counterinsurgents to

> exercise exceptional care when using airpower in the strike role. Bombing, even with the most precise weapons, can cause unintended civilian casualties. Effective leaders weigh the benefits of every air strike against its risks. An air strike can cause collateral damage that turns people against the host-nation (HN) government and provides insurgents with a major propaganda victory. Even when justified under the law of war, bombings that result in civilian casualties can bring media coverage that works to the insurgents' benefit.

Id. at Appendix E, para. E-5.

32. *See* CORDESMAN, *supra* note 14.

33. *See, e.g.*, *Iraq Study: Executions Are Leading Cause of Death*, USATODAY.COM, Apr. 15, 2009, http://www.usatoday.com/news/world/iraq/2009-04-15-iraq-civilian-deaths_N.htm ("Execution-style killings, not headline-grabbing bombings, have been the leading cause of death among civilians in the Iraq war").

34. Madelyn Hsiao-Rei Hicks et. al., *The Weapons That Kill Civilians – Deaths of Children and Noncombatants in Iraq 2003–2008*, NEW ENGLAND JOURNAL OF MEDICINE, Apr. 16, 2009, at 1585, 1586 *available at* http://content.nejm.org/cgi/reprint/360/16/1585.pdf.

35. *See, e.g.*, Walter Lewis, *In the Korean War*, THE REPORTER 113 (Special 50th Anniversary Edition 1999), *available at* http://www.afjag.af.mil/shared/media/document/AFD-090107-018 .pdf.

36. *See, e.g.*, David C. Morehouse, *A Year in Vietnam*, *id.* at 126–27.

37. AOCs are generally described in Chapter 7, Department of the Air Force, Air Force Doctrine Document 2, Operations and Doctrine 105 (2007), *available at* http://www.e-publishing.af.mil/shared/media/epubs/AFDD2.pdf.

38. PATRICIA A. KERNS, THE FIRST FIFTY YEARS: U.S. AIR FORCE JUDGE ADVOCATE GENERAL'S DEPARTMENT 138 (2001).

39. For a discussion of legal issues associated with no-fly zones, see generally Michael N. Schmitt, *Clipped Wings: Effective and Legal No-Fly Zone Rules of Engagement*, 20 LOYOLA OF LOS ANGELES INTERNATIONAL & COMPARATIVE LAW JOURNAL 727 (1998).

40. *See* BENJAMIN S. LAMBETH, AIRPOWER AGAINST TERROR: AMERICA'S CONDUCT OF OPERATION ENDURING FREEDOM 318 (2005). Although the involvement was reported by Lambeth as "heavy" in terms of influence, the support was largely provided by just three JAGs.

41. E-mail from Edward J. Monahan, JA Support at CAOC – OIF (June 8, 2009) (on file with author).

42. This is one of a number of AOC-related courses conducted by the 505th Training Squadron. *See generally* Department of the Air Force, 505th Training Squadron (Fact Sheet), http://www.505ccw.acc.af.mil/library/factsheets/factsheet.asp?id=5171 (last visited June 14, 2009).

43. DoD defines the air tasking order as a "method used to task and disseminate to components, subordinate units, and command and control agencies projected sorties, capabilities and/or forces to targets and specific missions. Normally provides specific instructions to include call signs, targets, controlling agencies, etc., as well as general instructions." *See* "air tasking order," DoD Dictionary, *supra* note 4, *available at* http://www.dtic.mil/doctrine/jel/doddict/data/a/9435.html.

44. E-mail from Major Mathew J. Mulbarger, Comments for Major General Dunlap on CAOC (June 9, 2009) (on file with author).

45. Monahan, *supra* note 41.

46. *See* Colin Kahl, Deputy Assistant Secretary of Defense for the Middle East, U.S. Department of Defense, Biography, DEFENSELINK, http://www.defenselink.mil/bios/biographydetail.aspx?biographyid=204 (last visited Oct. 12, 2009).

47. Colin H. Kahl, *How We Fight*, FOREIGN AFFAIRS, Nov./Dec. 2006, at 83, *available at* http://www.realclearpolitics.com/articles/2006/12/how_we_fight.html.

48. DoD defines rules of engagement as "[d]irectives issued by competent military authority that delineate the circumstances and limitations under which United States forces will initiate and/or continue combat engagement with other forces encountered." *See* "rules of engagement," DoD Dictionary, *supra* note 4, *available at* http://www.dtic.mil/doctrine/jel/doddict/data/r/6783.html.

49. Kahl, *supra* note 47.

50. Monahan, *supra* note 41.

51. *Id.*

52. Randon H. Draper, *Interview with a JFACC: A Commander's Perspective on the Legal Advisor's Role*, THE JAG WARRIOR, Autumn 2002, at 21–22.

53. Thom Shanker, *Civilian Risks Curb Airstrikes in Afghan War*, NYTIMES.COM, July 23, 2008, http://www.nytimes.com/2008/07/23/world/asia/23military.html.

54. *Id.*

55. DoD defines dynamic targeting as targeting "that prosecutes targets identified too late, or not selected for action in time to be included in deliberate targeting." *See* "dynamic targeting," DoD Dictionary, *supra* note 4, *available at* http://www.dtic.mil/doctrine/jel/doddict/data/d/19552.html.

56. DoD defines close air support as "[a]ir action by fixed- and rotary-wing aircraft against hostile targets that are in close proximity to friendly forces and that require detailed integration of each air mission with the fire and movement of those forces. Also called CAS." *See* "close air support," DoD Dictionary, *supra* note 4, *available at* http://www.dtic.mil/doctrine/jel/doddict/data/c/8823.html.

57. Monahan, *supra* note 41.

58. Shanker, *supra* note 53.

59. *Id.*

60. HUMAN RIGHTS WATCH, "TROOPS IN CONTACT": AIRSTRIKES AND CIVILIAN DEATHS IN AFGHANISTAN 4 (2008), *available at* http://hrw.org/reports/2008/afghanistan0908/afghanistan0908web.pdf (italics added).

61. Anna Mulrine, *Lawyers Review Airstrike Plans*, USNEWS.COM, May 29, 2008, http://www.usnews.com/articles/news/world/2008/05/29/lawyers-review-airstrike-plans.html.

62. In 2008, twenty-two judge advocates deployed to support air and space operations centers. *See JAG Corps Personnel in the Operational Setting*, THE REPORTER: THE YEAR IN REVIEW 118 (2008), *available at* http://www.afjag.af.mil/shared/media/document/AFD-090317-021.pdf.

63. P.W. SINGER, WIRED FOR WAR 391 (2009).

64. Rebecca Grant, *In Search of Lawful Targets*, AIR FORCE MAGAZINE, Feb. 2003, at 38, 40, *available at* http://www.airforce-magazine.com/MagazineArchive/Documents/2003/February%202003/02targets03.pdf.

65. SINGER, *supra* note 63, at 39.

66. William George Eckhardt, *Lawyering for Uncle Sam When He Draws His Sword*, 4 CHICAGO JOURNAL OF INTERNATIONAL LAW 431 (2003).

67. Charles J. Dunlap, Jr., *Lawfare: A Decisive Element of 21st-Century Conflicts?*, 54 JOINT FORCES QUARTERLY, 3rd Quarter 2009, at 34, *available at* http://www.ndu.edu/inss/Press/jfq_pages/editions/i54/12.pdf.

68. CORDESMAN, *supra* note 14.

69. Jim Garamone, *Gates Stresses Need to Curtail Civilian Casualties*, DEFENSELINK, June 12, 2008, http://www.defenselink.mil/news/newsarticle.aspx?id=54760.

70. *See* Press Conference, Secretary of Defense Robert Gates & Chairman, Joint Chiefs of Staff Michael Mullen, Leadership Changes in Afghanistan (transcript), DEFENSELINK, May 11, 2009, http://www.defenselink.mil/transcripts/transcript.aspx?transcriptid=4424.

71. *Compare* "intelligence preparation of the battlespace," which DoD defines as an

> analytical methodology employed to reduce uncertainties concerning the enemy, environment, and terrain for all types of operations. Intelligence preparation of the battlespace builds an extensive database for each potential area in which a unit may be required to operate. The database is then analyzed in detail to determine the impact of the enemy, environment, and terrain on operations and presents it in graphic form. Intelligence preparation of the battlespace is a continuing process.

See "intelligence preparation of the battlespace," DoD Dictionary, *supra* note 4, *available at* http://www.dtic.mil/doctrine/jel/doddict/data/i/8628.html.

72. *See, e.g.*, Protocol Additional to the Geneva Conventions of 12 August 1949, and Relating to the Protection of Victims of International Armed Conflicts art. 82, June 8, 1977, 1125 U.N.T.S. 3, *reprinted in* DOCUMENTS ON THE LAWS OF WAR 422 (Adam Roberts & Richard Guelff eds., 3d ed. 2000), *available at* http://www.unhchr.ch/html/menu3/b/93.html ("Parties to the conflict in time of armed conflict, shall ensure that legal advisers are available") [hereinafter Additional Protocol I].

73. Anna Mulrine, *Targeting the Enemy: A Look Inside the Air Force's Control Center for Iraq and Afghanistan*, U.S. NEWS & WORLD REPORT, June 9, 2008, at 26, *available at* http://www.usnews.com/articles/news/world/2008/05/29/a-look-inside-the-air-forces-control-center-for-iraq-and-afghanistan.html.

74. *See generally* "MCADRE 004 Joint Force Air Component Commander Course," Air University Catalogue Academic Year 2008–2009, Oct. 1, 2008, at 168, *available at* http://www.au.af.mil/au/cf/au_catalog_2008_09/AU_Catalog_Print_Version_1_Oct_08.pdf.

75. *See, e.g.*, Eric Schmitt & Thom Shanker, *U.S. Report Finds Errors in Afghan Airstrikes*, NEW YORK TIMES, June 3, 2009, at A1, *available at* http://www.nytimes.com/2009/06/03/world/asia/03military.html.

76. Barbara Opall-Rome, *Israelis Document Everything to Justify Strikes*, DEFENSE NEWS, Jan. 12, 2009, at 8.

77. Thomas Darnstadt & Christopher Schult, *Did Israel Commit War Crimes in Gaza?*, SPIEGELONLINE INTERNATIONAL, Jan. 26, 2009, http://www.spiegel.de/international/world/0,1518,603508,00.html.

78. This can be done in an effective way. *See, e.g.*, Defense Intelligence Agency, *Saddam's Use of Human Shields and Deceptive Sanctuaries: A Special Briefing for the Pentagon Press Corps*, DEFENSELINK, Feb. 2003, http://www.defenselink.mil/dodcmsshare/briefingslide/110/030226-D-9085M-020.pdf.

79. *See, e.g.*, Article 83 of Additional Protocol I to the 1949 Geneva Conventions. It provides:

> The High Contracting Parties undertake, in time of peace as in time of armed conflict, to disseminate the Conventions and this Protocol as widely as possible in their respective countries and, in particular, to include the study thereof in their programmes of military instruction and to encourage the study thereof by the civilian population, so that those instruments may become known to the armed forces and to the civilian population.

Additional Protocol I, *supra* note 72.

80. *Compare* Pamela Constable, *NATO Hopes to Undercut Taliban With 'Surge' of Projects*, WASHINGTON POST, Sept. 27, 2008, at A12, *available at* http://www.washingtonpost.com/wp-dyn/content/article/2008/09/26/AR2008092603452_pf.html (*quoting* Brigadier General Richard Blanchette, chief spokesman for NATO forces: "[i]f there is the likelihood of even one civilian casualty, we will not strike, not even if we think Osama bin Laden is down there").

81. *See, e.g.*, Additional Protocol I, *supra* note 72, art. 53.

82. Jim Garamone, *Taliban Forced Civilians to Remain in Targeted Buildings, Petraeus Says*, DEFENSELINK, May 10, 2009, http://www.defenselink.mil/news/newsarticle.aspx?id=54272.

83. *Compare* Constable, *supra* note 80 ("We need to weigh the effects and the proportionality of every action. If there is the likelihood of even one civilian casualty, we will not strike, not even if we think Osama bin Laden is down there," *quoting* Brigadier General Richard Blanchette, chief spokesman for NATO forces).

84. Consider the recent statement of US National Security Advisor General James Jones, USA (Ret.), during a recent interview:

> Stephanopoulos: You all had a busy week this week. The heads of Afghanistan and Pakistan came here to the United States to meet with the president—to meet with the president's entire team. And you seemed to be on the same page, yet after the meetings, the president of Afghanistan, Hamid Karzai, said that all airstrikes—all American airstrikes in Afghanistan must end. Will the U.S. comply with that demand?

> Jones: Well, I think that we're going to take a look at trying to make sure that we correct those things we can correct, but certainly to tie the hands of our commanders and say we're not going to conduct airstrikes, it would be imprudent.

See This Week, Interview with National Security Adviser General James Jones and Senator John McCain (ABC News television broadcast May 10, 2009) (transcript available at http://abcnews.go.com/ThisWeek/Story?id=7549797&page=1).

85. CENTER FOR PROFESSIONAL RESPONSIBILITY, AMERICAN BAR ASSOCIATION, MODEL RULES OF PROFESSIONAL CONDUCT Rule 2.1 (2007).

86. Michael Short, *Operation Allied Force from the Perspective of the NATO Air Commander, in* LEGAL AND ETHICAL LESSONS OF NATO'S KOSOVO CAMPAIGN 19, 26 (Andru E. Wall ed., 2002) (Vol. 78, US Naval War College International Law Studies).

87. JAGs are entitled by law to communicate directly with their JAG superiors, to include the Judge Advocate General. *See* 10 U.S.C. § 806 (2000).

88. Valor is one of the guiding principles of the Air Force JAG Corps. *See* Department of the Air Force, JAG Corps Values and Vision 2 (2006), *available at* http://www.afjag.af.mil/shared/media/document/AFD-080502-052.pdf.

89. MAX HASTINGS, WARRIORS: PORTRAITS FROM THE BATTLEFIELD xvii (2005) ("Physical bravery is found more often than the spiritual variety. Moral courage is rare . . . .").

90. Tom Brokaw, *Gen. Sanchez: Abu Ghraib 'clearly a defeat,'* MSNBC.COM, June 30, 2004, http://www.msnbc.msn.com/id/5333895/.

91. *See, e.g.*, Robert Burns, *Analysis: US must limit Afghan civilian deaths*, WASHINGTONPOST.COM, June 13, 2009, http://www.washingtonpost.com/wp-dyn/content/article/2009/06/13/AR2009061300246.html.

92. Some experts believe this quote is apocryphal. *See* CHURCHILL BY HIMSELF: THE DEFINITIVE COLLECTION OF QUOTATIONS 578 (Richard Langworth ed., 2008).

IX

The Iraq War: A Commander's Perspective

Michael L. Oates*

Introduction

It is a pleasure to be back in Newport and an honor to speak to you this afternoon. I have a lot of great memories from my days as a student here at the Naval War College; it was undoubtedly one of the most enjoyable experiences of my career, both from a personal and a professional standpoint.

When I visit places like this, I am often reminded that as military officers, we don't get enough opportunities during our careers to pause and think critically about our profession. To that end, I think it is important for military officers to spend time in academic environments such as this where they can read, write, listen to speakers, attend conferences like this one and interact with people who have different experiences, different points of view.

To you military officers in the audience today who are students here at the Naval War College, I say enjoy your time here, but make good use of it. Take some of those ideas that have been bouncing around in your head and share them with the rest of us. We have an old saying in the Army that a soldier should always improve his foxhole. I believe, as leaders, we have a similar obligation to our profession. That means having the courage to speak up and share ideas about how you think we can do things better. Granted, that is not always easy. People with innovative ideas often receive their fair share of pushback. But the flip side is you never know when one of your ideas will be the catalyst for real, meaningful change. As

* Major General, United States Army.

President John Quincy Adams said, "If your actions inspire others to dream more, learn more, do more, and become more, you are a leader."

Now that I have talked about the benefits of being in an academic setting, I have to poke a little fun at the folks who do this for a living. After spending the last thirteen months with my soldiers in Iraq—guys who use short sentences filled with colorful expletives, and for whom the word "*hooah*" is a noun, a verb and an all-purpose adjective—I had to chuckle when I saw the topic that the good people at the Naval War College asked me to address today in ninety minutes or less: "Provide a commander's perspective on the Iraq war. Discuss the principal military objectives and problems encountered in the offensive campaign, counterinsurgency operations, and the occupation and stability phases of the Iraq war."

Since I knew the audience would primarily be attorneys and academics, I asked my staff judge advocate, Mike Ryan, to explain the topic to me. Unfortunately, he spent thirteen months with me in Iraq, and I think it affected his ability to deal with complex subjects because when I asked for his help, he read the topic, shook his head and said: "Sir, I don't know what it means, but it sounds pretty *hooah*."

In all seriousness, let me start by saying that contrary to what you might think, I have no special insight about the war in Iraq. One thing I've learned over the years is that in Iraq, as in every war, a person's knowledge of things really depends on three things: when they were there, where they operated and their job. A soldier who fought in the Ia Drang Valley of Vietnam in 1965, for example, would have a much different perspective on the Vietnam War than, say, a Marine who fought in Northern I-Corps or a Navy pilot who flew bombing missions from an aircraft carrier. In much the same way, my experiences as an Assistant Division Commander for Operations in northern Iraq in 2006 and 2007 differed considerably from my experiences as a Division Commander in central and southern Iraq in 2008 and 2009. And, of course, neither of those two experiences resembled the time I spent as Chief of Staff to the Chief Operations Officer, Coalition Provisional Authority in Baghdad.

So what I have to say about Iraq today should probably be qualified to some extent since, like any other soldier, my remarks and opinions are based primarily on my own experiences during selected snapshots in time. Unlike a lot of folks who come to Iraq, receive a briefing in the Green Zone, then leave the country the next day, I will not claim to be an expert on Iraq.

The Initial Offensive Phase

As we all know, the war in Iraq began in March 2003 and it is still going on as we sit here today. Given the length of the war, and the infinite number of issues we could discuss, it should come as no surprise that in the next ninety minutes we will have to concentrate on a few key issues and try to hit just the wave tops. Also, I hope this will be more of a dialogue than a speech, so I will make a few key points on each issue and leave plenty of time for your questions and comments.

In keeping with the topics I was given, I will start by saying a few words about the initial offensive phase of the war. I think this is a subject worthy of discussion because it provides us with a number of important lessons learned.

I think the major lesson we learned during the initial phase of the war can be summed up by the age-old military maxim "you fight like you train." On that point, I would submit to you that prior to the invasion of Iraq no military in the world trained itself and its leaders for combat better than the US military. How we got to that level of proficiency is a remarkable story in and of itself and, as we will discuss later, it is a story that, in my opinion, is still instructive today.

In the post-Vietnam era, the men who commanded platoons and companies in Vietnam took a hard look at how the Vietnam War was conducted and what it did to the military. As they began to occupy positions of power they drew on those bitter experiences and said, "Never again." Those men—the ones author James Kitfield called the "prodigal soldiers"[1]—rolled up their sleeves and rebuilt the US military, taking an institution crippled by drug use, disciplinary problems, racial tensions, poor training and inadequate resources, and making it the best trained, best equipped, most professional fighting force the world has ever seen.

I have some personal experience with that time, having graduated from the US Military Academy in 1979. These days, when I hear younger officers complain about the Army, I am quick to remind them that I joined an Army that had just lost a war. Using words that are much too colorful for this forum, I go on to tell them that they simply cannot conceive how messed up that Army was then.

But in 2003, that was certainly not the case. As I noted a moment ago, what our military did best in the years leading up to the invasion of Iraq was train for combat. Our ground forces—the Army in particular—did this at our combat training centers: the National Training Center for our heavy forces and the Joint Readiness Training Center for our light fighters.

Because we were so well trained, so well equipped, so well led and so well resourced, we were able to invade Iraq in March 2003, defeat its military and topple its government in relatively short order using a force with less combat power than the one that liberated Kuwait during Operation Desert Storm. Putting aside the political reasons we invaded Iraq in 2003 and looking at things from a purely military standpoint, I think no fair-minded person can deny that our military was tremendously successful during the opening phase of the war. I believe that success was because we fought like we trained. What we did not know then—and if we are honest with ourselves, what we must admit now—is that as good as our combat training was, we were not well trained, well resourced or well prepared for the post-combat phase. To paraphrase the now famous quote from Secretary of State Colin Powell: we did a great job breaking Iraq, but we were not prepared for what happened once we bought it.

I say that understanding full well that hindsight is 20/20 and it is easy for me to stand here and critique operations after the fact. That is certainly not my intent. But part of making our military better is, as I mentioned at the outset, having the courage to look hard at ourselves in order to identify where we could have done things better and where we should change things in the future.

I sometimes tell my subordinates, "You're entitled to your own opinions, but you're not entitled to your own facts." In that vein, if we are fair and realistic, we have to say the facts with regard to the post-conflict phase speak for themselves, and what they tell is that the US military was neither trained nor resourced to be an occupying force in a country as large and complex as Iraq.

Even today, after all of the tremendous work the military has done in Iraq along the governance, economics, civil capacity and rule of law lines of effort, there are still those who argue that using the military for missions other than combat operations is like trying to hammer nails with a screwdriver. I have my own ideas on that point, some of which I will share with you later in this presentation.

Counterinsurgency Operations

Turning to counterinsurgency (COIN) operations, it is important to look at the situation that gave rise to the insurgency in the first place. As I noted previously, our initial invasion of Iraq was quick and successful militarily. However when the dust settled we looked around and realized that we were in charge of a country twice the size of Idaho; a country with six international borders and a population of over twenty-two million people from different religious, ethnic, cultural and tribal backgrounds. People who, as we soon found out, in many cases didn't like each other very much.

As if this situation were not challenging enough, the country we were in charge of had a long history of violence and oppression committed by a corrupt, dictatorial central government—a government that had systematically abused, neglected, stolen from and murdered its own citizens. It was a place where, in the best of cases, disputes were settled with decisions made by sheiks and tribal elders; in the worst of cases, they were settled with kidnapping, violence and murder. To make the problem even more interesting, the country we now controlled had no functioning police force or court system, and very little in the way of essential services like water, sewer, sanitation, medical care and electricity.

As someone with a background in physics, I can tell you that nature really does abhor a vacuum, and post-invasion Iraq was no exception. Accordingly, in little to no time, the power vacuums that existed in Iraq after the fall of the former regime were filled by a number of very dedicated and very aggressive groups, all vying for power and control.

Like most things in Iraq, the insurgency was split along religious, cultural and ethnic lines. Insurgents ranged from the Shiite groups like *Jaish al-Mahdi* (JAM) to the Sunni-led Al Qaeda in Iraq, and everything in between. In addition to their desire for power and control, most of these groups shared an intense hatred of the coalition forces, which they saw as occupiers. In the case of some of these groups, most notably Al Qaeda in Iraq, they were willing to commit horrific acts of violence and terrorism not only against military forces, but against anyone not aligned with their agenda, including Iraqi civilians.

So there we were, a relatively small military force being asked to confront a litany of problems—ones that would eventually take years to solve. We had to deal with everything from defeating a violent insurgency to meeting the basic human needs of the Iraqi civilian population and myriad problems falling between those two extremes. The challenges inherent in defeating the insurgency are something that could be talked about and debated for hours. In keeping with my "wave tops" approach to this talk, I will simply say that it took us a while to figure out the right approach.

How to defeat the insurgency in Iraq was something of a "chicken and egg" dilemma: do we concentrate on solving the problems of the Iraqi people—most notably things like essential services—first, or do we focus on killing and capturing the bad guys and, once things are secure, concentrate on making the Iraqis' daily lives better? Some, including many of our senior military leaders in Iraq during the first part of the war, advocated the former.

This "essential services first" school of thought argued that if the Iraqi people had electricity, clean water, trash pickup and schools for their children, they would be less likely to turn to a violent insurgency to solve their problems. It was a reasonable approach, one that makes sense on its face. We traveled along that line of drift for the first few years of the war, but what we eventually found was our successes were not really widespread or sustainable.

Again, I am not saying there is no merit at all to this approach. I will be the first one to tell you that you cannot kill your way out of a situation such as we had in Iraq. Attriting the enemy is undoubtedly important, but what we learned over time in Iraq was that success in a counterinsurgency campaign depends on more than just killing the enemy. There is a time and a place to do that for sure, but in counterinsurgency you have to take things a step further. To put it simply, you have to kill the right guys at the right places at the right times. Lethal operations have to disrupt networks and take out financiers. It's graduate-level stuff that goes well beyond the basic infantryman's ability to enter and clear a room.

I think another problem we had with defeating the insurgency relates in a way to the point I made in my initial remarks about fighting like we trained. What do I mean by that? Let me explain. The US military has always been at its best when it goes toe-to-toe with a definable, quantifiable enemy. In fact, many of our senior leaders during the first part of the Iraq war were guys who trained virtually all of their professional lives to defeat Soviet and Warsaw Pact armored formations coming through the Fulda Gap. In that kind of fighting, metrics and data are critically important: How many tanks am I up against? How many gallons of fuel do I have? How many BMPs,[2] tanks and artillery pieces do I have to kill before the enemy is combat ineffective? In my opinion, early in the war we often fell back on that mode of thinking, relying on numbers and metrics as a measure of our effectiveness.

Indeed, if you look back on the first few years of the war, our reports and briefings from that time were filled with statistics: number of patrols conducted, number of caches found and cleared, number of improvised explosive device (IED) or indirect fire attacks. With respect to the "essential services first" approach discussed a few moments ago, this love of numbers fit right into the template for success. We tracked the number of schools built, number of hours of electricity provided, number of Commander's Emergency Response Program projects initiated and number of dollars spent on those projects. With so many impressive statistics, pie charts and metrics on so many colorful PowerPoint slides, how could we be losing?

The problem was we *were* losing. To some extent, I attribute that to something that absolutely drives me around the bend: we were constantly looking at data without doing any analysis of what that data really means. To make matters worse, the data were often interpreted by people farthest from the source of the data—good people who through no fault of their own had no context whatsoever. When I think of those days, I am reminded of Secretary of Defense Robert McNamara, who said of Vietnam: "Every quantitative measurement we have shows we're winning this war."[3]

In my judgment, too often we relied on the raw numbers instead of thinking about what those numbers really meant. What I think we learned over time is that counterinsurgency is about people, not about data. It's not easy, as I indicated earlier when I addressed killing the enemy during COIN operations; it's graduate-level stuff. You have to do the hard work and take things a step further. You have to analyze people, relationships, networks and all kinds of complicated dynamics that take place between people on the ground and, in the case of Iraq, you have to understand the culture.

I think as a military force we became much more successful against the insurgency in Iraq when, under the leadership of General Petraeus and others who had taken a hard look at counterinsurgency, we realized that this fight was about people. People and relationships really are the center of gravity in a COIN fight. To get to know people, we had to get out of our forward operating bases, out of our vehicles and out of our comfort zones, and start talking to the Iraqis, developing relationships and partnering with the police and the army units we were over there trying to help.

Once we started talking to people, one of the first things we learned was that our "essential services first" approach was probably not the way to go. Under General Petraeus and General Odierno, we transitioned to the alternate view and began to secure the population. I think in many ways this helped us to tip the balance in our favor. Of course our success was enabled by a number of other factors, including the Anbar Awakening[4] and the Sons of Iraq,[5] the JAM ceasefire and, of course, the US troop surge. But none of those things, in my opinion, would have in and of itself brought us success without the change in direction and strategy, changes that forced us to stop looking at numbers and start talking to people.

Stability Operations

I would like to close my formal remarks by addressing our experience with stability operations in Iraq. In terms of recent experience, this is a subject I am very familiar with since the Army division I commanded in Iraq for the last year had governance, economics, civil capacity building and rule of law as its major lines of effort, especially during the second half of our tour.

When our division arrived in Iraq in May 2008, a number of us on the division staff had served in Iraq before. One of the first things that struck us all was the improvement in the security situation, especially in our area of operations, which encompassed most of central and southern Iraq. It was something that took us all a while to get used to.

In fact, during our first month in country, we were directed by our corps headquarters to assist the Iraqi army with retaking the city of Amarah, a large city in southeastern Iraq that had traditionally been a hotbed of *Jaish al-Mahdi* activity. Our staff worked hard on the plan. We spent considerable time looking in great detail at things like supporting fires, close air support, medical evacuation and detainee handling and processing. I even took my staff judge advocate with me to a joint planning meeting with the Iraqis at a place called Camp Sparrow Hawk near the city of Amarah because we were sure we would have to discuss rules of engagement, targeting and detainee issues with the Iraqi Army leadership.

To make a long story short, a few days later, Iraqi security forces (ISF) entered Amarah and retook the city without firing a single shot. For many of us who had been to Iraq before, the Amarah operation was something of a wake-up call. It demonstrated to us that things in Iraq really had changed. Now this is not to say Iraq is a safe place to be. It is still dangerous. During Task Force Mountain's tenure in Iraq we had fourteen soldiers killed and another sixty wounded. My point is that by the time we arrived, Iraqi security forces were well on their way to becoming a very proficient, capable force, and that, in my opinion, was one of the reasons we were able to focus our efforts on more non-kinetic missions.

In terms of stability operations, let me say just a few words about our work with Iraqi security forces. During our tour we partnered extensively with the Iraqi army, the Iraqi police, and the Iraqi Department of Border Enforcement. In fact, because I believed so strongly that a capable ISF is one of the major keys to stability in Iraq, I made ISF professionalization my division's main effort during the first half of the deployment.

Similar to what I addressed during the discussion on counterinsurgency, one of the things we found was that the better we got to know our ISF counterparts on a human level, the better we were able to teach, coach and mentor them, and the better they became. Our approach was simple—we made the ISF part of our formations. By that, I mean we did things like "shadow tracking" their supply, maintenance and personnel statistics so we could help them where they needed help the most. Not to put too fine a point on it, but I told my commanders and many of my staff from the start that I would judge their success by the success of their ISF partners.

I think the development of the ISF was the key to stability and I am proud to say our ISF partners developed into a tremendously capable force. By the middle part of our tour, for example, we stopped conducting unilateral operations in our division and began performing everything by, with and through the ISF. What we found was that as the ISF worked with us and became more professional, so did we. For their part, the ISF know the people, speak the language and can pick up on a lot of things we can't as Americans. For our part, we bring a wealth of knowledge on how to man, train and equip an army, along with a number of technologically advanced intelligence, surveillance and reconnaissance platforms and other enablers to which the ISF don't have access. By letting the ISF take the lead, we found the Iraqi people began to see them as a force that could be trusted—and trust is a critical component of Iraqi culture. As a measure of that trust, I will tell you that by the end of our tour over 90 percent of the tips we received about things like weapons caches and IEDs came from local nationals, usually through the ISF. I see that as a sign of real progress in the stability realm.

As I mentioned a moment ago, governance, economics, civil capacity building and rule of law were major lines of effort for us during Task Force Mountain's tour in Iraq—so much so that during our train up, we reorganized our fires and effects cell and devoted it almost entirely to governance, economics and reconstruction. I added a full-time political adviser from the Department of State to my staff and directed my Deputy Commanding General for Support to take the lead for all matters having to do with governance and civil capacity building. Given the time, resources and energy we put into those missions, I could talk about any one of them for hours, but since many of you in the audience are legal professionals, I will touch on some of our initiatives in the rule of law line of effort that I believe you will find interesting.

I think two things combined to jump-start our rule of law efforts during the last year. The first was the improved security situation that allowed us to focus on tasks and missions outside the security line of operation. The second was the implementation of the US-Iraq security agreement.[6]

For those of you unfamiliar with the security agreement, in January 2009 it replaced United Nations Security Council Resolution 1790[7] as the legal authority for US operations in Iraq. To my knowledge, the US-Iraq security agreement is the only status-of-forces-type agreement to which the United States is a party that authorizes US forces to conduct combat operations in the host nation. The caveat to that authorization is that our operations must be approved by and coordinated with the government of Iraq, and they must be conducted with full respect for Iraqi law and the Iraqi Constitution.

The requirement for us to conduct operations in accordance with Iraqi law has had a profound effect on the way we do things. In fact, many of you might be surprised to learn that the vast majority of US military operations in Iraq these days are conducted pursuant to arrest and search warrants issued by Iraqi judges.

By way of background, the Iraqi legal system is very similar to the US legal system with respect to criminal procedure. Before an arrest warrant can be issued, evidence must be presented to an Iraqi investigative judge. If the judge issues a warrant and the individual is apprehended, Iraqi law mandates that the person be brought before a judge within twenty-four hours for a detention hearing.

Because the security agreement requires US forces to abide by Iraqi law, we are bound by the rules I just described. In much the same way as I described how our efforts to professionalize the ISF were successful when we made them part of our formations, the security agreement's requirement that we work through the Iraqi legal system helped us make great strides in the rule of law. As we started moving actions through the Iraqi courts and dealing with Iraqi judges, we found that there was a certain amount of dysfunction in the Iraqi legal system, especially at the provincial level.

The police were often poorly trained, the judges were overworked and under-resourced, and the detention facilities had their share of issues. Based on the fact that we had to obtain warrants, our units had to develop better relationships with the police, the prosecutors and the judges in their local areas. In doing so, we were able to better identify gaps, seams and shortcomings in their training and in their systems that we were able to address.

One thing we found initially was that the Iraqi police and judges were not familiar with forensic evidence. Their legal system has always been testimony based. To help solve this problem we developed a number of innovative programs to train Iraqi judges and Iraqi prosecutors on forensic evidence. In a companion effort, US police training teams worked to train Iraqi police on basic crime scene investigation techniques and the fundamentals of actually securing forensic evidence. Finally, US explosive ordnance disposal experts have made great strides in teaching the Iraqi army how to collect basic forensic evidence at the sites of IED blasts and at the points of origin and points of impact of rocket and mortar attacks.

Since the implementation of the security agreement, US commanders have become well versed in obtaining arrest warrants and detention orders from investigative judges. To accomplish this task, most US divisions and brigades have formed law enforcement task forces made up of individuals with the relevant expertise. The organization of each task force varies slightly; however, most include judge advocates, military police officers, intelligence analysts, and one or more US contractors known as law enforcement professionals (LEPs). The LEPs are a relatively new addition to the fight in Iraq. Most are retired police officers from cities around the United States who are under contract to assist US forces with law enforcement–related tasks and training. The expertise and experience the LEPs have provided have been invaluable during the transition to warrant-based operations.

As you all know, one of the major keys to stability in any country is having a legal system the citizens can trust and depend on. Without a system for the peaceful resolution of disputes, order breaks down and people take the law into their own hands. I think our efforts in the rule of law arena have been a major driver of stability, especially in central and southern Iraq.

Conclusion

I will conclude by saying there is still a lot of hard work ahead of us in Iraq. By all indications, Iraq will turn out to be the longest war our nation has ever experienced and the effects of the war, especially on our military, remain to be seen.

For the military officers in the room today, I say be proud of what your profession has accomplished in Iraq. As I noted at the start, never stop thinking how to make things better. For our friends from other branches of public service and from the services of allied nations, I commend you. Very few citizens of any nation answer their country's call these days. Those of you who have should be immensely proud. For those of you from academia and non-governmental organizations, I hope you will keep thinking, keep writing and keep challenging us to do our jobs better. Without debate and constructive criticism, we in the military can get too comfortable with our own points of view.

It has been my pleasure to get the chance to spend time with you today. Thank you very much.

Notes

1. JAMES KITFIELD, PRODIGAL SOLDIERS: HOW THE GENERATION OF OFFICERS BORN OF VIETNAM REVOLUTIONIZED THE AMERICAN STYLE OF WAR (1995).
2. Russian tracked infantry combat vehicles.
3. NEIL SHEEHAN, A BRIGHT SHINING LIE 290 (1988).
4. For a discussion of the Anbar Awakening, see, e.g., Melinda Liu, *Gathering the Tribes: U.S. field commanders are finally beginning to tap the traditional networks that helped Saddam to stay in power*, NEWSWEEK, June 4, 2007, at 32; Martin Fletcher, *How life returned to the streets in a showpiece city that drove out al-Qaeda*, TIMES (London), Aug. 31, 2007, at 42.
5. For a discussion of the role of the Sons of Iraq in contributing to local security, see General David H. Petraeus, Commander, Multi-National Force–Iraq, Statement Before the Senate Armed Services Committee (Apr. 8, 2008), *available at* http://armed-services.senate.gov/statemnt/2008/April/Petraeus%2004-08-08.pdf.
6. Agreement Between the United States of America and the Republic of Iraq on the Withdrawal of United States Forces from Iraq and the Organization of Their Activities during Their Temporary Presence in Iraq, U.S.-Iraq, Nov. 17, 2008, *available at* http://graphics8.nytimes.com/packages/pdf/world/20081119_SOFA_FINAL_AGREED_TEXT.pdf.
7. S.C. Res. 1790, U.N. Doc. S/RES/1790 (Dec. 18, 2007).

X

The "Fog of Law": The Law of Armed Conflict in Operation Iraqi Freedom

Marc Warren*

The "fog of war" is a well-known combat experience. It is also an apt descriptor for how ambiguity in wartime can thwart the best military plans.[1] While the "fog of law"[2] is less documented, its effects may be just as profound. The "fog of law" is the ambiguity caused in wartime by the failure to clearly identify and follow established legal principles. It can frustrate deliberate planning, create confusion and lead to bad decisions that imperil mission accomplishment. When coupled with poor and inadequate planning, its effect can be near catastrophic. This article briefly explores the "fog of law" in Operation Iraqi Freedom (OIF) from before the war until the dissolution of the Coalition Provisional Authority (CPA) on June 28, 2004.

In OIF, the "fog of law" was created by positions taken at the strategic level that put conventional military forces in Iraq at needless disadvantage. Pejorative statements about the 1949 Geneva Conventions caused some soldiers to question their applicability in Iraq and gave credence to the false notion that the Conventions were deliberately disregarded by the military as a whole. Enhanced interrogation techniques used in Afghanistan and Guantanamo, and by some special operations and non-military forces in Iraq, contributed to a small number of detainee abuse cases and to the hyperbole that abuse was systematic. Reluctance to embrace the

* Colonel, JA, US Army (Ret.).

law of occupation and dedicate sufficient resources to its effective execution almost squandered a military victory.

Despite the effect of the "fog of law," conventional military forces in Iraq kept remarkable faith to the law of armed conflict. In general, this occurred in spite of, rather than because of, actions at the strategic level. In no small measure, this was due to the efforts of judge advocates who accompanied the forces into combat.[3] Judge advocates strove to overcome the "fog of law" in at least five areas: the application of the law of armed conflict, prisoners and detainees, interrogation policies, occupation and the rule of law.

The lesson of OIF is that legal ambiguity at the strategic level can imperil mission success. Conversely, legal clarity and compliance enhance military effectiveness, which in turn leads to more rapid mission success and reduced adverse impact on the civilian population in the combat zone. Old law is good law; the Geneva Conventions and the law of armed conflict in general are grounded in practicality and have retained remarkable vitality and utility. They should be embraced, not dismissed, and followed, not avoided. They must be explained to the media and to the civilian population generally. Failure to take and hold the legal high ground makes taking and holding the high ground on the battlefield much more difficult.

The Application of the Law of Armed Conflict in Iraq

The war in Iraq was an international armed conflict between two high contracting parties, followed by a state of belligerent occupation.[4] The law of armed conflict, including the Geneva Conventions, applied as a matter of law. The law of armed conflict and the Geneva Conventions were referenced in numerous operations plans, orders, policies and procedures issued by United States Central Command (USCENTCOM), the Combined Forces Land Component Command (CFLCC), V Corps and Combined Joint Task Force–7 (CJTF-7).[5] In his September 6, 2003 letter to the International Committee of the Red Cross (ICRC), the CJTF-7 commander wrote, "Coalition Forces remain committed to adherence to the spirit and letter of the Geneva Conventions."[6] Periodically, starting in September 2003, the CJTF-7 commander would issue by order specific policy memoranda reiterating the requirement for law of armed conflict compliance.

By contrast, US forces in Afghanistan were to "treat detainees humanely, and to the extent appropriate and consistent with military necessity, in a manner consistent with the principles of Geneva," a much less rigorous standard than adherence to the Conventions.[7] Moreover, some special operations and non-military forces engaged in the Global War on Terrorism (GWOT) operated under relaxed rules for detention, interrogation and prisoner transfer that were incompatible with the Geneva Conventions.[8] When units that had operated in Afghanistan were transferred to Iraq, some brought with them the less rigorous standards and relaxed rules, unfortunately reinforced by field application and standard operating procedures that they perceived had been validated in combat in Afghanistan. Countering the migration of these less rigorous standards and relaxed rules, once recognized, required constant vigilance and considerable effort. Unfortunately, the scope of the problem was not understood until months into OIF.[9]

Compounding the problem were muddled pronouncements at the operational and strategic levels about the characterization of the conflict ("we are liberators, not occupiers"),[10] a predisposition to view OIF as part of the larger GWOT, a reluctance to embrace the traditional and legitimate role of the military in occupation, and a tendency to apply policies developed for non-international military operations to an international armed conflict.[11]

Governments were not solely to blame for creating an ambiguous legal environment. Human rights and special interest groups further contributed to the "fog of law" during the occupation by declaring the illegality or immorality of the war, exaggerating and distorting breaches of discipline by coalition forces, and asserting the co-applicability of human rights law and the law of armed conflict.[12] The assertion of co-applicability diluted both and contributed, in part, to the lack of unity of effort between coalition forces and the CPA. While security deteriorated, the CPA expended its efforts to mandate changes to the Iraqi legal system, advance women's issues and influence other modest improvements to vague human rights.

Despite—or perhaps because of—the "fog of law," the principles of the Geneva Conventions are the bedrock of mandatory training for all soldiers and Marines, and they are the basis of "The Soldier's Rules" that are taught in basic training.[13] All of the training emphasizes practical application of the Conventions; it is not realistic to expect soldiers to follow the law of armed conflict simply because they are ordered to do so. Law of armed conflict refresher training was required as part of precombat training for Iraq. Several times during OIF, practical law of armed conflict refresher training was mandated down to the platoon level to address observed areas of concern, such as overzealous detention of civilians, and more nuanced law of armed conflict topics were briefed and discussed at commander's conferences held periodically in Baghdad.[14] In 2004, the ICRC's "Rules for Behavior in Combat" were incorporated into training packages for CJTF-7 soldiers.[15]

In exercises conducted before the war, considerable effort was put into training to apply the law of armed conflict in targeting decisions and in the rules of engagement (ROE). In January 2003, V Corps held a legal conference in Heidelberg to examine the ROE and to discuss targeting, prisoners of war and occupation. V Corps would be the coalition's main offensive effort in the ground campaign against Iraq. The V Corps commander spoke to the assembled judge advocates, including the staff judge advocates (SJAs) of the corps' subordinate wartime divisions, about the importance of adherence to the ROE and to the law of armed conflict.

Development of ROE extracts and pocket cards, and of ROE training vignettes, was a major focus of judge advocates assigned to forces staged in Kuwait before the start of the war. During February and March 2003, the draft ROE changed several times to add higher-level approval authorities for certain categories of targets and to require the use of complex collateral damage methodologies (CDM) for pre-planned targets. The unclassified ROE pocket cards issued to all US coalition personnel were replete with references to the law of armed conflict (the "law of war"). In fact, the first rule authorizing the attack of enemy military and paramilitary forces lists five constraints.[16]

While the ROE are not "law" per se, they must comply with the law of armed conflict as the commander's standards for the use of force.[17] Starting with the ROE development conference in London in November 2002, planners developed means to try to minimize collateral damage. The control of long-range fires was a large part of exercises in Poland in October 2002 and in Kuwait in November and December 2002. Judge advocates were placed in all corps- and division-level (and many brigade-level) fires centers to assist in the clearance of fires by ensuring compliance with the CDM, ROE and law of armed conflict. Within V Corps, judge advocates were placed down to the military police battalion level to help resolve prisoner of war and detainee issues.

Starting before hostilities commenced, V Corps and several of its subordinate divisions used ROE working groups composed of operators, intelligence officers and judge advocates to assess the ROE, recommend changes in their application and produce vignettes to train staffs and soldiers on how to apply the ROE on a dynamic battlefield. The ROE working group methodology continued at CJTF-7. Although the ROE remained unchanged until April 2004,[18] enemy tactics and other factors did change, necessitating more sophisticated discrimination in the application of force. For example, recognizing and targeting persons, none of whom wore uniforms or other identifying insignia, who were emplacing, watching over or detonating improvised explosive devices (IEDs) became a key part of ROE training.

Throughout the war, several targeting and ROE issues were recurrent vexing problems. First was the concept of "positive identification" (PID) of targets. The term "PID" had come into the ground ROE vernacular from air operations, to which it was far better suited. In an environment like Iraq, it implied a degree of precision impossible to attain as a matter of course, at least for conventional forces. Even though PID was defined to soldiers as a reasonable certainty that the target to be engaged was a legitimate military target,[19] it was often mischaracterized by commentators as requiring the pristine attack of military objects only, without mistake or collateral damage.[20]

Second, the fixation on discrimination led to the imposition of CDM on preplanned fires, including those supporting ground movements and affording suppression of enemy air defenses for rotary-wing operations. CDM was another concept better suited for air operations and it was added late to the ground ROE. Not only did it require conclusions not supported by adequate modeling tools available in ground unit headquarters, it contributed to the illusion that the effect of fires could be computed with precision. Operating forces made repeated requests to relieve fires supporting ground forces from the CDM or to exclude fires between the forward line of troops and the fire support coordination line from the CDM requirement, but the requests were denied by USCENTCOM or higher. The control measures to limit deliberate and shaping fires continued to masquerade as ROE, although fires in self-defense or in support of forces in contact were eventually exempted from the CDM burden.

Taken together, PID and CDM often required intellectual analysis in fires centers that presupposed that the reality on the ground comported with templates or with electronic means of surveillance. While there was certainly a good-faith analysis based on the best information available, it should not be confused with absolute certainty or precision. The analysis and clearance of fires are only as good as the information supporting the decision. This is particularly true with high-value and fleeting targets, where time is of the essence. While having judge advocates help review the information and provide advice on the legality of the fire mission adds rigor to the process, it seldom adds any degree of certainty or precision. Particularly with indirect fire from, and in support of, ground forces, precision is relative in any event.

The emphasis on discrimination had an insidious effect on interpretations of proportionality. Increasingly, proportionality was viewed as requiring a near-mathematical or ratio analysis of each particular target, rather than a balancing of the damage relative to the military advantage from a larger perspective. This played out for the most part in preplanned strikes from fixed-wing aircraft. After the march to Baghdad, an inordinate amount of command and staff activity was expended in convincing the combined air operations center that a strike was appropriate and that the ground commander would take responsibility for any unintended damage (i.e., "own the bomb"), even in cases where the strike was merely a bomb dropped in the desert nowhere near civilians as part of a show of force.

A third issue was created by the very nature of the enemy. Insurgents and terrorists don't wear uniforms or other distinctive insignia recognizable at a distance.

The ROE would allow engagement of persons who were members of certain specified groups or who were supporting those groups. Determining whether a person was a member of a specified group—and thus a member of a declared hostile force—relied on the quality of information and intelligence, particularly if the person was to be targeted at a time other than while directly participating in hostilities. Targeting a supporter could be even more problematic, as it required a determination as to the degree and materiality of support provided by the potential target, again based on information and intelligence.

Conventional forces are particularly likely to have difficulty in the deliberate targeting of members of specified groups and their supporters who are not wearing uniforms or otherwise recognizable at a distance. Typically, these difficulties exist because of missions executed at too low a level of command with insufficient intelligence analysis and inadequate decision-making processes. Put another way, if conventional forces are expected to conduct a raid against insurgents or terrorists, or their supporters, they must be supported by a reasoned intelligence-based decision made at an appropriately senior level of command. This point was not fully understood until well into the war. For too long, decisions on raids were made locally and individual engagement decisions were situational, essentially based on self-defense. This put lower-level commanders at risk of being second-guessed and soldiers at risk of being shot.

Fourth, coalition ROE in OIF were always a matter of frustration. As most coalition partners deployed to Iraq, their commanders and staffs would participate in ROE conferences, attended by CJTF-7 judge advocates, where they nearly uniformly expressed satisfaction with adopting the CJTF-7 ROE. However, once in country most coalition commanders were prohibited by their national leadership from employing their forces so as to fully apply the ROE. (British and Australian forces, committed in Iraq since the beginning of the war, were exceptions and had ROE that were compatible with the CJTF-7 ROE.) These "national red lines" lay dormant until April 2004, when Muqtada al-Sadr began attacking coalition forces and his Mahdi Army was designated as a declared hostile force.[21] Some coalition forces commanders simply refused to participate in offensive operations or even to maneuver their units in a way that might require them to use force in self-defense.[22]

Prisoners and Detainees

In 2002 and early 2003, planning for Iraqi prisoners of war occurred mostly at the USCENTCOM and CFLCC levels. At V Corps, enemy prisoners of war were generally viewed as a CFLCC responsibility, but there was detailed planning for handling capitulated forces. Although the assumption that Iraqi forces would capitulate *en masse* never became a reality, a key point in the planning was that these forces would enjoy the legal status of prisoners of war. Accordingly, the intricacies of the Third Geneva Convention were a frequently briefed and well-understood topic in the headquarters.

There was no meaningful planning at higher headquarters concerning prisoners other than enemy prisoners of war. In the absence of guidance, V Corps issued orders unilaterally. At the start of the war, one of the first fragmentary orders (FRAGO) issued by V Corps, Order Number 007, dealt with prisoners and detainees.[23] It cited the Third and Fourth Geneva Conventions and established a review and release mechanism for detainees that exceeded the requirements of the Fourth Convention, and adopted best practices from Haiti and Kosovo, including a review by a judge advocate of all detentions of civilians.[24] Of course, this was the first large-scale implementation by the United States of the Fourth Geneva Convention, new in 1949, and the sheer number of detainees would overwhelm the process. Regardless, in frequent interaction with the ICRC, there was never any dispute over the legal applicability of the Geneva Conventions, only in the ability of US forces to implement them completely.

Soon after closing on Baghdad in April 2003, one of the first organizational tasks was to separate common law criminals, prisoners of war and persons who had attacked coalition forces. In the crush of combat, prisoners had been commingled. Incredibly, coalition forces had not anticipated the impact of Saddam's general amnesty in November 2002 that had emptied the prisons and jails.[25] Thousands of criminals had been freed to prey upon the civilian population, and prisons and jails had been systematically looted. This caused countless problems as coalition troops not only captured prisoners of war and what were later called insurgents, but also detained thousands of common criminals. Some were detained in the act of committing violent crimes, some were turned in after the acts by local civilians, some were convicted criminals who had been granted amnesty, some were probably innocent of any wrongdoing and unjustly accused by a person holding a grudge; the result was a huge influx of prisoners, later termed criminal detainees, with precious few places to hold them, soldiers to guard them or courts to try them. The problem was compounded by soldiers using prisoner of war capture tags to document the apprehension of these persons; there were tags with "murderer" or "rapist" written on them and no more information.

In May 2003, US forces implemented CPA apprehension forms that required sworn statements from soldiers and witnesses on the circumstances of capture. This was met with some pushback from commanders and soldiers, but it helped ameliorate the situation and set conditions for future prosecutions. Using the model of the Fourth Geneva Convention, prisoners were classified into two categories: security internee and criminal detainee. The former were those who had engaged in hostilities and who would be held until the conclusion of hostilities or otherwise earlier released, perhaps through a parole or release guarantor agreement;[26] the latter were criminals who were held for trial or other disposition by the emerging Iraqi criminal justice system. The ICRC modified its capture cards in Iraq to recognize the two categories of prisoner.

For those whose status was in doubt, V Corps conducted tribunals under Article 5 of the Third Geneva Convention.[27] Commencing in June 2003, tribunals were held for all of the high-value detainees (HVDs), people like Deputy Prime Minister Tariq Aziz. The tribunals consisted of three judge advocates and determined whether the prisoners were prisoners of war, security internees or innocent civilians. None of the HVDs were deemed innocent civilians, but some were accorded prisoner of war status.

Despite these efforts, and the release of thousands of prisoners of war, the number of criminal detainees and security internees rose precipitously. On August 24, 2003, judge advocates from commands all over the country came to Baghdad for Operation Clean Sweep. Joined by a former Iraqi judge, judge advocates reviewed every single criminal detainee's file to determine who could be released outright or turned over to the emerging Iraqi courts for at least an investigative hearing. Nevertheless, the number of criminal detainees continued to grow. Iraqi courts were slow to open and Iraqi judges were reluctant to release prisoners once detained by coalition forces. Transporting prisoners from US detention facilities to Iraqi courthouses was a security, logistics, resource and accountability nightmare. CJTF-7 began holding criminal detainee review and release boards and simply released hundreds of prisoners, but most were bound over for disposition by the Iraqi criminal justice system.

In August 2003, CJTF-7 issued an order, nicknamed "The Mother of All FRAGOs" because of its size and sophistication, which established a review and appeal board as required by Article 78 of the Fourth Geneva Convention.[28] The process was initiated unilaterally, without orders or guidance from any headquarters above the level of CJTF-7 in Iraq. The new Article 78 review and appeal board could not keep pace with the volume of prisoners. It began to meet more frequently and soon expanded in size, eventually to be composed of permanent members whose full-time duty was board service.

The board struggled with commanders' opposition to release decisions, particularly from 4th Infantry Division, and with its own uncertainty over the meaning of the "imperative reasons of security" standard for internment under Article 78.[29] Over the year of OIF, the standard became more refined and the board required more detailed information concerning the threat posed by the prisoner. Early on, an imperative threat was presumed if the prisoner had been identified in post-capture screening as possessing intelligence information of value to coalition forces, which under the CFLCC ROE was a basis for detention. The shortage of skilled interrogators meant that the prisoner could remain under "intelligence hold" for weeks or months awaiting meaningful interrogation.[30] Later, the "intelligence hold" was prohibited as a means to establish the "imperative reasons of security" standard. Nevertheless, pressure from commanders not to release prisoners continued, despite briefings to the contrary at commander's conferences. On the other hand, the CPA frequently demanded the release of prisoners for political or public relations reasons, or based on anecdotal (and often inaccurate) humanitarian bases. The entire Article 78 review and appeal process was under constant tension.

Faced with the reality of continued detention of thousands of criminal detainees and security internees, the CJTF-7 SJA established and chaired the Detention Working Group in July 2003, which brought together legal, military police, military intelligence, medical, engineering and CPA assets in order to try to bring fusion and order to the chaotic situation. The first "Detainee Summit," held in August 2003 and chaired by the CJTF-7 SJA, identified serious shortfalls in detention operations expertise and recommended requesting additional subject matter experts and the establishment of a Detention and Interrogations Task Force, commanded by a brigadier general. These requests were transmitted to CFLCC and USCENTCOM in August 2003, but were not fully addressed until the creation of Task Force 134 in the spring of 2004.[31] Recognizing that the command was about to be overwhelmed by detainee operations, CJTF-7 requested additional legal support for the detention and interrogation mission in the summer of 2003,[32] as well as changes to the headquarters structure to provide judge advocates to the Joint Interrogation and Debriefing Center at the Abu Ghraib Central Detention Facility.[33] These requirements were not met until the formation of Multinational Forces–Iraq (MNF-I) and Multinational Corps–Iraq (MNC-I) in May 2004.[34]

In the interim, CJTF-7 created an additional legal support cell at Abu Ghraib, using attorneys and paralegals cobbled together from various sources. This cell provided general legal support to the detention mission and specific support to the internment process, including serving internment orders. Instead of sending the experts requested by CJTF-7, USCENTCOM sent an assessment team headed by the Provost Marshal General of the Army to study the situation.[35] The team ultimately produced a report in November 2003 that essentially corroborated and restated the issues and shortfalls previously identified by CJTF-7 months earlier.[36] Also in the fall of 2003, a team led by Major General Geoffrey Miller, former commander of the Guantanamo detention facility, came to Iraq to assess interrogation activities. The team recommended that military police soldiers take a more active role in setting conditions for interrogations and that experienced interrogators from Guantanamo train the interrogators at Abu Ghraib, many of whom were inexperienced reservists.[37]

In September 2003, judge advocates in Iraq envisioned and championed Operation Wolverine, which proposed the trial of captured Iraqi insurgents by military commission.[38] In October 2003, the proposal was modified to recommend a two-tiered approach, using the newly established Central Criminal Court of Iraq as the forum for most cases and general courts-martial where the cases involved attacks against US victims.[39] The proposal was not endorsed by USCENTCOM; the Secretary of Defense nevertheless approved the concept, but directed that all trials would be held in the Central Criminal Court of Iraq. A CPA order expanded the Court's jurisdiction and established case referral procedures.[40] Judge advocates and detailed Department of Justice attorneys reviewed case files to identify cases amenable to prosecution. Many files were classified or incomplete. There was real difficulty in turning classified intelligence information into prosecutable evidence, and there was often a paucity of significant information in the first place. However, by November 2003 the process had begun and convictions were eventually obtained for the murder of coalition soldiers and Iraqi civilians.[41]

This great demonstration of the law of armed conflict has been misrepresented by some as operating "beyond the confines" of the Geneva Conventions, because, they claim, CJTF-7 characterized those prosecuted as "unlawful combatants" in the manner of the Guantanamo prisoners.[42] Nothing could be more wrong. CJTF-7 never classified anyone in the manner of the Guantanamo prisoners. It developed and fielded a means to hold insurgents criminally accountable for their warlike acts violating Iraqi law or CPA ordinances committed without benefit of combatant immunity. Those insurgents prosecuted were still "protected persons" under the Fourth Geneva Convention, but they could be prosecuted because they had committed criminal offenses and were not lawful or privileged combatants. They did not meet the criteria of Article 4 of the Third Geneva Convention.[43] This result is not only clearly contemplated by the law of armed conflict, but a result reached only by strict adherence to the Third and Fourth Geneva Conventions, and with the approval of the US Department of Defense and the CPA.

Despite the trials, significant problems with detention continued. Military police support was limited and military police leadership in Iraq was junior and sporadic. Until several months into the occupation, the senior military police officer on the V Corps and CJTF-7 staff was a major. Even when the position of provost marshal was filled by a reserve colonel, his staff was inadequate.

In the summer and fall of 2003, troops dedicated to the detention and internment task were simply overwhelmed. The CJTF-7 SJA chaired a weekly meeting of military police, military intelligence, engineer, medical, legal and CPA representatives that attempted to synchronize and improve detention activities. Judge advocates did everything in their power to ensure that all prisoners were treated humanely and in accordance with the law. In many cases, judge advocates personally intervened to ensure that military authorities provided prisoners with adequate food, water, hygiene and shelter.[44]

Accountability of prisoners and transparency of the detention and internment system were continuing issues, even with assistance from the CPA. In cooperation with the CPA senior advisor to the Iraqi Ministry of Justice, CJTF-7 provided lists in Arabic of detainees and internees to civil-military operations centers and, in Baghdad, to courts and police stations.[45] Names of detainees and internees were provided to the ICRC through capture cards. However, routine delivery of the cards, as well as frequent interaction with the ICRC, was suspended after the ICRC moved its operations to Jordan in response to safety concerns stemming from the bombing of the United Nations headquarters building in Baghdad on August 19, 2003.

Also in the summer of 2003, the 800th Military Police Brigade, an Army reserve unit trained and validated to perform the detention and internment mission, and commanded by a brigadier general, deployed into Iraq and slowly established its headquarters in Baghdad. The unit was placed under the tactical control of CJTF-7, but remained under the command of CFLCC.[46] Initially viewed as the salvation of CJTF-7 in the areas of detention and internment, it quickly proved to be a disappointment. With few exceptions, the unit seemed unable to actually perform its mission, and breaches in accountability, discipline and standards were frequent.

In part, this was due to the status and composition of the unit. When its reserve component soldiers reached the end of their two-year mobilization commitment, they left the theater for deactivation and were not replaced. Soon after arriving in Baghdad, the experienced deputy commander of the brigade went home without a successor. The brigade command sergeant major, responsible for setting and enforcing soldier standards, was relieved and never replaced. This left the brigade without key senior leaders.

Assigned responsibility to run all larger detention facilities, including Abu Ghraib, and to provide support to the CPA in reestablishing prisons and jails throughout the country, the brigade was also assigned the mission to guard and administer Camp Ashraf, the cantonment area for the Mujahedin-e Khalq organization (MEK). The MEK was a military force of several thousand Iranians who had operated against Iran from bases in Iraq. The MEK was the only large-scale capitulation of the war—and its members weren't even Iraqis! They were, however, on the US list of designated foreign terrorist organizations[47] and CJTF-7 was directed not to process them under the Article 78 review and appeal process. After a year of interagency wrangling and debate, it was decided that they were simply "protected persons" under the Fourth Convention. During this year, the MEK members were kept under the control of the military police for screening, accountability and protection, a task that would have tested the capability of the 800th Military Police Brigade (or any other brigade) had that been its only mission.

The brigade struggled to maintain basic accountability of detainees and internees, to transport criminal detainees to court hearings and to guard prisoners generally without incident. Brigade soldiers shot several prisoners who had threatened them in crowded temporary detention facilities. In fact, the major reason Abu Ghraib was chosen as a detention facility despite its awful history under the Saddam regime was that it offered the only location in the Baghdad area to safely house prisoners. Judge advocates had been instrumental in locating and assessing the Abu Ghraib prison, and advocating its use for humanitarian reasons.[48]

The impact of special operations and non-military forces on detention operations was neither largely known nor understood at the time. In hindsight, some of the record-keeping and accountability problems experienced by the 800th Military Police Brigade were probably caused by special operations and non-military forces requesting that their prisoners held in conventional forces detention facilities be kept "off the books" and not reported to the ICRC. This problem was discovered by CJTF-7 during preparations for an ICRC visit to Abu Ghraib in January 2004.

After discovering prisoners who were not recorded, the CTJF-7 SJA went to the 205th Military Intelligence Brigade commander, who immediately directed that the prisoners be released from his custody, or properly recorded and reported to the ICRC. This was done the next day. The prisoners remaining in custody were deemed HVDs in a critical phase of interrogation. Accordingly, through the limited partial invocation of that portion of Article 143 of the Fourth Geneva Convention pertaining to imperative military necessity, the ICRC was precluded from conducting private interviews of the internees, but was given their names and allowed to observe them and the conditions of their captivity.[49] Additionally, the ICRC was informed that its delegates would be free to hold private meetings with the internees on any future visit, including a surprise visit.[50] Incredibly, even though the ICRC acknowledged the right of coalition forces to temporarily limit private interviews, this approach has been recklessly characterized by some as a "new plan to restrict" ICRC access to Abu Ghraib.[51]

Some special operations forces not under the command and control of CJTF-7 had their own long-term detention facilities.[52] USCENTCOM remained responsible for technical supervision, including legal supervision, of some special operations activities in Iraq. In almost all areas, CJTF-7 personnel, including judge advocates, were not even "read on" to their activities.

In at least two meetings with Central Intelligence Agency (CIA) representatives, including visiting CIA attorneys, the CJTF-7 SJA informed them of the applicability of the Geneva Conventions in Iraq ("this is not Afghanistan") and of the CJTF-7 order establishing the detention and internment process.[53] The representatives agreed to abide by the rules. The CJTF-7 legal staff strove to meet with all of the special operations legal advisors who rotated frequently in and out of the country, in order to brief them on the applicability of the Geneva Conventions and CJTF-7 orders in Iraq.

Removal of prisoners from Iraq to other countries was an occasional, but significant, point of friction with the CIA. CJTF-7's insistence that Article 49 of the Fourth Geneva Convention generally prohibited removing prisoners from Iraq was met with derision and skepticism.[54] On at least two occasions, USCENTCOM issued orders directing CJTF-7 to turn over non-Iraqi HVDs for transport to locations outside Iraq; the written orders were insisted upon by the command after judge advocates identified the issue. Despite its inapplicability in a belligerent occupation regulated by the Geneva Conventions, USCENTCOM continued to invoke the GWOT "global screening criteria" as authority to classify prisoners and to remove them from Iraq.[55] Direct requests from CIA representatives in Iraq were repeatedly declined by CJTF-7, but then renewed with the CPA. On May 2, 2004, the CJTF-7 SJA was summoned to the CIA station in Baghdad and shown a cable recounting standing interagency concurrence with transfers from Iraq as derogations under Article 5 of the Fourth Geneva Convention.[56] CJTF-7 nevertheless refused to alter its position that it would have to be ordered by USCENTCOM to turn over any prisoner for removal from Iraq.

When Saddam Hussein was captured on December 13, 2003, CJTF-7 took the position that he was a prisoner of war, which meant, among other things, that the command was obligated to report his capture to the ICRC and allow the ICRC to visit him. This characterization was met with reluctance, if not resistance, at higher levels, at least in part because of the mistaken notion that his status as a prisoner of war might accord him immunity from prosecution for his pre-capture criminal offenses. Ultimately, CJTF-7 prevailed in its position. Saddam's status as a prisoner of war was publicly acknowledged and the ICRC visited him in accordance with elaborate security precautions on numerous occasions, as did judge advocates.

Judge advocates helped the command reconcile the juxtaposition of Saddam's status as a prisoner of war with his status as the war's most high-profile captive. He was segregated for his own safety and security (as were other HVDs), but information about his capture, physical condition and demeanor was released to the public. As had been done with the bodies of his sons Uday and Qusay on July 24, 2003, a small number of Iraqi political leaders were allowed to observe Saddam under controlled circumstances in order to corroborate his identity. The public and military advantage to be gained from the observation was weighed against the general admonition of Article 13 of the Third Geneva Convention not to expose prisoners of war to public curiosity.[57] The balance tipped in favor of the observation; if Saddam's identity had not been confirmed to the satisfaction of the Iraqi people, he would have continued to be a shadow rallying point for the insurgency and his capture would have been dismissed as a hoax. Conversely, the CPA's insistence that "foreign fighters" should be placed on public display was rebuffed as a violation of the principles of Article 13.[58]

Not all significant prisoner issues were satisfactorily resolved. For example, a prisoner code-named "XXX" was held incommunicado on orders from USCENTCOM and he was neither reported to the ICRC nor subject to its observation. Judge advocates raised the issue of "XXX" early on and CJTF-7 demanded written orders from USCENTCOM to hold him in the specified manner. Periodically, CJTF-7 would request reissuance of the USCENTCOM order. The CJTF-7 SJA requested and received from the Joint Staff and the Department of Defense General Counsel's Office the authority and rationale for the USCENTCOM order: invocation of the derogation clause in Article 5 of the Fourth Convention concerning forfeiture of the rights of communication.[59] Although attorneys could disagree on the propriety of applying the derogation clause in this case, CJTF-7 had raised the issue and it had been determined at the highest level.

Interrogation Policies

A great deal of criticism has been leveled at the interrogation policies of conventional forces in Iraq.[60] Some of it is justified; most is not. One of the persistent assertions is that CJTF-7 promulgated many confusing and inconsistent interrogation policies.[61] Here are the facts: in 2003 there were two.[62] The first was developed in September 2003 in response to recommendations from Major General Miller's assessment team, as well as to regulate the interrogation approaches and techniques flowing in from Afghanistan and Guantanamo, and from non-military forces.[63] Many of these techniques appeared to be of the type used to teach interrogation resistance in survival, evasion, resistance and escape (SERE) programs.

The policy was transmitted to the USCENTCOM commander by memorandum stating that, unless otherwise directed, the CJTF-7 commander's intent was to implement it immediately.[64] Contrary to published reports, USCENTCOM did not direct otherwise.[65] Rather, the judge advocates at USCENTCOM and CJTF-7 engaged in a legal technical channel discourse, during which USCENTCOM (and CJTF-7) judge advocates raised concerns about the policy. This resulted in CJTF-7's rescission of the policy less than a month after it was issued.[66] This coordination was a great example of legal technical channel coordination concerning an extraordinarily difficult issue, accomplished amid the stress of combat by judge advocates working with inadequate rest under enormous pressure. In less than a month, judge advocates at USCENTCOM and CJTF-7 had worked through and resolved issues that continued to plague the military—and the US government—for several more years, at least until the passage of the Detainee Treatment Act[67] and publication of the new Army field manual on intelligence interrogations.[68]

On October 12, 2003, CJTF-7 implemented a second interrogation policy,[69] which essentially mirrored the interrogation approaches in Army *Field Manual 34-52*[70] and added additional safeguards, approvals and oversight mechanisms. The additions made the CJTF-7 interrogation policy more restrictive than that set forth in the *Field Manual*, which left much more to the judgment and discretion of the interrogator. The October 12 policy actually authorized two fewer techniques than did the *Field Manual*, although it did allow segregation in some instances.[71]

The facts have not prevented the media from exaggerated reporting and essentially blurring Iraq, Afghanistan and Guantanamo, and merging the actions of military and non-military forces. Conventional forces in general, and CJTF-7 in particular, have become, in the words of the old Iraqi saying, "the coat-hanger on which all the dirty laundry is hung." For example, a *Washington Post* editorial claimed that General Sanchez issued policies authorizing interrogation techniques "violating the Geneva Conventions, including painful shackling, sleep deprivation, and nudity."[72] This is false. The CJTF-7 policies authorized none of those techniques and did not violate the Geneva Conventions when used with the safeguards and oversight required by the policies.[73]

That said, the September policy, in effect for less than a month, was overbroad and made naive assumptions about some techniques based on assurances from the intelligence community.[74] These deficiencies were corrected in the October policy. Regardless, none of the CJTF-7 interrogation policies ever authorized, and would not allow, the use of shackling, sleep deprivation or nudity (or water boarding or the use of dogs[75] for that matter) as interrogation techniques. In fact, as was concluded by the Army's Chief Trial Judge in her exhaustive analysis of legal support to CJTF-7, had the CJTF-7 interrogation policies been followed, there would have been no abuses at Abu Ghraib.[76]

As an aside, while the entire Abu Ghraib incident is shameful and reprehensible, a point not commonly appreciated is that the individuals depicted being abused in the Abu Ghraib photographs were not security internees; they were criminal detainees—common criminals—who were not being (and would not be) interrogated in any event. Nevertheless, the Abu Ghraib scandal engulfed CJTF-7 in the late spring of 2004, diluting the command's focus and sapping its strength. This happened at the same time that al-Sadr's Shia militia attacked coalition forces; the Sunni insurgency exploded; Al Qaeda in Iraq emerged; Iranian adventurism increased; and key actions had to be taken to end the occupation, disestablish the CPA and enable the interim Iraqi government.

The scandal was a catastrophe.[77] It fueled propaganda for the enemy and was used to give credence to the myth of ambiguity about the applicability of the Geneva Conventions in Iraq. The myth was advanced by soldiers who, facing courts-martial for detainee abuse, asserted that they were confused over the rules (or, for that matter, who tried to raise the defense of superior orders or command policy to justify their actions).[78] Their assertions have been extensively covered and amplified in the media; they are the stuff of books and movies.[79] That the assertions have been spectacularly unsuccessful, despite the opportunity of extensive pretrial discovery to uncover any supporting evidence, has been much less widely reported.

But in fairness there is a point to be made concerning the possibility of confusion at the soldiers' level. There were soldiers who served in Afghanistan, where rules and principles were relaxed, and then redeployed to Iraq, where the Geneva Conventions fully applied.[80] There were also soldiers who interacted with special operations and non-military forces which operated under relaxed rules and principles, even in Iraq. So, it is possible that some soldiers at the junior level might have been confused about the applicability of the Geneva Conventions, at least until they received the refresher training on the law of armed conflict that was mandated by CJTF-7. But none of those soldiers should have reasonably believed that detainee abuse was ever authorized, and any who had questions should have sought clarification from a responsible leader.

Unfortunately, incidents of detainee abuse fueled inaccurate perceptions that US forces were ill disciplined and that the abuse of detainees was systematic or the norm.[81] The truth is that US forces were disciplined and detainee abuse cases were few.[82] Abu Ghraib was an awful and aberrant exception. It demonstrated the power of pictures[83] and the negative impact of the "strategic corporal."[84] Most detainee abuse cases occurred at point of capture, where tempers run high, frequently after an IED detonation or a firefight. The thresholds for classifying, reporting and documenting cases as detainee abuse were for a significant time very low in Iraq.[85] This led to an exaggeration of numbers.

Detainee abuse in Iraq, including the abuse at Abu Ghraib, occurred despite, and certainly not because of, military command policies and orders. There were huge problems caused by the sheer numbers of detainees and the unexpected crush of common law criminals. But the real root causes of the problem were the lack of relevant doctrine and training afforded to military intelligence interrogators; the absence of sufficient capable military police corps detention and correction expertise during the first year in Iraq; the failure of USCENTCOM to plan for, resource, and execute detention and interrogation operations in Iraq, even after previous experience in Afghanistan portended many of the same problems that were later repeated in Iraq;[86] and the broad interrogation authorities granted to non-military forces and to some special operations forces not under the command and control of CJTF-7, some of which were adopted by conventional forces in spite of orders and policies to the contrary.

Occupation

Worse than the inadequate planning and mixed messages on detention and interrogation was the utter confusion caused by the "fog of law" in the occupation of Iraq. The occupation was anticipated at the level of the operating forces. However, higher-level planning was inadequate or did not occur, strategic policy decisions were not made in a timely fashion and the requirements for occupation were not adequately resourced. The problem was not in failing to forecast the occupation as governed by the Fourth Geneva Convention; it was in failing to set the conditions for its meaningful execution. The situation was analogous to the dog chasing the car—the real difficulty comes when he catches it.

In January 2003, US Army, Europe hosted a legal conference in Heidelberg, at which an Israeli judge advocate who had experience in the administration of occupied territory talked about problems likely to face occupation forces. The conference augmented research on occupation law, including the study of materials from the US Army War College and the Center for Military History on US experiences after World War II. Also in early 2003, V Corps conducted an exercise named Victory Scrimmage in Grafenwöhr, Germany. In the exercise and its follow-on, V Corps war gamed what were termed "transitional occupation" issues, problems such as riots, criminal misconduct, looting, humanitarian relief requirements and civilian population movement that would impede offensive operations as coalition forces moved through Iraqi territory. These issues so concerned the V Corps commander, General Scott Wallace, that he directed an immediate follow-on exercise in Grafenwöhr to try to develop responses to the problems.

The result was stunning in several respects. First, it was clear that transitional occupation issues could appreciably slow offensive forces and potentially require substantial additional forces to deal with them. Unfortunately, it was also clear that these additional forces did not exist. V Corps had developed a time-phased force deployment list (TPFDL) over the past year of exercises and mission analyses. The

TPFDL identified the amount and flow of forces necessary to accomplish the mission. In Grafenwöhr, V Corps learned that the corps TPFDL had been scrapped and replaced by a much smaller force. The V Corps commander was deeply concerned about the reduction in combat power. The reduction meant that the V Corps commander had to do a "rolling start" of the ground offensive with forces available and with the expectation that additional divisions would arrive over time, instead of being able to mass all of his forces at once. The V Corps commander was also concerned about the cuts in combat support and combat service support forces, particularly military police units.

Second, Victory Scrimmage and its follow-on demonstrated a potentially huge planning and capability deficit if the assumptions concerning what was called Phase IV, the phase of the operation after decisive combat operations, proved to be invalid. These assumptions were premised on the belief that many Iraqi military forces would capitulate—that is, surrender *en masse* without a fight—and would be available to serve as a constabulary or security force; that Iraqi physical and social infrastructure would remain intact; and that a capable interim Iraqi government, probably under Ahmed Chalabi, would quickly emerge. If these assumptions were invalid (and, of course, every one of them proved to be invalid), and if US forces encountered problems like those identified in Victory Scrimmage (as they did), it was clear that there had to be a plan and resources for a sustained occupation. With regard to assumptions, it seems that the worst was assumed about Iraq's capabilities and intentions in deciding whether to go to war, and the best case was assumed as to what would happen once coalition forces crossed the Iraqi border.

Accordingly, V Corps dutifully identified numerous issues and requirements pertaining to occupation, and sent them up to higher headquarters. Some of V Corps' subordinate divisions, particularly 3d Infantry Division, did the same. In the legal arena, these included questions on the content of the occupation proclamation and ordinances, whether some Iraqi judges should be removed from the bench,[87] whether occupation courts with military judges could be convened by commanders and whether parts of the Iraqi Penal Code were to be suspended.[88] On a basic level, V Corps asked for an Iraq country law study and a translated copy of the Iraqi Penal Code. These questions and requests were received sympathetically by CFLCC in Kuwait, and the CFLCC SJA vigorously raised similar issues and questions, and joined in the requests until the war began. Unfortunately, the answer was that there were dedicated Phase IV planning cells at CFLCC and USCENTCOM, and in Washington, D.C., and that all of these matters were being addressed at "the national and coalition level."

The V Corps commander became so concerned about what was—or wasn't—being done at the Washington level that he sent the V Corps civilian political advisor to Washington to sit in on the meetings. Her report was that interagency planning for Phase IV was under way, but that it would not be called an "occupation." We would not be occupiers but "liberators," and "the 'O' word" was not to be used at all. Of course, this was ludicrous, as occupation is a fact, and the Fourth Geneva Convention and the older Hague Regulations establish the rights and obligations of an occupier as a matter of law.[89] This fact cannot be wished away or dismissed by using the euphemism of "liberator."

To make matters worse, the Corps' G-5, the civil affairs officer, had a heart attack in Grafenwöhr and could neither continue in the exercise nor deploy to Kuwait or on to Iraq. He was not replaced by a civil affairs officer. The position of G-5 was instead filled by the G-1, the personnel officer, who was a very competent officer, but a personnel specialist unschooled and inexperienced in civil affairs.

As coalition forces staged in Kuwait, planning for the occupation continued, albeit in a vacuum. In February 2003, the V Corps SJA section gave the corps commander a lengthy briefing on the rights and responsibilities of an occupier. The briefing concluded with the identification of numerous issues about which the operating forces required information and decisions. The V Corps commander directed the staff to coordinate with the Office of Reconstruction and Humanitarian Assistance (ORHA), which had recently established an element in Kuwait city. ORHA was the predecessor to the CPA.

The coordination revealed that ORHA had done little analysis and had devoted few resources to the effort. Not only did the organization not have any answers for V Corps, its staff had little awareness of many of the questions. In fairness, ORHA was designed for consequence management, not for the administration of occupied territory. ORHA assumed that the policy decisions so desperately needed would be issued from Washington.

At the start of combat operations and in the absence of guidance, but based on war-gaming and exercise experience, V Corps issued orders during the march to Baghdad regarding procedures and warnings at checkpoints (after a tragic incident early on in which an entire family had been killed as their van approached a checkpoint without slowing down, despite warning shots);[90] cordon and search operations; curfews; weapons, explosives and fuel possession controls; and the use of force against looters. The problem was that these were all issued as necessary at the tactical level and not as part of any cohesive plan. Efforts to try to address the problem in a comprehensive way were thwarted by a lack of fundamental policy decisions at a higher level. For example, an occupation proclamation and orders to civilians had been staffed, drafted, printed and prepositioned, but no order was ever given to release them.[91]

In Baghdad, there was inadequate troop strength to effectively control the city. The 3d Infantry Division had reached its culminating point. It had fought all the way to Baghdad and was exhausted; it just had little energy left to detain looters or guard key infrastructure. Orders were issued to protect museums, courthouses, police stations, power and water plants, and public records holding areas, but there were simply not enough troops to go around.[92] Even when troops were available, they frankly did not always follow through with their assigned tasks.[93]

For the first few weeks in Baghdad, ORHA was looked to as the occupation authority, although it was clear that only the military had the potential to exercise effective control. Despite its lack of a clear charter and sufficient resources, ORHA had two attributes: it did not interfere with the military and it trusted the judgment of military commanders. During the few weeks of ORHA's existence, the corps and division commanders were afforded freedom of action to engage the civilian population and restore security. The 101st Airborne Division (Air Assault), commanded by then–major general David Petraeus, was among the most successful in its initiatives to reestablish order and a semblance of normalcy in its assigned area of operations. Significant challenges continued in Baghdad, however.

The military recognized the importance of quickly addressing the issue of Ba'ath Party membership, which included most government workers, as well as teachers. V Corps suggested to ORHA that adopting a status-based policy that would disqualify Ba'ath Party members from government (and coalition forces) employment would cause massive practical problems and be counterproductive to efforts to quickly get the policeman back on the beat, the teacher back in the classroom and the municipal worker back on the street. Instead, V Corps advocated a conduct-based policy that would not prohibit employment of persons solely based on their membership in the Ba'ath Party, but would bar those persons who were suspected of crimes or other misconduct.

The policy required Iraqi government workers to sign an agreement renouncing and denouncing the Ba'ath Party, Saddam Hussein and his regime; promise to obey Iraqi law and military and CPA orders; and get back to work. Vetting of employees would take place over time. Judge advocates authored the conduct-based policy, implemented through an "Agreement to Disavow Party Affiliation."[94] General Wallace discussed it with retired Lieutenant General Jay Garner at ORHA, and the conduct-based approach with implementing renunciation agreement was approved. Thousands of agreements were printed and distributed, and the policy was implemented.

Less than ten days later, the CPA announced its de-Ba'athification policy, which took exactly the opposite tack.[95] The CPA policy was purely status-based and took thousands of people out of the work force, leaving them essentially unemployable and disaffected. Like the CPA order dissolving the Iraqi military, it was implemented with absolutely no coordination with the commanders on the ground and no consideration of what was already being done by the military, despite the fact that this decision would have a huge impact on law and order, security and stability, and reconciliation.[96]

The obligations of an occupier exist as a matter of law regardless of what the situation is called or what instrument is used to administer the territory. In this regard, the utility of the CPA is questionable as a matter of fact and suspect as a matter of law (at least until its authority was ratified by the UN Security Council).[97] Occupation is a military duty and the military has historical competence in occupation. The law of occupation is focused on the activities of the military and military government, and on the responsibilities of commanders. This law has developed for good reason.

When the CPA was established as a civilian entity, military commanders suffered a diminution of their authority to administer and exercise the rights of occupation, with no reduction in their legal responsibilities. As a practical matter, placing CJTF-7 in direct support of the CPA violated the military maxims of unity of command and unity of effort.[98] It was not clear who was in charge in Iraq, nor were the relative roles and responsibilities of the CPA and CJTF-7 clear.[99] What was obvious was that there was a diffusion of effort and the squandering of several golden months after a decisive military victory within which time most of the Iraqi population craved firm direction and before any insurgency could meaningfully develop.

The CPA concentrated on transformation outside the historical bounds of occupation: economic reform, developing the Iraqi stock market, reestablishing symphony orchestras and arts programs, judicial reform, building a criminal defense bar and promoting women's rights.[100] Many of these were nice things to do, but most did not contribute to stability and security. At best, many of the CPA's activities, even if successful, were irrelevant; many were setbacks. The CPA's effort to rebuild the Iraqi police force and army was haphazard and handicapped by its earlier dissolution of the Iraqi military. CJTF-7 had to bolster the CPA effort and establish parallel training programs and organizations, such as the Iraqi Civil Defense Corps, in order to field Iraqi security forces.[101]

Worse, some of the CPA's directives were a blatant interference with the military's warfighting mission. These included orders to release dangerous internees because of political considerations and extensive involvement in events in Fallujah in April 2004, including mandating peace talks, which culminated in CPA Administrator Bremer directing the CJTF-7 commander and the USCENTCOM commander, who was then present in Baghdad, to call off the attack on the city.[102] From the beginning, the CPA took an active role in military matters. On the day Administrator Bremer arrived in Iraq, he announced that US forces would shoot to kill all looters. This announcement was made without any coordination with the military in Iraq and no consideration of the ROE. Of course, the ROE rightly would not allow this and considerable time and effort had to be expended to issue clarifying orders and guidance to put this genie back in the bottle.[103]

The end of the CPA was as confused as its beginning. Its "transfer of sovereignty" to the interim Iraqi government was a complete mischaracterization of the authority the CPA held during the occupation. Occupation does not affect sovereignty and there was no sovereignty, only possession, to transfer back to the Iraqi government.[104]

There were bright spots in the CPA (its legal staff was brilliant). In general, however, it was a policy- and politics-laden bureaucracy that was a drain and distraction to the war effort. It contributed to both the "fog of law" and the "fog of war" in Iraq. In sum, the CPA was more hurtful than helpful.

Rule of Law

Although these were not termed rule of law activities at first, judge advocates began efforts to restore Iraqi judicial capability almost as soon as coalition forces entered the country. Judge advocates assigned to civil affairs units assessed courthouses in Basra and southern Iraq and assessments continued as the war progressed northward. Many court buildings had been looted. In some cases, however, judges and other court personnel had literally (and physically) protected their courthouses by remaining in the structures continuously.

In Baghdad, judge advocates unilaterally "deputized" court personnel as armed court police to guard many buildings and records. Not all buildings could be protected. In the main public records repository building in Baghdad where property and other records were stored, fires had been set in the document storage stacks. Courthouses, public records repositories and police stations were prime targets for arsonists.

Prior to the arrival of the first CPA senior advisor to the Ministry of Justice, there was no cohesive plan for interaction with the Iraqi judicial system. Until the establishment of the CPA, no questions about Iraqi law or the Iraqi legal system had been answered. One of the CPA's first decisions on the topic was to direct the application of the 1969 Iraqi Penal Code, with some suspended provisions.[105] The CPA also set priorities by directing that US forces were not to convene occupation courts, but would instead concentrate on revitalizing the Iraqi judicial system. On the topic of the Iraqi Penal Code, V Corps did not obtain an official version until it was in Iraq, and that thanks to the Center for Law and Military Operations at The Judge Advocate General's Legal Center and School in Charlottesville, Virginia. In the interim, one of V Corps' judge advocates, who happened to have been an Arabic linguist, had checked out a copy from the Kuwait city public library and began the tedious task of translating the code into English.

Without guidance, immediate actions were taken in accordance with the commander's intent using the Fourth Geneva Convention as a guide. The V Corps SJA went on the radio in Baghdad to order judges and court personnel to return to work. Maneuver unit judge advocates and civil affairs soldiers went all over the country to meet with judges, coax them to the bench and reestablish regular court sessions. This effort, a rudimentary rule of law program, was enthusiastically supported by commanders who saw the reopening of the courts as an essential aspect of restoring security, stability and public confidence.

Judge advocates and civilian attorneys working for the CPA routinely went to Iraqi courts, and even arranged for and executed payroll payments for judges and other Ministry of Justice personnel; they were under fire on a number of occasions as they did so. Later, judge advocates at the corps, division and brigade levels created and staffed Judicial Reconstruction Assistance Teams (called JRATs) and Ministry of Justice Offices (called MOJOs), and for almost a year managed the Baghdad and Mosul court dockets.

Despite these initiatives, rule of law activities in general remained disjointed, with responsibility shared by the CPA, civil affairs units and judge advocates assigned to maneuver units. Locally, rule of law efforts focused on opening Iraqi courthouses and increasing the pace of cases moving through them. Higher-level efforts concentrated on combating judicial corruption and improving the criminal justice system.[106] The CPA and military attorneys expended Herculean efforts and made progress, but synchronization of their efforts was uneven and clear rule of law performance measures and objectives were not defined.[107] Directive authority for overall rule of law activities was not fixed, and SJAs and CPA attorneys engaged in the activities commanded no assets. In the first year in Iraq, there were four CPA senior advisors to the Iraqi Ministry of Justice, not counting acting advisors who filled the gaps. This meant new philosophies, new approaches and redevelopment of personal bonds among all involved parties, including Iraqi ministers and judges.[108]

The lack of a coherent plan for rule of law activities is demonstrated by the arrival in the summer of 2003 of a distinguished team of judicial mentors from the United States. The team traveled around Iraq at great personal risk and presented a security and logistical burden to the military. Frequently unable to meet with Iraqi judges who were in hiding, or to travel to locations because of security concerns, the team returned to the United States having been frustrated in its mentoring mission. Fundamentally, the team should not have been in Iraq while security conditions were unstable and when Iraqi judges needed to hear one clear message from a single firm voice: return to the bench and move cases. Mentoring and other nuanced activities caused a confusion of message, complicated relationships and did not contribute to the most important task at hand, restoring security.

Conclusion

The "fog of law" is a needless and largely avoidable phenomenon. Soldiers deserve a clear and unambiguous legal framework. While their training and values will in most cases lead to soldiers doing the right thing at the tactical level of combat, they can be negatively impacted by the "fog of law" created at the operational and strategic levels. Its effects can undermine public support, provide propaganda to the enemy, create distractions, and contribute to false assumptions and bad decisions.

The "fog of law" can be lifted by applying these principles:

1. Follow the law. The law of armed conflict, including the Geneva Conventions, has developed over time for reasons of humanity and necessity and is grounded in pragmatism. Old law is still good law; the Geneva Conventions are neither quaint nor obsolete.[109] At a minimum, they can serve as guiding principles even when not applicable as a matter of law. When they do apply as a matter of law, as in Iraq, they have demonstrated their utility and ability to be meaningfully implemented in the new millennium.

2. The viability of the law of armed conflict must be demonstrated and explained to the media and to the civilian population generally. This necessitates public education programs, as well as timely and informed public briefings and reports when incidents occur. In this regard, the military has a practice of thorough investigation while striving to safeguard classified information, with the result being that the facts, as well as the military's perspective, are not made available to the public until long after the incident's notoriety has disappeared from public attention. In the interim, the enemy and special interest groups have had unimpeded freedom to manipulate the incident and control the public debate. The military simply must respond more quickly, definitively and publicly to suspected violations of the law of armed conflict or ROE, and to alleged breaches of discipline. There is a stable of pseudo-experts who

are immediately available to provide commentary—often wrong—on such matters. Distinguished outside experts should also be available to explain the law and principles at issue, and the military's perspective, to the media and public.[110] In appropriate cases, those experts should participate in investigations of high-profile incidents.

3. Disregard history at your peril. Decision makers would have benefited from a thorough study of occupation history, particularly the history of occupation in Germany and the Far East after World War II. It would have informed them greatly and potentially led them to avoid missteps about de-Ba'athification, restoration of law and order, and the resources and decisions necessary to implement an effective occupation. They would have also benefited from an analysis of past counterinsurgency and "nation-building" operations, such as the US occupation of the Philippines after the Spanish-American War, British counterinsurgency operations in Malaya, US military operations generally in Central America in the last century and British operations in Northern Ireland. Study of Israeli warfighting and occupation experience would have been particularly helpful. Among the things they would have discovered is that patience and adaptability are essential, and that missteps and mistakes are inevitable but recoverable.

4. Attempts to conflate the law of armed conflict, particularly the law of belligerent occupation, with human rights law are misguided, as they dilute both and erode the clarity of the well-developed law of armed conflict on which commanders and soldiers are trained. The interjection of human rights law into the wartime legal mix as a separate body of law causes confusion. However, it is equally misguided to completely dismiss the existence of overlaps between human rights law and the law of armed conflict, especially when including the aspects of Additional Protocol I that are customary international law.[111] The overlaps include those non-derogable human rights that are germane to wartime.[112] In those unusual cases where there are conflicts between overlapping human rights law and the law of armed conflict, the latter must prevail under the *lex specialis* rule.[113] In even rarer and more sophisticated cases, there may be gaps between human rights law and the law of armed conflict to which human rights law might apply. However, the application of human rights law in wartime should be a clear exception and occur only where justice necessitates that it address a gap such as when, for example, "the norms

governing belligerent occupation are silent or incomplete."[114] Otherwise, applying human rights law in wartime creates friction and confusion, while adding little except affording a means to obtain pecuniary damages and publicity. Nations—and legal theorists and politicians—would do well to concentrate on efforts to advance adherence to the law of armed conflict, particularly among non-State actors, before advocating the co-applicability of human rights law in wartime.

5. The principles of war and command, military doctrine, force ratios, troop-to-task ratios, and the military decision-making and orders processes all exist for a reason. Put another way, ignoring these things, whether done by senior military or civilian officials, is asking for trouble. In the legal arena, the long-developed concept of legal technical channels is important. Every SJA needs an SJA, and no attorney involved in military operations should be a solo practitioner.

6. The military must be responsible for occupation and, if necessary, administer occupied territory through a military government. The three most important legal, moral and military objectives in occupation are security, security and security.[115] Conventional wisdom now accepts that there should have been more interagency involvement in Iraq in the first year. This is wrong; in fact, there should have been less non-military presence in Iraq in the first year. There should have been more interagency planning before the war and a more responsive and cohesive interagency decision-making process before and during the war. But in Iraq the situation would have been drastically better had the military simply established a military government in order to stabilize the country, restore security, and reestablish infrastructure and institutions, and allow for the infusion of civilian experts and the re-emergence of an Iraqi government as conditions permitted. If it existed at all, the CPA should have been in support of the military, not vice versa, and the overall coalition occupation authority in Iraq should have been a military commander, perhaps with a civilian deputy or civilian senior advisor. Coalition forces would have had to endure the propaganda that they were occupiers, but how was this avoided by virtue of the CPA?

7. Modest rule of law activities are an essential and immediate instrument for the military to use to help reestablish security, order and public confidence.[116] Rule of law is a vague and relative term that requires clear

definition, assignment of responsibility and resources, and establishment of objectives and performance measures. There is no simple template for rule of law activities; the objectives and performance measures must be relative to the history, culture and reality on the ground.[117] The focus must be on the "Three Ps": police, prisons and prosecutors (courts). In an occupation, the Fourth Geneva Convention properly limits the scope of rule of law activities. More transformative and sophisticated rule of law activities, such as judicial mentoring, building a public defender system or helping to improve substantive law and procedure, should be delayed until security, legal and practical conditions permit.[118]

8. You play as you practice. For the military, this means that exercises must not end with the defeat of the enemy's military forces and intelligence preparation of the battlefield must include an analysis of the capability of the systems of government and public administration, as well as the enemy's order of battle. As much intellectual effort must go into planning for activities after decisive combat operations as is put into planning for fires and maneuver. This would include updating military doctrine and expanding the resources and capabilities for civil administration, military government and civil affairs in general.

9. There is a random spotlight of accountability for mistakes and misjudgments—whether real, exaggerated or even fabricated. The "fog of war" in battle is nothing compared to the fog of politics on Capitol Hill. This is unfair and capricious, particularly to professional soldiers who are political agnostics. In the legal arena, there has developed an unforeseen dark underbelly to operational law, and that is the notion that the SJA in the field is the "Guarantor General," the one person in the command who is somehow expected to have total awareness and perfect knowledge, to be read in to all activities, and to have the duty to identify, resolve and report all problems.[119] In general, conventional forces will continue to be held to account for the misconduct of special operations and non-military forces.

10. There cannot be different legal standards for soldiers and non-military forces, or even for soldiers operating in different operations or campaigns. It is too easy for the standards to be blurred and, as was the

case with interrogation policies between Afghanistan and Iraq, to migrate (perhaps a better term is to metastasize).

11. Some unified command SJAs should be general or flag officers, and selected judge advocate general and flag officers assigned to posts in the United States should be reassigned as legal advisors to commands in Iraq and Afghanistan. Most unified command SJA offices should be substantially larger and more capable. Despite some simply wrong assertions to the contrary,[120] judge advocates are a respected and proper source for legal and policy advice at all levels, and their presence and role with the operating forces sends a powerful message about a nation's commitment to the law of armed conflict.[121]

12. National leaders set a tone that can reach the individual soldier in the field. Whether in the executive or legislative branch, leaders should consider the impact of their words. It is as reckless for a politician to suggest that the law of armed conflict is no longer relevant as it is to suggest that torture and detainee abuse were pervasive in Iraq. Those responsible for setting national legal policies and tone would do well to hold themselves to the standard set for all coalition forces personnel in Iraq in 2003: "Respect for others, humane treatment of persons not taking part in hostilities, and adherence to the law of war and rules of engagement is a matter of discipline and values. It is what separates us from our enemies. I expect all leaders to reinforce this message."[122]

Notes

1. "The great uncertainty of all data in war is a particular difficulty, because all action must, to a certain extent, be planned in a mere twilight, which in addition not infrequently—like the effect of a fog or moonshine—gives to things exaggerated dimensions and unnatural appearance." CARL VON CLAUSEWITZ, ON WAR (Michael Howard & Peter Paret eds. & trans., Princeton University Press 1989) (1832).

2. The "fog of law" has been identified in other contexts, but application of the term to Iraq, and its corrosive effect in combat, was also noted by Professor Yoram Dinstein at the US Naval War College's 2009 International Law Conference, from which this "Blue Book" derives.

3. In November 2003, 154 officers (mostly judge advocates) and 180 paralegal noncommissioned officers (NCOs) and soldiers of the US Army's Judge Advocate General's Corps alone served in Iraq. Forty-one of the judge advocates and fifteen of the paralegal NCOs and soldiers were reservists. Briefing to The Judge Advocate General, US Army, CJTF-7 Legal Operations (Nov. 5, 2003).

4. S.C. Res. 1483, U.N. Doc. S/RES/1483 (May 22, 2003), *reprinted in* 42 INTERNATIONAL LEGAL MATERIALS 1016; *see also* YORAM DINSTEIN, THE INTERNATIONAL LAW OF BELLIGERENT OCCUPATION 12 (2009).

5. The law of armed conflict, including the Geneva Conventions and Hague Regulations, was cited in the legal annexes or appendices to the base operations plans and orders (Cobra II, most prominently), as well as in fragmentary orders that instructed soldiers to comply with the law of armed conflict. Representative of the orders were

(1) Fragmentary Order 946 (S) to CJTF-7 OPORD 03-036, dated 080425 OCT 03, which distributed the CJTF-7 Policy Memorandum to All Coalition Forces Personnel, Proper Treatment of the Iraqi People During Combat Operations (Oct. 5, 2003) [hereinafter Proper Treatment of the Iraqi People]. The order reemphasized adherence to the law of armed conflict ("the law of war"), directed that all coalition forces personnel would treat persons under their control with dignity and respect, and required dissemination of the memorandum down to the platoon level.

(2) Fragmentary Order 70 (S) to CJTF-7 OPORD 04-01, dated 160205 JAN 04, which reissued the October 5 memorandum and directed that all leaders reinforce its message.

(3) Fragmentary Order 388 (S) to CJTF-7 OPORD 04-01, dated 062325 MAR 04, which issued the "Rules for Proper Conduct During Combat Operations," reemphasized the responsibility of all coalition forces personnel to treat all persons with dignity and respect, reiterated the obligation of all coalition forces personnel to follow the law of armed conflict ("the law of war"), and directed that commanders and leaders use published training vignettes to train all personnel on these topics.

6. Letter from CJTF-7 Commander to Mr. Jean-Daniel Tauxe, Head of Delegation, ICRC Baghdad (Sept. 6, 2003) [hereinafter CJTF-7 Letter].

7. Memorandum from President George W. Bush to the Vice President et al., Humane Treatment of al Qaeda and Taliban Detainees (Feb. 7, 2002), *available at* http://www.aclu.org/files/assets/02072002_bushmemo_1.pdf.

8. Report of Senate Committee on Armed Services, Inquiry into the Treatment of Detainees in U.S. Custody, 110th Cong., 2d Sess. (Nov. 20, 2008).

9. The first indication was an August 2003 request from Alpha Company, 519th Military Intelligence Battalion for a review of interrogation techniques that were similar to those used in US survival, evasion, resistance and escape training. They were subsequently discovered to have been used by that unit with higher command approval in Afghanistan. The second indication was reporting from the ICRC which, unfortunately and for a number of reasons, was not given sufficient credence or attention.

10. *See, e.g.*, General Tommy Franks, Freedom Message to the Iraqi People (Apr. 16, 2003) ("Coalition Forces in Iraq have come as liberators, not as conquerors . . .").

11. US Deputy Secretary of Defense Memorandum, Global Screening Criteria for Detainees (Feb. 20, 2004) [hereinafter Global Screening Criteria].

12. Co-applicability of human rights law and the law of armed conflict is not an assertion limited to legal activists. It is a conclusion that has been reached by courts, including the International Court of Justice and the European Court of Human Rights. *See* DINSTEIN, *supra* note 4, at 69–71.

13. "The Soldier's Rules" are restated in Headquarters, Department of the Army, AR 350-1, Army Training and Leader Development para. G-21 (2009):

(1) Soldiers fight only enemy combatants.

(2) Soldiers do not harm enemies who surrender. They disarm them and turn them over to their superior.

(3) Soldiers do not kill or torture any personnel in their custody.
(4) Soldiers collect and care for the wounded, whether friend or foe.
(5) Soldiers do not attack medical personnel, facilities, or equipment.
(6) Soldiers destroy no more than the mission requires.
(7) Soldiers treat civilians humanely.
(8) Soldiers do not steal. Soldiers respect private property and possessions.
(9) Soldiers should do their best to prevent violations of the law of war.
(10) Soldiers report all violations of the law of war to their superior.

14. The law of armed conflict was an express or implied topic at all V Corps and CJTF-7 commander's conferences in Iraq during OIF, starting with the first one at Camp Victory in Baghdad in May 2004. All division and separate brigade commanders attended the conferences, along with the V Corps, then CJTF-7, senior staff. The March 27, 2004 conference, for example, included a presentation and discussion on "proper conduct during combat operations."

15. The training package was informally coordinated with the ICRC in Baghdad and issued by Fragmentary Order 388 to CJTF-7 OPORD 04-01, dated 062325 Mar 04. The order redistributed CJTF-7 Policy Memorandum Number 18, Proper Conduct During Combat Operations (Mar. 4, 2004), and added mandatory vignette-driven training on specific rules, including

(1) Follow the law of war.
(2) Use discipline in the use of force.
(3) Treat all persons with humanity, dignity and respect.
(4) Use judgment and discretion in detaining civilians.
(5) Respect private property.
(6) Treat journalists with dignity and respect.

16. CFLCC ROE Pocket Card, 252030 Nov 03. The pocket card, required to be carried at all times by US coalition forces personnel, states the following general rules:

(1) Treat all persons with respect and dignity.
(2) Conduct yourself with dignity and honor.
(3) Comply with the law of war. If you see a violation, report it.

17. Marc L. Warren, *Operational Law: A Concept Matures*, 152 MILITARY LAW REVIEW 33, 52 (1996).

18. The change in April 2004 was to make the Mahdi Army a declared hostile force. However, new CFLCC pocket cards were not issued, since the unclassified cards referred generically to "enemy military and paramilitary forces." (On April 29, 2003, USCENTCOM issued Supplemental ROE Measures that changed the combat ROE to the Phase IV (Civil-Military Operations) ROE; the order was rescinded the same day.)

19. CFLCC ROE Pocket Card, *supra* note 16.

20. Consider, e.g., the case of the Palestine Hotel in Baghdad, where two civilian cameramen were killed in an explosion caused by a round from the main gun of a US Abrams tank on April 8, 2003. The unit of which the tank was a part had been engaged in significant urban fighting, including repulsing an enemy counterattack on the day of the incident, and had received reports of enemy forward observers in high-rise buildings on the east side of the Tigris River. As the tank crossed the Al Jumhuriya Bridge, its crew spotted, and fired one round at, what appeared to be an enemy forward observer, but was in fact a civilian cameraman. The explosion killed Spanish cameraman Jose Couso and Reuters cameraman Taras Protsyuk, and wounded

three other journalists. US forces conducted an investigation and determined that the Palestine Hotel had been fortified by the enemy and was occupied by the enemy. The cameraman had been misidentified as an enemy forward observer, which was a reasonable mistake under the circumstances. The single round that killed the cameraman was thus fired with a reasonable certainty that the target was a legitimate military target, satisfying the requirements of the ROE, PID, and law of armed conflict. Nevertheless, the incident garnered criticism (*see, e.g.*, Committee to Protect Journalists, *Five years after deadly Palestine Hotel and Al-Jazeera strikes, unanswered questions linger* (Apr. 7, 2008), http://cpj.org/2008/04/five-years-after-deadly-palestine-hotel-and-aljaze.php) and led to criminal action by Spanish authorities seeking to hold the tank crew criminally accountable for the death of the Spanish cameraman.

21. The Mahdi Army was declared a hostile force on April 6, 2004. DONALD P. WRIGHT & TIMOTHY R. REESE, ON POINT II: TRANSITION TO THE NEW CAMPAIGN, THE UNITED STATES ARMY IN OPERATION IRAQI FREEDOM MAY 2003–JANUARY 2005, at 324 (2008), *available at* http://www.globalsecurity.org/military/library/report/2008/onpoint/index.html [hereinafter ON POINT II].

22. The US Army's history of OIF deals with the issue deftly and diplomatically: "The multinational units that had responsibility for the southern Shia cities—the Spanish, Salvadorans, and Ukrainians—were few and not prepared to act quickly against the uprising." *Id.*

23. *Id.* at 249.

24. Initially a five-day standard, review of detentions by a judge advocate magistrate was accelerated to seventy-two hours in the summer of 2003. Neither standard was required by law and both exceeded the standards imposed by Article 78 of the Fourth Geneva Convention, which requires only that decisions regarding internment shall be made according to a regular procedure that affords a right of appeal, to be decided with the least possible delay and, if denied, to be subject to periodic review conducted, if possible, every six months by a competent body. Convention Relative to the Protection of Civilian Persons in Time of War art. 78, Aug. 12, 1949, 6 U.S.T. 3516, 75 U.N.T.S. 287, *reprinted in* DOCUMENTS ON THE LAWS OF WAR 301 (Adam Roberts & Richard Guelff eds., 3d ed. 2000) [hereinafter GC]. US forces should have stressed that the reviews were neither required by law nor intended to be viewed as a right or as customary. The requirements of Article 78 were satisfied by the process specified in the "Mother of All FRAGOs." ON POINT II, *supra* note 21, at 249.

25. ON POINT II, *supra* note 21, at 248.

26. Parole agreements and guarantor agreements were used with mixed success as a means to release internees who were thought to present a continuing, but manageable, threat. The former would be signed by the internee at release; the latter would be signed by a person who was willing to assume responsibility for the released internee, usually a tribal elder. Significantly, while many prominent Iraqis would advocate for an internee's release, few would be willing to serve as a guarantor.

27. Article 5 states, in pertinent part:

> Should any doubt arise as to whether persons, having committed a belligerent act and having fallen into the hands of the enemy, belong to any of the categories enumerated in Article 4, such persons shall enjoy the protection of the present Convention until such time as their status has been determined by a competent tribunal.

Convention Relative to the Treatment of Prisoners of War art. 5, Aug. 12, 1949, 6 U.S.T. 3316, 75 U.N.T.S. 135, *reprinted in* DOCUMENTS ON THE LAWS OF WAR, *supra* note 24, at 244 [hereinafter GPW].

28. The FRAGO was issued on August 25, 2003 and replaced an earlier version issued on June 28, 2003. ON POINT II, *supra* note 21, at 248, 249.

29. The "imperative reasons of security" standard is not elaborated upon or defined in the article itself or in the official commentary to the Fourth Geneva Convention. COMMENTARY TO GENEVA CONVENTION IV RELATIVE TO THE PROTECTION OF CIVILIAN PERSONS IN TIME OF WAR 367 (Jean S. Pictet ed., 1958) [hereinafter ICRC COMMENTARY]. *See also* DINSTEIN, *supra* note 4, at 172–76.

30. The "intelligence hold" was not a category of detainee, but a descriptive term often used to satisfy the Article 78 "imperative reasons of security" requirement. Because of the accelerated pace of detentions and the shortage of interrogators, the number of detainees on intelligence hold grew from fewer than one hundred in July 2003 to more than twelve hundred in January 2004. ON POINT II, *supra* note 21, at 208.

31. *Id.* at 265.

32. In the summer of 2003, USCENTCOM denied requests for additional judge advocates. Meanwhile, mobilized reservists and CFLCC legal assets flowed out of Iraq, despite a burgeoning need for legal support. The CJTF-7 headquarters in general was chronically under-resourced. *Id.* at 157–61.

33. The fall 2003 proposal to make judge advocates part of the JIDC Joint Manning Document was not addressed until the spring of 2004.

34. ON POINT II, *supra* note 21, at 176.

35. Major General Donald Ryder, Assessment of Corrections and Detention Operations in Iraq (Nov. 6, 2003).

36. "A report that merely documents the problem will not be helpful." Memorandum from CJTF-7 Commander to Commander, USCENTCOM, Detention and Corrections Operations, Request for Assistance (Aug. 11, 2003).

37. ON POINT II, *supra* note 21, at 209, 210.

38. The genesis was an incident in which two soldiers of the US Army's 4th Infantry Division had been captured by insurgents at a checkpoint and then executed, their bodies dumped by the side of the road. The author flew to the scene with Lieutenant General Sanchez and there concluded that the command had to develop a legal process that could hold the perpetrators criminally accountable.

39. Memorandum from CJTF-7 SJA through Commander, CJTF-7, to Commander, USCENTCOM, on Prosecuting Iraqis for Security Offenses Against Coalition (Oct. 21, 2003).

40. CPA Order Number 13 (Revised) (Amended), The Central Criminal Court of Iraq, CPA/ORD/X2004/13 (Apr. 22, 2004), *available at* http://www.cpa-iraq.org/regulations/ (then The Central Criminal Court of Iraq (Revised) (Amended) hyperlink). The revised amended order contains the following language at section 19(1): "Prior to 1 July 2004, the Administrator retains the authority to refer cases to the CCCI [Central Criminal Court of Iraq]. . . . Cases referred by the Administrator will have priority."

41. Court sessions began in the late fall of 2003, but were hampered by a shortage of resources available to review and process cases. The pace quickened with the arrival of attorneys, paralegals and investigators of the Joint Services Law Enforcement Team in the spring of 2004. By July 2004, the CCCI had held thirty-seven trials for fifty-five defendants. ON POINT II, *supra* note 21, at 265.

42. JAMES R. SCHLESINGER, FINAL REPORT OF THE INDEPENDENT PANEL TO REVIEW DOD DETENTION OPERATIONS 82, 83 (2004) [hereinafter Schlesinger Report]. The report confused the term "unlawful combatant" used by CJTF-7 with the term "enemy combatant" used at Guantanamo. It is simply wrong when it states that "CJTF-7 concluded it had individuals in custody who met the criteria for unlawful combatants set out by the President and extended it in

Iraq to those who were not protected as combatants under the Geneva Conventions, based on [Office of Legal Counsel] opinions." *Id.* at 83.

43. Article 4 of the Third Geneva Convention establishes the criteria for prisoner of war status. The portion of Article 4A relevant to operations in Iraq after May 2003 states that prisoners of war include

> (2) [m]embers of other militias and members of other volunteer corps, including those of organized resistance movements, belonging to a Party to the conflict and operating in or outside their own territory, even if this territory is occupied, provided that such militias or volunteer corps, including such organized resistance movements, fulfill the following conditions:
>
> (a) that of being commanded by a person responsible for his subordinates;
>
> (b) that of having a fixed distinctive sign recognizable at a distance;
>
> (c) that of carrying arms openly;
>
> (d) that of conducting their operations in accordance with the laws and customs of war.

GPW, *supra* note 27, art. 4A(2).

44. ON POINT II, *supra* note 21, at 244. Judge advocates led the efforts to improve the Camp Cropper detention facility at the Baghdad International Airport and wrote orders to get tents, generators and other equipment for detention facilities throughout Iraq.

45. CJTF-7 Letter, *supra* note 6. By February 2004, the CPA had fielded an English and Arabic website, available to the public, that listed names and other key information pertaining to internees and detainees. ON POINT II, *supra* note 21, at 204.

46. ON POINT II, *supra* note 21, at 243.

47. The MEK remains on the list six years later. US Department of State, List of Designated Foreign Terrorist Organizations, July 7, 2009, http://www.state.gov/s/ct/rls/other/des/123085.htm.

48. Abu Ghraib was the only sizeable prison in the Baghdad area that remained largely intact, the rest having been looted to their bare foundations.

49. Article 143 of the Fourth Geneva Convention provides that representatives or delegates of the protecting powers "shall have access to all premises occupied by protected persons and shall be able to interview the latter without witnesses, personally or through an interpreter. Such visits may not be prohibited except for reasons of imperative military necessity, and then only as an exceptional and temporary measure." GC, *supra* note 24, art. 143.

50. The ICRC delegates accepted these conditions and made a return surprise visit in March 2004, when they were allowed to conduct private interviews with all of the detainees, except for one individual to whom access was erroneously denied. After the ICRC rightfully complained to the CJTF-7 SJA, the CJTF-7 C-2 directed that the ICRC be given unimpeded private access to the detainee. Department of the Army, Preliminary Screening Inquiry Report, Investigation of Legal Operations in CJTF-7, at 8 (Jan. 25, 2005) [hereinafter Preliminary Screening Inquiry Report].

51. Attachment A, paragraph (u) to congressional subpoena proposed by Senators Leahy and Feinstein, "Memorandum for MP and MI Personnel at Abu Ghraib from Colonel Marc Warren, the top legal advisor to Lt. General Ricardo Sanchez, New Plan to Restrict Access to Abu Ghraib (Jan. 2, 2004)." (The subpoena was defeated by the Senate Judiciary Committee on June 17, 2004.) There was no such document. In fact, every effort was being made in January 2004 to support and enable the ICRC's pending visit to Abu Ghraib after the disastrous visit in November 2003 (at which no judge advocates were present).

52. In December 2003, Colonel (retired) Stuart Herrington visited Iraq at the request of the US Department of Defense and gave a report to CJTF-7 that contained firsthand observations of abuse of detainees in a special operations detention facility. CJTF-7 sent the report to USCENTCOM, with the reminder that neither the command nor the facility at issue was under the command and control of CJTF-7. After some delay, USCENTCOM directed that CJTF-7 investigate the matter. This was done over protest. CJTF-7 had no superior command authority and its investigating officer was neither "read on" to the activities nor given full access to the facilities. The predictable (and predicted) result was that the investigation was inconclusive. The facility merited investigation and oversight. *See* Eric Schmitt & Carolyn Marshall, *Task Force 6-26: Before and After Abu Ghraib, a U.S. Unit Abused Detainees*, NEW YORK TIMES, Mar. 19, 2006, at A1.

53. These meetings took place in August 2003 and on January 21, 2004.

54. The first paragraph of Article 49 states: "Individual or mass forcible transfers, as well as *deportations of protected persons* from occupied territory to the territory of the Occupying Power or to that of any other country, occupied or not, *are prohibited, regardless of motive*" (emphasis added). This appears to be a total prohibition. This conclusion is reinforced in the official commentary to the Fourth Geneva Convention: "The prohibition is absolute and allows of no exceptions . . . ." ICRC COMMENTARY, *supra* note 29, at 279. However, persons may leave voluntarily or may be excluded. Exclusions occur most prominently in the case of infiltrators, such as persons who had entered Iraq unlawfully to take part in a *jihad* against coalition forces. "Infiltrators are simply not shielded by the Convention as protected persons." DINSTEIN, *supra* note 4, at 167. Exclusion could also be argued for persons such as the Palestinian terrorist Abu Abbas, who hijacked the cruise ship *Achille Lauro* and murdered US citizen Leon Klinghoffer in 1985. Abbas had been given sanctuary by Saddam Hussein and was living in Baghdad when captured by US forces. Had he not died of a heart attack while in custody in Iraq, he should have been amenable to removal from Iraq to face trial in the United States. A strong argument can be made that Article 49 could not have been intended to insulate criminals from the process of law in the manner of an extradition, especially where the crime occurred outside of the occupied territory and before the occupation. For a discussion of deportations and exclusions generally and the Israeli practice specifically, see *id.* at 160–68.

55. Global Screening Criteria, *supra* note 11.

56. Reliance in this circumstance on the broad derogation contained in the first paragraph of Article 5 appears to be misplaced. The first paragraph reads, "Where in the territory of a Party to the conflict . . . ." The next paragraph begins, "Where in occupied territory . . . ." The first paragraph thus refers to the territory of the occupying power, the second to occupied territory. Accordingly, the broad derogation resulting in the forfeiture of rights does not apply in occupied territory. Rather, only the more limited forfeiture of the "rights of communication under the present Convention" applies in occupied territory, and then only to "spies and saboteurs" and persons "under definite suspicion of activity hostile to the security of the Occupying Power." These categories certainly include insurgents captured in Iraq. Even still, the limited forfeiture was used sparingly by US coalition forces, and is still subject to the admonitions and requirements of the third paragraph of Article 5. GC, *supra* note 24, art. 5. *See also* DINSTEIN, *supra* note 4, at 63. A more accurate position would have been that the removal was the exclusion of a person not protected by the Fourth Geneva Convention, rather than of a protected person subject to derogation under Article 5. *See supra* note 54.

57. GPW, *supra* note 27, art. 13.

58. *But see* DINSTEIN, *supra* note 4, at 167: "Infiltrators are simply not shielded by the Convention as protected persons." Moreover, the foreign fighters were not accorded prisoner of war status.

59. The derogation is in the second paragraph of Article 5, which states:

> Where in occupied territory an individual protected person is detained as a spy or saboteur, or as a person under definite suspicion of activity hostile to the security of the Occupying Power, such person shall, in those cases where absolute military security so requires, be regarded as having forfeited rights of communication under the present Convention.

GC, *supra* note 24, art. 5.

60. *See, e.g.*, Schlesinger Report, *supra* note 42, at 61.

61. Major General George Fay & Lieutenant General Anthony R. Jones, Article 15-6 Investigation of the Abu Ghraib Prison and 205th Military Intelligence Brigade (2004), *available at* http://www.npr.org/iraq/2004/prison_abuse_report.pdf.

62. There was a third CJTF-7 memorandum on interrogation and counter-resistance policy issued on May 13, 2004. That memorandum remains classified as of the date of this writing.

63. Memorandum from Commander, CJTF-7, on Interrogation and Counter-Resistance Policy to Commander, US Central Command (Sept. 14, 2003), *available at* http://cup.columbia.edu/media/3738/jaffer-blog.pdf.

64. *Id.*

65. *See, e.g.*, Schlesinger Report, *supra* note 42, at 37; Senate Armed Services Committee Report, *supra* note 8.

66. Preliminary Screening Inquiry Report, *supra* note 50, at Tab 43 (Statement of Major Ricci-Smith).

67. Detainee Treatment Act of 2005, Pub. L. No. 109-148, 119 Stat. 2739 (2005). The Act is no panacea, however, as it continues to sanction "a parallel U.S. standard of detainee treatment and interrogation." David E. Graham, *The Dual U.S. Standard for the Treatment and Interrogation of Detainees: Unlawful and Unworkable*, 48 WASHBURN LAW JOURNAL 325, 346 (2009).

68. Headquarters, Department of the Army, FM 2-22.3, Human Intelligence Collector Operations (2006), *available at* http://www.fcnl.org/pdfs/civ_liberties/Field_Manual_Sept06.pdf.

69. Memorandum from Commander, CJTF-7, on CJTF-7 Interrogation and Counter-Resistance Policy to CJTF-7, C-2 et al. (Oct. 12, 2003), *available at* http://www1.umn.edu/humanrts/OathBetrayed/Taguba%20Annex%2028-A.pdf.

70. Headquarters, Department of the Army, FM 34-52, Intelligence Interrogation (1992), *available at* http://www.fas.org/irp/doddir/army/fm34-52.pdf. Although the 1992 version of the manual was in effect in 2003, judge advocates in Iraq used the 1987 version that was furnished to them by the CJTF-7 C-2 (Military Intelligence) section. Headquarters, Department of the Army, FM 34-52, Intelligence Interrogation (1987), *available at* http://www.loc.gov/rr/frd/Military_Law/pdf/intel_interrogation_may-1987.pdf. It was that version that was posted at the time on the official US Army publications website. Some investigators have concluded that the difference between the two versions was significant because the 1987 manual advised interrogators to "appear to be the one who controls all aspects of an interrogation, to include the lighting, heating and configuration of the interrogation room, as well as food, shelter, and clothing" given to detainees. *Id.* at 3-5. This language was omitted from the 1992 version and its inclusion in the CJTF-7 interrogation policy "clearly led to confusion on what practices were acceptable." Schlesinger Report, *supra* note 42, at 38. The conclusion is highly debatable, however, for at least two reasons. First, to assume that interrogators would study the text of a referenced manual presupposes an unlikely level of research and scholarship on their part. Second, since the 1987

manual applied to prisoner of war interrogations fully regulated by the Geneva Conventions, either the language was legally objectionable when promulgated (which is unlikely) or it refers only to the perception of the person being interrogated ("the interrogator should *appear* to be the one who controls all aspects of the interrogation") and it applies only to the control of aspects of the interrogation *above those required to satisfy the Geneva Conventions.*

71. Segregation in excess of 30 days required the approval of the CJTF-7 commander, after concurrence by the C-2 and legal review by the SJA. Legal Advisor to Chairman, Joint Chiefs of Staff, Interrogation Techniques Comparison Chart, May 2004.

72. Editorial, *A General's Dishonor*, WASHINGTON POST, Jan. 15, 2006, at B6.

73. "Neither the 14 September nor the 12 October CJTF-7 interrogation policies violated the Geneva Conventions." Preliminary Screening Inquiry Report, *supra* note 50, at 5.

74. The September (and subsequent) policies were staffed in the headquarters and with subordinate commands. In the staffing process, the term "stress positions" was discussed and was understood to have a different meaning in Iraq than elsewhere because of the application of the Geneva Conventions. Specifically, the example cited for the term was ordering a detainee to stand at attention or to remain sitting during an interrogation. During one staff discussion, a judge advocate asked a senior interrogator what would happen if a detainee refused the order. The interrogator answered, "Nothing. We can't touch a detainee." In fact, the September policy limited a "stress position" to one hour in duration and mandated that any technique must be "always applied in a humane and lawful manner with sufficient oversight by trained investigators or interrogators."

75. Military working dogs were authorized to provide security only, and had to be muzzled and under the positive control of a dog handler at all times. The infamous photographs of dogs snarling at a kneeling detainee at Abu Ghraib depicted military working dogs being used to quell a prison riot, not being used in an interrogation session.

76. "The CJTF-7 written interrogation policies did not cause or contribute to the abuse of detainees at Abu Ghraib. Had the policies been followed, the abuse would not have occurred. Abuse occurred in spite of the policies." Preliminary Screening Inquiry Report, *supra* note 50, at 6.

77. Charles J. Dunlap Jr., *Lawfare: A Decisive Element of 21st-Century Conflicts?*, 54 JOINT FORCE QUARTERLY, 3d Quarter 2009, at 34.

78. *See, e.g.*, Eric Schmitt, *Iraq Abuse Trial Is Again Limited to Lower Ranks*, NEW YORK TIMES, Mar. 23, 2006, at A1.

79. *See, e.g.*, GHOSTS OF ABU GHRAIB (Roxie Firecracker Film, HBO Documentary Film, 2007); and PHILIP GOUREVITCH & ERROL MORRIS, STANDARD OPERATING PROCEDURE (2008).

80. Ian Fishback, Editorial, *A Matter of Honor*, WASHINGTON POST, Sept. 28, 2005, at A21.

81. Although there was much exaggeration about detainee abuse, there were confirmed incidents and one case is too many. Perhaps the most disturbing—and extreme—case was the death of Iraqi Major General Abed Hamed Mowhoush during interrogation in November 2003, for which a US Army warrant officer was later convicted of negligent homicide. Josh White, *U.S. Army Officer Convicted in Death of Iraqi Detainee*, WASHINGTON POST, Jan. 23, 2006, at A2.

82. Through the first year of OIF, there were ninety-four "confirmed or possible" cases of prisoner abuse out of more than fifty thousand prisoners; 48 percent had occurred at point of capture. Inspector General, Department of the Army, Detainee Operations Inspection, at iv (July 21, 2004), *available at* http://www.gwu.edu/~nsarchiv/torturingdemocracy/documents/20040721.pdf. In all operations throughout the world, for calendar years 2002 through 2005, a total of 223 US Army soldiers had received adverse action (court-martial, non-judicial punishment, reprimand, separation or relief) for misconduct related to prisoner abuse. Department of the Army, Briefing, Detainee Abuse Disposition by Year Abuse Reported (2006).

83. In January 2004, after the Abu Ghraib photographs were turned over to the command, and before they were publicly known, the author informed ICRC delegates in Baghdad of the existence of the photographs, that the circumstances would be investigated and those responsible would be prosecuted, and that the command would tell the media about the abuse and about the existence of the photographs. (CJTF-7 informed the media in Baghdad about the abuse and the photographs in January 2004, some three months before the media frenzy ignited by the airing of the photographs on CBS's *60 Minutes II*.)

84. The term "strategic corporal" refers to "the devolution of command responsibility to lower rank levels in an era of instant communications and pervasive media images." Lynda Liddy, *The Strategic Corporal – Some Requirements in Training and Education,* AUSTRALIAN ARMY JOURNAL, Autumn 2005, at 139, 139, *available at* http://smallwarsjournal.com/documents/liddy.pdf. Of course, this responsibility may be exercised in a positive or negative fashion, each with magnified implications.

85. For a time, the reporting included all reported and suspected cases of detainee abuse, which meant that any complaint by a detainee was entered into the database, without regard to any legal or law enforcement threshold. During the period when the author participated in the weekly briefing to the Secretary of the Army concerning the topic of "detainee abuse," this low standard meant that cases tracked included complaints by detainees that the air conditioning had broken on a bus transporting them from Camp Bucca in southern Iraq to Baghdad. Moreover, some special interest groups would often jump to the conclusion that all detainee deaths in US custody were attributable to abuse or that all cases listed as "homicide" on criminal case reports were murders by US forces. (In fact, a "homicide" could be murder by another detainee or justifiable self-defense by a US soldier.)

86. After two detainees died in US forces custody at the Bagram, Afghanistan detention facility in December 2002, an investigation was conducted that found, among other problems, that the relationship between military intelligence interrogators and military police guards was blurred, that command and control of detention operations was not adequately defined, and that interrogation and disciplinary rules were not clear. These were exactly the problems repeated a year later in Iraq. Although the report of the investigation was known at USCENTCOM, it was not passed on to CJTF-7 and apparently no steps were taken to guard against recurrence in Iraq of the problems it documented.

87. Removal of judges is a prickly area, governed by Article 54 of the Fourth Geneva Convention, which affords special protection to public officials and judges by prohibiting the imposition of sanctions or other coercive measures against judges who "abstain from fulfilling their functions for reasons of conscience." GC, *supra* note 24, art. 54. However, Article 54 is tempered by its second paragraph reserving the right of the occupying power to remove public officials from their posts and by its explicit reference to Article 51, which accords the occupying power the right to order adult public servants to return to work. That the term "public officials" in Article 54 includes judges is clearly stated in the official commentary to the Fourth Geneva Convention. ICRC COMMENTARY, *supra* note 29, at 308.

88. Article 43 of the Hague Regulations states, in pertinent part, that the occupying power shall take measures to restore and ensure public order and safety, "while respecting, unless absolutely prevented, the laws in force in the country." Regulations Respecting the Laws and Customs of War on Land, Annexed to Convention No. II with Respect to the Laws and Customs of War on Land, July 29, 1899, 32 Stat. 1803; and Regulations Respecting the Laws and Customs of War on Land, annex to Convention No. IV Respecting the Laws and Customs of War on Land, Oct. 18, 1907, 36 Stat. 2227, *reprinted in* DOCUMENTS ON THE LAWS OF WAR, *supra* note 24, at 69. This rule is repeated in Article 64 of the Fourth Geneva Convention: "The penal laws of the occupied

territory shall remain in force, with the exception that they may be repealed or suspended by the Occupying Power in cases where they constitute a threat to its security or an obstacle to the application of the present Convention." GC, *supra* note 24, art. 64. In June 2003, the CPA suspended certain provisions of the 1969 Iraqi Penal Code "that the former regime used . . . as a tool of repression in violation of internationally recognized human rights standards" and suspended capital punishment. CPA Order Number 7, Penal Code, CPA/ORD/9 June 2003/07 (June 10, 2003), *available at* http://www.cpa-iraq.org/regulations/ (then Penal Code hyperlink).

89. Headquarters, Department of the Army, FM 27-10, The Law of Land Warfare para. 355 (1956) ("Occupation is a question of fact").

90. Checkpoint shootings plagued coalition forces. Judge advocates worked hard to find innovative ways to compensate civilians who had been inadvertently injured by US troops. The US Foreign Claims Act would not allow the payment of claims arising from broadly construed combat activities, such as most checkpoint shootings. Judge advocates convinced USCENTCOM to reverse its position prohibiting *solatia* or gratuitous payments, and helped draft the enabling language for the newly created Commanders' Emergency Response Program so as to allow payments for unintended combat damage. Judge advocates also established a meaningful foreign claims program after advocating that the Army, not the Air Force with its limited resources in country, should have single-service claims responsibility for Iraq.

91. An occupation proclamation is declaratory only and not legally necessary. DINSTEIN, *supra* note 4, at 48. In CPA Regulation 1 the CPA announced that it "shall exercise powers of government temporarily . . . . The CPA is vested with all executive, legislative, and judicial authority necessary to achieve its objectives." CPA Regulation 1, The Coalition Provisional Authority, CPA/REG/16 May 2003/01 (May 16, 2003), *available at* http://www.cpa-iraq.org/regulations/ (then The Coalition Provisional Authority hyperlink).

92. The commanding general of the US Army's 3d Infantry Division reported to the CFLCC deputy commander that he had too few troops to guard the specified facilities that he had been ordered to protect from looters. ON POINT II, *supra* note 21, at 148.

93. In April and May 2003, the author would often travel into central Baghdad to key facilities, particularly courthouses and police stations. There would often be no soldiers there, despite orders having been issued to secure the buildings.

94. ON POINT II, *supra* note 21, at 93.

95. CPA Order Number 1, De-Ba'athification of Iraqi Society and Government, CPA/ORD/16 May 2003/01 (May 16, 2003), *available at* http://www.cpa-iraq.org/regulations/ (then De-Ba'athification of Iraqi Society and Government hyperlink).

96. When combined with the order dissolving the Iraqi military (CPA Order Number 2, Dissolution of Entities, CPA/ORD/23 May 2003/02 (May 23, 2003), *available at* http://www.cpa-iraq.org/regulations/ (then Dissolution of Entities hyperlink)), the CPA's de-Ba'athification policy left hundreds of thousands of Sunni Arabs unemployed, while decapitating Iraq's governmental, security and education infrastructure.

97. In the case of the CPA, by S.C. Res. 1546, U.N. Doc. S/RES/1546 (June 8, 2004), *reprinted in* 43 INTERNATIONAL LEGAL MATERIALS 1459, which followed S.C. Res. 1483, *supra* note 4, which had recognized the United States and United Kingdom as occupying powers in Iraq.

98. The CJTF-7 mission statement read, in pertinent part: "Conduct offensive operations . . . in direct support of the Coalition Provisional Authority." ON POINT II, *supra* note 21, at 30.

99. An example of the chafing between CJTF-7 and the CPA was the inability to agree that USCENTCOM General Order Number 1, which among other things banned alcohol use and

possession in Iraq, applied to the CPA. This seems like a small issue, but it is a symptom of the lack of unity of, and confusion over, the chain of command. The CPA took the consistent position that the General Order was not applicable to either its civilian employees or its military personnel because it was effectively an embassy. Of course, it was not. The CPA was established as an instrument of the US Department of Defense (DoD), although its chain of command did switch from DoD to the National Security Council in November 2003. *Id.* at 181.

100. *See* K.H. Kaikobad, *Problems of Belligerent Occupation: The Scope of Powers Exercised by the Coalition Provisional Authority in Iraq, April/May 2003–June 2004*, 54 INTERNATIONAL AND COMPARATIVE LAW QUARTERLY 253 (2005).

101. ON POINT II, *supra* note 21, ch. 11.

102. *Id.* at 39.

103. There was much debate about whether US forces should have shot and killed civilian looters. Aside from the fact that most US troopers simply would not shoot an unarmed civilian who was not threatening them, the ROE would not allow it. The CFLCC ROE allowed soldiers and Marines to use deadly force to accomplish the mission against lawful targets (combatants), to protect themselves and others, and to protect designated property—but not to shoot a civilian walking down the street carrying a TV set. CFLCC ROE Pocket Card, *supra* note 16.

104. DINSTEIN, *supra* note 4, at 49.

105. CPA Order Number 7, *supra* note 88.

106. For an excellent primer on the CPA's rule of law activities, see Daniel L. Rubini, *Justice in Waiting: Developing Rule of Law in Iraq*, THE OFFICER, July–Aug. 2009, at 45.

107. Preliminary Screening Inquiry Report, *supra* note 50, at Tab 60 (End of Mission Report of Clint Williamson to the Administrator, CPA).

108. Also contributing was the secure video-teleconference, or SVTC. This technology allowed for personal communication between Iraq and Washington. The unfortunate reality was that it did not contribute much to common situational awareness or informed decision making; rather, it led to confusion as it sometimes trumped the military orders process and led to decisions that were not analyzed or thought through, and not coordinated with the military units that would have to implement them. The SVTC enabled policy from within the Beltway to be instantaneously injected into a theater of war—and that is normally not a good thing.

109. Memorandum to the President from Alberto R. Gonzales, Decision Re Application of the Geneva Convention on Prisoners of War to the Conflict with Al Qaeda and the Taliban (Jan. 25, 2002), *available at* http://www.slate.com/features/whatistorture/LegalMemos.html. In fairness to Mr. Gonzales, his references to the Geneva Conventions having been rendered quaint and obsolete were made in the context of the "new paradigm" of the war against terrorism and applied only to certain aspects of the Conventions, not to the Conventions as a whole.

110. This would also be in furtherance of the admonition to educate the civilian population on the principles of the Geneva Conventions.

> The High Contracting Parties undertake, in time of peace and in time of war, to disseminate the text of the present Convention as widely as possible in their respective countries, and, in particular, to include the study thereof in their programmes of military and, if possible, civil instruction, so that the principles thereof may become known to all their armed forces and to the entire population.

GPW, *supra* note 27, art. 127.

111. Protocol Additional to the Geneva Conventions of 1949, and Relating to the Protection of Victims of International Armed Conflicts, June 8, 1977, 1125 U.N.T.S. 3, *reprinted in* DOCUMENTS ON THE LAWS OF WAR, *supra* note 24, at 422 [hereinafter Additional Protocol I]. While the United States is not a party to Protocol I, it regards many of its provisions as customary

and binding international law. *See* Michael J. Matheson, *The United States Position on the Relation of Customary International Law to the 1977 Protocols Additional to the 1949 Geneva Conventions*, 2 AMERICAN UNIVERSITY JOURNAL OF INTERNATIONAL LAW & POLICY 419, 425 (1987).

112. DINSTEIN, *supra* note 4, at 81, 82.

113. *Lex specialis derogate lex generali* ("The *Lex Specialis* Rule"). *Id.* at 85.

114. *Id.* at 84.

115. The point was made by Professor Yoram Dinstein—"the three most important duties of the occupier are security, security and security"—in his closing remarks at the Naval War College's June 2009 conference.

116. Rebuilding the rule of law is a task too enthusiastically embraced in the US counterinsurgency field manual. Field Manual 3-24, Counterinsurgency (2006). A more realistic view of rule of law activities is found in CENTER FOR LAW AND MILITARY OPERATIONS, THE JUDGE ADVOCATE GENERAL'S LEGAL CENTER AND SCHOOL, RULE OF LAW HANDBOOK, A PRACTITIONER'S GUIDE FOR JUDGE ADVOCATES (2009).

117. *See* Rosa Ehrenreich Brooks, *The New Imperialism: Violence, Norms, and the "Rule of Law,"* 101 MICHIGAN LAW REVIEW 2275 (2003).

118. *See* Dan E. Stigall, *Comparative Law and State-Building: The "Organic Minimalist" Approach to Legal Reconstruction*, 29 LOYOLA OF LOS ANGELES INTERNATIONAL & COMPARATIVE LAW REVIEW 1, 30–31 (2007).

119. The term "Guarantor General" to describe the unrealistic expectations for the SJA was coined by Major General Mike Marchand when he was the Deputy Judge Advocate General, US Army, from 2001 to 2005.

120. *See* John Yoo & Glenn Sulmasy, *Challenges to Civilian Control of the Military: A Rational Choice Approach to the War on Terror*, 54 UCLA LAW REVIEW 1815 (2007).

121. Article 82, Legal advisers in armed forces, of Additional Protocol I states:

> The High Contracting Parties at all times, and the Parties to the conflict in time of armed conflict, shall ensure that legal advisers are available, when necessary, to advise military commanders at the appropriate level on the application of the Conventions and this Protocol and on the appropriate instruction to be given to the armed forces on this subject.

Additional Protocol I, *supra* note 111, art. 82.

122. Proper Treatment of the Iraqi People, *supra* note 5.

PART V

THE OCCUPATION OF IRAQ

XI

The Occupation of Iraq

Clyde J. Tate II*

This article addresses legal issues arising during occupation, specifically during the author's tenure as Staff Judge Advocate (SJA), III Corps and Multi-National Corps–Iraq (MNC-I). In doing so, personal thoughts will be recalled from days gone by on the legal issues which were dealt with at the operational—and at times tactical—level of war during the US occupation of Iraq, as well as during the key transitional period after occupation. It is hoped that these thoughts will inform future discussions by legal advisors facing similar challenges.

At the June 2009 conference from which this "Blue Book" derives, this presentation was billed as a retrospective. Such presentations can either be a travelogue with pictures of judge advocates (JAs) posed under the infamous Swords of Qadisiyah, or Hands of Victory, in Baghdad, or a series of "when I was in Iraq" vignettes. A retrospective is of most value to a legal practitioner, however, if it identifies key legal issues, shows how our institutions addressed those issues and explains what was learned from wrestling with them. Finally, this article tries to answer the most important question: how did lessons learned from our experiences at MNC-I during Operation Iraqi Freedom II (OIF II) aid commanders in accomplishing their mission? This author attempts to follow that path, then show how the work that was done led to significant changes that mitigated for future operations many of the issues confronted at MNC-I. The hope is that what is said

*Brigadier General, JA, U.S. Army.

will inform future discussions and encourage study, critical analysis and scholarly writings, all as enablers of change for the benefit of operational forces.

Putting the observations in context is important when you consider that the nature of the conflict and the issues confronted varied with each rotation of forces and, often, at different locales in theater during a single rotation. This author was the SJA for III Corps and MNC-I, and deployed to Iraq as part of OIF II, from May 2004 to February 2005. This author was preceded both in garrison and in theater by Army Colonel Karl Goetzke, who, despite very short notice, expertly trained, equipped and organized the III Corps Office of the Staff Judge Advocate (OSJA) while at Fort Hood and then deployed, serving as the SJA in theater from January 2004 to May 2004. Colonel Goetzke augmented both his garrison and theater team with mobilized US Army Reserve (USAR) judge advocates and paralegals; the mission could not have been accomplished without them. Remaining at Fort Hood, and serving as the Fort Hood installation SJA, was a mobilized USAR judge advocate.

The III Armored Corps is headquartered at Fort Hood, Texas, an expansive installation fondly referred to as "The Great Place." III Corps was activated in 1918 and, like so many corps in our Army's history, activated and deactivated many times over the years. As a corps, it last saw combat in 1945. It largely served as a training platform for armor units and was often in jest, but hardly to the liking of those serving near-entire careers at "The Great Place," referred to as America's most non-deployable corps.[1]

All that changed in September 2003 when the corps was notified of its upcoming deployment to Iraq in January 2004—only four months away! Its mission was to assume the tactical fight so that Combined Joint Task Force 7 (CJTF-7) could focus its efforts on the strategic fight.[2]

The initial role of III Corps in Iraq was to replace its V Corps counterparts across the CJTF-7 staff in anticipation of the activation of Multi-National Force–Iraq (MNF-I). The III Corps commander saw his role as a resource provider. He operated with a decentralized style enabling subordinate commanders to fight their fights in their areas of operations.[3] The corps had seven major subordinate commands, each with organic legal support:

- Multi-National Division (MND)–South (United Kingdom–led with one JA),
- MND–Central South (Polish-led with one coalition JA and one USAR JA),
- MND–Baghdad (led by the US Army's 1st Cavalry Division with a fully staffed OSJA),

• MND–North Central (led by the US Army's 1st Infantry Division with a fully staffed OSJA),

• I Marine Expeditionary Force (I MEF) in the west (with the I MEF OSJA team),

• MND–Northeast (Korean-led with a fully staffed legal section) and

• Multi-National Brigade–Northwest (led by a US Army Stryker brigade augmented to form Task Force Olympia with a thinly staffed but talented SJA section).

There were numerous geographically dispersed separate brigades in III Corps, each with its own judge advocate and paralegals. Members of the US Army Trial Defense Service, Region IX, also were present and fully engaged across the theater providing defense support. The III Corps OSJA deployed with thirty-five officers and fifteen enlisted soldiers, and formed the nucleus of the MNC-I OSJA. The office was complemented with one judge advocate from the Australian Defence Force, one judge advocate from the UK Directorate of Legal Services, one US Air Force judge advocate and one US Marine Corps judge advocate.

Within that broad context, several of the key events arising during OIF II will be highlighted. Each of these events adds to the context in which judge advocates provided legal support and presented unique issues that impacted our delivery of that support. Many of these key events overlapped major offensive operations, the latter of which are not the topic of this article but understandably presented separate legal issues. These include

• February 1, 2004: Transfer of authority from V Corps to III Corps.

• March 2004–May 2005: III Corps and MNC-I conducted the courts-martial related to the misconduct at Abu Ghraib, a topic discussed later.

• April 2004–June 2004: This period was described in *On Point II* as a time when the "caldron boils over."[4] Before this, there was relative calm after Saddam's 2003 capture. Also during this time, there was a significant transition of the units that would ultimately comprise OIF II.

• May 15, 2004: The activation of MNC-I and MNF-I. The latter command had a strategic focus, providing much needed interface with the Iraqi government ministries, the interim Iraqi government, and the Iraqi Governing Council. MNF-I was separately staffed with an OSJA. Also standing up at about that time was the Multi-National Security Transition Command and Joint Task Force 134, both with their own legal teams.

- June 28, 2004: The interim Iraqi government was established and the Transitional Administrative Law (TAL)[5] issued. A key task for the lawyers was to assess for the commanders how the TAL would impact ongoing combat operations.
- January 30, 2005: National elections held.
- February 10, 2005: Transfer of authority of MNC-I from III Corps to XVIIIth Airborne Corps.

The legal issues faced during this period are addressed by aligning those issues generally under the Army Judge Advocate General's Corps' core competencies.

Administrative and Civil Law

We quickly learned upon leaving garrison at Fort Hood that the deployment to Iraq did not mean administrative law issues were left behind. The most consuming of these tasks were investigations conducted under the provisions of Army Regulation 15-6[6] (generally similar to the Navy's JAGMAN (Manual of the Judge Advocate General) investigations). The high number of these investigations was quite surprising, but anecdotally every rotation from Operation Iraqi Freedom I through present operations has had the same realization. The investigation of incidents, though resource intensive, proved valuable to commanders, brought closure to soldiers involved in incidents, enhanced the safety of non-combat operations and demonstrated coalition forces' commitment to the rule of law.

Also in this core competency, we dealt with issues of unit historical property, including whether captured weapons could be preserved as part of the unit's history; war souvenirs; logistical support to the Army Air Force Exchange Service; so-called "friendly fire" incidents; joint and coalition investigations; Freedom of Information Act requests; and what were then known as Reports of Survey for lost or damaged US military property.

Military Justice

As with every rotation before and after, several high-profile military justice matters arose. Most notably, the author served as the legal advisor to the convening authority for courts-martial related to Abu Ghraib. Those courts-martial taught numerous lessons. Fortunately, this article is not about those courts-martial; these comments are thus aimed at the macro-level lessons. The Abu Ghraib cases demonstrated that the military justice system is fully exportable from garrison to the theater of operations as Congress intended it to be, even for complex cases. To that end, military judges, counsel—including trial counsel, and military and civilian defense counsel—and witnesses were brought into theater. This was a total JA-team support effort, beginning with the support we received from the OSJA, US Army Central in Kuwait. Other more fundamental adjustments were made to accommodate these trials, including equipping the renovated courtroom at Camp Victory on very short notice with the necessary technology to support expert witness and detainee depositions and testimonies, as well as cobbling together a consolidated team of trial personnel with the necessary workspace and support. Two cases were held at the Baghdad convention center, with its attendant security, transportation and logistics challenges. This was a massive logistical undertaking, but the convening authority allocated sufficient resources to ensure mission accomplishment.

Exportability is not without its limits, admittedly. Some of the cases were scheduled or likely scheduled to be tried at times when units were in major transition, or while key strategic events (such as upcoming January 2005 elections) were occurring. This meant that logistical support for the trials would have adversely impacted strategic operations or potential panel members were otherwise operationally engaged in those key events. Consequently, some cases were returned to the United States for trial and occurred both while the III Corps OSJA-Main was still deployed and after its return to Fort Hood. The consolidated trial team and the pending cases returned to Fort Hood to continue their work. The Abu Ghraib cases also taught the importance of dedicated trial resources for complex—and for Abu Ghraib, strategically significant—cases. It is naive to think that such litigation does not need to be viewed and resourced differently; far too much time was spent explaining in Army legal technical channels the need for additional personnel to support these trials.

The OSJA also dealt with, as has every rotation since, Washington's insatiable thirst for information on high-profile incidents. That desire for information will not diminish, so SJA offices have to consider how best to organize to satisfy that thirst without adversely impacting other, equally pressing matters.

Contract and Fiscal Law Issues

Contract and fiscal law was the subject area the OSJA was least equipped to address. There were simply insufficient numbers of experienced personnel to address the volume, magnitude and complexity of issues. This capability gap was not lost on those who followed on future rotations; they were much better trained and resourced to deal with the issues. One solution that has paid great dividends has been the Contract and Fiscal Law Reachback Group, nested within the Contract and Fiscal Law Division of the US Army Legal Services Agency and augmented, as an additional duty, by uniformed and civilian subject matter experts. "Reachback" means the ability to reach back to Washington, DC and consult with experts on difficult contract and fiscal law issues. This has ensured that both timely and correct advice was received.

Providing advice on the uses of Commanders' Emergency Response Program (CERP) funds proved challenging,[7] especially at a time of transition from seized CERP (with fewer restrictions on its expenditure) to appropriated CERP and its authorized uses. This transition prompted many efforts to educate commanders on how to adapt to the new, though more restrictive, uses of CERP.

Numerous issues arose involving contractors, contracted security and personal security details (PSDs) on the battlefield. One issue with which commanders at all levels struggled mightily was accountability for those persons, including these important questions: Who were these contractors? For whom did they work? Who was training them on rules of engagement (ROE) and rules for the use of force? A related question was what legal authority the civilians in these PSDs had to possess weapons: who, if anyone, had authorized them to have and carry firearms? Despite procedures to require weapons permits, it was never easy to determine if those procedures were followed. The procedures were an issue for MNF-I and higher command levels, but contractors failing to follow procedures and training on the rules became a challenge for commanders.

An issue dealt with daily was the proper role and use of contractors. We drew a firm and consistent line on questions regarding the use of contractors to provide forward operating base security, ensuring that commanders and contracting officers were "sensitive to the international law issues surrounding hiring a contractor to perform certain missions during military operations."[8]

A frequent challenge was the issue of weapons buyback and awards programs. There was a single awards program under the auspices of US Central Command (CENTCOM) but not every turned-in weapon qualified. This was sometimes a friction point with commanders who were unhappy when a particular weapon did not qualify for the CENTCOM awards program, since they perceived the effectiveness of such programs in pulling all weapons off the street. Without commenting here on the merit of weapons buyback programs, the OSJA legal opinion in these situations was consistent with the CENTCOM program.

Finally, any uncertainty about the authority to pay *solatia* payments was clarified in November 2004 when the Department of Defense's Deputy General Counsel issued a "no-objection" opinion to work done by CJTF-7 lawyers that had concluded that *solatia* payments could be made.[9] The authority to make such payments was widely welcomed by commanders who looked to offset injury and property damage caused to the local population.

Operational Law

Only a few of the many operational law issues confronted will be addressed. The ROE were virtually unchanged since the start of combat operations, yet there were numerous orders and messages related to the ROE that required even the most diligent of judge advocates and operators to look long and hard to ensure they had the latest guidance. The orders, numbering around thirty, addressed enemy tactics, techniques and procedures (also known as TTPs); indirect fires; troops in contact; and close air support. These orders were confusing, potentially contradictory when read in light of the ROE, and, in any event, simply not user friendly. Consequently, the 1st Cavalry Division OSJA led an effort to develop a consolidated ROE to ensure clarity, ease of use and relevance by bringing together key stakeholders to scrub the ROE and orders.

After June 28, 2004, the operational law team was fully engaged in drafting guidance for commanders to issue on how the TAL would impact ongoing operations. A balance was struck between conducting combat operations and demonstrating respect for the TAL, a balance which started to tip the scales in the direction of the situation as it currently exists under the US-Iraq security agreement.[10]

Key to training the ROE, and how the ROE applied to changing enemy TTPs, was the creation of ROE training vignettes. As TTPs changed, so did our vignettes, which were crafted to be immediately useful at the squad level, with or without the presence of a lawyer or paralegal to aid in the training.

Coalition ROE presented other challenges to the operational law team. Those issues and limitations were addressed primarily by understanding coalition partner ROE and respecting coalition ROE that could impact the roles in which those forces could be employed in operations.

At the conclusion of the occupation, coalition forces had to address how best to handle reports of abuse of detainees by Iraqi security forces (ISF). A "hands-off" approach was clearly unacceptable but the US role had to recognize the authority of the ISF in dealing with matters under their purview—and the larger issue of Iraqi sovereignty as a matter of international law. The command took a "stop-report-investigate" posture with regard to allegations of detainee abuse: stop the abuse, report it up the chain of command and investigate abuse allegations (if appropriate). That posture served commanders and soldiers well.

Operational law attorneys were engaged in these and all other issues across the full spectrum of legal support to operations, to include advice on interrogations, information operations, "friendly fire" incidents, foreign fighters, detainee operations, rule of law missions, application of the interim Iraqi government emergency measures to complement operations, synchronizing the legal assets of a multinational coalition and ISF ROE, all topics worthy of their own conference and separate discussion.

Conclusion

As alluded to at the outset of this survey of issues, the real value comes in assessing what was learned and what was done, across all our institutions, in response. This author is proud of how our institutions, aided by academic debate held in conferences and ensuing scholarly publications, responded to the challenges faced.

Since OIF II, Congress broadened the application of the Military Extraterritorial Jurisdiction Act, and the Department of Defense (DoD) issued policy and procedures related to its implementation.[11] Congress also amended Article 2 of the Uniform Code of Military Justice, broadening jurisdiction over DoD contractors and DoD civilians accompanying the force.[12] Greater guidance was issued regarding the roles of contractors on the battlefield, support to contractors and the possession of weapons by contractors.[13]

New organizations were established to support commanders, including the Joint Contracting Command–Iraq and Afghanistan, which is fully staffed by contracting, fiscal law and acquisition experts.

As discussed earlier, *solatia* provisions were clarified.[14]

As a result, at least in part, of the Army's experiences at Abu Ghraib, the Army rewrote its Interrogation Field Manual, which is now the standard for DoD.[15]

Training also has improved to better equip legal professionals. The Army implemented the Pre-deployment Preparation Program; the Brigade Judge Advocate Mission Primer, a three-day course held at the Pentagon; the Contract and Fiscal Law Reachback Group, which has proved invaluable; and a much larger contracting personnel "bench" as a result of the Gansler Commission.[16]

These changes are the result of our institutions adapting to the evolving requirements of the force and have, it is hoped, equipped current and future deployers with additional tools to address the challenges that will come their way. These changes also illustrate the value of conferences like the Naval War College's June 2009 conference—with their ensuing debate and scholarly publications—in enabling substantial and meaningful change.

Notes

1. The use of this moniker reached its zenith during the first Gulf War (1990–91), when both V Corps and VII Corps deployed to Saudi Arabia from Germany and XVIII Airborne Corps deployed to Saudi Arabia from the United States, while III Corps remained in Texas.

2. DONALD P. WRIGHT & TIMOTHY R. REESE, ON POINT II: TRANSITION TO THE NEW CAMPAIGN, THE UNITED STATES ARMY IN OPERATION IRAQI FREEDOM MAY 2003–JANUARY 2005, at 173 (2008), *available at* http://www.globalsecurity.org/military/library/report/2008/onpoint/index.html.

3. *See id.* at 174.

4. *Id.* at 38.

5. Law of Administration for the State of Iraq for the Transitional Period (2004) (describing the nature of the interim government and timetable for elections), *available at* http://www.cpa-iraq.org/government/TAL.html.

6. Headquarters, Department of the Army, AR 15-6, Procedures for Investigating Officers and Boards of Officers (2006), *available at* http://www.army.mil/USAPA/epubs/pdf/r15_6.pdf.

7. For a discussion of CERP, see Mark S. Martins, *The Commander's Emergency Response Program*, JOINT FORCE QUARTERLY, Apr. 2005, at 46.

8. *See generally* 2 CENTER FOR LAW AND MILITARY OPERATIONS, THE JUDGE ADVOCATE GENERAL'S LEGAL CENTER AND SCHOOL, LESSONS LEARNED FROM AFGHANISTAN AND IRAQ, FULL SPECTRUM OPERATIONS (1 MAY 2003–30 JUNE 2004) 106 (2005) [hereinafter LESSONS LEARNED].

9. *See* Memorandum from Charles A. Allen, Deputy General Counsel (International Affairs), Office of the General Counsel, Department of Defense, to the Staff Judge Advocate, US Central Command, Subject: Solatia (Nov. 26, 2004).

10. Agreement Between the United States of America and the Republic of Iraq on the Withdrawal of United States Forces from Iraq and the Organization of Their Activities during Their Temporary Presence in Iraq, U.S.-Iraq, Nov. 17, 2008, *available at* http://www.mnf-iraq.com/images/CGs_Messages/security_agreement.pdf.

11. The Military Extraterritorial Jurisdiction Act (MEJA) is codified at 18 U.S.C. §§ 3261–67 (2005). MEJA was amended in 2004 "to include employees, contractors (and subcontractors at any tier) and contractor employees [outside the United States] of any Federal agency or provisional authority whose employment relates to supporting the DoD mission." Ronald W. Reagan National Defense Authorization Act for Fiscal Year 2005, Pub. L. No. 108-375, § 1088, 118 Stat. 1811 (2004). This change was implemented by Department of Defense, Instruction 5525.11, Criminal Jurisdiction Over Civilians Employed By or Accompanying the Armed Forces Outside the United States, Certain Service Members, and Former Service Members (2005), *available at* http://www.dtic.mil/whs/directives/corres/pdf/552511p.pdf.

12. Article 2(a)(10), Uniform Code of Military Justice, was amended in 2006 to extend court-martial jurisdiction "[i]n time of declared war or a contingency operation, [to] persons serving with or accompanying an armed force in the field." John Warner National Defense Authorization Act for Fiscal Year 2007, Pub. L. No. 109-364, § 552, 120 Stat. 2083, 2217 (2006). This change was implemented by Memorandum from Secretary of Defense to Secretaries of the Military Departments et al., Subject: UCMJ Jurisdiction Over DoD Civilian Employees, DoD Contractor Personnel, and Other Persons Serving With or Accompanying the Armed Forces Overseas During Declared War or Contingency Operations (Mar. 10, 2008), *available at* http://www.dtic.mil/whs/directives/corres/pdf/sec080310ucmj.pdf.

13. LESSONS LEARNED, *supra* note 8, at 109. *See also* Department of Defense, Instruction 3020.41, Contractor Personnel Authorized to Accompany the U.S. Armed Forces (2005), *available at* http://www.dtic.mil/whs/directives/corres/pdf/302041p.pdf; Memorandum from Deputy Secretary of Defense to Secretaries of the Military Departments et al., Subject: Management of DoD

Contractors and Contractor Personnel Accompanying U.S. Armed Forces in Contingency Operations Outside the United States (Sept. 25, 2007), *available at* http://www.acq.osd.mil/dpap/pacc/cc/docs/DepSecDef%20Memo%20Mgt%20of%20Contractors %2025Sep07.pdf; Department of Defense, Instruction 3020.50, Private Security Contractors (PSCs) Operating in Contingency Operations (2009), *available at* http://www.dtic.mil/whs/directives/corres/pdf/302050p.pdf.

14. See *supra* text accompanying note 9.

15. Headquarters, Department of the Army, FM 2-22.3, Human Intelligence Collector Operations (Sept. 2006), *available at* http://www.fcnl.org/pdfs/civ_liberties/Field_Manual_Sept06.pdf.

16. Commission on Army Acquisition and Program Management in Expeditionary Operations, Urgent Reform Required: Army Expeditionary Contracting (Oct. 31, 2007), *available at* http://www.army.mil/docs/Gansler_Commission_Report_Final_071031.pdf.

XII

Occupation in Iraq: Issues on the Periphery and for the Future: A Rubik's Cube Problem?

George K. Walker*

Prior articles address occupation issues in 2003–9 coalition operations in Iraq from an international law perspective and legal and practical issues confronting coalition forces and their lawyers.

This article comments on legal issues at the periphery of the occupation, and problems that may arise in future occupations, whether governed by the UN Charter, special agreement or the law of armed conflict (LOAC). These include Charter-based law, *jus cogens* norms and other law (e.g., human rights law), international governmental organization (IGO) standards, the law of treaties and private law (e.g., admiralty law, torts, contracts) that may apply during occupations. These problems in single-State occupations, and even more so in multi-State occupations, can be vexing and complicated, like the solving of a Rubik's Cube puzzle.[1]

Geneva and Hague Law

The Fourth Convention,[2] one of the 1949 Geneva Conventions,[3] bears upon the LOAC governing occupations. Nearly all States are parties to them,[4] some with

* Professor of Law, Wake Forest University School of Law.

reservations or declarations.[5] Commentators and States say that some or all of the Fourth Convention recites customary law.[6] This has been so for 1907 Hague Convention IV[7] since the Nuremberg Judgment,[8] although one commentator says Hague IV has lost its normative value in the wake of post–World War II occupations.[9] However, unlike the other 1949 Conventions, the Fourth Convention declares that its rules supplement Hague IV and 1899 Hague Convention II for States not Hague IV parties[10] for hostilities (Section II) and military authority over hostile State territory (Section III).[11]

The first paragraph of Hague IV's Regulations, Article 23(h), part of Section II of that Convention, provides: "In addition to the prohibitions provided by special Conventions, it is especially forbidden . . . [t]o declare abolished, suspended, or inadmissible in a court of law the rights and actions of the nationals of the hostile party" during hostilities.[12] Thus even during armed conflict enemy nationals have rights guaranteed in court proceedings. The Regulations also protect courthouses and similar facilities that are public buildings.[13] Hague IV, Regulations, Article 43, in a commonly used English translation, is also pertinent to the analysis:

> The authority of the legitimate power having in fact passed into the hands of the occupant, the latter shall take all the measures in his power to restore, and ensure, as far as possible, public order and safety, while respecting, unless absolutely prevented, the laws in force in the country.[14]

Hague II, Regulations, Article 43, in an English translation, is similar:

> The authority of the legitimate power having actually passed into the hands of the occupant, the latter shall take all steps in his power to re-establish and insure, as far as possible, public order and safety, while respecting, unless absolutely prevented, the laws in force in the country.[15]

There is an apparent mistranslation from the authentic French text[16] of "l'ordre et la vie publics" in Hague IV, Regulations, Article 43, which should translate as "public order and life," implying "also the entire social and commercial life of the community,"[17] "public law and civil life,"[18] or "the entire social and economic life of the occupied region."[19] Since Hague II, Regulations, Article 43 uses the same phrase, "public order and safety," in an English version, comments on Hague IV should also apply to Hague II.[20]

The meaning of "laws in force" is also critical.[21] Can this phrase limit an occupier State to preserving the status quo, or has recent practice given it a more dynamic meaning?[22]

There are other differences. Hague IV's translation "in fact," compared with "actually" in Hague II, seems a minor distinction; "restore" in Hague IV seems to mean the same as "re-establish" in Hague II.[23] Whatever the correct translations, Article 43, seen by Benvenisti "as a sort of miniconstitution for the occupation administration," is important. Brussels Declaration Articles 2 and 3 were the origins of Article 43, but since 1874, and certainly since 1899 and 1907, central government's societal role has changed.[24]

Whether both treaties have the same language and practice under them is more than an academic issue. For example, among the States not party to Hague IV, fourteen are NATO Treaty[25] members and twelve are Rio Pact[26] members.[27] Those numbers are reduced to ten NATO members and three Rio Pact members who are not party to Hague II.[28] The result is that some of the members of the two alliances are, like the United States, party to both Hague II and Hague IV, others are party to one or the other, and still others are party to neither. All of the NATO States were or might be involved in collective self-defense responses in Afghanistan[29] and all members of both treaties could have participated in Iraqi coalition operations.

A message for future occupations is that participating States must consult their indexes of treaties in force,[30] particularly in multilateral operations, but even if one State is bound by Hague IV and the other by Hague II to compare differences in language, interpretation and application in practice. To be sure, Hague IV's Regulations are customary law,[31] and Hague II's and Hague IV's language is the same for this analysis,[32] but textual differences between the treaties or interpretation of them invite issues between occupier and occupied States or among occupier States, or if more than one State has been occupied.[33] This underscores customary law's importance but suggests diplomacy to persuade States to ratify Hague IV and eliminate the issue.[34] Moreover, if a State would emphasize treaty-based rules over custom-based norms, there is the possibility of a conflict on this score.

The narrow questions for this article are the meaning of "laws in force"[35] in an occupied State and how the exemption "unless absolutely prevented" fits into international law in the Charter era. May an occupier apply a "progressive development" principle,[36] including introducing, e.g., international human rights standards[37] not previously in force in an occupied State, or must it maintain existing law as an occupier found it? If an occupier State can introduce new measures,[38] how far can it go? After the 2003 invasion the Coalition Provisional Authority promulgated measures designed to reform domestic governance in Iraq.[39] Were these permitted under Article 43? When is an occupier "absolutely prevented" from applying an occupied State's law or using the exception clause to introduce new measures?[40] If human rights law would apply, whose perception of it counts, the occupier or occupied State's?[41] Dinstein proposes a "litmus test": if an occupier

State wishes to enact new legislation for the occupied State, "the decisive factor should be the existence of a parallel statute back home[,]" citing an example of requiring car seat belts where none had been required before occupation.[42] It is a useful test, but is it always appropriate? Take, e.g., another hypothetical from traffic laws. In the United States, an occupier State in Iraq, cars must be driven on the right side of a road. In the United Kingdom, the other major occupier, the opposite is true. In a desert country, does it make sense to require either if the previous rule had been no rule? Which rule should be an "improvement" if one must go into force? Should neighboring States' laws be taken into account?

Other commentators seem to take a different view, advocating abrogating occupied State laws incompatible with human rights law and promulgating progressive standards reflecting established human rights law norms and the like.[43] One military manual declares certain "human rights": "Respect for human rights—Family honour and rights, the lives of persons, and private property, as well as religious convictions and practices, must be respected."[44] For countries with similar military manual provisions labeling Hague-girded guarantees like this as human rights, an issue is whether the guarantee may be fleshed out through applying the current law of human rights. A more far-reaching issue is whether other human rights norms that do not fit under the Hague rubric may or must also be enforced.[45]

Commentators have raised the issue of self-determination, however it is defined.[46] Is it an occupier State's business to promote self-determination or the opposite during an occupation? Iraq is an amalgam of three former Ottoman Empire provinces: one that governed Kurds, a distinct ethnic group; another, with a Shiite Muslim population; and the third, a Sunni Muslim population. What positions should the occupiers have taken if claims for separate States for these three groups had arisen? By contrast, the UN governance of Kosovo before its independence concerned Kosovar self-determination. The UN interregnum had (and independent Kosovo today has) a Serb minority problem within Kosovo. Should Kosovo be a paradigm for future occupations? Is it an occupier's duty today, particularly in lengthy occupations, to promote self-determination?

An issue related to applying human rights law is the place of Martens clause principles, "usages . . . among civilized peoples, . . . the laws of humanity and the dictates of the public conscience."[47] What are these principles, which under the Fourth Convention and Protocol I, for States party to it,[48] may be further exceptions to applying an occupied State's laws? Are the clauses a statement of a general principle of international humanitarian law?[49] Are they a gate for applying human rights law, or is this another *lex specialis* situation demanding different norms, perhaps the same as human rights principles, but maybe different standards?

Might there be differing views of these issues between an occupier and an occupied State, which during an occupation would have little voice in the matter, but which might revert to earlier law after an occupier departs? Presumably the coalition reached consensus before initiating changes, but might there be issues within a coalition on what changes are appropriate?[50] If States leave or join a coalition during an occupation, how should consensus be maintained or achieved? If several States are under control of one or more occupier States, or if an occupied State is divided into administrative zones among occupier States, should the changes be the same throughout the occupied States, e.g., like Germany and Austria after World War II?[51] How would countries that are not occupier States view these matters, particularly if the occupier(s) proceed(s) as the coalition did during 2003–4 with wholesale changes,[52] but without benefit of UN law or similar support as was then[53] the case? There is also an issue of post-occupation law. If an occupier can impose beneficial changes, might an occupied State revert to its old ways after occupation ends by legislative changes, judicial construction or applying civil law principles on denial of precedent for prior cases[54] with resulting confusion (or worse) for the population? These are questions that should be asked and resolved in occupation situations.

The United Nations Charter

Before the 1949 Conventions went into force, States had begun ratifying the UN Charter. Its Article 103 declares that it trumps all treaties. Mandatory actions under the Charter have priority over treaty-based rules. Articles 25, 48 and 94 are sources[55] for Charter lawmaking; if the UN Security Council issues a "decision," it binds UN members.[56]

Article 51, preserving States' "inherent right" to exercise individual and collective self-defense until the Council acts on a situation threatening international peace and security, is another important rule.[57] An occupier must defend an occupied State from aggression as a Charter-based obligation under Articles 2(4) and 51 to preserve that State's territorial integrity and projected political independence in the future. A correlative to this is to assure, under a reasonableness standard, that an occupier does not compromise an occupied State's future by actions that leave it defenseless with insufficient security forces to protect it once it is no longer occupied. An occupied State's future territorial integrity and political independence must be assured. Occupiers should also be sure that municipal law changes do not have the same effect—e.g., transforming a formerly financially self-sufficient country into a weak State that cannot meet economic obligations, a circumstance that might reduce its armed forces to a level where self-defense would be impossible through inability to fund sufficient defense forces from taxes and other sources.

Other issues related to self-defense include applicable standards if personal or small-unit self-defense situations arise. An easy case is a response by occupier State units or individuals in circumstances like State v. State confrontations; international standards apply.[58] An example might be an occupier State soldier(s) confronted with State-sponsored border raiders from other countries invading an occupied State. Other relatively easy cases would be trying occupier State service members under its national military law,[59] trying an occupier State's citizen for offenses against occupier State security law[60] or trying an occupier State citizen tried in that State's courts;[61] in the first and third cases the accused's national law would apply if that State's legislation so provides.[62] Problems of perceptions of procedural justice might arise if the two States' self-defense standards are different, however.[63] More troublesome issues might come in "mixed" situations, e.g., a mob attack on occupier State forces where some mob members are occupied State citizens, some of whom participate in the mob action and others are human shields—i.e., unwilling mob members—and still others are, e.g., terrorists perhaps subject to international standards because they are outside-State-sponsored or operatives of organizations like al Qaeda.[64] If occupied State citizens are tried in occupied State courts, their national standards would seem to apply;[65] terrorists, if State-sponsored, would be subject to international law standards.[66] If the terrorists are, e.g., al Qaeda members, occupier State national standards like the US Military Commissions Act of 2006[67] might apply. The problem of perceptions (equal justice for a defense to the same alleged offense) here might be the greatest, particularly if one group mounts a successful self-defense claim and another does not. Yet another issue could arise if the confronted forces are members of different States' military services.[68] If a State or States operate(s) under UN auspices, issues of Charter-based rules may arise.[69] Finally, there is an issue of compliance with international human rights law standards, even for cases involving occupier nationals such as members of the occupier's armed forces, if human rights standards are more protective of personal rights.[70] What has been said about self-defense is, of course, a paradigm for other issues of law to be applied during occupations.

Other actions under Charter law may also articulate standards for occupation situations, i.e., "calls" for action by Council resolutions or General Assembly resolutions.[71] Whether these result in binding rules has been debated, most saying that the resolutions themselves do not bind members.[72] However, if many States accept a resolution as practice required by law, it can evolve into a customary norm, e.g., the Uniting for Peace Resolution.[73] To the extent that these resolutions' content recites general principles of law,[74] e.g., of humanity in Martens clauses,[75] they may strengthen these norms, particularly if a resolution cites a Geneva convention. How custom with genesis in *ipso facto* non-binding UN resolutions must be considered alongside mandatory Charter law is an open question.[76] The same is so for customary rules with a parallel, binding Charter rule, e.g., a customary right of self-defense alongside Article 51,[77] although in the latter case the logic is that such a customary rule can develop and might be different from the Article 51–supported norm.

After the 2003 invasion the Security Council approved Resolutions 1483[78] and 1546,[79] decisions[80] binding members. Resolution 1483, *inter alia*, declared that the US-led coalition (i.e., United Kingdom, United States) was the occupying power; Resolution 1546 welcomed the end of the occupation by June 30, 2004; then the LOAC applying to occupation ended, and governance of Iraq under the Interim Government began.[81] In the future, in other invasion and occupation situations, might there be non-binding resolutions, particularly as occupiers prepare to leave an occupied country? Since these non-binding resolutions can generate custom or restate general principles of law, do they as a sort of "super custom" thereby trump Fourth Convention treaty terms? If it is different from the letter of or practice under Hague Regulations, Article 43, does Charter-based law trump the practice? Probably so, but answers to these questions are far from clear.

Law of Other International Organizations

Another issue that can arise in the future is the impact of binding or non-binding agreements, resolutions or regulations of other IGOs, notably UN specialized agencies, and these documents' relationship with the LOAC governing occupations. The place of the work of IGOs is a related issue.

For example, the World Health Organization (WHO) Health Assembly, analogous to the UN General Assembly in that it has voting members from all States parties, has authority to adopt conventions or agreements within WHO's competence by a two-thirds vote. These conventions or agreements come into force for a member when accepted by the member in accordance with its constitutional processes. The Assembly can also adopt regulations for, e.g., sanitary and quarantine requirements and other procedures designed to prevent the international spread of disease. These regulations are in force for WHO members after the Assembly gives due notice,[82] except those notifying the WHO Director-General of their rejection of or reservation to the regulation within the time stated in the notice.[83]

If these WHO conventions, agreements or regulations are in force for an occupier State but not for an occupied country, or the other way around, how should they be applied in occupation situations under Article 43? Put more broadly, if an occupier is a member of other IGOs, but an occupied State is not, or the other way around, what law governs under Article 43? Health issues are likely to arise during armed conflict and an ensuing occupation. Other IGOs may have similar procedures for declaring binding rules. A further issue is whether these IGO regulations bind States not party to them, i.e., that they represent customary norms or perhaps general principles,[84] or by law of treaties principles binding third States.[85] And if not, should an occupier State introduce them as progressive development[86] under Article 43, so that an occupied State will be more forward-leaning in its international obligations and rights and national law when occupation ends? Or are these soft law[87] until an occupied State or an occupier chooses to accept the norms?

There is, of course, a possibility that otherwise-binding IGO-sponsored conventions, agreements or regulations may vary from UN law, e.g., self-defense under Charter Article 51 or the parallel customary right of self-defense,[88] or other binding UN law, e.g., Security Council decisions,[89] during an occupation. Here IGO rules must give way.[90]

A related issue is applying rules or principles from IGOs, i.e., soft law,[91] particularly if an occupied State and an occupier would differ on their application during occupation. To the extent that an IGO publishes rules purporting to restate custom or general principles acceptable under both States' laws, they should continue in force during occupation.[92] If they are not consistent, these standards may enter as secondary sources, i.e., research of scholars, in a source matrix.[93] If Charter law issues are at stake and these rules differ from IGO standards, analysis similar to that for IGO-based standards should apply.[94]

The Spectral Issue of Jus Cogens

Jus cogens, i.e., fundamental norms trumping treaty and customary law norms, and perhaps contrary general principles, has been a spectral source of law since World War II. Authorities differ on *jus cogens*' scope, ranging from a view that *jus cogens* does not exist to a Soviet author's position that the whole UN Charter restates *jus cogens*.[95] Be that divergence as it may, the International Court of Justice (ICJ) has twice said that Charter Article 2(4), which declares States entitled to their territorial and political integrity, "approaches" *jus cogens* status;[96] some argue that the right of self-defense also has *jus cogens* status.[97] The Vienna Convention on the Law of Treaties (Vienna Convention) declares rules for *jus cogens* in the law of treaties.[98] Perhaps not an issue related generally to occupation law today, *jus cogens* could create problems in the future, especially if an occupied State or other countries would claim a *jus cogens* violation and an occupier would not, or vice versa, or if a claimant argues that *jus cogens* supports its action when another claimant asserts a right under a treaty, customary law or general principles.

Law of Treaties Issues

Other law of treaties issues besides the law of *jus cogens* may apply in occupation situations.

Treaty succession principles have again become important as new States have emerged, sometimes after centuries (e.g., Belarus and Ukraine with the USSR's 1991 collapse) from the sovereignty of other countries. In other cases, new States have declared independence, e.g., some States emerging from the USSR's collapse. States have divided (e.g., Czechoslovakia) or merged (e.g., Germany).[99] Sometimes States' declarations recite what treaties of a former sovereign apply and, perhaps by inference, those that do not.[100] This can be relevant for occupation situations, e.g., involving applying Hague II or Hague IV or Protocol I.[101]

Vienna Convention Article 60(5) excludes application of its Convention material breach provisions to treaties providing for LOAC standards. Commentators argue over applying Article 60(5) to human rights treaties; most say it does not apply.[102] However, during occupations treaty breach issues for agreements other than those concerned with the LOAC may arise;[103] these could range from human rights treaties to those governing trade and the like. Recent ICJ decisions would say, however, that human rights law applies during armed conflict,[104] thus blunting the effect of Article 60(5) if construed to limit its application to LOAC treaties. There are advantages and disadvantages for applying the LOAC, customary or treaty-based, or human rights law.[105]

Impossibility of performance and fundamental change of circumstances are narrow exceptions for treaty non-performance.[106] This is particularly so in view of Vienna Convention Article 26's recitation of *pacta sunt servanda*, which restates a fundamental rule of the law of treaties.[107] Nevertheless, these claims may arise in contexts of compliance with treaties governing occupations, as well as other agreements binding occupier and/or occupied States. Are the exceptions in Hague II and Hague IV Regulations, Article 43, "unless absolutely prevented," or Hague IV, Regulations, Article 23(h)'s "especially forbidden" non-compliance statement, *lex specialis* rules to be used in place of general standards for impossibility and fundamental change of circumstances? Do rules on successive treaties apply?[108] Or are Vienna Convention standards the same as Geneva and Hague law? A common-sense answer is that they should be the same, or that *lex specialis* principles for applying Geneva/Hague law should govern, but the issue remains.

A similar issue is the relationship between rules for impossibility and fundamental change under the law of treaties and human rights treaties' derogation clauses.[109] War, or armed conflict, is the prototype of a public emergency threatening the life of a State, but that State may choose not to assert the derogation.[110] (There are certain non-derogable rights.[111]) Are these derogation clauses *lex specialis*, prevailing over general law of treaties rules for impossibility and fundamental change of circumstances? Like the LOAC exception clauses, it would seem that the answer should be yes. But do rules on successive treaties on the same subject apply, such that later in time standards govern?[112] Human rights treaties have a history contemporaneous with the Vienna Convention; sometimes one precedes the other to bind a particular country, and sometimes States may not have ratified the Convention. Some human rights treaties lack derogation clauses;[113] the customary law of treaties—i.e., States' rights to suspend or terminate treaties during armed conflict—applies to them unless these agreements apply during peace and war.[114] Or does it? For custom-based human rights law (e.g., if no treaty is in force), the analysis is problematic. By analogy to other customary norms now stated in treaties, e.g., the law of the sea,[115] the LOAC as a custom and treaty-based *lex specialis* should apply if human rights law and the LOAC squarely conflict.[116]

Suppose, during an occupation, armed conflict (e.g., invasion of an occupied State by a third State) between an occupied State and another country, or between an occupier State and a third State, erupts.[117] Do rules for suspending or ending treaties under customary law[118] or treaty provision[119] enter an occupier's decision matrix? Geneva and Hague law and the LOAC in general apply to States in armed conflict,[120] but the fate of other treaties (e.g., trade agreements or human rights treaties lacking derogation clauses) may be suspension or termination. In armed conflict situations, does the conflict provide another ground for suspending those human rights treaties with derogation clauses?[121] Other bases for suspending or terminating treaty obligations during conflict might be impossibility of performance or fundamental change of circumstances.[122] The answers to these questions are not clear, but an argument for suspending or terminating agreements without derogation clauses is that negotiators could have inserted them and for whatever reason chose not to include them, in view of similar agreements that have them or have clauses applying their terms in peace and war.[123] A rebuttal is that these agreements at least in part represent *jus cogens* and thus some rights under them are non-suspendable.[124]

Other Derogations from Applicable International Law

There are other derogations from applicable international law, sometimes treaty-based and sometimes grounded in custom, sometimes in both: state of necessity; reprisals; retorsions; reservations or understandings, interpretive statements and declarations under the law of treaties; treaty desuetude or obsolescence; and the persistent objector principle.

The International Law Commission's Draft Articles on State Responsibility, adopted in General Assembly Resolution 56/83 (2002),[125] restates the state of necessity doctrine in Article 25:

> 1. Necessity may not be invoked by a State as a ground for precluding the wrongfulness of an act not in conformity with an international obligation of that State unless the act:
>
> (a) is the only way for the State to safeguard an essential interest against a grave and imminent peril; and
>
> (b) does not seriously impair an essential interest of the State or States towards which the obligation exists, or of the international community as a whole.
>
> 2. In any case, necessity may not be invoked by a State as a ground for precluding wrongfulness if:
>
> (a) the international obligation in question excludes the possibility of invoking necessity; or
>
> (b) the State has contributed to the situation of necessity.

Article 25 commentary emphasizes the principle's narrow scope; it attempts to restate the rules of reprisal and declares that anticipatory self-defense is another example of justifiable rule-breaking under extraordinary circumstances.[126] Might necessity, under the extraordinary circumstances of the doctrine, justify breach of occupation law—customary or treaty-based—if an emergency ("grave and imminent peril") arises? Is "grave and imminent peril" the same as the Hague Article 43 "unless absolutely prevented" exception?[127] The same construction should apply to it as the language in Draft Article 25.[128] But what about the relationship between derogation clauses[129] and the necessity doctrine?

Reprisal rules say that prior notice of a breach of international law must be given an accused lawbreaker State with opportunity for it to bring its conduct into line with the law. If there is non-compliance, an aggrieved State may take measures, proportional to the circumstances but not necessarily in kind (e.g., economic measures to force human rights compliance), to bring a lawbreaker into line with the law.[130] Although reprisal situations could occur between a third State and an occupier or an occupied State, issues could arise between an occupier and the occupied State. Besides a problem of whose view of the law counts, there is a question of whether an occupier can act in its behalf or on behalf of an occupied State. The response to both questions is yes. Occupation law limits reprisals in some respects, e.g., forbidding reprisals against protected persons and their property.[131] A further question is whether reprisals not prohibited by the Fourth Convention can be imposed in light of human rights law.

Retorsions, an aggrieved State's unfriendly but proportional lawful acts to compel law compliance, may be invoked under general law[132] and the Fourth Convention.[133] What is proportional among States involved (occupier, occupied or third States) may arise, however.

Treaty reservations rules[134] must be consulted; States have reserved to the Geneva Conventions, for example.[135] Some treaties forbid reservations, e.g., the 1982 United Nations Convention on the Law of the Sea,[136] and there is a current debate on whether reservations to human rights treaties may be interposed, although they do not have no-reservations clauses.[137] Future legal battles over agreements forbidding reservations, or considered by their nature to bar them, may be over interpretive statements.[138]

Occupier and occupied States may have different views on desuetude or obsolescence, i.e., that a treaty is no longer in force because of longstanding non-observance of its terms.[139]

A correlative to treaty reservations rules is the persistent objector principle for customary law. Reports of its demise are premature; some, perhaps all, countries are active persistent objectors.[140] This principle may affect occupation law if an occupier State has views on custom different from those of an occupied State, or if occupier States have different views on custom.

Different International Law Standards for the Same General Body of Law, e.g., the Law of Armed Conflict among Occupier States

Prior analysis mostly considered LOAC occupation law issues in the context of a single occupier State, following the Fourth Convention format of addressing issues in the singular. If more than one State is an occupier for a country,[141] analysis can be more complex. If occupiers are part of a coalition or an alliance,[142] or a combination of alliance and coalition partners,[143] there is a further complexity. The reverse situation—if a State occupies more than one State, or a group of States (coalition or alliance) occupies more than one State after a conflict—presents more complications. Peoples within occupied territory may travel, perhaps subject to checkpoints, from one occupation zone to another. Even if they do not, local law,[144] public[145] and private,[146] of a subdivision (province or state as in the United States and other federal republics) of an occupied State may differ significantly.

Although the 1949 Geneva Conventions apply to nearly all States, and most of their principles are considered customary law, the same may or may not be true for the 1977 Protocols I and II[147] to them. The United States and other countries are not parties to one or both[148] and do not recognize all Protocol I and II provisions as customary law.[149] Protocol I supplements the Fourth Convention[150] and sometimes supersedes it.[151] The same issues may arise if Fourth Convention States interpret the Convention or custom differently.

Lack of universality is also true for other treaties, e.g., the Torture Convention,[152] although its rules prohibiting torture are considered at least customary law, if not *jus cogens*.[153]

If Charter law is involved, a problem may be interpreting or applying Article 51; some States involved in an occupation (typically occupier States) may adhere to a restrictive view of the valid scope of self-defense (i.e., reactive self-defense) and others may say anticipatory self-defense is lawful under the Charter and general international law. There may be differing views of what is lawful under either view, or what is valid when unit or individual self-defense is involved.[154] If the occupier(s) or occupied State(s) operate(s) under Security Council decisions or other UN and other IGO resolutions,[155] the same kind of definition and scope issues can arise.

Possible Solutions for These Problems

Today military forces operate under peacetime and war rules of engagement (ROE).[156] They have acted under ROE in the Iraq and Afghanistan occupations.[157] UN and other coalition and alliance operations have joint ROE and have used them in occupations.[158] ROE are used in law enforcement situations,[159] a major aspect of occupation law. ROE are not law but are options given commanders in conflict, potential conflict situations or similar circumstances like law enforcement, with a paramount right of self-defense. ROE are a confluence of diplomacy, policy and law.[160] ROE analysis suggests an analogous method to be considered for resolving questions raised for multiple levels of law, multiple sources of law within the same level of law and multi-State occupations.[161]

This author has suggested a factorial analysis, based on the *Restatement of the Law, Third, Foreign Relations Law of the United States*[162] *(Restatement (Third))* and *Restatement (Second) of Conflict of Laws*[163] *(Restatement (Second))* for these kinds of situations.[164] This analysis is based on choice of law or conflict of laws (private international law, as non-US commentators entitle it)[165] theories, although options are within a public international law context.[166] This is the kind of problem—choice of law and conflict of laws—albeit more complicated, in occupation law today, what with a hierarchy of sources atop traditional sources[167] and a possibility of many State actors, whether acting under the LOAC, UN law or general international law.

The author's *Restatement*-based analysis has not escaped criticism,[168] any more than the *Restatements*' use in US courts has met with universal approval and acceptance.[169] It is not useful for all occupation choice of law issues, notably ad hoc or fast-moving situations like self-defense[170] or operationally immediate decisions after occupation criteria have been satisfied.[171] Like planning for major military operations, it is time-intensive and can be cumbersome to use. But might a *Restatement*-style analysis be considered for "law planning" at an operational planning stage, perhaps with "law" options emerging, i.e., those for action below mandatory rules, e.g., self-defense, Security Council decisions where standards may be spelled out and the like?[172]

Even if it does not apply for public law issues, factorial analysis for conflict of laws questions may be an issue if courts consider private law issues,[173] e.g., maritime law claims arising from shipping to and from Iraqi docks on the Shatt al-Arab,[174] or medical supply contract issues involving WHO regulations for Afghanistan or Iraq if States concerned had adopted different WHO agreements or regulations.[175] Private law issues will arise in occupied State courts,[176] which may have conflict of laws questions before them.[177] If an occupier State can modify existing occupied State law on public law and private law[178] issues, can it or should it modify occupied State conflicts principles, perhaps through legislation, as has been the recent method for other countries, including those with common-law traditions?[179]

How the Restatement Analysis Works (Very Briefly)

After a decade of analysis in the American Law Institute,[180] *Restatement (Second)* appeared in 1971 and was partly revised in 1988. The *Restatement (Third)* appeared in 1987 after a similar process. The first step is to inquire whether there is a conflict of laws problem, i.e., is the law the same in both jurisdictions? If so, there is no conflict and the common standard applies.[181] This might be the circumstance where, e.g., human rights law and LOAC/occupation law standards are the same. If that is so, there is no need to analyze further; apply the common standard.

Each issue must be scrutinized (i.e., dépeçage) for possible conflicts, however.[182] The *Restatement (Second)* recites a major exclusion; if a jurisdiction has a statute governing conflict of laws, it must be used. If there is no legislation on point, a multifactor general analysis is interfaced with factors specific to an area of law, e.g., torts or contracts, or perhaps particular forms of torts or contracts.[183] There is little consideration of the international, or transnational, aspects of situations. Nevertheless, the *Restatement (Second)*'s explicit recognition of a higher rule, under construction principles in US law, is analogous to the command of the UN Charter on treaty law or a *jus cogens* mandate that may apply to an international situation.[184]

The *Restatement (Third)* does not list Charter law among its sources for public international law, but its comments note Charter supremacy in Chapter 1. Possible use of *jus cogens* is also mentioned.[185] The *Restatement* recites non-exclusive factors for applying particular law in Chapter 4, similar to the *Restatement (Second)* methodology.[186]

Besides US courts,[187] other institutions and countries have adopted similar factorial analyses for transnational conflict of laws. The European Union recognizes these principles, as do other States, among them US allies.[188] The US National Environmental Policy Act imposes factorial analysis for environmental impact statements.[189] The US Navy and other armed forces have used multifactor operational planning analysis.[190] What this author advocates is multifactor operational law planning analysis.

Is factorial analysis always necessary or useful? The answer is no; it will not work in rapid-response situations, like self-defense, although it might be used to plan for self-defense. It is not necessary in situations if competing laws are the same—the first requirement; if there is no conflict among competing laws, it is not necessary to go through the analysis.[191] Factorial analysis will not work for some law issues, e.g., treaty reservations or persistent objector situations;[192] the reservation or objection applies or it does not. It might help, e.g., with necessity, reprisal or retorsion situations[193] to promote thought on whether invoking necessity is appropriate, or the utility, kind and severity of action under necessity, reprisal or retorsion situations.

As experience through planning and execution proceeds, rules derived from repeated, similar situations that began with factorial analysis may be appropriate.[194] Applying this kind of analysis can lead to problems with a need to clarify the law with new rules,[195] but for military planning, might it be useful to think through conflicts problems before issuing black-letter recommendations for the command and an occupied State's citizens and institutions?

Conclusion: Analyzing Occupation Issues Thoroughly through "Operational Law Planning"

The relatively recent addition of operational law–trained attorneys to battle staffs and other commands has helped keep military operations within international and national law. As others have written, "lawfare"[196] is very much a part of those operations, particularly given the communications and media revolutions involving the Internet, television including 24-hour battlespace newscasting, radio broadcasting, e-mail, texting, facsimile, etc.[197] If John Paul Jones were alive today, he would say that international law is part of a commander's "tolerable Education."[198] But he might add: Consult your lawyer in planning or acting if it is feasible to do so under the circumstances. Put more prosaically, look before you leap. Perceptions of law compliance are part of today's battle problem.

A further problem, particularly for operations involving multilateral forces that may be involved in occupations of or involvement with more than one country, is a need to perceive conflict of laws issues that may arise. These may be "vertical" conflicts, e.g., between the LOAC and Charter-based law,[199] or "horizontal" law issues, e.g., among States involved in an occupation or, more subtly, a conflict between the law of the occupied State(s) as it stood when occupation began and the progress—or lack of it—of the law as occupiers and others believe it ought to be, or, at another level, the everyday rules of private orderings (torts, contracts, etc.).[200] For these issues, developing a factorial decision matrix, perhaps a general checklist for the "shelf" long before need arises or a campaign-specific one for particular military operations, perhaps based on conflict of laws (private international law) concepts[201] will help. If military staffs[202] plan for and solve complex occupation problems, whether in one-on-one situations or those with a number of States on either or both sides, operational law attorneys serving commanders can solve the complex, multilateral, multilayer legal problems involved. Using conflict of laws analysis may point toward clearer thinking about concrete solutions if multiple sets or layers of laws are or can be involved.[203] The proposed analytical method will not produce a black-letter "answer" or rule, but it should point toward more comprehensive, well-thought-out rules.

Like Rubik's Cube, the law puzzle for occupations is capable of solution, perhaps through factorial analysis in other than urgent situations (e.g., self-defense), for sometimes multilayer, multidimensional choice of law issues under Hague IV, Regulations, Article 43.[204]

Notes

1. Rubik's Cube is a three-dimensional puzzle Erno Rubik invented; a cube's six faces are covered by six colors (white, red, blue, orange, green, yellow) with nine smaller squares on the cube's sides. The challenge is to manipulate the cube pivot mechanism until all nine squares are the same color on each of the cube's six faces.

2. Convention Relative to the Protection of Civilian Persons in Time of War, Aug. 12, 1949, 6 U.S.T. 3516, 75 U.N.T.S. 287, *reprinted in* THE LAWS OF ARMED CONFLICTS 575 (Dietrich Schindler & Jiri Toman eds., 4th ed. 2004) [hereinafter Fourth Convention].

3. The others are Convention for the Amelioration of the Condition of the Wounded and Sick in Armed Forces in the Field, Aug. 12, 1949, 6 U.S.T. 3114, 75 U.N.T.S. 31 [hereinafter First Convention]; Convention for the Amelioration of the Condition of Wounded, Sick and Shipwrecked Members of Armed Forces at Sea, Aug. 12, 1949, 6 U.S.T. 3217, 75 U.N.T.S. 85 [hereinafter Second Convention]; Convention Relative to the Treatment of Prisoners of War, Aug. 12, 1949, 6 U.S.T. 3316, 75 U.N.T.S. 135 [hereinafter Third Convention]; all *reprinted in* THE LAWS OF ARMED CONFLICTS, *supra* note 2, at 459, 485, 507, respectively.

4. International Committee of the Red Cross, State Parties to the Following International Humanitarian Law and Other Related Treaties as of 14-Oct-2009, http://www.icrc.org/IHL.nsf/(SPF)/party_main_treaties/$File/IHL_and_other_related_Treaties.pdf [hereinafter State Parties], lists 194 parties to the 1949 Conventions.

5. *See id., supra* note 4; for a printed source, see THE LAWS OF ARMED CONFLICTS, *supra* note 2, at 635–88.

6. YUTAKA ARAI-TAKAHASHI, THE LAW OF OCCUPATION 59–64 (2009) (progression of Fourth Convention, *supra* note 2, from aspirational standards to mostly customary law); YORAM DINSTEIN, THE INTERNATIONAL LAW OF BELLIGERENT OCCUPATION 6–7 (2009) (possibility that some States may not see the 1949 Geneva Conventions as customary law or may not apply them as municipal law). International custom is general State practice accepted as law. Statute of the International Court of Justice art. 38(1)(b), June 26, 1945, 59 Stat. 1031, T.S. No. 993 [hereinafter ICJ Statute]; IAN BROWNLIE, PRINCIPLES OF PUBLIC INTERNATIONAL LAW 6–12 (7th ed. 2009); DINSTEIN, *supra* at 4; OPPENHEIM'S INTERNATIONAL LAW §§ 9–10 (Robert Jennings & Arthur Watts eds., 9th ed. 1992); RESTATEMENT (THIRD) OF THE FOREIGN RELATIONS LAW OF THE UNITED STATES §§ 102, 103(2)(d) & cmt. c (1987) [hereinafter RESTATEMENT].

7. Hague Convention No. IV Respecting the Laws and Customs of War on Land, Oct. 18, 1907, 36 Stat. 2227, *reprinted in* THE LAWS OF ARMED CONFLICTS, *supra* note 2, at 55 [hereinafter Hague IV].

8. Judgment, 1 Trial of the Major War Criminals Before the International Military Tribunal, Nuremberg, 14 November 1945–1 October 1946, at 253–54 (1947). The International Military Tribunal for the Far East, Judgment, 15 I.L.R. 356, 346–66 (1948) [hereinafter Tokyo trials] made the same holding. Two months after the Nuremberg trials ended, Affirmation of the Principles of International Law Recognized by the Charter of the Nuremberg Tribunal, G.A. Res. 95, 1 U.N. GAOR, 1st Sess., U.N. Doc. A/64/Add.1, at 188 (Dec. 11, 1946) [hereinafter Resolution 95], unanimously reaffirmed Nuremberg and Tokyo trials principles. Legality of the Threat or Use of Nuclear Weapons, Advisory Opinion, 1996 I.C.J. 226, 256 (July 8) [hereinafter Nuclear Weapons]; Armed Activities on the Territory of the Congo (Dem. Rep. Congo v. Uganda), 2005 I.C.J. 19, 70 (Dec. 19) [hereinafter 2005 Congo Case]; Legal Consequences of the Construction of a Wall in the Occupied Palestinian Territory, Advisory Opinion, 2004 I.C.J. 136, 172 (July 9) [hereinafter Wall Case] adopted Nuremberg principles; *see also* ARAI-TAKAHASHI, *supra* note 6, at 55, 57; DINSTEIN, *supra* note 6, at 5; ANNOTATED SUPPLEMENT TO THE COMMANDER'S HANDBOOK ON THE LAW OF NAVAL OPERATIONS ¶ 5.4.2 (A.R. Thomas & James C. Duncan eds., 1999) (Vol. 73, US Naval War College International Law Studies) [hereinafter NWP 1-14M ANNOTATED] (Hague general principles reflect customary law); UK MINISTRY OF DEFENCE, THE MANUAL OF THE LAW OF ARMED CONFLICT ¶ 1.25 (2005) [hereinafter UK MANUAL]; Christopher Greenwood, *Historical Development and Legal Basis, in* THE HANDBOOK OF HUMANITARIAN LAW IN ARMED CONFLICTS 1, 24 (Dieter Fleck ed., 1999) (Hague IV Regulations remain of "utmost importance"). These cases and the resolution, although secondary sources and not binding themselves, restate customary law. *See* ICJ Statute, *supra* note 6, arts. 38(1)(d), 59; BROWNLIE, *supra* note 6, at 15, 19–22; OPPENHEIM'S INTERNATIONAL LAW, *supra*

note 6, §§ 13, 16; RESTATEMENT, *supra* note 6, §§ 102, 103(2)(d) & cmt. c. Although the list of Hague IV parties is small compared with UN membership today, see THE LAWS OF ARMED CONFLICTS, *supra* note 2, at 85, and the treaty has an *inter se* clause, Hague IV, *supra* note 7, art. 2, treaty succession rules may apply Hague IV to other States. *See generally* Committee on Aspects of the Law of State Succession, Final Report, in International Law Association, Report of the Seventy-Third Conference Held in Rio de Janeiro, Brazil, August 17–21, 2008, at 250, 360–62 (2008) [hereinafter Final Report] (UN succession conventions' general acceptance; recent practice); OPPENHEIM'S INTERNATIONAL LAW, *supra* note 6, § 62, at 211–13; Symposium, *State Succession in the Former Soviet Union and in Eastern Europe*, 33 VIRGINIA JOURNAL OF INTERNATIONAL LAW 253 (1993); George K. Walker, *Integration and Disintegration in Europe: Reordering the Treaty Map of the Continent*, 6 THE TRANSNATIONAL LAWYER 1 (1993).

9. EYAL BENVENISTI, THE INTERNATIONAL LAW OF OCCUPATION 96–98, 190 (2d prtg. 2004). This claim must be evaluated in the light of Fourth Convention drafters' and negotiators' decisions to insert language in Article 154 that supplements Hague Convention (II) with Respect to Laws & Customs of War on Land, July 29, 1899, 32 Stat. 1803, *reprinted in* THE LAWS OF ARMED CONFLICTS, *supra* note 2, at 55 [hereinafter Hague II], and Hague IV, *supra* note 7, unlike language in analogous First, Second and Third Convention provisions. Another interpretation is that the Fourth Convention affirms Hague law. *See infra* notes 10–11 and accompanying text.

10. Hague II, *supra* note 9. Many States parties to Hague II are also Hague IV parties; eighteen are not. THE LAWS OF ARMED CONFLICTS, *supra* note 2, at 55. *Compare Convention of 1907*, *id.* at 85, *with Convention of 1899: Signatures, Ratifications and Accessions*, *id.* at 83. For States parties to both, Hague IV, Aricles 2 and 4 declare that it is substituted for Hague II, if all belligerents are parties. Treaty succession rules may bind many countries achieving independence since 1899. *See* Final Report, *supra* note 8; Symposium, *supra* note 8; Walker, *supra* note 8. Since the 1899 and 1907 Conventions recite the same terms at issue in this analysis in nearly identical language, Hague IV's status as custom, see *supra* notes 7–9 and accompanying text, applies to Hague II parties except persistent objectors. *See infra* note 140 and accompanying text. Hague II was not the first statement of occupation law. U.S. department of War, Instructions for the Government of Armies of the United States in the Field, General Orders No. 100 arts. 1–47, Apr. 24, 1863, *reprinted in* THE LAWS OF ARMED CONFLICTS, *supra* note 2, at 3, 4–9 [hereinafter Lieber Code]; Project of an International Declaration Concerning the Laws and Customs of War arts. 1–11, 36–42, Aug. 24, 1874, *reprinted in id.* at 21, 23–24, 27 [hereinafter Brussels Declaration]; INSTITUTE OF INTERNATIONAL LAW, THE LAWS OF WAR ON LAND arts. 41–60 (1880), *reprinted in id.* at 29, 35–37 [hereinafter OXFORD MANUAL], were its precursors. DINSTEIN, *supra* note 6, at 8–9.

11. The others say they supersede or are "complementary to" parts of prior treaties. *Compare* Fourth Convention, *supra* note 2, art. 154 *with* First Convention, *supra* note 3, art. 59 (replacing Convention for Amelioration of the Condition of Wounded in Armies in the Field, Aug. 22, 1864, 22 Stat. 940, *reprinted in* THE LAWS OF ARMED CONFLICTS, *supra* note 2, at 365; Convention for Amelioration of the Condition of Wounded and Sick in Armies in the Field, July 6, 1906, 35 Stat. 1885; Convention Relative to the Treatment of Prisoners of War, July 27, 1929, 47 Stat. 2021, *reprinted in id.* at 421 [hereinafter 1929 PW Convention]); Second Convention, *supra* note 3, art. 58, replacing Hague Convention No. X for the Adaptation to Maritime Warfare of the Principles of the Geneva Convention [of 1906], Oct. 18, 1907, 36 Stat. 2371, *reprinted in id.* at 397; Third Convention, *supra* note 3, arts. 134–35 (replacing 1929 PW Convention, *supra*, complementary to Hague II, *supra* note 9, Regulations; Hague IV, *supra* note 7, Regulations for *id.* ch. II [spies]); *see also* ARAI-TAKAHASHI, *supra* note 6, at 115–16; DINSTEIN, *supra* note 6, at 6–7; 1 JEAN S. PICTET, I CONVENTION COMMENTARY 407–8 (1952); 2 JEAN S. PICTET, II CONVENTION

COMMENTARY 277–78 (1960); 3 JEAN S. PICTET, III CONVENTION COMMENTARY 636–40 (1960); 4 JEAN S. PICTET, IV CONVENTION COMMENTARY (1958).

12. Hague IV, *supra* note 7, Regulations, art. 23(h), for which there is no comparable Hague II, *supra* note 9, provision. The *id.*, Regulations, art. 44 prohibition appears in the first paragraph of Hague IV, *supra* note 7, Regulations, art. 23(h) and is not relevant to this analysis. *See* United States, Department of the Army, FM 27-10: The Law of Land Warfare ¶ 372 (July 1956, Change No. 1, 1975) [hereinafter FM 27-10]; DINSTEIN, *supra* note 6, at 53, 195–96; *see also infra* notes 40, 108, 176 and accompanying text.

13. In today's world, presumably protection would extend to offices, e.g., of prosecutors, public defenders and poverty assistance attorneys in courthouses or similar buildings, as well as data centers, clerks' offices, etc. Hague II, *supra* note 9, Regulations, art. 56; Hague IV, *supra* note 7, Regulations, arts. 55, 56; *see also* Brussels Declaration, *supra* note 10, art. 7; FM 27-10, *supra* note 12, ¶ 400; OXFORD MANUAL, *supra* note 10, ¶ C(a) & art. 52; ARAI-TAKAHASHI, *supra* note 6, at 196–98, 206; DINSTEIN, *supra* note 6, at 213, 220. Hague II, *supra* note 9, Regulations, art. 55, does not refer to municipal property, unless its "communes" exception would apply, the French version of "municipalities," in Hague IV, *supra* note 7, Regulations, art. 55, which would treat such assets as private property; *see also* Brussels Declaration, *supra*, art. 8, referring to municipal assets as private property. *See also* DINSTEIN, *supra* note 6, at 220 n.1188. On the other hand, OXFORD MANUAL, *supra* note 10, art. 53, declares that municipal property cannot be seized. Lieber Code, *supra* note 10, art. 31, declared that title to occupied State-owned real property remained in that State; revenues from such property would go to the occupier; *id.* said nothing about public buildings, e.g., courthouses. *Id.* art. 39 would continue judges' salaries, to be paid from occupied state funds. Privately owned law offices and other law-related facilities or property, e.g., a privately operated poverty law center, are covered under Hague II, *supra* note 9, Regulations, arts. 52, 56; Hague IV, *supra* note 7, Regulations, arts. 52, 56 and may be requisitioned, but owners must be compensated; *see also* FM 27-10, *supra* note 12, ¶ 406; OXFORD MANUAL, *supra*, arts. 54, 56, 60; Lieber Code, *supra*, arts. 37–38; DINSTEIN, *supra* at 224–32. Some property of neutral-country nationals (ships, other means of transport) may be subject to angary, although Hague II, *supra* note 9, Regulations, art. 53; Hague IV, *supra* note 7, Regulations, art. 53 protect most property of neutrals' nationals, e.g., lawyers' property caught in an occupation situation. DINSTEIN, *supra* note 6, at 236–37. If a courthouse is, or is in, a historic building or a structure of cultural significance like some US courthouses, it would be protected during occupation as cultural property. Protocol Additional to the Geneva Conventions of 12 August 1949, and Relating to the Protection of Victims of International Armed Conflicts art. 53, June 8, 1977, 1125 U.N.T.S. 3, *reprinted in* THE LAWS OF ARMED CONFLICTS, *supra* note 2, at 711 [hereinafter Protocol I]; Convention for Protection of Cultural Property in the Event of Armed Conflict arts. 1(a), 4–5, May 14, 1954, 249 U.N.T.S. 240, *reprinted in id.* at 999 [hereinafter Cultural Property Convention]; Treaty on Protection of Artistic & Scientific Institutions & Historic Monuments, art. 1, Apr. 15, 1935, 49 Stat. 3267, 67 L.N.T.S. 290, *reprinted in id.* at 991; Hague IV, *supra* note 7, Regulations, arts. 27, 56; Hague II, *supra* note 9, Regulations, art. 56; OXFORD MANUAL, *supra*, art. 53; Brussels Declaration, *supra*, art. 8; FM 27-10, *supra* note 12, ¶¶ 45–46, 57, 405; UK MANUAL, *supra* note 8, ¶ 11.87.1; Lieber Code, *supra*, art. 34; *see generally* ARAI-TAKAHASHI, *supra* note 6, ch. 10; Hans-Peter Gasser, *Protection of the Civilian Population*, *in* THE HANDBOOK OF HUMANITARIAN LAW IN ARMED CONFLICTS, *supra* note 8, at 209, 262–63; JIRI TOMAN, THE PROTECTION OF CULTURAL PROPERTY IN THE EVENT OF ARMED CONFLICT (1996); Karl Josef Partsch, *Protection of Cultural Property*, *in* THE HANDBOOK OF HUMANITARIAN LAW IN ARMED CONFLICTS, *supra* note 8, at 377–97.

14. Hague IV, *supra* note 7, Regulations, art. 43.

15. Hague II, *supra* note 9, Regulations, art. 43. Earlier international authorities were similar in tone; promulgating new laws was forbidden unless "necessary." OXFORD MANUAL, *supra* note 10, art. 44; Brussels Declaration, *supra* note 10, art. 3. Lieber Code, *supra* note 10, art. 32, allowed occupiers to "suspend, change, or abolish, as far as the martial power extends . . ." an occupied State's laws, without the "necessity" limitation.

16. Authentic Text, *in* THE LAWS OF ARMED CONFLICTS, *supra* note 2, at 56 [hereinafter Authentic Text]. The final paragraph of Hague IV, *supra* note 7 ("Done in The Hague . . . "), says a single copy of the authentic text is filed with the Netherlands government.

17. DINSTEIN, *supra* note 6, at 89.

18. BENVENISTI, *supra* note 9, at 7; *see also* ARAI-TAKAHASHI, *supra* note 6, at 91 n.2, 96.

19. MYRES S. MCDOUGAL & FLORENTINO FELICIANO, LAW AND MINIMUM PUBLIC ORDER 746 (1961).

20. DINSTEIN, *supra* note 6, analyzes Hague IV, *supra* note 7, and cites Hague II, *supra* note 9, occasionally, DINSTEIN, *supra* at 4–6, 9, 53, 90, 231, 233, 287, but does not comment on this aspect of Hague II, *supra* note 9, Regulations, art. 43. ARAI-TAKAHASHI, *supra* note 6, and BENVENISTI, *supra* note 9, concentrate on Hague IV, *supra* note 7, as does FM 27-10, *supra* note 12. Like Hague IV, *supra* note 7, the authentic language of Hague II, *supra* note 9, is French, *see* Authentic Text, *supra* note 16, at 56; the final paragraph of Hague II, *supra* note 9 ("Done at The Hague . . . "), says a single copy of the authentic text is in Netherlands archives. Schindler & Toman, THE LAWS OF ARMED CONFLICTS, *supra* note 2, at 56, rely on THE HAGUE CONVENTIONS AND DECLARATIONS OF 1899 AND 1907, at 100-32 (James Brown Scott ed., 3d ed. 1918), that reproduced the US Department of State Convention translations in 22 Stat. 1803 and 36 Stat. 2227. The International Committee of the Red Cross website has had the erroneous version, as do ARAI-TAKAHASHI, *supra* note 6, at 91 and the long-influential 2 LASSA OPPENHEIM, INTERNATIONAL LAW § 169 n.4 (Hersch Lauterpacht ed., 1952). FM 27-10, *supra* note 12, *Foreword* recognizes that French is the Hague treaties' official language. *Id.* ¶ 363 recites the erroneous English-language Hague IV, *supra* note 7, Regulations, art. 43 version. UK MANUAL, *supra* note 8, ¶ 11.25 seems to rely on the erroneous translation.

US courts apply treaties' authentic language. Eastern Airlines v. Floyd, 499 U.S. 530, 534–37 (1991). The Executive and the Congress interpret treaties; courts may interpret them differently from either. *See, e.g.,* Hamdan v. Rumsfeld, 548 U.S. 557, 625–33 (2006) (Third Convention, *supra* note 3, arts. 2, 3); *see also* RESTATEMENT, *supra* note 6, § 326. It is the Supreme Court's interpretation of the laws that counts. United States v. Nixon, 418 U.S. 683, 703–5 (1974) (executive action review); Marbury v. Madison, 5 U.S. (1 Cranch) 137, 177 (1803) (US statute review). International court decisions, e.g., of the International Court of Justice (ICJ), are entitled to great respect, but they do not bind US courts. Medellin v. Texas, 128 S.Ct. 1346, 1358–60 (2008).

21. *See* ARAI-TAKAHASHI, *supra* note 6, at 97–98; BENVENISTI, *supra* note 9, at 12–18; DINSTEIN, *supra* note 6, at 108–9.

22. *See generally* ARAI-TAKAHASHI, *supra* note 6, at 98–113.

23. The French version is the same in both treaties; *compare* Hague II, *supra* note 9, Regulations, art. 43, 22 Stat. 1821, *with* Hague IV, *supra* note 7, Regulations, art. 43, 36 Stat. 2227. Since French is the authentic language of both treaties, it is not clear which is the more accurate English translation, or if a third and more precise English wording should be used. *See supra* notes 14–22 and accompanying text. I am not sufficiently fluent in French to offer comment.

24. ARAI-TAKAHASHI, *supra* note 6, at 93–96; BENVENISTI, *supra* note 9, at 9, 26–29, 182–83 (advocating change in the law if an occupied State's public at large supports it), 209–10. *See also* *id.* 9–14 for the Brussels Declaration and Hague IV, *supra* notes 7, 10, negotiations. Change in the

law based on public support can raise an issue of differences among groups within a State, e.g., different ethnic or religious groups that do not command a majority but are a vocal minority.

25. North Atlantic Treaty, Apr. 4, 1949, 61 Stat. 2241, 34 U.N.T.S. 243 [hereinafter NATO Treaty].

26. Inter-American Treaty of Reciprocal Assistance (Rio Treaty), Sept. 2, 1947, 62 Stat. 1681, 21 U.N.T.S. 77 [hereinafter Rio Pact].

27. Albania, Bulgaria, Croatia, Czech Republic, Estonia, Greece, Iceland, Italy, Latvia, Lithuania, Slovakia, Slovenia, Spain and Turkey are the NATO non-party States. Argentina, Bahamas, Chile, Colombia, Costa Rica, Ecuador, Honduras, Paraguay, Peru, Trinidad and Tobago, Uruguay and Venezuela are the Rio Pact non-party States. United States Department of State, Treaties in Force: A List of Treaties and Other International Agreements of the United States of America on January 1, 2009, at 410, 343–44, 438–40 (2009) [hereinafter TIF].

28. *Id.* at 438–40 (NATO: Albania, Croatia, Czech Republic, Estonia, Iceland, Latvia, Lithuania, Poland, Slovakia and Slovenia; Rio Pact: Bahamas, Costa Rica, and Trinidad and Tobago).

29. George K. Walker, *The Lawfulness of Operation Enduring Freedom's Self-Defense Responses*, 37 VALPARAISO LAW REVIEW 489, 498–500 (2003).

30. For the United States, TIF, *supra* note 27, printed annually but also on the Department of State website.

31. *See supra* notes 7–9 and accompanying text.

32. *See supra* notes 7–9, 14–15 and accompanying text.

33. The last scenario could have arisen in World War II; Bulgaria and Italy were Hague II, *supra* note 9, parties and not Hague IV, *supra* note 7, parties and were subject to occupation law for a while. When the Allies invaded and occupied Sicily and southern Italy, Italy was German's ally; when the Benito Mussolini government fell in Italy and a new Italian government declared war on Germany, the rest of northern Italy controlled by Germany became subject to occupation law under Germany and, as the Allies moved north into Italy, Allied occupation law under various sovereigns applied. BENVENISTI, *supra* note 9, at 84–91; DINSTEIN, *supra* note 6, at 37. As the Allies moved into Europe from the east (USSR forces) and the west (primarily UK, US forces), parts of other States allied with them—parts of Belgium, Denmark (Greenland), France until establishment of the Charles de Gaulle government, Greece, Iceland (first as a Denmark possession and later after its declaration of independence during World War II), Luxembourg, Netherlands, Poland, etc.—were subject to occupation by consent of governments in exile; belligerent occupation rules did not apply. The same applied to colonial areas Japan conquered that the Allies liberated in the Pacific theater; after annexing Manchuria, Japan established puppet governments for its conquests. The Allies restored colonies to their European sovereigns. BENVENISTI, *supra* note 9, at 60–66; DINSTEIN, *supra* note 6, at 37, 46–47. Italy's colonies and conquests were subjected to occupation. BENVENISTI, *supra* note 9, at 72–81.

34. Another issue is the scope of custom the Nuremberg and Tokyo judgments stated. Nuremberg was decided under Agreement for the Prosecution and Punishment of the Major War Criminals of the European Axis Powers and Charter of the International Military Tribunal, Aug. 8, 1945, 59 Stat. 1544, 82 U.N.T.S. 279; parties were France, Great Britain, the USSR and the United States. The International Tribunal tried high-ranking Nazi officials; other accuseds went before military commissions. For Japan, accuseds went before military commissions in Tokyo and elsewhere in Asia and territories Japan occupied during World War II. The US Navy conducted some. George E. Erickson, Jr., *United States Navy War Crimes Trials*, 5 WASHBURN LAW JOURNAL 89 (1965). Although it might be argued that only those States and their nationals involved in the trials were thereafter governed by customary rules the trials declared, Resolution 95, *supra* note 8, unanimously reaffirmed the Nuremberg and Tokyo principles. The *Nuclear*

Weapons, 2005 *Congo* and *Wall* Cases, *supra* note 8, shut the door on claims of lack of a customary norm or a variant on Nuremberg standards but do not erase issues of divergence, if any, between custom and Hague II and Hague IV and later interpretations of them. The three ICJ cases closed the gap, if it ever existed.

35. *See* DINSTEIN, *supra* note 6, at 90, 108–9, commenting on Hague IV, *supra* note 7, Regulations, art. 43. Since the Hague II, *supra* note 9, Regulations, art. 43 phrase is the same, the same construction should apply.

36. Progressive development is a term in the law of treaties; *see, e.g.*, IAN SINCLAIR, THE VIENNA CONVENTION ON THE LAW OF TREATIES 17–18 (2d ed. 1984) (comment on Vienna Convention on the Law of Treaties arts. 53, 64, 71, May 23, 1969, 1155 U.N.T.S. 331 [hereinafter Vienna Convention] status of standards for applying *jus cogens*). Progressive development, perhaps termed "innovative," can also be seen in secondary sources. *See, e.g.*, SAN REMO MANUAL ON INTERNATIONAL LAW APPLICABLE TO ARMED CONFLICTS AT SEA ¶ 136(g) & cmt. 136.1 (Louise Doswald-Beck ed., 1995) [hereinafter SAN REMO MANUAL]. *De lege ferenda*, sometimes styled *lex ferenda*, relates to the law as it should be; its antonym is *lex lata*, law as it presently is. Vienna Convention, *supra*, is in force for 109 States. Vienna Convention on the Law of Treaties Between States & International Organizations or Between International Organizations arts. 53, 64, 71, 73, 85, Mar. 21, 1986, 25 INTERNATIONAL LAW MATERIALS 543, is not in force but recites similar rules on this point and is subject to the Vienna Convention, *supra*. UN-related IGOs have ratified it, suggesting that it too must be considered if dealing with one of these IGOs. United Nations, Multilateral Treaties Deposited with the Secretary-General: Status of Treaties XXXIII-1, 3, http://treaties.un.org/Pages/Treaties.aspx?id=23&subid=A&lang=en (last visited Sept. 20, 2009) [hereinafter Multilateral Treaties].

37. Through Hague II and Hague IV, *supra* notes 7, 9, Regulations, art. 43's "laws" rules; *see supra* notes 14–21 and accompanying text. A debate, now maybe settled by ICJ judgments, continues on whether and under what circumstances human rights law applies during armed conflict, or whether the LOAC is *lex specialis*; i.e., in LOAC-governed situations, human rights law does not apply. *See infra* notes 104, 116 and accompanying text.

38. DINSTEIN, *supra* note 6, at 108–9 says that an occupied State's government can continue to legislate for occupied territory even after occupation begins. An occupier can concur with an occupied State's views, but the occupier has a full right to legislate for the territory.

39. BENVENISTI, *supra* note 9, at ix–x; DINSTEIN, *supra* note 6, at 12.

40. DINSTEIN, *supra* note 6, at 90–91, 110–16, advocates reading Fourth Convention, *supra* note 2, art. 64, to allow amending existing law, criminal or civil, if occupier security interests are at stake, occupied State law is inconsistent with Fourth Convention obligations, civilian population needs must be met ("Article 64's orderly government"), or maybe other changes under the Hague IV, *supra* note 7, Regulations, art. 43 "unless absolutely prevented" exception. FM 27-10, *supra* note 12, ¶¶ 369–70 recite Article 64 and say that "[i]n restoring public order and safety, the occupant will continue the ordinary civil and penal (criminal) laws of the occupied territory except to the extent it may be authorized by [Fourth Convention, *supra*, art. 64; Hague IV, *supra* note 7, Regulations, art. 43] . . . to alter, suspend, or repeal such laws," referring also to Hague IV, *supra* note 7, Regulations, art. 23(h). FM 27-10, *supra* note 12, ¶ 371 declares an occupier may

> alter, repeal, or suspend laws of the following types:
>
> *a.* Legislation constituting a threat to its security, such as laws relating to recruitment and the bearing of arms.
>
> *b.* Legislation dealing with political process, such as laws regarding the suffrage and of assembly.

c. Legislation the enforcement of which would be inconsistent with the duties of the occupant, such as laws establishing racial discrimination.

This seems to go further than Dinstein's interpretation and seems consistent with a view that occupiers may, by suppressing such laws, in effect promote human rights standards. *See, e.g.*, ARAI-TAKAHASHI, *supra* note 6, at 116–36; BENVENISTI, *supra* note 9, at 187–89, 210–11; MCDOUGAL & FELICIANO, *supra* note 19, at 767–71; 2 OPPENHEIM, *supra* note 20, §§ 172–72b. UK MANUAL, *supra* note 8, ¶¶ 11.19, 11.25.1 and 11.60, read together, seem to conclude similarly. Gasser, *supra* note 13, at 254–56, also citing Fourth Convention, *supra*, art. 64, says occupiers must keep national laws in force but that laws serving the purpose of warfare in the occupied territory or that are a threat to security or an obstacle to applying humanitarian law may be repealed or suspended, noting differing views. Gasser's view seems contradicted at Gasser, *supra* note 13, at 247–48 when he declares, following Protocol I, Article 75, that discrimination against civilians for reasons of race, nationality, language, religious convictions and practices, political opinion, social origin or position or similar considerations is unlawful. An occupier violates this rule if it keeps national laws of an occupied State in force that would inflict these kinds of discrimination.

41. *See* DINSTEIN, *supra* note 6, at 80–81.

42. *Id.* at 121.

43. BENVENISTI, *supra* note 9, at 14–15, 187–89, 210–11 (human rights standards may be guide for occupation law); *see also supra* note 40 (others seem to allow more progressive approach).

44. FM 27-10, *supra* note 12, ¶ 380, *quoting* Hague IV, *supra* note 7, Regulations, art. 46; *compare* Hague II, *supra* note 9, Regulations, art. 46; *see also* FM 27-10, *supra* note 12, ¶ 406. It must be noted, however, that citing Hague IV, *supra* note 7, and Fourth Convention, *supra* note 2, provisions in FM 27-10, *supra* note 12, ¶¶ 381–87 suggests that the drafters had a more restrictive view in 1956, i.e., what they meant was humanitarian law and not today's human rights law.

45. *E.g.*, FM 27-10, *supra* note 12, ¶ 377, declares an occupier's broad right to impose media censorship, without citing authority. International Covenant on Civil & Political Rights art. 19, Dec. 16, 1966, 999 U.N.T.S. 171 [hereinafter ICCPR], declares a right to expression of opinion in writing or in print, subject to "certain restrictions . . . provided by law and [which] are necessary." *Id.*, art. 4 allows derogations from this right "[i]n time of public emergency which threatens the life of the nation and the existence of which is officially proclaimed . . . to the extent strictly required by the exigencies of the situation . . . ," a derogation provision in human rights treaties. *See infra* notes 109–21 and accompanying text. How should an occupier apply censorship in the light of human rights law? Are the rules the same under occupation law and human rights law? A further problem, upon which authorities divide, is whether human rights law applies extraterritorially, such that occupier State personnel carry with them human rights obligations of their country into an occupied State. *Compare* ARAI-TAKAHASHI, *supra* note 6, ch. 21 (they do); DINSTEIN, *supra* note 6, at 70 (they do not).

46. ARAI-TAKAHASHI, *supra* note 6, at 65–67; BENVENISTI, *supra* note 9, at 184–87; DINSTEIN, *supra* note 6, at 51–52; *see also* U.N. Charter arts. 1(2), 55–56; LELAND F. GOODRICH ET AL., CHARTER OF THE UNITED NATIONS 29–34, 371–82 (3d rev. ed. 1969); Rudiger Wolfrum, *Self-Determination, in* THE CHARTER OF THE UNITED NATIONS 47–63 (Bruno Simma ed., 2d ed. 2002).

47. Fourth Convention, *supra* note 2, art. 158; *see also* First Convention, *supra* note 3, art. 63; Second Convention, *supra* note 3, art. 62; Third Convention, *supra* note 3, art. 142. As 1 PICTET, *supra* note 11, at 413; 2 PICTET, *supra* note 11, at 283; 3 PICTET, *supra* note 11, at 47, 648 and 4 PICTET, *supra* note 11, at 625, explain, Martens clauses bind Convention parties, even though they denounce the Convention(s), by the principles in them insofar as they express inalienable

and universal international law rules. *See also* Hague II, *supra* note 9, pmbl.; Hague IV, *supra* note 7, pmbl.; SAN REMO MANUAL, *supra* note 36, ¶ 2; INSTITUTE OF INTERNATIONAL LAW, THE APPLICATION OF INTERNATIONAL HUMANITARIAN LAW AND FUNDAMENTAL HUMAN RIGHTS IN ARMED CONFLICTS IN WHICH NON-STATE ENTITIES ARE PARTIES ¶ 4 (Aug. 25, 1999), *reprinted in* THE LAWS OF ARMED CONFLICTS, *supra* note 2, at 1205, 1207; INSTITUTE FOR HUMAN RIGHTS, DECLARATION OF MINIMUM HUMANITARIAN STANDARDS pmbl. (Nov. 30–Dec. 2, 1990), *reprinted in id.* at 1199, 1200; ARAI-TAKAHASHI, *supra* note 6, at 68–71(ICJ cases support view that clauses restate customary international law); MICHAEL BOTHE ET AL., NEW RULES FOR VICTIMS OF ARMED CONFLICT 44 (1982); LESLIE C. GREEN, THE CONTEMPORARY LAW OF ARMED CONFLICT 17–18, 34, 349 (2d ed. 2000); Greenwood, *supra* note 8, § 129(2) (clauses' impact difficult to assess). A preamble is not part of a treaty's binding language but may explicate its object and purpose. Vienna Convention, *supra* note 36, art. 31(2); *see also* ANTHONY AUST, MODERN TREATY LAW AND PRACTICE 235–38 (2d ed. 2007); SINCLAIR, *supra* note 36, at 127–28, 130.

48. Protocol I, *supra* note 13, art. 1(2) (customary law, Martens clause protection). State Parties, *supra* note 4, lists 168 States as Protocol I parties compared with 194 for the 1949 Conventions; many are or were US alliance or coalition partners in Afghanistan or Iraq. *See also* DINSTEIN, supra note 6, at 7 ("determined minority" of non-ratifying States for Protocol I); *supra* notes 25–28 and accompanying text.

49. ARAI-TAKAHASHI, *supra* note 6, at 71, 657–60 thinks so.

50. *Cf.* UK MANUAL, *supra* note 8, ¶ 11.3.3. The coalition had joint responsibility for areas under its effective control in Iraq during 2003–4. DINSTEIN, *supra* note 6, at 48.

51. If each occupying power has a separate zone to administer, as in Germany and Austria after World War II, each power is responsible under occupation law for its zone. *Id.* at 48–49. This does not respond to the issue of different interpretations and applications of the laws, including new legal regimes to replace what may have been laws like those in force in Nazi Germany. In zonal occupations, as in coalition occupations, the occupying powers should reach consensus on new legal regimes, looking to when an occupied State regains full sovereignty.

52. *See supra* note 39 and accompanying text.

53. *See infra* notes 69, 78–81 and accompanying text.

54. Although precedent (*stare decisis*) is an entrenched common law principle, States, including NATO and Rio Pact, *supra* notes 25, 26, countries, may adhere to a civil law standard like ICJ Statute, *supra* note 6, art. 59, declaring that a judgment only binds States before the Court and only for the particular case.

55. There are others, *e.g.*, U.N. Charter art. 17(1) (General Assembly must approve UN budget); *see also* GOODRICH ET AL., *supra* note 46, at 148–67; THE CHARTER OF THE UNITED NATIONS, *supra* note 46, at 334–36.

56. U.N. Charter arts. 25, 48, 94(2), 103; *see also* DINSTEIN, *supra* note 6, at 273; GOODRICH ET AL., *supra* note 46, at 207–11, 334–37, 555–59, 614–17; SAN REMO MANUAL, *supra* note 36, ¶¶ 7–9; THE CHARTER OF THE UNITED NATIONS, *supra* note 46, at 454–62, 776–80, 1174–79, 1292–1302; W. Michael Reisman, *The Constitutional Crisis in the United Nations*, 87 AMERICAN JOURNAL OF INTERNATIONAL LAW 83, 87 (1993) (principles from Council decisions under arts. 25, 48, 103 are treaty law binding UN members, overriding other treaty obligations).

57. U.N. Charter arts. 51, 103; *see also* GOODRICH ET AL., *supra* note 46, at 342–53; THE CHARTER OF THE UNITED NATIONS, *supra* note 46, at 778–806. U.N. Charter art. 2(1) recognizes the principle of State sovereignty, traditionally interpreted to mean that in the absence of governing law, States may act in their interest. *See also* GOODRICH ET AL., *supra* note 46, at 36–40; THE CHARTER OF THE UNITED NATIONS, *supra* note 46, at 68–91. In the case of self-defense, it

is more than self-interest; it is an inherent right the Charter enshrines under Articles 51 and 103. Debate continues on whether the right of self-defense includes a right of anticipatory self-defense and, more recently, claims of a right to take preemptive action. *See generally* George K. Walker, *Filling Some of the Gaps: The International Law Association (American Branch) Law of the Sea Definitions Project*, 32 FORDHAM INTERNATIONAL LAW JOURNAL 1336, 1355–56 nn.102–3 (2009).

National sovereignty, sometimes diminished or eroded, has been a fundamental principle since the Peace of Westphalia. Treaty of Peace of Münster, Fr.-Holy Rom. Empire, art. 64, Oct. 24, 1648, 1 Consol. T.S. 198, 319; Treaty of Peace of Osnabrück, Swed.-Holy Rom. Empire, art. 9, Oct. 24, 1648, *id.* at 119, 198; *see also* CHRISTIAN L. WIKTOR, MULTILATERAL TREATY CALENDAR 1648–1995, at 3 (1998). The Peace of Westphalia began the modern State system. Leo Gross, *The Peace of Westphalia, 1648–1948*, 42 AMERICAN JOURNAL OF INTERNATIONAL LAW 20 (1948). Treaties besides the U.N. Charter art. 2(1) ("sovereign equality" of UN members) and decisions invoking the sovereignty principle include the UN Convention on the Law of the Sea art. 157(3), Dec. 10, 1982, 1833 U.N.T.S. 3 [hereinafter LOS Convention]; Vienna Convention, *supra* note 36, pmbl.; S.S. Lotus (Fr. v. Turk.), 1927 P.C.I.J. (ser. A), No. 10, at 4, 18; S.S. Wimbledon (U.K. v. Ger.), 1923 *id.*, No. 1, at 15, 25; *see also* Declaration on Principles of International Law Concerning Friendly Relations & Co-Operation Among States in Accordance with the Charter of the United Nations, Principle 6, G.A. Res. 2625, U.N. GAOR, 25th Sess., Supp. No. 28, U.N. Doc. A/8028 (1970); Declaration on Inadmissibility of Intervention in Domestic Affairs of States & Protection of Their Independence & Sovereignty, G.A. Res. 2131, U.N. GAOR, 20th Sess., U.N. Doc. A/RES/2131 (1965); the Secretary-General, *A More Secure World: Our Shared Responsibility: Report of the Secretary-General's High-Level Panel on Threats, Challenges and Change*, ¶ 29, U.N. Doc. A/59/565 (2004) (States accepting UN Charter benefit of "privileges of sovereignty . . . [must] also accept its responsibilities"); the Secretary-General, *An Agenda for Peace: Report of the Secretary-General on the Work of the Organization*, U.N. Doc. A/49/277, S/24111 (1992); MICHAEL AKEHURST, A MODERN INTRODUCTION TO INTERNATIONAL LAW 21–23 (Brian Chapman ed., 3d ed. 1977); JAMES L. BRIERLY, THE LAW OF NATIONS 45–49 (Humphrey Waldock ed., 6th ed. 1963); BROWNLIE, *supra* note 6, at 287–89; GOODRICH ET AL., *supra* note 46, at 36–40; OPPENHEIM'S INTERNATIONAL LAW, *supra* note 6, §§ 37, 107; LORD MCNAIR, THE LAW OF TREATIES 754–66 (1961); RESTATEMENT, *supra* note 6, Part I, ch. 1, *Introductory Note*, 16 & 17; THE CHARTER OF THE UNITED NATIONS, *supra* at 70–91; R.P. Anand, *Sovereign Equality of States in International Law*, 197 RECUEIL DES COURS D'ACADEMIE DE DROIT INTERNATIONAL [R.C.A.D.I.] 9, 22–51 (1986); Boutros Boutros-Ghali, *Empowering the United Nations*, FOREIGN AFFAIRS, Winter 1992, at 89, 98–99; Jonathan I. Charney, *Universal International Law*, 87 AMERICAN JOURNAL OF INTERNATIONAL LAW 529, 539 (1993); Gerald Fitzmaurice, *The General Principles of International Law Considered from the Standpoint of the Rule of Law*, 92 RECUEIL DES COURS D'ACADEMIE DE DROIT INTERNATIONAL [R.C.A.D.I.] 1, 49–50 (1957); Louis Henkin, *International Law: Politics, Values and Functions*, 216, *id.* at 9, 46, 130 (1989); Oscar Schachter, *International Law in Theory and Practice*, 178, *id.* at 9, 32 (1982); C.H.M. Waldock, *General Course on Public International Law*, 106, *id.* at 1, 156–72 (1962). Sovereignty is a debatable issue today. HENRY KISSINGER, DOES AMERICA NEED A FOREIGN POLICY? TOWARD A DIPLOMACY FOR THE 21ST CENTURY 21–22, 235–37 (2001) declared that the sovereignty concept was in trouble; Henkin, *supra*, had earlier recognized sovereignty's force, but in LOUIS HENKIN, INTERNATIONAL LAW: POLITICS AND VALUES 8–10 (1995) denounced it.

58. There are differences among countries on the law of self-defense. *See supra* note 57 and accompanying text. Even this "easy" case might raise perceptions of equal justice. There are also

possibilities of renewed hostilities, or outbreak of new hostilities, where the LOAC, and not necessarily self-defense, is involved. *See generally* ARAI-TAKAHASHI, *supra* note 6, ch. 12.

59. *Cf.* Fourth Convention, *supra* note 2, arts. 64, 66; Hague II, *supra* note 9, Regulations, art. 43; Hague IV, *supra* note 7, Regulations, art. 43; FM 27-10, *supra* note 12, ¶ 374; ARAI-TAKAHASHI, *supra* note 6, at 157–62; DINSTEIN, *supra* note 6, at 137; 4 PICTET, *supra* note 11, at 334–37, 339–41; Gasser, *supra* note 13, at 273–77. For US forces and others subject to it, it is the Uniform Code of Military Justice, 10 U.S.C. §§ 801–946 (2009) [hereinafter UCMJ].

60. Fourth Convention, *supra* note 2, arts. 64, 66; Hague II, *supra* note 9, Regulations, art. 43; Hague IV, *supra* note 7, Regulations, art. 43; ARAI-TAKAHASHI, *supra* note 6, at 162–84; DINSTEIN, *supra* note 6, at 136–37; 4 PICTET, *supra* note 11, at 334–37, 339–41.

61. *Cf.* Fourth Convention, *supra* note 2, art. 64; Hague II, *supra* note 9, Regulations, art. 43; Hague IV, *supra* note 7, Regulations, art. 43; DINSTEIN, *supra* note 6, at 132–34; 4 PICTET, *supra* note 11, at 337; Gasser, *supra* note 13, at 271–72.

62. *E.g.*, UCMJ, *supra* note 59, art. 2, § 802, is premised on the nationality jurisdiction principle, i.e., a State's criminal laws follow those the Code covers wherever they go. BROWNLIE, *supra* note 6, at 300–304; OPPENHEIM'S INTERNATIONAL LAW, *supra* note 6, §§ 137–38; RESTATEMENT, *supra* note 6, §§ 402(1), 402(2).

63. To be sure, the differences can be erased in terms of law on the books if an occupier State promulgates changes to local law in conformity with its standards, but a perception might persist among an occupied State's legal community and its constituents, particularly if the differences are great. Local law refers to a jurisdiction's law exclusive of its conflict of laws, or private international law, principles. RESTATEMENT (SECOND) OF CONFLICT OF LAWS § 4(1) (1971, 1988 rev.) [hereinafter RESTATEMENT (SECOND)]; EUGENE F. SCOLES ET AL., CONFLICT OF LAWS § 2.1 (4th ed. 2004). Lieber Code, *supra* note 10, art. 43, declared prize money would be paid according to "local law," presumably the captor's law. *See also infra* note 144 and accompanying text.

64. DINSTEIN, *supra* note 6, at 99–107 (civilians can be Fourth Convention, *supra* note 2, art. 73, protected persons but become combatants subject to the LOAC if they participate as part of an attacking force, then revert to protected status as civilians).

65. This is subject to Fourth Convention authority to try them in special military courts and under lawful changes an occupier State might make in occupied State law. *See supra* note 60 and accompanying text.

66. S.C. Res. 1368, U.N. Doc. S/RES/1368 (Sept. 12, 2001); S.C. Res. 1373, U.N. Doc. S/RES/1373 (Sept. 28, 2001); United Nations Global Counter-Terrorism Strategy, G.A. Res. 60/288, U.N. Doc. A/RES/60/288 (Sept. 20, 2006); Protocol I, *supra* note 13, art. 51(2); Protocol Additional to the Geneva Conventions of 12 August 1949, and Relating to the Protection of Victims of Non-International Armed Conflicts arts. 4(2)(d), 13(2), June 8, 1977, 1125 U.N.T.S. 609, *reprinted in* THE LAWS OF ARMED CONFLICTS, *supra* note 2, at 775 [hereinafter Protocol II]; INSTITUTE FOR HUMAN RIGHTS, *supra* note 47, art. 6; Commission of Jurists, Hague Rules Concerning Air Warfare art. 22, Feb. 17, 1923, *reprinted in* THE LAWS OF ARMED CONFLICTS, *supra* note 2, at 315, 317; International Institute of Humanitarian Law, Declaration on the Rules of International Humanitarian Law Governing the Conduct of Hostilities in Non-International Armed Conflicts art. A2, Apr. 7, 1990, *in id.* at 1195, 1196; *see also* BOTHE ET AL., *supra* note 47, at 300–301, 677–78; BROWNLIE, *supra* note 6, at 745; OPPENHEIM'S INTERNATIONAL LAW, *supra* note 6, § 122, at 401–3; NWP 1-14M ANNOTATED, *supra* note 8, ¶¶ 8.5.1.2, 11.3; RESTATEMENT, *supra* note 6, § 404 (State-sponsored terrorism may be a universal crime); COMMENTARY ON THE ADDITIONAL PROTOCOLS OF 8 JUNE 1977 TO THE GENEVA CONVENTIONS OF 1977, at 618, 1375, 1453 (Yves Sandoz, Christophe Swinarski & Bruno Zimmerman eds., 1987). A caveat is

that terrorists' trials might be in special military courts or local courts in an occupied State under occupier or occupied State law, which might differ from international standards. *See supra* notes 60, 65, *infra* note 67 and accompanying text.

67. Pub. L. No. 109-366, 120 Stat. 2600, *inter alia* codified as 10 U.S.C. §§ 948a–950w (2009).

68. The problem can be largely eliminated in coalition or alliance operations if coalition or allied forces operate in defined areas, e.g., the UK and US sectors in Iraq and zones in occupied Germany and Austria after World War II, or if one country is the occupier State, as was the situation in Japan after World War II. There are no reported issues of this nature involving other States that sent forces to Iraq as part of the coalition. Agreements among occupier States, like status of forces agreements with rules on primary jurisdiction, might resolve issues among States, but a problem of occupied State and international perceptions might remain.

69. For the 2003 Iraq coalition, UN Security Council Resolutions 1483, S.C. Res. 1483, U.N. Doc. S/RES/1483 (May 22, 2003); 1511, S.C. Res. 1511, U.N. Doc. S/RES/1511 (Oct. 16, 2003); and 1546, S.C. Res. 1546, U.N. Doc. S/RES/1546 (June 8, 2004), were the chartering documents, recognizing the Coalition Provisional Authority and the occupation's end. For commentary on Iraq after occupation ended, *see generally* Andrea Carcano, *End of the Occupation in 2004? The Status of the Multinational Force in Iraq After the Transfer of Sovereignty to the Interim Iraqi Government*, 11 JOURNAL OF CONFLICT & SECURITY LAW 41 (2006), then (in 2005) arguing that the Interim Government did not meet sovereignty standards and that the coalition continued as occupiers. *See also infra* notes 78–81 and accompanying text.

70. *Cf.* BENVENISTI, *supra* note 9, at 20–21. An example is a criminal trial penalty phase where occupier State law allows the death penalty, perhaps under the LOAC, human rights law and occupied State law would not, following conviction for violating the law of war. *Cf.* FM 27-10, *supra* note 12, ¶ 508 (death penalty possible for grave breaches); *but see also* Fourth Convention, *supra* note 2, art. 75; Protocol I, *supra* note 13, art. 75(4); FM 27-10, *supra* note 12, ¶ 445; 4 PICTET, *supra* note 11, at 361–63; Gasser, *supra* note 13, at 274. A similar issue is if occupier State law allows capital punishment, human rights law does not, and occupier State law prescribes an execution method different from occupier State law. A common execution method under US law is lethal injection; other States might use methods not compatible with, *e.g.*, U.S. CONST. amend. VIII.

71. U.N. Charter arts. 10–11, 13–14 (provisions for Assembly recommendations), 33, 36–37 (Chapter VI provisions for possible Council action), 39–51 (Chapter VII provisions for situations involving breaches of the peace or threats to international peace and security and the inherent right of individual and collective self-defense and possible Council action).

72. SYDNEY D. BAILEY & SAM DAWS, THE PROCEDURE OF THE UN SECURITY COUNCIL 18–21, 236–37 (3d ed. 1998); BROWNLIE, *supra* note 6, at 14; JORGE CASTENADA, LEGAL EFFECTS OF UNITED NATIONS RESOLUTIONS 78–79 (Alba Amoia trans., 1969); GOODRICH ET AL., *supra* note 46, at 111–29, 133–44, 257–65, 277–87, 290–314; OPPENHEIM'S INTERNATIONAL LAW, *supra* note 6, § 16; RESTATEMENT, *supra* note 6, § 103(2)(d) & r.n.2; THE CHARTER OF THE UNITED NATIONS, *supra* note 46, at 257–87, 298–326, 583–94, 616–43, 717–49.

73. *See* W. Michael Reisman, *Acting Before Victims Become Victims: Preventing and Arresting Mass Murder*, 40 CASE WESTERN RESERVE JOURNAL OF INTERNATIONAL LAW 57, 72–73 (2007–2008), citing Uniting for Peace Resolution, G.A. Res. 377, ¶ 1, U.N. Doc. A.1775 (Nov. 3, 1950), employed during the Korean War to continue UN operations; Wall Case, *supra* note 8, 2004 I.C.J. at 148–51 (adv. op.); Certain Expenses of the United Nations, 1952 I.C.J. 151, 163–71 (adv. op.); *compare* Joseph Isanga, *Counter-Terrorism and Human Rights: The Emergence of a Rule of Customary International Law from U.N. Resolutions*, 32 DENVER JOURNAL OF INTERNATIONAL LAW & POLICY 233, 238–49 (2009), *also citing* 2005 Congo Case, *supra* note 8, 2005 I.C.J. at 53–54;

Nuclear Weapons, *supra* note 8, 1996 I.C.J. at 254–55; Military & Paramilitary Activities in & Against Nicaragua (Nicar. v. U.S.), 1986 I.C.J. 14, 99–108 (June 27) [hereinafter Nicaragua Case]. *See also* GEORGE K. WALKER, THE TANKER WAR, 1980–88: LAW AND POLICY 175–77 (2000) (Vol. 74, US Naval War College International Law Studies). Otherwise-non-binding Council resolutions, e.g., calls for action under Chapter VII, *supra* notes 55–57 and accompanying text, could evolve into a customary norm. Isanga, *supra* at 240, citing 2005 Congo Case, *supra* note 8, at 53–54; Wall Case, *supra* at 171.

The Supreme Court of the United States has held differently on another important General Assembly resolution, the Universal Declaration of Human Rights, G.A. Res. 217A, at 71, U.N. GAOR, 3d Sess., 1st plen. mtg., U.N. Doc. A/810 (Dec. 10, 1948). Sosa v. Alvarez-Machain, 542 U.S. 692, 734 n.12 (2004), declined to accept the Declaration as part of US customary international law because the US UN Permanent Representative, Eleanor Roosevelt, had declared the Declaration was not a binding standard. Filartiga v. Pena-Irala, 630 F.2d 876, 887 (2d Cir. 1980), reached a different conclusion on State-sponsored torture. DINSTEIN, *supra* note 6, at 68 and Committee on the Enforcement of Human Rights Law, International Law Association, *Final Report on the Status of the Universal Declaration of Human Rights in National and International Law*, Report of the 66th Conference 523, 544 (1994) say many Declaration provisions reflect customary international law. This illustrates dilemmas for US and other national decisionmakers; choices made in conformity with national law standards may not be the same as public international law norms or as the law as perceived by allied States. A related issue has been the growth of "soft law," i.e., standards, perhaps coming from an IGO, a non-binding agreement or a non-governmental organization (NGO), that deserve consideration, even if they may not have source of law status. AUST, *supra* note 47, at 52–53.

74. General principles of law are another primary international law source. ICJ Statute, *supra* note 6, art. 38(1)(c); BROWNLIE, *supra* note 6, at 19, 15–27; OPPENHEIM'S INTERNATIONAL LAW, *supra* note 6, § 12; *but see* RESTATEMENT, *supra* note 6, §§ 102(1)(c), 102(4) & cmt. *l* (general principles a subsidiary source).

75. *See supra* notes 47–49 and accompanying text.

76. Vienna Convention, *supra* note 36, art. 31(3)(b) may give an answer. It provides that subsequent practice under a treaty, and presumably an *ipso facto* binding UN resolution emanating from the Charter (which is a treaty), establishes the parties' agreement on application of the treaty. A longstanding view has been, however, that treaties and custom are coequal in status; *see* ICJ Statute, *supra* note 6, art. 38(1); RESTATEMENT, *supra* note 6, § 102. A custom coming later in time might trump an earlier, inconsistent treaty, particularly if it is in desuetude. AUST, *supra* note 47, at 14; BROWNLIE, *supra* note 6, at 5; RESTATEMENT, *supra* note 6, § 102 r.n.4. Whether these construction principles apply to Charter law situations is not clear. A reconciliation is that there may be a clear difference between the newer custom and the older treaty, such that Article 31(3)(b) does not apply.

77. *Cf.* Nicaragua Case, *supra* note 73, 1986 I.C.J. at 94.

78. S.C. Res. 1483, *supra* note 69.

79. S.C. Res. 1546, *supra* note 69; for questions related to self-defense issues possibly arising during an occupation, *see supra* notes 57–70 and accompanying text.

80. U.N. Charter arts. 25, 48, 103; *see also supra* notes 55–57 and accompanying text.

81. DINSTEIN, *supra* note 6, at 273. What began in 2004 was another kind of occupation—occupation by consent of the government of Iraq and not belligerent occupation under the LOAC, subject to Security Council Resolution 1546, *supra* note 69, standards. DINSTEIN, *supra* note 6, at 36 (citing pre-Charter examples), 273. The Fourth Convention/Hague IV, *supra* notes 2, 7, regime ended June 30, 2004. There can be UN forces occupation with host country consent

or in a kind of trusteeship; these are not belligerent occupations unless there is UN enforcement action, as distinguished from peacekeeping operations. DINSTEIN, *supra* note 6, at 38; Michael Bothe, *Peace-Keeping*, *in* THE CHARTER OF THE UNITED NATIONS, *supra* note 46, at 648, 683. These operations, often governed by Council decision but perhaps other UN resolutions, *see supra* notes 55–57 and accompanying text, may draw from the LOAC of belligerent occupation for their governance standards.

82. For analysis of "due notice" in the law of the sea (LOS) context, *see* LAW OF THE SEA COMMITTEE, *Report*, *in* PROCEEDINGS OF THE AMERICAN BRANCH OF THE INTERNATIONAL LAW ASSOCIATION 2007–2008, at 217–20 (2008) [hereinafter LOS Committee Report].

83. The Executive Board is WHO's executive arm, very roughly analogous to the UN Security Council. Constitution of the World Health Organization arts. 10, 19, 21–22, 24–37, 59–60, July 22, 1946, 62 Stat. 2679, 14 U.N.T.S. 185. E.g., Iraq, the United Kingdom and the United States are WHO members, but there may not be a common matrix of conventions, agreements or regulations among these countries. TIF, *supra* note 27, at 370–72.

84. *Cf.* BROWNLIE, *supra* note 6, at 691–92; OPPENHEIM'S INTERNATIONAL LAW, *supra* note 6, § 16; RESTATEMENT, *supra* note 6, §§ 102, 103(2)(c), cmt. c & r.n. 1; *supra* notes 73–74 and accompanying text.

85. Vienna Convention, *supra* note 36, arts. 34–38; AUST, *supra* note 47, ch. 14; BROWNLIE, *supra* note 6, at 627–29; OPPENHEIM'S INTERNATIONAL LAW, *supra* note 6, §§ 626–27; MCNAIR, *supra* note 57, ch. 16; RESTATEMENT, *supra* note 6, § 323.

86. *See supra* note 36 and accompanying text.

87. *See supra* note 73.

88. U.N. Charter arts. 51, 103; *see also supra* notes 55–57 and accompanying text. This is not as far-fetched as it might seem. In 1805 as part of Third Coalition actions against Napoleon Bonaparte, the commander of Austrian forces in the Italian peninsula established a cordon, "ostensibly" to protect against spread of yellow fever behind his defense lines. FREDERICK W. KAGAN, THE END OF THE OLD ORDER 501 (2006). Although this was a mask for Austrian troop buildup to await enemy attack if it came, suppose an occupier uses forces in self-defense in ways that have an incidental effect of violating health regulations but are reasonable under the circumstances. The right of self-defense would trump WHO rules. However, an occupier might use a factorial approach like that suggested *infra* notes 156–95 and accompanying text to implement self-defense to give partial or total effect to WHO rules.

89. *See supra* notes 55–57 and accompanying text.

90. U.N. Charter art. 103; *see also supra* notes 55–57, 71–73 and accompanying text.

91. *See supra* note 73.

92. An example from the law of naval warfare is the difference, sometimes subtle, between the SAN REMO MANUAL and NWP 1-14M ANNOTATED, *supra* notes 8, 36. Although both deal with LOAC rules for conflicts at sea, which had some resonance in the 2003–4 Iraq situation, another occupation might raise more of these issues.

93. ICJ Statute, *supra* note 6, art. 38(1)(d) (writings of scholars); BROWNLIE, *supra* note 6, at 691–92; OPPENHEIM'S INTERNATIONAL LAW, *supra* note 6, § 16; RESTATEMENT, *supra* note 6, §§ 102, 103(2)(c), cmt. c & r.n. 1,2.

94. *See supra* notes 88–90 and accompanying text.

95. *See generally* BROWNLIE, *supra* note 6, at 510–12 (*jus cogens*' content uncertain); T.O. ELIAS, THE MODERN LAW OF TREATIES 177–87 (1974) (same); OPPENHEIM'S INTERNATIONAL LAW, *supra* note 6, §§ 2, 642, 653 (same); MCNAIR, *supra* note 57, at 214–15 (same); RESTATEMENT, *supra* note 6, §§ 102 r.n. 6,323 cmt. b, 331(2), 338(2) (same); SHABTAI ROSENNE, DEVELOPMENTS IN THE LAW OF TREATIES 1945–1986, at 281–88 (1989); THE CHARTER OF THE

UNITED NATIONS, *supra* note 46, at 62 (dispute over self-determination as *jus cogens*); GRIGORII I. TUNKIN, THEORY OF INTERNATIONAL LAW 98 (William E. Butler trans., 1974) (all of the Charter is *jus cogens*); Levan Alexidze, *Legal Nature of* Jus Cogens *in Contemporary Law*, 172 RECUEIL DES COURS D'ACADEMIE DE DROIT INTERNATIONAL [R.C.A.D.I.] 219, 262–63 (1981); John N. Hazard, *Soviet Tactics in International Lawmaking*, 7 DENVER JOURNAL OF INTERNATIONAL LAW & POLICY 9, 25–29 (1977); Jimenez de Arechaga, *International Law in the Last Third of a Century*, 159 RECUEIL DES COURS D'ACADEMIE DE DROIT INTERNATIONAL [R.C.A.D.I.] 9, 64–67 (1978); Georg Schwarzenberger, *International* Jus Cogens?, 43 TEXAS LAW REVIEW 455 (1978) (*jus cogens* non-existent for self-defense, any other purpose); Dinah Shelton, *Normative Hierarchy in International Law*, 100 AMERICAN JOURNAL OF INTERNATIONAL LAW 291 (2006) (current analysis); Mark Weisburd, *The Emptiness of the Concept of* Jus Cogens, *As Illustrated by the War in Bosnia-Herzegovina*, 17 MICHIGAN JOURNAL OF INTERNATIONAL LAW 1 (1995) (criticizing the concept). An International Law Commission (ILC) study acknowledged primacy of UN Charter Article 103–based law and *jus cogens* but declined to list *jus cogens* norms. International Law Commission, Report on Its Fifty-Seventh Session (May 2–June 3 and July 11–August 5, 2005), U.N. GAOR, 60th Sess., Supp. No. 10, at 221–25, U.N. Doc. A/60/10 (2005) (2005 ILC Rep.); *see also* Michael J. Matheson, *The Fifty-Seventh Session of the International Law Commission*, 100 AMERICAN JOURNAL OF INTERNATIONAL LAW 416, 422 (2006).

96. Nuclear Weapons, *supra* note 8, 1996 I.C.J. at 245 ; Nicaragua Case, *supra* note 73, 1986 I.C.J. at 100–101; *see also Report of the International Law Commission on the Work of its Fifty-third Session*, U.N. GAOR, 56th Sess., Supp. No. 10, art. 50 and Commentary ¶¶ 1–5 at 247–49, U.N. Doc. A/56/10 (2001) [hereinafter Draft Articles on Responsibility of States for Internationally Wrongful Acts], *reprinted in* JAMES CRAWFORD, THE INTERNATIONAL LAW COMMISSION'S ARTICLES ON STATE RESPONSIBILITY 288–89 (2002) ("fundamental substantive obligations"); OPPENHEIM'S INTERNATIONAL LAW, *supra* note 6, § 2 (Art. 2(4) a fundamental norm); RESTATEMENT, *supra* note 6, §§ 102, cmts. h, k; 905(2) & cmt. g (same). The Court is bound by its sources rules, ICJ Statute, *supra* note 6, arts. 38, 59; maybe that is why it did not adopt *jus cogens* for the issue. Armed Activities on the Territory of the Congo (Dem. Rep. of Congo v. Rwanda), 2006 I.C.J. 3, 29–30, 49–50 (Feb. 3) (jurisdiction, admissibility of application) [hereinafter 2006 Congo Case] held a *jus cogens* violation allegation was not enough to deprive the Court of jurisdiction, preliminarily stating that Convention on Prevention & Punishment of Crime of Genocide, Dec. 9, 1948, 78 U.N.T.S. 277 [hereinafter Genocide Convention] represented *erga omnes* obligations; *see also* Application of Convention on Prevention & Punishment of Crime of Genocide (Bosn. & Herz. v. Serb. & Mont.), 2007 I.C.J. 191, ¶ 161 (Feb. 26) [hereinafter Genocide Case], citing 2006 *Congo Case*, *supra*. Vienna Convention, *supra* note 36, art. 53 (declaring *jus cogens* standards), was among other treaties 2006 *Congo Case*, *supra*, cited. While also citing *Nicaragua* and *Nuclear Weapons* cases, *supra* notes 8, 73, Shelton, *supra* note 95, at 305–306 says the 2006 *Congo Case* is the first ICJ case to recognize *jus cogens*, but its holding seems not quite the same as ruling on an issue and applying *jus cogens*. The case compromis included the Vienna Convention, *supra* note 36, which raises *jus cogens* issues that the Court could have decided under that law as well as traditional sources. ICJ Statute, *supra* note 6, arts. 36, 38, 59. Thus the issue technically remains whether the Court will apply *jus cogens* as a separate trumping norm, or whether it will apply *jus cogens* as stronger custom among competing primary sources—treaties, custom, general principles—under *id.*, art. 38(1). If the Court is true to its treaty-based rules, it should opt for the latter analysis. However, it is clear that a case will find the issue before the Court and it is reasonably clear that an appropriate case will find the Court declaring for *jus cogens*, perhaps as trumping custom under *id.*

97. Carin Kahgan, Jus Cogens *and the Inherent Right to Self-Defense,* 3 ILSA JOURNAL OF INTERNATIONAL & COMPARATIVE LAW 767, 823–27 (1997) (U.N. Charter art. 51 represents *jus cogens* norm); *but see* Schwarzenberger, *supra* note 95. Draft Articles on Responsibility of States for Internationally Wrongful Acts, *supra* note 96, art. 21 & Commentary, at 177–80, *reprinted in* CRAWFORD, *supra* note 96, at 166, resolves conflict between UN Charter Articles 2(4) and 51, saying that no Article 2(4) issues arise if there is a lawful self-defense claim, appearing to give Article 51 the same status as Article 2(4). If Article 2(4) has *jus cogens* status, and Article 51 does not, the result would be that a self-defense response, otherwise lawful under Charter or customary law, would violate a *jus cogens* norm in *id.* art. 2(4).

98. Vienna Convention, *supra* note 36, pmbl., arts. 53, 64, 71; *see also* AUST, *supra* note 47, at 319–20; RESTATEMENT, *supra* note 6, §§ 331(2)(b) & cmts. e, f; 338(2) & cmt. c; SINCLAIR, *supra* note 36, at 17–18, 218–26 (Vienna Convention, *supra*, principles considered progressive development in 1984).

99. *See generally* Final Report, *supra* note 8; Symposium, *supra* note 8; Walker, *supra* note 8.

100. TIF, *supra* note 27, is valuable if the United States is a party; Multilateral Treaties, *supra* note 36, may help if the UN Secretary-General is the depository; other treaties list other sites, and still others may be found on unofficial websites, e.g., State Parties, *supra* note 4. Contacting the US Department of State Office of the Legal Adviser (for US researchers) or a State's foreign ministry may also be useful, particularly if there are ongoing negotiations on what treaties are in force.

101. *See supra* notes 12–34, 48 and accompanying text.

102. Vienna Convention, *supra* note 36, art. 60(5). *See generally* Draft Articles on Responsibility of States for Internationally Wrongful Acts, *supra* note 96, art. 40 & Commentary ¶ 8, at 333, 336, *reprinted in* CRAWFORD, *supra* note 96, at 288, 290; AUST, *supra* note 47, at 295 (although negotiators had 1949 Conventions, *supra* notes 2, 3, in mind, Article 60[5] "would apply equally to other conventions of a humanitarian character, or to human rights treaties, since they create rights intended to protect individuals irrespective of the conduct of the parties to each other"); BROWNLIE, *supra* note 6, at 622–23; OPPENHEIM'S INTERNATIONAL LAW, *supra* note 6, § 649, at 1302; RESTATEMENT, *supra* note 6, § 335, cmt. c; SINCLAIR, *supra* note 36, at 190; Louise Doswald-Beck & Sylvain Vite, *International Humanitarian Law and Human Rights Law,* 293 INTERNATIONAL REVIEW OF THE RED CROSS 94 (1993); Crawford, *Introduction, in* CRAWFORD, *supra* note 96, at 41 (State cannot disregard human rights obligations because of another State's breach; no Vienna Convention, *supra* note 36, citation for the point); David Weissbrodt & Peggy L. Hicks, *Implementation of Human Rights and Humanitarian Law in Situations of Armed Conflict,* 293 Int'l Rev. Red Cross 120 (1993). AUST, *supra*, seems to be the only commentator applying Article 60(5) to human rights treaties; *see also* Crawford, *supra.* Preparatory works discussing other sources, *supra*, and Article 60(5)'s text ("treaties of a humanitarian character"), as distinguished from "treaties of a human rights character," which is not the Article 60(5) language, suggest a misstating of the law if distinctions between humanitarian and human rights law remain.

103. Vienna Convention, *supra* note 36, art. 60; Gabcikovo-Nagymoros Project (Hung. v. Slovk.), 1997 I.C.J. 7, 39, 64 (Sept. 25) (Article 60 customary law) [hereinafter Project Case]; Legal Consequences for States of the Continued Presence of South Africa in Namibia (South West Africa) Notwithstanding Security Council Resolution 276, Advisory Opinion, 1971 I.C.J. 16, 47 (June 21) (Article 60(3) customary law); Article 25 of *Harvard Draft Convention on the Law of Treaties* 27, 29 AMERICAN JOURNAL OF INTERNATIONAL LAW 657, 662, 1077–96 (Supp. 1935) [hereinafter Harvard Convention]; Draft Articles on Responsibility on States for Internationally Wrongful Acts, *supra* note 96, art. 42 & Commentary, at 294–301, *reprinted in* CRAWFORD, *supra*

note 96, at 255–60; AUST, *supra* note 47, at 293–96; BROWNLIE, *supra* note 6, at 622–23; OPPENHEIM'S INTERNATIONAL LAW, *supra* note 6, § 649; MCNAIR, *supra* note 57, ch. 36; RESTATEMENT, *supra* note 6, § 335; SINCLAIR, *supra* note 36, at 188–90; Jimenez de Arechaga, *supra* note 95, at 79–85.

104. 2005 Congo Case, *supra* note 8, 2005 I.C.J. at 60 (occupied territory); Wall Case, *supra* note 8, 2004 I.C.J. at 173–77 (occupied territory) (adv. op.); Nuclear Weapons, *supra* note 8, 1996 I.C.J. at 239 (armed conflict) (adv. op); *see also* DINSTEIN, *supra* note 6, at 69–71 (human rights apply to persons within a State's territory and subject to its authority). *Id.* 85–88 adds, however, that if the LOAC and human rights law conflict, LOAC as *lex specialis* governs. *See also* Wall Case, *supra* note 8, 2004 I.C.J. at 177–81 (human rights law also applies to areas subject to a State's jurisdiction but outside its sovereign territory, but possibility remains for applying LOAC as *lex specialis*); ARAI-TAKAHASHI, *supra* note 6, at 414–25; BENVENISTI, *supra* note 9, at 187–89. UK MANUAL, *supra* note 8, ¶ 11.8 states that the LOAC applies during occupations, but in paragraph in 11.19 declares that an occupier must enforce applicable human rights law and that if an occupier is a European Convention for Protection of Human Rights & Fundamental Freedoms, Nov. 4, 1950, 213 U.N.T.S. 221 [hereinafter European Convention], party the Convention as amended may apply in occupied territories. UK MANUAL, *supra* note 8, ¶ 11.60 adds that Universal Declaration of Human Rights, *supra* note 73, rules must also apply during Fourth Convention, *supra* note 2, Article 64–governed proceedings. The Declaration may fare differently in US courts. *See supra* note 73.

105. DINSTEIN, *supra* note 6, at 81–85.

106. Vienna Convention, *supra* note 36, arts. 61–62; *see also* Project Case, *supra* note 103, 1997 I.C.J. at 39 (Articles 61, 62 customary norms); Fisheries Jurisdiction (U.K. v. Ice.), 1973 I.C.J. 3, 18 (Feb. 2) (same for Article 62); AUST, *supra* note 47, at 296–300; BROWNLIE, *supra* note 6, at 623–25; ARIE E. DAVID, THE STRATEGY OF TREATY TERMINATION ch. 1 (1975); ELIAS, *supra* note 95, at 119–30; Harvard Convention, *supra* note 103, art. 28, at 1096–1126 (*rebus sic stantibus*); OPPENHEIM'S INTERNATIONAL LAW, *supra* note 6, §§ 650–51; RESTATEMENT, *supra* note 6, § 336; SINCLAIR, *supra* note 36, at 190–96; Report of the International Law Commission on the Work of Its Eighteenth Session, 21 U.N. GAOR, Supp. No. 9, U.N. Doc. A/6309/Rev. 1 (1966), *reprinted in* 2 (1966) YEAR BOOK OF THE INTERNATIONAL LAW COMMISSION 211, U.N. Doc. A/CN.4/Ser.A/1966/Add. 1, at 169, 255–58 [hereinafter 1966 ILC Rep.]; Gyorgy Haraszti, *Treaties and the Fundamental Change of Circumstances*, 146 RECUEIL DES COURS D'ACADEMIE DE DROIT INTERNATIONAL [R.C.A.D.I.] 1 (1975); Robert D. Kearney & Robert E. Dalton, *The Treaty on Treaties*, 64 AMERICAN JOURNAL OF INTERNATIONAL LAW 535, 541–44 (1970) (Vienna Convention, *supra* note 36, drafting negotiations); Oliver J. Lissitzyn, *Treaties and Changed Circumstances*, AMERICAN JOURNAL OF INTERNATIONAL LAW 895 (1967); Walker, *supra* note 8, at 65–68 (1993). MCNAIR, *supra* note 57, at 685 does not recognize a separate impossibility rule; some of his examples are impossibility situations and might be cited as such.

107. Vienna Convention, *supra* note 36, pmbl. ("... *pacta sunt servanda* rule [is] universally recognized"), art. 26; *see also* U.N. Charter pmbl. ("respect for obligations arising from treaties"); Project Case, *supra* note 103, ICJ at 78–79 ("What is required in the present case by ... *pacta sunt servanda*, as reflected in Article 26 of the [Vienna Convention, *supra*] is that the Parties find an agreed solution within the cooperative context of the Treaty."); AUST, *supra* note 47, at 144–45, 187; BROWNLIE, *supra* note 6, at 591–92 (general principle of law); Harvard Convention, *supra* note 103, art. 20, at 977 (rule of law); 1966 ILC Rep., *supra* note 106, at 211 (*pacta sunt servanda* a rule of law); OPPENHEIM'S INTERNATIONAL LAW, *supra* note 6, §§ 12, at 38, 584 (*pacta sunt servanda* a customary rule); HANS KELSEN, PURE THEORY OF LAW 214–17 (Max Knight trans., 2d rev. ed. 1967) (*pacta sunt servanda* comes from custom); MCNAIR, *supra* note 57, at

465, 493; RESTATEMENT, *supra* note 6, § 321 & cmt. a (*pacta sunt servanda* at core of law of international agreements and is "perhaps the most important principle of international law"); THE CHARTER OF THE UNITED NATIONS, *supra* note 46, at 35–36, 92–93, 96–97; SINCLAIR, *supra* note 36, at 83–84, 119 (no suggestion *pacta sunt servanda* a fundamental norm); Kearney & Dalton, *supra* note 106, at 516–17 (Vienna Convention, *supra* art. 26 negotiations analysis).

108. Vienna Convention, *supra* note 36, art. 30; AUST, *supra* note 47, ch. 12; BROWNLIE, *supra* note 6, at 629–30; Harvard Convention, *supra* note 103, art. 22, at 661–62, 1009–29; RESTATEMENT, *supra* note 6, § 323.

109. *E.g.*, ICCPR, *supra* note 45, art. 4; *see also* Nuclear Weapons, *supra* note 8, 1996 I.C.J. at 239 (adv. op.); INSTITUTE OF INTERNATIONAL LAW, *supra* note 47, art. 4; INSTITUTE FOR HUMAN RIGHTS, *supra* note 47, art. 18; SUBATARA ROY CHOWDHURY, RULE OF LAW IN A STATE OF EMERGENCY 12–13, 22–29, 59, 121–25, 210–11 (1989), analyzing International Law Association Minimum Standards of Human Rights Norms in a State of Emergency, 1984; Joan Fitzpatrick, *Protection Against Abuse of the Concept of "Emergency," in* HUMAN RIGHTS: AN AGENDA FOR THE NEXT CENTURY 203 (Louis Henkin & John Lawrence Hargrove eds., 1994); Louis Henkin, *International Human Rights as "Rights,"* 1 CARDOZO LAW REVIEW 446–47 (1979). Some human rights treaties apply in peace and war, *e.g.*, Convention Against Torture & Other Cruel, Inhuman or Degrading Treatment or Punishment art. 2(2), Dec. 18, 1984, 1468 U.N.T.S. 85 [hereinafter Torture Convention]; Genocide Convention, *supra* note 96, art. 1, whose terms are at least customary law. Reservations to Convention on Prevention & Punishment of Crime of Genocide, Advisory Opinion, 1951 I.C.J. 15, 23 (May 28); DINSTEIN, *supra* note 6, at 147; *supra* note 96 and accompanying text. Treaties can provide for armed conflict, *e.g.*, Convention on Rights of the Child arts. 38–39, Nov. 20, 1989, 1577 U.N.T.S. 3. Others have no derogation clauses, *e.g.*, International Covenant on Economic, Social & Cultural Rights, Dec. 16, 1966, 993 U.N.T.S. 3. Here law of treaties rules for armed conflict may apply. *See infra* note 118 and accompanying text.

110. DINSTEIN, *supra* note 6, at 71–74 (two regional human rights treaties, *e.g.*, European Convention, *supra* note 104, exclude application during armed conflict).

111. ICCPR, *supra* note 45, art. 4(2), listing Articles 6 (right to life, death penalty standards), 7 (prohibition against torture), 8(1) (prohibition against slavery), 8(2) (prohibition against servitude), 11 (imprisonment for contract breach barred), 15 (*ex post facto* criminal laws barred), 16 (recognition as a person before the law), 18 (freedom of thought, conscience, religion); *see also* ARAI-TAKAHASHI, *supra* note 6, ch. 19 ("expanding catalogue of human rights of non-derogable nature"); DINSTEIN, *supra* note 6, at 74–79 (other explicit, implicit limitations).

112. *See supra* note 108 and accompanying text.

113. *See supra* note 109.

114. This is so for the Genocide and Torture Conventions, *supra* notes 96, 109. There are others that lack derogation clauses. *See supra* note 109.

115. The LOS treaties except the LOAC from its rules through its "other rules" clauses. Before these treaties went into force, custom governed the LOS; alongside this custom, the LOAC in treaties, custom and general principles applied during armed conflict. *See infra* notes 118–19 and accompanying text.

116. DINSTEIN, *supra* note 6, at 85–88; *see also supra* note 104 and accompanying text. George K. Walker, *The 2006 Conflict in Lebanon, or What Are the Armed Conflict Rules When Legal Principles Collide?*, ch. 15, *in* ENEMY COMBATANTS, TERRORISM, AND ARMED CONFLICT LAW (David K. Linnan ed., 2008) proposes a factorial analysis for LOAC–human rights law and similar clashes based on private international law (conflict of laws) analysis; *see also* ARAI-TAKAHASHI, *supra* note 6, chs. 17–18, 24 for similar analysis; FERNANDO R. TESON, HUMANITARIAN

INTERVENTION: AN INQUIRY INTO LAW AND MORALITY (2d ed. 1997); John Norton Moore, *Toward an Applied Theory for the Regulation of Intervention*, *in* MOORE, LAW AND CIVIL WAR IN THE MODERN WORLD ch. 1 (1974) and sources *cited in* George K. Walker, *Principles for Collective Humanitarian Intervention to Succor Other Countries' Imperiled Indigenous Nationals*, 18 AMERICAN UNIVERSITY INTERNATIONAL LAW REVIEW 35, 56 n.111 (2002) (Kosovo), published in part as Walker, *Application of the Law of Armed Conflict During Operation Allied Force: Maritime Interdiction and Prisoner of War Issues*, *in* LEGAL AND ETHICAL LESSONS OF NATO'S KOSOVO CAMPAIGN 85 (Andru E. Wall ed., 2002) (Vol. 78, US Naval War College International Law Studies) (factorial approaches for intervention).

117. Under the LOAC occupation begins when enemy territory is placed under hostile forces' authority. Hague II, *supra* note 9, Regulations, art. 42; Hague IV, *supra* note 7, Regulations, art. 42. Occupation ends a year after military operations end under Fourth Convention, *supra* note 2, art. 6. Protocol I, *supra* note 13, art. 3 declares that occupation law standards continue until occupation ends, which could be more than a year. *See also* ARAI-TAKAHASHI, *supra* note 6, at 16–24; Bothe, *supra* note 81, at 59; DINSTEIN, *supra* note 6, at 42–45, 270–73; 4 PICTET, *supra* note 11, at 62–63; COMMENTARY ON THE ADDITIONAL PROTOCOLS, *supra* note 66, at 68. Although Nazi Germany disappeared as a sovereign State at World War II's end, States like Japan and Italy retained sovereignty and continued in occupation status after the war. The *debellatio* doctrine, *i.e.*, where a State disappears due to total subjugation in war, has been criticized as a principle of contemporary international law. *Compare* BENVENISTI, *supra* note 9, at 92–96, 183 (*debellatio* has no place in current international law) and ARAI-TAKAHASHI, *supra* at 34–40 (German sovereignty survived; argument against applying *debellatio*) *with* DINSTEIN, *supra* note 6, at 2, 32–33 (*debellatio* doctrine remains viable).

118. 5 GREEN H. HACKWORTH, DIGEST OF INTERNATIONAL LAW § 513, at 383–84 (1943); Harvard Convention, *supra* note 103, art. 35(a), at 664, 1183–1204; Institut de Droit International, *The Effects of Armed Conflicts on Treaties* (Resolution of the 1985 Helsinki Session) arts. 3–4, 61(2) ANNUAIRE 278, 280 (1986); Institut de Droit International, *Regulations Regarding the Effect of War on Treaties* (Approved at the 1912 Christiania Session) art. 5, *reprinted in* 7 AMERICAN JOURNAL OF INTERNATIONAL LAW 153, 154 (1913); AUST, *supra* note 47, at 308–11 (ILC's "ostrich-like" approach that a provision was unnecessary for Vienna Convention, *supra* note 36); BROWNLIE, *supra* note 6, at 620–21 (ongoing ILC work on the subject); OPPENHEIM'S INTERNATIONAL LAW, *supra* note 6, § 655; MCNAIR, *supra* note 57, ch. 43; RESTATEMENT, *supra* note 6, § 335, cmt. c; G.G. Fitzmaurice, *The Judicial Clauses of the Peace Treaties*, 73 RECUEIL DES COURS D'ACADEMIE DE DROIT INTERNATIONAL [R.C.A.D.I.] 255, 312 (1948); Cecil J.B. Hurst, *The Effect of War on Treaties*, 2 BRITISH YEARBOOK OF INTERNATIONAL LAW 37, 42 (1921); *see also* Vienna Convention, *supra* note 36, art. 60(5); *supra* notes 102–5 and accompanying text.

119. The LOS conventions' "other rules of international law" clauses are an example. *See* LOS Convention, *supra* note 57, pmbl., arts. 2(3) (territorial sea); 19, 21, 31 (territorial sea innocent passage); 34(2) (straits transit passage); 52(1) (archipelagic sea lanes passage; incorporation by reference of Articles 19, 21, 31); 58(1), 58(3) (exclusive economic zone, or EEZ); 78 (continental shelf; coastal State rights do not affect superjacent waters, i.e., territorial or high seas; coastal State cannot infringe or unjustifiably interfere with "navigation and other rights and freedoms of other States as provided in this Convention"); 87(1) (high seas); 138 (the Area); 293 (court or tribunal having jurisdiction for settling disputes must apply LOS Convention and "other rules of international law" not incompatible with the LOS Convention); 303(4) (archeological, historical objects found at sea, "other international agreements and rules of international law regarding the protection of objects of an archeological and historical nature"); Annex III, Article 21(1); Convention on the High Seas art. 2, Apr. 28, 1958, 13 U.S.T. 2312, 450 U.N.T.S. 92 [hereinafter High

Seas Convention]; Convention on the Territorial Sea and Contiguous Zone arts. 1(2), 22(2), Apr. 29, 1958, 15 U.S.T. 1606, 516 U.N.T.S. 205 [hereinafter Territorial Sea Convention]. Although the other 1958 LOS treaties do not have other-rules clauses, they declare that waters within their competence are high seas areas; the High Seas Convention, *supra*, art. 2 "other rules" clause applies. *See* Convention on the Continental Shelf art. 3, Apr. 29, 1958, 15 U.S.T. 471, 499 U.N.T.S. 311; Convention on Fishing & Conservation of the Living Resources of the High Seas arts. 1, 2, Apr. 29, 1958, 17 U.S.T. 138, 559 U.N.T.S. 285. The same is true for the contiguous zone next to the territorial sea; beyond the territorial sea, the contiguous zone is a high seas area. LOS Convention, *supra*, art. 33(1); Territorial Sea Convention, *supra*, art. 24(1). *See also* High Seas Convention, *supra*, art. 1, defining "high seas" as all parts of the sea not included in a State's territorial sea or internal waters. Like the territorial sea, airspace above it is part of a coastal State's sovereign territory. Convention on International Civil Aviation arts. 1, 2, Dec. 7, 1944, 61 Stat. 1180, 15 U.N.T.S. 295.

The longstanding consensus has been that these clauses mean that LOAC rules apply during armed conflict as between belligerents; neutrals' rights may also be affected, and as to neutrals' rights among themselves, the LOS, perhaps conditioned by the law of neutrality, prevails. There has been a minor trend toward citing the clauses for other than LOAC situations. LOS Committee Report, *supra* note 82, at 300–07.

The other- rules clauses confirm statements on applying belligerent occupation law beyond an occupied State's lands. Since all areas subject to the LOS have an exclusion for LOAC-governed situations, and occupation law is part of the LOAC, the result is that occupation law extends seaward to an occupied State's territorial sea and to its claims under other sea areas, e.g., its contiguous zone, continental shelf, EEZ, and fishing zones in addition to inland waters and airspace above its sovereign territory. DINSTEIN, *supra* note 6, at 47–48; INSTITUTE OF INTERNATIONAL LAW, OXFORD MANUAL OF NAVAL WAR art. 88 (1913), *reprinted in* THE LAWS OF ARMED CONFLICTS, *supra* note 2, at 1123, 1135; *see also* Fourth Convention, *supra* note 2, art. 2 (applies to total or partial occupation of Convention party's territory); 4 PICTET, *supra* note 11, at 21.

120. *See supra* notes 102–5 and accompanying text.

121. *See supra* notes 45, 109–16 and accompanying text.

122. *See supra* notes 106–16 and accompanying text.

123. *See supra* note 110 and accompanying text.

124. Not all customary human rights norms have *jus cogens* status. RESTATEMENT, *supra* note 6, § 702, cmt. 11. The important point is that law of treaties rules do not apply to custom-based rules. THEODOR MERON, HUMAN RIGHTS AND HUMANITARIAN NORMS AS CUSTOMARY LAW 3–10, 114–35 (1989). Custom also has limiting doctrines, e.g., the persistent objector principle. *See infra* note 140 and accompanying text.

125. G.A. Res. 56/83, U.N. Doc. A/RES/56/83 (Jan. 28, 2002).

126. Draft Articles on Responsibility of States for Internationally Wrongful Acts, *supra* note 96, art. 25 & Commentary, at 194–206, *reprinted in* CRAWFORD, *supra* note 96, at 178–86. State of necessity is not the same as necessity as a qualification for invoking the right of self-defense or as a qualification of standards for ordering an attack under the LOAC. States and commentators differ if anticipatory self-defense is lawful in the Charter era. *See supra* note 57; *see also* Thomas M. Franck, *On Proportionality of Countermeasures in International Law*, 102 AMERICAN JOURNAL OF INTERNATIONAL LAW 715, 719–37 (2008) (noting distinction between proportionality in self-defense and LOAC situations, and four other circumstances, including reprisals). *See also supra* notes 55–57 and accompanying text.

127. *See supra* notes 14–15, 35–42, 108 and accompanying text.

128. That seems to be the drafters' intent for Article 25. Draft Articles on Responsibility of States for Internationally Wrongful Acts, *supra* note 96, Commentary ¶¶ 2, 21 & notes 398, 435–36, although these do not refer to Hague IV, *supra* note 7, Regulations, art. 43. DINSTEIN, *supra* note 6, at 109, seems to agree, although he does not cite Draft Articles on Responsibility of States for Internationally Wrongful Acts, *supra* note 96, art. 25; he does note that Brussels Declaration, *supra* note 10, art. 3 uses "necessary."

129. *See supra* notes 35–42 and accompanying text.

130. *See generally* Franck, *supra* note 126, at 719–37.

131. Fourth Convention, *supra* note 2, art. 33; *see also* Protocol I, *supra* note 13, art. 73 (stateless persons); *compare* Hague II, *supra* note 9, Regulations, arts. 44–45 (occupied territory "population") *with* Hague IV, *supra* note 7, Regulations, arts. 44–45 (occupied territory "inhabitants"). *See* also ARAI-TAKAHASHI, *supra* note 6, at 285; BOTHE ET AL., *supra* note 47, at 446–50; DINSTEIN, *supra* note 6, at 61–63; FM 27-10, *supra* note 12, ¶¶ 272, 495(e), 497; NWP 1-14M ANNOTATED, *supra* note 8, ¶ 6.2.3.2 n.48; 4 PICTET, *supra* note 11, at 45–52, 227–29; COMMENTARY ON THE ADDITIONAL PROTOCOLS, *supra* note 66, at 845–55; Gasser, *supra* note 13, at 219–20, 248–49. The United States did not reserve to Article 33, *see* THE LAWS OF ARMED CONFLICTS, *supra* note 2, at 680–81, but the United States says it does not consider a comparable provision prohibiting reprisals against civilians in Protocol I, *supra* note 13, art. 51(6), as customary law insofar as it prohibits reprisals against civilians during armed conflict. NWP 1-14M ANNOTATED, *supra*, ¶ 6.2.3 n.36; *but see* ARAI-TAKAHASHI, *supra* note 6, at 285–89 (also noting the UK reservation to Protocol I, *supra* note 13, art. 51(6)); Frits Kalshoven, *Noncombatant Persons, in* The LAW OF NAVAL OPERATIONS 300, 306 (Horace B. Robertson Jr. ed., 1991) (Vol. 64, US Naval War College International Law Studies); Stefan Oeter, *Methods and Means of Combat, in* THE HANDBOOK OF HUMANITARIAN LAW IN ARMED CONFLICTS, *supra* note 8, at 105, 204–7. Protocol I's provision applies during armed conflict, not during occupations; it is recited in Protocol I, *supra* note 13, arts. 48–71, and not in Articles 72–79, which apply to the Fourth Convention, *supra* note 2. Article 4 of the Fourth Convention defines protected persons during armed conflict as those persons who find themselves, in case of a conflict or occupation, in the hands of a party to the conflict or an occupier State of which they are not nationals, i.e., the Convention covers persons not parties to a conflict. Nationals of States not bound by the Convention or of a neutral State without normal diplomatic representation with a State in whose hands they are, are not regarded as protected persons. Those the First, Second and Third Conventions, *supra* note 3, cover are also considered not to be protected persons. 4 PICTET, *supra* at 45–51. The upshot is that Article 33 does not cover reprisals against civilians of an opposing belligerent during armed conflict. Cultural Property Convention, *supra* note 13, art. 4(4) prohibits reprisals against cultural property; *see also* ARAI-TAKAHASHI, *supra* note 6, at 253–54; TOMAN, *supra* note 13, at 71.

132. BRIERLY, *supra* note 57, at 399; FRITS KALSHOVEN, BELLIGERENT REPRISALS 27 (1971); 2 CHARLES CHENEY HYDE, INTERNATIONAL LAW CHIEFLY AS INTERPRETED AND APPLIED BY THE UNITED STATES § 588 (3d ed. 1945–47); 2 OPPENHEIM, *supra* note 20, § 135; RESTATEMENT, *supra* note 6, § 905 & r.n. 8; JULIUS STONE, LEGAL CONTROLS OF INTERNATIONAL CONFLICT 288–89 (1959 rev.). Draft Articles on Responsibility of States for Internationally Wrongful Acts, *supra* note 96, Part 3, ch. 1, at 324–54, *reprinted in* CRAWFORD, *supra* note 96, at 281–302, charts a course apart from traditional reprisal and retorsion law, substituting a new term, countermeasures.

133. Although Fourth Convention, *supra* note 2, art. 33, bars reprisals against protected persons or property, it does not prohibit retorsions. 4 PICTET, *supra* note 11, at 224–29; *see also supra* notes 130–31 and accompanying text.

134. Vienna Convention, *supra* note 36, arts. 19–23; *see also* AUST, *supra* note 47, ch. 8; BROWNLIE, *supra* note 6, at 612–15; OPPENHEIM'S INTERNATIONAL LAW, *supra* note 6, §§ 614–19;

MCNAIR, *supra* note 57, ch. 9; RESTATEMENT, *supra* note 6, §§ 313–14; SINCLAIR, *supra* note 36, ch. 3.

135. *See Reservations and Declarations, in* THE LAWS OF ARMED CONFLICTS, *supra* note 2, at 650–88. It is also true for Protocol I, *supra* note 13. *Reservations and Declarations, in* THE LAWS OF ARMED CONFLICTS, *supra* note 2, at 792–818.

136. LOS Convention, *supra* note 57, art. 309. For possible application of this treaty, *see supra* note 119. It may also govern other occupation contexts as codified custom.

137. *Compare* the ILC reservations study, *Text of Draft Guidelines on Reservations to Treaties Provisionally Adopted So Far by the Commission, in* Report of the International Law Commission on the Work of its Fifty-fifth Session, 58 U.N. GAOR Supp. No. 10 at 50, U.N. Doc. A/58/10 (2003) and *Preliminary Conclusions of the International Law Commission on Reservations to Normative Multilateral Treaties Including Human Rights Treaties, in* Report of the International Law Commission on the Work of its Forty-Ninth Session, 52 U.N. GAOR Supp. No. 10 at ¶¶ 65–157, U.N. Doc. A/52/10 (1997), *available at* http://untreaty.un.org/ilc/documentation/english/A_52_10.pdf (last visited Sept. 20, 2009), which so far follows the Vienna Convention, *supra* note 36, approach, for Articles 19–23, *with* Human Rights Committee, General Comment Adopted by the Human Rights Committee Under Article 40, Paragraph 4, of the International Covenant on Civil and Political Rights, Addendum: Comment No. 24(52), General Comment on Issues Relating to Reservations Made Upon Ratification or Accession to the Covenant or the Optional Protocols Thereto, or in Relation to Declarations Under Article 41 of the Covenant, U.N. Doc. CCPR/C/21/Rev.1/Add.6 (Nov. 2, 1994), *reprinted in* 34 INTERNATIONAL LEGAL MATERIALS 839, 840, 842. This approach was criticized by United Kingdom, Observations of Franklin Berman, U.K. Foreign & Colonial Office Legal Adviser, to UN Human Rights Committee, July 20, 1995, *in United Kingdom Materials on International Law,* 66 BRITISH YEARBOOK OF INTERNATIONAL LAW 584, 655 (Gregory Marston ed., 1995); and Human Rights: 2001 Digest 305. Commentators differ on whether the Committee approach was beyond its competence. AUST, *supra* note 47, at 150–51; BROWNLIE, *supra* note 6, at 615; FRANK HORN, RESERVATIONS AND INTERPRETATIVE DECLARATIONS TO MULTILATERAL TREATIES 153–60 (1988); LIESBETH LIJNZAAD, RESERVATIONS TO UN–HUMAN RIGHTS TREATIES: RATIFY AND RUIN? ch. 3 (1995); Francesco Parisi & Catherine Sevcenko, *Treaty Reservations and the Economics of Article 21(1) of the Vienna Convention,* 21 BERKELEY INTERNATIONAL LAW JOURNAL 1, 20–22 (2003); Edward T. Swaine, *Reserving,* 31 YALE JOURNAL OF INTERNATIONAL LAW 307, 321–22 (2006). The ILC has been at work on the law of treaties related to multilateral reservations after receiving UN General Assembly endorsement for the project. G.A. Res. 48/31, U.N. Doc. A/RES/48/31 (Jan. 24, 1994); G.A. Res. 49/51, U.N. Doc. A/RES/49/51 (Feb. 17, 1995). For a short analysis through its 2005 session, see generally Matheson, *supra* note 95, 418–19; Swaine, *supra*. For counterpoint on Swaine's analysis, *see* Laurence R. Helfer, *Response: Not Fully Committed? Reservations, Risk, and Treaty Design,* 31 YALE JOURNAL OF INTERNATIONAL LAW 367 (2006). The Commission continues its work. *See generally* Alain Pellet, Special Rapporteur, International Law Commission, *Eleventh report on reservations to treaties,* U.N. Doc. A/CN.4/574 (Aug. 10, 2006).

Human rights law is relevant for occupations. *See supra* notes 43–49, 104–5, *infra* note 152 and accompanying text.

138. The law on these is vague. George K. Walker, *Professionals' Definitions and States' Interpretative Declarations (Understandings, Statements or Declarations) for the 1982 Law of the Sea Convention,* 21 EMORY INTERNATIONAL LAW REVIEW 461 (2007) offers solutions.

139. Vienna Convention, *supra* note 36, does not cover desuetude or obsolescence; its drafters considered these exceptions to performance fell under principles of parties' conduct to abandon a treaty, *id.,* art. 54(b). OPPENHEIM'S INTERNATIONAL LAW, *supra* note 6, § 646, at 1247; *see*

also AUST, *supra* note 47, at 306–7; MCNAIR, *supra* note 57, at 516–18; SINCLAIR, *supra* note 36, at 163–64 (drafters' explanation not entirely satisfactory); Richard Plender, *The Role of Consent in the Termination of Treaties*, 57 BRITISH YEARBOOK OF INTERNATIONAL LAW 133, 138–45 (1986). Desuetude claimants must take into account the *pacta sunt servanda* principle. Vienna Convention, *supra* note 36, art. 26; *see also supra* note 107 and accompanying text. Some LOAC treaties may be in desuetude. *See, e.g.*, SAN REMO MANUAL, *supra* note 36, ¶ 136 cmt. 136.2 (Convention Relating to Status of Enemy Merchant Ships at Outbreak of Hostilities, Oct. 18, 1907, 205 Consol. T.S. 305, in desuetude).

140. *See* Committee on Formation of Customary (General) International Law, *Final Report: Statement of Principles Applicable to the Formation of General Customary International Law, in* Final Report, *supra* note 8, at 712, 738–40; BROWNLIE, *supra* note 6, at 11; OPPENHEIM'S INTERNATIONAL LAW, *supra* note 6, § 10, at 29; NWP 1-14M ANNOTATED, *supra* note 8, ¶ 5.4.1; RESTATEMENT, *supra* note 6, § 102, cmts. b, d; Michael Akehurst, *Custom as a Source of Law,* 47 BRITISH YEARBOOK OF INTERNATIONAL LAW 1, 23–27; Waldock, *supra* note 57, at 49–52; 1 CUSTOMARY INTERNATIONAL HUMANITARIAN LAW xxxi–xlii (Marie Henckaerts & Louise Doswald-Beck eds., 2005) (no view on persistent objector doctrine, citing the doubts of Maurice H. Mendelson, *The Formation of Customary International Law,* 272 RECUEIL DES COURS D'ACADEMIE DE DROIT INTERNATIONAL [R.C.A.D.I.] 227–44 [1998]); *but see also* Charney, *supra* note 57, at 538–41 (persistent objector rule's existence open to serious doubt). J. ASHLEY ROACH & ROBERT W. SMITH, UNITED STATES RESPONSES TO EXCESSIVE MARITIME CLAIMS (2d ed. 1996), an exhaustive study of LOS claims protests, demonstrate that the rule is alive and well for LOS issues. Problems with studies of States' objections are that many lie buried in chancellery files because they seem to have little public research value when filed; they may be subject to national security concerns, *cf.* RESTATEMENT, *supra* note 6, § 312 r.n.5; there may be time delay rules barring publication until after a period of years; or States may have selective or non-publication policies like courts' unpublished opinion rules.

141. This was the situation in Austria and Germany after World War II; these countries were divided into four occupation zones. Germany had annexed Austria in 1938; the Third Reich ceased to exist as a State with surrender of German armed forces in May 1945.

142. Except perhaps Kuwait, which may have signed a bilateral self-defense agreement (up to now not published) with the United States, countries involved in the 1990–91 and 2003 Iraq conflicts were coalition partners. George K. Walker, *The Crisis Over Kuwait, August 1990–February 1991*, 1991 DUKE JOURNAL OF COMPARATIVE & INTERNATIONAL LAW 25, 30.

143. This has been the Afghanistan situation after 9/11; these have been NATO operations with separate US zones, although there has been no formal occupation. *See generally* Carcano, *supra* note 69, at 58; Walker, *supra* note 29, at 498–500 (participation under NATO Treaty, *supra* note 25; Rio Pact, *supra* note 26; Security Agreement (ANZUS Pact), Sept. 1, 1951, 3 U.S.T. 3420, 131 U.N.T.S. 83; bilateral agreements like Treaty of Mutual Cooperation & Security, with Agreed Minute & Exchange of Notes, Japan-U.S., Jan. 19, 1960, 11 U.S.T. 1632, 373 U.N.T.S. 179. By 2009 there was debate on whether it had become a non-international armed conflict or remained an international conflict. ARAI-TAKAHASHI, *supra* note 6, at 23–24.

144. Local law refers to a jurisdiction's law exclusive of its conflict of laws, or private international law, principles. *See supra* note 63.

145. This can range from general criminal law and different punishments for crime among these subdivisions to local government traffic laws and the like.

146. E.g., family law, contracts, torts, property.

147. Protocol I, *supra* note 13; Protocol II, *supra* note 66, governing conflicts like civil wars, for which the law of belligerent occupation does not apply unless a State fighting insurgents

recognizes their belligerency. Then the Fourth Convention, *supra* note 2, through its Common Article 3, applies. If a State is a party to Protocol I its Article 1(4) applies to self-determination conflicts. DINSTEIN, *supra* note 6, at 34; *see also* 4 PICTET, *supra* note 11, at 25–44.

148. State Parties, *supra* note 4, lists 164 States as Protocol II, *supra* note 66, parties, and 168 as Protocol I, *supra* note 13, parties; many are US alliance or coalition partners. State Parties, *supra* note 4, lists 194 States as 1949 Geneva Conventions parties.

149. *See, e.g., supra* note 48 and accompanying text.

150. Protocol I, *supra* note 13, arts. 1, 3, 49(4), 68, 72; *see also* BOTHE ET AL., *supra* note 47, at 37–52, 57–60, 291, 428–29, 441–45; COMMENTARY ON THE ADDITIONAL PROTOCOLS, *supra* note 66, at 34–56, 66–69, 606–8, 809–10, 841–44.

151. Protocol I, *supra* note 13, arts. 3 (extending Fourth Convention, *supra* note 2, art. 6, protections from a year after general close of military operations until occupation ends); 5(4) (parties to conflict must approve Protecting Power, amending Fourth Convention, *supra* note 2, art. 11); 43–44 (altering Contracting Parties in Third Convention, *supra* note 3, art. 4(A)(2)); 45(3) (greater protections for those taking part in hostilities not entitled to prisoner of war status, unless accused of espionage, extension of Fourth Convention, *supra* note 2, art. 5); 73 (prewar refugees, amending Fourth Convention, *supra* note 2, art. 4); *see also* DINSTEIN, *supra* note 6, at 7, 64–65, 96, 182, 281; 4 PICTET, *supra* note 11, at 45–64, 99–113.

152. Torture Convention, *supra* note 109. As Multilateral Treaties, *supra* note 36, at IV-9 suggests for this treaty in listing 146 parties, all States are not parties to every human rights treaty; the issue is whether custom or general principles bind non-party States. Beneath this general treaty web lie regional human rights treaties that must be consulted if States (occupier and occupied States alike) are parties. The issue here, like general treaties, is whether a regional treaty applies under law of treaties rules for territorial application. Vienna Convention, *supra* note 36, art. 29; AUST, *supra* note 47, at 202–5, 439–40; OPPENHEIM'S INTERNATIONAL LAW, *supra* note 6, § 621; MCNAIR, *supra* note 57, at 116–17; RESTATEMENT, *supra* note 6, § 322(b); SINCLAIR, *supra* note 36, at 87–92. If territorial rules do not apply, a question is whether a treaty applies to the person of one accused of a violation, under a treaty to which his/her country is a party, customary law, general principles of law or *jus cogens* standards. *See, e.g.,* ICCPR, *supra* note 45, art. 2; DINSTEIN, *supra* note 6, at 82, 147; OPPENHEIM'S INTERNATIONAL LAW, *supra* note 6, § 622; RESTATEMENT, *supra* note 6, § 322 r.n.3. Treaty succession principles may also govern territory rules; *see* Final Report, *supra* note 8; Symposium, *supra* note 8; Walker, *supra* note 8.

153. The same is true for the Genocide Convention, *supra* note 96. RESTATEMENT, *supra* note 6, §§ 702(a), 702(d) & cmts. a–b, d, g, o, r.n.1–3, 5; *see also supra* notes 95–98 and accompanying text.

154. *See supra* note 57 and accompanying text.

155. There may be similar issues under other Charter law or the law of IGOs and perhaps soft law norms derived from them or NGOs. *See supra* notes 55–57, 71–77, 82–94 and accompanying text.

156. *Cf., e.g.,* NWP 1-14M ANNOTATED, *supra* note 8, ¶¶ 3.11.5.1, 4.3.2.2, 5.5; *see also* BRADD C. HAYES, NAVAL RULES OF ENGAGEMENT: MANAGEMENT TOOLS FOR CRISIS (1989); D.P. O'CONNELL, THE INFLUENCE OF LAW ON SEA POWER 169–80 (1975); Christopher Craig, *Fighting by the Rules*, NAVAL WAR COLLEGE REVIEW, May–June 1984, at 23 (UK Wartime ROE, 1982 Falklands/Malvinas War); James C. Duncan, *The Commander's Role in Developing Rules of Engagement*, NAVAL WAR COLLEGE REVIEW, Summer 1999, at 76; Richard J. Grunawalt, *The JCS Standing Rules of Engagement: A Judge Advocate's Primer*, 42 AIR FORCE LAW REVIEW 245 (1997); J. Ashley Roach, *Rules of Engagement*, NAVAL WAR COLLEGE REVIEW, Jan.–Feb. 1983, at 46, *reprinted in* 14 SYRACUSE JOURNAL OF INTERNATIONAL LAW AND COMMERCE 865 (1988);

Ivan A. Shearer, *Rules of Engagement and the Implementation of the Law of Naval Warfare, id.* at 767.

157. Neil Brown, *Issues Arising from Coalition Operations: An Operational Lawyer's Perspective, in* INTERNATIONAL LAW AND MILITARY OPERATIONS 225, 228–31, 233 (Michael D. Carsten ed., 2008) (Vol. 84, Naval War College International Law Studies); Vickie McConachie, *Coalition Operations: A Compromise or an Accommodation, in id.*, ch. 12; Dale G. Stephens, *Coalition Warfare: Challenges and Opportunities, in* THE LAW OF WAR IN THE 21ST CENTURY: WEAPONRY AND THE USE OF FORCE 245 (Anthony M. Helm ed., 2006) (Vol. 82, Naval War College International Law Studies).

158. *See, e.g.*, Charles Dunlap, *Legal Issues in Coalition Warfare: A US Perspective, in* THE LAW OF WAR IN THE 21ST CENTURY, *supra* note 157, at 221, 224 (possibility of different interpretations by coalition partners); McConachie, *supra* note 157, at 242–43 (East Timor); Stephen A. Rose, *Crafting the Rules of Engagement for Haiti, in* THE LAW OF MILITARY OPERATIONS: LIBER AMICORUM PROFESSOR JACK GRUNAWALT 225 (Michael N. Schmitt ed., 1998) (Vol. 72, Naval War College International Law Studies). The International Institute of Humanitarian Law will publish draft multinational ROE in the near future.

159. *Cf.* NWP 1-14M ANNOTATED, *supra* note 8, ¶ 3.11.5.1 (US Coast Guard, Department of Defense units performing law enforcement duties).

160. Roach, *supra* note 156.

161. *See supra* notes 14–34, 50–54, 71–77, 82–98, 134–55 and accompanying text.

162. RESTATEMENT, *supra* note 6.

163. RESTATEMENT (SECOND), *supra* note 63.

164. WALKER, *supra* note 73, ch. 6 (environmental issues during armed conflict); Walker, *The 2006 Conflict in Lebanon, supra* note 116 (Israel-Lebanon-Hezbollah, 2006); Walker, *Principles, supra* note 116 (Kosovo).

165. "Conflict of laws" in US law instead of private international law or transnational law, ICJ Judge Philip C. Jessup's phrase for transactions and situations crossing national borders, results from the scholarship of US Supreme Court Justice Joseph Story. *See* PHILIP C. JESSUP, TRANSNATIONAL LAW (1956); JOSEPH STORY, COMMENTARIES ON THE CONFLICT OF LAWS (1834).

166. "Public international law," as contrasted with private international law or conflict of laws, is a term used throughout much of the world; in US law the field is known as international law. *Cf.* the title to BROWNLIE, *supra* note 6; *but see* the title to OPPENHEIM'S INTERNATIONAL LAW, *supra* note 6, representing older UK usage. Conflict of laws issues seldom arose in English courts before the end of the last century. SCOLES ET AL., *supra* note 63, §§ 1.1, 2.1.

167. Some UN law and *jus cogens* if the latter applies. RESTATEMENT (SECOND), *supra* note 63, § 6(1) gives primacy to statutes governing conflict of laws over common-law factorial analysis, an analogy to supremacy of Charter Articles 103 and 51 (the right of self-defense) and Security Council decisions under Articles 25, 48 and 94 over treaties. *See supra* notes 55–57 and accompanying text. In US courts state statutory or common-law conflict of laws rules must satisfy the Constitution's due process and full faith and credit provisions. Phillips Petrol. Co. v. Shutts, 472 U.S. 797, 816–23 (1985). This is another higher law analogy for Charter law supremacy on self-defense and Council decisions in public international law.

168. *E.g.*, Jane G. Dalton, *George K. Walker's The Tanker War, 1980–88: Law and Policy*, 96 AMERICAN JOURNAL OF INTERNATIONAL LAW 278 (2002) (book review).

169. Laker Airways v. Sabena, Belgian World Airways, 731 F.2d 909, 948–53 (D.C. Cir. 1984); Boudreau v. Baughman, 368 S.E.2d 849, 853–56 (N.C. 1988); SCOLES ET AL., *supra* note 63, §§ 2.19–2.24; WALKER, *supra* note 73, at 542. Other multifactor analyses have been criticized. *See, e.g.*,

John Norton Moore, *Prolegomenon to the Jurisprudence of Myres S. McDougal and Harold Lasswell*, 54 VIRGINIA LAW REVIEW 662 (1968), supporting the law-science-policy (LSP) decision-making approach Myres McDougal advocated but noting criticisms. LSP LOAC analysis, MCDOUGAL & FELICIANO, *supra* note 19, is still helpful. MYRES S. MCDOUGAL ET AL., HUMAN RIGHTS AND WORLD PUBLIC ORDER (1980) uses the analysis.

170. No one expects commanders, or an individual sailor, airman, soldier, Marine, or civilian supervisor, to seek legal advice on what to do in anticipatory or many reactive self-defense situations; here ROE give basic rules and declare the fundamental law of self-defense, and that is enough, if commanders act or acted on facts they know, or reasonably should have known. *See, e.g.*, Walker, *The 2006 Conflict in Lebanon, supra* note 116, at 258–59, 269.

171. Fourth Convention, *supra* note 2, arts. 2, 6; Hague II, *supra* note 9, Regulations, arts. 42–56; Hague IV, *supra* note 7, Regulations, arts. 42–56; ARAI-TAKAHASHI, *supra* note 6, at 16; BENVENISTI, *supra* note 9, ch. 2; DINSTEIN, *supra* note 6, ch. 2; FM 27-10, *supra* note 12, ¶¶ 351–61; 4 PICTET, *supra* note 11, at 17–25, 58–64; Gasser, *supra* note 13, at 240–46.

172. *See supra* notes 55–57 and accompanying text.

173. LSP analysis has been concerned with public order, i.e., public international law, issues, as titles to MCDOUGAL & FELICIANO and MCDOUGAL ET AL., *supra* notes 19, 169, suggest. *See also supra* note 169 and accompanying text.

174. If cargo loss claims come from voyages to or from US ports, US courts must apply US law, *i.e.*, the Carriage of Goods by Sea Act, 46 U.S.C. §§ 1300–15 (2006), modifying International Convention for Unification of Certain Rules Relating to Bills of Lading, Aug. 25, 1924, 51 Stat. 233, 120 L.N.T.S. 155 [hereinafter Brussels Convention]. Since the United States is not a party to, *e.g.*, Protocols, Feb. 23, 1968, 1412 U.N.T.S. 121, and Dec. 21, 1979, 1412 U.N.T.S. 121, to amend the Brussels Convention or the superseding United Nations Convention on Carriage of Goods by Sea, Mar. 31, 1978, 1695 U.N.T.S. 3, shipments to and from US ports are not governed by their terms. US courts might apply other treaty standards if litigants are nationals of States that are parties to these treaties, however.

175. *See supra* notes 82–87 and accompanying text.

176. Fourth Convention, *supra* note 2, art. 64; Hague II, *supra* note 9, Regulations, art. 43; Hague IV, *supra* note 7, Regulations, art. 43; *see also* 4 PICTET, *supra* note 11, at 335. Although the thrust of the Fourth Convention, *supra* note 2, is protecting accuseds in penal legislation—*see id.* arts. 64–78—DINSTEIN, *supra* note 6, at 128–29; 4 PICTET, *supra* at 335–69; UK MANUAL, *supra* note 8, ¶¶ 11.56–11.74 say Article 64 applies equally to private law claims. Even if Articles 64–78 would be held to apply only to criminal law, the first paragraph of Hague IV, *supra* note 7, Regulations, art. 23(h) declares that it is "especially forbidden . . . [t]o declare abolished, suspended, or inadmissible in a court of law the rights and actions of the nationals of the hostile party." Article 23(h) applies during occupations. DINSTEIN, *supra* at 135. The Article 23(h) prohibition is a customary norm. *See supra* notes 7–9 and accompanying text. There is no comparable Hague II, *supra* note 9, provision; *see supra* notes 12–13, 40 and accompanying text.

177. Conflict of laws, or private international law, is governed by *lex fori*, the law of the forum; it is "procedural" in nature, as distinguished from the "substantive" law of, e.g., contracts or torts.

178. *See supra* note 173 and accompanying text.

179. *See infra* note 188 and accompanying text.

180. The American Law Institute (ALI) is a non-profit corporation in Philadelphia. It elects US state and federal judges, academics and lawyers as members; there are *ex officio* members, e.g., US law school deans. The Institute works with the American Bar Association and the National Conference of Commissioners on Uniform State Laws on law-improvement projects. None of

these organizations is government-affiliated or sponsored. No government or court in the United States must accept and apply any standard these organizations publish unless, of course, higher authority, e.g., legislation, declares a restatement provision is the rule to be followed.

181. Phillips, *supra* note 167, 472 U.S. at 816; SCOLES ET AL., *supra* note 63, § 3.23. An analogy for this analysis is, e.g., if US national law and an international standard are the same. This occurs if US statutes implement a treaty without modifying treaty standards, *e.g.*, Hamdan, *supra* note 20, 548 U.S. at 627–33 (UCMJ, *supra* note 59, art. 21, 10 U.S.C. § 821 [2006] incorporates Third Convention, *supra* note 3, art. 3, rules without modification). It can also happen if courts agree that US judge-made law is the same as customary international law, *e.g.*, The Pacquete Habana, 175 U.S. 677, 686–700 (1900), whose rules for wartime capture of inshore fishing boats are the same in international law, Convention No. XI Relative to Certain Restrictions with Regard to the Exercise of the Right of Capture in Naval War art. 3, Oct. 18, 1907, 36 Stat. 2396. *Habana* general customary international law and scholarly research rules also remain the same for US courts. *Compare* Habana, 175 U.S. at 700 *with* Sosa, *supra* note 73, 542 U.S. at 734.

182. *See, e.g.*, RESTATEMENT (SECOND), *supra* note 63, §§ 6(1), 145, 187; *see also* SCOLES ET AL., *supra* note 63, §§ 2.14, 17.24, 18.8.

183. RESTATEMENT (SECOND), *supra* note 63, §§ 6, 145, 187–88. The *Restatement*'s drafters intended that the section 6 policies would be initially applied; some courts, if no statute is involved, examine the special provisions (*e.g., id.* §§ 145, 187–88) first, with review of section 6 factors next, or not at all. SCOLES ET AL., *supra* note 63, §§ 2.14, 2.19. The *Restatements'* black-letter section and Comment materials represent the ALI's official position. Reporters' notes after sections are not the ALI position but explain and amplify sections and Comments. *See also supra* note 180 and accompanying text.

184. U.N. Charter art. 103; *see also supra* notes 55–57 and accompanying text.

185. RESTATEMENT, *supra* note 6, § 102 & cmts. g, h, k; *see also supra* notes 55–57, 71–77, 95–98 and accompanying text.

186. The RESTATEMENT, *supra* note 6, also distinguishes between jurisdiction to prescribe, i.e., authority to legislate; jurisdiction to adjudicate, i.e., authority to subject people or things to court process; and jurisdiction to enforce, or executive authority to compel or induce compliance with law. It then gives factors for asserting kinds of jurisdiction, and for universal crimes, authority to prescribe rules and adjudicate issues connected with them. Compare *id.* §§ 102 & cmts. g, h, k; 401–4, 421, 423, 431–32 *with* RESTATEMENT (SECOND), *supra* note 63, § 6. Similar to *id.*, RESTATEMENT, *supra* note 6, has special factorial standards for selected transnational transactions, taxation and anti-competitive (i.e., anti-trust) activities; the RESTATEMENT (SECOND), *supra* note 63, purports to cover all areas of US law. *Compare* RESTATEMENT, *supra* note 6, §§ 411–16 *with, e.g.*, RESTATEMENT (SECOND), *supra* note 63, §§ 145, 187–88.

187. Many US jurisdictions apply RESTATEMENT (SECOND), *supra* note 63, methodologies. Some do analysis differently, e.g., examining a factor list (e.g., for torts), before considering RESTATEMENT (SECOND), *supra note* 63, § 6, the opposite of what the drafters intended. *See generally* SCOLES ET AL., *supra* note 63, § 2.19. US federal courts follow the RESTATEMENT (SECOND), *supra* note 63, if there is no statute, treaty or contrary precedent. *Compare, e.g.*, Harris v. Polskie Linie Lotnicze, 820 F.2d 1000, 1003–4 (9th Cir. 1987) (applying *Restatement [Second]* in Foreign Sovereign Immunities Act–governed case) *with* Oviessi v. Islamic Repub. of Iran, 573 F.3d 835, 841 (D.C. Cir. 2009) (applying state law in case under the Act to effectuate Congressional intent). Transnational or maritime law cases may cite RESTATEMENT, *supra* note 6, *e.g.*, F. Hoffman-La Roche Ltd. v. Empagran S.A., 542 U.S. 155, 163–67 (2004) (anti-trust); Neely v. Club Med Mgt. Serv., 63 F.3d 166, 183–98 (3d Cir. 1995) (maritime personal injury).

188. Changes have come through legislation or treaties. *See generally* PETER HAY ET AL., CONFLICT OF LAWS 538–45 (13th ed. 2009).

189. 42 U.S.C. § 4332 (2006). U.S. DEPARTMENT OF JUSTICE & FEDERAL TRADE COMMISSION, ANTITRUST ENFORCEMENT GUIDELINES FOR INTERNATIONAL OPERATIONS 20–22 (1995), *Reprinted in* 34 INTERNATIONAL LEGAL MATERIALS 1080, 1102–4, uses similar factorial analysis.

190. *Cf.* Frank M. Snyder, *Introduction, in* US NAVAL WAR COLLEGE, SOUND MILITARY DECISION (1992).

191. *See supra* note 181 and accompanying text.

192. A State can decline to invoke a reservation, inviting a claim of later practice inimical to the reservation. If a State has previously objected but does not do so in a particular situation, that could weaken an objection's "persistency." *See supra* note 140 and accompanying text. However, might a State recite, in publicly declining to invoke a reservation or objection, that its action in a particular occupation situation is subject to its prior reservation or objection in all other cases? There seems to be little law on this, *but cf.* Vienna Convention, *supra* note 36, art. 30(2) (treaty clause that it is subject to earlier treaty); *see supra* note 108 and accompanying text.

193. *See supra* notes 125–33 and accompanying text.

194. This has been the New York state experience, where its conflict of laws rules evolved from traditional vested rights rules to a factorial approach (contacts, interest analysis) for each issue in a case, *e.g.*, Babcock v. Jackson, 191 N.E.2d 279, 280–85 (N.Y. 1963) (which jurisdiction's guest passenger law should apply), to rules for variants on the issue, Neumeier v. Kuehner, 268 N.E.2d 454, 457–59 (N.Y. 1972), to applying these rules in other cases, *e.g.*, Cooney v. Osgood Mach., Inc., 612 N.E.2d 277, 279–84 (N.Y. 1993) (work-related injury), which also recognized the supremacy of the US Constitution's full faith and credit and due process principles, analogous to the UN Charter's primacy for public international law issues; *see supra* notes 55–57 and accompanying text. Less-than-critical analysis can cause results that many would think wrong, *e.g.*, Shultz v. Boy Scouts of America, 480 N.E.2d 679 (N.Y. 1985).

195. *See generally* Neumeier, *supra* note 194.

196. Dunlap, *supra* note 158, at 227–28.

197. These means of swift communications apply as well to coalition planning; indeed, one issue may be too many communications. It is a far cry from the courier system of two hundred years ago. *See, e.g.*, KAGAN, *supra* note 88, at 280–81 (communications difficulties for Third Coalition facing Napoleon, 1804–5).

198. Letter from John Paul Jones to Joseph Hewes (May 19, 1778), *in* SAMUEL ELIOT MORISON, JOHN PAUL JONES: A SAILOR'S BIOGRAPHY 55, 56 (1959).

199. This can also occur between the LOAC and law derived from other IGOs or NGO claims. *See supra* notes 55–57, 71–77, 82–90 and accompanying text.

200. Hague IV, *supra* note 7, Regulations, art. 43; *see also supra* notes 14–34, 50–54, 82–98, 134–55 and accompanying text.

201. *See supra* notes 156–93 and accompanying text.

202. KAGAN, *supra* note 88, at 279–80, discusses problems of staffing, planning and coordinating large-scale armies during the Napoleonic Wars, and separation of overall priorities and war planning in World War II. Might a similar division of tasks be appropriate for lawyers who serve commanders, particularly in occupation situations? E.g., US occupation planning spanned years before plans were put into effect after surrenders in Europe. *See generally* HARRY L. COLES & ALBERT K. WEINBERG, CIVIL AFFAIRS: SOLDIERS BECOME GOVERNORS ch. 1 (1964).

203. Having this analysis committed to records, electronic or otherwise and perhaps classified, may help justify ultimate actions commanders take, particularly if there are claims of legal liability, or if there are questions raised during later litigation, diplomacy or legislative investigations.

White House Counsel Alberto Gonzalez's unfortunate reference to the 1949 Geneva Conventions as "quaint" is a negative example of how these memoranda can hurt an author and those who supervise him or her as well as subordinates relying on them. The other side of the coin is that well-reasoned, thoughtful memoranda can be a positive support for action taken, even if the result is untoward. In self-defense and LOAC situations, and occupations as well, a commander or individual service member is bound by what he or she knew, or reasonably should have known, before acting. *See supra* note 170. Part of this reasonableness rule is advice on the law; solid analysis justifying how a choice of law was derived is critical to a record of that advice, even though results from action taken may not be seen as good in the eyes of some.

204. A peripheral issue is correctly translated treaties for clarity of interpretation and application. Some treaties have plurilingual texts, all of which are authentic, *see, e.g.*, U.N. Charter art. 111, and for which Vienna Convention, *supra* note 36, Article 33 rules apply. Others, like Hague II and IV, *supra* notes 7, 9, have one official language. Might it be appropriate for foreign or defense ministries to review treaties, particularly those in common use, to be sure of proper translation and note the problem in, e.g., military manuals? For Hague II and IV, the difference between, e.g., the official French text of Regulations, Article 43 and unofficial translations may be significant in occupations. There seem to be other translation issues. *See supra* notes 14–34 and accompanying text. *See also* AUST, *supra* note 47, at 253–55 (Article 33 recites custom); MCNAIR, *supra* note 57, at 30–31, ch. 25; RESTATEMENT, *supra* note 6, § 325, cmt. f & r.n. 2, § 326; SINCLAIR, *supra* note 36, at 147–53 (Article 33 recites custom). The more difficult problem is how to correct the problem. If over one hundred years have passed, and some States still adhere to Hague II, *supra* note 9, what chance is there for general acceptance of amending protocols? Might it be argued that parallel custom, *cf.* ICJ Statute, *supra* note 6, art. 38(1), supersedes the treaty rule, or that practice under the treaties, *see* Vienna Convention, *supra* note 36, art. 31(3)(b), cures the problem? Article 31(3)(b) is today a customary rule. *See generally* Genocide Case, *supra* note 96, 2007 I.C.J. ¶ 160; AUST, *supra* at 241; SINCLAIR, *supra* note 36, at 135–40. Another issue is considering review of national military manuals, e.g., FM 27-10, *supra* note 12, for correct translations and applying them. It is unlikely that States will negotiate amending protocols to correct mistranslations; manuals might note the problem and declare customary rules that have developed, either as superseding law or as practice under the treaties. Third, manuals should recognize developing principles that may apply to future occupations, e.g., Charter law, IGO-developed rules, *jus cogens* norms and human rights law. The influence of NGOs and soft law cannot be discounted, either.

XIII

The Occupation of Iraq: A Reassessment

Eyal Benvenisti and Guy Keinan*

I. Introduction

The invasion and subsequent occupation of Iraq in 2003 provided a rare opportunity to examine the viability in the twenty-first century of a legal doctrine rooted in the military and political circumstances of the nineteenth century.[1] The rarity of this opportunity is not a result of paucity of occupations, but of the prevalent disinclination of occupants to recognize their status as such.[2] This article reflects on several key questions concerning the occupation of Iraq, not in an attempt to evaluate the occupants for their compliance with the law, but rather to study contemporary challenges to the law and possibilities for adaptations in the twenty-first century. The article addresses the beginning and end of the occupation in Iraq and potential pre- and post-occupation responsibilities (Part II), and examines the scope of authority of the occupants and of the UN Security Council in Iraq (Part III). Part IV concludes.

II. The Time Frame of the Occupation in Iraq

The Beginning: When Was Iraq Occupied?

Background: When Does Occupation Begin?

This seemingly straightforward question has proven to be quite complex. It has always been complex, but for different reasons. In the nineteenth century, the

* Eyal Benvenisti, Anny and Paul Yanowicz Professor of Human Rights, Tel Aviv University, Faculty of Law, and Guy Keinan, LL.B. candidate, Tel Aviv University.

concern was that eager invaders would declare an area occupied prematurely. Because the law of occupation granted occupants control over key strategic resources, such as public property, invaders might be tempted to assert authority without actually controlling the area.[3] But over the years, and most notably since the adoption of Geneva Convention IV, which imposed on occupants extended obligations over civilians in occupied territories, and several human rights conventions that added to those obligations, occupants found little interest in asserting their status as occupants. The derogatory connotation that the term "occupation" has gained, particularly during the second half of the twentieth century, added to this reluctance. Moreover, the asymmetric nature of many of the recent conflicts has provided another incentive for the occupant to act through intermediaries or otherwise minimize its contact with particularly violent indigenous communities. Therefore, while the drafters of the original text on occupation law were concerned about overly assertive occupants, today's interpreters have to deal with occupants who try to evade this designation. With contemporary technology and weaponry that enables certain armies to control an area from a distance, a new challenge to the definition emerges.

Given the occupants' increasing ability and prevailing interest to control an area but not its population, it is important to note that the governing legal definitions seek to preclude this option and insist on the protection of individuals. The Hague Regulations emphasize the territorial test,[4] implying that whoever controls the territory has responsibility over the population, while Geneva Convention IV does not attempt a territorial definition, instead emphasizing the relations between the occupant and the "protected persons" who "find themselves . . . in the hands" of an occupying power[5] as the relevant test.

Some confusion, however, arises from the second sentence of Article 42 of the Hague Regulations, which stipulates that "[t]he occupation extends only to the territory where such authority has been established and can be exercised." This addition can at first sight be interpreted as suggesting that an occupant that manages to control only the land, but does not actually exercise authority over the civilian population, is freed from responsibility toward it. This reading is plainly wrong. It is wrong because the text was intended to exclude premature occupations, rather than to allow occupants to evade their responsibilities.[6] It is wrong also literally, because the reference in "such authority" is to the first sentence of the article, which discusses authority over *territory*, not over *the population* in the territory.[7] Finally, it is wrong because it lets occupants off the hook of responsibility toward the population. The better interpretation of the test for occupation therefore stipulates that occupation begins when the foreign army is in actual control *over enemy territory*, and is *in a position* to establish, if it so wishes, an authority of its own over the population. It is irrelevant whether or not the army *actually* does so. By assuming control over the land the occupant assumes responsibility over the population situated on that land.[8]

The same confusion is reflected in some States' military manuals. Whereas the German military manual accurately requires merely a *potential* to actually exercise authority,[9] the US military manual insists that the test for occupation is that the "invader has successfully substituted its own authority for that of the legitimate government in the territory invaded."[10] To add confusion, the British manual apparently contains an internal contradiction, as it appears to support both views. On the one hand, it stipulates that "the occupying power [must be] *in a position* to substitute its own authority for that of the former government" (paragraph 13.3), but later it indicates that occupation "depends on whether authority is actually being exercised over the civilian population."[11] In this confusing mist, the International Court of Justice (ICJ) adopted the "actual authority" test in the *Armed Activities* case.[12] Except for one district, where actual authority had been established and hence was regarded by the Court as occupied, the ICJ accepted Uganda's argument that in other areas it controlled only land, not people, and therefore did not "occupy" them.[13] In other words, in the ICJ's view, only direct authority *over a population* amounts to occupation. This is an unfortunate outcome.[14] It is unfortunate from the perspective of the local population, which is left with no accountable government in charge. It is also unfortunate from the perspective of neighboring States that are weary of geographical areas left without responsible State authority. An invader that is unaccountable for what transpires in an area it dominates is likely not to internalize the dangers emanating from the invaded territory, and, as a result, that area may become a source of regional, if not global, instability.

The Occupation of Iraq by the United States and the United Kingdom

It is quite obvious that the initial planning for the invasion of Iraq did not include plans to establish military administration whose authority would derive from the law of occupation. Months before the invasion, which began on March 20, 2003, officials in the US administration had been divided on the applicability of the law of occupation. While some of them believed it was appropriate, others viewed the situation not as occupation, but as mere "liberation."[15] Even after parts of Iraq had already been occupied and Baghdad was falling, President Bush and Prime Minister Blair emphasized this liberating role of their coalition and envisioned "the formation of an Iraqi Interim Authority, a transitional administration, run by Iraqis, until a permanent government is established by the people of Iraq."[16] Military officials still refused to speak of occupation in the legal, rather than colloquial, sense, and maintained that "occupation" in the legal sense required taking over an area "with the intent to run the government in that area,"[17] which, at the time, was not the case for the coalition forces in Iraq. But British jurists had a different view from the start. In a secret memorandum from late March, the British Attorney General, Lord Goldsmith, wrote that the United States and the United Kingdom would be bound by the law of occupation, unless the Security Council passed a specific resolution.[18]

These differences of opinion were reflected in a gradually changing attitude on the ground. The initial institution entrusted with administering occupied Iraqi territory was the US Office for Reconstruction and Humanitarian Assistance (ORHA), established two months before the ground invasion.[19] During the initial phase of the occupation, despite a late March Security Council resolution that had reminded coalition forces of an occupying power's responsibilities,[20] the coalition forces made efforts to set up an indigenous Iraqi regime. On April 15, Coalition officials held a meeting with Iraqi representatives in Nasiriyah, in which a thirteen-point statement on the political future of Iraq was adopted.[21] Together with a subsequent meeting, which took place on April 28 in Baghdad, these were part of "initial moves towards the establishment of a national conference, which could set up an interim authority and make progress towards constitutional change and the election of a new government."[22] But on April 16, only one day after the Nasiriyah meeting, without an explanation or a formal document setting it up,[23] the head of the ORHA announced the establishment of the Coalition Provisional Authority (CPA). Another three weeks passed until on May 8 the UK and US representatives to the UN sent a letter recognizing their obligations under the Hague Regulations and Geneva Convention IV.[24] L. Paul Bremer was appointed the US presidential envoy to Iraq on May 6 and the CPA Administrator on May 13.

The legal situation crystallized during the month of May as the occupying powers began seeking to establish their own government instead of setting up an interim Iraqi government. To do so they had to rely on authority under international law. While they did not explicitly acknowledge their status as occupants, they impliedly acknowledged the applicability of the Hague Regulations and Geneva Convention IV to their actions in Iraq. Explicit recognition of occupation law came later, when the British Foreign and Commonwealth Office relied on it expressly,[25] as did American legal advisors stationed in Iraq.[26]

Security Council Resolution 1483, of May 23, 2003, clarified the legal status of Iraq at the time. The Resolution "noted" the May 8 letter of the UK and US representatives, but continued to "recogniz[e] the specific authorities, responsibilities, and obligations under applicable international law of these States as *occupying powers* under unified command" (emphasis added).[27] The Resolution further "[*c*]*all*[*ed*] *upon* all concerned to comply fully with their obligations under international law including in particular the Geneva Conventions of 1949 and the Hague Regulations of 1907."[28]

But this was not meant to be a casebook example of occupation, because the occupants sought a broad Security Council mandate that went beyond the scope of authority recognized by international law.[29] The UN's role was meant to widen the authority of the CPA, while being instrumental—but without formal authority—in offering humanitarian relief and assistance to the CPA in the reconstruction of Iraq and the establishment of institutions for representative governance.[30]

Pre-occupation Responsibilities?

The traditional reading of the laws of armed conflict distinguishes between the hostilities and the post-hostilities phases. This distinction is also reflected in the different sections of the Hague Regulations. However, such a neat distinction can be questioned. As Dinstein notes, "[i]t is impossible to pinpoint an instant marking transition from an extended foray to a fledgling belligerent occupation."[31] Instead, it is possible to recognize the simultaneous applicability of both *in bello* and *post bellum* norms with respect to the obligations an enemy army has toward the local population.[32] Although it is beyond the scope of this article to explore this question in depth,[33] it can be noted that the obligations toward the population in enemy territory arise even before the establishment of firm control over territory and population. Given contemporary technology and weaponry, on the one hand, and the proliferation of weak or failing indigenous regimes, on the other, the neat allocation of responsibilities between occupant and occupied based on physical control of territory ("boots on the ground") does not serve humanitarian and global interests. It is necessary to impose legal restraints on any foreign power that effectively controls activity in a foreign area, even without having actual presence in the territory in the ancient form of full-fledged military administration. There is thus a need to redefine the rules of allocating responsibilities. The most sensible one would seem to be a rule that interprets authority as "power" (rather than "control" or "jurisdiction"), to be determined based on the consequences of the actual exercise of power in a given territory. A State that exercises its power in a foreign ungoverned or partly governed land will thus be regarded as bearing at least the basic obligations borne by an occupant.

This implies that pre-occupation obligations toward the local population need to be recognized, and they can derive, *inter alia*, from the obligations under Geneva Convention IV toward people who "find themselves . . . in the hands" of the invading army.[34] It would be ridiculous to suggest, for example, that Article 49 of that Convention, which proscribes deportations of enemy civilians, would be inapplicable unless the area has been occupied.[35] Similarly senseless would be the interpretation that only armies that actually substitute for the ousted government in a foreign territory are required to provide food and shelter to persons protected by Geneva Convention IV.

In the context of Iraq such questions were pertinent also to the failure to protect against looting. As in previous situations of invasions (e.g., Panama in 1989),[36] widespread looting followed the invasion and occupation of Iraq. On April 10, 2003, only one day after the fall of Baghdad to coalition forces, looting was already in progress.[37] But in Iraq the looting affected also art treasures and important archeological artifacts. The National Museum in Baghdad, for instance, lost around 15,000 artifacts.[38] Note that the Hague Convention on Cultural Property (1954)[39] obliges State parties[40] "to respect cultural property situated within their own territory as well as within the territory of other High Contracting Parties."[41] The Convention formally amplifies these duties during occupation, but they arguably apply also before the occupation stage.[42]

The End of Occupation

When Does Occupation Cease?

The occupation ends whenever the conditions of Article 42 of the Hague Regulations are no longer fulfilled.[43] Under the test of actual control, an occupation ends when the occupant no longer exercises its authority in the occupied territory. Under the test of potential control, the occupation ends when the occupant is no longer capable of exercising its authority. It is generally accepted that occupation continues as long as the occupying force can, within a reasonable time, send detachments of troops to make its authority felt within the occupied area.

In other words, an occupation ends as a result of the armed return of the ousted government, an indigenous uprising or a unilateral occupant withdrawal or as part of a peace agreement. The "legal oddity"[44] that is Article 6(3) of Geneva Convention IV does not affect the end of occupation. Although it stipulates that "the application of the present Convention shall cease one year after the general close of military operations," it does not regard the area as no longer occupied, and considers the occupant as bound by significant portions of the Convention,[45] as well as the Hague Regulations.[46]

A rather problematic question arises when the occupant transfers authority to an indigenous government that has no link to the ousted government. The law looks at such transfers with suspicion, because the concern is that the indigenous government might not be representative of the indigenous population and might be nothing but a puppet regime of the occupant. It is also worried about the commitment of the indigenous regime to respect the rights of the occupied population.[47] This is the challenge of what Roberts calls "transformative occupations," namely "occupations [that] aim at establishing a political order based on the principle of self-government."[48] In such occupations,

> determining at what point one can say that the transformation has been achieved, and the government of the occupied territory is in a position to exercise the powers of sovereignty, is genuinely difficult. . . . Where what is involved is a gradual transfer of powers to the indigenous authorities as their capacity to govern is built up, there is bound to be an arbitrary element in fixing on a single date as the symbolic ending of the occupation.[49]

Based on policy reasons and State practice, it can be said that "[t]he ultimate test for the legality of a regime installed by an occupant, is its approval in internationally monitored general elections, carried out without undue delay."[50]

The End of Occupation in Iraq

Although occupation is a matter of fact, its legal status can be subject to the determination of the Security Council acting under Chapter VII of the Charter as the ultimate arbiter of the law. Therefore, since Security Council Resolution 1546 stipulated that "by 30 June 2004, the occupation will end and the Coalition Provisional Authority will cease to exist, and that Iraq will reassert its full sovereignty,"[51] in the eyes of the law the occupation formally came to a close by June 30 despite the fact that the coalition forces were still exercising administrative authority in certain areas of Iraq.[52]

The discrepancy between the UN declaration on the reassertion of full Iraqi sovereignty and the actual state of affairs derives from the fact that at that point in time the fledgling Iraqi government was the construct of the occupation authority and was yet to be endorsed by a valid act of self-determination. Such an endorsement, which ended the occupation not only from the formal perspective, occurred only after the interim government of Iraq assumed full authority.[53]

Post-occupation Responsibilities?

If occupants may have pre-occupation responsibilities, they may be equally subject to post-occupation responsibilities to the extent that they continue to exert authority in the foreign territory. The previous occupant could also be responsible for ameliorating conditions it created in the previously occupied territory.[54]

Traditionally, in post-occupation situations, when former occupants were requested by the newly installed governments to maintain some authority, such authority was deemed to derive from the sovereigns' authorization, and hence was beyond the scope of the law of occupation. But this traditional view could be revisited. There may be sufficient ground to argue that even while exercising authority on the behest of an indigenous government, the entity that acts must comply with the international obligations to which it is bound. This is likely to be the case under international human rights law when the actor exercises authority over individuals who are under its control. This is also the case under international humanitarian law that stipulates minimal standards of treatment[55] under the national law of several countries.[56]

Such a view seems to find support in two recent judgments, related to the British occupation and post-occupation practices in Iraq. In the *Al-Jedda* case, the House of Lords ruled that even if the United Kingdom had been operating in Iraq on the UN's behalf (i.e., not as an occupant), it was still subject to its human rights obligations to the extent possible. As Lord Bingham noted, the United Kingdom could detain persons as authorized by the Security Council, "but must ensure that the detainee's rights . . . are not infringed to any greater extent than is inherent in such detention."[57] The same logic could apply to the post-occupation forces present in Iraq. More recently, the United Kingdom maintained that after the end of formal occupation, the British Army was merely an "executor" of decisions of Iraqi courts. Since prisoners were detained and transferred by the United Kingdom at the request of the Iraqi courts, the United Kingdom argued it did not exercise "any recognised extra-territorial authority."[58] The European Court of Human Rights (ECtHR), however, refused to regard that relationship between the British and the Iraqi government as one that excludes the applicability of the European Convention on Human Rights (ECHR) and the Court's jurisdiction. The gist of the idea is simple and convincing: acting under instructions of others cannot and does not relieve one of one's international obligations.

III. The Authority of the Occupants in Iraq

The Transformative Nature of the Occupation

Aiming to create a market-based democratic Iraq, the occupying powers introduced major administrative and legislative changes. These changes related not only to public order and security, to the "de-Ba'athification of Iraqi society," the overhauling of Iraqi criminal law and the judicial system, but also to areas often untouched during occupation, such as trade law,[59] company law,[60] securities law,[61] bankruptcy law,[62] and even intellectual property[63] and copyright laws.[64] The reasons usually given for these reforms were the need to promote human rights, efficiency, modernization and compliance with international standards. Because these reasons sometimes deviate from the traditional law of occupation, scholars referred to the occupation as "transformative."[65] This section reviews some of the more controversial changes introduced by the CPA. The subsequent section evaluates their compatibility with international law.

Among the many reforms taken by the occupants, it was the economic legislation that attracted the most criticism. Was it lawful, appropriate and needed to replace "all existing foreign investment law,"[66] to rewrite securities law almost completely,[67] to suspend all customs duties and tariffs,[68] and to profoundly change corporation law in a way that allows foreign citizens to acquire membership in companies?[69] The CPA sought to explain the motivation of these and other sweeping economic reforms by emphasizing indigenous endorsement. A key player in this indigenous participation was the Iraqi Governing Council, a "principal bod[y] of the Iraqi interim administration" established by the CPA on July 13, 2003.[70] The CPA emphasized that it "worked closely with the Governing Council to ensure that economic change occurs in a manner acceptable to the people of Iraq,"[71] and reiterated that the change was made "[i]n close consultation with and acting in coordination with the Governing Council."[72] In fact, the CPA attributed the foreign investment initiative to "the Governing Council's desire to bring about significant change to the Iraqi economic system."[73]

The CPA also relied on the UN authorization as an independent source of authority. Practically all orders issued by the CPA contained a preambular paragraph stressing their consistency with the laws and usages of war, as well as with the relevant Security Council resolutions. The CPA additionally relied on the report of the Secretary-General, which concerned "the need for the development of Iraq and its transition from a non-transparent centrally planned economy to a market economy characterized by sustainable economic growth,"[74] and often emphasized that it had "coordinated with the international financial institutions, as referenced in . . . U.N. Security Council Resolution 1483."[75]

Moreover, great efforts were made to show how the reforms would benefit Iraqi society. For example, the goal of foreign investment reforms was to "improve the conditions of life, technical skills, and opportunities for all Iraqis and to fight unemployment with its associated deleterious effect on public security."[76] The CPA saw itself obligated to "ensure the well being of the Iraqi people and to enable the social functions and normal transactions of every day [*sic*] life."[77]

The CPA didn't stop there. Economic modernity, fairness, efficiency, transparency, predictability and independence were invoked as justifications for several reforms.[78] Long-term policies were also mentioned: at one point, the CPA noted "the demonstrated interest of the Iraqi Governing Council for Iraq to become a full member in the international trading system, known as the World Trade Organization."[79]

The Lawfulness of the CPA Measures under International Law

The transformation of Iraq from a centralized dictatorship into a market-based democracy raised questions about the scope of authority of the CPA under international law. Some in the CPA really thought that the law of occupation allowed such wide-ranging reforms.[80] But British officials differed.[81] More generally, the British government distinguished "between *direct positive acts of government* and . . . the *facilitation of plans and efforts* of the nationals of the occupied territory for the development of governmental institutions,"[82] with only the latter being deemed permissible under occupation law.[83] To make reforms that go beyond the law of occupation, they maintained, "further authority in the form of a Security Council resolution would be required."[84] According to this view, with Security Council Resolution 1483 as the additional basis for the reforms, "the question of the UK's responsibilities in respect of political reform is no longer governed solely by the law of occupation."[85] Later the British discovered that they were expected to comply also with their international and European human rights obligations. As a consequence, in the occupation of Iraq there were three bodies of law—occupation law, human rights law and UN law—at play. This section analyzes the outcome.

Authority under the Law of Occupation

We begin with a succinct analysis of the scope of authority under the law of occupation. The request for authorization from the Security Council implies an acknowledgment of the limited authority granted to occupants under traditional occupation law. A textual reading of Article 43 of the Hague Regulations easily supports the conclusion that the occupant is bound by what Gregory Fox named "the conservationist principle."[86] The call for conservation of the *status quo ante bellum* is reflected in the admonition that the occupant has but de facto authority (whereas the ousted government is still the "legitimate power") in the restricted scope of authority "to restore, and ensure" public order and civil life, and in the obligation to respect the laws in force in the country "unless absolutely prevented."[87]

The term "unless absolutely prevented" was inserted during the First Peace Conference in 1899 to replace the term "unless necessary" at the insistence of the potentially occupied States to emphasize the occupant's obligation to also preserve the status quo in the legal sphere.[88] Whether this insertion was prudent is a different question. The restraint on the occupant's authority necessarily creates a tension with its authority and obligation to ensure public order and civil life. This restraint was significantly diluted by Article 64 of Geneva Convention IV, which replaced the negative test of "unless absolutely prevented" with a positive authorization for the occupant, which "may subject the population of the occupied territory to provisions which are essential to enable the Occupying Power to fulfill its obligations under the present Convention, to maintain the orderly government of the territory, and to ensure the security of the Occupying Power." The duties of the occupant under Geneva Convention IV are far more numerous than those stipulated in the Hague text. The Geneva text envisions the occupant no longer as the disinterested watch guard, but instead as a very involved regulator and provider.[89] Scholars in the post–World War II period readily conceded legitimate subjects for the occupant's lawmaking other than military necessity. The welfare of the population was deemed a worthy goal for the occupant to pursue.[90] Such an expansive view seems to be consonant with the prevalent view that the occupant is bound also by human rights obligations, and that in general it must "take measures to ensure respect for human rights and international humanitarian law in the occupied territories."[91]

The parallel applicability of international and, for the British troops, European human rights law raises additional questions regarding the authority of the occupants and the adequacy of the conservationist principle. It is beyond the scope of this article to explore the questions concerning the applicability of international and European human rights law to occupied territories, and the relationships between occupation law and human rights law. Still, international treaty bodies and tribunals,[92] as well as the majority of scholars,[93] are of the opinion that human rights law applies to occupied territories. The consequences of this parallel application would seem to support a modification of the conservationist principle when changes are necessary to ensure the enjoyment of human rights by the occupied population.[94]

Reflecting on the occupation of Iraq as a "transformative occupation," Adam Roberts noted that "occupying powers can justify certain transformative policies on the basis that these are the best way to meet certain goals and principles enshrined in international human rights law."[95] More generally, Roberts believes human rights conventions "can play an important role" in occupations, as they "may impose formal obligations on parties; be instrumental in political debate, as a basis for assessing the actions of external powers and local actors; provide legal procedures for taking action; or serve as one basis for pursuing transformative goals."[96] Other scholars accept this view with some insignificant nuances.

A particularly strong case can be made for extensive authorization to introduce significant changes in an occupied territory that had been governed by an unrepresentative regime that enjoyed little or no domestic support after being ousted by the occupant. The underlying premise of the law of occupation is, as was seen, that the legitimate power in the country retains the right to revert to its *ante bellum* position, unless it agrees to territorial changes. But when this power has already taken its last breath, or when its source of authority is contested by the indigenous population exercising its right to self-determination, the only legitimate power that seems relevant is the people itself and not the ousted regime. This is a situation where the "reversioner" is the people, and the occupant must take its interests and wishes, rather than those of the ousted regime, into account.[97] Such an argument can support the dismantling of the Ba'athist regime, which is evident in the CPA's first-ever legislative act, aptly titled "De-Ba'athification of Iraqi Society."[98] But it is important to keep in mind that even in such instances, reforms introduced by the occupant—as beneficial to the local population as they may be—are subject to the principle of self-determination. This principle may be "meaningful for the post-occupation society" only by refraining from making "overbroad systemic changes."[99] There is, therefore, ground to argue that the law of occupation, whether alone or together with the law on self-determination and human rights law, gave the occupants in Iraq a wide margin of discretion.[100]

It is noteworthy that the two occupants of Iraq did not wish to found their transformative occupation on their human rights obligations. In fact, they both rejected the applicability of human rights law in Iraq.[101] The US government has claimed that the International Covenant on Civil and Political Rights[102] does not apply outside its territory or during an international armed conflict.[103] In the midst of the Iraq conflict, the United States expressed its "firm belief" that humanitarian law is a "well-developed area of law conceptually distinct from international human rights law," and that the two cannot apply simultaneously.[104] The United Kingdom, as a party to the ECHR, had to face numerous petitions in relation to the ECHR's applicability in Iraq, and offered several reasons why it was not bound by that treaty[105]—reasons that did not impress the British courts[106] or the ECtHR.[107]

Authority under Security Council Resolution 1483

Security Council Resolution 1483 provided the framework for the coalition's actions in Iraq. On the one hand, it endorsed its authority over Iraq and the Iraqi people, and, on the other hand, it delineated the legal constraints and guidelines that this authority was bound by, namely "the Charter of the United Nations and other relevant international law,"[108] and other "obligations under international law including in particular the Geneva Conventions of 1949 and the Hague Regulations of 1907."[109] The President of the Security Council emphasized that the powers delegated by the Resolution "are not open-ended or unqualified," and should be exercised "in conformity with the Geneva Conventions and the Hague Regulations."[110] Concurrently, however, the Resolution clearly endorsed the transformative course of action that the CPA embarked upon immediately. The occupants, referred to as the "Authority" in the Resolution, are

> [*c*]*all*[*ed*] *upon*... consistent with the Charter of the United Nations and other relevant international law, to promote the welfare of the Iraqi people through the effective administration of the territory, including in particular working towards the restoration of conditions of security and stability and the creation of conditions in which the Iraqi people can freely determine their own political future....[111]

Furthermore, Resolution 1483 created a new position, the "Special Representative for Iraq," which would be independent of the occupying power and whose tasks would include assisting the people of Iraq, coordinating the activities of the United Nations in post-conflict processes in Iraq and with international agencies engaged in humanitarian assistance and reconstruction activities in Iraq, and promoting the protection of human rights.[112]

How should one read this Resolution? Does it endorse an expansive view of the law of occupation, or does it form an independent source of authority on the strength of Chapter VII law? Indeed, there are three possible interpretations of Resolution 1483. According to the first reading, the Resolution endorses an expansive reading, influenced by human rights law, of the occupant's authority under the law of occupation. A slightly different interpretation of the Resolution would suggest that the expansive reading of the occupant's powers applies only to the unique circumstances of Iraq as opposed to all other occupations. The third possible interpretation of the Resolution would be that the Resolution gave the occupants additional authority to transform Iraq that they would not have had otherwise. As mentioned above, at least British officials relied on the latter interpretation, having concluded that the law of occupation as such stopped short of granting them extensive authority.

In these authors' view, Resolution 1483 relates, of course, only to the specific situation in Iraq, but at the same time it signals an endorsement of a *general* view that regards modern occupants as subject to enhanced duties toward the occupied population and therefore also having the authority to fulfill such duties. "The call to administer the occupied area 'effectively' acknowledges the several duties that the occupants must perform to protect the occupied population. It precludes the occupant from hiding behind the limits imposed on its powers as a pretext for inaction."[113] Indeed, an evolutionary reading of the law of occupation in an era heavily informed by human rights concerns cannot reach a different conclusion.[114]

This interpretation is based not only on the Resolution or the evolutionary interpretation of the law of occupation. It is also based on the authority of the Security Council when acting under Chapter VII of the UN Charter. This authority is not limitless but subject at least to compliance with *jus cogens*.[115] One of the central *jus cogens* norms is the right of peoples to self-determination.[116] The law of occupation internalizes a delicate balance between conflicting interests of occupant and occupied, and is heavily influenced by the effort not to alienate the indigenous people's right to continue to exercise its right to self-determination.[117] The law of occupation has always been intimately linked to the concept of national sovereignty. "Indeed, the evolution of the concept of occupation can be seen as the mirror-image of the development of the concept of sovereignty."[118] Therefore, authorizing an occupant to derogate from its responsibilities under the law of occupation and thereby limit and shape the political choices of an occupied sovereign people carries the danger of effectively infringing the right to self-determination, which might be beyond the authority of the Council.[119]

Obviously, not every limitation of the right to self-determination is an impermissible infringement of a *jus cogens* right. There may be solid reasons to interfere in the exercise of the right to self-determination to ensure that the process is practical, inclusive and fair. It is also reasonable to argue that the Security Council is more trustworthy than the occupant to be entrusted with such a complex matter, and therefore it may be granted the authority to limit or influence the exercise of the right to self-determination to a greater extent than the occupant would, as is the case in territories directly administered by the UN.[120] The Security Council is clearly less prone to bias than the occupant, if only because of its diverse composition and lack of immediate interest.[121] It therefore makes eminent sense to recognize that the Security Council would have the authority under Chapter VII of the Charter to authorize the transformation of a regime under occupation beyond what the law of occupation would otherwise allow, but this could not be an unfettered discretion delegated to interested parties without monitoring them. If the Security Council wished to extend such an authorization to the occupant, it would have to remain closely involved, through ample supervisory mechanisms, effectively approving and reviewing the actual transformation process. Because such mechanisms were not employed in the case of Iraq, the CPA having acted with limited monitoring by the Council,[122] one could understand its attitude either as carelessness that bordered on infringement of its *jus cogens* obligations or as a reflection of its general attitude toward the occupant's powers under the law of occupation.

IV. Conclusion: The Legacy of the Occupation of Iraq

The occupation of Iraq raises a host of questions beyond the scope of a single article. In addition to questions regarding the timing of the occupation, pre- and post-occupation responsibilities, and the scope of authority of the occupant in transformative occupation, the occupation of Iraq gave rise to queries regarding the definition of protected persons[123] and the proper interpretation of Article 49 of the Fourth Geneva Convention,[124] in addition to the proper treatment of detainees and the responsibility for their shameful abuse. The management by the occupants of public property, including natural resources such as oil and freshwater, was also subject to legal analyses.[125] Overall it is almost astounding to observe how a nineteenth-century doctrine that during the last half century almost reached the stage of desuetude due to lack of adherence was suddenly revived in unanticipated circumstances. Critics could argue that its invocation was nothing more than an afterthought, a sort of "Plan B" that was put in motion after the effort to install a "genuine" indigenous regime failed. Nevertheless, the doctrine was there ready to be applied, flexible enough to be adapted to twenty-first-century contemporary circumstances and challenges, as well as current legal and political perceptions.

Resolution 1483 marks the first time the Security Council resorted to the concept of occupation to describe, authorize and delimit the authority of foreign troops in control of enemy territory. The recognition of the applicability of the law on occupations refuted the claim that occupation, as such, is illegal, and revived the neutral connotation of the doctrine, at least from a legal perspective. At the same time, the broad mandate recognized by the Security Council as pertaining to the occupants to transform Iraq into a market-based democracy, although commendable and probably lawful under UN Charter law, also tested the limits of the law of occupation and the Security Council's own authority to shape the way the Iraqi people exercised their inalienable right to self-determination.

Notes

1. On the history of the law of occupation, see Eyal Benvenisti, *The Origins of the Concept of Belligerent Occupation*, 26 LAW & HISTORY REVIEW 621 (2008); Nehal Bhuta, *The Antinomies of Transformative Occupation*, 16 EUROPEAN JOURNAL OF INTERNATIONAL LAW 721 (2005).

2. EYAL BENVENISTI, THE INTERNATIONAL LAW OF OCCUPATION 5 (1993).

3. For this reason, "to extend the rights of occupation by mere intention, implication or proclamation, without the military power to enforce occupation, would be establishing a paper occupation infinitely more objectionable in its character and effect than a paper blockade." DORIS APPEL GRABER, THE DEVELOPMENT OF THE LAW OF BELLIGERENT OCCUPATION 1863–1914: A HISTORICAL SURVEY 56 (1949).

4. Regulations Respecting the Laws and Customs of War on Land, Annexed to Convention No. IV Respecting the Laws and Customs of War on Land art. 42, Oct. 18, 1907, 36 Stat. 2227, *reprinted in* DOCUMENTS ON THE LAWS OF WAR 69, 80 (Adam Roberts & Richard Guelff eds., 3d ed. 2000) ("Territory is considered occupied when it is actually placed under the authority of the hostile army. The occupation extends only to the territory where such authority has been established and can be exercised") [hereinafter Hague Regulations].

5. Convention Relative to the Protection of Civilian Persons in Time of War art. 4, Aug. 12, 1949, 6 U.S.T. 3516, 75 U.N.T.S. 287, *reprinted in id.* at 301, 302 [hereinafter Geneva Convention IV].

6. Suggestions in the Hague conference of 1899 to remove the second sentence had been rejected, as it was seen as crucial to the understanding of the first sentence. The Belgian representative insisted that the second sentence's absence might lead to premature proclamations of occupation. *See* GRABER, *supra* note 3, at 60.

7. "Territory is considered occupied when *it* is actually placed under the authority of the hostile army" (authors' emphasis).

8. *See* Armed Activities on the Territory of the Congo (Dem. Rep. Congo v. Uganda), 2005 I.C.J. 116 (Dec. 19) (separate opinion of Judge Kooijmans, ¶ 49) ("I am, therefore, of the opinion that it is irrelevant from a legal point of view whether [Uganda] exercised this authority directly or left much of it to local forces or local authorities. As long as it effectively occupied *the locations* which the DRC Government would have needed to re-establish its authority, Uganda had *effective*, and thus factual, authority" (first emphasis added)).

9. Federal Ministry of Defense of the Federal Republic of Germany, ZDv 15/2, Humanitarian Law in Armed Conflicts: Manual ¶ 526 (1992) ("[T]he occupying power must *be able to* actually exercise its *authority*" (first emphasis added)).

10. DEPARTMENT OF THE ARMY, FM 27-10, THE LAW OF LAND WARFARE ¶ 355 (1956).

11. UNITED KINGDOM MINISTRY OF DEFENCE, THE MANUAL OF THE LAW OF ARMED CONFLICT ¶¶ 13.3, 13.3.2 (2004) (authors' emphases).

12. Armed Activities on the Territory of the Congo (Dem. Rep. Congo v. Uganda), 2005 I.C.J. 116, ¶ 173 (Dec. 19) ("the Court must examine whether . . . the said authority was in fact established and exercised") [hereinafter Armed Activities case].

13. *Id.*, ¶ 170.

14. See the critical comments of Judge Kooijmans in his separate opinion, *supra* note 8, ¶¶ 40–41.

15. David Scheffer, *The Security Council and International Law on Military Occupations*, *in* THE UNITED NATIONS SECURITY COUNCIL AND WAR: THE EVOLUTION OF THOUGHT AND PRACTICE SINCE 1945, at 597 (Vaughan Lowe et al. eds., 2008); Adam Roberts, *Transformative Military Occupation: Applying the Laws of War and Human Rights*, 100 AMERICAN JOURNAL OF INTERNATIONAL LAW 580, 608–9 (2006).

16. Joint Statement by President George W. Bush and Prime Minister Tony Blair on Iraq, 1 PUBLIC PAPERS 328 (Apr. 8, 2003), *available at* http://usa.usembassy.de/etexts/docs/bush080403.htm ("The Interim Authority will be broad-based and fully representative, with members from all of Iraq's ethnic groups, regions and diaspora. The Interim Authority will be established first and foremost by the Iraqi people, with the help of the members of the Coalition, and working with the Secretary General of the United Nations").

17. United States Department of Defense News Transcript, Briefing on Geneva Convention, EPW's and War Crimes (Apr. 7, 2003), http://www.au.af.mil/au/awc/awcgate/dod/t04072003_t407genv.html. When asked whether the United States was an occupying power in Iraq, W. Hays Parks, Special Assistant to the Army Judge Advocate General, replied: "Obviously, we occupy a great deal of Iraq at this time. But we are not, in the technical sense of the law of war, a military occupier or occupation force."

18. John Kampfner, *Blair Was Told It Would Be Illegal to Occupy Iraq*, NEW STATESMAN, May 26, 2003, *available at* http://www.newstatesman.com/200305260010.

19. L. Elaine Halchin, Congressional Research Service, *The Coalition Provisional Authority (CPA): Origin, Characteristics, and Institutional Authorities* 1–2 (Apr. 29, 2004), *available at* http://www.fas.org/man/crs/RL32370.pdf.

20. S.C. Res. 1472, U.N. Doc. S/RES/1472 (Mar. 28, 2003). However, this Resolution was ambiguous and did not expressly say that the occupation had begun.

21. Plan Unveiled for Iraq (Apr. 15, 2003), http://www.abc.net.au/news/stories/2003/04/15/832822.htm. Principle 13 stated: "The Iraqi participation in the Nasiriyah meeting voted that there should be another meeting in 10 days in a location to be determined with additional Iraqi participants and to discuss procedures for developing an Iraqi interim authority."

22. Paul Bowers, Iraq: Law of Occupation, House of Commons Library Research Paper 03/51 (June 2, 2003), *available at* http://www.parliament.uk/commons/lib/research/rp2003/rp03-051.pdf [hereinafter Research Paper 03/51].

23. Roberts, *supra* note 15, at 610 n.12. It is not clear *how* the CPA was legally established. *See* Halchin, *supra* note 19, at 4.

24. Letter Dated 8 May 2003 from the Permanent Representatives of the United Kingdom of Great Britain and Northern Ireland and the United States of America to the United Nations Addressed to the President of the Security Council, U.N. Doc. S/2003/538 (May 8, 2003).

25. Committee on Foreign Affairs Written Evidence, Memorandum from the Foreign and Commonwealth Office (May 13, 22, 2003), *available at* http://www.publications.parliament.uk/pa/cm200203/cmselect/cmfaff/405/405we04.htm.

26. NOAH FELDMAN, WHAT WE OWE IRAQ: WAR AND THE ETHICS OF NATION BUILDING 54–56 (2004).

27. S.C. Res. 1483, U.N. Doc. S/RES/1483 (May 23, 2003). As a "unified command," the countries operating in Iraq "bear the brunt of joint responsibility for what is happening within the area subject to their combined effective control." YORAM DINSTEIN, THE INTERNATIONAL LAW OF BELLIGERENT OCCUPATION 48 (2009). This unified command eventually took the form of the Coalition Provisional Authority. For a discussion of the Authority's creation and structure, see Halchin, *supra* note 19. For an explanation of how the CPA fits in the legal framework of the Hague Regulations, see Michael A. Newton, *The Iraqi Special Tribunal: A Human Rights Perspective*, 38 CORNELL INTERNATIONAL LAW JOURNAL 863, 872 (2005).

28. S.C. Res. 1483, *supra* note 27, ¶ 5.

29. *See infra* pp. 274–76. The two States sought to obtain a UN mandate in order to "evade legal difficulties if [they] sought to move beyond the limited rights conferred by the Hague Regulations and Geneva Convention IV to vary existing arrangements." *See* Research Paper 03/51, *supra* note 22, at 16.

30. S.C. Res. 1483, *supra* note 27, pmbl.

31. DINSTEIN, *supra* note 27, at 39.

32. This arguably applies also to questions concerning the rules of engagement, which are beyond the scope of this article.

33. *See* Eyal Benvenisti, *The Law on Asymmetric Warfare*, *in* LOOKING TO THE FUTURE: ESSAYS ON INTERNATIONAL LAW IN HONOR OF W. MICHAEL REISMAN (Mahnoush Arsanjani, Jacob Cogan, Robert Sloane & Siegfried Wiessner eds. (forthcoming 2010)).

34. Geneva Convention IV, *supra* note 5, art. 4.

35. See the determination of the International Criminal Tribunal for the former Yugoslavia (ICTY) Trial Chamber in Prosecutor v. Naletilić & Martinović, Case No. IT-98-34-T, Judgment, ¶ 221 (Mar. 31, 2003) (reasoning that "[o]therwise civilians would be left, during an intermediate period, with less protection than that attached to them once occupation is established").

36. For the US military's failure to prevent the looting in Panama, see DONALD P. WRIGHT & TIMOTHY R. REESE, ON POINT II: TRANSITION TO THE NEW CAMPAIGN: THE UNITED STATES ARMY IN OPERATION IRAQI FREEDOM, MAY 2003–JANUARY 2005, at 55 (2008), *available at* http://www.globalsecurity.org/military/library/report/2008/onpoint/chap02-02.htm.

37. Frank Rich, *And Now: 'Operation Iraqi Looting*,' NEW YORK TIMES, Apr. 27, 2003, § 2, at 1, *available at* http://www.nytimes.com/2003/04/27/arts/and-now-operation-iraqi-looting.html.

38. Roger Cohen, *The Ghost in the Baghdad Museum*, NEW YORK TIMES, Apr. 2, 2006, § 2, at 1, *available at* http://www.nytimes.com/2006/04/02/arts/design/02cohe.html.

39. Convention for the Protection of Cultural Property in the Event of Armed Conflict, May 14, 1954, 249 U.N.T.S. 240, *reprinted in* DOCUMENTS ON THE LAWS OF WAR, *supra* note 4, at 373, *available at* http://www.icrc.org/IHL.NSF/FULL/400?OpenDocument [hereinafter Hague Convention on Cultural Property].

40. The Convention is relevant to the Iraq war assuming the Convention, which currently has 123 parties, is customary law. When the war began, the United States and the United Kingdom were merely signatories (US ratification came on March 13, 2009); Iraq was a party.

41. Hague Convention on Cultural Property, *supra* note 39, art. 4(1).

42. The occupant is required to "support the competent national authorities of the occupied country in safeguarding and preserving its cultural property" and "take the most necessary measures of preservation" (*id.*, art. 5). Since lootings often erupt in the post-invasion, pre-occupation phase, it is sensible to give cultural property a higher degree of protection, usually pertinent in occupations, and oblige the invading power to actively secure art, archeology and similarly endangered resources.

43. For these conditions see pp. 263–64 *supra*, as well as the ICTY's determination in Naletilić & Martinović, *supra* note 35, ¶ 215. *See also* Prosecutor v. Kordić & Čerkez, Case No. IT-95-14/2-T, Judgment, ¶ 338–39 (Feb. 26, 2001).

44. The "one year after" rule probably never reflected customary law but was instead understood as a specific reference to the post-WWII occupations in Germany and Japan. Adam Roberts, *Prolonged Military Occupation: The Israeli-Occupied Territories since 1967*, 84 AMERICAN JOURNAL OF INTERNATIONAL LAW 44, 57 (1990) ("In general, the 'one year after' provision of 1949 must be viewed as a legal oddity"). Professor Bothe and his fellow authors say:

> Article 6(3) of the Fourth Convention . . . was a special ad hoc provision for certain actual cases, namely the occupation of Germany and Japan after World War II. There is no reason to continue to keep in force such provisions designed for specific historic cases. In 1972 the majority of government experts expressed a wish to abolish these time limits.

MICHAEL BOTHE ET AL., NEW RULES FOR VICTIMS OF ARMED CONFLICTS: COMMENTARY ON THE TWO 1977 PROTOCOLS ADDITIONAL TO THE GENEVA CONVENTIONS OF 1949, at 59 (1982). According to Article 3(b) of Additional Protocol I, occupation law ceases to apply "on the termination of the occupation." Protocol Additional to the Geneva Conventions of 12 August 1949, and Relating to the Protection of Victims of International Armed Conflicts, June 8, 1977, 1125 U.N.T.S. 3, *reprinted in* DOCUMENTS ON THE LAWS OF WAR, *supra* note 4, at 422. The ICJ referred to Article 6(3) as relevant in the *Wall* advisory opinion (Legal Consequences of the Construction of a Wall in the Occupied Palestinian Territory, Advisory Opinion, 2004 I.C.J. 136, 185 (July 9) [hereinafter Wall Advisory Opinion]), but it is widely accepted that this reference was seriously flawed. *See* Michael J. Dennis, *Application of Human Rights Treaties Extraterritorially in Times of Armed Conflict and Military Occupation*, 99 AMERICAN JOURNAL OF INTERNATIONAL LAW 119, 134 (2005); Roberts, *supra* note 15, at 597; Ardi Imseis, *Critical Reflections on the International Humanitarian Law Aspects of the ICJ Wall Advisory Opinion*, 99 AMERICAN JOURNAL OF INTERNATIONAL LAW 102, 105–9 (2005).

45. This is clear from the text of Article 6(3) itself, which reads:

> [*I*]*n the case of occupied territory*, the *application* of the present Convention shall cease one year after the general close of military operations; however, the Occupying Power shall be bound, for the duration of the occupation, to the extent that such Power exercises the functions of government in such territory, by the provisions of the

following Articles of the present Convention: 1 to 12, 27, 29 to 34, 47, 49, 51, 52, 53, 59, 61 to 77, 143 [emphasis added].

In other words, occupation continues, but it is no longer subject to the entirety of the Convention.

46. See Geneva Convention IV, *supra* note 5, art. 154, discussing the relationship between the Geneva and Hague texts.

47. *See, e.g.*, *id.*, art. 47.

48. Roberts, *supra* note 15, at 616.

49. *Id.*

50. BENVENISTI, *supra* note 2, at 173.

51. S.C. Res. 1546, ¶ 2, U.N. Doc. S/RES/1546 (June 8, 2004).

52. DINSTEIN, *supra* note 27, at 273 (the occupation ended "only 'notionally'"). While Sassòli agrees that this was the legal effect of Resolution 1546, he criticizes it and calls it a "dangerous precedent." Marco Sassòli, *Legislation and Maintenance of Public Order and Civil Life by Occupying Powers*, 16 EUROPEAN JOURNAL OF INTERNATIONAL LAW 661, 684 (2005).

53. It is hard to point at a specific time when that happened. The assumption of authority was gradual, just as the occupation did not end overnight. See Adam Roberts, *The End of Occupation: Iraq 2004*, 54 INTERNATIONAL & COMPARATIVE LAW QUARTERLY 27, 46 (2005), discussing Iraq's status after June 28, 2003 ("The Interim Government, while exercising a wide range of governmental decision-making powers, is constrained in key respects by its essentially caretaker character, the formal restrictions as regards 'taking any decisions affecting Iraq's destiny', the limitations on its treaty-making powers, and its weaknesses in certain areas when compared to the position of external powers in Iraq").

54. *See* Eyal Benvenisti, *The Law on the Unilateral Termination of Occupation*, *in* A WISER CENTURY? JUDICIAL DISPUTE SETTLEMENT, DISARMAMENT AND THE LAWS OF WAR 100 YEARS AFTER THE SECOND HAGUE PEACE CONFERENCE 371, 379 (Thomas Giegerich ed., 2009).

55. For example, coalition forces must respect Common Article 3 of the Geneva Conventions, as well as Article 75 of Additional Protocol I (both providing fundamental guarantees), as long as they continue to participate in an armed conflict.

56. American and British laws may bind American and British soldiers, respectively, even when the soldiers are stationed abroad. See Justice Barak's reasoning in HCJ 393/82 Jama'it Askan Alma'amun v. Commander of IDF Forces [1983] IsrSC 37(4) 785, 810 ("Every Israeli soldier carries in his backpack the customary rules of public international law relating to the laws of war, as well as the basic rules of Israeli administrative law").

57. R (on the application of Al-Jedda) v. The Secretary of State for Defence [2007] UKHL 58, ¶ 39 [hereinafter Al-Jedda case].

58. Al-Saadoon and Mufdhi v. United Kingdom, App. No. 61498/08 (admissibility decision), ¶ 79, http://www.echr.coe.int/eng ("The applicants were detained and transferred by United Kingdom forces solely on the basis of decisions taken unilaterally by the Iraqi courts") [hereinafter Al-Saadoon case]. The ECtHR had determined that this argument was not "material" to the admissibility decision, and would be discussed in relation to the merits of the case. *See id.*, ¶ 89.

59. CPA Order No. 54, Trade Liberalization Policy 2004 with Annex A (Feb. 24, 2004). All CPA orders, regulations and memoranda are available at http://www.cpa-iraq.org/regulations/ (then hyperlink by name of order, regulation or memorandum).

60. CPA Order No. 64, Amendment to the Company Law No. 21 of 1997 with Annex A (Feb. 29, 2004).

61. CPA Order No. 74, Interim Law on Security Markets (Apr. 18, 2004).

62. CPA Order No. 78, Facilitation of Court-supervised Debt Resolution Procedures (Apr. 19, 2004).

63. CPA Order No. 80, Amendment to the Trademarks and Descriptions Law No. 21 of 1957 (Apr. 26, 2004).

64. CPA Order No. 83, Amendment to the Copyright Law (Apr. 29, 2004).

65. *E.g.*, Roberts, *supra* note 15; Gregory Fox, *The Occupation of Iraq*, 36 GEORGETOWN JOURNAL OF INTERNATIONAL LAW 195 (2005).

66. CPA Order No. 39, Foreign Investment (Sept. 19, 2003).

67. CPA Order No. 74, *supra* note 61.

68. CPA Order No. 56, Central Bank Law with Annex A (Feb. 24, 2004).

69. CPA Order No. 64, *supra* note 60.

70. CPA Regulation No. 6, Governing Council of Iraq (July 13, 2003). *See also* S.C. Res. 1511, ¶ 4, U.N. Doc. S/RES/1511 (Oct. 6, 2003) ("the Governing Council and its ministers are the principal bodies of the Iraqi interim administration, which, without prejudice to its further evolution, embodies the sovereignty of the State of Iraq during the transitional period until an internationally recognized, representative government is established and assumes the responsibilities of the Authority"). The Governing Council was dissolved on June 1, 2004 (CPA Regulation No. 9, Governing Council's Dissolution (June 9, 2004)) and replaced by the interim government of Iraq (CPA Order No. 100, Transition of Laws, Regulations, Orders, and Directives Issued by the CPA (June 28, 2004)).

71. CPA Order No. 39, *supra* note 66, pmbl.

72. *Id.*

73. *Id.*

74. As articulated by CPA Order No. 78, *supra* note 62.

75. CPA Order No. 40, Bank Law with Annex A (Sept. 19, 2003).

76. CPA Order No. 39, *supra* note 66, pmbl.

77. *Id.*

78. See, for instance, CPA Orders No. 64, *supra* note 60; No. 74, *supra* note 61; No. 80, *supra* note 63; No. 83, *supra* note 64.

79. CPA Order No. 80, *supra* note 63.

80. Theodore W. Kassinger & Dylan J. Williams, *Commercial Law Reform Issues in the Reconstruction of Iraq*, 33 GEORGIA JOURNAL OF INTERNATIONAL & COMPARATIVE LAW 217, 218–19 (2004).

81. Or as the Attorney General put it in late March 2003, "[T]he imposition of major structural economic reforms would not be authorised by international law." Kampfner, *supra* note 18.

82. Kayian Homi Kaikobad, *Problems of Belligerent Occupation: The Scope of Powers Exercised by the Coalition Provisional Authority in Iraq, April/May 2003–June 2004*, 54 INTERNATIONAL & COMPARATIVE LAW QUARTERLY 253, 260 (2005) (emphasis in original).

83. Committee on Foreign Affairs Written Evidence, *supra* note 25 ("Whilst the introduction of democratic changes in government can not be imposed by the Occupying Powers, this does not affect the rights of the Iraqi people themselves to develop their own systems of government. It is therefore permissible for the Occupying Powers to play a facilitating role in relation to reforms genuinely undertaken by the people of Iraq themselves").

84. *Id.*

85. *Id.*

86. Fox, *supra* note 65, at 263.

87. Hague Regulations, *supra* note 4, art. 43 ("The authority of the legitimate power having in fact passed into the hands of the occupant, the latter shall take all the measures in his power to restore, and ensure, as far as possible, public order and safety, while respecting, unless absolutely prevented, the laws in force in the country").

88. Benvenisti, *supra* note 1, at 646–47.

89. The occupant is required to ensure the humane treatment of protected persons, without discriminating among them, and to respect, among other things, the protected persons' honor, family rights, religious convictions and practices, and manners and customs. Geneva Convention IV, *supra* note 5, art. 27. Additionally, it is required to facilitate the proper working of all institutions devoted to the care and education of children (*id.*, art. 51), provide specific labor conditions (*id.*, art. 52), ensure food and medical supplies to the population (*id.*, art. 55), maintain medical services (*id.*, art. 56), and agree to relief schemes and to facilitate them by all means at its disposal (*id.*, art. 59).

90. GERHARD VON GLAHN, THE OCCUPATION OF ENEMY TERRITORY: A COMMENTARY ON THE LAW AND PRACTICE OF BELLIGERENT OCCUPATION 97 (1957); MORRIS GREENSPAN, THE MODERN LAW OF LAND WARFARE 224 (1959); MYRES S. MCDOUGAL & FLORENTINO P. FELICIANO, LAW AND MINIMUM WORLD PUBLIC ORDER 767, 770 (1961); ODILE DEBBASCH, *L'OCCUPATION MILITAIRE: POUVOIRS RECONNUS AUX FORCES ARMÉES HORS DE LEUR TERRITOIRE NATIONAL* 172 (1962); LORD MCNAIR & ARNOLD DUNCAN WATTS, LEGAL EFFECTS OF WAR 369 (1966). For a more conservative view, see Michael Bothe, *Belligerent Occupation*, *in* 4 ENCYCLOPEDIA OF PUBLIC INTERNATIONAL LAW 65 (Rudolf Bernhardt ed., 1982); RÜDIGER WOLFRUM, DEVELOPMENTS OF INTERNATIONAL LAW IN TREATY MAKING 9 (2005).

91. Armed Activities case, *supra* note 12, ¶ 211.

92. ICJ (Wall Advisory Opinion, *supra* note 44); ECtHR (Loizidou v. Turkey, App. No. 15318/89, 23 Eur. H.R. Rep. 513 (1996) (merits) (the European Convention on Human Rights applies to the part of Cyprus occupied by Turkey)); UN Human Rights Committee (Concluding Observations of the Human Rights Committee: Israel, U.N. Doc. CCPR/C/79/Add.93 (Aug. 18, 1998), *available at* http://www1.umn.edu/humanrts/hrcommittee/israel1998.html).

93. *See, e.g.*, Roberts, *supra* note 44, at 70 ("the scope-of-application provisions of human rights accords do not exclude their applicability in principle, even if they do, as noted below, permit certain derogations in time of emergency"); ESTHER COHEN, HUMAN RIGHTS IN THE ISRAELI-OCCUPIED TERRITORIES 1967–1982, at 28–29 (1985); BENVENISTI, *supra* note 2, at 187–89. *But see* Yoram Dinstein, *Human Rights in Armed Conflict: International Humanitarian Law*, *in* HUMAN RIGHTS IN INTERNATIONAL LAW 345, 350–52 (Theodor Meron ed., 1985) (stipulating that most human rights exist in peacetime but may disappear completely in wartime; Dinstein later supported the simultaneous applicability of human rights law. *See* DINSTEIN, *supra* note 27, 69–71).

94. DINSTEIN, *supra* note 27, at 113 (an occupant may repeal existing legislation that is inconsistent with binding norms of international law such as Geneva Convention IV), 115 (the occupant may legislate "at the behest" of the local population), 116 (the occupant has a "right to revise and even reform legislation in consonance with new developments"). Sassòli endorses an expansive authority to legislate and he does so with the local population's best interests in mind. Aside from the usual exceptions to the conservationist principle, he supports occupant legislation that is "essential for the implementation of IHL [international humanitarian law]" and that realizes human rights law or maintains civil life (Sassòli, *supra* note 52, at 675–77). In his view,

> [t]he occupying power . . . has an obligation to abolish legislation and institutions which contravene international human rights standards. . . . [I]t may introduce only as many changes as is absolutely necessary under its human rights obligations and must

stay as close as possible to similar local standards and the local cultural, legal and economic traditions.

Id. at 676–77.

95. Roberts, *supra* note 15, at 620. One such scenario is when "the occupant and/or international bodies properly refer to human rights law as providing a legal basis for changing certain laws of the occupied territory, or even as setting goals for a transformative occupation." *Id.* at 601.

96. *Id.* at 600.

97. Melissa Patterson, Note, *Who's Got the Title? or, The Remnants of Debellatio in Post-Invasion Iraq*, 47 HARVARD INTERNATIONAL LAW JOURNAL 467 (2006).

98. CPA Order No. 1, De-Ba'athification of Iraqi Society (May 16, 2003). *See also* CPA Memorandum No. 1, Implementation of De-Ba'athification Order No. 1 (June 3, 2003).

99. Fox, *supra* note 65, at 277.

100. An alternative basis for the applicability of international human rights treaties in occupied territories would be the law of occupation itself. Article 43 of the Hague Regulations requires the occupant to respect "the laws in force in the country." To the extent that international treaties, including human rights treaties, form part of the local law, the occupant is bound to respect them as well. Hague Regulations, *supra* note 4, art. 43.

101. That did not keep the CPA from taking human rights considerations into account—e.g., CPA Order No. 19, Freedom of Assembly (July 9, 2003) ("*Determined* to remove the unacceptable restrictions on human rights of the former Iraqi Ba`ath Party regime . . .").

102. International Covenant on Civil and Political Rights, Dec. 16, 1966, 999 U.N.T.S. 171, *reprinted in* 6 INTERNATIONAL LEGAL MATERIALS 368 (1967).

103. United States Department of Defense, Working Group Report on Detainee Interrogations in the Global War on Terrorism: Assessment of Legal, Historical, Policy, and Operational Considerations 6 (Apr. 4, 2003), *available at* http://www.dod.gov/pubs/foi/detainees/working_grp_report_detainee_interrogations.pdf. *See also* Brief for Appellees at 41–42, Al Odah v. U.S., 321 F.3d 1134 (D.C. Cir. 2003) (No. 02-5251), *available at* http://www.aclu.org/hrc/Post911_AlAdah_v_US.pdf.

104. Press Release, U.S. Mission to the U.N. in Geneva, General Comments of the United States on Basic Principles and Guideline on the Right to a Remedy for Victims of Violations of International Human Rights and Humanitarian Law (Aug. 15, 2003), *cited in* Michael J. Kelly, *Critical Analysis of the International Court of Justice Ruling on Israel's Security Barrier*, 29 FORDHAM INTERNATIONAL LAW JOURNAL 181, 205 (2005).

105. The government maintained that the ECHR was "intended to apply in a regional context in the legal space of the Contracting States." Letter from Adam Ingram, MP, UK Armed Forces Minister, to Adam Price, MP (Apr. 7, 2004), *cited in* Ralph Wilde, *The Applicability of International Human Rights Law to the Coalition Provisional Authority (CPA) and Foreign Military Presence in Iraq*, 11 ILSA JOURNAL OF INTERNATIONAL & COMPARATIVE LAW 485, 488–89 (2005). On that basis, the United Kingdom argued that, although it was an occupying power in Iraq, it did not possess the needed degree of effective control for the ECHR to apply, and that there was no general doctrine of "personal jurisdiction" in relation to the ECHR. Al-Skeini and others v. Secretary of State for Defence [2004] EWHC 2911, ¶ 287 [hereinafter Al-Skeini [2004]]. Later, the United Kingdom maintained that its actions in Iraq were attributable to the United Nations, thereby absolving it of any responsibility under the ECHR (Al-Jedda case, *supra* note 57, at ¶ 3, ¶ 49).

106. Al-Skeini [2004], *supra* note 105, ¶ 287; Al-Skeini and others v. Secretary of State for Defence [2007] UKHL 26, ¶ 132.

107. Al-Saadoon case, *supra* note 58, ¶ 88.

108. S.C. Res. 1483, *supra* note 27, ¶ 4.
109. *Id.*, ¶ 5.
110. U.N. SCOR, 58th Sess., 4761st mtg. at 11–12, U.N. Doc. S/PV.4761 (May 22, 2003).
111. S.C. Res. 1483, *supra* note 27, ¶ 4.
112. *Id.*, ¶ 8.
113. Eyal Benvenisti, *Water Conflicts during the Occupation of Iraq*, 97 AMERICAN JOURNAL OF INTERNATIONAL LAW 860, 863 (2004).
114. For the rise of human rights in international law, see THEODOR MERON, THE HUMANIZATION OF INTERNATIONAL LAW (2006). For an evolutionary interpretation of treaties, see Legal Consequences for States of the Continued Presence of South Africa in Namibia (South West Africa) Notwithstanding Security Council Resolution 276 (1970), Advisory Opinion, 1971 I.C.J. 16, 31 (June 21); World Trade Organization, Appellate Body Report, *United States—Import Prohibition of Certain Shrimp and Shrimp Products* ¶¶ 129–30, WT/DS58/AB/R (Oct. 12, 1998); RICHARD GARDINER, TREATY INTERPRETATION 251–56 (2008).
115. For a discussion of derogation from *jus cogens* rights by the Council, see Case T-315/1, Yassin Abdullah Kadi v. Council of European Union and European Commission, [2005] ECR II-3649, ¶ 230; Erika De Wet, *The Role of Human Rights in Limiting the Enforcement Power of the Security Council: A Principled View*, *in* REVIEW OF THE SECURITY COUNCIL BY MEMBER STATES 7, 22 (Erika De Wet et al. eds., 2003); Dapo Akande, *The International Court of Justice and the Security Council: Is There Room for Judicial Control of Decisions of the Political Organs of the United Nations?*, 46 INTERNATIONAL & COMPARATIVE LAW QUARTERLY 309, 322 (1997). *See also* Marten Zwanenburg, *Existentialism in Iraq: Security Council Resolution 1483 and the Law of Occupation*, 86 INTERNATIONAL REVIEW OF THE RED CROSS 745, 760–66 (2004). *But see* GREG FOX, HUMANITARIAN OCCUPATION 211–13 (2008).
116. For the principle of self-determination as an *erga omnes* obligation, see East Timor (Port. v. Austl.), 1995 I.C.J. 90, 102 (June 30). For the principle as also a *jus cogens* right, see Draft Articles on Responsibility of States for Internationally Wrongful Acts, Report of the International Law Commission on the Work of its Fifty-third Session 113, U.N. GAOR, 56th Sess., Supp. No. 10, at 48, U.N. Doc. A/56/10 (2001), *available at* http://untreaty.un.org/ilc/texts/instruments/english/draft%20articles/9_6_2001.pdf; ANTONIO CASSESE, SELF-DETERMINATION OF PEOPLES: A LEGAL REAPPRAISAL 320 (1995).
117. BENVENISTI, *supra* note 2, at 213–14.
118. Benvenisti, *supra* note 1, at 623.
119. *See also* Yehuda Z. Blum, *UN Membership of the "New" Yugoslavia: Continuity or Break?*, 86 AMERICAN JOURNAL OF INTERNATIONAL LAW 830, 833 (1992) ("Yugoslavia has been *suspended* from the General Assembly, pending reconsideration of the matter by the Council . . ., in a manner not foreseen by the Charter . . .").
120. On these, see RALPH WILDE, INTERNATIONAL TERRITORIAL ADMINISTRATION: HOW TRUSTEESHIP AND THE CIVILIZING MISSION NEVER WENT AWAY (2008); CARSTEN STAHN, THE LAW AND PRACTICE OF INTERNATIONAL TERRITORIAL ADMINISTRATION: VERSAILLES TO IRAQ AND BEYOND (2008).
121. While the United States and the United Kingdom were both occupants in Iraq and permanent members of the Council, their interests were balanced by the presence of other permanent members, most notably China and Russia.
122. The occupants were merely "encourage[d]" to "inform the [Security] Council at regular intervals of their efforts . . ." (S.C. Res. 1483, *supra* note 27, ¶ 24). There is no evidence of such regular notifications.

123. Memorandum Opinion from Jack L. Goldsmith III, Assistant Attorney General, to the Counsel to the President, "Protected Person" Status in Occupied Iraq under the Fourth Geneva Convention (Mar. 18, 2004), *available at* http://www.usdoj.gov/olc/2004/gc4mar18.pdf.

124. Memorandum from Jack L. Goldsmith III, Assistant Attorney General, to William H. Taft, General Counsel, Department of State, Re: Draft Opinion Concerning Permissibility of Relocating Certain "Protected Persons" in Occupied Iraq (Mar. 19, 2004), *available at* http://www.washingtonpost.com/wp-srv/nation/documents/doj_memo031904.pdf; Leila Nadya Sadat, *Ghost Prisoners and Black Sites: Extraordinary Rendition under International Law*, 37 CASE WESTERN RESERVE JOURNAL OF INTERNATIONAL LAW 309, 324–38 (2006); David Weissbrodt & Amy Bergquist, *Extraordinary Rendition and the Humanitarian Law of War and Occupation*, 47 VIRGINIA JOURNAL OF INTERNATIONAL LAW 295, 320–43 (2007).

125. Michael Ottolenghi, *The Stars and Stripes in Al-Fardos Square: The Implications for the International Law of Belligerent Occupation*, 72 FORDHAM LAW REVIEW 2177, 2205–10 (2004) (discussing the use of Iraqi oil); Frederick Lorenz, *Strategic Water for Iraq: The Need for Planning and Action*, 24 AMERICAN JOURNAL OF INTERNATIONAL LAW 275, 280, 285, 296–98 (2008); Amy Hardberger, *Whose Job Is It Anyway? Governmental Obligations Created by the Human Right to Water*, 41 TEXAS JOURNAL OF INTERNATIONAL LAW JOURNAL 533, 561–63 (2006).

PART VI

STABILITY OPERATIONS IN IRAQ

XIV

Counterinsurgency and Stability Operations: A New Approach to Legal Interpretation

Dale Stephens*

Introduction

We live in the postmodern era of warfare,[1] where small-scale, intra-State conflict is increasingly becoming the norm. While the modern era conceived of war and warfighting as a large-scale, inter-State conflict waged between massed professional armies,[2] the postmodern era perceives conflict as "war among the people"[3] where technological advantage, massive firepower and physical maneuver can count for little in the struggle for ascendancy.[4] It turns out that such conflict can be as deadly and as strategically significant as conventional warfare.

The US military in its recent reconceptualization of how such wars are to be effectively engaged (and how victory is to be meaningfully measured) has embraced the realities of the emergent postmodern style of warfare. The recently published *U.S. Army/Marine Corps Counterinsurgency Field Manual*[5] and its companion volume, *The U.S. Army Stability Operations Field Manual*,[6] portray a somewhat counterintuitive model for prevailing in these postmodern conflicts. Significantly, the methodologies these manuals espouse are written against the background of bitter experience of conflict in Iraq and Afghanistan. Indeed, partially through necessity, these doctrines emerged from reflection about these conflicts and took

* Captain, CSM, Royal Australian Navy. All views expressed in this article are solely those of the author and do not necessarily reflect the views of the Australian government, Department of Defence or Royal Australian Navy.

account of "counterinsurgency best practice."[7] The tactics and doctrine reflected in these manuals worked to stave off near defeat, especially in the Iraq theater of operations during the 2007 "surge."[8]

Paradoxically, while military doctrine has managed a self-conscious leap in perspective regarding means and methods of warfare, there has been a correlative lack of innovation within established mainstream legal thinking, at least in the prevailing literature.[9] A formalist methodology of interpretation and a continued commitment to the attritional focus of the law of armed conflict (LOAC) remain the prevalent orthodoxy, notwithstanding that such binary thinking has proven to have had limited utility within counterinsurgency (COIN) and stabilization operations. There is plainly a need for renewed thinking, or at least an appreciation of the direction warfare is going, so that interpretative techniques employed in LOAC may be reimagined and recalibrated in order to remain relevant to operational realities. This paper seeks to facilitate that process.

Part I of the paper will survey the themes contained in the counterinsurgency/stability operations manuals and will contrast these to the prevailing intellectual framework which underpins LOAC. Part II examines the key principles of "distinction" and "proportionality" under LOAC and argues that a reconceptualized interpretative approach to implementing these principles is required. A particular emphasis will be placed on the rules/standards dichotomy in order to better reveal the limits of formalist thinking. Finally, Part III will canvass the challenges and choices available to an operational legal advisor when operating during COIN/stability operations consistently with revised doctrine.

Part I. COIN and Stability Operations: A New Doctrinal Paradigm

Counterinsurgency Doctrine

The strategic-political realities of the Cold War prompted preparation for large-scale, inter-State "industrial" warfare.[10] Technology, firepower and maneuver were key elements in designing effective and efficient combat for massed professional armies. Rationalist strategizing provided the necessary gestalt and the "tools of modernity"[11] were expected to deliver operational success. According to Lieutenant General Sir John Kiszely, it was a model that relied upon "more advanced technology, firepower, lethality, speed, stealth, digitization, logistics, network-centric warfare [and] hi-tech 'shock and awe.'"[12] These features still underpin the requirements of fighting conventional warfare. Indeed, conventional warfare still occurs, but is not the likely anticipated scenario for future warfighting.

The reality of postmodern warfare is what has been occurring in "post-conflict" Iraq and Afghanistan in recent years. Such conflicts are mostly non-international in character and are typically manifested as small internecine warfare where non-State actors employ asymmetric means against State military forces. The environment in which this warfare is undertaken is one of mixed peace and war. The deployment of armed State forces within such conflicts has been difficult to reconcile with "first order" conventional warfare training and preparation. Such conflict has been variously described as, *inter alia*, "military operations other than war" (MOOTW), peacekeeping, peace enforcement, "wider peacekeeping," low intensity conflict and "gray area operations."[13] These terms are not interchangeable, as they differ according to legal and doctrinal authority and the nature of the deployment, but they all share common elements which separate them from conceptions of conventional warfare. These operations have required different and more nuanced skills, though it was thought that conventional warfare training could be "ratcheted down" to apply to such operations.[14] Such assumptions were not well placed.

The US *COIN Manual* grapples with the new realities of postmodern war and recommends decisive change. Indeed, the introduction to the manual makes it very clear that it is intended to be "paradigm shattering."[15] Within the first paragraph of the introduction, the point is forcefully made that "[t]hose who fail to see the manual as radical probably don't understand it, or at least understand what it's up against."[16] The manual provides that while all insurgencies are *sui generis,* there are common characteristics that apply to all and there are patterns of operational response that have been proven to be effective. The manual evidently borrows from classic counterinsurgency works relating to the British experience in Malaya[17] and the French experience in Algeria,[18] and it also updates the work that had been undertaken during the Vietnam conflict.[19] Most significantly, it draws upon contemporary experience in Iraq and Afghanistan in detailing a number of principles labeled "paradoxes of counterinsurgency operations"[20] that provide a conceptual framework for operational planning.

In very clear terms the manual outlines the elements of an insurgency and identifies the requirements that must be met in order to prevail. The doctrine is confrontational and counterintuitive to that which is required for conventional warfare. The manual painstakingly describes that an insurgency is fundamentally a political struggle, where the center of gravity is the population, which remains "the deciding factor in the struggle."[21] It is asserted that insurgents invariably use unlawful means to intimidate the population and discredit the legitimate government. Such unlawful means are designed to bring about an overreaction by counterinsurgent forces. Violence is the currency of an insurgency and destabilizing the legitimacy of the host-nation government and its supporting counterinsurgent forces a strategic goal.[22] Provoking violation of counterinsurgent ethics and values in reacting to an insurgency is a means to secure that goal. This perspective is highlighted by counterinsurgent specialist David Kilcullen when describing the operational *modus operandi* of Al Qaida in Iraq as one that relies upon provocation, intimidation, protraction and exhaustion, and drawing the majority of its strength from the "backlash engendered by counter-insurgent overreaction rather than genuine popular support."[23] The *COIN Manual* describes that "[t]he real battle is for civilian support for, or acquiescence to, the counterinsurgents and host nation government. The population waits to be convinced. Who will help them more, hurt them less, stay the longest, earn their trust?"[24] Thus the primary purpose of a counterinsurgency is "securing the civilian, rather than destroying the enemy."[25]

In countering an insurgency, traditional thinking regarding combat and the application of overwhelming force acts as a negative factor. "Cartesian or reductionist"[26] logic that is so ingrained in military staff training as the primary means for problem solving offers little assistance. The temptation to act, "to do something,"[27] is likely the wrong response; rather, the better solution in a tactical sense may be to exercise patience, "to do nothing."[28] Such an approach is challenging to the military ethos; Sir John Kiszely notes that counterinsurgency "requires . . . warriors to acquire some decidedly un-warrior-like attributes, such as emotional intelligence, empathy with one's opponents, tolerance, patience, subtlety, sophistication, nuance and political adroitness."[29] The battle is not conceived in the ordinary "formulaic and mechanistic"[30] sense but rather is more conceptual, relying heavily upon sociological and psychological inputs. Kiszely reinforces the need to work smarter rather than harder when conceptualizing the counterinsurgency strategy, noting in tandem with the *COIN Manual* that depriving the insurgents of popular support and winning it oneself is the key objective:

> [T]he contest takes place not on a field of battle, but in a complex civilian environment . . . . Nor is it a primarily military contest . . . . The war, is in large part a war of ideas, the battle largely one for perception, and the key battleground is in the mind—the minds of the indigenous population, and the minds of regional and world opinion.[31]

Kiszely approvingly cites classic counterinsurgency expert David Galula's estimation of effort in battling an insurgency as "twenty percent military, eighty percent political [as] a formula that reflects the truth."[32] The psychological imperatives are reiterated in General Rupert Smith's analysis in *The Utility of Force* when he observes that "[w]ar amongst the people is different: it is the reality in which the people in the streets and houses and fields—all the people, anywhere—are the battlefield."[33] Kilcullen notes more pragmatically that "[i]n [a] population-centric strategy, what matters is providing security and order for the population, rather than directly targeting the enemy—though this type of strategy will also effectively marginalize them."[34]

The implications of the revised COIN doctrine are far-reaching. The manual lists a number of contemporary counterinsurgency imperatives that should guide planning and execution.[35] These principles have been replicated in operational guidelines within Multi-National Force–Iraq (MNF-I) protocols[36] and have, in fact, become operationalized over the past few years. Their import is significant with respect to both military ethos and public expectation, and, as will be demonstrated *infra*, also with respect to classic legal reasoning under LOAC. The principles of legal relevance recognized within the manual include the following contemporary "paradoxes":

- "Sometimes, the more you protect your force, the less secure you may be,"[37]
- "Some of the best weapons for counterinsurgents do not shoot,"[38]
- "Sometimes, the more force is used, the less effective it is,"[39] and
- "The more successful the counterinsurgency is, the less force can be used and the more risk must be accepted."[40]

It is evident that COIN doctrine does knowingly place greater physical risk on counterinsurgent forces. It concedes that choices will need to be made that will result in higher counterinsurgent casualties. These truisms necessarily test resolve,[41] as well as public expectation. The questions of insurgent targeting and the formulation of collateral/incidental damage/injury assessments in this new intellectual environment play a pivotal part of the COIN strategy. Significantly, they do so in a manner that reverses expectations and conventional reasoning. As will be discussed *infra*, a revised interpretative lens must be applied when grappling with these legal tests. Such analysis reconfigures the current self-contained ethical certainties currently underpinning traditional LOAC reasoning.

Stability Operations

Stability operations are incorporated into modern COIN[42] and form part of the so-called "full-spectrum operations" operational design. COIN and stability operations are likely to be conducted conjointly but emphasize different aspects of the continuum. Stability operations doctrine shares the COIN aversion to kinetic operations though it is more dedicated to broader capacity building.[43] Stability operations are defined within US joint doctrine as follows:

> [Stability operations encompass] various military missions, tasks, and activities conducted outside the United States in coordination with other instruments of national power to maintain or reestablish a safe and secure environment, provide

> essential governmental services, emergency infrastructure reconstruction, and humanitarian relief.[44]

Despite the overwhelming emphasis previously placed upon conventional warfare preparation, the *Stability Operations Manual* notes that the US military has, in fact, only been involved in eleven conventional conflicts during its entire history.[45] Conversely it has been involved in hundreds of operations that may be identified as stability operations. Significantly, since the fall of the Berlin Wall alone, the manual notes that US forces have been involved in fifteen stability operations.[46] The *Stability Operations Manual* represents a decisive "moment" where such operations are squarely addressed and where doctrine is both tailor-made and comprehensive.

Stability operations are principally concerned with post-conflict operations. The (in)famous phase IV element of the Operation Iraqi Freedom campaign plan, for example, was not accorded a particularly high priority during the planning and execution phases of the Iraqi conflict,[47] and yet was supposed to deal with stabilization. The failure to implement a comprehensive stabilization policy self-evidently represented a significant strategic failure. As a result of that experience, and the recalibration of enlightened doctrinal thinking, stability operations have been formally accorded a high priority within the planning framework. US Department of Defense Directive 3000.05 stipulates that

> Stability Operations are a core U.S. military mission that the Department of Defense shall be prepared to conduct and support. They shall be given priority comparable to combat operations and be explicitly addressed and integrated across all [Department of Defense] activities including doctrine, organizations, training, education, exercises, material, leadership, personnel, facilities, and planning.[48]

Stability operations are predicated upon the strategic proposition that in the contemporary environment, US security is threatened more by weak and failing States, which can act as sanctuaries for multinational terrorist networks, than by traditional strong nation-State entities.[49] The institutional design that underpins stability operations is the creation in a post-conflict State of an environment that facilitates reconciliation; establishes the development of political, legal, social and economic institutions; and facilitates transition to a legitimate civil authority operating under the rule of law.[50] It does deal with capacity building (indeed, embracing the previously maligned notion of "nation building") and procedurally adopts an interagency focus.[51] Doctrinally, the US military's role in stability operations is to assist the US Department of State, which is to lead in these efforts,[52] but also principally to provide the necessary security to permit these conditions to manifest.

The stability operations doctrine has, not surprisingly, been dismissed as utopian in design.[53] The doctrine's precepts of providing "basic public services, physical reconstruction, the hope of economic development and social amelioration"[54] have been criticized by commentators such as Edward Luttwak, who query whether models of Western liberal democracy (and the efforts required to create such societies) are really the only political structures that will provide sufficient stability for US security interests.

Notwithstanding these criticisms, stability operations doctrine and the integral capacity-building elements have been strongly identified by counterinsurgency experts as being a critical factor in effectively combating an insurgency. In describing the factors that contributed to the success of the 2007 Iraq "surge," for example, Kilcullen notes, "[W]e conducted operations to support the rule of law, which helped deal with 'accelerants,' and we introduced what we might call 'decelerants' such as political reconciliation and building competent, nonsectarian governance and national institutions, which helped slow and reduce the intensity of the violence."[55] Indeed, Kilcullen criticizes the prevalent thinking that underpinned the original Operation Iraqi Freedom planning for failing to anticipate the military leverage required to facilitate Iraqi governmental capacity to ameliorate sectarian tendencies: "[B]ecause our focus was on transition rather than stabilization, on getting ourselves out no matter what the situation was on the ground, we lacked the presence or relevance to generate that leverage."[56]

Like the COIN doctrine, the *Stability Operations Manual* implicitly acknowledges that there is a finite limit in the ability of military force to achieve societal outcomes. It has become a necessary feature of postmodern conflict today that such recognition of the limitations of force is indispensible to strategic success. These lessons are learned over and over and yet have been demonstrated to achieve success in the context of multiple UN peace operations where stability-type functions have formed a core element of Security Council peace-keeping/peace-enforcement mandates.[57]

There remains considerable debate on the meaning of "rule of law" within the academic literature and how it may be measured. Some perceive it as the external indicia of a functioning legal system—that is, the establishment of police forces and stations, courthouses and prisons—namely an institutionalist perspective,[58] whereas other more substantively based conceptions equate rule of law success to the acquisition of internal values within the society and especially the power elites.[59] This too may draw the critique of imperialism, especially in its emphasis upon international human rights (HR) standards being externally imposed upon a prevailing culture.[60] Notwithstanding these critiques, the implementation of a rule of law program is seen, under stability operations doctrine, as a fundamental feature in building host-State legitimacy,[61] though as will be subsequently addressed, it is not without its own operationally significant difficulties.

Part II. The Law of Armed Conflict: Interpretative Paradigms in COIN/Stability Operations

The law of armed conflict reflects an amorphous panoply of historical influences. Sovereignty is represented in its preeminent, as well as disaggregated, forms, as are the humanitarian impulses that act as a counterbalance to sovereign military rights. In form, it displays a jumble of sharp distinctions, positivist freedom, humanitarian obligations and, of course, the perennial interpretative interplay between rules and standards.

The interdependence of rules and standards and between law and policy forms the foundational structure and the basic intellectual framework for tackling the paradoxes of restraint and freedom under the law. In discerning the correct interpretative valence of the law of armed conflict either in conventional warfare or under the more attenuated circumstances of COIN/stability operations, it is especially critical to investigate the well rehearsed "dialectic"[62] reasoning that is employed when reconciling the advantages and disadvantages of employing rules and standards and their respective modalities.

The purpose of this Part, therefore, is to survey interpretative techniques under the framework of the rules/standards dichotomy as applicable to the law of armed conflict. As the previous Part has demonstrated, there is a decisive shift in reimagining the way the law should be applied in COIN/stability operations in order to achieve definitive military goals. Rules necessarily carry with them a level of rigidity that potentially resists incorporation of "policy," whereas standards have always been open to a more intuitive application of socio-legal norms. In the COIN environment these traditional approaches have been upended somewhat, especially in relation to the LOAC concepts of distinction (a rule) and proportionality (a standard). This author will argue that in shaking these *prima facie* perspectives, the COIN doctrine has created a fissure that reveals the limits of the traditional certainties concerning interpretative valence. Simultaneously, however, we get an extremely insightful glimpse into the policy/legal interplay that underpins all international law and which offers a unique opportunity for a more normatively based and savvy approach to interpretation.

Rules and Standards

In his seminal article "Form and Substance in Private Law Adjudication"[63] Duncan Kennedy provides an illuminating account of the jurisprudence of rules and standards. Kennedy notes that such jurisprudence is "premised on the notion that the choice between standards and rules of different degrees of generality is significant, and can be analyzed in isolation from the substantive issues that the rules or standards respond to."[64] Dealing first with rules, Kennedy identifies particularly the dimension of "formal realizability,"[65] which acts to give rules their "ruleness."[66] Hence a rule may be construed as a directive that is issued in language that directs action in a determinate way to test factually distinguishable situations.[67] Standards, on the other hand, are more fluid and refer to directives that relate directly to one of the substantive objectives of the legal order. Kennedy notes that examples of standards are found in principles of "good faith," "due care," "fairness," etc.[68] Thus, when dealing with a standard, a judge is required to "both discover the facts of a particular situation and to assess them in terms of purpose or social values embodied in the standard."[69] This process is plainly a more freewheeling exercise where underpinning values intentionally play a bigger role in the *ex post* reasoning that is required under this regime. It also allows for a more instrumental application of the law.

Pierre Schlag offers a similar, if more fused, explanation, identifying both rules and standards as directives comprised of two parts, namely a "trigger" and a "response."[70] The "trigger" may be empirical or evaluative.[71] A rule paradigmatically comprises a hard empirical trigger and a hard determinate response; hence he offers that a rule may be stated as follows: "sounds above 70 decibels shall be punished by a ten dollar fine."[72] In contrast, Schlag defines standards as having a soft evaluative trigger and a soft modulated response, identifying an example of a standard as "excessive loudness shall be enjoinable upon a showing of irreparable harm."[73] Rules and standards may both be general or particular, may be conditional or absolute, narrow or broad, weak or strong.[74] Rules are thought to be more costly in terms of their development with legislators or courts, employing greater work in anticipating future variables they wish covered, and are perceived to be less cost intensive in their application. Standards, on the other hand, offer a reverse cost/benefit symmetry, being less costly to develop and more costly to apply in each instance, requiring greater analysis and appreciation of both particular and surrounding circumstances.[75]

The acknowledged benefits of rules are that they encourage certainty and guard against official arbitrariness.[76] Individuals may thus plan their affairs more confidently knowing the boundaries of permissible and forbidden conduct. This may, however, permit "close sailing" to social limits by canny individuals who are able to more precisely order their activities to follow, but not exceed, strict limits.[77] This may, in turn, foster more socially suspect behavior as a "fixed cost" of doing business.[78] Standards, on the other hand, require individualized judgments about substantive compliance/violation that permit endorsed policy considerations to play a significant role in the balancing that invariably takes place.[79] Conversely, the ambiguity about where the limits may lie within a standard can have a "chilling effect" upon individuals, who may desist from socially useful or desirable activities because of self-imposed margins of appreciation to assumed limits.[80] Standards lack the certainty of rules and determinations having little precedential value are usually the result.

Because rules can also be general, judges (and other decisionmakers) may end up providing ad hoc exceptions and variations to their interpretations that act over time to seriously undermine the certainties anticipated.[81] There may be other rules that are more particular in character and which act to contradict general rules, or at least carve out specific areas of independent operation. Indeed, the historic positivist/realist debate revolves around the very choices permitted when interpreting rules. H.L.A. Hart's "soft positivism," for example, anticipates a broad settled "core" of meaning in the interpretation of rules and a smaller "penumbra" of debatable meaning.[82] Legal realists find Hart's assertions to be somewhat overstated, at least in the context of appeal cases, and, while equally relying upon the positivist frame of rules as having determinative effect, find greater discretion within legal culture when applying particularized canons of interpretation to reach socially cognizable outcomes.[83]

The Law of Armed Conflict Interpretative Structure

Evidencing its evolutionary historical development, the modern law of armed conflict displays ample evidence of both hard empirical rules and more fluid evaluative standards within its structure. These were products of different historical attitudes toward questions of sovereignty and more recently reflect questions of legitimacy.[84] Given the historical longevity of this body of law, fulsome positive freedoms are invariably argued in favor of military discretion and the prevailing treaty rules, especially those from the nineteenth and early twentieth centuries, tend to accommodate such advocacy. It needs to be recalled that a great proportion of the modern law of armed conflict was fashioned at a time when international jurisprudence was reluctant to presume limitations upon sovereignty.[85] Against this backdrop it is not altogether surprising that humanitarian advocates modified their strategy in the post–World War Two environment to introduce a new narrative to the substance of the law. The incorporation of standards into the LOAC lexicon was anticipated to better achieve humanitarian outcomes within orthodox interpretative attitudes.[86] Moreover it seemed to permit greater partnership with military voices in exercising statecraft.[87]

Mainstream LOAC literature tends toward a classic "soft positivism" in its interpretative valence. Language is parsed carefully and the pedigree of legal norms assessed very carefully.[88] It has largely been a "closed system" of interpretative analysis, where there are exclusive relationships between legal ideas[89] and where language and its syllogistic interpellation play a key role in divining legal meaning. Under this theory, legal practitioners and judges alike are able to skillfully employ these interpretative techniques to arrive at the "correct" legal answer in each case. Of course, it axiomatically reflects the "Hartian" themes of interpretation. It is this author's contention that such a methodological view has its unacknowledged limitations especially in the context of COIN/stability operations. This article examines the key LOAC principles of distinction and proportionality under the aegis of the new doctrinal orientation applicable to postmodern warfare and will make a case for acknowledging a revised measure of interpretative approach.

The Principle of Distinction

The principle of distinction has been described as a "cardinal" principle of the law of armed conflict by the International Court of Justice (ICJ).[90] Indeed, the principle as reflected in Additional Protocol I to the 1949 Geneva Conventions (GPI) [91] is titled the "Basic Rule" in Article 48, which states:

> In order to ensure respect for and protection of the civilian population and civilian objects, the Parties to the conflict shall at all times distinguish between the civilian population and combatants and between civilian objects and military objectives and accordingly shall direct their operations only against military objectives.

Violation of Article 48 is deemed a "grave breach" by virtue of Article 85(3)(a) of GPI,[92] and under Article 85(5) is further defined as a "war crime"[93] that "High Contracting" parties have a duty to repress and for which they have a duty to ensure appropriate penal and disciplinary consequences are imposed. These obligations extend to both subordinates and superiors who come within the ambit of command responsibility.[94] Given the central place of the principle of distinction in the LOAC firmament, it is not surprising that it has been accorded such stature.

The terms of Article 48 appear clearly to be a "rule." Invoking Kennedy's criteria, it is clear that there is a high degree of formal realizability in its terms. A distinction "at all times" is to be made between "combatants" and the "civilian population," as well as "military objectives" and "civilian objects," and parties are obliged to "direct operations only against military objectives" and, by implication, "combatants." The directive plainly contains the hard empirical trigger and hard determinative response. Combatants and military objectives only may be attacked and civilians and civilian objects may not. Violation of this "Basic Rule" is deemed both a "grave breach" and a "war crime."

As with all generally stated directives, this rule is both under- and over-inclusive.[95] The operation of other provisions within GPI[96] (as well as Additional Protocol II (GPII) for non-international armed conflict [97]) make an exception for the rule against attacking civilians in the case of those civilians who take a "direct part" in hostilities, for "such time as they take a direct part."[98] International dialogue on the issue of direct participation in hostilities (DPH) has, over recent years, mapped out a series of functional categories for those civilians who may lose their immunity.[99] The consensus view would seem to be that DPH extends down the causal chain from primary "shooter" or "bomb layer" to include (among others) civilian planners and tactical facilitators, at least in relation to organized armed groups whose members assume a "continuous combat function" in non-international armed conflict.[100] Such expansion exceeds what the original drafters of the GPI seemed to anticipate,[101] though the expansion does reflect emergent operational realities and associated State practice. Current perspectives have nonetheless set what appear to be policy limits on the breadth of the loss of immunity (despite the logic of "continuous combat function" extending down the causal chain). Hence financiers and those inciting such participation through propaganda are not considered to come within the DPH rubric,[102] notwithstanding that such activity has great strategic and operational significance on sustaining a conflict, especially in an insurgency.[103] Thus, by virtue of a combination of legal construction and the artifice of applied policy, certain civilians lose their immunity and others don't under the DPH formula. Some determinations are based upon a logical deduction from what "direct participation" connotes, and others are based upon policy reasons which seek to exclude those who might otherwise be caught by logically assessing their functional impacts in inciting or sustaining an insurgency.[104] These categories have been relatively clearly defined and articulated, and have been subject to close superior court scrutiny in at least one domestic legal system.[105] They may also be reasonably appreciated in any "kill-capture" targeting methodology undertaken by an opposing military force. It is, to paraphrase Kennedy, a relatively classic application of a list of distinguishable factual criteria that allows intervention in a determinate way. One is able to compile a "list" from a review of authoritative legal materials and can verify via this list whether an individual's function puts him/her inside or outside the veil of immunity.

Accordingly, there appears to have been the development of a rule that, while still relatively general, permits a confident appreciation of boundary. Military action based upon this directive may be executed to the limits tolerated by the law and, of course, canny military/legal planning may indeed permit "close sailing" while still purchasing the "moral absolutism" that "complying with the law" provides.

While providing a firm lawful basis for the conduct of "kill-capture" operations, the law itself is predicated upon a different theoretical model from that which applies in the context of COIN/stability operations. Accordingly, as a template for military action its assumptions may lack the necessary operational acuity for postmodern success. The primary corpus of modern LOAC was developed in the immediate aftermath of the Second World War. The law, as comprised in the four 1949 Geneva Conventions, complemented the pre-existing Hague Law, which dealt mostly with "means and methods." This collective body of law anticipated State-on-State "industrial" warfare[106] to be the prototypical norm, where attrition is the primary means by which to defeat military adversaries. The subsequent Vietnam conflict provided significant impetus to the development of the 1977 Additional Protocols that acted to partially fuse Geneva and Hague law with a more contemporary relevance. Nonetheless, there was still a significant emphasis placed upon a linear conception of warfare between sovereign equals and the model for military triumph was still most assuredly one of attrition. Admittedly, GPI expressly recognizes particular non-State fighters participating in conflicts relating specifically to colonial and alien domination and against racist regimes in their exercise of self-determination.[107] However, they were not treated in any original manner; rather such fighters were "elevated" in status akin to that of soldiers within State forces. Similarly, while non-international conflicts were specifically dealt with under GPII, the preeminent model was one that anticipated organized dissident armed forces controlling territory and exercising State-like powers with respect to that territory in order to implement the Protocol, as well as exercising "responsible command" over such forces in order to conduct "sustained and concerted military operations."[108]

The framework for engaging in conflict during COIN/stability operations eschews these norms. The strategies and tactics for COIN/stability operations are profoundly more nuanced than what the law provides. The COIN doctrine counsels greater restraint when confronting and targeting individuals who come squarely within the criteria of DPH targeting. It has become clear that functional categorization of individuals and the validity of the norm are not the complete answer for lawful targeting—just as it has become clear that a state cannot kill its way out of an insurgency. The success of the Iraqi surge in 2007 was dependent on an extremely nuanced and politically aware strategy of engagement, where efforts were made to reconcile with those who were otherwise targetable under the DPH formula. The COIN guidance applicable to MNF-I makes it clear that discretion is to be carefully exercised with respect to the application of force. Non-kinetic options have a decisive strategic role; hence under the point titled "Promote reconciliation" the MNF-I guidance notes:

> We cannot kill our way out of this endeavor. We and our Iraqi partners must identify and separate the "reconcilables" from the "irreconcilables" through engagement, population control measures, information operations, kinetic operations, and political activities. We must strive to make reconcilables a part of the solution, even as we identify, pursue, and kill, capture, or drive out the irreconcilables.[109]

The guidance for who may be "reconcilable" within the policy is not defined with any great clarity. The criteria nonetheless require greater consideration of individual identity and broader sociopolitical considerations relating to the individual and the sectarian/tribal/regional connections he/she may be entwined within. Kilcullen identifies such potentially "reconcilable" persons as "accidental guerillas,"[110] individuals who find themselves manipulated into insurgent activity but without the hard-core ideological drive. "Reconcilables" are also plainly those persons who may be turned against their terrorist sponsors and who may offer both intelligence and cooperation with the counterinsurgency effort. The turning of the "Sons of Iraq," predominantly within Al Anbar province during the surge, for example, has been identified as a key outcome in addressing the insurgency.[111]

When the objective of a successful COIN/stability operation campaign is to "win the population," rather than "kill-capture" the insurgents,[112] a different orientation to legal interpretation is required. In reflecting on his experiences in Iraq, former MNF-I Commander General David Petraeus acknowledged that when engaged in COIN a sophisticated risk/benefit calculation is mandated when dealing with the consequences of targeting. He implicitly acknowledges that such an analysis may transcend traditional LOAC thinking in terms of determining who may be targeted when he notes:

> [W]e should *analyze costs and benefits of operations before each operation* . . . [by answering] a question we developed over time and used to ask before the conduct of operations: "Will this operation," we asked, "take more bad guys off the street than it creates by the way it is conducted?" If the answer to that question was, "No," then we took a very hard look at the operation before proceeding.[113]

In reinforcing this point, General Petraeus refers to lessons learned by previous US commanders, commenting that

> [i]n 1986, General John Galvin, then Commander in Chief of the U.S. Southern Command (which was supporting the counterinsurgency effort in El Salvador),

> described the challenge captured in this observation very effectively: "The . . . burden on the military institution is large. Not only must it subdue an armed adversary while attempting to provide security to the civilian population, it must also avoid furthering the insurgents' cause. If, for example, the military's actions in killing 50 guerrillas cause 200 previously uncommitted citizens to join the insurgent cause, the use of force will have been counterproductive."[114]

The law of armed conflict doesn't deal well with these questions. With respect to the principle of distinction, it requires consideration of whether the person is targetable, not whether the person should in fact be targeted and what such targeting will do in the broader strategic environment. How do we rationalize this? It may be that formalist conceptions of legal interpretation under LOAC are not indicted under this new doctrinal focus and the principle of distinction may still retain its binary certainty. One might regard considerations of individual "reconcilability" and cost/benefit analysis as mere "policy" overlays. A conscientious lawyer will therefore guard against crossing the line, will ensure that he/she carefully stays within the confines of "the law" and will know where the seam of true legal advice must end. To do so, though, seems a bit disingenuous. The policy overlay that is mandated by the COIN/stability operations doctrine requires consideration of variables concerning individual identity, of affiliation and role, and of sociopolitical context. It does so because it has been proven to work in achieving the military goals sought. A responsible lawyer must take these things into account when dispensing meaningful legal advice. Once these elements are put into the balance, the rule regarding distinction becomes less an empirical exercise and more of an evaluative process. The rule begins to transform into a standard. On the one hand is the requirement to determine whether or not the person is in fact targetable under the general DPH formula and then on the other is the issue of individually specific criteria to determine whether or not the person is "reconcilable" or his targeting otherwise has greater operational implications. Under this standard, the responsible lawyer is permitted to have broader regard to the purposes and social values the doctrine is propagating. Thus, in undertaking this exercise the role of policy becomes heavily implicated in the interpretation of the "rule." This in turn shapes the quality of legal advice that must be reached. The issue is equally attenuated when dealing with the cognate principle of proportionality, which will now be addressed.

The Principle of Proportionality

The principle of proportionality as outlined in GPI is provided in the following relevant recitation of Article 51(5)(b) under the heading "Protection of the civilian population." Article 51(5)(b) prohibits indiscriminate attacks, defined as "[a]n attack which may be expected to cause incidental loss of civilian life, injury to civilians, damage to civilian objects, or a combination thereof, which would be excessive in relation to the concrete and direct military advantage anticipated." The principle is also contained in Article 57(2)(b), which is listed under the chapeau of "Precautions in attack."

The principle plainly introduces a standard whose factors concerning collateral damage to property and incidental injury to civilians need to be balanced and weighed against concrete and direct military advantage. The principle is one that has not easily been reconciled. Professor Dinstein notes, for example, that there has always been a fundamental disconnect between balancing military considerations against civilian losses, as they are "dissimilar considerations."[115] Major General Rogers poignantly notes that "[t]he rule is more easily stated than applied in practice."[116]

Numerous States parties to GPI have made declarations seeking to assure a more expansive (and militarily advantageous) formalist architecture, including, for example, declarations that the security of the attacking force may be a factor that may be taken into account when balancing against "excessive" civilian loss and that proportionality assessments should be undertaken with respect to the "attack as a whole" and not individualized aspects of the attack.[117] Dinstein notes the criticism leveled at the principle as elaborated within GPI as permitting possibly too great a subjective assessment by military commanders when undertaking the balancing requirement.[118] As with the principle of distinction, a somewhat linear formulation of assessment is undertaken. Hence civilians and civilian objects are accorded a "value" and an exchange is processed along consequentialist lines, whereby an attack may proceed on the basis that "anticipated concrete and direct military advantage" outweighs, by even the smallest of margins, the expected civilian loss.

Against this background the *COIN Manual* signals a self-conscious revision of the application of the proportionality principle in accordance with its stated "paradoxes" of counterinsurgency. Hence the manual states:

> In conventional operations, proportionality is usually calculated in simple utilitarian terms: civilian lives and property lost versus enemy destroyed and military advantage gained. But in COIN operations, [military] advantage is best calculated not in terms of how many insurgents are killed or detained, but rather which enemies are killed or detained . . . . In COIN environments, the number of civilian lives lost and property destroyed needs to be measured against how much harm the targeted insurgent could do if allowed to escape.[119]

The commentary subsequently notes that the principles of discrimination and proportionality may have an additional sociopolitical significance, stating that "[f]ires that cause unnecessary harm or death to noncombatants may create more resistance and increase the insurgency's appeal—especially if the populace perceives a lack of discrimination in their use."[120]

The formulation of military advantage and express reference to the political and social implications of the use of force aren't easily reconciled with classic recitations of the parameters for assessing military advantage over civilian cost. The *COIN Manual* commentary cited above focuses on the individual identity of the insurgent, requires assessment of future potential harm such a person may inflict (harm that the insurgent "could do") and seeks to measure that against potential civilian loss in terms of civilian reaction in relation to ongoing support for the insurgency and the associated risk of alienation. Such prescriptions plainly fit within a model of "winning the population" under the COIN strategy by designing a sociopsychological "barrier" between the population and insurgents, but do not seem to square with the commentary offered on this principle arising out of the negotiations that produced the Additional Protocols. Thus the International Committee of the Red Cross (ICRC) *Commentary* to the negotiations notes that the proportionality principle is to be viewed in the tactical context, not strategic, commenting that the military advantage should be "substantial and close"[121] and that advantages that "would only appear in the long term should be disregarded."[122] Similarly, the ICRC *Commentary* rejects any notion of "political" advantage as coming within a formalistic reading of what the term "military advantage" anticipates.[123] This is not the type of calculation that the *COIN Manual* mandates.

The ICRC *Commentary* naturally presumes that the balancing anticipates that incidental loss of civilian life is to be weighed (and sacrificed) against military advantage and seeks to impose finite humanitarian limits on that equation. The COIN orientation of this formula, however, ends up conflating minimization of incidental civilian loss with military advantage. Ganesh Sitaraman concludes his analysis of this phenomenon by stating that there is a unification of both humanitarian concerns and strategic self-interest.[124] As a standard, the proportionality principle more openly permits recourse to social purposes as an interpretative tool. The ICRC *Commentary* reinforces this perspective by invoking the standard-like obligations of "good faith"[125] and "equity"[126] as criteria that must apply to decision making under the proportionality principle. Has, in fact, the COIN direction to assess second- and third-order effects under the proportionality equation rendered the proportionality standard more "rule-like" with respect to weighing the humanitarian side of the equation? Certainly, the trend in international tribunal decision making has been to continually highlight humanitarian interests in LOAC[127] and this author has argued elsewhere that the ICJ has proposed a formula for proportionality that does accord a perceptible weighting for humanitarian requirements.[128]

A military decisionmaker is obliged under the COIN doctrine to assess the civilian loss occasioned by an attack in broader operational and strategic terms. This is not mandated under the terminology of Articles 51 and 57 of GPI but nonetheless from the perspective of the military decisionmaker is a norm that now has authoritative effect. Akin to the status of a domestic law "regulation" the revised *COIN Manual* has definitive de facto impact. A strict formalist approach to this issue may disregard such doctrine as mere "policy." As discussed previously, however, it would be a foolish military lawyer who would adopt such a posture. The COIN doctrine has an empirical rigidity that necessarily influences the manner in which the principle of proportionality is applied. As Sarah Sewall emphasizes:

> [I]n this context, killing the civilian is no longer just collateral damage. The harm cannot be easily dismissed as unintended. Civilian casualties tangibly undermine the counterinsurgent's goals . . . . [T]he fact or perception of civilian deaths at the hands of their nominal protectors can change popular attitudes from neutrality to anger and active opposition.[129]

Indeed, so strategically significant is the issue of incidental injury in the COIN context that the commanding general in Afghanistan recently issued a directive detailing very limited and prescribed circumstances under which close air support and indirect fire can be undertaken in residential areas.[130] Such circumstances start to resemble a "list" approach to when incidental injury may be occasioned. The fact of incidental injury, however justified under formalist recitations of the law, has proven to be a strategically intractable problem. Military policy has imposed a high value on civilian loss that effectively weights the proportionality formula in favor of the humanitarian side, not because it is the "nice" thing to do, but rather as Kilcullen notes, "our approach was based upon a clear-eyed appreciation of certain basic facts"[131] concerning the nature and quality of fighting an insurgency.

Rules/Standards and Legal Reasoning

The law of armed conflict sets, throughout its structure, the principles of military necessity and humanitarian considerations in equipoise.[132] The humanitarian strategy of relying upon both rules and standards to advance humanitarian priorities under this body of law is a considered, and a not-so-surprising, outcome. We find hard empirically based rules to ensure a firm separation between combatants and civilians under the principle of distinction and a more evaluative standard for undertaking proportionality calculations where incidental injury is anticipated. As we have seen, under prevailing canons of interpretation, rules provide a requisite level of certainty and objectivity, whereas employment of standards mandates that "all perspectives"[133] be taken into account, making "visible and accountable the inevitable weighing process that rules obscure."[134] The proportionality standard thus requires that an express incorporation and open balancing of civilian lives be made in the decision-making calculus.

As previously discussed, the COIN doctrine has inverted these truisms by rendering the principle of distinction more standard-like and the principle of proportionality more rule-like. It seems ironic that the purpose of this inversion is to actually advance humanitarian considerations, albeit under a self-interested strategy of ensuring military success. Should this be a problem? It would seem to be problematic from a formalistic perspective. Focusing solely upon military (and political) effect under the law rather than upon traditional functional categories has the potential to obscure the integrity of the "equipoise" established under the law. The evolution of "effects-based targeting" methodology, for example, which similarly applies a much more instrumentalist approach to targeting decisions, has been resisted by international legal scholars because of its potential to undermine the traditional legal distinctions between civilian and combatant.[135] The fear is that if military effectiveness becomes a viable benchmark for confidence then civilian protection will be progressively eroded.

There remains a strong professional adherence to the existing formalist tenor of the law of armed conflict, even when deviation from its terms can actually increase the probability of humanitarian outcomes. Gabriella Blum has, for example, surveyed a range of case studies where utilitarian reasoning under the law would lessen humanitarian risk, though she has also demonstrated powerful resistance to the employment of such reasoning.[136] Her review of the "early warning procedure" decision by the Israeli Supreme Court in the case of *Adalah v. IDF*[137] is particularly instructive. The case concerned the use of Palestinian civilians by the Israel Defense Forces (IDF) to provide early warning of an imminent arrest in order to facilitate potential surrender and evacuation of innocent persons. Empirical evidence adduced by Blum tends to support the conclusion that use of such volunteers has reduced casualties of both military and civilians when undertaking such arrests, though concomitantly the use of such procedures is *prima facie* contrary to a number of provisions of LOAC. The Israeli Supreme Court unanimously rejected IDF use of this technique, holding that this procedure was contrary to the law of armed conflict, reiterating "the IHL prohibition on using the civilian population for the military needs of the occupying army, and also the obligation to distance innocent civilians from the zone of hostilities."[138] It appears that the pragmatic humanitarian outcomes that the IDF policy sought to optimize weren't significant enough to obviate the risk of forensic violation of LOAC principles.

Unlike the choices faced by the Israeli Supreme Court in the *Adalah* case, the reasoning applied under the COIN/stability operations doctrine doesn't constitute a direct affront to the existing humanitarian principles underpinning the LOAC; rather it demands a variegated reasoning process. Such reasoning can exist within traditional categories by providing a narrower band of who may be targeted (distinction) and when incidental injury is permissible (proportionality) and may thus meet with less resistance. These goals are certainly consistent with humanitarian priorities but they demand a more policy/political-oriented interpretative approach in individual cases, and, of course, they serve specific military ends. If nothing else it demonstrates yet again the indeterminacy of the law and the artificiality of formalist legal reasoning. H.L.A. Hart himself acknowledged that principles, policies and purposes can inform reasoning within the penumbral region of rules and the more open context of standards. He remained adamant that such "law making" occurred only at the "fringe"[139] with respect to rules and was nonetheless still subject to "indisputable" measures of correctness with respect to standards.[140] This marginalization of principles, policies and purposes to inform legal reasoning has been at the center of jurisprudential debate for many years. It was Hans Morgenthau who advocated a more direct assimilation of policy and law over sixty years ago. His functionalist advocacy required "precepts of international law" to be interpreted in the light of "ethico-legal principles"[141] with a strong reference to "social"[142] context if law was to escape its formalistic orientation and become more relevant to international discourse. In the COIN doctrine we see the realization of this concept. Doctrine applies to reshape rules and standards alike, such modification being consciously directed under specific means/ends rationality. It remains to be seen whether this development is accepted for what it is, or whether it will be reconciled and explained away within existing canons of interpretation, no matter how artificial and unsatisfying that explanation. In representing an affront to interpretative approaches to rule formalism, it may also be resisted for what it presages. Conflating military effectiveness with humanitarian protection is surely sound but, as in the *Adalah* case, the acceptance of this proposition strikes deep into judicial sensitivities and runs the perceived risk of opening the door to accepting a deeply instrumentalist approach to the law that risks elevating military effectiveness as an interpretative benchmark.

Alternatively, the combination of rules and standards methodologies under COIN/stability operations doctrine can operate to better inform ethical judgment. In his critique of the principle of LOAC's concept of distinction, David Kennedy queries whether the purpose of the classic rule is "ethical distinction" or "instrumental calculation."[143] The same critique may, of course, apply to the principle of proportionality. According to Kennedy, the combination of invoking a formalist style of interpretation in conjunction with an underlying utilitarian orientation allows for a "proceduralization" of bloodshed that permits the avoidance of any real sense of personal responsibility.[144] The new COIN/stability operations doctrine, which demands sociopolitical analysis in any targeting solution under the law, meets these criticisms. However, it carries with it a particular cognitive risk. Once individuals are assessed on criteria of "reconcilability" rather than on the more formulaic DPH criteria, it animates both cognitive and emotional processing of information. Thus, from an emotional perspective, whether a targeting action is an instance of lawful engagement or "murder" has the potential for initiating significant cognitive dissonance. It is an omnipresent feature in individual decisions under the law and the "firewall" between such concepts is adequately maintained through a functional DPH category approach. The requirement for individual assessment based upon socio-legal considerations, even when a person comes within the DPH criteria, threatens to unravel this ethical "distance" that the existing law establishes.

In warfare, military lawyers effectively undertake the judicial decision-making role. Military lawyers will provide a multitude of interpretations and advice to commanders on what always seem to be cascading legal problems. This advice is always time sensitive and always undertaken in the shadow of the law. The COIN/stability operations policy approach to questions of targeting imposes a definitive high "value" on civilian life that is heavily weighted on achieving advantageous militarily strategic outcomes. This policy can in fact be reconciled with existing formulations of distinction and proportionality, but we should be aware of the way this policy is guiding selection of legal canons of interpretation. The malleability of interpretative devices, of turning rules into standards and vice versa, exposes the apparent structural "certainties" of formalism and threatens incorporation of the traditional risks of arbitrariness, subjectivity and inflexibility associated with the rules/standards dichotomy in a compounded manner. It would be wrong to read too much into this phenomenon, however. Indeterminacy is more of a feature of the law than we might like to think. The realist movement and its "critical legal studies" successors have long been dedicated to ascertaining the inchoate policy preferences of judicial decision making. Here, ironically, the role of humanitarian considerations has been "imposed" as an express preference in the interpretation of the principles of distinction and proportionality. It is both an ethical distinction and an instrumental calculation. It also speaks the language of legitimacy, which is fast becoming the currency of the law of armed conflict but, as stated, is not without its cognitive risks.

Part III. Legal Plurality in COIN/Stability Operations

The COIN/stability operations manuals emphasize the critical need for intervening forces to assume a particularized form of ethical orientation, one that displays demonstrable compliance with the law and its underlying humanitarian ethos and also accepts greater risk in achieving the military goals that have been set. Acting with "rectitude" has become a key theme in establishing the necessary legitimacy to underpin COIN/stability operations.[145] The role of "soft power" has been highlighted as a fundamental tenet of success. In this regard Kilcullen notes, "America's international reputation, moral authority, diplomatic weight, persuasive ability, cultural attractiveness, and strategic credibility—its 'soft power'—is not some optional adjunct to military strength. Rather, it is a critical enabler for a permissive operating environment."[146] In the working environment of COIN/stability operations this throws up numerous legal conundrums. The perennial question of the interplay between LOAC and human rights law within a conflict zone is one of these. Another is the choice between invocation of the full conventional apparatus of the law of armed conflict when dealing with, for example, "irreconcilables," as against resort to law enforcement measures and associated criminal justice procedures to be undertaken primarily by domestic national forces.

The dilemmas facing the legal advisor in a "post-conflict" conflict are multifaceted and perhaps more challenging than in a straightforward conventional war context. At what point, for example, does the LOAC framework give way to human rights norms and the application of domestic criminal law standards? Is it a sliding scale? Are there particular categories of actor or context where the break is more abrupt? COIN and stability operations doctrine makes it plain that counterintuitive principles are critical to success, though conventional LOAC interpretative methodologies still have their place. The challenge is discerning when one is to be preferred over the other. In all post-conflict societies where intervening military forces are operating, there is a strong will for emerging national institutions to assert their understandable desire for sovereign independence. Concomitantly, a stated counterinsurgency "paradox" principle is "[t]he host nation doing something tolerably is normally better than us doing it well."[147] Establishing the legitimacy of domestic institutions is a key factor in COIN/stability operations doctrine, though what if the probable cost of forbearance is the loss of life in one's own forces? Moreover, what if complying with civil law processes (warrant-based arrests, for example) will likely result in greater casualties for your forces though resort to available LOAC avenues of action to "kill-capture," which minimize that risk, are equally available? Which legal option is the right one to take? Post-conflict societies are often in a mixed state of war and peace, and the reality of complying with civil law enforcement measures is not like that in Western democratic societies. When is the assumption of greater risk, which COIN/stability operations doctrine mandates, not appropriate, especially when other legal regimes that mitigate that risk (though not without some cost to legitimacy) are equally applicable and equally valid?

The Interaction of LOAC and International Human Rights Law in COIN/Stability Operations

The interaction of the law of armed conflict and international HR law, which is so much a staple of contemporary mainstream academic debate, has its operationalization in the very contexts that COIN and stability operations doctrine anticipates. This requires practical disentangling on the ground. While the framework established by the ICJ in the *Nuclear Weapons* advisory opinion[148] for reconciling these questions makes plain that LOAC (referred to by the Court as international humanitarian law (IHL)) and HR law can both apply during a time of armed conflict, the maxim of *lex specialis* will determine the content of prevailing obligation. In that instance, dealing with the right to life and the prohibition of arbitrary deprivation, in issuing its advisory opinion the Court found that IHL represented the *lex specialis*.[149] The ICJ's subsequent pronouncement in the 2004 *Wall* advisory opinion[150] provided less than exacting guidance when determining that "some rights may be exclusively matters of IHL; others may be exclusively matters of human rights law; yet others may be matters of both these branches of international law."[151]

The question of resolution between these two bodies of international law may, however, be more prosaically tackled. Rather than a mighty clash of strategic principle where one body of law *in toto* trumps the other, there appears to be a more nuanced assimilation that is occurring in practice. For certain coalition partners either policy or domestic legal directives will directly or indirectly apply human rights norms to their operational activities. They are rarely formally expressed at the ground level as being one or the other and to the soldier on the ground the distinction is of little import. Hence, with respect to detention operations, which are plainly a significant component of COIN operations, it is evident that the influence of domestic law, such as the UK Human Rights Act (which in turn incorporates the European Convention on Human Rights) will continue to have application for activities occurring during armed conflict. As the *Al-Skeini* case[152] has established, these norms can have decisive legal application in a conflict so as to compel observance by particular forces with respect to particular fact circumstances.[153] While courts will invariably rely upon a careful recitation of facts and circumstances when formulating such standards, government and military policy will usually provide for a broader degree of "margin" to ensure lawful and socially legitimate/acceptable behavior. Hence the impact of this UK legislative authority (as judicially interpreted) has an assimilative effect in terms of standard operating procedures (SOPs) written for such operations, ones that other coalition partners are required to respect and observe when engaging in combined operations. Whether the guidance derives from LOAC or HR law, from domestic or international law, the impact upon operations on the ground and the indirect policy do influence behavior and act as socializing agents between forces acting in concert. Thus in the event of COIN operations within Iraq or Afghanistan, should non-UK forces wish to utilize UK detention facilities there is a requirement for compliance with UK legal and policy preferences. Given the specificity of such obligations the question of *lex specialis* becomes, in effect, one of HR obligations providing definitive guidance.

The Orientation of Legal Advice

Grappling with the reality of legal plurality within an operational context, especially when looking at both the horizontal and vertical planes of interaction in a COIN environment, provides unique challenges. Lawyers are used to compartmentalizing legal concepts and applying time-tested forensic skills and "disciplined, intuitive"[154] legal reasoning to the resolution of problems. The law of armed conflict provides a particularized intellectual structure. Counterinsurgency inverts most of the truisms associated with such formalist thinking. When defeat was staring the coalition in the eyes in Iraq in 2007, a radical new strategy was developed that recognized the need for a more careful and judicious application of force ("We cannot kill our way out of this endeavor"). Classic legal prescriptions under LOAC don't quite match the objectives being sought, or at least don't synchronize with the new "means" as easily, except in the pressing case of targeting "irreconcilables."

The legal advisors in both Iraq and Afghanistan over the past few years have been dealing with the classic "three-block war" concept.[155] In these instances, the forces were engaged in antiterrorism, as well as counterinsurgency, while simultaneously trying to build capacity and ensuring compliance with the multifaceted rule of law foundation that COIN/stability operations doctrine demands.[156] Legal problems in these contexts are not so easily compartmentalized; these issues are too deeply interconnected. Choices need to be made holistically with the net result possibly being the loss of one's own soldiers through compliance with what appears to be abstract and aberrant policy. It is clear, though, that the new doctrine reflected in the COIN/stability operations is actually working in the strategic sense.

Doctrine plays a decisive role in military decision making and there is evidence that operational planning teams have socialized the new directions mandated in effectively fighting this postmodern warfare. As previously mentioned, there is not a lot of evidence that the legal community has been as ready to internalize these fundamental changes. Lawyers have a tendency to interpret factual problems in accordance with extant legal prescriptions and prevailing models, and seek to manipulate facts to ensure a sense of legal integrity when dispensing advice. Perhaps the dissociative mechanism of distinguishing between law and policy that lawyers readily employ to temper challenges to formalist orthodoxy in the area of operational law will again prevail. Perhaps the law of armed conflict will retain its perceived ideational integrity, though stepping back from this, there is something unsettling in trying to conform postmodern approaches into a legal framework that predominantly dates back to the post–World War Two era (in fact, back to the nineteenth century). It seems to set the stage for legal marginalization. The better accommodation may be one that retains the substance of the law but is more open to a modified interpretative valence.

Part IV. Conclusion

The body of the modern law of armed conflict is "the result of an equitable balance between the necessities of war and humanitarian requirements."[157] Through the mechanism of hard-line empirical rules, as well as flexible evaluative standards, this fundamental military/humanitarian balance is in perpetual creative tension. The adoption of a shared vocabulary within the law has allowed an intersection of dialogue between military professionals and humanitarian advocates that has, in fact, empowered both camps. It is of no small measure, for example, that the principle of proportionality may be celebrated as a desirable union of both military economy and humanitarian restraint. The principle provides a moral and political convergence: only "direct and concrete military advantage" and non-"excessive" civilian loss are permitted. Yet, the simple mechanics and elegant mathematical confidence of the proportionality principle seem to permit avoidance of broader ethical questions. As David Kennedy has observed, mechanically complying with the law can allow the avoidance of "ethical jeopardy" and the minimization of personal responsibility.[158] The recognition of the specifics of individual identity and anticipating the second- and third-order effects of a "proportionate attack" are not matters that have occupied much legal time in any planning analysis, and yet, as we have seen in COIN, they can have enormous strategic policy significance.

The postmodern era of warfare challenges old legal orthodoxies. Concepts such as avoiding incidental civilian injury in terms that far exceed legal limits and requiring greater precision in targeting than merely verifying the relevant civilian/combatant categories of privilege (and its loss) represent a powerful transformative approach to conducting operations. The COIN/stability operations doctrine predicates are largely counterintuitive and at odds with traditional approaches to legal interpretation. When, for example, has "emotional intelligence," as General Kiszely identifies,[159] ever been relevant to disciplined legal analysis? It is evident that the weight of operational doctrine and increasing assimilation of human rights norms into multi-splintered SOPs require a reconsideration of prevailing approaches to interpretative valence. Perhaps issues such as human rights norms applying to operations and the conflation of military advantage with preserving civilian lives under age-old formulas may be rationalized and distinguished as "mere" policy. Perhaps legal advisors can continue to insist on a "Hartian" template for interpretative rectitude and can answer all the relevant constituencies "out there" with a robust assertion that it "is the law" that justifies and rationalizes actions, and as lawyers we must be vigilant to remain strictly within its boundaries. Or perhaps not. Could it be that policy has always infiltrated legal reasoning in ways that are not openly acknowledged? Perhaps the American realists of the interwar period[160] did have it right and legal analysis can be much more flexible and accommodating of policy inputs than what we might want to admit and, moreover, may do so without impugning the integrity of the law. Perhaps the law of armed conflict still retains all we need to ensure military success, we just need to be mindful of what we mean by such success and be conscious of how we can get there. Either way, a real revolution in military affairs is under way and it does implicate the law in fundamental ways. The coming storm offers a rare opportunity to recalibrate the interpretative valence of the law in a spirit of self-awareness made all the more ironic by the fact that it is operational pragmatism that has sparked this phenomenon.

Notes

1. John Kiszely, *Post-Modern Challenges for Modern Warriors*, AUSTRALIAN ARMY JOURNAL, Winter 2008, at 177.
2. *Id.* at 178.
3. RUPERT SMITH, THE UTILITY OF FORCE: THE ART OF WAR IN THE MODERN WORLD 5 (2007).
4. Kiszely, *supra* note 1; COIN Manual, *infra* note 5, at iii.
5. HEADQUARTERS, DEPARTMENT OF THE ARMY & HEADQUARTERS, MARINE CORPS COMBAT DEVELOPMENT COMMAND, FM 3-24/MCWP 3-33.5, THE U.S. ARMY/MARINE CORPS COUNTERINSURGENCY FIELD MANUAL (University of Chicago Press 2007) (2006) [hereinafter COIN Manual].
6. HEADQUARTERS, DEPARTMENT OF THE ARMY, FM 3-07, THE U.S. ARMY STABILITY OPERATIONS FIELD MANUAL (University of Michigan Press 2009) (2008) [hereinafter Stability Operations Manual].
7. DAVID KILCULLEN, THE ACCIDENTAL GUERRILLA 129 (2009).
8. *Id.* at 128–54.
9. Ganesh Sitaraman, *Counterinsurgency, the War on Terror, and the Laws of War*, 95 VIRGINIA LAW REVIEW 1745, 1747 (2009) ("despite counterinsurgency's ubiquity in military and policy circles, legal scholars have almost completely ignored it").

10. SMITH, *supra* note 3, at 5.
11. Kiszely, *supra* note 1, at 179.
12. *Id.*
13. There has been a strong sense of ad hoc doctrinal "catch-up" to synchronize with these non-conventional operations especially during the 1990s. *See, e.g.*, Peter Viggo Jakobsen, *The Emerging Consensus on Grey Area Peace Operations Doctrine: Will It Last and Enhance Operational Effectiveness?*, INTERNATIONAL PEACE-KEEPING, Autumn 2000, at 36; Michael Stopford, *Peace-Keeping or Peace-Enforcement: Stark Choices for Grey Areas*, 73 UNIVERSITY OF DETROIT MERCY LAW REVIEW 499 (1996); INTERNATIONAL & OPERATIONAL LAW DEPARTMENT, THE JUDGE ADVOCATE GENERAL'S SCHOOL, OPERATIONAL LAW HANDBOOK ch. 23 (2001).
14. Kiszely, *supra* note 1, at 185–86.
15. COIN Manual, *supra* note 5, at xxxv.
16. *Id.* at xxi.
17. *Id.* at 234–35.
18. *Id.* at 13 & 252 ("Lose Moral Legitimacy, Lose the War").
19. *Id.* at 11–14.
20. *Id.* at 47–51.
21. *Id.* at xxv.
22. *Id.* at 37–39, 42–43, 49–50; Stability Operations Manual, *supra* note 6, at 1-29.
23. KILCULLEN, *supra* note 7, at 30–34.
24. COIN Manual, *supra* note 5, at xxv.
25. *Id.*
26. Kiszely, *supra* note 1, at 182.
27. *Id.*
28. COIN Manual, *supra* note 5, at 49.
29. Kiszely, *supra* note 1, at 184.
30. *Id.* at 179.
31. *Id.* at 180.
32. *Id.*
33. SMITH, *supra* note 3, at 6.
34. KILCULLEN, *supra* note 7, at 129–30.
35. COIN Manual, *supra* note 5, at 44–47.
36. MNF-I Commander's Counterinsurgency Guidance (June 21, 2008), *reprinted in* THOMAS E. RICKS, THE GAMBLE 369 (2009), *available at* http://www.mnf-iraq.com/images/CGs_Messages/080621_coin_%20guidance.pdf [hereinafter MNF-I Guidelines].
37. COIN Manual, *supra* note 5, para. 1-149, at 48.
38. *Id.*, para. 1-153, at 49.
39. *Id.*, para. 1-150, at 48.
40. *Id.*, para. 1-151, at 48.
41. "Resolve" is identified in many accounts of COIN as being the key counterinsurgent vulnerability. *See, e.g.*, Jim Molan, *Thoughts of a Practitioner*, AUSTRALIAN ARMY JOURNAL, Winter 2008, at 215, 220.
42. COIN Manual, *supra* note 5, at xxiii.
43. Given the natural interaction between COIN and stability operations doctrine, I will be referring to both as COIN/stability operations. The main point is that they are doctrinally distinct from conventional warfare.
44. Stability Operations Manual, *supra* note 6, at viii.
45. *Id.* at 1-1.

46. *Id.* at 1-3.

47. See DONALD P. WRIGHT & TIMOTHY R. REESE, ON POINT II: TRANSITION TO THE NEW CAMPAIGN, THE UNITED STATES ARMY IN OPERATION IRAQI FREEDOM MAY 2003–JANUARY 2005 ch. 2 (2008), *available at* http://www.globalsecurity.org/military/library/report/2008/onpoint/index.html, where the following is stated:

> Clearly, the PH [phase] IV planning efforts by ORHA [Office of Reconstruction and Humanitarian Assistance], the Joint Staff, and CENTCOM attest to the fact that many within the US Government and the DOD community realized the need to plan for operations after the fall of the Saddam regime. . . . Nonetheless, as in the planning process for Operation JUST CAUSE, the emphasis within the major US commands, as well as within the DOD, was on planning the first three phases of the campaign. As stated earlier in this chapter, the Office of the Secretary of Defense focused the CENTCOM and CFLCC [combined force land component commander] staffs on these phases. The CENTCOM staff spent a greater amount of time on the preparation for the staging of forces in Kuwait and initial offensive operations than it did on what might happen after the toppling of the Saddam regime. At the CFLCC level, Benson, the chief CFLCC planner, asserted that he was not able to induce McKiernan to spend a significant amount of time on the planning for stability and support operations. . . . Not surprisingly, Benson felt somewhat overwhelmed by the task of PH IV operations given the lack of resources he had. He underlined the problem created by Army planners who gave most of their attention to conventional operations, saying, "We were extraordinarily focused on Phase III. There should have been more than just one Army colonel, me, really worrying about the details of Phase IV."

48. Stability Operations Manual, *supra* note 6, at ix.

49. *Id.* at vii.

50. US Department of Defense policy is as follows:

> Stability operations are conducted to help establish order that advances U.S. interests and values. The immediate goal often is to provide the local populace with security, restore essential services, and meet humanitarian needs. The long-term goal is to help develop indigenous capacity for securing essential services, a viable market economy, rule of law, democratic institutions, and a robust civil society.

US Department of Defense, Directive 3000.05, Military Support for Stability, Security, Transition, and Reconstruction (SSTR) Operations para. 4.2 (Nov. 28, 2005), *available at* http://www.dtic.mil/whs/directives/corres/pdf/300005p.pdf [hereinafter DoD Directive 3000.05].

51. Stability Operations Manual, *supra* note 6, at 1-22, 1-23.

52. National Security Presidential Directive/NSPD-44 (2005), *available at* http://www.fas.org/irp/offdocs/nspd/nspd-44.html; Stability Operations Manual, *supra* note 6, para. 1-66, at 1-22. DoD Directive 3000.05, *supra* note 50, para. 1-73, at 1-15, emphasizes, however, that military force "will assume responsibility" for stability operations tasks even in the absence of civilian capacity or preparedness to undertake such activities.

53. William Easterly, *J'accuse: The US Army Development Delusions*, AID WATCH, June 18, 2009, *available at* http://www.press.umich.edu/pdf/9780472033904-review1.pdf, where the author states: "The 2009 US Army Stability Operations Field Manual is remarkably full of utopian dreams of transforming other societies into oases of prosperity, peace, and democracy through the coordinated use of military force, foreign aid, and expert knowledge."

54. Edward Luttwak, *Dead End: Counterinsurgency Warfare as Military Malpractice*, HARPER'S MAGAZINE, Feb. 2007, at 33, *available at* http://www.harpers.org/archive/2007/02/0081384.

55. KILCULLEN, *supra* note 7, at 143.

56. *Id.* at 126.

57. See S.C. Res. 1272, para. 2, U.N. Doc. S/RES/1272 (Oct. 25, 1999), which provided that the mandate of the United Nations Transitional Administration in East Timor was comprised of the following elements:

(a) To provide security and maintain law and order throughout the territory of East Timor;
(b) To establish an effective administration;
(c) To assist in the development of civil and social services;
(d) To ensure the coordination and delivery of humanitarian assistance, rehabilitation and development assistance;
(e) To support capacity-building for self-government; [and]
(f) To assist in the establishment of conditions for sustainable development.

58. Tonya Jankunis, *Military Strategists Are from Mars, Rule of Law Theorists Are from Venus: Why Imposition of the Rule of Law Requires a Goldwater-Nichols Modeled Interagency Reform*, 197 MILITARY LAW REVIEW 16, 41–42 (2008).

59. *Id.* at 42.

60. Dan E. Stigall, *The Rule of Law: A Primer and a Proposal*, 189 MILITARY LAW REVIEW 92, 97–98 (2006).

61. Stability Operations Manual, *supra* note 6, at 1-40–1-46.

62. Pierre Schlag, *Rules and Standards*, 33 UCLA LAW REVIEW 379, 383 (1985).

63. Duncan Kennedy, *Form and Substance in Private Law Adjudication*, 89 HARVARD LAW REVIEW 1685 (1976).

64. *Id.* at 1687.

65. *Id.*

66. *Id.*

67. *Id.*

68. *Id.* at 1688.

69. *Id.*

70. Schlag, *supra* note 62, at 381.

71. *Id.* at 382.

72. *Id.* at 383.

73. *Id.*

74. *Id.* at 381–82.

75. *See generally* Louis Kaplow, *Rules versus Standards*, 42 DUKE LAW JOURNAL 557 (1992).

76. Kennedy, *supra* note 63, at 1688.

77. Schlag, *supra* note 62, at 379–80.

78. *Id.* at 385.

79. Kennedy, *supra* note 63, at 1688.

80. Schlag, *supra* note 62, at 385.

81. Kennedy, *supra* note 63, at 1701.

82. H.L.A. HART, THE CONCEPT OF LAW 134 (2d ed. 1994).

83. Brian Leiter, *American Legal Realism*, *in* PHILOSOPHY OF LAW AND LEGAL THEORY 64 (Martin P. Golding & William A. Edmundson eds., 2009).

84. DAVID KENNEDY, OF WAR AND LAW 134–38, 156–57 (2006).

85. S.S. Lotus (Fr. v. Turk.), 1927 P.C.I.J. (ser. A) No. 10 (Sept. 7).

86. DAVID KENNEDY, THE DARK SIDES OF VIRTUE: REASSESSING INTERNATIONAL HUMANITARIANISM 267 (2004).

87. KENNEDY, *supra* note 84, at 104.

88. *Id.* at 91.

89. RICHARD POSNER, THE PROBLEMS OF JURISPRUDENCE 434–46 (1990).

90. Legality of the Threat or Use of Nuclear Weapons, Advisory Opinion, 1996 I.C.J. 226, para. 78 (July 8) ("The cardinal principles contained in the texts constituting the fabric of humanitarian law are the following. The first is aimed at the protection of the civilian population and civilian objects and establishes the distinction between combatants and non-combatants; States must never make civilians the object of attack . . . .") [hereinafter Nuclear Weapons case].

91. Protocol Additional to the Geneva Conventions of 12 August 1949, and Relating to the Protection of Victims of International Armed Conflicts, June 8, 1977, 1125 U.N.T.S. 3, *reprinted in* DOCUMENTS ON THE LAWS OF WAR 422 (Adam Roberts & Richard Guelff eds., 3d ed. 2000) [hereinafter GPI].

92. *Id.*, art. 85(3)(a), provides that "the following acts shall be regarded as grave breaches of this Protocol, . . . (a) making the civilian population or individual civilians the object of attack."

93. *Id.*, art. 85(5), provides that "[w]ithout prejudice to the application of the Conventions and of this Protocol, grave breaches of these instruments shall be regarded as war crimes."

94. *Id.*, art. 86(2), provides that

> [t]he fact that a breach of the Conventions or of this Protocol was committed by a subordinate does not absolve his superiors from penal or disciplinary responsibility . . . if they knew, or had information which should have enabled them to conclude in the circumstances at the time, that he was committing or was going to commit such a breach . . . .

95. Kennedy, *supra* note 63, at 1695.

96. GPI, *supra* note 91, art. 51(3), states that "[c]ivilians shall enjoy the protection afforded by this Section, unless and for such time as they take a direct part in hostilities."

97. Protocol Additional to the Geneva Conventions of 12 August 1949, and Relating to the Protection of Victims of Non-International Armed Conflicts, June 8, 1977, 1125 U.N.T.S. 609, *reprinted in* DOCUMENTS ON THE LAWS OF WAR, *supra* note 91, at 483 [hereinafter GPII]; GPII's Article 13(3)'s terms are substantively identical to those in GPI, *id.*

98. GPI, *supra* note 91.

99. The International Committee of the Red Cross (ICRC), in conjunction with the TMC Asser Institute, has, since 2003, engaged in an ongoing study of the "direct participation in hostilities" concept with a number of experts in the field and through this process has made a valuable contribution to the ongoing debate with its successive yearly release of reports of proceedings. *See also* Michael N. Schmitt, *Humanitarian Law and Direct Participation in Hostilities by Private Contractors or Civilian Employees*, 5 CHICAGO JOURNAL OF INTERNATIONAL LAW 511 (2005); and Dale Stephens & Angeline Lewis, *The Targeting of Civilian Contractors in Armed Conflict*, 9 YEARBOOK OF INTERNATIONAL HUMANITARIAN LAW 25 (2006).

100. Based on the study of "direct participation in hostilies," the ICRC recommended that the LOAC be interpreted as follows: "In non-international armed conflict, organized armed groups constitute the armed forces of a non-State party to the conflict and consist only of individuals whose continuous function it is to take a direct part in hostilities ('continuous combat function')"; and commented that "[t]hus, individuals whose continuous function involves the preparation, execution or command of acts or operations amounting to direct participation in hostilities are assuming a continuous combat function." NILS MELZER, INTERPRETIVE GUIDANCE

ON THE NOTION OF DIRECT PARTICIPATION IN HOSTILITIES UNDER INTERNATIONAL HUMANITARIAN LAW 16, 34 (2009), *available at* http://www.icrc.org/Web/eng/siteeng0.nsf/htmlall/direct-participation-report_res/$File/direct-participation-guidance-2009-icrc.pdf [hereinafter ICRC Interpretative Guidance].

101. COMMENTARY ON THE ADDITIONAL PROTOCOLS of 8 JUNE 1977 TO THE GENEVA CONVENTIONS OF 12 AUGUST 1949 para. 1659, at 516 (Yves Sandoz, Christophe Swinarski & Bruno Zimmermann eds., 1987) [hereinafter ICRC Commentary], states that "[d]irect participation in hostilities implies a direct causal relationship between the activity engaged in and the harm done to the enemy at the time and place where the activity takes place."

102. The Supreme Court of Israel expressly excluded financiers from its determination of persons who directly participate in hostilities. HCJ 769/02 Public Committee against Torture in Israel v. Government of Israel, Judgment, para. 35 [Dec. 13, 2006] (not yet published), *available at* http://elyon1.court.gov.il/files_eng/02/690/007/a34/02007690.a34.pdf. *See also* ICRC Interpretative Guidance, *supra* note 100, at 51–52.

103. Sitaraman, *supra* note 9 ("A civilian engaged in spreading propaganda may be highly effective in contributing to the defeat of the counterinsurgents, even though his actions are not intended to cause harm to physical forces"; and he observes, "A television or radio station is a much greater force multiplier for an insurgency than a few additional recruited combatants").

104. INTERNATIONAL COMMITTEE OF THE RED CROSS, DIRECT PARTICIPATION IN HOSTILITIES UNDER INTERNATIONAL HUMANITARIAN LAW 2 (Sept. 2003), *available at* http://www.icrc.org/Web/ara/sitearaO nsf/htmlall/participation-hostilities-ihl-311205/$File/Direct_participation_in_hostilities_Sept_2003_eng.pdf; and NILS MELZER, THIRD EXPERT MEETING ON THE NOTION OF DIRECT PARTICIPATION IN HOSTILITIES: SUMMARY REPORT 17–36 (Oct. 2005), *available at* http://www.icrc.org/Web/eng/siteeng0.nsf/htmlall/participation-hostilities-ihl-311205/$File/Direct_participation_in_hostilities_2005_eng.pdf.

105. Public Committee against Torture in Israel, *supra* note 102.

106. SMITH, *supra* note 3, at 5.

107. GPI, *supra* note 91, art. 1(4).

108. GPII, *supra* note 97, art. 1.

109. MNF-I Guidelines, *supra* note 36.

110. KILCULLEN, *supra* note 7, at 38.

111. RICKS, *supra* note 36, at 264.

112. Sitaraman, *supra* note 9, at 1777 ("Counterinsurgency is defined by a win-the-population strategy for victory, not a kill-capture strategy for victory. It shifts the goals of war from destroying the enemy to protecting the population and building an orderly, functioning society").

113. David H. Petraeus, *Learning Counterinsurgency: Observations from Soldiering in Iraq*, AUSTRALIAN ARMY JOURNAL, Winter 2008, at 57, 63 (2008).

114. *Id.*

115. YORAM DINSTEIN, THE CONDUCT OF HOSTILITIES UNDER THE LAW OF INTERNATIONAL ARMED CONFLICT 122 (2004).

116. A.P.V. ROGERS, LAW ON THE BATTLEFIELD 20 (2d ed. 2004).

117. See, e.g., the following declarations:

> Australia: In relation to paragraph 5(b) of Article 51 and to paragraph 2(a)(iii) of Article 57, it is the understanding of Australia that references to the "military advantage" are intended to mean the advantage anticipated from the military attack considered as a whole and not only from isolated or particular parts of that attack.
>
> United Kingdom: In relation to paragraph 5(b) of Article 51 and paragraph (2)(a)(iii) of Article 57, that the military advantage anticipated from an attack is intended to refer

to the advantage anticipated from the attack considered as a whole and not only from isolated or particular parts of the attack.

The complete text of all reservations and declarations is available at http://www.icrc.org/ihl.nsf/WebSign?ReadForm&id=470&ps=P#res.

118. DINSTEIN, *supra* note 115, at 122.

119. COIN Manual, *supra* note 5, at 247–48.

120. *Id.* at 249.

121. ICRC Commentary, *supra* note 101, para. 2209, at 684.

122. *Id.*

123. *Id.*, para. 2218, at 685 ("there can be no question of creating conditions conducive to surrender by means of attacks which incidentally harm the civilian population").

124. Sitaraman, *supra* note 9, at 1781 ("proportionality, a principle that in counterinsurgency unifies humanity and strategic self-interest").

125. ICRC Commentary, *supra* note 101, para. 2208, at 683.

126. *Id.*, para. 2206, at 683.

127. See, e.g., the International Court for the former Yugoslavia's judgment in *Prosecutor v. Kupreskic*, Case No. IT-95-16-T (Jan. 14, 2000), where both the Martens clause (para. 527) and human rights law (para. 529) are cited to signal the "profound transformation of humanitarian law" to permit the imposition of more humanitarian standards. For a contextualized analysis of these factors, see Gabriella Blum, *The Laws of War and the "Lesser Evil,"* 35 YALE JOURNAL OF INTERNATIONAL LAW 1 (2010), where the author identifies a structural resistance by courts/tribunals to permit military forces to depart from the terms of IHL's formalist terms even where a greater humanitarian outcome would be anticipated from such departure.

128. *See* Dale Stephens, *Human Rights and Armed Conflict: The Advisory Opinion of the International Court of Justice in the Nuclear Weapons Case*, 6 YALE HUMAN RIGHTS AND DEVELOPMENT LAW JOURNAL 1, 14–15 (2006).

129. COIN Manual, *supra* note 5, at xxv.

130. Headquarters, International Security Force, Tactical Directive (July 6, 2009), *available at* http://www.nato.int/isaf/docu/official_texts/Tactical_Directive_090706.pdf.

131. KILCULLEN, *supra* note 7, at 145.

132. Michael N. Schmitt, *The Vanishing Law of War: Reflections on Law and War in the 21st Century*, HARVARD INTERNATIONAL REVIEW, Spring 2009, at 64, *available at* http://www.entrepreneur.com/tradejournals/article/200271861.html.

133. Kathleen Sullivan, *Foreword: The Justice of Rules and Standards*, 106 HARVARD LAW REVIEW 22, 69 (1992).

134. *Id.* at 67.

135. *See* Dale Stephens & Michael W. Lewis, *The Law of Armed Conflict—A Contemporary Critique*, 6 MELBOURNE JOURNAL OF INTERNATIONAL LAW 55, 82–83 (2005), *available at* http://mjil.law.unimelb.edu.au/issues/archive/2005(1)/03Stephens.pdf.

136. Blum, *supra* note 127.

137. HCJ 3799/02 Adalah v. GOC Central Command [2005] (not yet published), English trans. *available at* http://elyon1.court.gov.il/Files_ENG/02/990/037/a32/02037990.a32.pdf.

138. Blum, *supra* note 127, at 17.

139. HART, *supra* note 82, at 133.

140. *Id.* at 131.

141. Hans Morgenthau, *Positivism, Functionalism and International Law*, 34 AMERICAN JOURNAL OF INTERNATIONAL LAW 260, 269 (1940).

142. *Id.* at 270.

143. KENNEDY, *supra* note 84, at 117.

144. *Id.* at 169.

145. MARK O'NEILL, *Back to the Future: The Enduring Characteristics of Insurgency and Counterinsurgency*, AUSTRALIAN ARMY JOURNAL, Winter 2008, at 41, 53 (2008).

146. KILCULLEN, *supra* note 7, at 14.

147. COIN Manual, *supra* note 5, at 49–50.

148. Nuclear Weapons case, *supra* note 90.

149. *Id.*, para. 25.

150. Legal Consequences of the Construction of a Wall in the Occupied Palestinian Territory, Advisory Opinion, 2004 I.C.J. 136 (July 9), *reprinted in* 43 INTERNATIONAL LEGAL MATERIALS 1009 (2004).

151. *Id.*, para. 106, at 97. The Court also determined that the application of the International Covenant on Civil and Political Rights, International Covenant on Economic, Social and Cultural Rights and the Convention on the Rights of the Child also adhered to occupied territory (paras. 111, 112 & 113).

152. Al-Skeini & Others v. Secretary of State for Defence [2007] UKHL 26.

153. In this instance, the House of Lords determined that UK forces could be held accountable for the violation of rights of detainees when held by them in a UK military installation abroad under the UK Human Rights Act, even during a time of armed conflict, on the basis of a constructive territoriality.

154. Charles Fried, *The Artificial Reason of the Law or: What Lawyers Know*, 60 TEXAS LAW REVIEW 35, 57 (1981).

155. Kiszely, *supra* note 1, at 185. The concept of the "three-block war" was promulgated by General Charles Krulak when he was Commandant of the Marine Corps, from 1995 to 1999. He used the phrase in the realization that on the modern battlefield Marines could be called upon to perform very different missions simultaneously. *See* Charles C. Krulak, *The Strategic Corporal: Leadership in the Three Block War*, MARINES MAGAZINE, Jan. 1999, at 3, *available at* http://www.au.af.mil/au/awc/awcgate/usmc/strategic_corporal.htm.

156. KILCULLEN, *supra* note 7, at 152 ("prosecuting the campaign demands an agile mixing of counterinsurgency, counterterrorism, border security, nation-building, and peace enforcement operations").

157. ICRC Commentary, *supra* note 101, para. 2206, at 683.

158. KENNEDY, *supra* note 84, at 169.

159. Kiszely, *supra* note 1, at 184.

160. Referring generally to 1918–39, the period between the end of World War One and the beginning of World War Two.

XV

Rule of Law Capacity Building in Iraq

Richard Pregent*

Introduction

This article discusses the US efforts to assist the government of Iraq (GOI) in establishing the rule of law (ROL). It focuses on the period from the summer of 2008 to the summer of 2009, and the perspective is that of a military lawyer seconded to the US Embassy in Iraq. Although dated, the events and observations set forth may provide useful lessons as the United States continues its reconstruction and stabilization efforts in Iraq and elsewhere. Before beginning a detailed review of ROL capacity building in Iraq, the basic concept must be placed within a broader context.

ROL capacity building is one aspect of a broader national strategic goal of reconstruction and stabilization of "fragile, conflict-prone, and post-conflict states."[1] Whether the premise that "weak and failed states are per se among the most significant threats to the United States"[2] is valid or not is beyond the scope of this discussion; it is simply accepted as true. Within the Department of Defense (DoD) the reconstruction and stabilization mission is described as "stability operations"; ROL capacity building is one part of those operations.[3] In a typical post-conflict situation a State's ability to keep the peace by enforcing the law has been compromised. Police, courts and detention capacity may be limited or not exist at all. The ROL plays a key role in establishing and maintaining stability, particularly in disciplining the actions of the State. It is, however, only one part of the good governance

* Colonel, JA, US Army.

needed to help stabilize and rebuild a weakened State. Just as important to stability operations is the State's ability to provide for the essential needs of its citizenry: clean water, adequate food and shelter, a secure environment and a functioning economy with legitimate employment opportunities.

For the purposes of this discussion, the definition of the rule of law set forth in the US Army's *Rule of Law Handbook* has been adopted:

> Rule of Law is a principle of governance in which all persons, institutions and entities, public and private, including the state itself, are accountable to laws that are publicly promulgated, equally enforced, and independently adjudicated, and which are consistent with international human rights norms and standards.
>
> That principle can be broken down into seven effects:
>
> - The state monopolizes the use of force in resolution of disputes.
> - Individuals are secure in their persons and property.
> - The state is itself bound by law and does not act arbitrarily.
> - The law can be readily determined and is stable enough to allow individuals to plan their affairs.
> - Individuals have meaningful access to an effective and impartial legal system.
> - Human rights and fundamental freedoms are protected by the state.
> - Individuals rely on the existence of legal institutions and the content of the law in the conduct of their daily lives.[4]

This definition was adopted by both the US Mission–Iraq (the Mission) and Multi-National Forces–Iraq (MNF-I) in their joint campaign plan.

It must also be recognized that ROL capacity building cannot be conducted in an operational vacuum. Some degree of security must exist for technical advisors to focus on a State's compliance with its own laws, building a functional court system, protecting the due process rights of pretrial detainees and the many other ROL capacity-building missions. There will be instances in which security and the types of protections associated with the rule of law will come into tension. In those cases senior leaders will have to make the strategic decision to improve security that some may criticize as compromising the rule of law. Particularly during an active counterinsurgency there will be times when the long-term goals of the rule of law mission will of necessity be a lower priority than establishing and maintaining security.

Finally, US ROL capacity-building efforts are hampered by a lack of both unity of command and unity of effort. The DoD stability operations doctrine tries to reconcile two conflicting facts: that reconstruction and stabilization efforts are best conducted and led by civilians, and that military personnel will oftentimes be the only assets available to perform these tasks.[5] At times this conflict has defined the US government's (USG) ad hoc reconstruction and stabilization efforts in Iraq since the invasion.

This article will first discuss the tensions that occasionally arose between security operations and ROL capacity-building efforts, and then focus on the roles the Departments of State (DoS), Defense and Justice (DoJ) played in ROL capacity building in Iraq. Finally, there will be an assessment of the effectiveness of the current USG approach with specific recommendations for improvements.

Security and the Rule of Law

The Awakening

In 2007 many of the Sunni insurgency leaders realized that it was in their best interest to come to terms with the coalition forces (CF) and government in Iraq.[6] The movement began in Anbar province and became known as the Awakening. As the movement spread, MNF-I entered into agreements with regional Awakening leaders, literally bringing former Sunni insurgents, the Sons of Iraq (SOI), into a contractual relationship with CF. The SOI were paid salaries by CF and were incorporated into CF security plans and operations. Some observers believe this development was a greater contributor to the improvement in security than the increase in combat forces, commonly referred to as the Surge, ordered by the Bush administration in 2007.[7]

In late 2007 the Awakening began to bear political fruit: MNF-I negotiated an agreement with the GOI to incorporate a portion of the SOI into government positions.[8] SOI members were hired into positions at the Ministry of Interior (MOI) and brought into the Iraqi army. This partial "reconciliation" between the GOI and former insurgents was strategically key to improving security across the country; wherever these agreements were put in place acts of violence decreased dramatically. Even though the agreements were effective, they were also extraordinarily difficult to maintain politically for both the Sunni insurgency leadership and the primarily Shia elected government officials. Elected leaders felt the SOI had boycotted earlier national elections and chosen to become terrorists, while the SOI felt the elected government had been complicit in the vicious sectarian ethnic cleansing that had convulsed the country since the Samarra mosque bombing in

February 2006.[9] Thus this political compromise was both strategically crucial and extremely fragile.

As insurgents, many of the SOI had committed criminal acts before this reconciliation. In many cases arrest warrants had been legally issued by Iraqi judges. These arrest warrants were not withdrawn with the advent of the Awakening nor when CF—and later the GOI—entered into agreements with the SOI. In 2008 there were several instances of Iraqi security forces (ISF) arresting senior Sunni Awakening leaders based upon these pre-Awakening warrants. These arrests led the SOI to believe the GOI was breaking faith with their agreements, creating a very real risk that the security situation would backslide as the SOI turned back to the insurgency. Although the arrests on their face were lawful, they also created the strategic risk of destabilizing fragile political agreements.

At first glance, CF and Mission leadership seemed to be placed in the position of having to choose between supporting the arrest and prosecution of Sunni leaders for criminal acts or discouraging this enforcement of the law—essentially encouraging Iraqi officials to ignore judicial arrest warrants—in order to support a political agreement that improved the nation's short-term security. In fact, there was no choice in the matter; the realities on the ground dictated that security be maintained and the warrants not be executed. Given the circumstances in Iraq at the time, short-term security necessarily took priority over long-term realization of the principles underlying the rule of law.

The resolution was that the Awakening leadership would not be prosecuted for allegations of criminal acts related to the insurgency that preceded their agreements with CF and the GOI. Criminal allegations that arose for acts committed after the conclusion of these agreements, however, did result in arrests and prosecutions. This political resolution was not formally approved by the Iraqi Parliament; an Awakening amnesty was never enacted. The executive branch simply did not execute the legally valid arrest warrants issued by the courts. In principle, this undercut the rule of law in Iraq. In reality, it made it possible for the SOI to begin a reconciliation process with the GOI and improved security nationwide. The improved security environment made it possible for the GOI, USG and the international community to expand their reconstruction efforts, to include trying to establish the rule of law. Ultimately, the leadership realized that the rule of law capacity-building mission must not block political accommodations between factions that make stability possible.

UN Security Council Resolution Detainees

Another example of the tension between ROL capacity building and maintaining security can be found in the disposition of legacy detainees. These individuals were detained by CF under the authority of a series of UN Security Council Resolutions (UNSCRs), the last being UNSCR 1790,[10] which expired December 31, 2008. It was replaced by the US/Iraq security agreement (SA), which took effect the next day.[11] Article 22 of the security agreement states:

> Upon entry into force of this Agreement, the United States Forces shall provide to the Government of Iraq available information on all detainees who are being held by them. Competent Iraqi authorities shall issue arrest warrants for persons who are wanted by them. The United States Forces shall act in full and effective coordination with the Government of Iraq to turn over custody of such wanted detainees to Iraqi authorities pursuant to a valid Iraqi arrest warrant and shall release all remaining detainees in a safe and orderly manner, unless otherwise requested by the Government of Iraq and in accordance with Article 4 of this Agreement.[12]

On January 1, 2009 when the SA came into effect, US forces held in excess of 15,000 detainees. The challenge was to devise a process that complied with the SA without undercutting security, and in a way that supported the establishment of the ROL. The end result was a qualified success.

Under the SA, detainees either had to be prosecuted pursuant to Iraqi criminal law or had to be released. At the time, nearly two thousand detainees held by CF under the authority of the UNSCRs were in some stage of criminal prosecution in an Iraqi court. These detainees could be transferred into the Iraqi pretrial detention system as space became available. Both the GOI and CF were concerned that releasing the remaining thousands of detainees at one time could not be done "in a safe and orderly manner."[13] It would put hard-earned security improvements at risk. CF established a review and release plan for the remaining detainees.

Lists of detainees were given to the GOI each month with releasable information that supported the detentions. Frequently the information supporting detention was classified so very little evidence was provided. Most disclosures consisted of a conclusory statement that the detainee was involved in supporting the insurgency. The GOI in turn either acceded to the releases or provided warrants for the arrests of the detainees. To the surprise of many, the GOI began to produce hundreds of warrants for detainees CF intended to release. It quickly became evident that the GOI was not issuing warrants as the result of independent assessments of evidence in accordance with Iraqi criminal and constitutional law. The warrants were being mass-produced by the GOI to effect the transfer of legacy detainees from US custody into Iraqi pretrial detention.

Many within the GOI leadership believed that the detainees CF held were security threats and their release would destabilize the country. Many within the US forces leadership felt the same. Because a warrant enabled CF to transfer the detainees into the Iraqi criminal justice system rather than release the detainees into Iraqi society, many US military leaders welcomed the flood of Iraqi warrants as a positive development rather than a violation of the principles underlying the rule of law. US forces made no effort to encourage the GOI to issue warrants that were based upon adequate evidence. Keeping these detainees off the streets was deemed more important than ensuring that their deprivation of liberty was done in accordance with the law. The result was moving even more pretrial detainees into a criminal justice system that was already glutted and dysfunctional.

One of the many organizations that worked closely with Iraqi officials to help establish the ROL, the Law and Order Task Force (LAOTF), had studied the detainee population records at Rusafa prison, Iraq's largest detention facility. This prison held over 20 percent of Iraq's entire detainee population and would house the vast majority of detainees transferred from US custody. LAOTF's study showed that over 20 percent of the prison population had been arrested by the Iraqi army and no action had been taken on their cases since their detention order. Over 500 of these detainees had been in pretrial confinement more than a year without any action taken on their cases; over 290 of these had been in pretrial confinement for over two years with no action taken. This study highlighted violations of Iraqi law and a significant cause of the constant overcrowding and inhumane conditions for the detainees. The United States was quick to bring this to the attention of the Minister of Justice for corrective action.

Despite this information, US detention leaders chose to continue to equate warrants with success. The warrants enabled the United States to transfer detainees into a broken Iraqi pretrial detention system. This exacerbated the overcrowding and continued to overwhelm the Iraqi courts. Many argued that the warrants were valid on their face, that the United States had no authority to question them and that the SA gave the United States no choice but to transfer the detainees. While each of these statements was true, the reality was that the US leadership made no effort to ensure that Iraq was taking these actions against US-held detainees in accordance with Iraqi law.

The vast majority of the detainees transferred were Sunni, a reflection of the fact that 80 percent of the detainee population was Sunni. It remains to be seen whether the USG detention leaders have created a longer-term strategic risk. Will these detainees be treated like those detained by the Iraqi army and remain in pretrial confinement with no action being taken on their cases for years? If so, will it undercut efforts at reconciliation and radicalize the detainees and their families and tribes once again?

Unlike the case of not executing arrest warrants against the leadership of the Awakening, the decision to transfer thousands of Sunni detainees from US detention into Iraqi custody without some effort to ensure the integrity of the judicial process was a mistake. These wholesale transfers were expedient from a security point of view. The focus on security, however, has arguably led the United States to be complicit in what is de facto security detention. It is impossible to predict the impact these actions will have on establishing the rule of law in Iraq. The least that can be said is that this was a lost opportunity to encourage the executive branch of the GOI to comply with its own laws.

The Counter-Terrorism Bureau

In 2006 and 2007 Iraq's security forces were virtually incapable of conducting effective counterterrorism operations. The Ministry of Interior in particular had been infiltrated by criminal elements involved in sectarian violence. Iraqi special operations forces (ISOF) were often hamstrung by an inefficient command structure and a lack of funding. In response, and with the support of CF, the Prime Minister (PM) established the Counter-Terrorism Bureau (CTB). The CTB was intended to develop anti-terrorism strategies for the government, as well as conduct counterterrorism operations.[14] The PM removed ISOF from the Ministry of Defense (MOD) and placed them under his direct control. Initially this was done within the context of a statement of emergency (SOE) announced by the PM and approved by the Iraqi Council of Representatives (COR) in accordance with the Iraqi Constitution. The Constitution, however, states that an SOE may only be declared for a period of thirty days and must be extended for similar periods with the COR's approval for each period.[15] The original SOE lapsed and has never been approved again by the COR in accordance with the Constitution.

With the technical assistance of CF, the CTB proved to be an effective counter-terrorism force. There were incidents, however, where the CTB appeared to be undisciplined and acting from a sectarian bias. Since it was not part of a ministry, it was not subject to ministerial oversight. Tensions arose between the executive branch and the COR during 2008 as the PM pressed to have legislation enacted legitimizing the CTB.[16] The proposed legislation, however, would have approved the status quo and did not include oversight processes that were independent of the PM's office. In early 2009 the COR passed a statute that prohibited expending funds on any quasi-governmental institutions that were created or operated outside of established legal institutions. This was directly aimed at forcing the executive branch to institutionalize the CTB. Critics were concerned that the CTB, which had grown to nine ISOF brigades located across the country, could become the PM's personal militia.

US forces were intimately involved in the development of the CTB and helped ensure its fighting effectiveness. The CTB in fact made significant contributions to the counterterrorism fight in Iraq, and was an important factor in creating and maintaining security. The CTB did not, however, have a legitimate basis in Iraqi law. The executive branch had built it unilaterally without concern for the law. The CF and US Mission leadership once again felt the tension of security versus the rule of law. It had helped create an effective fighting force, but one that was operating outside the authorities of the Iraqi Constitution and Iraqi laws. This tension was primarily one between branches of Iraqi government and the US ability to influence that debate grew less as Security Council Resolution 1790 lapsed and the security agreement took effect. To date this internal Iraqi debate has not been resolved.

During the counterinsurgency fight US forces must be mindful that the capabilities it helps the host nation develop are consistent with that nation's legal structure. Supporting the PM's effort to fight the insurgency and terrorism cannot be done in such a way that it undercuts the balance of powers established by that State's constitution. To do so could result in the re-establishment of a strongman State rather than a State governed by the rule of law.

Rule of Law Capacity Building

In 2008 both MNF-I and the Mission were anticipating the expiration of UN Security Council Resolution 1790 at the end of the calendar year.[17] This would bring to an end the United Nations Chapter VII authority for coalition forces to conduct military operations in Iraq as they had since the formal end of occupation in June 2004. Without the consent of the government of Iraq, the host nation, there would no longer be legal authority for CF to be present on Iraqi territory, never mind conduct unilateral military operations. Bilateral negotiations had begun seeking an arrangement that would respect Iraq's sovereignty and growing sense of nationalism, while simultaneously allowing for the support and technical assistance provided by US forces—assistance both sides recognized as absolutely essential to maintain and improve security.

It was in this context that a periodic review of progress in achieving the goals of the joint campaign plan (JCP) was conducted for the ambassador and MNF-I commander in the summer of 2008. At that time the JCP focused on four lines of operation: security, economic, political and diplomatic. The Awakening, the surge of US forces and the increases in the capabilities of Iraqi security forces had resulted in a dramatic improvement in the security environment; by virtually every statistical measure acts of violence had reached levels last seen in 2003. Economically, Iraq was facing a budget surplus. This was due primarily to record high prices for oil (approximately 95 percent of the Iraqi economy is based upon oil revenues). Another contributing factor was government inefficiency; ministries simply could not execute their budgets. While oil production was still inefficient, it was envisioned that the budget surplus would provide the opportunity to make needed capital investments to improve output. On the political front, progress had been made by the COR in passing some "benchmark" legislation,[18] the executive branch appeared to be making efforts to conduct security operations and govern in a generally non-sectarian manner, and preparations were on track for provincial elections in December 2008. Finally, in the diplomatic arena, Iraq's international relations were progressing. More nations, particularly regional neighbors, were sending delegations to, and opening missions in, Iraq, and Iraq was increasing its participation in regional and international forums. Thus, impressive progress had been achieved in each line of operation. The same could not be said for the establishment of the rule of law.

While the Iraqi judiciary was legally independent of the other branches of government, it was also overwhelmed. The High Judicial Council recognized a need for 3,000 judges;[19] there were only about 1,250. Judicial security was a significant problem; dozens of judges had been assassinated since 2003. These problems led to significant backlogs of cases, which exacerbated the existing pretrial detention challenges. Pretrial detention conditions rarely met the most basic international standards. Conditions of overcrowding, inadequate hygiene facilities and very limited medical support—in some cases there was none—existed in nearly every pretrial detention facility. Forcing confessions from prisoners was a well-established police practice. MNF-I police training teams reported scores of detainee abuse cases at Iraqi detention facilities every month, supported by physical evidence. In addition, there were significant challenges beyond "courts, cops, and corrections," the areas military forces traditionally focus on during post-conflict operations. Official corruption was endemic and the GOI had not developed the oversight mechanisms needed to combat it. The ministry inspectors general were neither resourced nor empowered to act. The Board of Supreme Audit and the Commission on Integrity were similarly hampered. Most problematic was Article 136b of the Criminal Procedure Code, which gave individual ministers the authority to block the criminal prosecution of any member of their ministries. After this periodic review the ambassador and MNF-I commander decided to make the rule of law a separate line of operation of the JCP.

The persons tasked to lead the lines of operations were the senior officers responsible for the US government efforts in those areas: the MNF-I Deputy Commanding General for Operations for the security line, and the Mission's senior political, economic and diplomatic officers for those lines. The lead for the rule of law line of operation was shared by the Mission's Rule of Law Coordinator (ROLC) and the MNF-I Staff Judge Advocate (SJA), a US Army colonel. This was a reflection of both the realities on the ground and the manner in which the United States had conducted operations in Iraq since the invasion. While the ambassador was the senior representative of the United States, there was an overwhelming military presence. In August 2008 there were over 160,000 coalition forces in Iraq, with nearly as many contractors supporting the military presence. These military and civilian assets were spread across the country. The number of Mission personnel and contractors was a small fraction by comparison, and most were concentrated in Baghdad.

Civilian-Led Rule of Law Capacity-Building Assets

The ROLC was a senior executive service officer seconded to the Mission from the Department of Justice. It should be noted that rule of law capacity building was only part of his responsibilities. Both DoJ and the Mission looked to that person to oversee all USG justice activity in Iraq, the ROLC basically serving the role of legal attaché, as well as rule of law coordinator. In August 2008 the number of personnel under the ROLC's technical supervision included personnel from the US Marshals Service, the Federal Bureau of Investigation and Department of Homeland Security, but few of these assets were in Iraq to support the ROL capacity-building mission. ROLC personnel dedicated to the ROL mission included the ROLC deputy, one action officer and liaisons to the Ministry of Justice (MOJ), Ministry of Interior (MOI), the Iraqi High Tribunal (IHT), the Bureau of International Narcotics and Law Enforcement (INL) office, and the International Criminal Investigative Training Assistance Program (ICITAP) office. There were also resident legal advisors (RLAs) located with most of the Provincial Reconstruction Teams (PRTs). The numbers and sizes of PRT offices fluctuated frequently, but in the summer of 2008 there were about twenty-six PRTs spread across the country. There were several in Baghdad and some of the eighteen provinces had two or more, while the Kurdistan region had only one. The PRTs and their RLAs fell under the authority of the Chief of the Office of Provincial Reconstruction (OPR) and not the ROLC.

The ROLC MOJ and MOI liaisons had limited impact. The capacity-building mission for the MOI rested with MNF-I.[20] Thus the Mission's liaison was an observer of events within the Ministry of Interior and developed a network within the ministry to arrange key leader engagements. This was an important function, but did not make a critical contribution to ROL capacity building. Regarding the MOJ liaison, it must be noted that, in the summer of 2008, the acting Minister of Justice, who had been in place for nearly a year, refused to cooperate with either CF or the Mission. This continued until early 2009 when a new minister was appointed. Thus, the Mission's MOJ liaison could accomplish very little. The IHT liaison office was known as the Regime Crimes Liaison Office from 2003 to 2007. In the earlier years it had a larger staff and provided significant amounts of technical assistance to the IHT. By 2008 the IHT was well established and the liaison office was reduced to a single officer who observed the court's activities and provided technical assistance as needed. The bulk of the ROL capacity-building contributions by the ROLC were made by ICITAP, INL and the RLAs with the PRTs.

ICITAP's role was to provide technical assistance to the GOI to improve the quality of correctional facilities and the professionalism of the Iraqi Corrections Service. ICITAP had been present in Iraq since 2003 and helped the GOI make enormous strides in its correctional system. In 2008 it had a senior corrections professional in the ROLC managing over eighty contractors divided into teams spread across eleven prisons and six detention facilities. Although ICITAP's focus was on post-trial detention facilities, it maintained a presence in some pretrial facilities. ICITAP worked closely with MNF-I's Task Force (TF) 134 to train Iraqi corrections officers and help the GOI institutionalize this training capacity. The ICITAP contractors were the USG's eyes and ears into Iraqi corrections facilities. ICITAP was greatly responsible for the fact that by 2008 MOJ-run facilities usually met international standards and rarely generated allegations of detainee abuse. As discussed later, conditions in pretrial detention facilities were appalling, but most of those facilities were run by the MOI.

The RLAs focused on rule of law capacity building at the provincial level and below. As previously indicated, they were part of the PRTs, falling under the authority of the embassy's Office of Provincial Reconstruction, not the ROLC. The PRTs had the broader reconstruction and stabilization goals of supporting good governance by improving the local governments' ability to provide essential services, employment and educational opportunities, and health services, as well as increasing the transparency of government to battle corruption. The RLAs focused on the rule of law aspect of reconstruction and stabilization, tailoring their efforts to the needs of a given region. The RLAs frequently served in austere and dangerous environments, and relied on MNF-I assets for security and movement support. Several RLAs were retired military lawyers or assistant US attorneys on detail and served for at least a year.

Although the INL office had no rule of law capacity-building practitioners, it controlled the funding for the civilian rule of law capacity-building efforts and managed related contracts. INL funded ICITAP, most of the RLAs, Iraqi judicial and law enforcement assistance programs, various information technology initiatives and the construction of five prisons. INL also managed a $400 million contract for the DoD to provide over 750 police and border advisors. The ROLC had no authority over the director of the INL office. This was a significant source of friction in the Mission's rule of law capacity-building efforts. Frequently, the INL office would act independently without coordinating its actions with the ROLC. At other times, the INL office would disagree with the rule of law priorities set by the ROLC and refuse to fund them. The tension between these offices reflected the greater tension between the Department of Justice and Department of State. DoS lacked subject-matter expertise in rule of law capacity building and turned to DoJ for this support. Yet DoS refused to give that officer authority over the funding of rule of law capacity building. This fundamental gap between DoS capabilities and responsibilities is at the heart of USG failings in reconstruction and stabilization efforts.

Military-Led Rule of Law Capacity-Building Assets

By comparison to the civilian-led effort the US military applied far more assets to the stabilization and reconstruction mission, including rule of law capacity building. In 2004, then–major general Petraeus built the Multi-National Security Transition Command–Iraq (MNSTC-I), consolidating US government efforts to provide technical assistance to the GOI in rebuilding the Ministries of Defense and Interior, as well as the Iraqi military and police forces. In its early years MNSTC-I focused on force generation to increase the number of ISF available to conduct counterinsurgency operations. As the security situation improved in 2008, MNSTC-I began to shift its focus to professionalizing those forces and improving their respective ministries' ability to support and oversee their operations. MNSTC-I assisted both the MOI and MOD in developing codes of conduct, and establishing open and transparent internal court systems to discipline their forces. Dozens of MNSTC-I advisors and contractors worked within the ministries to institutionalize oversight mechanisms (inspectors general and human rights offices) and at the training bases to assist in establishing training standards that included respect for basic human rights and the rule of law. These advisors also worked to "train the trainers," helping to develop a cadre of Iraqis who understood the subjects and who had developed the skills needed to pass that knowledge on to new trainees. MNSTC-I also trained CF training teams that were then assigned to the field commanders within Multi-National Corps–Iraq (MNC-I), MNF-I's subordinate, operational command.

In 2008, MNC-I had 120 military training teams, 35 national police training teams and 244 police training teams operating in Iraq. These teams were partnered with Iraqi units and worked with them on a daily basis to provide technical assistance in conducting operations and professionalizing the forces. MNC-I required each subordinate command to inspect all Iraqi detention facilities within its area of responsibility every quarter. Training teams were often used to conduct these assessments. Monthly reports were provided to the MNC-I Provost Marshal and proved to be an invaluable tool to identify the areas with the most significant problems. MNC-I also had a contract for law enforcement support in addition to the $400 million contract managed by INL referred to above. About 150 civilian law enforcement professionals were provided under this contract and were distributed down to the battalion level to work with the police training teams and partnered Iraqi units. In 2008 over two hundred military lawyers and paralegals were serving within MNC-I. Many of them worked with the PRT RLAs and local Iraqi judicial and law enforcement officers on various rule of law capacity-building projects.

TF 134 was created in 2004 to manage detention operations for CF. Although the task force's principal mission was running detention facilities at Camps Cropper and Bucca, which housed thousands of security detainees, it also made significant contributions to rule of law capacity building. The TF 134 legal office was staffed with dozens of attorneys whose mission was to support the prosecution of security detainees in the Central Criminal Court of Iraq. These lawyers marshaled the evidence and provided it to the investigating judge in an effort to turn security detainees held under the authority of Security Council Resolution 1790 into prisoners convicted and sentenced under Iraqi criminal law. Although this effort was intended primarily to prosecute and punish those who attacked CF, it had the added benefit of improving to some degree the efficiency and professionalism of one of Iraq's largest criminal courts.[21]

TF 134 also conducted inspections of Iraqi prison facilities to ensure that the facilities met basic standards before transferring detainees that were charged with, or convicted of, committing offenses under Iraqi law. In addition, TF 134 trained Iraqi corrections officers and integrated them into the guard force rotations at Camps Cropper and Bucca, providing carefully supervised on-the-job training. In 2009, TF 134 initiated and oversaw, in coordination with ICITAP, the construction of a multimillion-dollar training center near Camp Cropper. This effort included the development of programs of instruction and training Iraqi trainers. Despite the downsizing of MNF-I in 2009, TF 134 also built a capability to field nine corrections assistance transition teams. Much like the police training teams described earlier, these teams travel to Iraqi detention facilities ICITAP cannot support, and provide technical assistance to the Iraqi guard force and facility managers.

MNF-I created the Law and Order Task Force (LAOTF) in 2008. It was intended to help build "Iraqi capacity for independent, evidence based, and transparent investigation and trial of major and other crimes before the Central Criminal Court of Iraq."[22] LAOTF was located at Forward Operating Base Shield near Rusafa prison, Iraq's largest detention facility, and the Rusafa criminal courts. Rusafa prison included both sentenced prisoners and pretrial detainees. Although the conditions were better than most Iraqi pretrial detention facilities, it was notoriously overcrowded. The detention facility was poorly managed; corruption and sectarian bias were rampant. ICITAP's efforts to improve prison conditions were frequently frustrated by the inertia of the Rusafa criminal courts. In August 2008 the courts were so slow that it would take three years to retire the backlog of cases. Thousands of pretrial detainees languished awaiting trial. LAOTF's mission was to improve the Rusafa criminal court's throughput.

LAOTF was initially staffed with US military lawyers, and criminal investigators from Australia, the United Kingdom and US armed forces. It was intended that the criminal investigators be paired with Iraqi criminal investigators to improve the quality and efficiency of their investigations. The military lawyers were titled "mentors" for the Iraqi investigative and trial judges.[23] LAOTF also established Iraq's first defense clinic near the prison. The clinic was run by an experienced US DoJ civilian attorney and a military judge advocate. It was comprised of about twenty Iraqi defense counsel who were "mentored" on how to provide support to Rusafa detainees. It must be noted that the Iraqi criminal justice system is inquisitorial rather than adversarial, leaving a very limited role for defense counsel. Most Western-trained attorneys found it difficult to accept that the investigative judge served the roles of prosecutor and defense counsel, as well as that of independent judge.[24] The goal of the defense clinic was not to change Iraqi criminal law or practice, but a more modest one of providing detainees with advocates who might be able to move their cases through the investigative process more quickly.

LAOTF also assumed a role in coordinating Iraqi judicial support to military operations following the expiration of Resolution 1790. As the expiration date approached, MNF-I conventional forces began to conduct all operations "by, through, and with" their Iraqi counterparts. These operations were based upon warrants issued by Iraqi criminal courts. LAOTF worked closely with the units and Central Criminal Court of Iraq judges to assist in the presentation of evidence supporting the issuance of warrants and the follow-on prosecution of those cases. This support helped to some degree in disciplining the operations of the Iraqi security forces who were not accustomed to conducting counterinsurgency operations with a goal of criminally prosecuting the detainees, an important rule of law goal.

Rule of Law Coordinating Center

As the importance of rule of law capacity building was being recognized by the Mission and MNF-I leadership by making it a separate line of operation in the joint campaign plan, the ROLC and MNF-I Staff Judge Advocate recognized that there were numerous actors working in the field. They also recognized that those efforts were being conducted by separate commands and agencies; there was no unity of command. Trying to achieve a unity of effort, they decided to create the Interagency Rule of Law Coordinating Center (IROCC).

The IROCC was intended to coordinate and synchronize rule of law capacity building. In military parlance, it would serve the role of a fusion cell. The concept of the IROCC was initially opposed by the senior DoS leadership in the Mission, a result of the ingrained institutional concern about the "militarization of diplomacy." Only after repeated assurances that the IROCC would have no authority over any DoS assets did the Mission relent.

The concept was that the IROCC would be staffed with action officers from the ROLC office and the MNF-I SJA's rule of law office. Those officers would continue to work on rule of law issues but do so together in one office ensuring that all would have a broad situational awareness, avoiding redundancies and achieving synergies. The IROCC would be led by an Army judge advocate colonel working for both the ROLC and the MNF-I SJA. When the draft fragmentary order (FRAGO) was initially staffed, civilians within the ROLC office who would be working within the IROCC objected. These were DoJ employees who balked at working within an organization led by a military officer. Once again, it was reiterated that the IROCC was a coordinating body and had no tasking authority over either DoS or DoJ personnel.

Once the FRAGO was issued by the MNF-I commander,[25] the military entities involved in rule of law capacity building (MNC-I, MNSTC-I, TF 134 and LAOTF) immediately engaged in the coordination process led by the IROCC. Mission representatives (ROLC, OPR, ICITAP, MOJ and MOI liaisons, INL, Baghdad PRT RLAs) also participated. At the action officer level it was quickly discovered that the IROCC was a useful (and non-threatening) coordinating body. Weekly video-teleconferences were held with all rule of law capacity builders at the operational level and above participating.

Initially the IROCC focused on Iraqi detention facility inspections. A central database, accessible to all ROL capacity builders, was developed for inspection reports, as was a central inspection/assessment calendar to de-conflict the oversight process. MNSTC-I advisors to the Ministry of Defense Human Rights Office and Ministry of Interior Inspector General offices were able to better coordinate logistical support for Iraqi inspections of Iraqi detention facilities. MNC-I was able to more quickly provide reports of inspections and serious incident reports to the MNSTC-I liaison officers to ensure inspection reports were not stale and could be investigated by the Iraqis. The results of all inspections were more efficiently and broadly shared across the inspecting community. Significant incidents or particularly bad conditions could be quickly brought to the attention of both the Mission and MNF-I leadership. The IROCC supported a "targeting" process for key leader engagements.

The IROCC became the established mechanism for USG rule of law capacity builders to coordinate and de-conflict their efforts. During the weekly meetings rule of law capacity-building initiatives were presented, ranging from real property dispute resolution to coupons for legal representation for the indigent. The IROCC held a separate forensics forum, gathering subject-matter experts from MNSTC-I, MNC-I, ROLC, MNF-I, LAOTF and TF 134, and the UK Mission, to discuss initiatives to help the Iraqis develop a forensic capability within its Ministry of Interior and courts. It was quickly discovered that there were overlapping efforts and opportunities that had not been identified earlier. The forum helped the leadership dispel "urban legends" that the Iraqi courts would not accept forensic evidence, and to focus their efforts on the weakest link in the forensic arena—police training. The IROCC also held an information technology forum during which it gathered all those who were developing databases or information management systems for the Iraqis (TF 134, LAOTF, INL and MNC-I). The goal was to achieve compatibility and avoid creating a series of separate, unique and incompatible information management systems.

The International Committee of the Red Cross attended several IROCC meetings, as did the UK Mission legal advisors. After six months the IROCC attempted to engage with the international community to coordinate ROL capacity-building efforts there as well. The Mission leadership objected, saying that this was the exclusive province of the DoS and the ROLC office. It should be noted that to date there is no organization comparable to the IROCC within the international community in Iraq.

Despite the bureaucratic hesitation, the IROCC proved to be a useful coordinating mechanism. It remains to be seen whether the various agencies involved in reconstruction and stabilization operations in the future will embrace the concept of a fusion cell in the field.

State Department Leadership in Reconstruction and Stabilization

The concept of "nation building," widely criticized during the 1990s with US involvements in Somalia, Rwanda, Bosnia-Herzegovina and Kosovo, took on a new legitimacy after the attacks of 9/11. During those earlier peacekeeping and humanitarian operations, US support to the capacity-building efforts fell to the military because of both a lack of interest on the part of policymakers within the Clinton administration and a lack of capacity within the Department of State. After 9/11 many now viewed weak and failing States as potential threats to the United States because of their inability to deny safe haven to transnational terrorists, or, as in the case of the Taliban, a willingness to provide such a haven.[26] The lack of a civilian capacity to plan, coordinate and execute post-conflict governance and capacity building became clear after the invasion of Iraq and the toppling of the Saddam Hussein regime.

In 2004 the State Department established the Office of the Coordinator for Reconstruction and Stabilization (S/CRS). In the same year Congress supported the creation of the S/CRS with funding in its Consolidated Appropriations Act for fiscal year 2005. The congressional language set forth a broad stability and reconstruction leadership role for DoS, including developing a readily deployable capability of civilian subject-matter experts to lead reconstruction activities in regions or countries trying to overcome crises.[27] In December 2005 President Bush signed National Security Presidential Directive 44 (NSPD 44), explicitly tasking the Secretary of State to lead and coordinate all US government stabilization and reconstruction efforts.[28] The Secretary of State was given the responsibility to not simply lead the interagency process on this subject, but also develop a strong civilian response capacity for post-conflict situations.

Over the last four years the S/CRS established an Active Component (CRC-A) and Standby Component. The S/CRS's goal is to have 250 government personnel working in the CRC-A full-time and 2,000 working in other federal agencies outside DoS but available for surge requirements. The S/CRS also seeks to create a reserve force of up to two thousand persons not employed by the government but available for deployments.[29] This force structure has not been authorized or funded to date. The Bush administration proposed a Civilian Stabilization Initiative for fiscal year 2009, requesting $248.6 million to finance the first year of the initiative. This sum represents a small fraction of the monies expended by the USG in Iraq each year for stabilization and reconstruction.[30] In the last two years a very limited number of DoS personnel have been deployed by the S/CRS to support capacity-building initiatives in Sudan, Haiti, Chad and Liberia.[31] It must be noted that, since its creation in 2004, the S/CRS has had no significant involvement in Iraq and has made virtually no contribution to the reconstruction and stabilization efforts there.

Virtually all USG rule of law practitioners currently working in Iraq are military, DoJ or contractor personnel. Although INL and the United States Agency for International Development (USAID) administer many large ROL-related contracts, neither organization has a DoS rule of law subject-matter expert serving in Iraq. It is particularly noteworthy that the Mission's Rule of Law Coordinator is seconded to the Mission from DoJ. In Iraq, the State Department outsources the management of rule of law capacity building and contracts out all reconstruction and stabilization efforts. It is unclear whether either DoS or USAID has the subject-matter expertise on staff to manage these contracts.

In the fall of 2008 the American Academy of Diplomacy issued a report on what it described as a "crisis in diplomatic readiness."[32] The report recognizes that DoS is incapable of performing the missions given it by NSPD 44 and acknowledges that the military has assumed a greater role in diplomacy as a result: "The 'militarization of diplomacy' is noticeably expanding as DoD personnel assume public diplomacy and assistance responsibilities that the civilian agencies do not have the trained staff to fill."[33] The report illustrates DoS problems in several areas. In 2008 there was a 2,400 personnel shortfall; in 2006, 29 percent of the positions that required language proficiency were filled with persons without those skills. Additionally, USAID has 2,200 persons to administer $8 billion in development funds, while in 1990 they had 3,500 to manage $5 billion annually. The report makes specific recommendations to deal with the problems, including increasing staffing authorizations by more than 4,700, increasing funding by hundreds of millions of dollars and transferring authority over security assistance programs from DoD to DoS.[34]

Department of Defense Stability Operations

In 2005 the Department of Defense made stability operations a core military mission.[35] This was a fundamental change to US military doctrine; DoD had accepted that it had an important role in post-conflict reconstruction and stability operations. The directive tasked the development of doctrine and force structure. It acknowledged that the immediate goals of these operations were establishing security and providing for the population's humanitarian needs. The longer-term goals were developing indigenous security capacity, a market economy, rule of law, democratic institutions and a civil society. The directive also stated that "integrated civilian and military efforts are key to successful stability operations."[36] Most important, the directive fundamentally changed US military doctrine by elevating stability operations to the same level of importance as traditional combat operations.[37]

The US Army published Field Manual 3-07,[38] its stability operations doctrine, in October 2008. The doctrine was developed to implement the DoD stability operations directive and provide guidance on how US forces and personnel would contribute to achieving the reconstruction and stabilization goals of the national strategy[39] and NSPD 44 missions. Field Manual 3-07 sets out a series of security, stabilization and reconstruction tasks that must be accomplished in post-conflict situations; rule of law capacity building is included with the provision of essential services for the general populace. Echoing the directive, Field Manual 3-07 acknowledges that many of the stability operations tasks would be most effectively performed by host-nation or USG civilian personnel, but recognizes that civilians may not be available to perform these tasks: "In the event civilians are not prepared to perform those tasks, military forces will assume that responsibility."[40] While Field Manual 3-07 appears to recognize the reality of the limited USG civilian reconstruction and stabilization capabilities, it arguably creates more problems than it resolves.

How does the Department of Defense plan for the inability or unwillingness of the Department of State to accomplish its mission? Does the State Department's inability to field stability and reconstruction experts to perform and manage those efforts in Iraq justify DoD's development of the force structure, doctrine, training and funding to meet another agency's responsibilities? Will Congress allow DoD to develop a budget that is to some extent a contingency plan for DoS failures?

Mission Definition

Finally, the inability to clearly define the rule of law capacity-building mission in Iraq must be addressed. A mission's goal must be defined with some degree of clarity before resources can be allocated in a disciplined manner and objective metrics developed to assess progress. In Iraq this was the function of the joint campaign plan. As noted earlier, rule of law became a line of operation in the new plan published in December of 2008. The challenge with the rule of law annex was how to define success or measure progress. The annex identified six broad areas to focus rule of law capacity-building efforts. The first two dealt with detainees and are beyond the scope of this discussion. The last four focused on judicial security, Iraqi detention conditions and capacity, corruption, and improving the civil and criminal justice systems.

At the beginning of a post-conflict operation, rule of law goals can often be quantified. For example, immediately after the overthrow of the Saddam Hussein regime, police stations, courts and detention facilities needed to be reopened. This required physical structures and trained staffs. Objective metrics can be used to determine if there is sufficient bed space, or adequate numbers of judges or police. This was true in Iraq for the first several years. The greater challenge is in trying to quantify progress in "establishing the rule of law." By 2008 the rule of law planners in Iraq were frequently faced with trying to quantify the unquantifiable. How efficient must the courts be? How well trained must the police be? How "modern" must the law be?

The end result was a rule of law annex that set forth broad goals with intermediate steps that might assist the Iraqis in enhancing the rule of law. The annex was broad enough that it could consume whatever military or civilian assets might be available; the only constraint was the Iraqi willingness to accept the technical support. The rule of law annex identified where MNF-I and the Mission needed to make an effort in rule of law capacity building, but failed to define what the level of effort should be. The result is that the rule of law capacity-building mission in Iraq could be a never-ending saga; it is capable of absorbing an infinite amount of resources.

Recommendations

A. The State Department should embrace its responsibilities in reconstruction and stabilization operations. The S/CRS has no presence in Iraq. If that organization is responsible for reconstruction and stabilization efforts, it should fill the rule of law coordinator post at the US Mission in Baghdad. DoS has spent five years developing a very limited capacity and missed the opportunity to develop subject-matter expertise by practice. DoS needs to focus on existing operations, as well as developing a capacity for the future.

B. The rule of law mission in Iraq must be clearly defined by DoS in coordination with DoD. Only then can requirements be defined and specific metrics developed. DoS must lead this effort and not outsource its responsibilities.

C. Congress should fully fund the Civilian Stabilization Initiative, as well as the recommendations of the American Academy of Diplomacy.

D. As DoS develops the civilian capacity to plan, coordinate and execute reconstruction and stabilization operations, DoD and other government agencies should continue to fill the voids in the field.

E. Until DoS develops this capacity, DoS should accept the need for DoD to accomplish the mission. The two departments must work together cooperatively until DoS can assume the lead and DoD can assume a supporting role.

F. An annual report to Congress should be required cataloguing these interagency contributions, as well as DoS progress or lack of progress in developing the capabilities needed to meet its responsibilities.

Conclusion

The US rule of law capacity-building efforts in Iraq have been, and continue to be, extensive in terms of both manpower and funding. These efforts have been well intentioned, and in many areas have accomplished a great deal. This said, it must be noted that the USG rule of law capacity-building community in Iraq lacks unity of command. This is a result of DoS's lack of will, as well as capacity, to assume its leadership role. The institutional concern over the "militarization of diplomacy" focuses on DoD's intrusion into what DoS believes is its area of responsibility. It fails to recognize, however, that DoD is filling a void caused by DoS's lack of capacity.

Rule of law capacity-building missions must be clearly defined. Without that clarity resourcing will never be adequate nor will progress be quantifiable. These missions must be defined, planned for and executed under the leadership of an adequately funded and empowered State Department.

Notes

1. Nina M. Serafino, Congressional Research Service, *Peacekeeping/Stabilization and Conflict Transitions: Background and Congressional Action on the Civilian Response/Reserve Corps and Other Civilian Stabilization and Reconstruction Capabilities*, No. RL32862 (July 23, 2009), at 3, *available at* http://assets.opencrs.com/rpts/RL32862_20090723.pdf.
2. *Id.* at 10.
3. Headquarters, Department of the Army, FM 3-07, Stability Operations paras. 1-40–1-43, at 1-9 (2008), *available at* http://downloads.army.mil/docs/fm_3-07.pdf [hereinafter FM 3-07].
4. THE RULE OF LAW HANDBOOK: A PRACTITIONER'S GUIDE FOR JUDGE ADVOCATES 5–6 (Katherine Gorove & Thomas B. Nachbar eds., 2008).
5. US Department of Defense, Directive 3000.05, Military Support for Stability, Security, Transition and Reconstruction (SSTR) Operations para. 4.3 (2005), *available at* http://www.dtic.mil/whs/directives/corres/pdf/300005p.pdf [hereinafter DoD Directive 3000.05]; Chairman of the Joint Chiefs of Staff, Joint Publication 3-0, Joint Operations, at V-24 (2006), *available at* http://www.dtic.mil/doctrine/jel/new_pubs/jp3_0.pdf ("US military forces should be prepared to lead the activities necessary to [secure and safeguard the populace, reestablish civil law and order, protect or rebuild key infrastructure, and restore public services] when indigenous civil, USG, multinational or international capacity does not exist or is incapable of assuming responsibility").
6. Thomas Ricks & Stephen Biddle, *"The Gamble": Did the Surge Work?*, WASHINGTONPOST.COM, Feb. 23, 2006, http://www.washingtonpost.com/wp-dyn/content/discussion/2009/02/05/DI2009020502774.html.
7. *See id.*
8. Greg Bruno, *Finding a Place for the 'Sons of Iraq,'* CFR.ORG, Jan. 9, 2009, http://www.cfr.org/publication/16088/#p7.

9. Ellen Knickmeyer & K.I. Ibrahim, *Bombing Shatters Mosque in Iraq*, WASHINGTONPOST.COM, Feb. 23, 2006, http://www.washingtonpost.com/wp-dyn/content/article/2006/02/22/AR2006022200454.html.

10. S.C. Res. 1790, U.N. Doc. S/RES/1790 (Dec. 18, 2007).

11. Agreement Between the United States of America and the Republic of Iraq on the Withdrawal of United States Forces from Iraq and the Organization of Their Activities during Their Temporary Presence in Iraq, U.S.-Iraq, Nov. 17, 2008, *available at* http://www.mnf-iraq.com/images/CGs _Messages/security_agreement.pdf.

12. *See id.*, art. 22.

13. *See id.*

14. US Department of Defense, Measuring Stability and Security in Iraq: Report to Congress (Mar. 7, 2008).

15. Iraq Const. art. 61, para. 9 (2005), *available at* http://www.uniraq.org/documents/iraqi_constitution.pdf.

16. Jim Michaels, *Chain of command concerns raised in Iraq*, USATODAY.COM, Feb. 23, 2009, http://www.usatoday.com/news/world/iraq/2009-02-23-maliki_N.htm.

17. S.C. Res. 1790, *supra* note 10.

18. In 2007 the USG identified eighteen specific areas it believed Iraq needed to address, including reconciliation, oil revenue sharing, transparent elections and corruption. *See* U.S. Troop Readiness, Veterans' Care, Katrina Recovery, and Iraq Accountability Appropriations Act, 2007, Pub. L. No. 110-28 (2007).

19. Iraqi High Judicial Council Five Year Strategic Plan (undated) (on file with the MNF-I Office of the Staff Judge Advocate).

20. In the summer of 2009 an assessment was conducted to determine how this might be shifted to the Mission, but to date providing technical assistance to the MOI remains with the military.

21. TF 134–supported prosecutions maintained about a 50 percent conviction rate, while the rest of Iraqi criminal courts' conviction rate hovered around 10 percent.

22. MNF-I Commander's Memorandum on Areas of Focus for LAOTF (Mar. 15, 2008) (on file with the MNF-I Office of the Staff Judge Advocate).

23. It must be noted that none of these military lawyers could speak Arabic nor were they experienced or schooled in Iraqi law. Thus the title "mentor" was presumptuous. Accepting this criticism, the judge advocates assigned to these duties normally established close ties with the Iraqi judges, who took pride in teaching the US lawyers about their legal system and traditions. The judge advocates also shared with the Iraqi jurists US legal practices and traditions. The end results included small improvements in Iraqi judicial efficiency and work ethics. Like so many areas within rule of law capacity building, however, these incremental improvements are nearly impossible to measure.

24. Of particular note is the lack of a right to be warned against self-incrimination. For a detailed analysis of the issue and the "corrective" action taken during the occupation by the Coalition Provisional Authority, see Dan E. Stigall, *Comparative Law and State-Building: The "Organic Minimalist" Approach to Legal Reconstruction*, 29 LOYOLA OF LOS ANGELES INTERNATIONAL & COMPARATIVE LAW REVIEW 1, 30–31 (2007).

25. Fragmentary Order (FRAGO) Transitional Justice (Aug. 16, 2008) (copy on file with the Center for Law and Military Operations, The US Army Judge Advocate General's School and Law Center).

26. Serafino, *supra* note 1.

27. Consolidated Appropriations Act of 2005, Pub. L. No. 108-447, 118 Stat. 2809 (2004).

28. National Security Presidential Directive/NSPD 44, Management of Interagency Efforts Concerning Reconstruction and Stabilization (Dec. 7, 2005), *available at* http://www.fas.org/irp/offdocs/nspd/nspd-44.html.

29. AMERICAN ACADEMY OF DIPLOMACY, A FOREIGN AFFAIRS BUDGET FOR THE FUTURE: FIXING THE CRISIS IN DIPLOMATIC READINESS 21 (2008), *available at* http://www.stimson.org/budgeting/Publications/Long_Final_11_08.pdf [hereinafter FIXING THE CRISIS].

30. Accurate figures for the costs of reconstruction and stabilization efforts in Iraq are not readily available. For the purposes of this discussion it is worth noting that this funding proposal does not even match the cost of one contract for law enforcement professionals discussed above. Each year DoD funds and INL administers that $400 million dollar effort, which represents a relatively small part of the overall rule of law capacity-building effort—and rule of law capacity building is only one part of reconstruction and stabilization in Iraq.

31. FIXING THE CRISIS, *supra* note 29, at 43.

32. *Id.*

33. *Id.* at 3.

34. *Id.* at 4.

35. DoD Directive 3000.05, *supra* note 5.

36. *Id.*, para. 4.c.

37. *Id.*, para. 4.a.

38. FM 3-07, *supra* note 3.

39. Defined as follows:

> 1-48. National strategy is based on a distinctly American policy of internationalism that reflects the interests and values of the country. It clearly aims to make the world a safer, better place, where a community of nations lives in relative peace. To that end, the *National Security Strategy* and subordinate supporting strategies focus on a path to progress that promotes political and economic freedom, peaceful relations with other nations, and universal respect for human dignity.
>
> 1-49. The body of security strategy that shapes the conduct of stability operations includes the *National Security Strategy*, the *National Defense Strategy*, and *The National Military Strategy of the United States of America* (known as the *National Military Strategy*). Related strategies include the *National Strategy for Combating Terrorism*, the *National Strategy for Homeland Security*, and the *National Strategy to Combat Weapons of Mass Destruction*. Together with national policy, strategy provides the broad direction necessary to conduct operations to support national interests.

Id., paras. 1-48, 1-49, at 1-10.

40. *Id.*, para. 1-73, at 1-15.

PART VII

HUMAN RIGHTS AND THE LAW OF WAR IN IRAQ

XVI

The Dark Sides of Convergence: A Pro-civilian Critique of the Extraterritorial Application of Human Rights Law in Armed Conflict

Naz K. Modirzadeh*

Introduction

International human rights academics and activists rarely have a great deal to celebrate. Compared to their colleagues in private international law or domestic law, they are faced with creating a convincing account of "real" law. They often work on the most horrifying atrocities committed against individuals around the world, struggling to draw the world's and the international community's attention to the plight of subjugated and silenced masses. Like their colleagues who work in the field of international humanitarian law (IHL, or law of armed conflict), they focus on history's darkest moments, when humanity seems lost or forgotten.

Yet, in the last decade, human rights scholars and advocates working at the cutting edges of academia and litigation have led a tremendous amount of innovation in the literature and in courtrooms and UN committees around the world. They have managed to transform a long-accepted truism of international law, and to

* Senior Associate and Head of Policy, Harvard Program on Humanitarian Policy and Conflict Research (HPCR). The opinions expressed in this article do not represent HPCR, and all errors are those of the author.

challenge States and their militaries to fundamentally reconsider the nature and scope of their obligations on the battlefield.

Indeed, the idea of co-application of international humanitarian law[1] and human rights law has drawn a tremendous amount of academic attention and a huge amount of innovation in international and domestic jurisprudence. This transformation, this much-touted shift in the field of international law, is often referred to as the "humanization of humanitarian law"[2] and, more technically, the "convergence"[3] of international human rights law (IHRL) and international humanitarian law. Yet in the current headlong approach into convergence, rights and rights institutions may carry risks to the very goals many humanitarian-minded international lawyers seek to achieve.

The current debates around the applicability of human rights during conflict, the extraterritorial applicability of human rights and the *post facto* enforcement of human rights claims against military personnel engaged in armed combat appear to avoid the central question of whether adding human rights to the legal terrain of war is good—good for civilians, good for the longevity of legal constraints on conduct during conflict and good for the promotion of human rights. Underlying the huge number of scholarly papers on the issue of parallel application of IHRL and IHL,[4] as well as the increasingly pro-convergence jurisprudence of key international courts, is an assumption that more human rights (in a formal sense) always equal more *enjoyment* of basic rights. To the extent that a major scholarly project seems to be intent on demonstrating that human rights law was always meant to apply during armed conflict and that the main challenge before us is the specific and detailed enforcement of discrete rules of IHRL, we need an honest assessment of what we want human rights law to *do* for us and how the pragmatic and tactical deployment of human rights arguments will affect the overall fate of rights discourse in war.

The goal of this article is not to delve into the legal complexities of various courts' interpretations of the details of the application of human rights law in war, but rather to take a bird's-eye view of the debate and to question whether it is a good thing to insist on the extraterritorial applicability of human rights to armed conflict situations. The tone of the many articles and commentaries on the topic of "convergence" suggests that if only the views of various UN treaty bodies and forward-thinking courts were applied fully by the military, it is obvious that the experience of civilians caught up in armed conflict would be improved, that detention would be more humane, that accountability for violations would be increased—that, in short, outcomes would be more *humanitarian*. I aim to question that assumption, and to raise questions about whether even the full realization of the aspirations of human rights scholars and advocates would actually be better for civilians in war.

The real desired impact of insisting on the co-application of human rights law with IHL is far more limited than a frank reading of most of this scholarship would suggest. Indeed, it seems that rather than transforming the very legal framework within which armed conflict occurs the main upshot of promoting parallel application is to increase the available legal forums and accountability measures to which States can be subject *after* alleged violations occur. This article questions whether promotion of full parallel application, with the intent of only changing the framework of *post facto* accountability, actually harms the capacity for law to protect civilians in war. This paper argues that the formalist machinations currently employed to argue that violations of IHL should come within the jurisdictional ambit of human rights instruments and courts may be harmful to the very aims liberal international lawyers seek to achieve. My argument is that parallel application is equally as bad for the Iraqi civilian as it is for the American soldier. As we pull back the layers of legalistic argumentation, the real role of rights discourse and the real function of human rights law on the battlefield seem much less thought-out than leading scholars suggest, and the implications for this new approach to international law seem much more problematic than the current debate on the issue presents.

For the civilian and the soldier, the vague overlap of these two bodies of law is at best incoherent, and at worst raises expectations that cannot be met. The civilian in Basra during the occupation would be told that he might have some human rights claims against the British (in the event that they have a certain kind of control over him), no human rights claims against US forces (because they refuse to recognize the applicability of the law), full human rights claims vis-à-vis the Iraqi transitional government (depending on what stage of the Iraqi transitional government we would be looking at, and depending on the interpretation of what it would mean for human rights obligations to continue to apply to Iraq even after the invasion toppled its pre-existing government), and moderate human rights claims vis-à-vis any European States party to the European Convention on Human Rights that would happen to have any control over an individual Iraqi in the south. Contrary to IHL, where the civilian (or prisoner of war or enemy combatant) is not a rights-holder but a person to whom obligations are owed by a party to the conflict (and therefore where we would look to the behavior of the party to the conflict in order to determine whether there has been a violation of the rules), IHRL raises the expectation that there is a clear duty-bearer who is capable of responding to the rights claim held by any individual on a given territory.

From the perspective of the commander seeking to provide regulations to the soldier based on the State's relevant obligations under international law, rules of warfare and doctrine on the battlefield must be whittled down to clear and brief rules of engagement. While senior commanders, military policymakers and military lawyers advising high-ranking officers may (and often do) take policy, politics and additional bodies of law into account, the rules that ultimately govern conduct and determine whether soldiers are subject to criminal liability must be those that are clearly recognized by the State in question as applicable to a particular conflict.

Part I sketches the background of the development of IHL and IHRL, and provides an overview of the stakes in the debate over extraterritorial applicability of IHRL in armed conflict. Part II presents a list of ten concerns one might have about the current accepted consensus toward convergence. Part III concludes with a view toward possible pathways forward.

Part I: Background to the Relationship between IHL and IHRL

In this section, I hope to lay out the key signposts in the debate on convergence, pointing out the actors in each salient aspect of the discussion on convergence. My purpose is not to go into the detailed and complex questions involved in each aspect of the debate, but to provide a bird's-eye view of the key questions and the practical implications of a given position. In particular, I want to draw attention to the increasingly common reference in the scholarly literature to a "consensus" or "settled issue" on the first-order questions relating to the applicability of human rights law in conflict.

It may be useful before delving into the key signposts of the debate to review the generic narrative of the question of convergence, one that seems to be accepted by all sides. In presenting this narrative, I am hoping to foreshadow some of the seemingly innocuous assumptions within it that will come back to be important in our critique of contemporary positions on the convergence question.

The first question in the debate over convergence, one that is largely treated in the past tense in contemporary scholarly literature, is whether human rights law applies *at all* during armed conflict. Here, there is usually a reference to the "traditional" or "classical" position of international law, in which human rights was the "law of peace," and IHL the "law of war," with a clear and unquestioned separation between the two. In the "good/bad old days" (depending on who is presenting the intellectual history) of international law, it was clear that the law of peace could not apply during armed conflict because the law of peace addressed the relationship between the State and the citizen/territorial subject during the normal conditions of peace, whereas IHL was a highly specialized legal regime created in close consultation with military personnel for the purposes of regulating the state of exception from day-to-day governance that characterizes warfare. This traditional understanding of the clean separation between the law of peace (human rights) and the law of war (IHL) accepts that when we are talking about a situation of armed conflict, we will necessarily be in a context where human rights will be impossible to apply, and where there will be little to no accountability for human rights violations. In addition, underlying this "traditional" position seems to be an understanding that those who must deal with the law, enforce it on the ground and be accountable for compliance are very different.

So, if we imagine that the line below is the overall span of a human life, from birth to death,

human rights law addresses every possible way in which this human life might encounter the State, and even how the individual might encounter other private actors *within* the State: the right to education,[5] the right to basic health care,[6] the right to shelter,[7] the right to marry the person of one's choosing,[8] the right to parent according to one's values,[9] regulation of encounters with police and the courts,[10] regulation of one's encounter with imprisonment, structuring of paid labor and equality of labor,[11] political participation,[12] and religious participation,[13] among others. The historic singularity of human rights law, and its revolutionary transformation of traditional Westphalian sovereignty, is the notion that the individual has rights on the international stage—that international law can reach into the State and regulate the relationship between the individual and her government. In vesting the individual with rights by virtue of her personhood, IHRL empowers the individual to imagine and pursue a full, rich, emancipated, politically vital existence. IHRL is unlimited in its scope and potential; it quickly moves beyond the basic necessities of bare human sustenance and provides the constitution for a society built on individual choice and engagement. So, we might see our individual's lifetime as legally covered by IHRL in this manner,

IHRL

where the scope of IHRL's influence on the individual's relationship with the State and public life is limited only by the development and expansion of IHRL itself.

The traditional model conceives that if, in the span of this individual's life, her State should enter into armed conflict, it is at this very moment that IHRL ceases to be relevant to her relationship to the State and, instead, IHL alone regulates her relationship to belligerent actors until the end of hostilities.

Again, in this model, IHRL is merely suspended for the duration of armed conflict and is immediately "reactivated" once the State returns to a normal state of governance of its own territory.

At its most basic level, the concept of convergence suggests that because IHRL always applies to individuals in their relationships to the State (except in the limited cases of derogation as allowed under the International Covenant on Civil and Political Rights (ICCPR) but not under a number of other IHRL treaties), it continues to apply during armed conflict, but may be limited or refined by IHL as the *lex specialis*. Convergence argues that IHRL cannot be arbitrarily suspended simply because an armed conflict has broken out on the territory of a State with international obligations under human rights law, but that it may be *limited* in its application by IHL. So, in our individual's timeline,

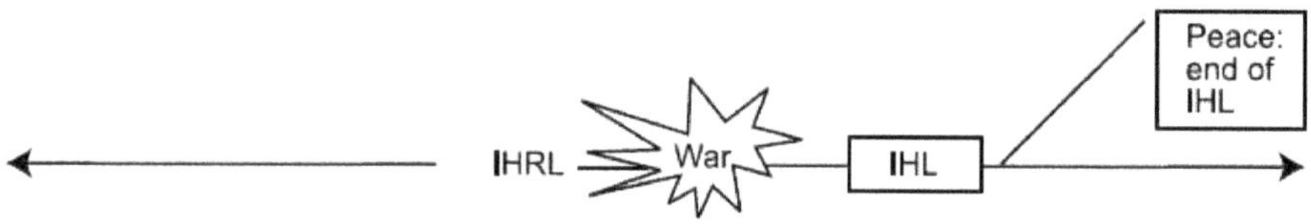

IHRL continues to apply *in parallel* to IHL for the duration of the armed conflict, and as before IHL ceases to apply once the armed conflict is over. Theoretically, this would apply for any and all discrete human rights obligations of the State in question: so if a State has ratified the ICCPR; International Covenant on Economic, Social and Cultural Rights (ICESCR); Convention on the Elimination of All Forms of Discrimination against Women; Convention against Torture (CAT) and Convention on the Rights of Children (CRC), then that State would remain responsible for its obligations within those treaties (and vis-à-vis the relevant treaty bodies) during the armed conflict, except insofar as particular obligations are altered or limited by the function of IHL. As a result, in the event that our individual's State finds itself fighting off an invasion from a neighboring enemy, the State would continue to be responsible for the human rights of individuals on its territory for the duration of the armed conflict, while both the State *and* the invading nation would be responsible for IHL vis-à-vis the population.

The first-order question of the convergence debate is whether IHRL and IHL should apply side by side during armed conflict, and how that parallel application can be articulated in theoretical terms and put into practice. As we will see, while the theoretical or principled position for parallel application seems to be dominant (and even wholly uncontroversial at this stage), the question of *how* these bodies of law should apply in tandem, what provisions of human rights law continue to apply to the State and what additional obligations are created by the operation of human rights law are hotly contested.

Assuming the theoretical applicability of human rights law is accepted, the second major question in the debate focuses on extraterritorial applicability of human rights law during armed conflict. This asks whether a given State *carries* its human rights obligations abroad on the backs of its military forces. IHL is by its nature extraterritorial: IHL follows fighting forces and its applicability in a given situation is generally determined by a factual assessment of the circumstances at a given time. For its part, human rights law has traditionally been closely tied to the particular institutions and systems of governance of the State that brings human rights regulations upon itself. The broad question of extraterritorial application of human rights law (within which armed conflict is but a particular instance) concerns whether a State can ever have obligations under its various human rights treaty (or customary law) obligations that extend beyond its territorial borders, its territorial jurisdiction and some limited understanding of foreign territories in which it enforces jurisdiction (such as embassies abroad).

We could imagine this question as having an impact on all sorts of contemporary situations: States could be held responsible for the human rights violations committed by multinational corporations acting abroad, and they could be responsible for violations committed by international financial institutions of which they are members. Here the debate goes beyond whether human rights law continues to apply during armed conflict and its concomitant concerns: whether a State would be responsible to control the human rights violations of an armed group carrying out violations on its territories in a non-international armed conflict; whether a State would be responsible for violations of various civil and political rights while defending itself against an invasion; and whether a State would have obligations to provide humanitarian access under the right to food or other provisions of ICESCR. The question then becomes whether IHRL obligations of a particular State *travel with* that State when it is engaged in military actions abroad. If they do, do they carry the full scope of human rights obligations, or some minimal "core" of rights? Is the State responsible for the institutional context in which individuals enjoy their rights in foreign lands, or only for those encounters between foreign individuals and the State's representatives? And what is the reach of national or regional human rights bodies in determining whether States have complied with their human rights obligations in the course of armed conflict?

For the growing number of international bodies, courts and States that argue that, at least in principle, human rights law does travel with the obligated State, the bulk of the legal debate turns to the question of what *level of control* or military involvement is required before the application of human rights law is triggered. Is mere presence enough? Is effective control rising to the level of occupation required? Is the level of control required more constraining than the standard for occupation? Must an individual be in the custody of a State before that State's human rights obligations extend to that individual on foreign soil? These questions—whether human rights law applies extraterritorially to some extent, and, if so, what jurisdictional reach is provided—are at the core of the debate over convergence.[14] Current human rights scholarship and lawyering strongly support the extraterritorial application of human rights law in armed conflict, a position slowly gaining recognition in key domestic and international jurisprudence.[15]

Having provided a narrative summary of the development of these areas of law, it may be useful to now provide an overview of the ways that the two bodies of law function. IHL is, if nothing else, grounded in and justified on the basis of its practicality, its intimate connection to military professionals and what they are asked to do in the heat of battle. The defense of IHL against the charge that it is not protective enough, or that it skews the calculus of life and death toward the needs and entitlements of the military, is that this state of affairs is the only way to maintain the legitimacy of the law in the eyes of commanders, that we must be modest in our aims for complex legal restraints during the most brutal and unregulated fog of war. As such, IHL offers three key moments for the law to act: *prior to conflict*, IHL is the basis for military doctrine and training on protection of civilians, proportionality, distinction and other key restraints on warfare; *during conflict*, its provisions allow commanders and instructors to create simple, concrete rules for conduct, and the battle-relevant aspects of IHL provide commanders with the limits on what military personnel may do in the pursuit of their objectives, and clear provisions for the treatment of various categories of individuals; *after hostilities*, IHL provides the grounds for disciplining troops who violate the rules according to national military law grounded in international norms, as well as creates the legal framework for accountability of military personnel and others in the command structure in other legal forums (such as international tribunals, national high courts, the International Criminal Court, etc.).

In practical terms, it is in the first two areas that IHL is most impactful: it has often been noted that *post facto* accountability for IHL is extremely difficult to establish.[16] Liability for violations of provisions related to proportionality, distinction and other obligations under IHL that involve balancing or a reasonable-commander standard is, in practical terms, usually established only in the most extreme cases of violation.[17] In this sense, the rules of IHL emphasize *a priori* prevention of violations, and focus on the basic protections owed to those individuals *hors de combat* as well as a pragmatic set of detailed rules for treatment of prisoners of war and others detained by parties to the armed conflict. The provisions of IHL are ideally suited for being diluted and distributed in simple terms to military professionals in the battlefield: indeed, the interpretation of IHL rules is often based in the practicality of application in the heat of battle.[18]

IHRL is based on a different set of assumptions about the way that States act, and the capacity of the international community to regulate that behavior. Human rights law functions as an agreement by States with other States ratifying not only a set of obligations vis-à-vis those they govern, but also laying out a specific and detailed set of rights claims that can be activated by the population of the ratifying State. Whereas IHL focuses on the obligations of the high contracting parties, focusing on the statuses of those who enjoy particular protections or are owed specific levels of care (with no reference to rights-holders or individuals in a position to make claims against legal obligations), IHRL identifies a broad scope of rights spanning civil and political life; economic, social and cultural rights; and a series of more specific individual rights where the State is expected to take positive action as well as refrain from certain behavior.[19] IHRL sees the greatest potential for achievement of human rights in national implementation of international norms by encouraging domestic absorption of treaty provisions and amendment of domestic laws and practices that potentially violate human rights obligations. Unlike IHL, human rights law very rarely sets out a balancing equation between the entitlements of the State and the rights of the individual: while there are specific arenas in which the interests of the State are weighed against the enjoyment of the right (such as when the government seeks to limit rights during a state of emergency under the derogation provisions of the ICCPR or when States are entitled to limit free expression for public morals or public order reasons), IHRL strictly regulates the actions of the State and insists on the consistent provision of judicial and due process protections for individuals. Perhaps most significantly, international human rights law imagines its arena of application as that of a State in full control of its systems of governance, constantly negotiating—through domestic institutions—its role within the environment of a particular culture and approach to citizenship. Unlike IHL, which assumes the tragic and destructive backdrop of war and is thus modest in its ambition, human rights law lays out the full vision for a future community of the governed endowed with increasingly substantial claims against those in power.

Part II: A Preliminary List of Critiques: Is More Human Rights Law Always a Good Thing?

A common theme in writing and debate on the subject of the parallel application of IHRL and IHL in wartime, particularly regarding extraterritorial applicability of human rights obligations, is the notion that we are witnessing a now-inevitable trend of progress toward more human rights, that the question of convergence is no longer a question of "whether" as much as "how far." As one author notes, in summarizing a range of articles on the debate, "With respect to the differing opinions, it is submitted here that the continued applicability of IHRL during armed conflict is by now firmly determined."[20] Another leading commentator concludes, albeit with apparent hesitation,

> How these two bodies of law, which were not originally meant to come into such close contact, will live in harmony in the broader framework of international law remains to be seen over time. But one thing is clear: there is no going back to a complete separation of the two realms. Potentially, a coherent approach to the interpretation of human rights and humanitarian law—maintaining their distinct features—can only contribute to greater protection of individuals in armed conflict.[21]

One striking aspect of the huge volume of scholarship celebrating and analyzing the co-applicability of IHL and IHRL in armed conflict is the lack of critique of the concepts and assumptions underlying this new legal order. While a number of scholars do seem to recognize the *technical* challenges posed to those responsible for enforcing human rights in battle, the field has not been subject to critical thinking on the possible costs of bringing human rights discourse and human rights frameworks into the realm of war. Given that the very few examples of scholarship rejecting or limiting the applicability of human rights law in war are drafted by those sympathetic to States that object to extraterritorial application of their human rights obligations,[22] it is appealing to dismiss critics of convergence as either seeking to avoid regulation of conduct or seeking to maintain the most permissive legal regime possible for troops. Indeed, most scholars and practitioners working on this issue—whether in human rights litigation or those taking a strong academic position favoring convergence—seem to assume that the only possible stance against convergence could be either from States protecting their own interests and the entitlements of the military (read the United States and Israel),[23] or from those military commanders who fear that it will be practically impossible to implement human rights law on the ground. For those engaged in this debate, the very appeal of this rapidly growing genre of scholarship may well be the seemingly clear fault lines: it seems rather intuitive that the "good guys," the liberal, pro–human rights lawyers and scholars concerned with States that justify their behavior in the framework of permanent war, would be in favor of the expansion of the human rights regime by any means possible, and through any legal contortions necessary. Equally, it seems clear that the "bad guys," States that reject these very laws because they are overly restraining or expose them to liability for horrific violations, or conservative scholars and lawyers sympathetic to the military, would be against the application of human rights in the battlefield and would engage in anachronistic arguments about the glorious past of international law when things were clear and laws stayed in their appropriate spaces. Given these alternatives, one would want to be on the side of progress, the future, the best use of the international legal system for the increasing realm of human rights application.

In this sense, the debate over extraterritoriality and convergence, when mapped onto debates over the "war on terror," and treatment of detainees in the wars of Afghanistan and Iraq, has taken on a politicized tone: it seems natural that those in favor of human rights, humane treatment of individuals in detention and increased regulation of warfare would be on the side of more convergence, while those on the side of powerful States, limitation of individual rights in favor of national security and protection of the entitlements of the military against the involvement of the international community are on the side of discrete application and strong use of the *lex specialis* principle to privilege IHL over IHRL during armed conflict.

In the rest of this section, I would like to unpack these assumptions and take a step back from the overwhelming tone of victory and inevitability that seems to characterize the bulk of scholarship and litigation on the topic of parallel application. I want to ask whether there are reasons why those in favor of human rights law, strengthening enforcement and legitimacy of international law in armed conflict, and holding States accountable for their obligations when they act militarily ought to question the enthusiastic embrace of convergence. Rather than suggesting a particular posture such scholars or lawyers ought to take on the issue, I hope to argue that there must be more principled debate over the issue of whether convergence is a good thing for human rights, for IHL and for the role of international law in armed conflict. It is possible that the remarkably limited amount of critical scholarship on this topic (other than papers drafted by those who take a clear contra-convergence position) reflects the fact that there is nothing concerning here, that indeed there is no aspect of convergence that should raise critical questions. It may be that, when we look at the weight of evidence and legal analysis on the topic, there are no real costs to convergence, and only benefits to be gained—but maybe not.

Below, I present a partial list of concerns I think we ought to have about the move toward extraterritorial application of human rights law in armed conflict, in the form of ten critiques of and questions on the currently dominant approach.

The list is not meant to be exhaustive, nor does every critique apply to every possible instance of parallel application on the ground. Rather, the purpose of the list is to open up space for a pro-rights, pro-civilian protection objection to full-scale convergence, and to encourage a more critical approach to the issue by lawyers and scholars engaged in these two fields.

Rights at the End of a Gun: Do Divergent Foundations Matter?

As though referring to long-lost cousins who have recently become friendly, many scholars and courts discussing the question of convergent application begin or end their analyses by noting that IHRL and IHL have very different backgrounds.[24] The common approach to this issue is to articulate that at one time (in the early days of both bodies of law) it was thought that the two were completely distinct, and that they indeed have very different "upbringings" in the context of international law, but that, throughout the 1970s and beyond, this foundational difference has come to matter less and less as IHL and IHRL first were recognized as "complementary" in armed conflict and are now increasingly recognized as "convergent." This common story of progress acknowledges that there are important normative distinctions between the bodies of law,[25] but that as key UN bodies and international courts have come to recognize co-application, these original differences have been surpassed by the recognition that both generally serve to protect "humanity."[26]

The debate here tends to focus on two key issues: first, some authors and jurists look to the detailed pedigree of each body of law to determine whether drafters and early commentators in fact envisioned any future convergence. Such authors look to *travaux préparatoires*, early conferences on human rights law, and commentaries on the Geneva Conventions and Additional Protocols in order to argue either that the two bodies of law were never intended to commingle and that convergence is a dangerous departure from foundational intent, or (more commonly) to argue that the seeds of harmonization were present both from the very early days of post–World War II IHL and in the intent of drafters and key commentators alike. This latter group argues that while foundational differences were present, and normative differences persist, early drafters imagined a future where both bodies of law could be utilized to enhance the overall humanitarian goals of international law.[27] The second aspect of the debate looks to institutions, on the one hand, pointing out that the early institutional history of the two legal regimes kept them separate and encouraged the creation of two distinct professional fields (often turning to early institutional history of human rights law within the UN and of IHL within the International Committee of the Red Cross (ICRC) and in State conferences), and, on the other, looking to the claims of contemporary institutions about the increased capacity for human rights bodies to engage with IHL.[28]

For strict separationists, such as those supporting the US position, the foundations of the laws and their differing origins support the sentiment that IHL displaces IHRL and that human rights obligations were certainly not meant to be applied when States act militarily outside of their territories.[29] In mining the foundations and historical origins of the two bodies of law from this perspective, the widely acknowledged difference in the spirit and purpose of the laws informs their initial codification as well as their normative and institutional development, pointing to the intent that they be kept separate as the laws of war and the laws of peace. For pro-convergence commentators, the origins of the law, particularly the *travaux préparatoires* of the two Additional Protocols to the 1949 Geneva Conventions, as well as the text of various UN conferences (often noting the 1968 Tehran Conference as a key turning point toward convergence), and the progressive movement of human rights treaties away from any notion of strictly territorial jurisdiction, point to early support for the eventual merging or co-applicability of IHRL and IHL for States when acting outside of their territorial jurisdictions.

To this point, we can see how the profoundly different roots and early articulations of IHRL and IHL could play into the conclusions of either side: either the origins clearly should show us the intended walls between the two bodies of law or the historic and normative differences were only a point on a spectrum toward a more humane and rights-oriented approach to international law in general. Here, I want to suggest that we step back from this perspective of origins and foundations and instead question to what extent the extremely divergent underpinnings and moral philosophies of IHRL and IHL ought to compel critical thinking about supporting the extraterritorial applicability of human rights treaties in armed conflict. That is, rather than pointing to origins as an argument for or against the drafters' *intent* that States should incorporate human rights law into their legal frameworks when fighting or detaining or occupying abroad, I wonder if we should look to origins and foundations to question whether today we *should* promote this type of human rights enforcement.

I want to suggest that the current debate on origins has shied away from the more difficult question of whether human rights law belongs on the battlefield, and whether the foundations of the law should constrain and limit scholars and jurists from moving forward too boldly in articulating the human rights obligations of States at war. In later sections I will ask whether human rights law translates into battle rules in the same way as IHL, but here I want to ask, do we want it to? What costs might be borne by human rights law and the human rights movement if extraterritorial applicability of human rights in armed conflict is taken seriously in the years to come?

It is commonly noted that the history of international humanitarian law rests on a number of factors that explain and ensure its widely recognized universality and legitimacy within a diversity of States. The law, rooted in early notions of chivalry and professional military conduct, was drafted in close coordination with military experts and senior military personnel, and is promulgated with a close eye to the practical challenges faced by military forces. Part of this story of IHL is also about the morbid calculus of the rules, whether we rely on Colonel Draper's retelling of how cynics see the law of war, namely "how to kill your fellow human beings in a nice way,"[30] or look to the ways in which IHL allows the lawful killing of combatants and does not make illegal the killing of civilians and those *hors de combat* as long as their deaths are incidental to a lawful attack and not disproportionate to the military advantage anticipated. Despite the very legitimate criticisms of this aspect of IHL—its apparent *in*humanity, its willingness to allow (or at least not punish) horrific bloodshed of those not involved in hostilities, its blindness to the killing of combatants—it is clear in its objective and simple to understand in its compromises. It is a body of law specifically crafted to regulate moments in human history and relationships between States that have often been thought ungovernable, and it does not pretend to be anything other than the most plausible set of rules for an admittedly terrible context.

One of the differences between IHRL and IHL is that the latter only recognizes obligations of the State toward those who fit into a particular status: protection and rules regarding rights and responsibilities are purely status based, not deriving from one's basic humanity as in human rights law. This is often raised as a point of weakness of IHL, but one could also argue that this aspect of the law of war—the delimitation of a set of protections for the nationals of the enemy—is precise and intentionally limited in its understanding of the ugly nature of the relationship between an invading/attacking State and the enemy population.[31] There are obligations to those individuals, yes, but it is understood that those obligations are in an environment of duress, fear and belligerency. IHL does not pretend that this relationship, between the forces of the invading military and the civilians of the invaded territory, is anything other than tense and hostile. It does not allow us to assume or pay heed to the claims of the invading forces as to their purposes for invading or their intentions toward the civilian population. It simply sets out the baseline obligations of the enemy military to protect the civilian population and those *hors de combat*, both in active hostilities and under occupied control.

I want to suggest that once we introduce rights talk to this equation, we begin to reshape the relationship of the military forces to the enemy population, perhaps in ways that are not imagined by those who support the extraterritorial applicability of human rights law and its convergence with IHL.

In the voluminous literature on when human rights law begins to apply extraterritorially, the most agreed-upon baseline for the initiation of human rights law obligations is the "effective control" test. The basic argument comes down to exactly at what point an enemy military force begins to have human rights obligations toward a foreign population on the territory of that population. Most scholars agree that under current law, that test—while still unclear and somewhat confusing—relies on a demonstration that the military has "effective control" over a person or territory (and possibly whether the State is responsible for a particular violation—the so-called "cause and effect" test of jurisdiction), which seems to be similar to (though not identical to) the test of occupation.

Again, rather than burrowing into the wide-ranging debates over appropriate activation of extraterritorial jurisdiction I want to argue that whatever our test for the control required for human rights jurisdiction (identical to occupation, capacity to exercise civil administration, physical presence, control over a territorial space analogous to an embassy),[32] such application of IHRL in armed conflict locates the moment when human rights start to oblige the State in question on the use of military force. Rather than focusing on the question of the type of control that is being used, or the type of administration that the foreign party can or cannot exercise, I am concerned that *no matter what formulation of extraterritorial jurisdiction is used*, the pro-convergence position bases the applicability of human rights law on the use of armed force in a foreign land.

Should those interested in the long-term development of human rights law encourage such a vision of rights? To what extent does this approach to human rights jurisdiction undermine the very foundations of human rights law, and open up its most basic tenets to being questioned? The relationship imagined between the soldier and the enemy civilian in IHL, and that between the government agent and the "citizen"[33] in IHRL are central to the way the law sets out both obligations and claims, in the ways that the bodies of law create accountability for violations and in the way they task ratifying States with ensuring compliance. In armed conflict, much of the determination of appropriate treatment lies in the mind of the reasonable commander in recognition of the necessity of creating rules that must be able to function and be considered legitimate during combat. In a regular governance context, the determination of rights-respecting conduct lies with a web of institutions, domestic judicial guarantees and international bodies.

A civilian who is made aware of the basic (and rather minimal) obligations of the armed forces of an enemy State for her protection clearly understands the purpose of IHL: to ensure that in the very worst imaginable context, she is guaranteed a basic level of protection—not to be directly targeted if she does not participate in hostilities, not to be tortured if she is detained, to have access to basic lifesaving humanitarian relief, etc. The logic behind the law is also apparent: this is not a long-term relationship, and the law does not provide the grounds for a good society or interactions based on trust and due process. Rather, this is a set of rules that restricts the military forces while they fight, while recognizing that they *will* fight, and that people (even those not involved in the fighting) will die in the process. The addition of human rights law to this clear and honest (albeit stark) framing of roles and relationships runs the risk of confusing all actors and (more important) raising expectations that can never be met.

It is worthwhile here to look at the language of the much discussed and often criticized UK House of Lords decision in *Al-Skeini*,[34] a case where many commentators felt that the Lords did not go far enough in recognizing extraterritorial responsibility, and were overly deferential to the ECtHR decision in *Bankovic* in construing jurisdiction.[35] The approach of Lord Brown of Eaton-under-Heywood is worth examining as an exemplar of what many commentators would see as an overly restrictive reading of jurisdiction (and one allowing the military to avoid responsibility for particular acts). Lord Brown begins by setting forth his reading of the *Bankovic* decision as to Article 1, noting the few "circumstances in which the Court has exceptionally recognized the extraterritorial exercise of jurisdiction by a State," which include

> [w]here the State "through the effective control of the relevant territory and its inhabitants abroad as a consequence of military occupation or through the consent, invitation or acquiescence of the government of that territory, exercises all or some of the public powers normally to be exercised by [the government of that territory]" (para 71) (ie when otherwise there would be a vacuum within a Council of Europe country, the government of that country itself being unable "to fulfil the obligations it had undertaken under the Convention" (para 80) (as in Northern Cyprus[)].[36]

Based on this reading of *Bankovic*, and arguing that the appellants' approach to jurisdiction would "stretch to breaking point the concept of jurisdiction extending extra-territorially to those subject to a state's 'authority and control,'" Lord Brown concludes that

> except where a State really does have effective control of a territory, it cannot hope to secure Convention rights within that territory and, unless it is within the area of the Council of Europe, it is unlikely in any event to find certain of the Convention rights it is bound to secure reconcilable with the customs of the resident population. Indeed it goes further than that. During the period in question here it is common ground that the UK was an occupying power in Southern Iraq and bound as such by Geneva IV and the Hague Regulations. Article 43 of the Hague Regulations provides that the occupant "shall take all measures in his power to restore and ensure, as far as possible, public

> order and safety, while respecting, unless absolutely prevented, the laws in force in the country." The appellants argue that occupation within the meaning of the Hague Regulations necessarily involves the occupant having effective control of the area and so being responsible for securing there all Convention rights and freedoms. So far as this being the case, however, the occupants' obligation is to respect "the laws in force," not to introduce laws and the means to enforce them (for example, courts and a justice system) such as to satisfy the requirements of the Convention.[37]

My point here is that even if we apply the exact same jurisdictional test for extraterritorial application as we would apply for the application of occupation law (the factual test derived from a combination of Hague and Geneva law), doing away with a great deal of the confusion addressed by courts trying to work through this issue, we have not done away with the core problem of extraterritorial applicability during armed conflict. Military occupation is a situation of caretaker governance directly following an invasion or war in which the occupied population has been subjected to the control of the belligerent enemy force because its own government has lost the war. It is inherently temporary and has stringent limitations on the capacity for the State to govern precisely because the drafters of the Fourth Geneva Convention recognized that many occupying States would attempt to create the impression that the population welcomed their presence, that they had created a legitimate governing regime, that they were liberators. Occupation law reminds everyone involved that the relationship is fundamentally one of a dominant, victorious military force and a vanquished, unequal population of "protected persons." While these persons may hold discrete "rights" vis-à-vis the occupiers,[38] the law not only consistently recalls the security needs of the occupying military, it allows the use of force, arbitrary detention and other security measures.

This is not simply a technical *lex specialis* issue, where lawyers can parse out which human rights can be overlooked by the more specific function of a given provision of IHL (such as security detention or limitation of rights to trial). Rather, this is at the very heart of the difference—the critical and necessary difference—between IHRL and IHL. It seems that the pro-convergence argument would hold that occupation is exactly the situation in which human rights law applies extraterritorially (even courts that have restrained extraterritorial jurisdiction during armed conflict acknowledge that occupation may be the archetypal context for extraterritorial human rights obligations to hold). But life under occupation was never meant to be like life in one's country governed by one's own leader(s): occupation law secures the minimum protections of the occupied, but it also acts to prevent the occupying power from slipping into the position of the legitimate (read national, territorial) government. Its provisions ensure that the occupying power is *not* able to control the State lawmaking and governance infrastructure in such a way that would facilitate meaningful human rights compliance. Whatever the specific function of these restraints in a given occupation situation, the normative spirit of the law, the message that it communicates to the occupied population, is clear: the international community does not believe that the occupier is in your country for your good or benefit, and its stay is temporary, potentially difficult, violent and limited. Whatever criticism one has of occupation law, its advantage is that it does not allow us to forget that we are in armed conflict. It does not allow us to pretend that we are in peace, or that the population has consented to its situation.[39]

My point here is not that it is legally impossible to imagine that an occupying power could be in a position to apply human rights standards: obviously, for the majority of human rights provisions, the occupied territory would already be obliged to respect key rights under its own ratifications, and as the caretaker regime, the occupying power would have a pre-existing IHL obligation to respect those agreements. As Ralph Wilde argues, in criticizing the *Al-Skeini* decision's jurisdictional formula,

> In the first place, it is assumed that human rights law properly applied, with all the advantages of limitation clauses, derogations, and, for the ECHR [European Convention on Human Rights], the margin of appreciation, would actually oblige the State to exercise public authority both generally and in particular in a manner that would put it at odds with obligations under the law of occupation. . . . [T]hese assertions presuppose the validity of a particular approach to the relationship between different areas of international law, without having explained the basis for this validity. A clash between two areas of law is feared, and a solution to this clash offered by defining the applicability of one area of law so as to remove it from being in play, without explaining the basis for choosing this particular method of norm clash resolution.[40]

Wilde continues, arguing that the law does not make it clear that human rights law should be rendered inapplicable through the functioning of occupation law's limitation on the governing power of the occupier,

> An equally plausible scenario, of course, in light of both the ECHR itself and its relationship to other areas of law, is that a relatively modest set of substantive obligations would actually subsist, qualitatively and quantitatively different from those in play in the State's own territory, even if derived from the same legal source.[41]

This argument builds on the idea that those States (primarily the United States and the United Kingdom) who are worried about extraterritorial human rights jurisdiction have little reason to worry, because the actual law-added impact of human rights would be minimal. Wilde approvingly quotes the dictum of Lord Justice Sedley in the *Al-Skeini* decision at the Court of Appeal level, a quote that merits close reading, as it captures the message one encounters frequently in the convergence literature,

> If effective control in the jurisprudence of the [European Court of Human Rights] marches with international humanitarian law and the law of armed conflict, as it clearly seeks to do, it involves two key things: the de facto assumption of civil power by an occupying State and a concomitant obligation to do all that is possible to keep order and protect essential civil rights. It does not make the occupying power the guarantor of rights; nor therefore does it demand sufficient control for all such purposes. What it does is place an obligation on the occupier to do all it can. If this is right, it is not an answer to say that the UK, because it is unable to do everything, is required to guarantee nothing.[42]

This argument seems like an appealing solution to the problems posed by convergence and extraterritorial applicability. It suggests that clearly the occupying power would not be required to apply the entirety of human rights norms, or *really* be obligated to respect and apply human rights law in the same way that it would at home, but rather to do its best. While this is of course a laudable principle, and we might wish that all occupiers would act in this manner, I question the legal argument and the plausibility of such a solution to the practical challenge of identifying what exactly is the function of human rights law on the battlefield. What rights do the people in this situation actually have against the occupying power? How can we know whether an occupier is doing "all it can"?

Before we enter into the pragmatic and practical problems raised by such a vague legal standard (and I believe there are many), it is worth considering whether one reason we find it so difficult to blend these two bodies of law in practice, even in such a narrow context as envisioned by the *Bankovic* or *Al-Skeini* courts, is that the true import of the genetic difference between IHRL and IHL was not properly heeded. That is, the issue of differing origins, differing foundational philosophies, and differing imagined communities of the law is not simply a historical artifact to be overcome by progress; it reflects the wisdom of not pretending that armed conflict is anything other than what it is: unpredictable, often cruel, bloody and unjust. In valuing foundations and origins in a different light, we are able to see that one reason that human rights law was not originally drafted to apply in extraterritorial exertions of military force and occupation is precisely because the relationship necessary for the spirit and letter of human rights law to hold does not exist between the invaders and the invaded. Nor should it.

Dismissing Dilemmas as "Technical": Leaving the Hard Cases Untheorized

It is striking how many scholarly articles on convergence and court decisions on the issue of extraterritorial applicability of human rights in armed conflict reference the challenge of practically applying this body of law on top of, through or in addition to IHL. An oft-referenced paragraph from the International Court of Justice's (ICJ) *Wall* advisory opinion serves as a useful starting point:

> As regards the relationship between international humanitarian law and human rights law, there are thus three possible situations: some rights may be exclusively matters of international humanitarian law; others may be exclusively matters of human rights law; yet others may be matters of both these branches of international law.[43]

Many commentators have noted that this paragraph, and the Court's subsequent reliance on the *lex specialis* principle to determine which body of law will hold on a particular set of facts, is an unsatisfying and confusing way to approach the actual application of human rights law during armed conflict. The Court does not go on to provide any examples of such a division of applicable law, and its subsequent decision on the issue does little to build on this paragraph's language. As one scholar has argued, the actual functioning of the *lex specialis* principle is notoriously elusive and provides little in the way of concrete interpretive guidance for solving conflict of laws problems in this arena.[44]

While many scholars and jurists acknowledge the tremendous current confusion on how the convergence principle applies in practice (while reiterating that the current law is indeed that both bodies of law apply in all armed conflicts), few tackle *how* human rights law will actually be applied in the day-to-day military operations that characterize armed action abroad.[45] These questions are often referred to in an offhand manner as technical matters to be dealt with by those who will be made responsible for applying the vague principles of convergence.[46] In this section, I want to ask whether this leaves the job of courts and theorists half done: to what extent must human rights law theory be transformed in order to make convergence a coherent reality? To what extent do the possible changes to human rights law that would be wrought by true extraterritorial application have implications for how we think about and theorize human rights norms today? If soldiers become human rights enforcers, if military commanders acting outside the territory of the State party to the human rights treaty are put on the front lines of interpreting human rights provisions, how do these technical and pragmatic choices impact our understanding of rights?

Once again, long-standing differences between IHRL and IHL should inform our understanding of this issue. IHL theory treats the practical realm as sacrosanct:

most serious scholarship or jurisprudence on the laws of war supplements any theoretical argument or model with a claim for why the posited theory is practicable, pragmatically sound, and capable of being applied by the military and to soldiers. For most IHL scholars putting forth theoretical or normative arguments, plausibility to the military planner, the reasonable commander and the military lawyer is almost as important as acceptance by fellow scholars and policymakers.[47] Human rights scholars, with their focus on a State's obligations to control and shape its own institutions in its own seat of power (its government, its means of coercion, its courts, its police, its school system, its national budget and financial decisions), are not so constrained.

Avoiding the difficult question of practice and operations seems like more than an oversight or a decision to leave those matters to future scholarship and jurisprudence.[48] While a number of scholars seem to recognize the significant problems posed by convergence to actual military practice during armed conflict, referencing in particular the dilemmas faced by coalition forces that may have different interpretations of the applicability of human rights law (as was the case in Iraq), as well as the means by which the military would be asked to make human rights–based decisions, few present a coherent theory of *how* their ideas can be realized. My sense is that this derives from two underlying problems with the current debate. First, due to the sense that those arguing for convergence are clearly on the "right" side of the debate and that they are obviously making arguments for more humanity and more protection, there is little pressure for those making convergence arguments to normatively justify their positions and ground these normative claims in an understanding of how convergence will actually improve the status of civilians caught up in armed conflict. The operating assumption of pro-convergence scholarship is that more human rights obligations on the battlefield will mean more human rights enjoyment for the affected population. Second, the ubiquitous claim that the main legal battle has been won, that with the three key ICJ decisions (the *Nuclear Weapons* and *Wall* advisory opinions and the *Congo* decision) international law today simply *demands* convergence, makes it easier to avoid the hard cases of how these vague opinions can be translated into operational guidelines for soldiers.[49]

I question whether this reliance on hyper-positivism is enough to solve the problem. While article after article analyzes the same judicial and quasi-judicial material (the *Loizidou* line of cases at the ECtHR, leading through *Issa*; the key decisions of the IACHR; the ICJ decisions; and the Human Rights Committee's relevant views and General Comment 31) in an effort to meticulously demonstrate exactly how well-founded is the claim that convergence is in fact law, these analyses rarely move into exactly which human rights provisions would converge with which international humanitarian law norms, how detention operations on the ground would materially change, how commanders would embed human rights interpretation into their orders, how decisions around targeting would be impacted, and how the balance between security of forces and civilians would be struck.[50] It is worth considering that the reason we see so little of this type of discussion in the voluminous debate on convergence is that the main contribution to battlefield regulation envisioned by those who advocate convergence actually has very little to do with the key areas that IHL regulates. Perhaps advocates of convergence have spent so little time theorizing what exactly will converge—how military lawyers should incorporate human rights law into their advice to commanders, how military planners should use human rights law in their preplanned targeting and how occupation authorities should consider human rights in detention operations—not because these are insignificant concerns, but because they actually imagine that the payoff of activating extraterritorial obligations of human rights will be in the aftermath of war. It is worth remembering that the clear texts of the oft-cited decisions of the ICJ, the ECtHR and the Human Rights Committee certainly do not limit convergence in this manner: the formalist reading of the current majority position seems right—human rights law *does* apply, and it applies extraterritorially.

I would argue that now that advocates of convergence seem to have won the formalist legal battle, they have a responsibility to begin work on the hard cases that have been left to footnotes and marginalia. They must begin to articulate a theory of exactly how human rights go to war, and make a link between vague declarations of applicability and detailed recommendations for practice and operations. Foreshadowing some of the critiques that will follow, I would argue that this work will be fraught with tensions and difficult choices that have not been properly considered and weighed by advocates thus far.

Lowest-Common-Denominator Governance: Creating a False Sense of Rule of Law

Much of the jurisprudence and literature on extraterritorial application and convergence focuses on the level of effective control required in order for human rights obligations to apply to the State engaging militarily beyond its borders.[51] The upshot of the current approach seems to lie between the "cause and effect" doctrine (rejected in *Bankovic*, but revived in other cases and still promoted by a number of scholars) and the idea that a State acting extraterritorially during armed conflict would have human rights obligations consequent to its degree of control of the territory and population of the invaded State. While the current law is far from clear, most of it seems to agree that the degree of obligation would increase as a State asserted more control, culminating in detention of persons as the clearest example of control for human rights applicability purposes.

Assuming that this interpretation of contemporary international law is correct, it seems to me that this encourages us to take a lowest-common-denominator approach to governance, and the ways in which human rights are respected in a real place with an actual population.[52] It is important to note here that IHL is not a legal regime that is concerned with governance: while of course there are provisions in occupation law about how an occupying power should engage in the act of administering a territory that it controls, those rules do not purport to promote a good governance agenda, or to lay the foundations for democratic or rights-respecting statecraft.

When we make the move to add human rights law (and, its important corollary, the *expectation* and *reliance* of the members of the population that they have legitimate human rights claims against various foreign State entities as represented through their militaries) in concert with increasing degrees of effective control, it strikes me that we treat governance as something that can be parceled out, diminished to some set of basics, and diluted to a generic palette of tasks that could be equally borne and applied by any actor who happens to be part of the invading/occupying forces. The reliance on control as the central mechanism by which human rights law applies extraterritorially during armed conflict seems to threaten the very core of human rights principles: that they are intimately tied to the way in which a State governs, the ways in which it communicates its system of governance to its people, and the means by which it demonstrates its accountability to their rights claims and rights enjoyment over time. How can enemy soldiers step into this governance function? What is lost when we minimize the act of governing to the levers of control that may or may not be in place at a given time? Unlike targeting decisions, orders regarding proportionality assessments or civil-military cooperation in humanitarian assistance operations, rights do not function in minute-by-minute decisions taken by commanders and soldiers; they are based on a relationship, a two-way exchange between the rights-holder and the duty-bearer. How can building a prison, erecting a checkpoint or detaining a group of young men provide the appropriate foundations for human rights to function?[53]

It seems worth considering that this approach to human rights applicability encourages us to see governance as synonymous with control: whoever happens to be able to exert brute force over the civilians at a given moment in the conflict such that they have some sliding degree of control will have some sliding degree of human rights obligations. I am not making a pragmatic argument here (see the above critique for that point), though there are clearly many ways in which this system seems patently unworkable in actual conflict. Rather, I want to put forward the argument that such an approach to human rights obligations *and* human rights claims (meaning what the civilians hold in their hand, what they are able to understand, who they are able to turn to in real time) harms human rights law in ways that are not currently being measured by proponents of convergence.

Lowest-common-denominator governance has costs in the ways I have discussed above, but I think the inclusion of rights talk in effective military control also allows us to avoid the ways in which armed conflict actually impacts how people caught in its chaos experience justice. As documented extensively elsewhere, efforts to foster and sustain the rule of law in Iraq have not proved effective.[54] To the extent that any semblance of rule of law existed prior to the 2003 invasion, the war, subsequent occupation and conflict between armed groups have devastated the ability of Iraqi citizens to access and rely upon the legal system. Human rights law is at the core of the concept of rule of law, especially in the sense that it grounds this often-nebulous concept to a set of treaties and mechanisms. Human rights imagine the full human being living her day-to-day life and interacting with organs of the state in a myriad of ways.

The legal claim that human rights law now applies extraterritorially to States in armed conflict, and the increasing embrace of convergence in the practice of international non-governmental organizations (INGOs),[55] humanitarian organizations, UN agencies[56] and other key actors on the ground, allows us to feel that we are doing something to improve the experience of rule of law in countries like Iraq, or that we are increasing the capacity of the population to raise claims against the invading or occupying army. While we know that the actual legal system of Iraq has been decimated by years of conflict, sanctions, and now occupation and internal conflict, the use of rights talk—and the constant reference to the human rights obligations of coalition actors—masks the real cost that this has on the capacity of Iraqis to enjoy human rights by emphasizing international obligations and fancy legal argumentation. But replacing the domestic legal system with "the international community" or with the legal system of another country (the domestically accepted human rights obligations of the Netherlands, United Kingdom, Canada, etc.) does not necessarily improve the experience of law or the accountability of actors vis-à-vis the Iraqi civilian.

International rights mean little without local law and order. Pretending otherwise, or focusing energies on supporting rare "impact litigation" connecting a handful of victims with prominent human rights lawyers in Europe or civil rights organizations in the United States, does not change that. Such litigation, and findings of individual liability of soldiers for human rights violations, may improve the Dutch, British or Canadian legal order and it may over time improve the behavior of these States' militaries in actions around the world, but it does not necessarily increase the rights enjoyment of Iraqis.

My point here is not to say that such cases are unimportant or that we should not value their potential for positive transformation of military behavior and public attitudes back home toward the actions of their States abroad. My concern is that the increasing sense among human rights lawyers and scholars that there is "no difference" between IHL and IHRL is disconnected from reality as experienced by civilians in the countries most affected by these debates.[57] Furthermore, the increasingly legalistic insistence on convergence allows us to pretend that international law is doing more for civilians in armed conflict than it actually does (or can). IHL, which renders discussions of governance and rule of law as (at best) out of place and (at worst) insulting, prohibits us from making such a slide, and forces us to properly ascertain the horrible impact of war on affected populations' experience of day-to-day justice.

Can the Moral Force of Human Rights Withstand Their Formal Application in Armed Conflict? Setting Human Rights Up to Fail

The current focus on legalistic convergence (as opposed to actual operational practice and concrete examples of parallel application) undermines the moral power of human rights law, and threatens to diminish the hard-fought gains of human rights norms and rights discourse in the past several decades. To put it simply, we all know at an intuitive level that an Iraqi in Iraq under occupation cannot possibly enjoy the same human rights as I can as an American citizen in the United States. Yet, there is no way (so far) to translate that basic commonsense idea in discussions of international legal application. If the Iraqi cannot have the same rights during conflict or occupation as I do during peacetime in my home State, but human rights lawyers want to argue that he "has human rights," what rights should he have? What does human rights mean if we strip it down this way, if we pick at which rights can be enforced in which circumstances by particular armies at particular times?

As I have noted above in a different context, claiming that international law now recognizes the (full) applicability of IHRL to States fighting outside of their own borders creates expectations among the civilian population (as well it should). If I am told I have a bundle of rights, who has the duties? How do I claim them? Where do I go? This is a very different matter from explaining to the civilian population that the armed forces or the occupying power have an obligation to minimize civilian harm, to provide adequate access to basic lifesaving goods and not to attack civilians. Human rights is a set of negative *and* positive obligations, but more than that it is a manner of relating, one that is anathema to the relationship between soldiers and enemy civilians. The call for extraterritorial human rights application in armed conflict implicates human rights language and the promise of human rights in the very ugly business of control by an enemy military. Can this be expressed to the civilian population in a way that does not permanently pervert that population's appreciation for human rights law? After the conflict is over, and the enemy forces are gone, will the civilians—now again citizens, no longer categorized by their status—be able to see human rights law in the same light? If convergence fails to deliver in any meaningful way in terms of material changes to the experience of civilians in armed conflict (and, given the lack of development of concrete operational rules for how military lawyers, planners and commanders might change their behavior as a result of adding human rights law to IHL, we have good reason to believe this might be the case), will human rights law and rights discourse suffer lasting damage?

It is worth noting that the international community has invested tremendous resources in increasing the awareness of and respect for human rights among populations in the developing world—particularly in the Middle East[58]—against significant cultural and religious objections to universal rights. Human rights law has a long way to go before it is accepted as the framework for the relationship between the governed and the governors: how is this regime affected by the declaration that any military force that happens to act on the territory has human rights obligations equivalent to those held by the home State?

This is another way in which the distinction between IHL and IHRL reflects a serious and deep difference. As reflected in emerging scholarship, IHL has not historically had a "culture problem": one finds very few debates in the post–World War II writing on IHL discussing cultural relativism versus universalism, multiple or plural interpretations of proportionality and distinction based on local norms, or different approaches to detention based on custom.[59] Whether well-founded or not, IHL has generally been able to comfortably claim universal adherence and acceptance based on its practical credentials, its lack of the "name and shame" approach to enforcement and monitoring, and its profound respect for the sovereign. IHL focuses (with some important exceptions) on the behavior of the professional military, and relies on its very limited scope of application and limited relevance to how States govern people's daily lives to assert its relatively unchallenged dominance over the norms regulating armed conflict.

In this light, if we consider the objections of the United Kingdom to full extraterritorial application of the CAT, arguing that it "could not have taken legislative or judicial measures of the kind required by Article 2 of the CAT in Iraq since legislative authority was in the hands of the Coalition Provisional Authority and judicial authority was in the hands of the Iraqi courts,"[60] it seems that the current pro-convergence position would ask us to respond by accusing the British of seeking to maximize their military entitlements as an occupying power (including the power to interrogate security detainees or keep individuals in administrative detention with very minimal fair trial guarantees), while actively trying to avoid the increased protective and rights-based regulations of the CAT. However, one could also argue that there would be valid concern on the part of an Iraqi that the British ability to craft and make decisions based on human rights *ought to be* limited, precisely because we would not want the British—as a military occupier—to have the kind of influence over Iraqi institutions that would arguably be necessary to fully respect human rights law vis-à-vis Iraqi individuals who find themselves before the courts. IHL keeps the British position limited: they have responsibility over their own actions vis-à-vis enemy civilians when they are taken into custody, when they are on the opposite end of a gun and when they are within the range of a bomb.

Human rights law asks that the State with obligations to an individual takes real steps to permanently transform institutions that structurally violate rights. How will the still-fragile worldwide acceptance of human rights law and rights discourse fare as military forces are encouraged to take the helm of such transformations? Do we want to encourage foreign invading States to promote a human rights agenda vis-à-vis the population under attack? Can human rights law be respected in this manner, and would the population accept such an articulation of human rights? To put it another way, while I understand the short-term gains of demanding that the British respect human rights law in their actions in Iraq (one could perhaps argue that it would result in better trials, or less torture, though again this has yet to be convincingly demonstrated by any argument about *how* human rights law would materially change the current panoply of rules under IHL), I do not *want* an occupying power that has invaded my State to be recognized by the international community as having a "rights-based" relationship with my population. I do not want that State to be in a position to argue that it has to engage in certain institutional changes in order to be able to comply with its human rights obligations back home. I do not want a State that has no relationship to civil society in my country, has no long-term understanding of my population, its history, its religious values, etc., to have a hand in shaping its human rights framework simply by virtue of its choice to invade.

Seen in this light, the aggressive promotion of full convergence by some human rights bodies and human rights lawyers seems to flip the legitimacy of the rights regime. One might argue that the current interpretation of extraterritorial applicability of IHRL in armed conflict is much more limited than I am suggesting—that human rights really apply only when the invading/attacking/belligerent State is in a quasi-governing stance vis-à-vis my population. But, given that there are no coherent legal grounds for this limitation, the concerns raised here should give pause to the march toward convergence. If convergence applies to detention today, how can we know whether it will be said to apply to speech, religion, education and elections tomorrow? What if it is argued (as one could well imagine in Iraq) that the invading or occupying State is in fact far better suited and experienced to enforce human rights law in these sectors than the host State?

In this sense, in a context where human rights norms are currently under attack in much of the world for representing the wish of Western States to change developing countries, and where human rights discourse has recently had to defend itself after being marshaled by those who used human rights arguments to support the invasion of Iraq, the dilemmas of convergence raised here ought to be considered as serious threats to the legitimacy of the human rights project. The pro-convergence position imagines a world in which the duty-bearers of rights held by individuals have an exchangeable responsibility that can be shifted between States, coalitions of States and even international organizations that happen to be acting upon a civilian population at any given time during armed conflict. Today, my human rights might be owed by the armed forces that happen to be transferring through my village, tomorrow by my own State, the next day by the coalition forces that will occupy for several months. Something is lost in this shift, in this exchange. The governor-governed relationship that is central to the corpus of human rights, and central to rights talk and rights advocacy, is not only about who is held responsible before an international court, or what State holds the *duty*. It also empowers the rights-holder, and provides the central logic for the legitimacy of human rights law in gaining State consent and popular universality: the bonds of trust, geography, home, kinship, culture, refuge and family that create the context in which the governor-governed relationship takes shape mean that the rights-holder has a clear sense of *who* owes him respect of his rights, and *why*. It gives the rights-holder the agency to *change* and *impact* the duty-bearer. IHL not only has no such provisions; it is inherently opposed to such a conception of relations.[61] The admixture of what makes IHL legitimate and what makes IHRL legitimate may delegitimize both bodies of law, and impact the ways in which the law is able to regulate.

The Call for "Basic" Rights: Reintroducing a Hierarchy of Rights?

A survey of the scholarly literature on the parallel application of IHRL and IHL, as well as the key judicial and quasi-judicial documents on this fiercely debated topic, reveals the repeated use of phrases such as "basic" rights, "hard-core" rights or "core" provisions of human rights law.[62] This language seems appealing, in that it appears to refer to some previously agreed-upon, truly vital subset of human rights provisions, and to argue that we must simply take that agreed-upon set of "super-rights" and insist that they apply extraterritorially to States engaged in armed conflict. However, this language, and this frequent invocation of "basic" rights, is deeply problematic, and goes against the dominant (and, until now, victorious) trend in human rights law and scholarship to insist that human rights are indivisible and cannot be picked apart or prioritized on the basis of which rights are more "serious" or "urgent" than others.[63] Indeed, it is often noted that part of the reason that the derogation clause of the ICCPR was not replicated in subsequent human rights treaties is for the precise reason that it seemed to encourage a sense that there were some rights that were considered more important by the international community than others. It is surprising to see human rights proponents referencing a return to some vague conception of basic or fluid rights, insofar as the human rights movement spent many years convincing States that such an approach to their obligations was unacceptable and went against the spirit of key treaties.

From a legal interpretation perspective, the problem of how to respond to the human rights lawyers who claim that only some rights must be applied by States acting abroad has been recognized by a number of courts. As the much-criticized *Bankovic* court points out in rejecting the "cause and effect" theory of extraterritorial IHRL applicability, the obligations of the ECHR should not be "divided and tailored in accordance with the particular circumstances of the extra-territorial act in question."[64] The *Al-Skeini* decision (also disputed by proponents of convergence for not going far enough in recognizing extraterritorial obligations in armed conflict) references this language of the ECtHR and states,

> In other words, the whole package of rights applies and must be secured where a contracting state has jurisdiction. This merely reflects the normal understanding that a contracting state cannot pick and choose among the rights in the Convention: it must secure them all to everyone within its jurisdiction. If that is so, then it suggests that the obligation under article 1 can arise only where the contracting state has such effective control of the territory of another state that it could secure to everyone in the territory all the rights and freedoms in Section 1 of the Convention.[65]

Similarly, the recent Canada Federal Court of Appeal decision rejecting extraterritorial application of the Canadian Charter of Rights and Freedoms to Canadian Forces in Afghanistan states,

> Surely, Canadian law, including the *Canadian Charter of Rights and Freedoms*, either applies in relation to the detention of individuals by the Canadian Forces in Afghanistan, or it does not. It cannot be that the Charter will not apply where the

> breach of a detainee's purported Charter rights is of a minor or technical nature, but will apply where the breach puts the detainee's fundamental rights at risk.
>
> That is, it cannot be that it is the nature or quality of the Charter breach that creates extraterritorial jurisdiction, where it does not otherwise exist. This would be a completely unprincipled approach to the exercise of extraterritorial jurisdiction.[66]

Yet, from a practical and strategic perspective, convergence (in the extraterritorial application sense) makes it virtually impossible *not* to prioritize rights or reintroduce the long-dead notion of a hierarchy of rights. As the Court of Appeal in *Al-Skeini* notes, "No doubt it is absurd to expect occupying forces in the near-chaos of Iraq to enforce the right to marry vouchsafed by Art. 12 or the equality guarantees vouchsafed by Art. 14. But I do not think effective control involves this."[67] Indeed, the argument for parallel application would be incredibly difficult to make to States (and their militaries) without some degree of limitation on the entire scope of rights provided in the relevant treaties (particularly when advocates of extraterritorial application argue that rights would increase with the level of control, suggesting that some minimal rights would apply with minimal control or during active hostilities). This reference to some inherent limitation to which human rights would actually oblige States acting militarily abroad (which has a very weak legal basis outside of the non-derogable provisions of the ICCPR) seems directed to those States (mainly the United States and United Kingdom) concerned about extraterritorial jurisdiction, assuring them that there is no actual expectation that they would be required to apply many of the relevant treaty obligations.

This may be a good strategic approach for arguing that extraterritorial application of IHRL in armed conflict is a reasonable expectation, or one that we can imagine taking hold in practice, but it is exceptionally difficult to uphold from both a legal *and* principled perspective. What would it look like to actually determine which rights apply with a given level of control? Who would determine which are "core" rights and which are those rights that could be left out of the equation? The military? The UN treaty body? Again, some seem to argue that States would be required to apply only the non-derogable provisions of the ICCPR, but what about the many other treaties implicated when courts speak of the applicability of "international human rights law"?[68] More important perhaps, to what extent do these arguments—once put into practice—threaten the indivisibility principle of human rights law? Do we open the door for States to argue that *other* situations would justify applying rights obligations on a sliding scale? This seems like a difficult conundrum to escape from: once advocates argue for the parallel applicability of international human rights law in armed conflict, once courts recognize that these rights apply according to some degree of control, the temptation to pick and choose rights is almost unavoidable. Such a move comes with real risks for the coherence of human rights law and its stability.

Lex Specialis as Everything and Nothing: Diluting the Clarity of IHL?

One response to the above critique is to rely on the *lex specialis* principle to determine when IHRL will fill gaps in IHL, on using IHRL as a supplementary legal regime that is often overridden by the laws of war.[69] While the principle presents an appealing mechanism, it seems to be utilized by scholars and jurists across the spectrum of views on convergence to advocate for their approach to the dilemma. As one author notes, "[E]ven more worrying is the fact that the broadness of this principle allows manipulation of the law, a maneuvering of the law that supports diametrically opposed arguments from supporters that are both for and against the compartmentalization of international humanitarian law and international human rights law."[70]

Some would argue that the actual impact of convergence and extraterritorial applicability as recognized by courts is strongly limited by this principle—that when we seek to actually make sense of how rules and behavior would be impacted by the decisions of the ICJ the changes in rules that apply in combat would be minimal. Proponents of this view would argue that, for example, in developing rules of engagement for a particular theater, military planners and lawyers would almost always find themselves in a situation where IHL addresses the behavior they seek to address. In this way, *lex specialis* functions to render relatively meaningless the legal principle of convergence: yes, the laws may formally apply simultaneously during armed conflict, but in any given factual situation the relevant human rights norm (freedom of movement, freedom from torture, the right to life, freedom from arbitrary detention) would be trumped by the more specific or more clearly applicable IHL rule (military necessity, proportionality, distinction, prohibition on torture, treatment of prisoners).[71]

Such an approach might serve to address the lack of clarity and minimal operational guidance provided by current legal interpretations of convergence and extraterritorial applicability, and might allow States to continue to craft rules that are seen as compliant with the law while the norms are still being figured out. However, as a long-term approach to the question of parallel application, particularly for States and military professionals seeking to comply with changing norms, as well as for the coherence of both legal systems, this way of looking at the problem seems lacking in a number of ways. First, such an approach would seem to gut the very notion of convergence, and render the claim that both bodies of law apply somewhat incredulous. Second, there may well be situations of substantive law where a human rights claim could be made and not dismissed by the *lex specialis* of IHL. This might be the case where IHL is completely silent on a matter that is explicitly addressed by IHRL,[72] or where human rights law provides much richer detail on a given situation than the basic rule of IHL (such as in detention situations).[73]

As noted in the introduction to this article, however, the bulk of the power of IHL to regulate and to protect lies in the development of clear rules and clear guidance to commanders and soldiers *before* combat decisions are made.[74] To the extent that even the most sophisticated scholars of international law seem to find the principle of *lex specialis* difficult to work with and lacking in specifics, it seems unlikely that an approach that relies heavily on this principle will serve to protect rights *or* enhance the clarity of existing rules. Indeed, one risk of the current lack of practice-oriented theories for understanding and interpreting State obligations to apply and differentiate the two bodies of law is not only that human rights law will not actually be added to the rules in any meaningful way, but also that the clarity of IHL rules will be blurred in the process.

One-Way Convergence? The Question of Distinct Professional Cultures and Languages

One needs only to attend any academic conference or panel on IHL and IHRL in order to observe the vast differences between the professions, academic cultures and approaches to theory, lawyering and practice. Without claiming that these are essential characteristics, or that there is never overlap between those who focus on either of these bodies of law, I want to argue there that these professional identities matter and have an impact on how we ought to understand the implications of convergence in practice as the field emerges.

Before the very recent trend toward seeing IHRL and IHL as subsets of the same legal field, the educational and professional choices leading to becoming a practitioner or specialist in either field were quite divergent. While both are, of course, fields of public international law and share affinities of background and training to some extent, the "typical" IHRL scholar/lawyer and IHL expert are two rather different characters. Traditionally, those interested in IHL have had professional experience in the military, in government or with the ICRC. Many scholars who have had such professional experience remain closely connected to the relatively small community of IHL practitioners and scholars, often meeting at the same academic conferences and relatively familiar with the range of perspectives within their ranks on the key debates. Many IHL scholars remain actively engaged in the application of principles, either through advising States or international tribunals, contributing to ICRC and other expert processes, or working closely with those who train military lawyers and humanitarian actors. While there have been significant efforts to increase the training and academic development of IHL in the developing world, most scholarship, commentary and expertise on this body of law continues to stem from the West.

Human rights lawyers, advocates and practitioners are a much less well-defined group, and represent a much larger body of professionals. Firstly, not all human rights practitioners are lawyers, and many have professional backgrounds in advocacy organizations, non-governmental groups, domestic civil rights and human rights organizations, and community-based organizations. Scholars of human rights law are also drawn not only from the legal discipline, but also from philosophy, political science and anthropology. There is no institution in human rights that matches the history, power and influence of the ICRC, and while there are some leading global non-governmental organizations (NGOs), they enjoy less of a direct link to State policymaking than their counterparts at the ICRC. While today there are a number of State-based human rights institutions and departments in ministries of foreign affairs, many human rights lawyers consider themselves to be advocates of victims against the State and its machinery. As human rights law has enjoyed tremendous popularity as a field of study in the global south, its lawyers, scholars and experts represent a diverse group of leading thinkers and practitioners around the world.

The above caricatures are just that, caricatures, but they serve to emphasize that as these two fields merge more and more, and as convergence begins to trickle through to lawyering, scholarship, training and implementation, there may be real differences of approach, engagement and professional styles that are under-appreciated in the current debate. As more and more prominent human rights organizations (such as Human Rights Watch and Amnesty International) take on IHL in their monitoring, reporting and advocacy,[75] it remains to be seen whether a third professional community of those who work specifically on convergence will emerge. Alternatively IHL may have to expand its ranks to include human rights lawyers that may have wildly different perceptions of the laws of armed conflict, how its rules are and should be interpreted and applied, and how practitioners concerned with either or both bodies of law should engage with State actors and the military.

One might argue that there is real value in the two professions remaining distinct and maintaining their divergent internal cultures. To the extent that human rights lawyers and advocates come to speak in the language of IHL, with its acceptance of civilian deaths that are not excessive in relation to the military advantage anticipated, its recognition of the massive destruction to military objects waged in war, its constant balancing of humanity against the powerful argument of military necessity, and its faith in the decision making of the reasonable commander, will something be lost in the advocacy for the rights of individuals? Will the moral core of human rights lawyering, and its insistence on the promise of aspirational goals, be lost as these lawyers and scholars immerse themselves in the technicalities of warfighting? Do we want to maintain a space in international law and policy for the voice of human rights advocates that speak purely in the language of human rights and do not need to acquiesce to military entitlements in the same way that IHL lawyers and scholars must? In the sense that convergence focuses on how human rights law comes into the realm controlled by IHL, will the conversation and conversion go only one way, without demanding the IHL lawyers and scholars also become conversant with human rights law and its tremendous history of internal theoretical debates?

To some extent, the substance of human rights claims, as well as the style of human rights argumentation and advocacy, currently seems incongruous with the substance and approach of IHL. Today, the human rights advocate would stick out at a meeting of IHL experts. The human rights lawyer would probably make awkward references to peace, bring up questions of *jus ad bellum*,[76] passionately emphasize the rights of individuals to their claims, and stress the obligation of States to investigate and punish every act of State-sponsored killing. Most IHL lawyers would likely be polite, but see little opportunity to engage on the technicalities of targeting, on the number of civilians who could be killed in an otherwise legal attack without giving rise to liability or on the highly detailed debate over when civilians can be said to be directly participating in hostilities.[77] The convergence of the two bodies of law could dramatically change this conversation: it could foster a new group of professionals who would be wholly comfortable with such language, and who could easily discuss which human rights rules would be trumped during an air campaign. This might ease the integration of the two bodies of law, it might even lead to solutions to some of the critiques I have listed here. But it might also diminish the capacity of the human rights movement to speak with a clear voice and to advocate on behalf of individuals against States. Both professions are vital to the protection of civilians in armed conflict *and* to the lives those civilians are able to lead once armed conflict has ended. My argument is not that one is morally superior to the other, but rather that their distinction, even their distaste for one another's approach to the key issues, to States and to the military, is vital to the functioning of the separate bodies of law, and to their capacity to marshal future lawyers and professionals to their ranks.

Human Rights Bodies in the Chain of Command: Incompatible Systems of Accountability?

To the extent that convergence suggests that IHRL applies during armed conflict and side by side with IHL, how can we understand the ways in which human rights bodies will come to address States engaged in armed conflict, and how might the military enforcement structure incorporate human rights law?

IHL relies on its own internal governance and enforcement structures: the reason that it travels so well is that it relies on the training, command structure and disciplinary machinery of the military. Theoretically at least, IHL should apply just as efficiently and effectively in a jungle war with little to no judicial mechanisms as in a prolonged air war over an enemy capital. IHRL, on the other hand, is rooted in institutions, in the particular infrastructure of a State's approach to governance, in the transformation—over time—of a State into a more human rights–respecting and rights-enforcing space. This transformative goal is geographically bound. It relates to shifts in culture, to alterations in domestic law that reflect the incorporation of human rights norms into the national system, and to the development of a long-term relationship between the State and international treaty bodies and other human rights mechanisms.

As the two merge, and as the conception of human rights jurisdiction expands, various (and perhaps all) human rights bodies will be in a position to consider the application of their particular treaties to situations of armed conflict, perhaps simultaneously addressing a State's compliance with human rights norms on its own territory, as well as its behavior in a far-off conflict. To the extent that the function of human rights law during armed conflict opens up the conflict to the inquiry and interpretation of human rights bodies, the more those bodies will be in a position to pass judgment not only on a State's compliance with a given human rights treaty, but also on that State's compliance with IHL *as interpreted through the lens of human rights law*. That is, in order to determine exactly *how* a given human rights treaty applies in a situation of armed conflict outside the territory of the obligated State, a given treaty body would need to first assess that there is in fact an armed conflict, use either *lex specialis* or some other mechanism in order to determine which body of rules applies to the situation before it, determine whether human rights law applies to those areas where IHL is (supposedly) silent, and then determine what level of violation of a human rights provision has occurred and what remedy should be made available to the claimant.

Such a scenario involves a number of significant steps. First, it suggests that human rights bodies will increasingly be getting involved in the notoriously difficult task of classification of conflict. Second, they would need to—at the very least—engage in enough analysis of IHL in order to determine which facts and legal issues are relevant and within their scope of review (in individual complaint cases, in court cases and in assessing State party reports). And finally, depending on their answers to these questions, the human rights bodies would be in a position to interpret, reflect upon and judge military behavior that falls within both categories of law, or where IHL is (supposedly) silent (targeting of civilians taking a direct part in hostilities, curfew regulations, treatment of women in detention, judicial due process of administrative detainees, etc.).[78]

This might be something to celebrate: one might argue that this opens up the traditionally insular field of IHL to a much broader scope of interrogation and analysis, and that it extends the conversation on IHL compliance beyond military tribunals or special courts. However, as such jurisprudence and quasi-jurisprudence develops in the Human Rights Committee; the Committee against Torture; the Committee on Economic, Social and Cultural Rights; the ECtHR; the IACHR; and other venues, we might ask whether such varied analysis and feedback to States on detailed issues of IHL is in fact *good* for the protection of civilians in armed conflict. Depending on the State, they may be subject to the views of a range of treaty bodies, which may have wide-ranging assessments of the critical issues listed above. How should States respond to this? At what level would we measure compliance?

The cost is not just in the possibility for a cacophony of conflicting or incoherent views on issues such as classification or direct participation in hostilities. It is also the possibility that these bodies would not be seen as legitimate to provide detailed analysis of legal issues seen as the province of military professionals. Would all human rights bodies begin to seek out IHL experts to bring specialization on these issues to their ranks? How would their views be weighed against domestic State interpretations of IHL? The more we move away from broad, vague generalities ("human rights law applies during armed conflict") and toward specific assessments of military conduct in conflict, the more we must ask whether human rights bodies are the appropriate or competent organs to address issues of IHL. What are the risks to the legitimacy of both these bodies *and* human rights law if States disregard much of their analysis (as has arguably been the case with the Human Rights Committee's General Comment No. 31)?

Undermining Sovereignty and Long-Term Rights Development

While scholars and human rights bodies have explored the obligations of non-State or private actors, ultimately human rights law centers on the sovereign State as the only entity with legal obligations under the law. This is more than a legalistic matter of jurisdiction or obligation; it is also critical to how human rights law develops, and its long-term vision for transforming those States that subject themselves to the human rights regime. It recognizes that as States open themselves to the scrutiny of human rights bodies, as they engage with NGOs and other human rights actors, as their domestic courts and internal State regulations come to absorb human rights norms, the relationship between the governor and the governed improves by becoming more transparent, accountable and democratic. For many States, their compliance with human rights law has been linked to their economic development, their good relations with other States and their reputations on the international stage.

One dilemma that has received little or no attention in the literature on convergence and in the work of human rights lawyers encouraging an expansion of extraterritorial applicability of human rights law is how these developments endanger the sovereignty of those States on which foreign militaries act, and how in turn this impacts the long-term development and growth of human rights enjoyment. While there has been so much focus on chastising those powerful States that reject or severely limit extraterritorial applicability, there seems to have been very little attention paid to those States that have been or will be invaded, occupied, bombed and otherwise subjected to the possibility of extraterritorial application of *other States' human rights obligations.* I imagine that part of the reason for this is that the sovereignty argument is easily manipulable by States such as the United States that reject extraterritorial applicability or like the United Kingdom, which is seeking to limit the contexts in which human rights principles would apply to the military. Another reason may be that thus far specially impacted States (almost uniformly in the developing world) have not verbalized a concern about this matter.

The *Al-Skeini* court touches on this issue with language that has been widely criticized by scholars. First, in approvingly citing the *Bankovic* court's finding that the ECHR is "essentially regional," and deeply rooted in the notion of the cultural and legal space of the Council of Europe, the House of Lords notes,

> The essentially regional nature of the Convention is relevant to the way that the court operates. It has judges elected from all the contracting states, not from anywhere else. The judges purport to interpret and apply the various rights in the Convention in accordance with what they conceive to be developments in prevailing attitudes of the contracting states. This is obvious from the court's jurisprudence on such matters as the death penalty, sex discrimination, homosexuality and transsexuals. The result is a body of law which may reflect the values of the contracting states, but which most certainly does not reflect those in many other parts of the world. So the idea that the United Kingdom was obliged to secure observance of all the rights and freedoms as interpreted by the European Court in the utterly different society of southern Iraq is manifestly absurd. Hence, as noted in *Bankovic* [citation omitted], the court had "so far" recognised jurisdiction based on effective control only in the case of territory which would normally be covered by the Convention. If it went further, the court

> would run the risk not only of colliding with the jurisdiction of other human rights bodies but of being accused of human rights imperialism.[79]

In the latter part of the decision, again in language that seems to have been dismissed by scholars,[80] Lord Brown, in citing the Article 43 Hague constraints on transformation of the territory by an occupying power, notes,

> The appellants argue that occupation within the meaning of the Hague Regulations necessarily involves the occupant having effective control of the area and so being responsible for securing there all Convention rights and freedoms. So far as this being the case, however, the occupants' obligation is to respect "the laws in force," not to introduce laws and means to enforce them (for example, courts and a justice system) such as to satisfy the requirements of the Convention. Often (for example where Sharia law is in force) Convention rights would clearly be incompatible with the laws of the territory occupied.[81]

Lord Brown later refers to the reasoning behind the general limitation on extraterritorial application of domestic laws: "The essential rationale underlying the presumption against extraterritoriality is that ordinarily it is inappropriate for one sovereign legislature to intrude upon the preserve of another."[82]

Ralph Wilde may well be correct that these positions represent "crude chauvinism,"[83] or "orientalist positioning of Islam and Europe as normative opposites."[84] He might even be right that "subjecting the UK presence in Iraq to the regulation of human rights law would have the effect of mitigating, not exacerbating, the colonial nature of the occupation."[85] I am not seeking to defend the actual position of either the Lord Justice, or to comment on the possible conflicts between Shari'a (or any other domestic or regional set of norms) and international human rights law.[86] Rather, I want to argue that human rights lawyers and those seeking to expand extraterritorial applicability of human rights law have been surprisingly silent on this issue. It seems that, taken from the perspective of a State (and its population) on which extraterritorial application of human rights would play out, the risk of human rights imperialism, or colonialism and transformation buttressed with the language of human rights (and imposed through the means of military control), may be neither preposterous nor ill founded.

This is one of the ways in which the lack of rigor and clarity in the arguments for extraterritoriality has a cost in understanding the risks posed by its increasing application. It is important to be very clear here about what is actually envisioned when we speak of extraterritorial applicability of human rights law in armed conflict. I raise this because it is very common to dismiss the above concern by noting that "most of the rights" would apply regardless of extraterritorial applicability due to the legal obligations of the invaded or occupied State. This is a faulty argument, and it slides over the more transformative and radical implications of extraterritoriality. Of course an occupying power would be responsible to apply the human rights norms that the occupied State has consented to, as well as all *jus cogens* and customary norms that the State would equally be obliged to respect. But that is *not* the grounds for triggering human rights obligations as imagined by proponents of convergence. Rather, the strong convergence argument suggests that an invading State brings with it its own human rights obligations, as well as its own *domestic* interpretations of how those human rights apply. Any other conclusion would go against the very purpose of extraterritorial jurisdiction.

This is less a claim about culture than it is one of the dangerous potential for undermining not only the sovereignty of invaded States, but more specifically their own domestic understandings of the interpretation and application of international human rights law. If we take extraterritoriality seriously, if we assume that advocates of convergence are being honest when they suggest that the full range of human rights obligations should apply in armed conflict, then how can this problem be avoided? Here, those who favor extraterritoriality tend to make an appealing and emotional argument that one sees repeated in both the literature and recent court decisions. In the widely cited language from the ECtHR's *Issa* decision (which many convergence scholars see as moving away from *Bankovic*), the Court states,

> Moreover, a State may also be held accountable for violation of the Convention rights and freedoms of persons who are in the territory of another State but who are found to be under the former State's authority and control through its agents operating—whether lawfully or unlawfully—in the latter State [citations omitted]. Accountability in such situations stems from *the fact that Article 1 of the Convention cannot be interpreted so as to allow a State party to perpetrate violations of the Convention on the territory of another State, which it could not perpetrate on its own territory.*[87]

A scholarly assessment of this language in *Issa* adds, "It is a strange idea, indeed, to suggest that a country's law cannot apply to criminal conduct of its nationals, to say nothing of its very agents, just because they are abroad when they violate the law."[88] One can see why this is such a compelling argument, and why it urges us to rally around the applicability of the law. It seems to say, "If extraterritoriality is not enforced, it would make a mockery of human rights, it would allow States to run rampant simply because they acted outside of their own territories." This is, however, a deeply flawed argument, and it takes our attention away from the real costs at stake here. First, we must clearly distinguish extraterritorial application of human rights law from State responsibility for the acts of its agents, which is regulated through rules on State responsibility, attribution and domestic criminal law. We do not need the extraterritorial application of human rights law in armed conflict to create criminal liability for agents of the State that commit crimes abroad while acting with the color of State authority. Second, and this point is often lost in the discussion, extraterritorial application of full human rights treaties in armed conflict makes a significant jump from existing narrow exceptions to territorial jurisdiction by addressing the conduct of the State and its agents vis-à-vis the nationals of *another* State, a State with its own human rights relationship to individuals on its territory. And finally, of course, it is not as though States acting abroad in armed conflict would be engaging in unregulated mayhem were it not for the extraterritorial application of human rights law, would be free to commit wanton crimes against the population of another State by virtue of their border-crossing. Indeed, the bulk of the entire field of international humanitarian law is dedicated to the regulation of exactly the moment when one State crosses the border of another State and engages in armed conflict there.

If extraterritorial applicability of human rights law in armed conflict grows and expands in the ways promoted by convergence advocates, these dilemmas go beyond the level of the abstract, and position weak States at a tremendous disadvantage in understanding and consenting to the laws that would be in force on their territories to their peoples. In an important recent Canadian case regarding detention and transfer of detainees in Afghanistan, we see this argument playing out in greater detail than anywhere else. The human rights lawyers arguing for the applicability of the Canadian Charter of Human Rights and Freedoms to Canadian detention operations make a curious argument to overcome the sovereignty problem, claiming, as Justice Mactavish states,

> [t]hat the Government of Afghanistan has implicitly consented to an extension of Canadian jurisdiction to its soil. As evidence of this, the applicants point to the fact that Afghanistan has surrendered significant powers to Canada, including, most importantly, the usual State monopoly over the use of coercive power within its territory.[89]

I can understand that as a tactical maneuver this approach may have extended the applicability of the law. However, from a principled perspective, I wonder how many human rights advocates would want to share with their colleagues in Afghanistan (or Iraq or Pakistan) that due to their State's "consent" to the presence of foreign military forces on their territory, they had in fact ceded sovereignty over the laws applicable to their own citizens to the governments controlling those foreign militaries? Relying on Canadian precedent on the question of extraterritorial jurisdiction generally, Justice Mactavish rejects this aspect of the argument, noting that "there has been no consent by the Government of Afghanistan to having Canadian Charter rights conferred on its citizens, within its territory."[90]

It may be that human rights advocates have shied away from acknowledging this critique, or engaging seriously with the costs posed to human rights law and third-world sovereignty by the extraterritoriality argument, because some of the claims I have posed above (the local laws problem, the sovereignty problem, and the colonialism problem) seem to be (perhaps disingenuously) cited by those who oppose extraterritoriality from the posture of defending the US or Israeli positions.[91] It may well be that opposing or questioning extraterritorial application of human rights law in armed conflict makes for strange or distasteful bedfellows in some cases. However, this is no reason to avoid critical inquiries into the implications of the arguments currently posed before courts and human rights bodies and in scholarship promoting a more robust application of one State's legal obligations and interpretations on the territory of another, particularly in light of contemporary politics around the misappropriation of human rights discourse by military interventionists.

Once human rights lawyers in the West go down this road, it may be very difficult to pull back and limit the sweeping legal arguments that are currently being made. One could imagine that beyond the dilemmas raised above, this could pose real risks to the long-term development of human rights law in countries that experience this type of extraterritorial jurisdiction being claimed and played out on their territories—though, significantly, not actually litigated on their territories or by their courts or judges.

Bad Lawyering? Asking IHRL to Do the Hard Work of Transforming IHL and Global Politics

A final concern relates to some of the issues raised immediately above, but goes to the heart of what proponents of convergence claim in legal argumentation, and what they actually seem to be seeking in terms of outcomes.

A first critique focuses on the gap between the legal claim that the full scope of human rights law applies once extraterritorial jurisdiction is activated in armed conflict, and the actual cases and examples we see brought forward by human rights lawyers and scholars. As I have noted above, as a matter of legal interpretation, it is difficult to identify any intrinsic limitation on the scope of human rights obligations that would apply to a State once we determine that extraterritoriality applies. That is, while scholars seem to want to argue that we should not worry, that the actual scope of human rights law implied in convergence is narrow or reasonable, this goes against the principle of indivisibility and leaves open the determination of which rights apply when (allowing States to pick and choose, to argue that "positive" obligations do not apply, or that only certain "negative" obligations are truly binding).

As I have argued above, in order for extraterritoriality to mean anything, and in order for *lex specialis* to be able to function as between two bodies of law, then human rights law must substantively add something to the current set of obligations and protections laid out in IHL. This seems only logical. If scholars and advocates are vigorously fighting for human rights law, arguing that the lack of application of this law would allow States to commit violations they would otherwise be prevented from committing at home, or that the true spirit of human rights law means that it must be applicable to an obliged State wherever it chooses to extend its authority, then surely they must believe that there are real, material aspects from the corpus of human rights law that will add to, transform, enhance or build upon the existing obligations of IHL. Yet, curiously, very few scholars or advocates have put forward such concrete proposals or examples of the substantive, normative contribution of human rights law application.

Instead, in the range of cases where advocates have sought to hold States accountable for their domestic human rights obligations in military action abroad, they seem to focus on substantive rules of human rights that have their exact corollaries in the protections of IHL. Most of the cases focus on torture or death in detention, transfer of detainees to custody where there is a risk of torture, targeting of civilians alleged to be participating in hostilities and killing of civilians. There is an excellent tactical reason for this: of all the differences between IHL and IHRL, perhaps the most important in this arena is that human rights law provides standing for individuals to claim their rights under international law, and to seek redress and remedy for violations against them. IHL, on the contrary, provides no such standing, and currently provides no avenues for individual complaints of violation under international humanitarian law or any obligation for violating States to provide redress or remedy to those against whom war crimes or grave breaches have been perpetrated.

Thus, the convergence of IHRL and IHL, and the extraterritorial application of human rights law in armed conflict, provides a crucially important and potentially revolutionary ability for individuals and their advocates to bring cases against States for violations. Because of the way that *lex specialis* functions, the procedural opening—the granting of standing to individuals—allows courts to assess and provide remedy for violations that are simultaneously contrary to a State's obligations both under IHRL *and* under IHL. Looking at the current cases, it may well be that the most important takeaway of all of this technical, lengthy debate over extraterritoriality, formal applicability of human rights law and parallel obligations comes down to, in practical terms, the possibility to bring individual claims against the State for damages or other remedy.

One might argue that this will have incredibly powerful implications for the protection of civilians in armed conflict. The more States are on alert that they may be subject to liability and findings for remedy in human rights bodies or under their domestic human rights law, the more they will improve their standards, limit violations of IHL, and take greater care with proportionality and distinction. Yet, it seems to me that such a position involves making tremendous sacrifices and ignoring considerable risks in order to gain the rare opportunity to bring such cases before courts. If human rights advocates are claiming that the true vision of extraterritorial applicability of human rights in armed conflict is that States will now be bound by the full panoply of human rights in their relationships with individuals on the territories they invade, but with the real intention of using these arguments to open up the opportunity to bring individual cases that involve violations of IHL, these advocates risk being blind to how the full force of their arguments will impact human rights law and practice in the long term.

In this light, the actual practice of convergence and extraterritoriality (as opposed to the soaring claims of its proponents) seems to be the best attempt at a workable solution to the problem of the lack of serious enforcement of IHL, and the lack of any capacity for individuals to demand that States recompense them for the damages wrought during war. While instrumentalizing human rights in this manner may provide short-term payoffs (one victim may receive compensation, one family may ensure that its son is not transferred to brutal detention conditions), it leaves unaddressed and untheorized the broader implications for how law functions in war. Also, this approach seems to make a promise that human rights lawyers do not intend to keep: it signals to individuals on the territory of an invaded State that those military forces who invade, occupy or detain have a qualitatively different relationship with them than that provided by IHL; it suggests that these individuals ought to expect a different type of behavior by these forces. Part of the reason we do not see much discussion of how this vision of the law will work in practice may be that there is actually little intent to develop rules for battlefield lawyering or training of soldiers, but only to create a mechanism for accountability *after* violations have taken place. This abdicates the responsibility set up by speaking in the language of human rights. Ultimately, having human rights *claims* means being able to know whom to go to to get the water turned on, to get food for your children, and to complain to when the police harass you or when your political party is shut down.

The paltry literature on what exactly a war imbued with human rights looks like *for the people living through it* leaves us wondering whether convergence can ever live up to its formalist promise that the law will be there, that the parties must apply all (or some?) of their human rights obligations in addition to their international humanitarian law responsibilities. What claims will people have in the midst of conflict? To whom should they take these claims? In coalition situations, which party is responsible to answer to the valid (at least legally) rights claims that convergence seems to encourage? Inviting reliance by civilians can be good for their human rights enjoyment only if we have some sense of the way in which the system will work. If the only purpose is to create claims after violations have occurred in a far-off land, it is not clear how this actually respects the human rights that convergence seeks to identify and demand.

Using human rights law, and the broad legal claim of extraterritoriality for this much narrower purpose, avoids doing the hard work of actually transforming and re-envisioning IHL in the way that most advocates would want. It allows lawyers to turn to the legalistic machinations of jurisdiction instead of advocating for the wholesale reconsideration of accountability in the laws of war. This is an important debate, one that must be had and one that is surely influenced by the ways that human rights law has transformed our global legal culture. As long as we pretend that the debate is about the full application of human rights law, when it is primarily about accountability mechanisms and remedies for victims of IHL violations, I would argue that we are not having the challenging and critical political battles that need to be fought in order to achieve the deeper ends of extraterritoriality. In this way, extraterritoriality takes energy away from the efforts to strengthen IHL and to make States more accountable for their actions in armed conflict.

A similar critique, and one that will likely be popular with those who oppose extraterritoriality on grounds of protecting military entitlements, is that the arguments for convergence and extraterritorial application can sometimes shade into backdoor pacifism. That is, to the extent that over-regulating the battlespace is not actually meant to develop a robust set of actual human rights obligations and their interpretations when taken to war, but instead meant to change the calculus for States when entering into armed conflict, joining coalitions or contributing troops to peace enforcement operations, this strikes me also as a misuse of human rights law and language. If advocates believe that human rights law (standing on its own, as applied to States on their own territories and through traditional mechanisms of human rights monitoring and enforcement) should in fact *prevent* States from going to war, or that it adds serious considerations to the *jus ad bellum* questions of the legality of war, then they should say so, and they should expand the provisions of human rights law that seem to support such an outcome.[92] Advocating for an unclear, vague, confusing admixture of human rights and IHL on the battlefield with the ultimate goal of influencing *jus ad bellum* encourages bad lawyering and avoids the much more compelling debates that could be taking place within human rights law about the costs of war itself.

Part III. Looking Ahead

If scholars and practitioners weigh the costs and risks I have discussed above, they should consider new approaches that address these dilemmas honestly and rigorously. With the goal of increasing protection of civilians in armed conflict, securing the human rights of all individuals, and enhancing the clarity and effectiveness of the regulations of parties to armed conflict, how might the field react to some of the above critiques? In this section, I want to propose some possible ways forward, not necessarily as pragmatic solutions to knotty legal problems, but to recast the question of how human rights law impacts the role of law in armed conflict.

There is no question that the interplay between international human rights law and international humanitarian law is here to stay. There is no going back to a clean separation between the two fields, if such a separation ever existed. More and more the key actors in armed conflict (militaries, State policymakers, humanitarian organizations, human rights groups) are merging the two discourses and identifying tools that draw on rules and mechanisms from both fields. How might we imagine paths ahead that recast the question of convergence? These four paths forward are not actually meant to be a practical list of approaches that I am necessarily advocating, or a list that does not entail dilemmas of its own. But, given the critiques above, and assuming we want to be more honest and rigorous about what we are doing in this area of law and policy, these possibilities suggest some ways that we might rethink the entire question of extraterritorial application of human rights in armed conflict.

Create New, Leaner Body of "Human Rights at War"

One possibility is that human rights scholars and practitioners, rather than focusing on the rules of international humanitarian law or how human rights law can directly interact with those rules, develop and expand a new field of "human rights at war." Such a project might take a number of forms. The central feature would be that it would focus on building consensus around the key aspects of human rights law that could practically apply during armed conflict, and focus on the ways in which human rights bodies and mechanisms could interpret and enhance such tools.

At the most ambitious level, this would involve strengthening or redrafting those aspects of human rights law that would severely limit the capacity of States to enter into armed conflict, and would develop the rules of IHRL to take a strong position on *jus ad bellum* determinations. As some scholars have suggested, there is much in the corpus and drafting background of human rights law that suggests a strongly contra-conflict posture. Here, lawyers and policymakers would identify and build upon those trends within the law, working with States to highlight the ways in which their human rights obligations bind them to limit their engagement in armed action altogether.

Such a human rights law of war, unhindered by the constraints of IHL, might even be proposed as a direct challenge to IHL—rethinking central assumptions and concepts that structure our contemporary thinking on justice in war. A law of human rights at war might directly question current understandings of proportionality, distinction, precautionary measures, occupation and treatment of detainees, using the drastically different language and approach of human rights law to rethink these categories in a far more civilian-protective mode. One could imagine that such a development of human rights would blend legal understandings of *jus ad bellum*, *jus in bello*, and post-conflict and stability operations to create an overall set of obligations for States that fight.[93]

While such an approach would certainly face a profound challenge in implementing a transformation of this scale, efforts in this direction would sharpen arguments *between* IHL and IHRL, and would insist on keeping in the foreground the serious (and I would argue, necessary) tensions between the two fields. Indeed, debates between States and scholars on such an approach could illuminate the ways in which human rights law and practice, outside of the well-defined and narrow discourse of IHL, might reshape our understanding of the normative constraints on armed conflict and the duties owed to civilians.

A less ambitious approach within this category would be a project among State parties to human rights treaties, human rights bodies and scholars to actively identify a subset of human rights provisions that create the toolkit of "human rights at war." Here, human rights advocates and scholars would have to be honest in acknowledging that they do not foresee the entirety of human rights law applying in armed conflict. Rather, they would identify the key provisions of human rights law that, different from protections and obligations already enshrined in IHL, would substantively add to what civilians could expect from State parties to armed conflict, and what civilians could demand under human rights law. This might involve a gathering of States to clarify consensus around key provisions, moving away from the current confusion of multiple layers of litigation, regional human rights bodies and domestic interpretations of convergence, providing support for this leaner, thinner body of human rights law.

Such an approach would provide an opportunity for the development of a new cadre of professionals: individuals with experience, background and influence in both IHL and IHRL, equipped with the tools of fact-finding and advocacy common to human rights, but also able to engage with military professionals and State policymakers in discussing the difficult choices that must be made during armed conflict. State involvement, buy-in and consent would be critical to such an enterprise, mitigating some of the legitimacy challenges discussed above.

While perhaps more pragmatic than the current approach, such a step would involve the risk of diminishing and narrowing human rights protections, and conceding that indivisibility would have to give way to the desire to introduce at least some robust human rights protections that all States understand must be operationalized and applied throughout their military planning and practice. Further, such an approach might lead to new engagements between human rights advocates and military professionals, focusing on those legal provisions that—through negotiation—are seen as applying in parallel to IHL provisions.

Develop and Strengthen Accountability Mechanisms in IHL

A second possible approach to the dilemmas discussed above might focus entirely on innovating around accountability mechanisms in IHL. Perhaps inspired by the ICJ's vague call for parallel application of the two bodies of law, such an approach might involve efforts to enhance existing accountability mechanisms within IHL (most existing Geneva Convention mechanisms are currently moribund) or to introduce some of the monitoring and accountability mechanisms present in the human rights system to IHL.[94]

At the strongest level, this could involve introducing a mechanism for individual complaints or individual standing under IHL at the international level. Examples might include creating mechanisms for individuals to make claims against the State domestically, or a centrally located international body that would hear claims, interpret the rules of IHL according to specific fact situations, and provide decisions, remedies and redress. Such a development would be outside of, and in addition to, existing mechanisms for internal military discipline, domestic war crimes legislation and international criminal law. Rather, such a body would focus solely on individual complaints against the State for violations of IHL in armed conflict (because this would not involve substantive human rights law, the mechanism would by nature have extraterritorial reach, applicable to any States engaging in the armed conflict at issue in the case).[95] In addition to hearing complaints and adjudicating cases, one could imagine that such a mechanism could also have a body that would oversee and interpret the rules of IHL in the same vein as many of the UN human rights treaty bodies.

Such an approach would involve a new drafting process, perhaps similar to the optional protocols created subsequent to a number of human rights treaties, seeking the consent of States to such a mechanism and creating new procedures for individual complaints cognizant of the particular needs of the IHL system, and calibrated to the realities of armed conflict. Given the deep dilemmas present in making the current legal interpretations of convergence a reality, one might argue that such an approach, while requiring major efforts at bringing together States and initiating a new process, holds a greater promise of long-term success and real results for victims than the divergent and often conflicting approaches of individual States to extraterritorial application of human rights in armed conflict.

This approach would have the advantage of creating a standardized mechanism for monitoring and accountability. Rather than relying on rare cases brought on behalf of individuals in foreign courts, States would be required to implement the necessary procedures within their armed forces to monitor compliance, investigate violations and alter behavior in response to findings of the new accountability mechanism. Because the military would necessarily be involved in such a process, the incentives to comply and participate would also be higher than the current approach of extraterritorial human rights application.

Finally, such an approach would have an additional advantage compared to the jurisdiction of human rights bodies: because it would be working with IHL, which binds non-State actors, it may also be in a position to hear individual claims against armed groups. While seeking redress or compensation from such groups would provide a major obstacle, the legal framework would exist to explore ways in which non-State parties to an armed conflict could also be brought into the accountability system.

Strengthen Territorial-State Mechanisms for Holding Actors Accountable for Violations

A third approach would indeed look to convergence, but a different breed of this argument than I have challenged in this paper. This possibility would seek to strengthen and embolden domestic human rights obligations and mechanisms during armed conflict (whether non-international or international). That is, this approach would focus on the continued parallel application of human rights law during armed conflict per the current dominant legal consensus, but *not* extraterritorial application of these rules.

As human rights advocates have pointed out in arguing for extraterritorial application of human rights law as a means (the only means) for accountability, we see contemporary cases where the United States and other States deny that they are engaged in an international armed conflict in countries such as Iraq, creating a gap in protective rules. As many have pointed out, the rules of non-international armed conflict are ill-suited to these contemporary situations, where major States are involved in massive combat, stability and State-building operations on the territory of another State, but without the rule framework of international armed conflict or occupation. In such a situation, it is less clear that IHL by itself is able to cover adequately the encounters between troops and Iraqis, or provide a clear set of roles and responsibilities for all actors involved. At first glance, it *does* appear that extraterritoriality, applied through the home State of the military forces, is the only available answer. Yet here it seems that advocates of extraterritoriality forget the role of the territorial State.

One approach to increasing protection in these contexts would be to insist that host States harness their power to hold all parties on their territory accountable for compliance with IHRL. In Iraq today, it is the Iraqi government that has the clearest and most well understood human rights obligations vis-à-vis the Iraqi people. This obligation to protect the rights of the people extends not only to the acts of the Iraqi State, but also implies that the government will protect Iraqis from any threats to their human rights that occur in Iraq.

In this model, human rights advocates and scholars would focus their energies not on extraterritorial application of human rights law in armed conflict, but rather on the ways that parallel application and convergence strengthen the hand of invaded States to insist that all actors comply with the *territorial State's* human rights obligations. Here, one could imagine that advocates could work with territorial-State courts and human rights bodies, strengthen their power to monitor and investigate abuses, and monitor closely the bilateral agreements and immunity clauses entered into by the territorial State with foreign States and their troops.

Of course, the reality is that the legal systems in many countries in the midst of or recovering from armed conflict are not well equipped to monitor and enforce human rights law. And for most Iraqis, the foreign military forces on their territory are not seen as accountable to Iraq, its government or its people. I am not suggesting that turning to Iraqi institutions to enforce and investigate human rights violations by those on its territory or within its jurisdiction would necessarily provide better results in the short term. It probably would not. Not only do Iraqi human rights organs and courts lack the capacity to adequately investigate alleged human rights violations by military forces or private military contractors, but they are faced with various immunity agreements, as well as the political impossibility of taking on a tremendous power imbalance. However, such efforts would allow the citizens and civilians in the State to understand what human rights law can actually promise them, and would provide a much more clear-eyed understanding of the current state of how human rights law applies in armed conflict.

Rather than drawing our attention to impractical legal claims for extraterritorial application, or emphasizing legal formality with no real intention of altering the substantive rules affecting invading State behavior, such an approach would build on human rights obligations where they are strongest, and empower the affected State to enhance accountability and transparency in the long term. Even if efforts to investigate and hold accountable foreign States fail, such a process, and such a public debate within the country itself, would make real the true promise of what human rights law and human rights discourse can do in a situation of conflict. To the extent that the current insistence on extraterritoriality is a tactical attempt to take advantage of more sophisticated and better understood courts in Europe, the United States and Canada in order to litigate complex human rights issues, it denies those who hold the rights in question the power to truly take ownership of their claims.

Indeed, this approach might flip the current power dynamic of human rights advocacy, shifting the center of gravity of the debate and its language away from Western capitals and toward the States most impacted by armed conflict (such as Iraq, Afghanistan and Pakistan). We might imagine that local human rights organizations and advocates would take the lead on determining how to craft human rights strategies appropriate to armed conflict, building their capacity to work with both human rights and IHL, and working with domestic lawyers and laws to enhance enforcement. This approach would also have the payoff of building up these domestic institutions for the long term: as parallel application of human rights and IHL would always be in the background, domestic human rights and legal mechanisms would increase their capacity to deal not only with foreign militaries, but also with the violations committed by internal armed groups operating within the State.

Move from Law to Policy, Emphasizing Pragmatism over Formal Legal Rules

In this final path, human rights advocates and scholars would need to get their hands dirty in actual military policymaking and planning. Rather than insisting on formal normative consensus, or repeatedly citing unclear and relatively impractical legal definitions of "effective control," "cause and effect" and other grounds for human rights jurisdiction, those following this approach would make a definitive turn away from law and toward policy.

Leaving behind the normative certainty of convergence and the trump card of rights talk, advocates and scholars might instead seek to formulate human rights in the language of military policy and planning. We increasingly see that the military references much of its behavior on policy grounds. Thus, detainee treatment going above the standards of IHL (such as providing advocates for detainees going before boards, or providing compensation for civilian victims of attacks) is often explained not on the basis of IHL (where States would normally deny that they have such obligations) or formal human rights obligation, but rather as a matter of policy (a policy that may well be presented as influenced by a number of factors including human rights, counterterrorism and nation building).

It may well be that human rights talk and rights culture have, to varying degrees based on the country in question and its domestic rhetoric around rights and international law, been absorbed into military and State thinking on strategic and policy decisions on the ground. Indeed, one could likely trace the human rights origins of key provisions in individual coalition member's detention policies in Iraq and Afghanistan, or in important paragraphs of their bilateral security arrangements with those nations. Human rights actors and scholars can and should be proud of such impact on strategy and policymaking, and that the absorption of human rights norms into bilateral agreements,[96] detention policies, rules of engagement, counterinsurgency doctrine[97] and even individual orders in the field may well result in improved conditions and treatment of civilians and prisoners inspired by the content of human rights instruments.

But we should not forget that there is a difference between decision making and conduct on the basis of policy, and obligations to act as a matter of law. At the margins, and in areas where interpretations of law are wildly divergent, formalism may still matter. To the extent that concerns about the specifics of applying convergence, or "operationalizing" its norms, are dismissed by States with claims that human rights law is already applied as a matter of policy, or that it is already part and parcel of any on-the-ground decision-making environment, it is worth pointing out that when a detainee brings a claim for remedy on the basis of international human rights law, or when a humanitarian organization is attempting to understand its roles and responsibilities on the ground, actual legal obligations will determine outcomes.

However, this approach could be the most impactful of all in terms of real change to State and military behavior, and tangible increases in protection, treatment and respect for basic rights. While it involves considerable sacrifices in terms of the types of argumentation available to human rights advocates, and while it moves away from the current focus on litigation, this approach would facilitate more fluid negotiations with the military planners and decisionmakers on the ground and at the capital level, leaving law and obligations out of the room and focusing on the practical ways in which States can improve their outcomes by incorporating human rights principles into the day-to-day operations of soldiers. I imagine that one reason this approach would be unattractive to many human rights advocates is that it would involve, first, promoting human rights in a context that might involve justifying these principles on the basis of counterterrorism, counterinsurgency, increased cooperation of the population with the military, increased acquiescence of the population to the policy desires of foreign States, etc. Second, such an approach would necessarily mean getting involved with the ugly realities of military decision making, accepting that not all legal rights–holders will be granted protections in the same way, and that military security will likely always trump policy-based rights and protections. Finally, contrary to much of human rights advocacy that relies on soliciting public support and eliciting public outrage, this approach would likely need to be confidential, involving little engagement with the public and focusing on identifying compelling and practical tools that will convince States that it is in their interests to embrace aspects of human rights into their military policies, rules of engagement and orders.

That said, this approach may facilitate a discussion and practical engagement with human rights in armed conflict that moves out of academic scholarship and discussions at conferences over *lex specialis*, and shifts to the real choices human rights advocates expect military leaders and soldiers to make on the ground. Rather than engaging in an adversarial conversation mediated by courts or human rights bodies, this approach would ask that human rights advocates envision rights through the prism of armed conflict, and from the perspective of the military. This raises a number of serious concerns about the extent to which this would still be human rights advocacy as we know it, but it may also pave the way for actual and significant changes in on-the-ground decisions, and in the ability of individuals caught in armed conflict to lead more dignified lives.

Notes

1. I will use IHL and LOAC (law of armed conflict) interchangeably throughout, while acknowledging and appreciating Yoram Dinstein's call to refer to this body of law as LOAC exclusively. YORAM DINSTEIN, THE CONDUCT OF HOSTILITIES UNDER THE INTERNATIONAL LAW OF ARMED CONFLICT 13–14 (2004).

2. Theodor Meron, *The Humanization of Humanitarian Law*, 94 AMERICAN JOURNAL OF INTERNATIONAL LAW 239, 243–44 (2000). Meron's article was part of the first wave of work on this issue, and did not call for the full implementation of human rights in international armed conflict as it is sometimes imagined today.

3. I will be using the terms "convergence," "parallel application" and "co-application" interchangeably to refer to the concept that international human rights law and international humanitarian law are applicable simultaneously during armed conflict, and that States are obligated to comply with obligations under both bodies of law (including obligations to report to relevant legal bodies, cooperate with organizations, etc.), and that to some extent, individual soldiers can potentially be liable for violations of either or both bodies of law for their conduct during hostilities outside of the territorial State. While it could be argued that "convergence" and "parallel application" represent different methods of co-applicability, with the former indicating a sudden

moment when both bodies of law come together and create a single legal framework blending provisions from both regimes, and the latter representing dual and *distinct* legal frameworks that apply independently of one another until and unless they come into direct contact, the literature seems to treat the two terms as having the same meaning and resulting in similar implications in terms of legal framework.

4. Any argument that attempts to take on a topic on which there has been so much scholarship runs the risk of becoming mired in a literature review or a rehashing of existing material. There is a tremendous amount of writing on both the general topic of overlap between IHRL and IHL, and the various subtopics within the broad issue of convergence. Indeed, two recent full volumes of law journals were dedicated exactly to this issue. *See* 40 ISRAEL LAW REVIEW (2007); 90 INTERNATIONAL REVIEW OF THE RED CROSS (2008). For an understanding of the broad issues related to overlap and convergence, see, e.g., Noam Lubell, *Parallel Application of International Humanitarian Law and International Human Rights Law: An Examination of the Debate*, 40 ISRAEL LAW REVIEW 648 (2007); for a focus on human rights law in occupation, see Aeyal M. Gross, *Human Proportions: Are Human Rights the Emperor's New Clothes of the International Law of Occupation?*, 18 EUROPEAN JOURNAL OF INTERNATIONAL LAW 1, 8 (2007); Danio Campanelli, *The Law of Military Occupation Put to the Test of Human Rights Law*, 90 INTERNATIONAL REVIEW OF THE RED CROSS 653 (2008); for a clear articulation of the contra-convergence position, see Michael J. Dennis, *Non-Application of Civil and Political Rights Treaties Extraterritorially During Times of International Armed Conflict*, 40 ISRAEL LAW REVIEW 453 (2007); for a very useful and comprehensive review of the relevant international jurisprudence on the debate, see John Cerone, *Human Dignity in the Line of Fire: The Application of International Human Rights Law During Armed Conflict, Occupation, and Peace Operations*, 39 VANDERBILT JOURNAL OF TRANSNATIONAL LAW 1447 (2006); for the leading analysis of how human rights norms might impact right to life and use of force issues, see Kenneth Watkin, *Controlling the Use of Force: A Role for Human Rights Norms in Contemporary Armed Conflict*, 98 AMERICAN JOURNAL OF INTERNATIONAL LAW 1, 9 (2004).

5. International Covenant on Economic, Social and Cultural Rights art. 13, G.A. Res. 2200A (XXI), U.N. Doc. A/6316 (Dec. 16, 1966), 993 U.N.T.S. 3 [hereinafter ICESCR].

6. *Id.*, art. 12.

7. *Id.*, art. 11.

8. *Id.*, art. 10(1).

9. International Covenant on Civil and Political Rights art. 18, G.A. Res. 2200A (XXI), U.N. Doc. A/6316 (Dec. 16, 1966), 999 U.N.T.S. 171 [hereinafter ICCPR].

10. *Id.*, arts. 9, 14.

11. ICESCR, *supra* note 5, art. 8.

12. ICCPR, *supra* note 9, art. 25.

13. *Id.*, art. 18.

14. Because of the sheer volume of writing on this issue in recent years, my goal here is not to do justice to the many contributions on the question of convergence, nor to focus on the nuance within each sub-issue of the debate. Rather, I want to try to give a rough map of the key issues in the debate, before moving into the critique. For a more detailed review of the current debate, see Lubell, *supra* note 4.

15. Armed Activities on the Territory of the Congo (Dem. Rep. Congo v. Uganda), 2005 I.C.J. 116, ¶ 216 (Dec. 19); Legal Consequences of the Construction of a Wall in the Occupied Palestinian Territory, Advisory Opinion, 2004 I.C.J. 136, ¶ 106 (July 9) [hereinafter Wall Advisory Opinion]; Issa and Others v. Turkey, App. No. 31821/96, 41 Eur. Ct. H.R. Rep. 567 (2004) [hereinafter Issa]; U.N. Human Rights Committee, *General Comment No. 31: The Nature of the*

General Legal Obligation Imposed on States Parties to the Covenant, ¶ 10, U.N. Doc. CCPR/C/21/Rev.1/Add.13 (May 26, 2004) [hereinafter General Comment No. 31]; Françoise J. Hampson, *The Relationship between International Humanitarian Law and Human Rights Law from the Perspective of a Human Rights Treaty Body*, 90 INTERNATIONAL REVIEW OF THE RED CROSS 549 (2008).

16. *See generally* Dieter Fleck, *Individual and State Responsibility for Violations of the Ius in Bello: An Imperfect Balance*, *in* INTERNATIONAL HUMANITARIAN LAW FACING NEW CHALLENGES (SYMPOSIUM IN HONOUR OF KNUT IPSEN) 171 (Wolff Heintschel von Heinegg & Volker Epping eds., 2007). Fleck notes,

> It is not only the *lex specialis* character of international humanitarian law, but even more so the particular deficiencies of law application in international armed conflicts, non-international armed conflicts and internal disturbances which makes the exercise of individual and international responsibility a complex, difficult and often hopeless task. Lawyers, tasked to find appropriate remedies for violations of international humanitarian law, are navigating in foggy areas in which relevant provisions are not too systematic and more than often competing interests obscure what should be achieved for restoring peace and justice.

Id. at 173.

17. *E.g.*, Prosecutor v. Galic, Case No. IT-98-29-T, Judgment and Order, ¶¶ 706, 719 (Dec. 5, 2003).

18. See, e.g., COMMENTARY ON THE ADDITIONAL PROTOCOLS OF 8 JUNE 1977 TO THE GENEVA CONVENTIONS OF 12 AUGUST 1949, at 950, ¶ 3346 (Yves Sandoz, Christophe Swinarski & Bruno Zimmermann eds., 1987), which notes,

> Thus historically, the law of armed conflict was created largely in the heat of battle, and the weight and obligation of its implementation and development rests primarily on the shoulders of those who exercise military command in the field. To withdraw this fundamental responsibility—which has always been that of military commanders—from them, would undoubtedly have constituted a serious error, and the Protocol was careful to avoid this.

19. *E.g.*, ICCPR, *supra* note 9, arts. 18, 19; ICESCR, *supra* note 5, arts. 9, 11; Convention on the Elimination of All Forms of Discrimination against Women arts. 13, 14, Dec. 18, 1979, 1249 U.N.T.S. 13; International Convention on the Elimination of All Forms of Racial Discrimination arts. 2, 5, Mar. 7, 1966, 660 U.N.T.S. 195 [hereinafter CERD].

20. Lubell, *supra* note 4, at 650.

21. Cordula Droege, *Elective Affinities? Human Rights and Humanitarian Law*, 90 INTERNATIONAL REVIEW OF THE RED CROSS 501, 548 (2008). See also Lubell, *supra* note 4, at 660, which concludes, using the analogy of a difficult but worthwhile romantic relationship that seems common in this genre of scholarship:

> It is clear that while International Humanitarian Law and International Human Rights Law have been engaged in a relationship for many years, there are still some rocky patches that need to be navigated before we can be assured that the two branches of law can live together happily ever after.

22. *See, e.g.*, Dennis, *supra* note 4, at 453–502. Mr. Dennis is a long-standing attorney in the Office of the Legal Adviser, US Department of State.

23. One author notes, "Few states have contested, vis-à-vis the human rights bodies, the application of the human rights treaties abroad. Apart from Israel, it is doubtful whether any state

has consistently objected to the extraterritorial application of human rights instruments." Droege, *supra* note 21, at 519.

24. *See, e.g.*, Watkin, *supra* note 4, at 9 (noting that "[t]he normative framework of international humanitarian law differs in many respects from that of international human rights law"). The relative or married couple metaphor is seen often in writing on this topic. *See, e.g.*, Robert Kolb, *The Relationship between International Humanitarian Law and Human Rights Law: A Brief History of the 1948 Universal Declaration of Human Rights and the 1949 Geneva Conventions*, 80 INTERNATIONAL REVIEW OF THE RED CROSS, 409 (1998) (noting, "Today there can no longer be any doubt: international humanitarian law and international human rights law are near relations"). *See also* Louise Doswald-Beck & Sylvain Vité, *International Humanitarian Law and Human Rights Law*, 293 INTERNATIONAL REVIEW OF THE RED CROSS (1993) 94–119, at 94 (stating that "as human rights law and humanitarian law have totally different historical origins, the codification of these laws has until very recently followed entirely different lines").

25. Dennis, *supra* note 4, at 453.

26. *See, e.g.*, Prosecutor v. Furundzija, Case No. IT-95-17/1-T, Judgment, ¶ 183 (Dec. 10, 1998) (noting that "[t]he general principle of respect for human dignity is the basic underpinning and indeed the very *raison d'etre* of international humanitarian law and human rights law").

27. Meron, *supra* note 2, at 239.

28. Hampson, *supra* note 15, at 561. *See also* Nancie Prud'homme, Lex Specialis: *Oversimplifying a More Complex and Multifaceted Relationship?*, 40 ISRAEL LAW REVIEW 356 (2007).

29. Dennis, *supra* note 4, at 453.

30. G.I.A.D. Draper, *The Relationship between the Human Rights Regime and the Law of Armed Conflict*, 1 ISRAEL YEARBOOK OF HUMAN RIGHTS 191 (1971).

31. *See* Dan E. Stigall, Christopher L. Blakesley & Chris Jenks, *Human Rights and Military Decisions: Counterinsurgency and Trends in the International Law of Armed Conflict*, 30 UNIVERSITY OF PENNSYLVANIA JOURNAL OF INTERNATIONAL LAW 1367, 1370 (2009) [hereinafter Stigall et al.].

32. *See, e.g.*, Ralph Wilde, *Triggering State Obligations Extraterritorially: The Spatial Test in Certain Human Rights Treaties*, 40 ISRAEL LAW REVIEW 503, 516 (2007).

33. Human rights are not based on the status of citizenship in any formal sense; I use the term here to denote the concept of a member of a community, a person in a society that relates to a government, a member of a civil polity. While, of course, human rights protections extend to individuals who find themselves on the territory of an obliged State even for a short period of time, the bulk of human rights law, jurisprudence and scholarship focuses on the relationship between the governed and the governors, those who are part of a society for the long term and those who are in power in that society.

34. Al-Skeini v. Secretary of State for Defence [2007] UKHL 26 [hereinafter Al-Skeini (HL)].

35. See, e.g., Wilde, *supra* note 32, and Hampson, *supra* note 15, for critiques of the Al-Skeini (HL) decision.

36. Al-Skeini (HL), *supra* note 34, ¶ 109.

37. *Id.*, ¶¶ 127, 129.

38. *See* DINSTEIN, *supra* note 1, at 21–22.

39. One of the rare articles to take a critical view of convergence theories from the perspective of concern for civilians (as opposed to from a military or State entitlement perspective) is an important piece by Tel Aviv University Professor Aeyal Gross, questioning the application of human rights law in the most long-standing military occupation in contemporary history, that of Israel in the Occupied Palestinian Territory. Gross argues that

> [rights] analysis is usually best at identifying and treating individual localized violations, which are deemed the exception in a regime where democracy and human rights are the norm. In the context of occupation, where the norm is the denial of rights and the lack of democracy, rights analysis may distort the picture by pointing to rights denial as the exception rather than the norm. Rights analysis is weak at creating structural changes. The result, even if the rights of the people living under occupation prevail in specific cases, may often be the legitimation of rights' denial rather than the opposite: cases where individuals win rights' victories may create the myth of a "benign occupation" that protects human rights even though they are mostly denied.

Gross, *supra* note 4, at 8. Gross's significant article seems to have gained little notice in the literature on convergence, and I hope to argue here that his analysis can and should be expanded to include situations beyond the Israeli/Palestinian conflict, and the specifics of long-term occupation.

40. Wilde, *supra* note 32, at 518–19.

41. *Id.* at 519.

42. Al-Skeini v. Sec. of State for Defence [2005] EWCA 1609 (Civ.), ¶¶ 196–97, *quoted in* Wilde, *supra* note 32, at 519 [hereinafter Al-Skeini (Civ.)].

43. Wall Advisory Opinion, *supra* note 15, ¶ 106.

44. Prud'homme, *supra* note 28.

45. The *Al-Skeini* decision recognizes the problem in reviewing existing ECtHR decisions, noting,

> The problem which the House has to face, quite squarely, is that the judgments and decisions of the European Court do not speak with one voice. If the differences were merely in emphasis, they could be shrugged off as being of no great significance. In reality, however, some of them appear much more serious and so present considerable difficulties for national courts which have to try to follow the jurisprudence of the European Court.

Al-Skeini (HL), *supra* note 34, ¶ 67.

In its leading case on this issue, the Canada Federal Court of Appeal also recognizes the challenge posed to national courts attempting to understand the current interpretation of the law on this issue, noting that "the current state of international jurisprudence in this area is somewhat uncertain." Amnesty International Canada v. Canada (Chief of the Defence Staff), [2008] 4 F.C. 546, ¶ 214 [hereinafter Amnesty v. Canada]. A range of scholars across the spectrum of the debate has also recognized the lack of clarity on this issue. *See, e.g.*, Dennis, *supra* note 4, at 482 (noting that "there is no clear understanding concerning the precise manner in which the obligations assumed by states under international human rights treaties interact with the *lex specialis* of international humanitarian law, if it is assumed the former apply extraterritorially during periods of armed conflict and military occupation"); Françoise Hampson, *Is Human Rights Law of Any Relevance to Military Operations in Afghanistan?*, *in* THE WAR IN AFGHANISTAN: A LEGAL ANALYSIS 485, 510 (Michael N. Schmitt ed., 2009) (Vol. 85, US Naval War College International Law Studies) (noting that "[h]uman rights bodies and the ICJ are of the view that [human rights law] also applies to cases of military occupation but it is not clear how human rights bodies understand the concept of occupation, and the application of human rights law is not free of theoretical and practical difficulties. What is wholly unclear is the extent to which and the manner in which it applies in other extraterritorial circumstances, particularly to the conduct of military operations"); Stigall et al., *supra* note 31, at 1372 (stating that "various countries, regional organizations and international organizations differ in their position on the proper extraterritorial application or jurisdictional scope of their own and international human rights norms"); Droege, *supra* note 21, at 502 (reiterating the current confusion over how the two bodies of law can apply coherently, and stating that "[j]urisprudence on concrete cases will, hopefully, provide more clarity over time. . . . [S]ome areas are becoming clearer and in other areas patterns are emerging but are not consolidated").

46. This is not a new observation, and is certainly not a critique that applies equally across the board. Several scholars, particularly in the newest iterations of the debate, do seek to propose improved theoretical models for applying *lex specialis*, for harmonizing IHRL and IHL. In addition, some recognize the current paucity of thinking within pro-convergence scholarship on application. Citing another notoriously vague phrase in the (quasi-)jurisprudence on the issue, the UN Human Rights Committee's language in General Comment 31 noting that "[w]hile in respect of certain Covenant rights, more specific rules of international humanitarian law may be specially relevant for the purposes of the interpretation of Covenant rights, both spheres of law are complementary, not mutually exclusive," the author notes,

> Such generalizations are unlikely to offer solace to those tasked with the responsibility for implementation of the complementarity principle in the field. Thus, given the adoption of this doctrine, there would appear to be merit in exploring the capacity for a joint general comment between the Committee bodies, which could offer guidance on how to address the challenges and obstacles associated with the application of human rights norms during armed conflict and their relationship with international humanitarian law. In the absence of such direction, the clarity and precision necessary to implement complementarity will remain missing.

John Tobin, *Seeking Clarity in Relation to the Principle of Complementarity: Reflections on the Recent Contributions of Some International Bodies*, 8 MELBOURNE JOURNAL OF INTERNATIONAL LAW 356, 366 (2007).

47. Michelle A. Hansen, *Preventing the Emasculation of Warfare: Halting the Expansion of Human Rights Law into Armed Conflict*, 194 MILITARY LAW REVIEW 1, 51 (2007).

48. In a striking example, one scholar states, "This article holds that, undoubtedly, human rights law speaks about and to armed conflict," and then appends the following footnote to the sentence: "Admittedly such an application does raise some difficulties." Karima Bennoune, *Toward a Human Rights Approach to Armed Conflict: Iraq 2003*, 11 UC DAVIS JOURNAL OF INTERNATIONAL LAW AND POLICY 171, 196 n.125 (2004).

49. I am not suggesting that human rights law is necessarily more difficult to translate into military application or that it would be impossible to craft tactical battle rules based on human rights law—rather that this work seems not to have been done by many promoting extraterritorial applicability. Dale Stephens addresses this issue elegantly in his analysis of the debate over the relationship between the two bodies of law. Dale Stephens, *Human Rights and Armed Conflict: The Advisory Opinion of the International Court of Justice in the Nuclear Weapons Case*, 4 YALE HUMAN RIGHTS & DEVELOPMENT LAW JOURNAL 1 (2001).

50. It is telling that the two leading articles providing such a clear-eyed and practical-minded overview of how LOAC practice and theory would be impacted by co-application are written by senior military law scholars. Watkin, *supra* note 4, at 9; and Stephens, *supra* note 49.

51. Wall Advisory Opinion, *supra* note 15, ¶ 111; General Comment No. 31, *supra* note 15, ¶ 10; Bankovic v. Belgium et al., App. No. 52207/99, 2001-XII Eur. Ct. H.R. 333; Issa *supra* note 15; Coard et al. v. the United States, Case 10.951, Inter-Am. C.H.R., Report No. 109/99, Sept. 29, 1999.

52. Françoise Hampson's assessment is incredibly useful to keep in mind here. She notes, "Human rights more generally refers to values and precepts that may (or should) be the basis of

policy decisions, such as the rule of law, democracy, participation, transparency and accountability. Human rights in this sense is part of the 'good governance' agenda." Hampson, *supra* note 45, at 486.

53. One scholar, after providing an exhaustive review of the relevant case law, concludes,

> It thus appears that states remain bound by human rights law even when engaged in hostilities far from their home territories. Even during the invasion phase of an armed conflict, it would seem that a state would exercise sufficient control over any individuals with whom its forces come in contact for those individuals to fall within the scope of beneficiaries of that state's human rights obligations. This, however, does not mean that the content of those obligations would be the same as if the individuals in question were within the home territory of that state. The scope of the obligation, at least in terms of the level of obligation as explained above, will vary with the degree of control exercised in the circumstances. Once an individual is taken into detention by the state, the degree of control over the individual will clearly have increased.

Cerone, *supra* note 4, at 1507.

54. Haider Ala Hamoudi, *Reconsidering the 'Rule of Law' in Iraq*, JURIST, Sept. 8, 2009, http://jurist.law.pitt.edu/forumy/2009/09/reconsidering-rule-of-law-in-iraq.php.

55. *See, e.g.*, Brief for Interights et al. as Amici Curiae Supporting Appellants and Respondents, Al-Skeini (HL), *available at* http://www.interights.org/view-document/index.htm?id=245; *see generally* Rachel Brett, *Non-governmental Human Rights Organizations and International Humanitarian Law*, 80 INTERNATIONAL REVIEW OF THE RED CROSS 531–36 (1998).

56. S.C. Res. 1894, U.N. Doc. S/RES/1894 (Nov. 11, 2009) (noting "that the deliberate targeting of civilians as such and other protected persons, and the commission of systematic, flagrant and widespread violations of applicable international humanitarian and human rights law in situations of armed conflict may constitute a threat to international peace and security . . ."); GERARD MCHUGH, STRENGTHENING PROTECTION OF CHILDREN THROUGH ACCOUNTABILITY: THE ROLE OF THE UN SECURITY COUNCIL IN HOLDING TO ACCOUNT PERSISTENT VIOLATORS OF CHILDREN'S RIGHTS AND PROTECTIONS IN SITUATIONS OF ARMED CONFLICT (2009) (in a report discussing the role of the UN Security Council in holding violators of children's rights and protections in armed conflict accountable, noting that "[t]he term '*children's rights and protections*' is used throughout this report to include the human rights of children as specified in the Convention on the Rights of the Child and other international human rights Covenants and treaties, as well as the protections afforded to children (by virtue of the obligations to parties to armed conflict) in situations of armed conflict under applicable treaty-based and customary international humanitarian law").

57. Program on Humanitarian Policy and Conflict Research at Harvard University, Live Seminar: Human Rights in the Battlefield: Litigating Violations in Iraq (Sept. 22, 2009), http://ihlforum.ning.com/events/human-rights-in-the (password required).

58. *See, e.g.*, Office of the United Nations High Commissioner for Human Rights, *Summary of National Initiatives Undertaken within the World Programme for Human Rights Education (2005–Ongoing)*, http://www2.ohchr.org/english/issues/education/training/Summary-national-initiatives2005-2009.htm (last visited Nov. 16, 2009); Alfred M. Boll, *The Asian Values Debate and Its Relevance to International Humanitarian Law*, 83 INTERNATIONAL REVIEW OF THE RED CROSS 45 (2001).

59. *See, e.g.*, René Provost, *International Committee of the Red Widget? The Diversity Debate and International Humanitarian Law*, 40 ISRAEL LAW REVIEW 614 (2007); Ramesh Thakur, *Global Norms and International Humanitarian Law: An Asian Perspective*, 83 INTERNATIONAL REVIEW OF THE RED CROSS 19 (2001).

60. Al-Skeini v. Secretary of State for Defence [2004] EWHC 2911 ¶ 103 (Admin.).

61. A slightly different way of thinking about this is presented in the excellent and thought-provoking piece by Aeyal Gross, who notes,

> [G]overnment-governed relationships exist during occupation as well, although they assume a different nature because the ruled have not given their consent and the ruler is not accountable. Transplanting human rights to a situation of occupation may thus blur its inherently undemocratic rights-denying nature, and confer upon it the perceived legitimacy of an accountable regime.

Gross, *supra* note 4, at 33.

62. *See, e.g.*, Bennoune, *supra* note 48, at 205 (noting specific rights that would apply in the Iraq war); Cerone, *supra* note 4, at 1498–1507 (arguing that the level of obligation of States acting abroad varies in current legal interpretation, and that there is likely a "variable scope of obligation," where so-called negative rights would apply frequently extraterritorially, and so-called positive rights might apply according to a reasonableness test where "the adoption of affirmative measures is only required when and to the extent that the relevant party de jure or de facto enjoys a position of control that would make the adoption of such measures reasonable." *Id.* at 1505); Stigall et al., *supra* note 31, at 1375 (arguing that "[t]he proper rule in situations of military occupation or control is to apply basic human rights norms extraterritorially . . .").

63. World Conference on Human Rights, June 14–25, 1993, *Vienna Declaration and Programme of Action* art. 5, U.N. Doc. A/CONF.157/24 pt. 1 (July 12, 1993) (declaring that "[a]ll human rights are universal, indivisible and interdependent and interrelated"); International Conference on Human Rights, April 22–May 13, 1968, *Proclamation of Teheran* art. 3, U.N. Doc. A/CONF. 32/41 (May 13, 1968) ("Since human rights and fundamental freedoms are indivisible, the full realization of civil and political rights without the enjoyment of economic, social and cultural rights is impossible").

64. Bankovic, *supra* note 51, ¶ 75.

65. Al-Skeini (HL), *supra* note 34, ¶ 79.

66. Amnesty v. Canada, *supra* note 45, ¶¶ 310, 311.

67. Al-Skeini (Civ.), *supra* note 42, ¶ 196.

68. I am not addressing here the question of an occupying power's (in the IHL sense) obligation to apply the laws in force in the occupied territory. In reality, of course, most of the "core" rights that are regularly referenced as applying extraterritorially would indeed apply through this mechanism. But the convergence argument seems to want to avoid limiting the extraterritorial applicability of IHRL to situations of military occupation, and indeed its insistence on the additional application of IHRL would suggest that its proponents believe that *some* obligations would be added on top of the already existing obligations under IHL.

69. Many authors refer to the principle as one tool for resolving the problems that arise from parallel application. For a comprehensive treatment of the history of this principle in addressing convergence, *see* Prud'homme, *supra* note 28, at 355–78.

70. *Id.* at 383.

71. There remains, of course, the major issue of accountability and enforcement mechanisms (human rights principles that would not be negated by even the most muscular use of *lex specialis*), which I will address in below sections.

72. *See* Hampson, *supra* note 15, at 560.

73. For a useful attempt at clarifying the various ways in which the rules would interact, and how *lex specialis* might operate in context, see Orna Ben-Naftali & Yuval Shany, *Living in Denial: The Co-application of Humanitarian Law and Human Rights Law to the Occupied Territories*, 37 ISRAEL LAW REVIEW 17 (2004).

74. Hampson notes,

> The solution to the *lex specialis* problem in practice has to be capable of being applied by those involved at the time they act or take decisions. It cannot be determined after the event, even if that is when it is enforced. . . . Some way needs to be found to develop a coherent approach to the problem.

Hampson, *supra* note 15, at 562.

75. One scholar notes,

> A further explanation for the increased interest in IHL among human rights groups has been the increasingly technocratic and professional nature of some international human rights work. Becoming versed in the intricacies of IHL has allowed human rights advocates to talk like experts and to find a place at the table with military officials and government representatives, debating the choice of targets. This was a pragmatic endeavor which in many ways made sense. Still, too many important concessions can be made for a place at the table when the terms of the discussion held there have already been set.

Bennoune, *supra* note 48, at 222.

76. *See id.* at 214 (noting that "when a war is patently illegal, . . . if the only mode of analyzing the conflict is humanitarian law, then the central illegality, which is the wellspring of all other violations, will be overlooked"). An interesting argument is made by William A. Schabas, in one of the very few analyses critiquing the impact that convergence might have on human rights law and practice, who notes, in illustrating how IHL does not consider the "legitimate aim" (in a human rights law sense) of a State in assessing the legality of a military attack,

> This is where the attempts to marry international human rights law and international humanitarian law break down. International human rights law is not indifferent and does not look favorably upon unjust war. Indeed, it might be said that there is an anti-war or pacifist dimension to international human rights law that is largely absent—for understandable and logical reasons—from international humanitarian law.

William A. Schabas, Lex Specialis? *Belt and Suspenders? The Parallel Operation of Human Rights Law and the Law of Armed Conflict, and the Conundrum of* Jus Ad Bellum, 40 ISRAEL LAW REVIEW 592, 607 (2007).

77. By way of example, one former Pentagon targeting specialist who went on to become a military analyst at Human Rights Watch has noted that "[t]he administration of President George W. Bush sanctioned up to 30 civilian deaths for each attack on a high-value target in the Iraq war." Suzanne Koelbl, *The Pentagon Official Who Came in from the Cold*, SPIEGEL ONLINE INTERNATIONAL, Apr. 3, 2009, http://www.spiegel.de/international/world/0,1518,617279,00.html (last visited Nov. 11, 2009). Whether or not this is an accurate number, the point is that IHL forces us to speak in such terms, and its language is often focused on precisely such an impossible calculus. Many human rights lawyers and advocates find this very concept repugnant; indeed, they find such an approach anathema to the notion of human rights. Human rights lawyers' arguments and claims, *outside of IHL*, may be critical to ultimately changing the way States understand armed conflict, or the degree of support that home-State populations are willing to grant for political decisions taken to go to war or behavior in war. The more they are brought into the language and discourse of IHL, the more they are complicit in the balancing of military necessity and humanity, the less they are able to fulfill this vital function. *See* Sharon Otterman, The Calculus of Civilian Casualties, NEW YORK TIMES NEWS BLOG, http://thelede.blogs.nytimes.com/2009/01/06/the-calculus-of-civilian-casualties/ (Jan. 6, 2009) (noting that

the acceptance of thirty civilian deaths per high-value target was also reiterated by General T. Michael Moseley).

78. In her subtle and pragmatic analysis of the issues facing human rights bodies that take on issues of international humanitarian law, Françoise Hampson sets out the dilemmas the current array of legal options presents to human rights bodies seeking to utilize *lex specialis*, engaging in classification and determining in what instances human rights law would demand a higher level of protection than international humanitarian law. She is ultimately critical of the current approach of human rights courts to the issue of extraterritorial application (to the extent that the interpretation is limited to situations of occupation, however defined, and situations of detention) for ignoring the ICJ decision that human rights law continues to apply in armed conflict and because it would allow States a much broader leeway than they would receive from the same human rights courts in situations of non-international armed conflict. Ultimately, despite the significant challenges she illuminates, Hampson is optimistic (I would argue overly so), noting that "[t]he test for any solution is that it must be both coherent and practical and should seek to avoid diminishing existing protection. It ought to be possible to achieve consensus on the implications in practice on the simultaneous applicability of IHL and human rights law." Hampson, *supra* note 15, at 572.

79. Al-Skeini (HL), *supra* note 34, ¶ 78.

80. *See, e.g.*, Stigall et al., *supra* note 31, at 1375 (stating that "[t]he suggestion that application of these norms extraterritorially is a form of cultural imperialism is preposterous").

81. Al-Skeini (HL), *supra* note 34, ¶ 129.

82. *Id.*, ¶ 141.

83. Wilde, *supra* note 32, at 522.

84. *Id.* at 521.

85. *Id.* at 522.

86. For an analysis of the relationship between Islamic law and international human rights law, see Naz K. Modirzadeh, *Taking Islamic Law Seriously: INGOs and the Battle for Muslim Hearts and Minds*, 19 HARVARD HUMAN RIGHTS JOURNAL 181 (2004).

87. Issa, *supra* note 15, ¶ 71 [emphasis added].

88. Stigall et al., *supra* note 31, at 1375.

89. Amnesty v. Canada, *supra* note 45, ¶ 152.

90. *Id.*, ¶ 172.

91. *See, e.g.*, Dennis, *supra* note 4, at 471–72.

92. Two scholars discussed above do make such a bold claim, and wisely bypass the well-trod convergence/extraterritoriality arguments in order to argue that human rights law actually demands that States avoid war. *See* Schabas, *supra* note 76; Bennoune, *supra* note 48.

93. There is some development in this direction in recent scholarship, providing an aggressive frontal challenge to IHL and its underpinnings from the perspective of human rights law and moral philosophy. *See* David S. Koller, *The Moral Imperative: Toward a Human Rights–Based Law of War*, 46 HARVARD INTERNATIONAL LAW JOURNAL 231 (2005) (stating that "the commonly shared understanding of the concept of human rights provides a solid basis for drafting replacements for the IHL principles of discrimination, and proportionality, resulting in a human rights–based law of war." *Id.* at 243–44). *See also* Bennoune, discussed *supra* note 48.

94. *See* Watkin, *supra* note 4, at 9 (noting that "[t]he approach to the control of force in armed conflict as the exclusive domain of international humanitarian law is facing an intensified effort to have it encompass human rights norms and their associated accountability structure").

95. One scholar considers such a possibility, but ultimately rejects it:

> It might be tempting to propose a radical solution: the creation of a right of individual petition for violations of IHL which would be submitted to a new dispute settlement mechanism, and the exclusion of such cases from human rights bodies. This would only work if the ICJ accepted that a rigid distinction had been created between IHL and human rights law.

Hampson, *supra* note 15, at 572.

96. Arrangement for the Transfer of Detainees Between the Government of Canada and the Government of the Islamic Republic of Afghanistan, Can.-Afg., May 3, 2007, *available at* http://www.afghanistan.gc.ca/canada-afghanistan/documents/arrangement_detainee.aspx?lang=eng.

97. *See* HEADQUARTERS, DEPARTMENT OF THE ARMY & HEADQUARTERS, MARINE CORPS COMBAT DEVELOPMENT COMMAND, FM 3-24/MCWP 3-33.5, THE US ARMY/MARINE CORPS COUNTERINSURGENCY FIELD MANUAL (University of Chicago Press 2007) (2006).

XVII

Detention Operations in Iraq: A View from the Ground

Brian J. Bill*

Introduction

For many, detention operations in Iraq will be forever linked with the criminal abuses that occurred in Abu Ghraib.[1] The ensuing efforts to assign personal responsibility to those involved satisfied some proportion of the public and left others demanding more. As the story eventually faded from the front pages, public interest in detention operations in Iraq faded as well, and many could be forgiven the assumption that such operations had all but ended in the wake of Abu Ghraib.

Yet detention operations did not end in Iraq. Indeed, they expanded well beyond the scope that many believed possible earlier. At their height in late 2007, coalition forces[2] were detaining in excess of 26,000 persons within Iraq. But like the dog that didn't bark, the later operations failed to attract any significant notice, despite their extensive nature. This article will attempt to shed some light on subsequent detention operations conducted by the coalition forces, focusing on those aspects associated with the legal authorities to detain and release detainees.

Part I will discuss the legal background against which detention of persons is authorized during conflicts and other operations. Part II will describe in some detail the command structure of the operation and the applicable regulatory guidance, and then will explain the various review processes by which detainees were initially interned and then eventually released. Because the author's experience in

---

*Captain, JAGC, US Navy.

detention operations was in 2007 and 2008, the processes discussed will necessarily be limited to that time period. This need not be a significant liability, as that period offered both already-developed and innovative processes that deserve study, and potential emulation in similar situations in the future, with which Part III will be mostly concerned.

Part I—The Law

The detention operation with which this article is primarily concerned is that under the auspices of relevant resolutions of the United Nations Security Council. The authorities granted there did not arise in a vacuum, however, and the international laws applicable to earlier phases of the operations in Iraq still retained some degree of authority. Accordingly, a review of those applicable laws will be presented.

A. Combat Operations

Following the initiation of combat operations[3] on March 20, 2003,[4] Common Article 2 of the Geneva Conventions[5] was triggered, and therefore all the provisions of the Conventions applied to operations that followed. In addition, the *jus in bello* provisions relating to targeting of persons on the battlefield[6] were also applicable. Accordingly, combat forces were permitted to use lethal force against combatants, and required to refrain from the use of force against non-combatants. Persons captured on the battlefield would be assessed to fall into one of several categories, and their subsequent treatments depended on the applicable categories.

Combatants would normally be considered prisoners of war. Article 4 of the Geneva Convention Relative to the Treatment of Prisoners of War (PW Convention) sets out the criteria for prisoner of war status, the predominant categories being members of the enemy's armed forces and members of organized militias who are under responsible command, wearing a distinctive sign, carrying their arms openly, and observing the law of war.[7] Assuming the person fits into one of these categories, he is immediately treated as a prisoner of war in accordance with the remainder of the PW Convention, and he is detained for the remainder of the conflict.[8] The detaining power is under no obligation to review the status of the prisoner of war nor to release him until after the cessation of hostilities.

If there is doubt about the detained person's status as a prisoner of war, the detaining power shall convene a tribunal to make the determination in accordance with Article 5 of the PW Convention.[9] Article 5 provides very little guidance as to the nature of the tribunal; the practice of the United States is to set up an administrative panel of three officers to hear the evidence, with no involvement of counsel for the person in question.[10] The charter of the Article 5 tribunal is a limited one:

does the person whose case is before it (there is no requirement that the person be physically present before the tribunal) meet one of the criteria of Article 4? The tribunal need not determine that the person is a lawful combatant, though it will likely do so in making a determination of status. The text of Article 5 supports this conclusion, beginning, "Should any doubt arise as to whether persons, *having committed a belligerent act* and having fallen into the hands of the enemy . . . ."[11] This verbal formulation indicates that it is, by this point, a given the person has committed a belligerent act, though who has made that determination is nowhere stated. The Article 5 tribunal, therefore, does not determine whether the person's detention will continue, but merely decides whether the provisions of the PW Convention will apply to that detention. Another implication is that the drafters may have thought that doubt would *only* arise in the case of a potential illegal combatant, for in the other categories—for example, the armed forces—it is not necessary that the service member ever commit a belligerent act to receive prisoner of war protection.

Should the person be determined *not* to be a prisoner of war, the next step in the legal analysis is one of some controversy, brought into prominence by the decision of the United States to detain persons in Guantanamo. That decision is not the focus of this article, so the respective positions will merely be summarized. The US position is that there is a gap in coverage between the PW Convention and the Geneva Convention Relative to the Protection of Civilian Persons in Time of War (Civilians Convention), into which persons characterized variously as illegal combatants, unprivileged belligerents, or, as used in Guantanamo, enemy combatants fall. Customary international law permits the detention of all combatants, legal or illegal, for the pendency of the conflict. The characterization of a combatant as "illegal" renders him liable for prosecution without the benefit of combatant immunity, while also depriving him of protection under the PW Convention. The contrary position is that there are no gaps between the 1949 Conventions, and that a detained person who does not benefit under the PW Convention must necessarily benefit from the Civilians Convention.

Assuming the "no-gaps" position as a matter of convenience of discussion, the detaining power next turns to the Civilians Convention to determine whether detention is available. The first issue is whether the person is a "protected person" under Article 4 of the Civilians Convention.[12] In short, Article 4 declares all non-national (of the detaining power) civilians to be protected persons, then excepts certain subclasses from that protection.[13] Non-protected persons benefit only from the general protections set forth in Part II of the Civilians Convention,[14] and from the general standards of humane treatment contained in Common Article 3.[15] Protected persons benefit from the more substantive protections contained in Part III of the Civilians Convention. In the context of detention, the legal analysis depends on *where* the protected person is being detained, though the practical effect between the two is not great.

Part III of the Civilians Convention is entitled "Status and Treatment of Protected Persons." The first section is entitled "Provisions Common to the Territories of the Parties to the Conflict and to Occupied Territories." This section provides protections that, while more specific than those set out in Common Article 3, are not appreciably greater.[16] The next two sections are split in their coverage between that afforded to protected persons in the home territory of the detaining power and those who are detained in occupied territory.[17] As regards the power to detain protected persons, the applicable articles provide similar, though not identical, protections and procedures.

Article 41, which applies to protected persons in the detaining power's home territory, permits internment or assigned residence[18] of protected persons if "other methods of control mentioned in the present Convention [are] inadequate."[19] Article 42 goes on to provide that internment may only be ordered "if the security of the detaining power makes it absolutely necessary."[20] Article 43 provides for reviews of the initial decision to order internment, with reconsideration of the decision occurring "as soon as possible by an appropriate court or administrative board," and a further review accruing twice yearly.[21]

In occupied territories, all the provisions related to internment are in a single article, Article 78. There is a slightly different standard from that espoused in Article 42; under Article 78, internment is possible "for imperative reasons of security."[22] Unlike Article 42, which is silent on the procedures by which the detaining power makes the initial determination to intern, Article 78 provides that such a decision must be made "according to a regular procedure to be prescribed by the Occupying Power."[23] The Article 43 "reconsideration" is in Article 78 restyled as an "appeal," to be decided "with the least possible delay."[24] Further review of continued internment is to be "if possible every six months,"[25] which is probably a better formulation that the "twice yearly" formulation in Article 43. This section of Article 78 concludes with the requirement that the review be by a "competent body"[26] set up by the detaining power, which is much less rigorous than the court suggested by Article 43, though maybe about the same as the administrative board option also provided in Article 43.

B. Occupation Phase

President Bush announced the end of combat operations on May 1, 2003.[27] This date marks the beginning of the occupation phase in Iraq. Common Article 2 remained applicable at this time,[28] and the Geneva Conventions therefore continued in full applicability as a matter of law. Accordingly, the legal authorities to detain civilians were unchanged during this period.

Shortly after the occupation began, the Coalition Provisional Authority (CPA) was established to function as the interim government of Iraq.[29] The CPA issued various orders codifying some of the procedures affecting detention operations. These will be discussed in some detail later. It is necessary to note now, however, that the CPA pronounced that its orders and regulations would remain binding Iraqi law after the dissolution of the CPA.[30] This is important because some of the procedures used in later detention operations continued to trace their authority from CPA issuances, as the Iraqis had neither rescinded nor repealed them.

C. United Nations Mandate

With the imminent standing up of the new Iraqi government, the United Nations Security Council provided a different legal authority for continued combat and detention operations, apart from the previously explicit reliance on Geneva Conventions rules related to international armed conflict or occupation.

United Nations Security Council Resolution (UNSCR) 1546[31] was passed on June 8, 2004, in anticipation of Iraqi resumption of sovereignty on June 30, 2004. It is explicitly a Chapter VII[32] resolution by which the Security Council acts in its mandatory, international law–making role. For present purposes, paragraph 10 contains the following, where the Security Council

> [d]ecides that the multinational force[[33]] shall have the authority to take all necessary measures to contribute to the maintenance of security and stability in Iraq in accordance with the letters annexed to this resolution expressing, inter alia, the Iraqi request for the continued presence of the multinational force and setting out its tasks . . . .[34]

Two letters are annexed to the resolution. The first was from the Prime Minister of the Interim Government of Iraq, Dr. Allawi, in which he wrote:

> Until we are able to provide security for ourselves, including the defense of Iraq's land, sea and air space, we ask for the support of the Security Council and the international community in this endeavour. We seek a new resolution on the Multinational Force (MNF) mandate to contribute to maintaining security in Iraq, including through the tasks and arrangements set out in the letter from Secretary of State Colin Powell to the President of the United Nations Security Council.[35]

Secretary Powell's letter contains the critical language:

> Under the agreed arrangement, the MNF stands ready to continue to undertake a broad range of tasks to contribute to the maintenance of security and to ensure force protection. These include activities necessary to counter ongoing security threats posed by forces seeking to influence Iraq's political future through violence. This will include combat operations against members of these groups, *internment where this is necessary for imperative reasons of security*, and the continued search for and securing of weapons that threaten Iraqi security.[36]

UNSCR 1546 therefore authorized internment for imperative reasons of security, and while it may have been preferable to have had such language in the resolution proper,[37] it nevertheless included the authorization through this internal chain of references. The authority to intern was not dependent on any other international law authorities; that is, with the resumption of Iraqi sovereignty it was recognized that that the occupation, and the ability to intern through Article 78, had ended. Rather, this is an example of the Security Council making binding international law.

By its terms, UNSCR 1546 was to expire at the conclusion of the process of forming an Iraqi government;[38] prior to the national voting that took place on December 15, 2005, the Security Council acted again in UNSCR 1637[39] to extend the mandate until December 31, 2006. UNSCR 1723[40] extended it yet again to December 31, 2007, and UNSCR 1790[41] further extended it to December 31, 2008. In each of these subsequent resolutions no explicit reference was made to combat operations or internment. Rather, each reaffirmed the authorizations contained in UNSCR 1546, which itself contained the combat and internment authorizations.

Returning to the authorization for internment, the language chosen for Secretary Powell's letter—internment for imperative reasons of security—appears to be taken directly from Article 78 of the Civilians Convention as the closest legal analogy. Whether that was objectively true or not, and whether it was the intention of the Security Council, it was Article 78 and associated articles to which coalition forces looked in designing the operation to be later described.

D. Post-mandate Authority

Prior to the Security Council action in UNSCR 1790,[42] it was already recognized that the UN mandate would end after December 31, 2008.[43] After long negotiations throughout 2008, two agreements were signed on November 17, 2008.[44] The Strategic Framework Agreement[45] set forth a number of aspirational principles to guide future relationships between the United States and Iraq. The Security Agreement[46] sets forth the rules to be followed by US forces beginning on January 1, 2009. Very decidedly, the broad mandate of the UNSCR era had ended. In regard to detention operations, the Security Agreement moved away from the "imperative threat" administrative internment model to one that is based on criminal detention overseen by the Iraqi judiciary.[47] Those detainees whose detentions predated January 1, 2009 (i.e., those who had been detained under authority of the Security Council resolutions) are to be released "in a safe and orderly manner" unless the Iraqis are able to charge them criminally, in which case the Iraqis will assume custody.[48]

Part II—Description of Detention Operations

A. Structure

In this section, the practical application of the law, such as it was, to actual detention operations will be described. It will begin with a short explanation of the command relationships as they existed at the time. Although such details usually appeal only to military professionals, a familiarity with the various units and officials will help in understanding the interplay of the various procedures used in detention operations in Iraq.

The combatant commander with responsibility for Iraq is the Commander, US Central Command,[49] headquartered in Tampa, Florida. Central Command issued numerous orders containing policies and guidance that were utilized in detention operations.

The senior coalition force commander in Iraq was designated as Commander, Multi-National Forces–Iraq, often abbreviated as MNF-I. The commander has always been a US Army four-star general; the commanders during the period to be discussed below were Generals David Petraeus and Raymond Odierno.[50] The relevant major subordinate commanders to MNF-I were Multi-National Corps–Iraq, or MNC-I, and the Deputy Commanding General for Detention Operations (DCG-DO), who was also designated as the Commander, Task Force 134 (TF 134).[51]

MNC-I, commanded by a three-star Army general, contained all of the operating forces in Iraq. Iraq was divided by MNC-I into subregions, each of which was commanded by a two-star general.[52] Though the boundaries between them changed, there were, during the times relevant for this article, six subregions, designated as Multi-National Divisions–North, Baghdad, and Central, and Multi-National Force–West,[53] all of which were US commands; any detainees from these units would go into US detention. The remaining regions were Multi-National Division–Center-South, comprising a small region commanded by the Polish, and Multi-National Force–Southeast, most notably containing Basra, commanded by the British.[54] Few detainees were taken in Multi-National Division–Center-South, though they would eventually wind up in US detention facilities. The British ran their own detention facilities.

The position of the Deputy Commanding General for Detention Operations was an unusual one. As a result of the abuses uncovered at Abu Ghraib,[55] the DCG-DO was established as a two-star general position, reporting directly to the Commander, MNF-I. The DCG-DO was responsible for setting and implementing detention policy throughout Iraq. Anomalously, a two-star general was in the position to make policy that a three-star (MNC-I) was to follow. Although in practice this unusual power relationship proved no problem, there were occasions, mostly related to policies associated with the release of detainees, where the interests of MNC-I and DCG-DO clashed. Unless the situation was otherwise resolved, the Commander, MNF-I, made the final decision.

The DCG-DO also commanded TF 134,[56] and it was in this position that the commander spent the great majority of his time.[57] The primary responsibility of TF 134 was the proper care and custody of the detainees in centralized facilities, known as theater internment facilities (TIFs).[58] Subsidiary responsibilities included the lawful interrogation of detainees and the provision of due process hearings to the detainees regarding their continued detention.

TF 134 was itself largely made up of individual augmentees and ad hoc units. Unlike the multinational divisions, where the commanding general would deploy to Iraq with most of his normal staff, the commander of TF 134 was ordered individually to his position. The rest of the headquarters staff consisted of active-duty officers and enlisted personnel from all of the armed services, or mobilized members of the reserves or National Guard. Many were volunteers, serving tour lengths of four to twelve months, though six months was the norm. Under the headquarters staff were subordinate organizations, though only the major organizations applicable to this article will be discussed.

1. Care and Custody

Doctrinally, care and custody of detainees is a military police (MP) function,[59] and MP commanders were placed in charge of the theater internment facilities. This was an instance where an existing staff, normally an MP brigade headquarters, would deploy in full.[60] Their staff would be augmented in theater by individual augmentees. The guards in the compounds would come from other existing MP companies, most of which were in the reserve or National Guard,[61] or from provisional units of airmen or sailors whose specialties were anything but MP-related duties.[62] Redundant layers of command were necessary to ensure that this diverse guard force, with its vastly different service experiences, functioned as a cohesive and professional force in an environment that permitted no mistakes.

2. Interrogations

All interrogations of detainees within a theater internment facility were conducted by the Joint Intelligence and Debriefing Center (JIDC). The JIDC was commanded by a colonel of the military intelligence branch, who reported directly to the Commander, TF 134. The personnel under the JIDC commander comprised a military intelligence brigade headquarters element, typically from the Army reserves or Army National Guard, heavily supported by individual augmentees from other services, as well as by various contractors.

Every security detainee, shortly after his arrival at the theater internment facility and while still being processed into the facility, would undergo a screening interview by JIDC interrogators.[63] The purpose of the screening was to gather basic biographical information, and to generally assess the detainee's knowledge and cooperation.[64] Although the facts and circumstances that led to the detainee's capture and internment would be discussed, the screener's task was not to attempt to prove or disprove the facts underlying the capture; rather, he was to assess whether the detainee knew anything that would be of future tactical or strategic importance. For example, if a detainee was captured while emplacing an improvised explosive device, or IED, the screener would undoubtedly ask about the circumstances surrounding that act, but would focus his questioning on whether this detainee knew where the device was made, or who was in charge of the network responsible for IEDs in that region, and so on. If the screener believed that the detainee had information on these areas, he would schedule the detainee for further interrogation at a later time. Most detainees, however, were screened as having little intelligence value, and were never again interrogated.

The follow-on interrogations which did occur were conducted in accordance with Army Field Manual 2-22.3,[65] as had been made mandatory by the Detainee Treatment Act of 2005.[66] The field manual lists the approved "approaches" an interrogator may take with any detainee;[67] anything not listed is per se unauthorized and the manual makes clear that certain actions are always prohibited.[68] Though there was concern that, by explicitly setting out the approaches that would be used, the quantity and quality of the intelligence gained from interrogations would suffer, anecdotal indications are that the fears have been unjustified.[69]

3. Legal Reviews

The legal section of TF 134 was uniquely structured, and had a very limited and defined mission. In a normal military command, the judge advocate to a commander is responsible for providing advice on many topics: military justice, administrative law, fiscal issues, ethics, operational law and contracts, among others. The commander of TF 134, however, did not have such a judge advocate on his staff; rather, the Staff Judge Advocate to the Commander, MNF-I, was tasked to provide him advice in all of these areas. The head of the TF 134 legal office was instead denominated as the Legal Advisor to TF 134; his mission was solely the legal processing of detainees.[70]

The TF 134 legal office was staffed exclusively by individual augmentees, predominantly from the Air Force and Navy, with a very few from the Army (mostly reserve or National Guard), Marine Corps and Coast Guard. At its height in late 2007, the TF 134 legal office had approximately 150 personnel assigned. Of these, approximately one-third were judge advocate officers, with the remainder made up of enlisted paralegal specialists, information technology specialists and investigators. As the number of detainees decreased throughout 2008, so did the size of the TF 134 legal office.

The TF 134 legal office was structured largely along functional lines. Each of the review boards was assigned a number of judge advocates and enlisted support personnel. The Central Criminal Court of Iraq liaison office was similarly staffed. A headquarters element section was also established to coordinate the actions of the other sections and to process special cases. Each section reported to a designated officer-in-charge, who reported to the Legal Advisor, who in turn reported to the DCG-DO.

B. Legal Guidance

As discussed in Part I, the "law" under which the United States operated was the Security Council resolutions permitting detention for imperative reasons of security; the Geneva Convention for the Protection of Civilians, specifically Article 78, would be applied by analogy. In the absence of other binding law,[71] policy and regulatory guidance filled the void. However, in the discussion that follows, it will be noted that there are few citations to authority, for the following reason: there was little binding authority.

Department of Defense Directive 2310.01E[72] contains overarching guidance for all US detainee programs. The directive mandates humane treatment for all detainees[73] and, regardless of the detainee's legal status, requires that the protections contained in Common Article 3 be applied as a minimum.[74] It also provides that detainees who are not prisoners of war "shall have the basis of their detention reviewed periodically by competent authority."[75] The directive otherwise provides little specific guidance.

The Coalition Provisional Authority required, in its Memorandum 3,[76] certain procedures to be followed in the detention of security detainees. Detainees whose detention lasted more than seventy-two hours would be entitled to a review of the decision to intern,[77] and that review had to occur within seven days.[78]

Further reviews were required "periodically," with the first review required within six months.[79]

Using these directives as a base, Commander, US Central Command, issued several supplemental orders which governed detention operations in general and the legal review process in particular.[80] The Commander, MNF-I, further implemented the Central Command orders, especially when the Central Command order permitted the Commander, MNF-I, to delegate certain of the powers that had been bestowed upon him.[81] These orders were still written at a relatively high level of generality. When they were more detailed, they were usually descriptive of the procedures already developed within TF 134. Put another way, TF 134 developed practices and procedures which were thought to best implement the overarching guidance, though hardly as unconstrained actors, as both Central Command and MNF-I were always aware of what was going on in TF 134. When the time came to revise the Central Command and MNF-I orders, those responsible for the revisions were usually quite satisfied with making directive the procedures being used. A prime example of this was the Multi-National Force Review Committee (MNFRC).[82] This was a TF 134 initiative to improve the Combined Review and Release Board (CRRB), but it was not mentioned at the time of its implementation in either the Central Command or MNF-I directives. When updated, both directives ordered the implementation of the Multi-National Force Review Committee in the form in which it was already being used.

This lack of detailed guidance provided a useful degree of flexibility and permitted TF 134 legal personnel, who were dealing with issues on a day-by-day basis, to adopt procedures best suited to the circumstances. It should not be characterized as a totally ad hoc process, changeable at will and subject to no oversight. Procedures were not changed unless they yielded improvements and then only after consultation with the chain of command.

Although the procedures occasionally changed, the substantive standard used throughout all legal reviews was always the same: whether the detainee was an imperative threat to security. This critical standard never received any further elaboration in any of guidance discussed above and so the term was used in its colloquial sense.[83]

C. Practice

1. Preliminary Matters

Detention begins when a soldier on the ground determines that a person is a threat. Coalition forces in Iraq had been authorized the power to detain persons, but had also been authorized the power to engage in combat operations, which imply the use of force (up to and including deadly force): detention on the battlefield is an application of authorized force. The soldier may decide to subsequently release the person captured or may decide that he presents a more lasting threat, in which case he would return to his unit with the detainee in custody. The detainee will be enrolled in the unit's internment facility and if qualified interrogators are available will be questioned. Within a short period, normally fourteen days, the unit must decide to release him, or to seek longer-term detention in the theater internment facility. If the latter, the decision must be approved by a brigade commander.

The detainee is then is either convoyed or flown by the capturing unit to Camp Cropper TIF,[84] which is located within Victory Base Complex.[85] At Camp Cropper, the capturing unit turns over all personal effects of the detainees. These effects are warehoused until they are returned to the detainee upon his release. The capturing unit personnel also turn in whatever evidence they have to support continued detention. At a minimum, this must include a completed standard form, which contains, among other things, identifying information about the detainee, a short synopsis of the conduct which led to his capture and identification of relevant witnesses. In addition, two sworn statements describing the capture or other circumstances are required. In most cases, more information would be included, such as pictures, charts and other relevant statements. Assuming these items were all produced, TIF personnel "sign" for the detainee and his personal effects, and the capturing unit is relieved of any further responsibility for both.

Administrative in-processing consists of a medical screening and treatment if required; clothing and supplies issue; and various briefings related to rules and regulations inside the TIF. Importantly, it is at this point that the detainee is assigned an internment security number, or ISN;[86] it is by this six-digit number that the detainee will be referred to throughout his period of detention. This entire process may take two or three days, during which the detainees are segregated from the general population within the TIF. It is also during this period the JIDC would perform the initial interrogation screening interview. At the conclusion of the in-processing, the detainee would be assigned to a compound within Camp Bucca or Camp Cropper TIFs.

Contemporaneous with the detainee's in-processing, the detainee's legal file will be put together. This all-important file will often serve as a proxy for the detainee himself. Initially it consists only of the paperwork delivered by the capturing unit, together with the results of the interrogation screening and medical screening. It is delivered to the Task Force 134 Magistrate Cell for further processing.

At the Magistrate Cell, personnel place the paperwork into standard six-part folders, labeling the outside of the folder with the detainee's ISN. The various parts—standard forms, statements, other evidence, intelligence information, if any, and process paperwork—are arbitrarily chosen and only serve to make examining a particular file for a certain piece of information easier. The file normally contains only paper, though occasionally capturing units will include a CD-ROM or DVD which might contain video or scans of additional documents. Real evidence, to the extent that it still exists,[87] is referred to in the file but is physically housed within the Camp Cropper TIF warehouse.

Though a file would seem to be only a file, the detainee file has a few unusual features that are worth discussing, if only because they affect future reviews.

First, there are portions of the file that are classified, and the entire folder is therefore marked as containing classified information, usually at the secret level. This is rarely an issue in normal processing because all US personnel whose jobs involve these files have a secret clearance. Indeed, in general terms it was possible to share most classified material with coalition force personnel in the course of duties; Iraqi members of the Combined Review and Release Board[88] were also permitted access to some classified data. The problem arose when it was necessary to convey information from the file to the detainee, either in written form or in person, during the Multi-National Force Review Committee.[89] No classified material could be shared with the detainee. In those instances, it was necessary to convey information in more general terms that were not classified. A further problem with classification was that some of the material in the file would be classified as prohibiting dissemination to all, or most, other countries; the shorthand would be that the information was classified as NOFORN, meaning no foreign dissemination. Iraqi members of the Combined Review and Release Board were not permitted access to NOFORN material. Accordingly, part of the process of putting the files together in the Magistrate Cell was to segregate NOFORN materials into yet another file folder that was contained within the normal six-part folder. When the time came to provide the file to an Iraqi member, for example, the NOFORN folder would be pulled out, and at the conclusion of the hearings the NOFORN folder would be returned to the six-part folder for storage.

It should be noted that no sustained effort was attempted to translate all of the information contained in the file into Arabic. Such a task was beyond the capabilities of the already overworked translators. Certain material (e.g., detainee or witness written statements) would start in Arabic and be translated into English; the Arabic material remained in the file. Any correspondence with the detainee was translated into Arabic, and both the English and Arabic versions were included in the file. But US service member statements, intelligence and interrogation reports, and any other documents remained in English only. At the boards where the Iraqi members did not speak English (a significant number did), the interpreter assigned to the board would go through the file and provide an on-the-spot translation of the relevant documents. This was not a perfect solution, but under the circumstances, it was the best that could be done.

The final comment about the files in general concerns one of the most troublesome types of evidence—the Iraqi informant. Sectarian violence was often higher than violence directed against coalition forces. Even within particular sects, there are the lawless and the law-abiding. Iraqis almost always knew who the "bad guys" were. It took a personal act of courage by an Iraqi to provide a statement to coalition forces implicating his or her neighbor in insurgent acts. Sometimes these statements would be the basis upon which targeting decisions would be made. In other cases, after a person was detained coalition forces would canvass the village soliciting statements in the hopes that the prospect of the person's continued detention would encourage informants to come forward. In either case, it was necessary to provide the informant with a measure of confidentiality, as any other course put the informant's life in great danger. Some units would protect the informant's name by assigning him a number, which is all that would be reflected in the file.[90] If the informant number was not enough to protect him, perhaps because he gave information that would otherwise reveal his identity, the report might be classified at some level, which led to the classification problems discussed above.

There were two great difficulties with these statements. First, there was no realistic way to test their veracity. Most would be characterized as sworn statements, yet it was never clear who was administering the oath, and whether the informant believed that swearing to an American or his designee carried the same weight that swearing before an Iraqi official would. More important, once the informant provided his statement, he had no further relationship to the case as it progressed through the various levels of review. Both the sheer number of detainee cases and the dangerous security situation in the field made it unlikely that informants would be interviewed a second time about a particular case, and the format of the reviews, being administrative rather than criminal, did not require any personal participation by the informant. So, the informant's statement had to be taken at face value. If the informant had provided truthful information in the past (this was often noted by the capturing unit in the paperwork they provided),[91] the board assessing the information might give it more credence. On the other hand, an informant of unknown reliability might be viewed with skepticism. The detail provided by the informant could be another indicator of truth, as might the informant's averment that he personally witnessed some action on the part of the detainee as opposed to merely hearing about it. Corroboration among various informant statements might also help.

The second problem flowed from the first. It became evident, at least as early as the time in which the detainee population was growing rapidly, that certain Iraqis were informing on their neighbors for personal reasons. The so-called "grudge informer" isn't a new phenomenon.[92] If coalition forces received information, credible on its face, that a person was an insurgent, they would obligingly pick up the neighbor and whisk him away. In Iraq at the time, there was no effective sanction for bearing false witness against a neighbor. If subsequently released, the former detainee would not know the identity of the informant against him so there was no risk. As boards became more experienced with assessing the validity of informant statements, these types of statements tended to stand out, but not always.[93]

2. Magistrate Cell Review

The Magistrate Cell was staffed with an officer-in-charge and ten to twelve attorneys, slightly more enlisted paralegals and several interpreters. From the middle of 2007 until the middle of 2008, it operated around the clock, with two shifts working twelve hours each. This coincided with the surge in troops in Iraq, hence the greatest influx of detainees. In the fall of 2007, more than sixty detainees, on average would arrive every day at Camp Cropper TIF and require review by the magistrate. The attorney magistrates would typically review cases from a single operational area; for example, two attorneys might be assigned to cases coming from Multi-National Division Central. The benefit of this arrangement was that the reviewing attorney was better able to become familiar with the method of processing the evidence used by that unit and build a relationship with those responsible for the processing at the operational level.

Through policy, the Magistrate Cell review was to be complete within seven days of the detainee's arriving at the TIF.[94] Accordingly, the attorney magistrates would begin working on the cases as they came in and the file folders were assembled. In practice, the seven-day limit was rarely violated, despite the overwhelming number of cases arriving daily.

The procedure used by the magistrate was unremarkable: did the evidence contained in the folder[95] support the belief that this person was an imperative threat to security? If the magistrate's answer was yes, a notification was prepared for the detainee and his detention would continue, subject to subsequent reviews. If no, the capturing unit was given notification of the intent to release the detainee and invited to submit additional evidence that might not have been included in the original package. The magistrate would also frequently contact the capturing unit asking for clarification of materials in the package; for example, if there is a reference in the file to a witness statement that was not there, the magistrate would call and ask for it. The intent was not to perfect the case for continued detention, but only to ensure that all the available facts were in front of the decisionmaker. If, after these efforts, the evidence was still insufficient the detainee would be processed for release.

The attorney magistrate's decision was, in general effect, final. There were too many cases coming through the office for the officer-in-charge to do anything more than random quality assurance checks and the TF 134 Legal Advisor was even less able to oversee individual cases. Insofar as these attorneys would process many hundreds of cases during their tours, their judgment became quite refined.

An additional decision made by the attorney magistrate was whether there was sufficient competent evidence in the file to merit prosecution at the Central Criminal Court of Iraq.[96] As seen, the paper file was sufficient for the purposes of deciding on continued detention, but the file alone, to the extent that its contents could even be shared given its often classified nature, would not prevail in a prosecution in Iraqi court where witnesses and physical evidence were necessary. Accordingly, the magistrate would refer those cases that appeared to contain the requisite unclassified and available evidence to the TF 134 legal office charged with assisting with prosecutions. The magistrates were instructed to be liberal in referring cases, since cases could be non-referred, but there was no effective mechanism to prosecute cases which had not been referred in the first place. Even with this liberal practice, the referral rate for prosecution was fairly constant at only 15 to 20 percent.

The notification of continued detention prepared when the magistrate decided that continued detention was appropriate was additionally styled as an advisement of appeal rights, with an invitation to the detainee to choose to appeal, and, if he did so, to submit reasons why he was not an imperative threat to security. These notifications were delivered to the detainees in translated form and read to those who were illiterate.[97] Written appeals were translated back into English and entered into the file for review by the next board.

3. Combined Review and Release Board Review

Regardless of whether the detainee elected to appeal his continued detention, his case would be reviewed automatically by the appellate body, called the Combined Review and Release Board, or CRRB. To put it another way, the CRRB reviewed every case that passed through the Magistrate Cell. The CRRB was to review the case within ninety days,[98] though in practice, especially once the Multi-National Force Review Committee came into being, the CRRB review was completed within two or three weeks of the magistrate's decision to continue detention. Until it was replaced by the Multi-National Force Review Committee, discussed below, the CRRB also performed the six-month periodic review of every detainee's case. The

CRRB procedures were the same, whether the case before it was an initial appeal or later periodic review.

The CRRB was a panel made up of both Iraqi and coalition force officials. The Iraqi members were generally civilian employees from the Ministries of the Interior, Justice and Human Rights. The coalition forces members were always US military officers, usually drawn from MNF-I staff elements. The panels were composed so that each had an Iraqi majority, although due to absences, that was not always possible. The lack of an Iraqi majority did not invalidate the board. To permit the attendance of the Iraqi members, the CRRB convened in the International Zone. The members were already working elsewhere in the International Zone, and were provided with passes, or were met and escorted, which permitted their entrance to the US Embassy Annex within the International Zone.

The process was overseen by the CRRB office of the TF 134 legal office, with an officer-in-charge and four to six attorneys, together with paralegal and interpreter support. The CRRB office was responsible for "docketing" all the cases and preparing the files for review. The file would be reviewed to ensure its completeness and the reviewing attorney would write a summary of the case, which would be translated into Arabic. Material which could not be shared with the Iraqis because of its classification as NOFORN would be placed in a separate folder within the larger detainee folder if it had not already been done beforehand. Boards were held up to five days a week, depending on the cases ready for review and member availability.

On the day of any particular board, the files would be brought to a conference room where the members had been assembled. A CRRB attorney and interpreter would accompany the files. There was little ceremony. If there were no Iraqi members, or if the Iraqis read and understood English, as many did, each member would read through the file on his own and provisionally vote whether there was sufficient evidence to consider the detainee an imperative threat to security or not. Discussion of the cases was encouraged, though it was up to the members how much they did, if at all. At the end of the consideration and discussion, the votes would be tallied; a majority prevailed. If the Iraqi members did not understand English, the interpreter would perform an ad hoc translation of the relevant evidentiary documents in the file as it was impossible, due to the volume of cases and chronic shortage of skilled interpreters, to translate everything in every file other than the CRRB attorney-prepared summary of the case. Discussion of the cases had to be through the medium of the interpreter, but it still occurred. The CRRB attorney played little role in the board other than ensuring that all the files were considered and the voting was taking place.

The historic recommended-for-release rate at the CRRB was approximately 12 to 15 percent, especially when it was the only board conducting periodic reviews.

Once the CRRB became the initial appeal–only board, the recommended-for-release rate increased, but only marginally, never reaching 20 percent.

4. Multi-National Force Review Committee Review

The CRRB was an efficient, though not necessarily effective, tool for determining whether a detainee was an imperative threat to security. Chief among the problems was the file on which the reviews were based: there was little or no change in the file from review to review. The evidence supporting the detainee's initial detention, assuming that it was sufficient to pass through previous boards, was more likely than not to also prove sufficient to pass through any subsequent boards. Indeed, the only real differences among the boards were the change in the membership reviewing the file; different members might reach different conclusions based on the same evidence in the file. The CRRB was also, perversely, too efficient, especially when members, most notably the Iraqi members, were long-term members. As with any task, the longer one works on it, the better and faster one becomes. The detainee files were often quite thick, but among all the paper there were usually only a couple of very important pieces of relevant information. Ignoring the trivia, an experienced member knew what to look for, but it occasionally happened that the trivia contained information that could have a bearing on the outcome. Nevertheless, as the board had a hundred or more files before it every day, careful consideration of each was usually sacrificed for speed. A factor in this as well was that the review became that of the file, not the underlying person whom the file represented. Each file had, as its first page, a picture of the detainee, and occasionally had other photographs of him as part of the evidence, but this was not always enough to impress upon the members that they were dealing with a real person, not just an ISN.

The file-only method of review had a more practical downside: disruption in the TIFs. General Stone, the DCG-DO at the time, would often liken the situation to that of the movie *The Gods Must Be Crazy*, in which a Coke bottle, discarded from a passing airplane, lands near an African tribesman, and he then attempts to return this gift of the gods. Releases from the TIFs were almost as haphazard, at least from the detainees' point of view. One day a detainee would be tapped on the shoulder and told that he was about to be released: he didn't know how that decision was reached or why. Likewise, those detainees around him, who didn't get the tap, were equally mystified about why they too were not being released. Detainee discontent resulted in riots and near-riots becoming increasingly common in Camp Bucca.[99]

For all these reasons, the DCG-DO decided to institute a new review procedure, which was named the Multi-National Force Review Committee. The single biggest innovation was that the detainee was to appear before the board and participate in the hearing. This led to many other practical changes.

First, because transportation of large numbers of detainees was impossible, the detainees could not come to the boards. Instead, the boards had to go to the detainees. Accordingly, all boards would henceforth be held within the TIFs in order to facilitate easy and secure detainee movement. Space to hold the boards was initially a problem, but was solved relatively quickly. Camp Cropper only required a single board to handle its volume of boards and a trailer in the TIF proved adequate to the need. At Camp Bucca, with its much larger detainee population, a suite of trailers was eventually installed to comprise what became known as the "Justice Complex." It included several board rooms, administrative spaces and a holding area for the detainees.

Second, whereas the CRRB was able to work through a hundred or more cases in a day, any reasonable board procedure involving the detainee would have to accept many fewer completed boards per day. With a detainee population during this period exceeding 20,000, topping out at more than 26,000 in the fall of 2007, it was necessary to complete just under one thousand boards per week in order to ensure that all detainees were provided a review every six months (or twenty-six weeks). This necessitated greatly expanding the number of boards running every day. Various combinations were tried, with nine boards (eight at Camp Bucca, one at Camp Cropper) hearing twenty cases per day, with boards held six days a week finally being settled upon. This gave a theoretic capacity of over one thousand cases per week, though that capacity was never reached as boards would often be cancelled and rescheduled due to administrative difficulties with moving files, detainee unavailability due to sickness, difficulty in finding sufficient members to sit on the boards or security issues beyond control (e.g., a security operation or exercise run by TIF leadership). As many as thirty boards per day were tried, but that proved to be too many, exhausting the board members. As the detainee population decreased, the number of hearings per day per board was decreased. It was found that anything less than fifteen hearings per day was too "easy" on the members, when the standard workday in Iraq was twelve hours. The solution was to slowly decrease the number of boards, maintaining fifteen to twenty hearings for each.

Third, because of the increased number of boards, there was an increased need for members. Recall that the CRRB was a joint Iraqi–coalition forces board. With that in mind, the Iraqis were approached prior to the first MNFRC, briefed on the concept, and asked whether they would like to participate as members. Although they were supportive of the new board system and expressed an interest in sending members, no Iraqi members ever participated. This could be explained by a number of reasons. The CRRB was held in the International Zone, close to the ministry offices of the Iraqi members. Gaining access to the Embassy Annex complex through security was a challenge, but one that was met. Now the boards were being held at the TIFs. Daily travel to Camp Cropper from the International Zone was possible, but only in armored convoys. Travel to Camp Bucca was all but impossible for the Iraqis on their own, and spending an extended period at that very remote location, once they got there, would not have appealed to any of the potential Iraqi members. While the Iraqis would have been welcomed as members, their absence did lead to many administrative conveniences, as there was no need to worry about access to classified material in the files that could not be shared with the Iraqis and no material in the files needed to be translated by the interpreters.

The question was where to find the other members. MNC-I was initially invited to send members prior to the first boards, but declined, although as will be discussed it did send members later. With no Iraqis, no MNC-I members, and no extant ability to task other units to provide members, all MNFRC members were at first drawn from TF 134. Officers from throughout Camp Bucca were tasked with sitting on the boards, without being relieved of their normal duties. Senior officers in the grade of O-4 and above to sit as president of each board were in especially short supply and therefore those that were available were tasked disproportionately. The TF 134 chief of staff decreed that all TF 134 staff officers assigned to the headquarters would travel to Camp Bucca to sit on boards for two weeks. This helped, though wasn't a full solution. TF 134 also requested, and was granted, the assignment of a group of officers and senior enlisted personnel whose sole job in Iraq would be as MNFRC members. They reported administratively to the Legal Advisor. Their presence greatly relieved the burden on personnel assigned to the TIF staff from sitting as members. Additionally, as these permanent MNFRC members heard more and more cases their expertise greatly increased, improving decisions. Nevertheless, the "TF 134–only" boards were responsible for the lack of acceptance of the results early in the process.

With no prior practice to consult in the design of the MNFRC, the procedures utilized for an Article 5 tribunal,[100] set forth in the Army regulation providing policy and procedures for the treatment of, *inter alia*, detainees,[101] were used by analogy. The board was composed of three members. The president was a senior officer, O-4 or above. One of the other members could be a senior enlisted person, in the grade of E-7 or above.[102] Each member was provided with a memorandum entitled "Instruction to Members," signed by the DCG-DO, which set forth his expectations for their performance and his thanks for their serving as members.[103] Each member signed the memorandum indicating he or she had read and understood the contents. MNFRC staff members would also provide training on the process, especially on how to read and understand the detainee files.

The night before the board the members were required to read the files, taking notes as necessary. The boards began early in the morning and ran until all were completed. Each board was held in a separate hearing room, minimally configured with a table in the front for the members, a table for the detainee, a seat for the interpreter and several chairs in the back for any observers. A guard was always present, in whose physical custody the detainee always remained.

The hearing followed a script. The president began by explaining the nature of the hearing and its purpose, paying special attention to an explanation of the standard of imperative threat to security that the board would be using to arrive at its decision. The detainee was told that he could offer evidence of any kind. He could make a statement, but was not compelled to do so. If he consented to make a statement and to answer questions, he was encouraged to speak truthfully; to this end he was sworn in in an appropriate manner. The preliminaries over, the president detailed the nature of the evidence against the detainee. The detainee then had the opportunity to rebut the evidence.[104] The board members would then ask questions, usually about the detainee's pre-capture conduct, but also about his conduct within the TIF and often his intentions once he was released. At the conclusion of this portion, the president would return to the script, remind the detainee that the board would be voting on whether the detainee presented an imperative threat to security, and dismiss him back to the TIF. The members would deliberate and vote; a majority vote won. Each member would sign the voting sheet and a short description of why the board voted as it did was written on it. The dissenting member, if any, also had the opportunity to write a short statement. The MNFRC staff member collected the voting sheet and file, and set up the next board.

The critical role of the interpreter must be mentioned here. Accurate, faithful interpretation was required but occasionally not delivered. All interpreters were hired by a government contractor, which certified as proficient all those it hired. Some were clearly more proficient than others,[105] but in a theater where interpreters of *any* proficiency were in short supply, the MNFRC staff was happy to have every one it had. Another problem that sometimes occurred was that the interpreter took on too much of an expanded role, propounding questions that weren't asked by the assigned members or embellishing answers made by the detainee. In certain situations, this made sense; for example, if the detainee didn't understand the question as phrased by the member, the interpreter could more reasonably ask it in a different manner or as a series of questions. At other times, the interpreter's intrusion was improper and was stopped.

The MNFRC result yielded a recommendation to the DCG-DO on the status of the detainee: its vote to release did not itself effect a release. All recommendations for release had to be approved by the DCG-DO,[106] who was free in theory and practice to disregard the recommendation of the MNFRC or that of any of the other boards earlier discussed. This was a continued complaint of the International

Committee of the Red Cross (ICRC) representatives. In the ICRC's view, the board deciding the appeal under either Article 43 or 78 of the Civilians Convention needed to be "independent," and to have the final authority on release.[107] The complaint had two strands. One was that the members of the boards needed to be independent of the DCG-DO; because the members all worked for TF 134, they were not independent. The response was always that, as a practical matter, the DCG-DO had little interest in, and absolutely no direct input into, any board. His interest was merely institutional: Was the procedure fair and being followed? Were the members being exposed to all the evidence and were they voting their conscience? If so, results in any particular case were a matter outside of the DCG-DO's notice. Never were magistrates or board members upbraided for their recommendations and so they were independent in reality, even if not in theory.

There was no good answer to the second strand of the complaint about the DCG-DO's final authority. The regulations delegating release authority to the DCG-DO did not permit further delegation to a lower level such as a board nor would the DCG-DO have been inclined to do so even if possible. His ability to provide quality assurance provided some level of comfort in the operating forces that releases were appropriate.[108] In the great majority of cases, the recommendation of the MNFRC (or any other review board) was followed, and the detainee released. In those instances when the recommendation was not followed, it was because of additional information being brought forward that convinced the DCG-DO that the detainee remained an imperative threat.[109]

From the beginning, the MNFRC yielded a higher release rate than the CRRB. The institutional response progressed from expectation, through mild alarm, to final acceptance. Some explanation is in order. When the MNFRC was first instituted, it had a minimum number of boards; the CRRB still functioned as the primary six-month review mechanism. It happened at a time that there was an independent requirement for major releases of detainees (e.g., the coalition generally released a number of detainees during Ramadan as a gesture of goodwill). To "harvest" these increased numbers of releases, the early boards were "seeded" with cases of detainees who were thought to represent lower threats. The resulting release recommendation rate for these MNFRCs was just under 25 percent, compared with 12 to 15 percent for the CRRB, fulfilling the need for releases. The rate was high, but expected. However, once the "seeding" stopped and regular cases came before the boards, the recommended release rate stayed at around 25 percent, and actually began increasing, until it reached a relatively steady rate of over 40 percent. This was the alarm phase, mostly on the part of the operating forces, which increasingly came to view the MNFRC as merely a release board. Within the TF 134 staff, the increasing recommended release rate was troubling only if it indicated that either the process was bad, or the members were not taking their duties seriously. Investigation proved neither to be true. Put another way, the TF 134 staff's view was that if the process was fair—and was followed—the recommended release rate was merely whatever it was. The substantial increase over that of the CRRB was attributed to three factors. The first was the presence of the detainee. As a simple matter of human nature, having a real person in front of you, instead of merely a file with his picture, is more likely to engender empathy, and, in close cases, may make the difference. Second, though the detainee's evidence was nearly always just his statement and answers to questions, it was more than what was in the paper file. Finally, a board process, following a script, lent itself to greater deliberation on each case. Matters which might have escaped the notice of the CRRB could be discovered by a board which had more time to review the case.

Final acceptance of the MNFRC process, and the higher recommended release rate, took more time. In the beginning of 2008, MNC-I members began to participate on the MNFRC. At the direction of MNF-I, MNFRC panels would have two MNC-I members each, giving them the majority vote. The results were instructive. On the first Saturday[110] with MNC-I members, the recommended release rate "dropped" to around 20 percent. On Sunday, it increased to maybe 24 percent, and so on, upward every day, until by Thursday it was again near 40 percent. On Saturday, new members would be seated, and the process repeated. Eventually, Saturday's rate began increasing, and within several months, the new boards were consistently recommending releases at around 40 percent, regardless of the day.[111] The reasons could only be discovered anecdotally. In the beginning, hostility toward the process was clearly evident; that hostility waned as individual members' tenures wore on and waned organizationally as MNC-I recognized that these results were attributable to their own members. In the end, the operating forces, through their participation in the release process, took an ownership stake, which led to their acceptance of the results.

Although the MNFRC received many improvements—a more focused script, permanent members, MNC-I members—one of the more interesting was the assignment of personal representatives to some of the detainees. The credit belongs to the ICRC representatives who first proposed the idea. As indicated, detainees appeared before the MNFRC alone. Among the population of detainees was a significant number of juveniles.[112] The ICRC asked whether it was possible to help the juvenile detainees at their MNFRC review for it would be a very important, but also forbidding, process for them. The ICRC representative initially suggested assigning counsel to the juveniles. A compromise was reached, modeling the concept on that of the personal representative assigned to persons appearing before a Combatant Status Review Tribunal.[113] The personal representative was not a lawyer; his or her role was not to act as an advocate during the hearing. Rather, the representative's role was to assist the detainee in preparing for the hearing, explaining the process and appearing with him at the hearing. The personal representative could make a statement for the detainee and could suggest to the members questions that might be relevant, but he or she was not to offer argument in the manner of counsel.

The implementation of providing a personal representative for juveniles began in late 2007. One of the officers assigned as a permanent MNFRC member was reassigned as the juvenile personal representative. A naval reservist, whose civilian job was as a school teacher with significant counseling experience, was chosen for the position; experience showed that she was an excellent choice. Experience also showed, as reported by MNFRC members and juvenile detainees alike, that the initiative was a success. The ICRC next asked to expand the program to represent other vulnerable populations, to include female detainees, third-country nationals (i.e., detainees who were not citizens of Iraq) and those detainees with diminished mental capacity. These, too, were successfully implemented, mostly because of the overall limited numbers.[114] Expanding the program further was explored with the ICRC, but no other discrete population that needed representation was identified. The ICRC was unapologetic in its request that *every* detainee receive the benefit, but that was logistically and administratively impractical. Indeed, the ICRC, while happy enough with the limited personal representation, never hid its ambition to push the MNFRC process until, step-by-step, legal counsel were assigned to all detainees at every hearing.

Though not part of the MNFRC process, some mention should be made of the programs offered to the detainees within the TIF, as participation in some of these could have a positive impact on the detainee's case. In mid-2007, when faced with rising numbers of detainees and rising discontent among them, the DCG-DO decided to implement a set of formal programs that eventually became known as Theater Internment Facility Reconciliation Center, or TIFRC, services.[115] The services included literacy programs (well over half of the detainee population was illiterate), limited vocational training, work programs and religious engagement classes.[116] Though these programs could be viewed as a kind of social work, the focus was on reducing the threat a participating detainee presented, thereby facilitating his earlier release from custody. The programs had two main purposes. The first responded to the finding that a majority of the detainees had joined the insurgency for money: they had no jobs and were willing to take cash to emplace IEDs, etc. The vocational training and work programs were designed to address that problem. The second purpose responded to the belief that insurgent extremists were misusing Islam to encourage insurgent acts as a religious duty. Once the detainees learned to read, they could study the Quran, with the help of Iraqi clerics contracted by US forces, and determine for themselves that Islam teaches quite the opposite. The hope was that completion of the programs would change a former security threat into no threat at all.

The TIFRC concept was developed contemporaneously with the MNFRC, and integrated into the MNFRC's process. MNFRC members were specifically directed to consider the detainee's participation, if any, in the TIFRC services in making their determination on whether he presented an imperative threat. It was to be considered merely as a factor among many: there was no pressure to recommend release for successful participants, and failure to participate was not to be considered negatively. Additionally, the MNFRC members had the opportunity to recommend for future TIFRC participation those detainees whose detention they decided to continue but who might benefit, next time, from having gone through the programs. Providing them with this recommendatory power was valuable early in the TIFRC process when the services were just beginning. When the services became more widely available to all detainees, the MNFRCs were no longer given the option of "retain, with TIFRC."

5. Special Release Processing

The discussion up to this point has focused on regularly scheduled reviews, from the initial review at the Magistrate Cell through the CRRB and MNFRC. However, there was another significant method by which detainees' cases would be reviewed, and detainees released—that was through special release processing. Although there were many ways that the special release process could be initiated, the single constant was that the DCG-DO made an individual decision whether to grant the release.

Special release requests originated from many sources. Some came from Iraqi officials. It was a rare meeting with Iraqi government officials, or other important personages, such as influential sheiks, where the DCG-DO did not return with a list of detainees to consider for special release. Other requests would come from within the coalition: officials from the battalion through the MNF-I level would often ask for releases to further their engagement efforts. A somewhat separate category included those requests from doctors, asking for the compassionate release of detainees with terminal or serious medical conditions.

These requests were individually processed.[117] Attorneys within the headquarters element of the TF 134 legal office would be designated as "Special Release Attorneys," whose job would be to research the case, write a memo detailing the relevant facts, and make a recommendation as to whether the request should be granted or not. The memo was staffed through the Legal Advisor to the DCG-DO, who would make the final decision. The standard against which the decisions were made remained the same—imperative threat to security—but there was a willingness to accept more risk in these releases than with normal periodic reviews. This was most evident for requests which originated from within the coalition: if a ground commander, with knowledge of the detainee's background,[118] was willing to accept him back within his battlespace, with reluctance the request was often granted. There was generally less tolerance of risk with requests from Iraqi officials, though the political considerations associated with such requests could often tip the balance.

6. Criminal Prosecution

CPA Memo 3 provided that coalition forces could detain two classes of persons: those "suspected of having committed criminal acts and [who] are not considered security threats,"[119] and others "for imperative reasons of security in accordance with the mandate set out in UNSCR 1546."[120] To the extent the authority to detain persons for criminal acts had been used earlier, by 2007 it was exceptionally rare for coalition forces to apprehend and hold a person who presented only a criminal threat. Rather, all detainees processed into the TIF went through the Magistrate Cell and were assessed as imperative threats to security as already described. That is not to say that criminal prosecutions did not occur, for that was another major operation that must be discussed, albeit briefly.[121]

CPA Order 13[122] established a national-level court called the Central Criminal Court of Iraq, or CCCI. The Court's jurisdiction extended to all criminal violations, misdemeanor or felony, though in its discretionary jurisdiction it was encouraged to concentrate on the most serious cases, such as terrorism, acts intended to destabilize democratic institutions, and violence based on race, nationality, ethnicity or religion.[123] The CCCI sat in Baghdad in a building just outside the International Zone. It was the court to which all coalition force detainee criminal cases were referred.

Within the TF 134 legal office there was a CCCI liaison office, which was tasked to prepare cases for eventual prosecution at CCCI. Attorneys within that office would receive the files forwarded to it from the Magistrate Cell and determine, based on their experience with the Court, whether prosecution was worthwhile, based on either the nature of the misconduct alleged or the state of the evidence and availability of witnesses. A case for which prosecution was not deemed worthwhile was "non-referred," after which the detainee's case would be returned for review by the CRRB or MNFRC, as appropriate, to determine whether he remained an imperative threat.

Those cases that warranted prosecution were prepared for prosecution by the CCCI liaison office attorney, and then presented to the Iraqi prosecutor and investigative judge for proceedings in accordance with the Iraqi criminal code. It is important to note that the CCCI liaison office attorneys did not themselves prosecute any case; however, their role hardly ended with passing off a prepared case file. The CCCI liaison office attorney would collect all physical evidence, summarize all other evidence, arrange the presence of witnesses and ensure that the detainee defendant appeared. The attorney would be present for the investigative hearing and subsequent trial, and would be responsive to any questions or requests for evidence from the judges. Investigative judges would often solicit from the attorney questions that they (the judges) might want to ask. If the CCCI liaison office attorney didn't act as the prosecutor, he or she was certainly a very active "shadow" prosecutor.

Convictions resulted in just less than 60 percent of the cases. Compared to those of any normal US jurisdiction, where conviction rates regularly exceed 90 percent, these results were not particularly impressive. However, there were several reasons to be satisfied with the results. The Iraqi system did not engage in any type of plea bargaining, so a powerful incentive to plead guilty to charges was removed. A defendant taking his chances at trial is occasionally rewarded. CCCI liaison attorneys were also forced to take cases to trial they knew would not result in conviction. For example, assume coalition forces raid a house and find a cache of illegal weapons, IED-making materials, etc. They detain all of the military-aged males in the house. CCCI liaison attorneys would have to bring all of these persons to the joint trial, knowing that the Court was likely to convict only the owner of the house or someone else who could be said to have possessed the weapons, acquitting the rest. If even one of the persons found during the raid was not brought to trial, all defendants would point to the missing person as the possessor of the weapons and the Court would find no one guilty.

Those convicted would be transferred to Iraqi custody as soon as possible but due to the overcrowding of Iraqi facilities it often did not happen quickly. These detainees remained in the TIF, though in a separate compound, while awaiting eventual transfer. They were otherwise treated the same as all other detainees, other than that their periodic reviews ended because they were considered to have begun serving their sentences.

If the Court failed to convict the detainee defendant, the criminal proceeding ended but the person was still a security detainee. These cases would be immediately reviewed by the CRRB or MNFRC for its recommendation. In the case where the file contained information that could not be shared with the Court because of its classification, the board could well conclude that the detainee remained a threat and recommend his continued detention despite the acquittal. This was a source of confusion for the detainee and of tension with the Court, though most of the judges understood the separate security-based detention authority.

Part III—Applications for the Future

This article has presented a description of the detainee operations during a portion of coalition operations in Iraq, and may prove to be of some limited value in the documentation of that experience. However, more important, the lessons learned may prove to be useful in future operations. The following comments and recommendations are offered in that hope.

Before offering such comments, it is important to insist that the practices described earlier or recommended below should not be taken as establishing custom that will bind the United States or others in similar situations. The law, such as it was applied by analogy to detainee operations, is not very detailed nor, in some ways, very demanding. This author is confident that the reviews of the cases of detained persons went beyond what the law required. The United States was able to set the conditions for the practices described by devoting substantial financial and personnel resources to the detention mission in Iraq; those generous resources may not be available in a future operation, and thus it may become necessary to adhere only to the more minimal requirements of the positive law. Other nations may not have the resources under any circumstances to enable them to provide more than the law requires and the US practices should not force them, through a claim of a new customary international law obligation, to try.

A. Detainee Personal Appearance

All things being equal, a review at which the detainee appears and speaks is likely to be better than one in which he is not given that opportunity. "Better" in this context means more likely to arrive at a correct assessment of the level of threat the detainee presents. Detention is costly: to the detaining power in resources and personnel; to the detainee and his family, which often suffers; and to the occupied or host nation, depending on the legal authority for the detention, which needs to move beyond civilian internment as it reasserts its own sovereignty. Of course, in a situation in which civilian internment is permitted in any form, things are not always equal. The somewhat relaxed requirements for hearings under the Geneva Conventions clearly recognize that in a conflict certain unavoidable impositions on individual rights will occur and that even a minimal process will, if followed, be better than no process at all.

Nevertheless, if resources permit, it would be worthwhile to permit the detainee to appear at all levels of review. The MNFRC proved successful, and if it worked with over twenty thousand detainees, it would certainly work in smaller-scale detention operations. The CRRB would have been replaced totally by the MNFRC in its reduced role as the ninety-day appeal board but for the Iraqi participation.

Insofar as Iraqi participation on the MNFRC was unable to be arranged and the CRRB was the only time when the Iraqis did participate, it was determined to be politically inexpedient to abolish it. However, a future detention operation need not be constrained by these considerations, and the appeal and subsequent review board could be designed from the beginning with the appropriate membership.

Permitting a personal appearance at the initial review stage, at the point where the Magistrate Cell functioned, need not require an MNFRC-like panel (though it could); it is quite possible for the magistrate to conduct the hearing, and make the decision, alone. Consideration was given to permitting detainees to personally appear before the Magistrate Cell, but insufficient manning prevented that from occurring. The attorneys assigned as magistrates were already employed full-time in preparing and perfecting the files, writing summaries, and so on, and levying an additional requirement upon them to hold a hearing for each of those same cases would have been impossible. But, as stated before, with greater personnel resources, or with fewer cases, it would have been possible and beneficial.

The problem with this recommendation is that it is essentially irrevocable during the remainder of that operation. Should personal appearance be the standard set at the beginning, and the operational tempo dramatically increases or the security situation deteriorates, it will be difficult to revert to a file-only review, mostly because of the negative reaction from the detainees,[124] and possibly by organizations, such as the ICRC, monitoring the process. There is a certain appeal, therefore, in starting with the minimums and improving them once a steady state has been realized.

B. Personal Representatives

The decision to grant a personal representative to the detainees, or any subgroups thereof, must be based on the perceived need and the availability of resources. It may yield better results and will help the perception of fairness by the detainees. Efforts to turn any of the hearings into a fully adversarial process, with or without the involvement of counsel, should be resisted until such time as national policymakers direct a different course, and then only after debating the compatibility of such a procedure in an area of conflict.

C. Technology

Better uses of technology may not have directly benefited the quality of the reviews, but certainly would have eased the administrative burdens associated with the hearings. Consider the role of the detainee file. It was the centerpiece of every review, even at the MNFRC. If the file was lost or missing, nothing could be done with that detainee. (In almost all cases, the file could often be reassembled from its constituent parts scattered throughout the force.) The logistical effort to track and move the files was impressive. The files were assembled at the Magistrate Cell, and when their review was complete, they were boxed up and convoyed to the International Zone, where they would be collected by the CRRB (and a more limited number by the CCCI liaison office). Upon completion of the CRRB review, they were boxed up again, convoyed back to Victory Base, put on a plane at Baghdad International Airport, flown to Basra, and convoyed to Camp Bucca. If the file was needed for special release processing, it would return along that path to Victory Base Complex, and maybe back to Camp Bucca again later before it returned to another way station in this possibly unending process.

Ideally, files would begin their lives as scanned images, using a program such as Adobe Acrobat to organize the pages in a standardized manner similar to the six-part folders. New material (e.g., the results of a periodic review) could be inserted at the appropriate place in the electronic file. The files would reside on a central server, with visibility throughout the force. Board members would each have computers with which to read the electronic files.

Many efforts were made to reach this ideal, but the sheer number of files in existence made it impractical with the then-current resources. Scanning can be time consuming and quality assurance must be strict if all paper documents are to be destroyed. Each resulting file often exceeds twenty-five megabytes in size. While storage requirements are considerable, though manageable, bandwidth considerations are not so easily solved. Some method must be reached to ensure the "originality" of a single version (the paper file system has this obvious advantage) that can be changed only by those authorized to do so. None of these problems are intractable—bandwidth will likely be the most difficult challenge, as it is always in short supply, especially in an area of conflict—and future technological innovation may make their solutions so much easier.

Another technological solution, one which was investigated but not implemented mostly due to lack of bandwidth again, was "virtual" hearings, at which one or more of the members might participate from a remote location. Such a system would have much appeal, eliminating the onerous travel to a remote location such as Camp Bucca.[125] The quality of the resulting hearing, however, would be correlated to the quality of the video-teleconference link, as the visual aspects of a hearing are often more important than the aural. Compare, for example, a situation where the members appeared to the detainee, and the detainee to the members, on a laptop screen using a webcam versus a full-motion, wide-screen presentation. A virtual presence is always inferior to real presence; the issue is always how much degradation is acceptable.

D. Broad Participation Membership

Boards, specifically the MNFRC, worked well with "general purpose" officers, yet as the process matured and the types of persons who sat on the boards broadened the process improved. When designing a review panel for a future board, it would be best to begin with the broadest possible participation.

In an operation which permits the involvement of representatives of the host nation, the benefit of having them participate will likely outweigh the administrative burdens (clearances and disclosure predominantly). They need not be given the majority vote, such as was the case in the CRRB, though the political situation, especially one in which the visiting force's presence is based on host-nation consent, may warrant that concession. The cultural sensitivities and awareness that such members bring to the board cannot be otherwise replicated.

Concerning own-force members, senior enlisted members are always a valuable addition, despite an otherwise pervasive preference for officers only.[126] Members from the operating forces must participate. In addition to their wealth of experience resulting from seeing the same type of incidents that have resulted in detention occur firsthand, their involvement helps to lend an ownership stake in the process to the operating forces.[127] Permanent members, if they are available, will almost certainly have little or no operating exposure, but their experience reviewing many, many boards will help to establish some parity of treatment across the process.

E. Programs within the TIF

Administrative detention has been recognized as necessary during the types of operations described. The conditions under which the detainees are held must comport with enumerated standards: these responsibilities are doctrinally exercised by the military police, and help to maintain the peace and order of the detainee camps. However, the same conditions may also have a direct bearing on the legal reviews. Programs such as those of the TF 134 TIFRC discussed above are designed to reduce the threat the detainees present post-capture. Participation in these programs by the detainee must be highlighted to the board reviewing his continued detention and assessed as one additional factor among many in determining whether the detainee remains an imperative threat. If members, educated about the TIFRC programs, are according them no weight in their decisions, the programs should be changed or cancelled, except to the extent that they serve a separate military police function within the TIF. On the other hand, programs which have a positive effect on board decisions should be expanded, with the hope of greater numbers of releases of those who are no longer threats.

Conclusion

Detention, in some form, is a reality in every operation, just as the application of force, in some form, often including deadly force, is also a reality. The availability of detention to soldiers in a conflict may tend to reduce the amount of force that would otherwise be used to complete a mission: without detention available, the soldier can either shoot to kill or let the targeted person run away to fight again tomorrow. Detention is hardly cost-free, and its very availability can often lead to abuses of the authority that allows it. The law regarding detention attempts to strike the appropriate balance in often general terms, explicitly relying upon the good faith of the parties in applying the law to facts on the ground.

The detention operations described in this article represent an evolution over several years. They were characterized by an overall good-faith effort to apply the letter and spirit of the law, but they were far from perfect. The damage caused by Abu Ghraib is incalculable, but it focused command attention on detention operations and made incredible resources available to improve them, and so resulted in a much better product. Procedures were developed and conscientiously applied, but mistakes are likely in any system. Many were detained, and for too long, who did not deserve to be detained. The process eventually found them, and they were released. Many were released who should not have been released, either through oversight, failure to synthesize all available information or by misjudgments by the reviewing board; some returned to the insurgency and killed coalition force members or Iraqi citizens, and this too is a tragedy. Mistakes on either side are inevitable; the best systems can only hope to minimize them.

Appendix

(TF 134 Letterhead)

Reply to Attention of
MNFI-DCG-DO 5 August 2007
MEMORANDUM FOR MULTI-NATIONAL FORCE REVIEW COMMITTEE MEMBERS
SUBJECT: Multi-National Force Review Committee Instructions

1. You have been selected for important duty as a member of the Multi-National Force Review Committee (MNFRC). This duty is a critical part of the efforts of the Multi-National Force, and vital to a measured and steady reintegration of security internees back into Iraqi society. While assigned, this will be your primary duty, until your assignment ends. You should review this letter and other instructional material that will be made available to you prior to your first board.

2. The persons who appear before you are security detainees. We detain them under the authority of the United Nations Security Council Resolutions which permit us to hold those who present imperative threats to coalition forces or the Iraqi people. Although in many cases their conduct could be characterized as criminal, it is not necessary to our detention that they be charged with, or convicted of, a crime. Similarly, the detainees are not serving a sentence. Rather, they are held because they have been determined to be security threats.

3. Your task is to determine whether the detainee remains an imperative threat to security. You must believe that there are reasonable grounds to sustain that finding. "Reasonable grounds" consist of sufficient indicators to lead a reasonable person to believe that detention is necessary for imperative reasons of security.

4. You should consider the following factors in arriving at this determination:

- Your focus should be on the threat the detainee presents today, not the threat he posed when he was captured. Pre-capture conduct may be important as an indicator of the detainee's threat level now, and in the future, but it is not the sole indicator. The detainee will have undergone several legal reviews prior to appearing before you. You are in no way bound by their findings and recommendations.

• You will have access to classified and unclassified information associated with the case. As you review the information, focus on facts, not on the conclusions of others: it is your job to draw the conclusions.

• You should understand that time spent in the Theater Internment Facility (TIF) can change a person—for good or for bad. It is your job to assess that change, and apply it to your threat determination. In this regard, you will be provided with a "report card" for each detainee. It will detail his performance in the TIF, including: any disciplinary infractions; any instances of positive performance; participation in educational classes, religious enlightenment courses, or in various vocational training courses. Be aware that a detainee may engage in negative or group behaviors in a prison-like environment for self-preservation. You will be provided with various assessments of the detainee by counselors, psychologists, and religious leaders. Take all of these items into account when you make your decision.

• You will have the opportunity to question the detainee. Make use of it, but be mindful of disclosing classified information, especially sources and methods of collection. It is up to you to determine the detainee's credibility, and what weight you give his answers. Be aware that cultural differences may complicate this challenge. A cultural advisor will be available to help you in this regard.

• Treat the detainee with respect. Show no bias to his regional or religious background. Don't be affected by his manner of dress or personal appearance. Finally, remember that, although you will be participating in many of these boards, he only gets to appear before this one, and your decision is going to have a profound impact on his life.

5. At the conclusion of the hearing, you will be able to discuss the case with your fellow members, and vote. Each member's vote is equally weighted. Senior members will not unduly influence junior members. You must decide first whether the detainee is an imperative threat to security. If he is not, you should vote to Release; if he is, you should vote to Retain. Majority rules. If the majority votes to Retain, you next vote whether the detainee should be recommended for participation in TIFRIC, or TIF Re-Integration Center. This program is described more fully in information available to you, but is generally for those detainees whom you feel will benefit from the suite of services offered on their way to eventual release. Again, majority rules.

6. If you have any questions about this duty, contact the TF 134 Legal Advisor or his MNFRC Representative.

7. Thank you for participating in this process. You are making a difference in our efforts to ensure the safety and stability of Iraq, and the success of the Coalition Force mission.

/signed/
DOUGLAS M. STONE
Major General, USMC
Deputy Commanding General for
Detainee Operations

I hereby acknowledge receipt of these instructions and will comply with all of the above:

____

Signature and date

Notes

1. *See, e.g.*, Seymour M. Hersch, *The Annals of National Security: Torture at Abu Ghraib*, THE NEW YORKER, May 10, 2004, at 42, *available at* http://www.newyorker.com/archive/2004/05/10/040510fa_fact.

2. As will be discussed, though technically a coalition operation among many nations, the primary actor, and in most cases the only actor, in the detention operations discussed in this article was the United States. Nevertheless, since some aspects of the operation did involve the coalition in the broader sense, the term "coalition forces" will be used as a shorthand.

3. Note that this article will not discuss the legal basis for initiating conflict, or *jus ad bellum*. For such a discussion, see Andru E. Wall, *Was the 2003 Invasion of Iraq Legal?*, which is Chapter IV in this volume, at 69.

4. *See* President George W. Bush, President Bush Addresses the Nation (Mar. 19, 2003), http://georgewbush-whitehouse.archives.gov/news/releases/2003/03/20030319-17.html (announcing that combat operations had begun in Iraq as of March 19, 2003, in Washington, DC, but March 20 in Iraq due to the time difference).

5. Article 2 is common to all four Geneva Conventions. *See* Convention for the Amelioration of the Condition of the Wounded and Sick in Armed Forces in the Field art. 2, Aug. 12, 1949, 6 U.S.T. 3114, 75 U.N.T.S. 31 [hereinafter Wounded and Sick Convention]; Convention for the Amelioration of the Condition of Wounded, Sick and Shipwrecked Members of Armed Forces at Sea art. 2, Aug. 12, 1949, 6 U.S.T. 3217, 75 U.N.T.S. 85 [hereinafter Shipwrecked Convention]; Convention Relative to the Protection of Prisoners of War art. 2, Aug. 12, 1949, 6 U.S.T. 3316, 75 U.N.T.S. 135 [hereinafter PW Convention]; Convention Relative to the Protection of Civilian Persons in Time of War art. 2, Aug. 12, 1949, 6 U.S.T. 3516, 75 U.N.T.S. 287 [hereinafter Civilians Convention]; all *reprinted in* DOCUMENTS ON THE LAWS OF WAR (Adam Roberts & Richard Guelff eds., 3d ed. 2000) at 197, 198; 222, 223; 244, 245; and 301, 302; respectively. Common Article 2 states: "[T]he present Convention shall apply to all cases of declared war or of any other armed conflict which may arise between two or more of the High Contracting Parties . . . ."

6. *See generally* Regulations Respecting the Laws and Customs of War on Land, annexed to Convention Respecting the Law and Customs of War on Land, Oct. 18, 1907, 36 Stat. 2277, *reprinted in* DOCUMENTS ON THE LAWS OF WAR, *supra* note 5, at 73. *See also* Protocol Additional to the Geneva Conventions of 12 August 1949, and Relating to the Protection of Victims of International Armed Conflicts, June 8, 1977, 1125 U.N.T.S. 3, *reprinted in* DOCUMENTS ON THE LAWS OF WAR, *supra* note 5, at 422.

7. PW Convention, *supra* note 5, art. 4. The remaining categories of persons eligible for prisoner of war status include armed forces of a government not recognized by the detaining power, civilians accompanying the force, certain merchant mariners, and civilians comprising mass levies. *Id.* For a discussion suggesting additional inferred conditions over the four enumerated in the text, see YORAM DINSTEIN, THE CONDUCT OF HOSTILITIES UNDER THE LAW OF INTERNATIONAL ARMED CONFLICT 36 (2004).

8. PW Convention, *supra* note 5, art. 118.

9. *Id.*, art. 5.

10. *See* Headquarters, Department of the Army, Reg. 190-8, Enemy Prisoners of War, Retained Personnel, Civilian Internees and Other Detainees (1997) [hereinafter AR 190-8]. AR 190-8 has applicability among all four US services: the Air Force, Marine Corps and Navy have each provided AR 190-8 a designation within their own systems of regulations.

11. PW Convention, *supra* note 5, art. 5 (emphasis added).

12. Civilians Convention, *supra* note 5, art. 4.

13. The exceptions from protected-person status include nationals of a country not a party to the Convention, and nationals of neutral States in the territory of the detaining State, and nationals of cobelligerents anywhere, so long as the neutral or cobelligerent State has normal diplomatic relations with the detaining State. *Id.*

14. Part II is entitled "General Protection of Populations Against Certain Consequences of War." *Id.*, Part II. The articles therein (Articles 13–26) generally protect hospitals, medical personnel and transports associated with the same, and encourage the parties to specially protect certain vulnerable populations (expectant women, children, etc.). *Id.*

15. Like Article 2, Article 3 is common to all the Geneva Conventions. *See* Wounded and Sick Convention, *supra* note 5, art. 3; Shipwrecked Convention, *supra* note 5, art. 3; PW Convention, *supra* note 5, art. 3; Civilians Convention, *supra* note 5, art. 3. Although by its terms Common Article 3 applies only to armed conflicts "not of an international character occurring in the territory of one of the High Contracting Parties," the ICRC *Commentary* makes clear that these same standards were intended to apply to all armed conflicts. The *Commentary* states:

> The value of the provision [sub-paragraph (1) of Common Article 3] is not limited to the field within Article 3. Representing, as it does, the minimum which must be applied in the least determinate of conflicts, its terms must *a fortiori* be respected in international armed conflicts proper, when all the provisions of the Convention are applicable. For "the greater obligation must include the lesser," as one might say.

COMMENTARY ON GENEVA CONVENTION III RELATIVE TO THE TREATMENT OF PRISONERS OF WAR 38 (Jean S. Pictet ed., 1958) [hereinafter ICRC COMMENTARY].

16. *Compare, e.g.,* Civilians Convention, *supra* note 5, Article 27 requirement of humane treatment without adverse distinctions *with* a similar provision in Common Article 3, paragraph 1, *id.*; Article 32's, *id.*, prohibition of murder and torture *with* Common Article 3, *id.*, paragraph 1(a); and Article 34's, *id.*, prohibition on the taking of hostages *with* Common Article 3, paragraph 1(b), *id.*

17. Section II is entitled "Aliens in the Territory of a Party to the Conflict," *id.*; Section III is "Occupied Territories," *id.*

18. Although the Civilians Convention typically discusses internment along with assigned residence, the focus of this article is only on internment, and therefore any references to assigned residence will be henceforth disregarded.

19. Civilians Convention, *supra* note 5, art. 41. The text of the article is actually written to make clear that nothing *more severe* than assigned residence or internment is possible; by clear implication, assigned residence or internment is therefore permissible.

20. *Id.*, art. 42.

21. *Id.*, art. 43.

22. *Id.*, art. 78. The ICRC *Commentary* suggests that the "imperative reasons of security" standard of Article 78 is more stringent than the "absolutely necessary" standard of Article 42, even though their colloquial meanings seem substantially equivalent. Comparing Article 78 to Article 42, the *Commentary* states:

> In occupied territories the internment of protected persons should be even more exceptional than it is inside the territory of the Parties to the conflict; for in the former case the question of nationality does not arise. That is why Article 78 speaks of imperative reasons of security; there can be no question of taking collective measures: each case must be decided separately.

ICRC COMMENTARY, *supra* note 15, at 367. The observation is resolved in the commentary to Article 41: "[T]here might be situations—a threat of invasion for example—which would force a government to act without delay to prevent hostile acts, and to take measures against certain categories without always finding it possible to consider individual cases." *Id.* at 256.

23. Civilians Convention, *supra* note 5, art. 78. In discussing the content of the "regular procedure" to be followed, the *Commentary* refers the reader to the "precise and detailed procedure to be followed" set out in Article 43. ICRC COMMENTARY, *supra* note 15, at 368. However, the promised detail is lacking both in the text of Article 43 and its accompanying commentary; both are written at the same level of generality as Article 78. *See* Civilians Convention, *supra* note 5, art. 43; ICRC COMMENTARY, *supra* note 15, at 261.

24. Civilians Convention, *supra* note 5, art. 78.

25. *Id.*

26. *Id.* The commentary to Article 78 offers the observation that the reviewing body must be more than a single individual. ICRC COMMENTARY, *supra* note 15, at 369. *But see* YORAM DINSTEIN, THE INTERNATIONAL LAW OF BELLIGERENT OCCUPATION 175 (2009), where Professor Dinstein discusses, approvingly, Israel's decision to have Article 78 appeals decided by a single judge.

27. *See* President George W. Bush, President Bush Announces Major Combat Operations in Iraq Have Ended (May 1, 2003), http://georgewbush-whitehouse.archives.gov/news/releases/2003/05/20030501-15.html.

28. "The Convention shall also apply to all cases of partial or total occupation . . . ." Civilians Convention, *supra* note 5, art. 3, para. 2.

29. CPA Regulation No. 1, issued on May 16, 2003, is the means by which the CPA established itself. Section 1 declared that "[t]he CPA shall exercise powers of government temporarily in order to provide for the effective administration of Iraq during the period of transitional administration . . . ." "The CPA is vested with all executive, legislative, and judicial authority necessary to achieve its objectives . . . ." Coalition Provisional Authority Regulation No. 1, CPA/REG/16 May 2003/01 (May 16, 2003), sec. 1, *available at* http://www.cpa-iraq.org/regulations/20030516_CPAREG_1_The_Coalition_Provisional_Authority_.pdf.

30. CPA Regulation No. 1 states, "Regulations and Orders will remain in force until repealed by the Administrator or superseded by legislation issued by democratic institutions of Iraq." *Id.*,

sec. 3(1). Throughout its existence, the CPA also issued various memoranda. These are defined as interpretive guides to regulations and orders, *id.*, sec. 4(1); as such, they cannot be considered "law" in the same sense as regulations and orders.

31. S.C. Res. 1546, U.N. Doc. S/RES/1546 (June 8, 2004).

32. U.N. Charter chap. VII (Action with Respect to Threats to the Peace, Breaches of the Peace, and Acts of Aggression).

33. S.C. Res 1511, U.N. Doc. S/RES/1511 (Oct. 16, 2003), also a resolution under Chapter VII, previously authorized "a multinational force under unified command to take all necessary measures to contribute to the maintenance of security and stability in Iraq." *Id.*, para. 13.

34. S.C. Res. 1546, *supra* note 31, para. 10.

35. *Id.* at 8.

36. *Id.* at 11 (emphasis added).

37. The public statements of many Security Council representatives adverted to the importance of the explicit Iraqi request for assistance to their voting for the resolution. *See* Press Release, Security Council, Security Council Endorses Formation of Sovereign Interim Government in Iraq; Welcomes End of Occupation by 30 June, Democratic Elections by January 2005, U.N. Doc. SC/8117 (June 8, 2004), *available at* http://www.un.org/News/Press/docs/2004/sc8117.doc.htm. Accordingly, the annexation of the Allawi letter to the resolution no doubt served a political purpose.

38. S.C. Res. 1546, *supra* note 31, para. 12.

39. S.C. Res. 1637, U.N. Doc. S/RES/1637 (Nov. 11, 2005).

40. S.C. Res. 1723, U.N. Doc. S/RES/1723 (Nov. 28, 2006).

41. S.C. Res. 1790, U.N. Doc. S/RES/1790 (Dec. 18, 2007).

42. *Id.*

43. *See* The White House, Fact Sheet: U.S.-Iraq Declaration of Principles for Friendship and Cooperation (Nov. 26, 2007), *available at* http://georgewbush-whitehouse.archives.gov/news/releases/2007/11/20071126-1.html. Among the principles contained in the declaration are "Iraqis have expressed a desire to move past a Chapter VII MNFI mandate and we are committed to helping them achieve this objective," and "[a]fter the Chapter VII mandate is renewed for one year, we will begin negotiation of a framework that will govern the future of our bilateral relationship." *Id.*

44. For a more detailed treatment of the two agreements, see Trevor A. Rush, *Don't Call It a SOFA!: An Overview of the U.S.-Iraq Security Agreement*, ARMY LAWYER, May 2009, at 34.

45. Strategic Framework Agreement for a Relationship of Friendship and Cooperation between the United States of America and the Republic of Iraq, Nov. 17, 2008, *available at* http://www.mnf-iraq.com/images/CGs_Messages/strategic_framework_agreement.pdf.

46. Agreement Between the United States of America and the Republic of Iraq on the Withdrawal of United States Forces from Iraq and the Organization of Their Activities during Their Temporary Presence in Iraq, Nov. 17, 2008, *available at* http://www.mnf-iraq.com/images/CGs_Messages/security_agreement.pdf [hereinafter Security Agreement].

47. *See id.*, art. 22. *See also* Rush, *supra* note 44, at 42–46.

48. Security Agreement, *supra* note 46, art. 22.

49. The area of responsibility for Central Command included Iraq, Afghanistan, the Horn of Africa, Iran and Pakistan. *See* United States Central Command, AOR Countries, http://www.centcom.mil/en/countries/aor/ (last visited Aug. 31, 2009). Needless to say, each of these countries assigned to the commander of Central Command presented significant military challenges.

50. General Petraeus assumed the position of Commander, MNF-I, on February 10, 2007. *See* Multi-National Force–Iraq, Petraeus Assumes MNF-I Command, http://www.mnf-iraq.com (search "petraeus assumes command," All Words option) (last visited Aug. 31, 2009). General Odierno assumed command on September 16, 2008. *See* Multi-National Force–Iraq, Odierno Assumes Command of Coalition Forces in Iraq, http://www.mnf-iraq.com (search "odierno assumes command," All Words option) (last visited Aug. 31, 2009).

51. The other major subordinate command, Multi-National Security Transition Command–Iraq, was not involved in detention operations.

52. These were usually division commanders in their normally assigned, non-deployed billet.

53. Multi-National Force–West was the region commanded by a Marine Corps general, the operating forces of which were predominantly, but not exclusively, Marines. The different name—"Multi-National Force" versus "Division"—is the remnant of an earlier command relationship by which the Marine commander, then a three-star general, was independent of MNC-I and reported directly to MNF-I.

54. As the Polish and British forces departed from Iraq, their areas of responsibility were assumed by Multi-National Division–Central, which was re-designated as Multi-National Division–South. *See* Multi-National Force–Iraq, MND-C, MND-SE Operating Areas Combine to Create MND-South, http://www.mnf-iraq.com (search "mnd south british," All Words option) (last visited Aug. 31, 2009).

55. *See* Antonio M. Taguba, Army Regulation 15-6 Investigation of the 800th Military Police Brigade (certified on June 4, 2004), *available at* http://www.npr.org/iraq/2004/prison_abuse_report.pdf [hereinafter Taguba Report]. General Taguba recommended "[t]hat a single commander in CJTF-7 be responsible for overall detainee operations throughout the Iraq Theater of Operations." *Id.* at 21. CJTF-7 was the predecessor command to MNF-I.

56. The genesis of the name of the task force came simply from the name of the building—Building 134 on Camp Victory—at which the task force was initially headquartered.

57. As will be seen below, the execution of the detention operation mission was overwhelmingly more time consuming than that of creating policy. In recognition of that, all of the commander's staff resided in TF 134; there was no identified staff for the DCG-DO.

58. Operating units, such as divisions and brigades, would also operate small internment facilities, at which detainees would be held for a limited period of time before being transferred to the theater internment facility. The operations at the lower-level facilities are not the focus of this article.

59. Headquarters, Department of the Army, FM 3-19.40, Internment/Resettlement Operations para. 3-12 (Sept. 4, 2007). In accordance with US Department of Defense, Directive 2310.01E, The Department of Defense Detainee Program para. 1.2 (Sept. 5, 2006), *available at* http://www.dtic.mil/whs/directives/corres/pdf/231001p.pdf [hereinafter DoDD 2310.01E], the Secretary of the Army is designated the Executive Agent for Detention Operations. As such, doctrinal publications such as FM 3-19.40 have applicability across service lines.

60. TF 134 benefited from having both active-duty brigade elements, commanded by a colonel (O-6), and reserve or National Guard units, commanded by brigadier generals (O-7).

61. One of the consequences of the extensive detention operation missions in Iraq and Afghanistan was that active-duty MP units were heavily stressed, and therefore in short supply.

62. For example, Navy provisional units might be made up of aviation mechanics, sonarmen or boatswain's mates, and be commanded by a surface warfare officer. All were individual augmentees, who would form into units in the United States, train for a period of time, deploy and then upon redeployment return to their original units.

63. Headquarters, Department of the Army, FM 2-22.3, Human Intelligence Collector Operations para. 6-13 (Sept. 2006), *available at* http://www.fcnl.org/pdfs/civ_liberties/Field_Manual_Sept06.pdf [hereinafter FM 2-22.3].

64. *Id.*, para. 3-24.

65. FM 2-22.3, *supra* note 63.

66. Detainee Treatment Act of 2005, Div. A, Title X, § 1002, Pub. L. No. 109-148, 119 Stat. 2680 (codified at 10 U.S.C.S. § 801 Note (LexisNexis 2009)) [hereinafter DTA]. The Act provides: "No person in the custody or under the effective control of the Department of Defense or under detention in a Department of Defense facility shall be subject to any treatment or technique of interrogation not authorized by and listed in the United States Army Field Manual on Intelligence Interrogation." *Id.*, § 1002(a). In essence, the DTA "enacted" certain portions of FM 2-22.3, *supra* note 63, into positive law. The decision was welcomed by many as a means of providing transparency to interrogation operations, and criticized by others on constitutional grounds or the practical ground that by limiting interrogation methods to those publicly disseminated, potential enemies may benefit by developing effective resistance techniques. *See* James A. Barkei, *Legislating Military Doctrine: Congressional Usurping of Executive Authority Through Detainee Interrogations*, 193 MILITARY LAW REVIEW 97 (2007) (arguing that the DTA impermissibly intrudes upon the President's powers).

67. FM 2-22.3, *supra* note 63, chap. 8.

68. *Id.*, para. 5-75.

69. As a participant in many briefings to distinguished visitors, among them congressional leaders and Department of Defense officials, at TF 134, this author heard many questions about the effect of the Detainee Treatment Act/FM 2-22.3 scheme. The JIDC commander and his head interrogator always responded that they supported the policy and believed that it did not adversely affect their ability to harvest useful intelligence.

70. This position was another result of the recommendations of General Taguba. *See* Taguba Report, *supra* note 55, at 21, where it was recommended "[t]hat it is critical that the proponent for detainee operations is assigned a dedicated Senior Judge Advocate, with specialized training and knowledge of international and operational law, to assist and advise on matters of detainee operations."

71. It is argued that human rights law is equally applicable and binding to the detention operations in Iraq conducted by the United States. For purposes of this article the author will simply espouse the US government position that human rights law did not apply.

72. DoDD 2310.01E, *supra* note 59.

73. *Id.*, para. 4.1.

74. *Id.*, para. 4.2.

75. *Id.*, para. 4.8.

76. Coalition Provisional Authority Memorandum No. 3 (Revised), Criminal Procedures, CPA/MEM/27 June 2004/03 (June 27, 2004), *available at* http://www.cpa-iraq.org/regulations/20040627_CPAMEMO_3_Criminal_Procedures__Rev_.pdf [hereinafter CPA Memo 3].

77. *Id.*, sec. 4.1.

78. *Id.*, sec. 4.2.

79. *Id.*, sec. 4.3.

80. US Central Command promulgated its orders in many areas, to include those applicable to detention operations, as Fragmentary Orders (or FRAGOs), in recognition that the FRAGO modified a previously issued overarching order. The FRAGOs changed with some regularity and, more important, were always classified, so they defy easy citation. The general provisions discussed here, however, are unclassified.

81. MNF-I issued its order in this area in memorandum form. Like the Central Command FRAGOs, the memorandum order was classified, and citation to it, even if possible, would not be helpful.

82. *See infra* Part II.C.4.

83. S.C. Res. 1546, *supra* note 31, merely puts forth the standard of "imperative reasons of security," echoing the same language in Article 78, Civilians Convention, *supra* note 5. The ICRC *Commentary* makes it clear that it should be a high standard, but struggles to provide further coherent guidance as to its meaning. Internment under Article 78 is said to be "even more exceptional" than that under Articles 41 and 42, though only in the sense that internment must be applied individually as opposed to collectively. ICRC COMMENTARY, *supra* note 15, at 367. *See* discussion, *supra*, in note 22. In a comment to Article 42, it is offered that in order to intern "the State must have good reason to think that the person concerned, by his activities, knowledge or qualifications, represents a real threat to its present or future security." The footnote to this assertion reads: "The fact that a man is of military age should not necessarily be considered as justifying the application of these measures, unless there is a danger of him being able to join the enemy armed forces." *Id.* at 258. The *Commentary* raises as many questions as its solves. Interning a person for his "activities" is straightforward, and is the normal basis on which detention would depend. "Knowledge" and "qualifications" are less clear: is it possible to intern a person for merely knowing how to make or emplace an IED? And what to make of the footnote regarding those of military age? It begins by saying that being of military age is not a reason for internment, but then says that it can be such a reason if there is a danger of the person being *able* to join the opposing force, regardless of any intention of doing so. Other commentators have also struggled with the quality of the standard. *See, e.g.*, DINSTEIN, *supra* note 26, at 173 (citing various Israeli court cases construing the "imperative threat" standard, revealing only different verbal formulations, with little additional specificity); Ashley S. Deeks, *Administrative Detention in Armed Conflict*, 40 CASE WESTERN RESERVE JOURNAL OF INTERNATIONAL LAW 403, 406 (noting only that Article 78 establishes a "high" standard, representing a balance between the needs of the State for security and individual liberty).

84. TF 134 owned two camps containing TIFs. Camp Cropper is the facility through which every detainee first passed. It was at Camp Cropper that all administrative processing and initial interrogations would be conducted. Some detainees would remain at Camp Cropper; others would be sent to Camp Bucca in southern Iraq close to the border with Kuwait. Camp Bucca was built solely for the purpose of holding detainees. It was administratively subdivided into two and then three individual TIFs, mostly for the purpose of command and control, but for this paper, it will be treated as a single facility.

85. Victory Base Complex surrounds Baghdad International Airport and extended to most of the area that was known as the Al Faw Palace complex. This is a different area from the International Zone, popularly known as the "Green Zone," which comprises an area on the western bank of the Euphrates River. The US Embassy is located in the International Zone; first housed in Saddam Hussein's former presidential palace, it has since moved to a new building elsewhere in the zone. Certain of the review boards discussed later were conducted in the International Zone. Victory Base Complex and the International Zone are separated by approximately seven miles. To get from one to the other required either a military convoy or a helicopter flight.

86. *See* DoDD 2310.01E, *supra* note 59, para. 4.4.1.

87. As will be evident throughout this article, detainee operations are neither premised upon nor necessarily directed toward successful criminal prosecution. Soldiers are not criminal investigators and the uncertain security situation rarely permitted any forensic exploitation of the capture site. To take the clearest case, detainees would often be found in possession of dangerous

weapons; after taking pictures of them, the weapons were usually destroyed in the field in the interest of safety and force protection.

88. *See* discussion *infra* Part II.C.3.

89. *See* discussion *infra* Part II.C.4.

90. The unit would maintain the information permitting a correlation between the assigned number and the informant's actual identity.

91. *See* FM 2-22.3, *supra* note 63, at 6-10, for a discussion of the "rating" system used to assess cooperation and knowledge of detainees or other informants.

92. *See* David Dyzenhaus, *Symposium: The Hart-Fuller Debate at Fifty: The Grudge Informer Case Revisited*, 83 NEW YORK UNIVERSITY LAW REVIEW 1000 (2008).

93. An anecdote might be helpful. Detainee A was picked up and held on the strength of the statement of a neighbor that implicated Detainee A in various insurgent activities. Detainee A later claimed, truthfully in the eyes of the board which voted for his release, that he was feuding with this neighbor because he (Detainee A) had accused the neighbor's daughter of immoral behavior. Detainee B, whose case happened to come up for review at the same time, was also the victim of the same neighbor's complaints; in this case, Detainee B stated he had complained to the authorities that the neighbor was running a bordello, after which he was detained by coalition forces. Detainee B was also voted for release. Although the results in each of these cases may have been release if viewed individually, the happenstance of them both being reviewed at the same time made the truth clearer.

94. *See* CPA Memo 3, *supra* note 76, sec. 4.2. It was generally assumed that the Magistrate Cell review was the review required by the guidance, though an argument could be made that the review at the brigade level by the commander and his staff complied with the requirement.

95. The detainee did not appear before the magistrate. See the discussion in Part III, *infra*, about efforts made to explore the possibility of detainee involvement at this stage.

96. *See* discussion, *infra* Part II.C.6, on the process followed for criminal prosecutions.

97. All correspondence was delivered by a TF 134 organization called the Detainee Assistance Center. Minimally staffed with an attorney or two, as many paralegals, and several interpreters, its main task was to answer any questions the detainees had about their legal situations.

98. Article 78 required that the detention procedure "shall include a right of appeal for the parties concerned. Appeals shall be decided with the least possible delay." Civilians Convention, *supra* note 5, art. 78. CPA Memo 3 did not include a requirement for an appeal; the six-month review was the first required review subsequent to the initial seven-day review. CPA Memo 3, *supra* note 76, sec. 6. The ninety-day review was clearly established in written guidance and actual practice by 2007, but its genesis is unclear.

99. Certainly detainee disturbances were not caused solely by the review system utilized, though it was a contributing factor. An additional factor was the work of detainee provocateurs, generally identified as extremists, who continued to carry on the insurgency from within the internment facilities.

100. PW Convention, *supra* note 5, art. 5.

101. AR 190-8, *supra* note 10, para. 1-6, entitled "Tribunals."

102. This was one of the divergences from AR 190-8 (the other was that no written record, aside from the written voting sheet, was prepared). AR 190-8 states that all members are to be commissioned officers. *Id.* The decision was that senior enlisted personnel, with their significant military experience and maturity, would often be better members than would very junior officers. In other military administrative boards, such as boards to administratively separate members from the service, the three-member panel may include a senior enlisted member; *see, e.g.*, Headquarters, Department of the Army, Reg. 635-200, Active Duty Enlisted Administrative Separations

para. 2-7.a (June 6, 2005); Bureau of Naval Personnel, Department of the Navy, Naval Military Personnel Manual art. 1910-502 (June 21, 2008). A less principled reason was the need to increase the pool of members from which TF 134 drew.

103. The text of the "Instructions to Members" is included as an appendix, *infra*.

104. I offer no claim here that these hearings were contests among equals. The military detainers had many resources to draw upon to collect evidence, while the detainee often had little more in his defense than his own statement and answers to questions.

105. Common to any operation which relied upon interpreters, the quality of the interpretation provided could only be assessed by other interpreters, whose own proficiency could be as questionable.

106. As the DCG-DO was exercising delegated power from MNF-I, the Commanding General, MNF-I, also had the power to order a release, which he exercised occasionally.

107. Admittedly, neither the text to either of the articles nor the *Commentary* specifically makes these a requirement. *See* Civilians Convention, *supra* note 5, arts. 43, 78; ICRC COMMENTARY, *supra* note 15, at 260, 368. The ICRC's position was based more on practical realities. For a board to be fair, it had to be able to arrive at an independent decision. For a board to be worthwhile, it had to have a final effect and not be merely recommendatory.

108. This is hardly a legal argument. Rather, it is a concession to the need to relieve some of the natural tension that exists between the operating forces which capture and detain persons and an organization such as TF 134 charged with holding, and releasing, those same detainees. In very general terms, the operating forces would prefer that no detainees were released: they were threats when captured, and would be threats again if released. It is too easy, in their view, for garrison-based organizations, such as TF 134, to release detainees, because they aren't likely to encounter them again on the street. Having a general officer make the final decision reduced some amount of the public recrimination.

109. The process followed was this: every MNFRC release recommendation was vetted through the capturing unit for comment. If the capturing unit had no comment or objection, the release would be approved. If the unit objected, it was required to provide additional information about the detainee that might not have been available in the file. Once received, the detainee would appear before a second MNFRC, which had the benefit of the new evidence. This second board (which, in the mania for acronyms, was called the P-MNFRC, for Post-MNFRC) was unconstrained by the results of the first, and its new recommendation would be followed in the same manner as a regular MNFRC.

110. No boards were held on Friday, the Islamic holy day. The MNFRC work week began on Saturday.

111. The rates provided here are rough averages and reflect the trend of the data reported to the DCG-DO, who reported it in turn to MNF-I. The actual data are now unavailable and irretrievable.

112. CPA Memo 3, in the section discussing security internment, stated: "Any person under the age of 18 interned at any time shall in all cases be released not later than twelve months after the initial date of internment." CPA Memo 3, *supra* note 76, sec. 6.5. Determining a detainee's age was often difficult, as many did not know their birthdates, and documentation was rarely available. Those under age eighteen who had been detained for one year were released with no other process necessary. Those who turned eighteen while in custody did not, TF 134 reasoned, benefit from the CPA Memo 3 provision, and their detentions continued until they were otherwise released.

113. *See* Memorandum from the Deputy Secretary of Defense to the Secretaries of the Military Departments et al., Implementation of Combatant Status Review Tribunal Procedures for

Enemy Combatants Detained at U.S. Naval Base Guantanamo Bay, Cuba (July 14, 2006) (Encl. 3, Personal Representatives Qualifications, Roles and Responsibilities), *available at* http://www.defenselink.mil/news/Aug2006/d20060809CSRTProcedures.pdf.

114. TF 134 held several hundred juveniles, though because of the ability to hold them for only one year, they appeared usually only once each before an MNFRC. *See* discussion *supra* note 112. There were usually fewer than two hundred third-country national detainees, and female detainees never exceeded twenty at any one time, and were usually fewer than five. There was no established method for identifying those with diminished mental capacity. The medical command planned at one time to screen every detainee for mental ability for its own treatment purposes. TF 134 would have used whatever list they provided, but little came of it. Identification of those in this last category was therefore ad hoc. Because of the limited numbers, only two personal representatives were necessary at a time: one at Camp Cropper, where all juveniles and females were held, and one at Camp Bucca for anyone else.

115. Early in his tenure as DCG-DO, which began in May 2007, General Stone had a vision of moving away from the warehouse model used at Camp Bucca to smaller, regionally based TIFs. These would be designed and built as TIFs first and foremost, but with facilities to permit the services discussed in the text. Initially denominated as TIF Re-Integration Centers (TIFRIC), the name was later changed to TIFRC. Two TIFRCs were planned, one in Ramadi in western Iraq, and one in Taji, just north of Baghdad; only Taji was completed in late 2008. While awaiting these facilities, Camps Cropper and Bucca TIFs were reconfigured to offer the same services, so that they became TIFRCs in the same sense.

116. Naming the religious component proved very difficult. It could not appear to be the US government encouraging religion from the point of view of a US audience nor the United States "teaching" Islam to an Iraqi audience. Religious "engagement" was chosen as a somewhat neutral term.

117. When large-scale requests were received, it was impractical to consider each individual as described in the text. For example, it was not unusual to receive a list of ISNs from Iraqi officials that ran into the hundreds of detainees. In those cases, the cases would be sent immediately to an out-of-cycle MNFRC; the members were made aware of the reason for the special hearing. The results of the MNFRC would then substitute for the recommendation usually made by the special release attorney for the DCG-DO's decision on release.

118. One of the consequences of regular unit rotations through the theater was that successor units often had little information about "their" detainees (in the sense that the detainees had been captured in, and would return to, their areas of operation). Departing units would sometimes box up all detainee files and bring them back with them to their home bases in the United States or elsewhere; sometimes they would be stored in a warehouse on a base in Iraq with no easy means of retrieving individual files. It would occasionally happen that a unit would ask for the release of a detainee about whom it had little information, and when more fully acquainted with the facts underlying the original detention, it withdrew its request.

119. CPA Memo 3, *supra* note 76, sec. 5.1.

120. *Id.*, sec. 6.1.

121. For a more detailed description of the procedures used in criminal prosecutions by authors who were assigned to TF 134, see Michael J. Frank, *Trying Times: The Prosecution of Terrorists in the Central Criminal Court of Iraq*, 18 FLORIDA JOURNAL OF INTERNATIONAL LAW 1 (2006); W. James Annexstad, *The Detention and Prosecution of Insurgents and Other Non-Traditional Combatants—A Look at the Task Force 134 Process and the Future of Detainee Prosecutions*, ARMY LAWYER, July 2007, at 72.

122. Coalition Provisional Authority Order No. 13 (Revised)(Amended), The Central Criminal Court of Iraq, CPA/ORD/X 2004/13 (Apr. 22, 2004), *available at* http://www.cpa-iraq.org/regulations/20040422_CPAORD_13_Revised_Amended.pdf.

123. *Id.*, sec. 18.

124. The MNFRC was designed, in part, to address detainee discontent. *See* discussion *supra* note 99 and accompanying text. The MNFRC largely fulfilled its promise, and was often credited, by the DCG-DO and other officials, with being the single biggest factor in subsequent TIF "calming." Detainees finally saw that reviews were ongoing, and participated in the hearing of their own cases. Increased numbers of detainees were being released. As time went on, the calming effect dissipated, for there were detainees who appeared before MNFRC and yet were not being released. Had the MNFRC simply been ended, and the CRRB reinstituted, we could have expected much worse.

125. A species of this worked successfully at CCCI. Those US service members who were witnesses in a CCCI case, but who had rotated back to the United States, were permitted to testify before the investigative judge via video teleconference.

126. Two anecdotes may help illustrate the point. General Petraeus observed an MNFRC at Camp Bucca several months after they had begun running. He sat in on a case in which the detainee was alleged to have been involved with an IED attack on coalition force soldiers. After the explosion the soldiers traced the wire used to initiate the IED to the house in which they found the detainee. General Petraeus sat through the entire hearing and remained—quietly—as the members deliberated. Unanimously they provisionally voted to retain. General Petraeus got up to leave, and said something to the effect of "If I was voting, I would vote to release" and left. Two of the members—the two officers—then changed their votes. The sole enlisted member stood his ground; that is why they are invaluable to a process such as this. The other anecdote relates to comments members would make at the conclusion of their service on the MNFRC. Senior enlisted members would often say that they were going to go back to their units and make sure they did things correctly in the future, and were able to do so in a way that officers cannot.

127. As with many matters discussed, this is a recommendation based on practicalities, not the law. In the abstract, detainees should be released or detained based solely on the quality of the evidence; the operating forces, in a military hierarchy, must acknowledge that. Nevertheless, it must be recognized that the operating force's lack of acceptance of the process can ultimately frustrate the entire effort. A process in which they are given a voice may avoid that result.

XVIII

The Role of the International Committee of the Red Cross in Stability Operations

Laurent Colassis*

I. Introduction

What is the role of the International Committee of the Red Cross (ICRC) in stability operations in Iraq? In order to answer this question, it is necessary to examine the ICRC's mandate, its main activities in Iraq and the major legal challenges it faces as it conducts its activities.

II. The ICRC's Mandate

The ICRC is a neutral, impartial and independent humanitarian organization formally mandated by States party to the Geneva Conventions (GC)[1] to ensure, among other activities, assistance to, and protection of, victims of armed conflicts or other situations of violence.[2] Its work is firmly rooted in public international law. The Statutes of the International Red Cross and Red Crescent Movement[3] and resolutions of the International Conference of the Red Cross and Red Crescent underscore the legitimacy of the ICRC's work. States have also given the ICRC the responsibility to monitor the application of international humanitarian law (IHL).[4] As the guardian of IHL, the ICRC takes measures to ensure respect for, promote,

* Deputy Head of the Legal Division of the International Committee of the Red Cross (ICRC), Geneva. The views expressed in this article are those of the author and do not necessarily reflect those of the ICRC.

reaffirm and even clarify and develop this body of law.[5] The ICRC is also "particularly concerned about a possible erosion of IHL and takes bilateral, multilateral or public steps to promote respect for and development of the law."[6]

In order to carry out its activities in international armed conflicts, the ICRC has been granted an explicit right to regular access to prisoners of war under Geneva Convention III (GC III)[7] and to civilians protected by Geneva Convention IV (GC IV).[8] The ICRC also enjoys a broad right of initiative for other humanitarian activities.[9] In non-international armed conflict, the ICRC may offer its services to the parties to the conflict under Common Article 3 of the 1949 Geneva Conventions. In situations that have not reached the threshold of an armed conflict, the ICRC "may take any humanitarian initiative which comes within its role as a specifically neutral and independent institution and intermediary."[10]

III. ICRC Activities in Iraq

The ICRC has been present in Iraq since the outbreak of the Iran-Iraq war in 1980.[11] During these years, it maintained a permanent presence in the country, even in March 2003 at the start of the international armed conflict between the US-led coalition and the regime of Saddam Hussein.[12]

As of this writing, the security situation in Iraq is still fragile. Some five hundred people are killed on average every month and two thousand people are wounded in indiscriminate attacks and mass explosions that occur predominantly in Baghdad, Ninewa and Diyala governorates.[13] Security has improved, however, as compared to the situation between May 2006 and August 2007 when two thousand to three thousand civilians died each month because of the armed conflict.[14] Thanks to this improvement, the ICRC has been able to expand its activities and its presence inside the country. After running a mainly remote-control operation for a few years, the ICRC delegation for Iraq has returned to direct implementation of all its activities[15] and can now access large parts of the country.

ICRC delegates are based in Baghdad, Najaf, Basra, Erbil, Suleymanieh and Dohuk, and regular visits are made to offices in Khanaqin and Ramadi.[16] In 2008, Iraq was the ICRC's third-largest operation in the world, preceded only by Sudan and Somalia, representing an expenditure of US$88.5 million. The budget remains about the same for 2009.[17] More than 530 staff are based in Iraq and in Amman, Jordan, 91 of whom are expatriates.[18] In the current context, priority is given to protection activities, with a particular focus on persons detained[19] or interned[20] by the Multi-National Force–Iraq (MNF-I) in Iraq and by the Iraqi authorities.

In 2008, ICRC delegates carried out

- twenty visits in ten places of detention under the authority of the MNF-I—a total of 33,000 internees and detainees were visited and 3,500 were followed up individually;
- twenty-one visits to eight places of detention holding 9,500 detainees under the authority of the Iraqi government; and
- visits to twenty-six places of detention holding almost 3,000 detainees under the authority of the Kurdistan Regional Government.[21]

Besides visiting detainees, the ICRC helps to maintain the links between them and their families. In 2008, thousands of people deprived of their liberty were visited by the ICRC and were able to restore and maintain contact with their families by receiving visits from their families or exchanging news through Red Cross messages (RCMs) and phone calls. Almost 311,000 messages were exchanged with the support of the Iraqi Red Crescent Society. The ICRC also supported families visiting their relatives interned at Camp Bucca near Basra by covering part of their travel expenses and providing financial support for 69,600 visits to 20,550 internees. At their requests, twenty-nine detainees released from detention were repatriated to their countries of origin under the auspices of the ICRC. In addition, 805 detention certificates were issued to former detainees, enabling them to qualify for social welfare benefits. The ICRC also established a "helpline" for families in Iraq seeking information about family members in MNF-I custody. This helpline received an average of 1,800 calls a week from families who wanted to locate detained relatives or send RCMs.[22]

The conflict has also resulted in widespread displacement throughout Iraq, mainly for sectarian reasons. Around 10 percent of the population has been internally displaced.[23] The ICRC provided monthly food and hygiene assistance to 98,000 internally displaced persons in 2008.[24]

During 2009, the ICRC continues to try to determine the fate of those who went missing during the successive conflicts involving Iraq since 1980. The civilian population affected by the armed conflict is also provided with assistance. Assistance activities include providing emergency relief, support to seventeen hospitals and twelve primary health care centers, and emergency repair work on health, water and sanitation infrastructure.[25] The ICRC's priority in Iraq during 2009 remains visiting detainees. Regular visits are made to more than twenty-seven thousand detainees held by the Iraqi central government, the MNF-I and the Kurdistan Regional Government.[26] However, this does not reflect the total number of persons currently held in the country. The ICRC will continue to assess the security conditions in Iraq in order to increase the number of places where it can visit detainees in order to support the Iraqi government in strengthening its detention systems and meeting international standards regarding conditions of detention and treatment. In 2008, the ICRC reached oral agreements with all Iraqi ministries that have places of detention under their authority, and the ICRC is negotiating an overall agreement with the Ministry of Foreign Affairs regarding visits to all places of detention in the country.

IV. Legal Challenges Arising from Detention/Internment by a Multinational Force in a "Host" Country

The ICRC classified the situation in Iraq as an international armed conflict between March 2003 and mid-2004, when the hostilities were inter-State. After the handover of power from the Coalition Provisional Authority to the interim Iraqi government on June 28, 2004, following UN Security Council Resolution (UNSCR) 1546,[27] the legal situation changed. The hostilities became non-international in character, involving a group of States on one side, and non-State armed groups on the other.[28] The explicit, valid and genuine consent of the Iraqi government to the continuous presence of foreign forces in Iraq is the key element that led to this requalification of the conflict since it has transformed hostile armies (in the sense of Article 42 of the 1907 Hague Regulations)[29] into friendly armies. Despite the improvement of the security conditions in Iraq and the common perception that the armed conflict in Iraq is largely over, widespread violence and a lack of respect for human life continue to affect the Iraqi people.[30] Indiscriminate attacks kill or injure dozens of people every day. Because of the level of intensity of the armed confrontations and the degree of organization of the parties involved,[31] the ICRC continues to characterize the situation in Iraq as an internationalized internal armed conflict,[32] or as a multinational non-international armed conflict, governed by rules applicable to non-international armed conflicts, particularly Common Article 3 of the Geneva Conventions, the rules of customary international law applicable in non-international armed conflicts, international human rights law and Iraqi domestic law insofar as it complies with international law.[33]

Detaining insurgents is one of the main activities carried out by the allied foreign forces in Iraq. Detention by a multinational force in a "host" country poses significant legal and practical challenges, which are discussed below.

Legal Basis for Detention/Internment in a Multinational Non-international Armed Conflict

There is no debate that UNSCR 1546, adopted on June 8, 2004 under Chapter VII of the UN Charter, and the exchange of letters annexed thereto provided a legal basis for internment.[34] This right of the MNF-I to intern, for imperative reasons of security, was extended in UNSCRs 1637 (2005),[35] 1723 (2006)[36] and 1790 (2007),[37] but ended on December 31, 2008 with the expiration of UNSCR 1790. This led to significant changes in the conduct of detention operations by the MNF-I in Iraq.

On November 17, 2008 the United States and Iraq signed a security agreement on the withdrawal of US troops from Iraq and the organization of their activities during their remaining time in the country.[38] This agreement, which entered into effect on January 1, 2009, does not provide a legal basis for the United States to intern people, nor does it include any provision regarding the continuation of internment.

Internment is a form of deprivation of liberty that is an inevitable and lawful result of armed conflict.[39] The fact that Common Article 3 neither expressly mentions internment, nor elaborates on permissible grounds or process, has become a source of different positions on the legal basis for internment in a multinational non-international armed conflict. In the ICRC's view, both treaty and customary international humanitarian law[40] contain an inherent power to intern and thus may be said to provide a legal basis for internment in non-international armed conflicts. However, in the absence of any specific provision of Common Article 3 or of 1977 Additional Protocol II (GP II) on the grounds for internment or on the process to be followed, the ICRC believes that an international agreement between the multinational force and the "host" State should be concluded—or domestic law adopted—specifying grounds and process for internment in keeping with the principle of legality. It is the ICRC's understanding that neither internment nor administrative detention[41] is permitted under Iraqi law. The transfer of internees to the Iraqi government to continue internment activities is therefore not an option.

It has been announced that the security agreement would be supplemented with standard operating procedures or other procedures. It is also the ICRC's view that these would not provide the multinational force sufficient legal basis for internment as they do not have the force of law. As a result, internees will have to be either released or charged under Iraqi law.

In the event that some internees are not released, but are handed over to the Iraqi authorities to be criminally prosecuted, they must be transferred in accordance with Iraqi criminal procedure. To this end, the security agreement stipulates that "[t]he United States Forces shall act in full and effective coordination with the government of Iraq to turn over custody of such wanted detainees to Iraqi authorities pursuant to a valid Iraqi arrest warrant."[42]

In addition, the security agreement stipulates that Iraqi authorities can also ask the MNF-I to arrest wanted individuals;[43] thus US authorities continue to detain some individuals.

Release of Persons from MNF-I Detention/Internment

Another important humanitarian and legal concern follows from the release of persons from MNF-I internment. All the detainees who are not transferred to Iraqi authorities by US authorities shall be released in a safe and orderly manner, unless otherwise requested by the government of Iraq in accordance with the security agreement.[44]

Holding internees beyond the date on which they have been authorized for release cannot be justified, as it is without legal basis.[45] Given the high number of internees still present in US internment facilities, the MNF-I is facing serious logistical and security-related difficulties in carrying out this task. As a result, there are some delays in releasing internees, a problem that also partly lies with the Iraqi authorities, since they review all the files. Considering these practical constraints, the ICRC recommended avoiding unnecessary delays of releases and promptly informing each internee selected for release of the reasons for any delay in his or her release.

After they were released at their places of capture, some internees suffered incidents of revenge. Guidance could be drawn from Article 5(4) of GP II, which requires that necessary measures shall be taken to ensure the safety of released persons[46] in order to organize release in a safe environment. To this end, the ICRC asked US authorities to establish a system for safe release, leaving the choice of the location to be released to the greatest extent possible to the concerned internee himself/herself, based on a detailed assessment of his/her fears. The ICRC considered that such a system would address the fears generally expressed about releases at the points of capture.

Transfer of Internees and Criminal Detainees

In addition to the concerns with regard to the release of individuals, the transfer of persons between States in situations where multinational forces are detaining persons in the territory of a "host" State has given rise to a range of legal—and practical—issues, particularly the respect for the principle of *non-refoulement.*

Non-refoulement is the principle of international law that precludes a State from transferring a person within its control to another State if there are substantial grounds to believe that this person faces a risk of certain fundamental human rights violations—notably torture, other forms of ill-treatment, persecution or arbitrary deprivation of life.[47]

An obligation to respect the principle of *non-refoulement* expressly appears in IHL in the context of international armed conflicts, as reflected in Article 45(4), GC IV.[48] Furthermore, broader restrictions on transfer between detaining powers can be found in Article 12(2), GC III and Article 45(3), GC IV,[49] which prohibit transfer of persons deprived of liberty in any situation where the Geneva Conventions would not be observed by the receiving State, without limiting this prohibition to the restrictive case of *non-refoulement.*

Most pertinent to the situation in Iraq and US obligations in this context is the rule as it exists under human rights law.[50] The principle of *non-refoulement* is explicitly recognized in a number of human rights instruments, e.g., in Article 3 of the Convention against Torture and Other Cruel, Inhuman or Degrading Treatment or Punishment (CAT).[51] While not explicitly contained in the International Covenant on Civil and Political Rights (ICCPR),[52] it is the ICRC's understanding that the principle of *non-refoulement* constitutes a fundamental component of the absolute prohibitions of arbitrary deprivation of life and of torture, cruel, inhuman or degrading treatment provided for in Articles 6 and 7 of the ICCPR.[53] This interpretation is based on the view that the rights in question are of such fundamental importance that a State cannot circumvent its obligations by turning a blind eye to the risk that a person will be subjected to ill-treatment or arbitrary deprivation of life as a result of its own authorities' decision on transfer. In practical terms, these obligations require the United States to refrain from transferring to Iraqi authorities or to any other State any person in its custody who risks being subjected to torture or other forms of ill-treatment, or who faces the possibility of the imposition or execution of the death penalty following a trial that does not respect fundamental guarantees. These obligations apply not only when a person is in the territory of a State, but also extraterritorially when a person is in the power, or under the effective control, of the State's authorities.[54]

One of the questions that has arisen in the context of Iraq is whether the principle of *non-refoulement* applies even though persons are transferred from one State to another without actually crossing an international border. In other words, does the principle of *non-refoulement* also apply when persons are transferred from the MNF-I to Iraqi authorities within the territory of Iraq? Both the wording of existing treaty law provisions and the rationale of the principle of *non-refoulement* are relevant in determining whether *non-refoulement* applies only to transfer across an international border or not. Article 3 of the CAT refers to *refoulement* "to another State" only. Article 45(4), GC IV refers to transfer "to a country" and Articles 12(2), GC III and 45(3), GC IV refer to transfer "by the Detaining Power to a Power which is party to the Convention." None of these formulations explicitly suggests that an international border must be crossed. In addition to the wording, the rationale for the principle of *non-refoulement* is critical to its interpretation. The idea behind the principle is to protect persons from transfers if there is a risk that some of their fundamental rights may be violated. The material question, therefore, should not be whether a transferred person crosses an international border, but whether the individual is put at real risk of violations of his/her fundamental rights as a result of transfer to the effective control of another State. If crossing a physical border were the decisive criteria, the principle of *non-refoulement* could be easily circumvented through a simple formality. For instance, a detainee could be transferred from Guantanamo Bay to the US internment facility at Bagram in Afghanistan, and then from Bagram to the Afghan authorities. The principle of *non-refoulement* would obviously not apply to the first step of the transfer (from Guantanamo Bay to Bagram) as the detainee would remain under the control of US authorities. Requiring the physical crossing of a border in order to recognize the applicability of the principle of *non-refoulement* to the second step of this transfer would lead to the absurd conclusion that the principle of *non-refoulement* cannot apply to transfers of detainees between two States when they are carried out in two phases. Thus, the real issue is whether a person has been transferred from the control of a detaining State to the control or jurisdiction of another State, regardless of whether the individual has crossed an international border.[55]

Contrary to the explicit obligation of *non-refoulement* in international armed conflicts (Article 45(4), GC IV), there is no such provision for non-international armed conflicts. Nonetheless, the humanitarian principles enshrined in Article 12(2), GC III and Article 45(3), GC IV, namely that a detaining State transferring a detainee to an ally shall ensure that the transferred detainee will be treated in accordance with the Geneva Conventions by the receiving State, should also be taken into account when foreign troops intervene on the side of the government to which they transfer their detainees.[56] In these situations of multinational non-international armed conflict, such as the current one in Iraq, the underlying logic that an individual protected by IHL should not lose his or her protection through a transfer between allies should be the same as the one governing international armed conflicts. In addition, Common Article 3 of the Geneva Conventions absolutely prohibits murder, as well as torture and other forms of ill-treatment. A State would act in contradiction of Common Article 3 when it transferred a detainee to another State if there were substantial grounds to believe that the transferred person would be ill-treated or arbitrarily deprived of life. Just as the Geneva Conventions prohibit circumvention of the protections owed to protected persons by transfer to a non-compliant State (Articles 12(2), GC III and 45(3), GC IV), IHL applicable in non-international armed conflict should not be circumvented by transferring internees to a State that will not respect its obligations under Common Article 3. Furthermore,

> [t]his provision should be interpreted in the light of the interpretation given to the parallel provisions in human rights law. If the absolute human rights law prohibition of

> torture and other forms of ill-treatment precludes the transfer of a person at risk of such treatment, there is no reason why the absolute prohibition in humanitarian law should not be interpreted in the same way.[57]

In any event, these existing norms of IHL applying to transfers would not preclude application of the principle of *non-refoulement* under human rights law,[58] as the rights concerned are non-derogable.

An additional problem is created by the fact that the United States has an obligation to transfer detained persons to Iraq pursuant to the security agreement.[59] Thus, the practical challenges that the application of the principle of *non-refoulement* can create must be recognized, and should not be underestimated. There are, however, solutions that respect the principle of *non-refoulement*. They include, among others, monitoring, or even joint administration, of places of detention in order to follow up on transferred persons. Moreover, respecting the principle of *non-refoulement* does not impede the transfer of thousands of persons as it only applies to those specific individuals who face a real risk that certain of their fundamental rights may be violated. In the context of transfers between multinational forces and the "host" country, practical solutions must be found that take into consideration the balance between, on the one hand, a transferring State's security concerns and material limitations to detain persons who should normally be detained by the host country, and, on the other hand, the need to provide real protection against ill-treatment or arbitrary deprivation of life. In striking this balance, particular respect must be given to the principle of *non-refoulement*, keeping in mind the overriding humanitarian purpose of IHL.[60]

In order for a person to be able to challenge his or her transfer meaningfully, a number of procedural guarantees are essential.[61] If there is a risk of violations of fundamental rights, the person must not be transferred. If it is determined that there is no such risk, the transferring State must

- inform the concerned person in a timely manner of the intended transfer;
- give the person the opportunity to express any fears that he or she may have about the transfer;
- give the person the opportunity to challenge the transfer before a body that is independent from the one that made the decision to transfer;
- give the person the option to explain why he or she would be at risk in the receiving State to the independent body that reviews whether his or her fears are well founded;
- assess the existence of the risk on a case-by-case basis; and

- suspend the transfer during the independent review of whether such fears are well founded because of the irreversible harm that would be caused if the person were indeed at risk.[62]

In the course of its visits to persons deprived of their liberty in Iraq, the ICRC conducts pre-departure interviews with certain detainees subject to transfer or release in order to be able to transmit any fears the detainees might have to the transferring authorities. It is not the ICRC's mandate to assess whether a person's fear of being transferred is well-founded. This responsibility rests with the transferring authority, which must interview the detainee as part of its own assessment of the risk for the person concerned.

In addition, the ICRC frequently lends its services to facilitate the return of detainees to their places of origin or their transfer to third States.[63] In this respect, each foreigner (third-country national) is met individually and asked whether he or she wants his/her State of nationality to be notified. If he or she agrees, the ICRC informs his/her embassy about his/her presence in the detention facility. Upon request, the ICRC carries out repatriation of released foreigners. In 2008, twenty-nine detainees released from MNF-I (twenty-three), central Iraqi (three) and regional Kurdish (three) custody were repatriated to their countries of origin under the auspices of the ICRC. The ICRC will not facilitate a transfer if it thinks that it would be contrary to international legal requirements. Moreover, as a matter of general policy, the ICRC only assists persons who wish to be transferred; that is, those who have given their informed consent to transfer, since it would be incompatible with its humanitarian mandate to assist in a transfer which, even if lawful, is against the will of the person concerned.[64]

Post-transfer Responsibilities

Another important issue related to the transfer between allies is whether the transferring authority retains some responsibilities after the transfer.

If a transfer takes place, the responsibility for the transferred person rests with the receiving State. The sending State might, however, have a number of post-transfer responsibilities, even in cases where the transfer is carried out with full respect given to the principle of *non-refoulement*.[65] For instance, Article 12(3), GC III (prisoners of war) and Article 45(3), GC IV (protected persons) contain strong post-transfer responsibilities under which the transferring State has to assure itself that the receiving State will respect the Convention. Article 12 provides:

> If that Power [to which the prisoners of war are transferred] fails to carry out the provisions of the Convention in any important respect, the Power by whom the prisoners of war were transferred shall, upon being notified by the Protecting Power,

> take effective measures to correct the situation or shall request the return of the prisoners of war/protected persons. Such requests must be complied with.

Similarly, Article 45(3) provides:

> If that Power [to which the protected persons are transferred] fails to carry out the provisions of the Convention in any important respect, the Power by which the protected persons were transferred shall, upon being so notified by the Protecting Power, take effective measures to correct the situation or shall request the return of the protected persons. Such requests must be complied with.

As stated by the *Commentary* on GC III, the States "adopted a system of subsidiary responsibility, subject to certain specific conditions."[66] The *Commentary* adds that "[t]he general conditions of internment stipulated in the Convention must be respected: quarters, food, hygiene. . . . If the receiving Power fails to carry out these provisions in any 'important' respect, the responsibility of the transferring Power is again involved."[67]

There is no equivalent provision for post-transfer responsibilities in non-international armed conflicts. A situation in which a person captured in a non-international armed conflict would be transferred between different States was probably not considered in 1949 when the Conventions were drafted. Now, however, in a multinational non-international armed conflict like the one in Iraq, the protection needs of a transferee can be very similar to—or probably even greater than—those envisaged in GC III and GC IV in circumstances such as when an Iraqi detainee is transferred from the MNF-I to his/her State of nationality. While in international armed conflict the general assumption is that a repatriated protected person is not at risk in his/her country of nationality, in non-international armed conflict the situation is different because the transferred person may have been fighting against the authorities of his/her country of nationality and therefore may face reprisals. Thus, the considerations of Articles 12(3), GC III and 45(3), GC IV should also be taken into account in transfers between allied powers in the context of multinational non-international armed conflicts in order to ensure that transferred persons are protected from violations of IHL.[68]

Such post-transfer responsibilities would also correspond to States' obligation to ensure respect for IHL as provided for in Common Article 1 of the Geneva Conventions.[69] This duty entails a responsibility for all States to take feasible and appropriate measures to ensure that the rules of IHL are respected by the parties to an armed conflict.[70] It is a commitment to promote compliance with IHL.[71] Transferring States, in particular, have greater means to ensure respect in contexts where they have a strong diplomatic and military presence in the receiving State, as is the case with the United States in Iraq. They can engage in a dialogue on the treatment of detainees and undertake other measures, such as post-transfer follow-up or capacity building at the different levels of the chain of custody, to ensure that the receiving State abides by its obligations.

Judicial Guarantees

An additional legal challenge for the MNF-I stems from the disrupted Iraqi judicial system.[72] US authorities continue to give custodial support to Iraqi authorities, thus effectively retaining control over some criminal detainees on behalf of Iraqi authorities, including those arrested in 2009.[73] US authorities must therefore ensure that such custody complies with the requirements of Iraqi national legislation and internationally recognized standards, particularly judicial guarantees.

To this end, US authorities should use their influence to ensure that

- all persons arrested in 2009 benefit from safeguards under Iraqi law (e.g., the requirements for arrest warrants, detention orders and appearances before a judge within 24 hours), provided these safeguards are in compliance with internationally recognized standards;
- information obtained by US forces without observing the safeguards provided for in Iraqi criminal law, in particular in those instances where the person is without legal assistance, is not transmitted to the Iraqi authorities; and
- the time spent in MNF-I internment is deducted from the sentences imposed by Iraqi courts if the reasons for criminal imprisonment are based on facts that led to the internment.[74]

Given the concerns about the capacity of an already overstretched Iraqi judicial system to efficiently and promptly absorb such an important new caseload of detainees, the influence exercised by the United States and the support provided to Iraqi authorities are crucial to ensuring those authorities have the ability to train correctional staff to meet international standards.[75] In addition, this US support should ensure that basic judicial guarantees are respected so that persons transferred to the Iraqi criminal system can benefit from fair trials.

V. Conclusion

Despite significant security and political improvements, conditions in Iraq are volatile and unpredictable, and security remains one of the ICRC's first concerns. Even if its operations in Iraq remain driven by security constraints, the ICRC wants to continue to maintain a sufficient level of activities to identify and address the needs of the most vulnerable people in the country:

> The recent experience of the ICRC in Iraq . . . made a difference to the lives of many hundreds of thousands of Iraqis. Maintaining a presence and proximity on the ground, taking action wherever possible, not only allows [the ICRC] to carry out humanitarian work but also serves as a basis for increasing [its] knowledge and understanding of a complex situation and keeping track of humanitarian needs. . . . A presence on the ground provides opportunities for humanitarian dialogue, on which a positive perception and consequent acceptance often heavily depend. Such a presence on a broader scale also enables a balanced stance to be maintained among the various communities by addressing their needs, however different they may be from one place to another.[76]

If its presence on the ground is crucial to enabling the ICRC to protect and assist persons covered by IHL, in accordance with its international mandate and its own commitment to do so, the relevance and the credibility of the ICRC also come from its operational approach. Through its neutral, impartial and independent humanitarian action,[77] i.e., remaining distinct from political interests and not taking sides, the ICRC can better reach those persons in need and act on their behalf. In a polarized world, such an approach may also reduce tension and contribute to the stability of a devastated country like Iraq. In 2007, Toni Pfanner stated:

> Perhaps one way back to a stable Iraq, one that would serve equally the needs of its entire people, is through the unanimous acceptance of impartial humanitarian action. Such action, which makes no distinction between victims, could foster reconciliation and serve to counter the pernicious idea that human lives must inevitably be sacrificed—an idea that will only further encourage hatred and then more hatred, revenge followed by more revenge.[78]

Today, some two years later, that statement still shows the best way forward.

The ICRC is also confronted with complex legal issues arising from detention activities in Iraq. These legal challenges are numerous, and the ICRC's role is to help the various parties to the armed conflict abide by their obligations under IHL. Rules protect. The purpose of ICRC activities in this area is precisely to ensure that the rules laid down by IHL are respected so that violations are prevented. As Professor Sandoz indicated,

> Surely respect for every human being, and compassion for those who suffer, are values on which the future of the world must be built. By defending these values even in war, the guardian of international humanitarian law is also combating the feelings of helplessness and fear that make peoples indifferent to each other and drive them into isolation.[79]

Adherence to the law enhances security and facilitates national reconciliation and a return to peace, which are the likely long-term goals of most parties to non-international armed conflicts.[80] In this sense, it can be also said that the ICRC contributes to the stabilization of Iraq, as well as of any other place in the world where the ICRC works for the faithful application of IHL. Respect for IHL protects people, their well-being and their dignity. Apart from the importance of respecting the fundamental values embodied in IHL to protect human beings, respecting those values in times of armed conflict can also facilitate the resumption of dialogue between the parties to the conflict and ultimately the restoration of peace. It is of utmost importance that all those involved in the Iraqi conflict recognize that compliance with the law is also a necessary component of a broader political process that could one day lead to the end of the tragedy in Iraq.

Notes

1. *See, e.g.*, Convention Relative to the Protection of Civilian Persons in Time of War art. 10, Aug. 12, 1949, 6 U.S.T. 3516, 75 U.N.T.S. 287, *reprinted in* DOCUMENTS ON THE LAWS OF WAR 301 (Adam Roberts & Richard Guelff eds., 3d ed. 2000) [hereinafter GC IV]. The Geneva Conventions are universally ratified (194 States parties).

2. Statutes of the International Red Cross and Red Crescent Movement art. 5(2)(d), Oct. 31, 1986, as amended, http://www.icrc.org/Web/eng/siteeng0.nsf/htmlall/statutes-movement-220506/$File/Statutes-EN-A5.pdf [hereinafter Statutes of the Movement].

3. These Statutes were adopted during the 25th International Conference of the Movement that States parties to the Geneva Conventions attended as full members.

4. Statutes of the Movement, *supra* note 2, art. 5(2)(c).

5. *See* Yves Sandoz, *The International Committee of the Red Cross as Guardian of International Humanitarian Law*, Dec. 31, 1998, http://www.icrc.org/web/eng/siteeng0.nsf/html/about-the-icrc-311298.

6. INTERNATIONAL COMMITTEE OF THE RED CROSS, THE ICRC: ITS MISSION AND WORK 7 (2009), *available at* http://www.icrc.org/Web/Eng/siteeng0.nsf/htmlall/p0963/$File/ICRC_002_0963.PDF.

7. Convention Relative to the Treatment of Prisoners of War art. 126, Aug. 12, 1949, 6 U.S.T. 3316, 75 U.N.T.S. 135, *reprinted in* DOCUMENTS ON THE LAWS OF WAR, *supra* note 1, at 244 [hereinafter GC III].

8. GC IV, *supra* note 1, arts. 76, 143.

9. *See, e.g.*, GC IV, *supra* note 1, art. 10; GC III, *supra* note 7, art. 9. Similar provisions appear in Article 9 of the two first Geneva Conventions.

10. Statutes of the Movement, *supra* note 2, art. 5(3) (which grants the ICRC a very broad statutory right of initiative).

11. Karl Mattli & Jörg Gasser, *A Neutral, Impartial and Independent Approach: Key to ICRC's Acceptance in Iraq*, 90 INTERNATIONAL REVIEW OF THE RED CROSS 153, 167 (2008), *available at* http://www.icrc.org/Web/eng/siteeng0.nsf/htmlall/review-869-p153/$File/irrc-869_Mattli.pdf; INTERNATIONAL COMMITTEE OF THE RED CROSS, ANNUAL REPORT 2008, at 342 (2009), *available at* http://www.icrc.org/web/eng/siteeng0.nsf/htmlall/section_annual_report _2008?OpenDocument.

12. However, it should not be forgotten that the repeated US and UK airstrikes in the air exclusion zone of southern Iraq, which resumed in September 1996 after three years of interruption, already constituted an international armed conflict.

13. ICRC Field Newsletter, Iraq: Civilians without Protection 1 (Aug. 13, 2009), http://www.icrc.org/web/eng/siteeng0.nsf/htmlall/iraq-newsletter-120809.

14. Iraq Body Count, Documented Civilian Deaths from Violence: Monthly Table, http://www.iraqbodycount.org/database/ (last visited Sept. 4, 2009). Despite their limitations, the figures in the Iraq Body Count database are sufficient. Beth Osborne Daponte, *Wartime Estimates of Iraqi Civilian Casualties*, 89 INTERNATIONAL REVIEW OF THE RED CROSS 943, 957 (2007), *available at* http://www.icrc.org/Web/eng/siteeng0.nsf/htmlall/review-868-p943/$File/irrc-868_Daponte.pdf.

15. Direct implementation entails on-site ICRC supervision and often on-site ICRC involvement, at least in certain project phases, such as evaluation and assessment. The ICRC only applies the remote-control procedure to types of projects that meet strict technical and financial risk criteria and are well known from previous interventions, thus enabling the organization to draw on its firsthand experience in the project decision-making process. The remote-control model is based on the mobilization of an extensive network of competent local contractors and consultants, working in close collaboration with ICRC engineers. The key to the success of the remote-control model is based on the following factors:

- highly experienced, motivated and committed ICRC Iraqi employees;
- strong collaboration with and ownership by the relevant local authorities;
- an extensive network of local contractors/consultants throughout the country; and
- strong control mechanisms, whereby separate entities are involved in needs assessment and project design, implementation, monitoring and evaluation.

Mattli & Gasser, *supra* note 11, at 162.

16. ICRC setup at the time of this writing (September 2009).

17. INTERNATIONAL COMMITTEE OF THE RED CROSS, OVERVIEW OF OPERATIONS 2009, at 49 (2008), *available at* http://www.icrc.org/Web/eng/siteeng0.nsf/htmlall/appeals-overview-181108/$File/2009_OverviewOperations.pdf.

18. ICRC, The ICRC in Iraq, http://www.icrc.org/web/eng/siteeng0.nsf/htmlall/iraq?opendocument#Operational%20update (last accessed Sept. 14, 2009).

19. "Detained person" or "detainee" is used in this article to cover all persons deprived of their liberty for reasons related to the armed conflict in Iraq regardless of any specific legal basis. Thus, it includes persons who have taken a direct part in hostilities and who have fallen into the power of the adversary party, as well as those detained on criminal charges or for security reasons, provided that there is a link between the armed conflict and their deprivation of liberty.

20. An "interned person" or an "internee" is generally deprived of liberty following an order by the executive authorities when no specific criminal charge is brought against the individual concerned. COMMENTARY ON THE ADDITIONAL PROTOCOLS OF 8 JUNE 1977 TO THE GENEVA CONVENTIONS OF 12 AUGUST 1949, at 875 (Yves Sandoz, Christophe Swinarski & Bruno Zimmermann eds., 1987) [hereinafter ICRC Commentary]. For the sake of simplification, the terms "detained person" and "detainee" are sometimes used in this article in a generic sense to cover also "interned persons" or "internees," *id.*

21. International Committee of the Red Cross, The International Committee of the Red Cross in Iraq: 2008 Facts and Figures 2, http://www.icrc.org/Web/eng/siteeng0.nsf/htmlall/iraq-newsletter-311209/$File/2008-iraq-eng.pdf (last visited Sept. 14, 2009) [hereinafter Iraq 2008 Facts and Figures].

22. *Id.*

23. Internal Displacement Monitoring Centre, Challenges of Forced Displacement within Iraq (Dec. 31, 2008), http://www.internal-displacement.org/countries/iraq.

24. Iraq 2008 Facts and Figures, *supra* note 21, at 5.

25. International Committee of the Red Cross, Operational Update: Iraq—Indiscriminate Attacks Take Heavy Toll on Civilians (Aug. 15, 2009), http://www.icrc.org/Web/eng/siteeng0.nsf/html/iraq-update-150909 [hereinafter Indiscriminate Attacks Take Heavy Toll].

26. News Release 09/57, International Committee of the Red Cross, Iraq: Civilians Still Facing Hardship Every Day (Mar. 19, 2009), http://www.icrc.org/web/eng/siteeng0.nsf/htmlall/iraq-news-190309?opendocument.

27. S.C. Res. 1546, U.N. Doc. S/RES/1546 (June 8, 2004).

28. ICRC, Iraq post 28 June 2004: Protecting Persons Deprived of Freedom Remains a Priority, Aug. 5, 2004, http://www.icrc.org/web/eng/siteeng0.nsf/htmlall/63kkj8?opendocument.

29. Regulations Respecting the Laws and Customs of War on Land, Annex to Convention No. IV Respecting the Laws and Customs of War on Land art. 42, Oct. 18, 1907, 36 Stat. 2227, *reprinted in* DOCUMENTS ON THE LAWS OF WAR, *supra* note 1, at 69 ("Territory is considered occupied when it is actually placed under the authority of the hostile army").

30. Indiscriminate Attacks Take Heavy Toll, *supra* note 25.

31. International Committee of the Red Cross, Opinion Paper, How is the Term "Armed Conflict" Defined in International Humanitarian Law? (Mar. 2008), http://www.icrc.org/web/eng/siteeng0.nsf/htmlall/armed-conflict-article-170308/$file/Opinion-paper-armed-conflict.pdf.

32. For a more detailed analysis of internationalized internal armed conflicts to which the law of non-international armed conflict applies, see Hans-Peter Gasser, *Internationalized Non-international Armed Conflicts: Case Studies of Afghanistan, Kampuchea and Lebanon*, 33 AMERICAN UNIVERSITY LAW REVIEW 145, 147 (1983); Dietrich Schindler, *International Humanitarian Law and Internationalized Internal Armed Conflicts*, 22 INTERNATIONAL REVIEW OF THE RED CROSS 255 (1982); Michael Bothe, *Völkerrechtliche Aspekte des Angola-Konflikts*, 37 HEIDELBERG JOURNAL OF INTERNATIONAL LAW 572, 590–91 (1977), *available at* http://www.hjil.de/37_1977/37_1977_3_4_a_572_603.pdf; Jelena Pejic, *Status of Armed Conflicts*, *in* PERSPECTIVES ON THE STUDY OF CUSTOMARY INTERNATIONAL LAW 77, 89–94 (Elizabeth Wilmshurst & Susan C. Breau eds., 2007); Sylvain Vité, *Typology of Armed Conflicts in International Humanitarian Law: Legal Concepts and Actual Situations*, 91 INTERNATIONAL REVIEW OF THE RED CROSS 69, 85–87 (2009), *available at* http://www.icrc.org/Web/eng/siteeng0.nsf/htmlall/review-873-p69/$File/irrc-873-Vite.pdf.

33. For a more detailed analysis on the classification of the Iraqi conflict, see Knut Dörmann & Laurent Colassis, *International Humanitarian Law in the Iraq Conflict*, 47 GERMAN YEARBOOK OF INTERNATIONAL LAW 293, 307–14 (2004).

34. S.C. Res. 1546, *supra* note 27, ¶ 10 ("*Decides* that the multinational force shall have the authority to take all necessary measures to contribute to the maintenance of security and stability in Iraq in accordance with the letters annexed to this resolution expressing, inter alia, the Iraqi request for the continued presence of the multinational force and setting out its tasks, including by preventing and deterring terrorism" (emphasis in original)).

35. S.C. Res. 1637, ¶ 1, U.N. Doc. S/RES/1637 (Nov. 11, 2005) ("*Notes* that the presence of the multinational force in Iraq is at the request of the Government of Iraq and, having regard to

the letters annexed to this resolution, *reaffirms* the authorization for the multinational force as set forth in resolution 1546 (2004) and *decides* to extend the mandate of the multinational force as set forth in that resolution until 31 December 2006" (emphasis in original)).

36. S.C. Res. 1723, ¶ 1, U.N. Doc. S/RES/1723 (Nov. 28, 2006) ("*Notes* that the presence of the multinational force in Iraq is at the request of the Government of Iraq and *reaffirms* the authorization for the multinational force as set forth in resolution 1546 (2004) and *decides* to extend the mandate of the multinational force as set forth in that resolution until 31 December 2007, taking into consideration the Iraqi Prime Minister's letter dated 11 November 2006 and the United States Secretary of State's letter dated 17 November 2006" (emphasis in original)).

37. S.C. Res. 1790, ¶ 1, U.N. Doc. S/RES/1790 (Dec. 18, 2007) ("*Notes* that the presence of the multinational force in Iraq is at the request of the Government of Iraq and *reaffirms* the authorization for the multinational force as set forth in resolution 1546 (2004) and *decides* to extend the mandate as set forth in that resolution until 31 December 2008, taking into consideration the Iraqi Prime Minister's letter dated 7 December 2007, including all of the objectives highlighted therein, and the United States Secretary of State's letter dated 10 December 2007" (emphasis in original)).

38. Agreement between the United States of America and the Republic of Iraq on the Withdrawal of United States Forces from Iraq and the Organization of Their Activities during Their Temporary Presence in Iraq, U.S.-Iraq, Nov. 17, 2008, *available at* http://georgewbush-whitehouse.archives.gov/infocus/iraq/SE_SOFA.pdf [hereinafter Security Agreement].

39. *See* GC IV, *supra* note 1, arts. 41(1), 78(1). *See also* Protocol Additional to the Geneva Conventions of 12 August 1949, and Relating to the Protection of Victims of Non-International Armed Conflicts arts. 5, 6, June 8, 1977, 1125 U.N.T.S. 609, *reprinted in* DOCUMENTS ON THE LAWS OF WAR, *supra* note 1, at 483.

40. CUSTOMARY INTERNATIONAL HUMANITARIAN LAW vol. I, 344–52 (2 volumes: Vol. I, Rules; Vol. II, Practice (2 Parts)) (Jean-Marie Henckaerts & Louise Doswald-Beck eds., 2005).

41. The terms "internment" and "administrative detention" are used interchangeably, although the former is the term used in situations of armed conflict whereas the latter is the term used in situations outside armed conflict.

42. Security Agreement, *supra* note 38, art. 22(4).

43. *Id.*, art. 22(3).

44. *Id.*, art. 22(4).

45. *See* Jelena Pejic, *Procedural Principles and Safeguards for Internment/Administrative Detention in Armed Conflict and Other Situations of Violence*, 87 INTERNATIONAL REVIEW OF THE RED CROSS 375, 382 (2005), *available at* http://www.icrc.org/Web/eng/siteeng0.nsf/htmlall/review-858-p375/$File/irrc_858_Pejic.pdf.

46.
> Release should not take place if it proves impossible to take the necessary measures to ensure the safety of the persons concerned. It is not indicated for how long such conditions of safety should be envisaged. It *seems* reasonable to suppose that this should be until the released persons have reached an area where they are no longer considered as enemies or otherwise until they are back home, as the case may be.

ICRC Commentary, *supra* note 20, at 1393–94 (emphasis added).

47. An extensive analysis of the principle of *non-refoulement* can be found in Emanuela-Chiara Gillard, *There's No Place Like Home: States' Obligations in Relation to Transfers of Persons*, 90 INTERNATIONAL REVIEW OF THE RED CROSS 703 (2008), *available at* http://www.icrc.org/Web/eng/siteeng0.nsf/htmlall/review-871-p703/$File/irrc-871-Gillard.pdf. *See also* Elihu Lauterpacht & Daniel Bethlehem, *The Scope and Content of the Principle of Non-refoulement: Opinion*, *in*

REFUGEE PROTECTION IN INTERNATIONAL LAW 87 (Erika Feller, Volker Türk & Frances Nicholson eds., 2003), *available at* http://www.unhcr.org/4a1ba1aa6.html.

48. GC IV, *supra* note 1, art. 45(4), stipulates that "[i]n no circumstances shall a protected person be transferred to a country where he or she may have reason to fear persecution for his or her political opinions or religious beliefs."

49. GC III, *supra* note 7, art. 12(2) ("[p]risoners of war may only be transferred by the Detaining Power to a Power which is a party to the Convention and after the Detaining Power has satisfied itself of the willingness and ability of such transferee Power to apply the Convention. When prisoners of war are transferred under such circumstances, responsibility for the application of the Convention rests on the Power accepting them while they are in its custody"). This provision is mirrored in Article 45(3) of GC IV, *supra* note 1.

50. For an analysis of the application of the principle of *non-refoulement* under human rights law, see Gillard, *supra* note 47, at 708–10, 716–23; Cordula Droege, *Transfers of Detainees: Legal Framework,* Non-refoulement *and Contemporary Challenges*, 90 INTERNATIONAL REVIEW OF THE RED CROSS 669, 671–73 (2008), *available at* http://www.icrc.org/Web/eng/siteeng0.nsf/htmlall/review-871-p669/$File/irrc-871-Droege2.pdf.

51. Convention against Torture and Other Cruel, Inhuman or Degrading Treatment or Punishment, G.A. Res. 39/46, annex, 39 U.N. GAOR Supp. (No. 51) at 197, U.N. Doc. A/39/51 (1984).

52. International Covenant on Civil and Political Rights, Dec. 16, 1966, 999 U.N.T.S. 171.

53. *See* U.N. Secretariat, Compilation of General Comments and General Recommendations Adopted by Human Rights Treaty Bodies, *General Comment No. 20, Prohibition of Torture, or Other Cruel, Inhuman or Degrading Treatment or Punishment* 31, ¶ 9, U.N. Doc. HRI/GEN/1/Rev. 1 (July 28, 1994); U.N. Human Rights Committee, *General Comment No. 31, Nature of the General Legal Obligation Imposed on States Parties to the Covenant*, ¶ 12, U.N. Doc. CCPR/C/21/Rev. 1/Add. 13 (May 26, 2004) [hereinafter General Comment 31]. For case law concerning member States of the Council of Europe, see the European Court of Human Rights judgments since Soering v. United Kingdom, 161 Eur. Ct. H.R. (ser. A) ¶ 91 (1989), *reprinted in* 28 INTERNATIONAL LEGAL MATERIALS 1063.

54. Legal Consequences of the Construction of a Wall in the Occupied Palestinian Territory, Advisory Opinion, 2004 I.C.J. 136, ¶¶ 108–11 (July 9), *reprinted in* 43 INTERNATIONAL LEGAL MATERIALS 1009 (2004); Armed Activities on the Territory of the Congo (Dem. Rep. Congo v. Uganda), 2005 I.C.J. 116, ¶ 119 (Dec. 19); U.N. Committee against Torture, *Consideration of Reports Submitted by States Parties Under Article 19 of the Convention*, ¶ 15, U.N. Doc. CAT/C/USA/CO/2 (July 25, 2006); U.N. Human Rights Committee, Communication No. 52/1979 *López Burgos v. Uruguay, Views of the Human Rights Committee*, ¶ 12.3, U.N. Doc. CCPR/C/13/D/52/1979 (July 29, 1981); General Comment No. 31, *supra* note 53, ¶ 10.

55. Droege, *supra* note 50, at 677, 683; Gillard, *supra* note 47, at 712–15.

56. Droege, *supra* note 50, at 675.

57. *Id.*

58. *Id.* at 671–73; Gillard, *supra* note 47, at 708–10, 716–23.

59. Security Agreement, *supra* note 38, art. 22.

60. Droege, *supra* note 50, at 701.

61. The procedural dimension is especially emphasized in Lauterpacht & Bethlehem, *supra* note 47, ¶¶ 159 *et seq.*

62. Droege, *supra* note 50, at 679–80; Gillard, *supra* note 47, at 738.

63. *See, e.g.*, Indiscriminate Attacks Take Heavy Toll, *supra* note 25.

64. Droege, *supra* note 50, at 680–81.

65. For an analysis of responsibilities following a transfer in violation of the principle of *non-refoulement*, see Gillard, *supra* note 47, at 738–40.

66. COMMENTARY III ON THE GENEVA CONVENTIONS OF 12 AUGUST 1949, at 137 (Jean Pictet ed., 1960) [hereinafter Commentary III].

67. *Id.* at 138.

68. *See* Droege, *supra* note 50, at 698.

69. *See* International Committee of the Red Cross, *Summary Report: Improving Compliance with International Humanitarian Law—ICRC Expert Seminars, in* INTERNATIONAL COMMITTEE OF THE RED CROSS, INTERNATIONAL HUMANITARIAN LAW AND THE CHALLENGES OF CONTEMPORARY ARMED CONFLICTS annex 3 at 46, 48–49 (2003), *available at* http://www.icrc.org/Web/eng/siteeng0.nsf/htmlall/5XRDCC/$File/IHLcontemp_armedconflicts_FINAL_ANG.pdf (The ICRC, in cooperation with other institutions and organizations, organized a series of regional expert seminars on the topic "Improving Compliance with International Humanitarian Law" as part of the preparation for the 28th International Conference of the Red Cross and Red Crescent. Regarding Common Article 1, seminar participants confirmed that it entails an obligation, both on States party to an armed conflict and on third States not involved in an ongoing armed conflict. In addition to a clear legal obligation on States to "respect and ensure respect" for international humanitarian law within their own domestic contexts, third States are bound by a negative legal obligation to neither encourage a party to an armed conflict to violate international humanitarian law nor take action that would assist in such violations. Furthermore, third States have a positive obligation to take appropriate action—unilaterally or collectively—against parties to a conflict who are violating international humanitarian law. All participants affirmed that this positive action is at minimum a moral responsibility and that States have the right to take such measures, with the majority of participants agreeing that it constitutes a legal obligation under Common Article 1. This is not to be construed as an obligation to reach a specific result, but rather an "obligation of means" on States to take all appropriate measures possible, in an attempt to end international humanitarian law violations).

70. *See* INTERNATIONAL COMMITTEE OF THE RED CROSS, INTERNATIONAL HUMANITARIAN LAW AND THE CHALLENGES OF CONTEMPORARY ARMED CONFLICTS (2003), *reprinted in* 86 INTERNATIONAL REVIEW OF THE RED CROSS 213, 237–39 (2004).

71. See intervention by Mr. Pilloud from the ICRC at the 1949 Diplomatic Conference. II-B Final Record of the Diplomatic Conference of Geneva of 1949, at 39. *See also* INTERNATIONAL COMMITTEE OF THE RED CROSS, DRAFT RULES FOR THE LIMITATION OF DANGERS INCURRED BY THE CIVILIAN POPULATION IN TIME OF WAR 129 (2d ed. 1958); Commentary III, *supra* note 66, at 18.

72. *See* Eric Stover, Miranda Sissons, Phuong Pham & Patrick Vinck, *Justice on Hold: Accountability and Social Reconstruction in Iraq*, 90 INTERNATIONAL REVIEW OF THE RED CROSS 5 (2008), *available at* http://www.icrc.org/Web/eng/siteeng0.nsf/htmlall/review-869-p5/$File/irrc-869_Stover.pdf.

73. *See* Security Agreement, *supra* note 38, art. 22.

74. Internment/administrative detention is a measure of control aimed at dealing with persons who pose a real threat to State security, currently or in the future, in situations of armed conflict, or to State security or public order in non-conflict situations; it is not a measure that is meant to replace criminal proceedings. . . . Unless internment/administrative detention and penal repression are organized as strictly separate regimes there is a danger that internment might be used as a substandard system of penal repression in the hands of the executive power,

> bypassing the one sanctioned by a country's legislature and courts. The rights of criminal suspects would thus be gravely undermined.

Pejic, *supra* note 45, at 381.

75. [There are] many problems afflicting Iraq's legal system. They include the large number of detainees that has resulted from the surge of US and Iraqi military operations, allegations of the use of torture to extract confessions and concerns about the impartiality of some court officials. This state of affairs hardly bodes well for the promotion of national reconciliation in Iraq. Nor is it conducive to the development of an independent, transparent and accessible judicial system, which is a key component of social reconstruction.

Stover, Sissons, Pham & Vinck, *supra* note 72, at 27.

76. Mattli & Gasser, *supra* note 11, at 168.

77. For a more detailed analysis of the ICRC's neutral, impartial and independent humanitarian action, see Pierre Krähenbühl, *The ICRC's Approach to Contemporary Security Challenges: A Future for Independent and Neutral Humanitarian Action*, 86 INTERNATIONAL REVIEW OF THE RED CROSS 505 (2004), *available at* http://www.icrc.org/Web/eng/siteeng0.nsf/htmlall/66CM82/$File/irrc_855_Krahenbuhl.pdf.

78. Toni Pfanner, *Editorial*, 89 INTERNATIONAL REVIEW OF THE RED CROSS 779, 783 (2007), *available at* http://www.icrc.org/Web/Eng/siteeng0.nsf/html/review-868-p779.

79. Sandoz, *supra* note 5.

80. *See* MICHELLE MACK & JELENA PEJIC, INCREASING RESPECT FOR INTERNATIONAL HUMANITARIAN LAW IN NON-INTERNATIONAL ARMED CONFLICTS 31 (2008), *available at* http://www.icrc.org/Web/Eng/siteeng0.nsf/htmlall/p0923/$File/ICRC_002_0923.PDF.

PART VIII

CLOSING ADDRESS

XIX

Concluding Observations: The Influence of the Conflict in Iraq on International Law

Yoram Dinstein*

The conference from which these articles derive was an exceptionally successful and multilayered one in which a rich lode of legal insights and lessons learned (based, in many instances, on firsthand experience in the field) was truly struck. I cannot do justice to all the contributions to the conference and to this volume; I will simply focus on ten points that look particularly apposite to me.

A. "Lawfare" versus Warfare

The first point relates to the dichotomy between the laws of warfare and the war of "lawfare." The term "lawfare"—apparently coined, and certainly popularized, by Major General Dunlap—is not just a clever play of words. We live at a time when the shrewd use of law as a weapon in the marketplace of public relations may often counterbalance the successful employment of weapons in the battlefield. In the debate, General Dunlap has suggested that it may be a good idea to educate the civilian population, which is potentially subject to aerial bombardment, to reconcile itself to the inevitability of some collateral damage being engendered by almost any attack. My own submission is that before you undertake the massive (and perhaps impossible) task of teaching the enemy population to accept death as a fact of life, it

* Professor Emeritus, Tel Aviv University, Israel.

may be more productive to educate the general public on our side of the aisle—and especially the media and the non-governmental organizations (NGOs)—to face up to the ineluctable consequences of war.

Speaking of the media, it cannot be ignored that they report armed conflicts with little understanding of the legal niceties, and this has a serious impact on the perceptions of the public at large. The very availability of precision-guided munitions (PGMs) at this moment in history—a subject matter that I shall return to *infra* C—has made commentators jump to the hasty conclusion that every attack can be surgical, that every payload may acquire the target "on the nose" and that no collateral damage should be viewed as immaculate anymore. As a matter of fact, in April of this year, a major West Coast newspaper deemed fit to state that "[y]ou can kill all the combatants you want. What you are not allowed to do is cause collateral damage—civilian casualties."[1] Astonishingly, the authority cited for this implausible assertion is supposed to be no other than yours truly! I hope that I do not have to persuade those present here that, in fact, I have always argued otherwise, i.e., that there is no way to avert altogether collateral damage to civilians. But the real issue is not the misleading authority: it is the misleading statement.

What is to be done about such misrepresentations of the law of armed conflict (LOAC)? In my opinion, there are three practical steps that should be taken:

- In the daily briefings provided to the media during hostilities, it is indispensable to incorporate some legal interpretation. In other words, it is not enough to describe what happened, or even to include real-time visual (camera or video) coverage of Air Force missions and similar highlights of the military operations. It is absolutely necessary to offer the media a legal appraisal of the events or, in other words, a bit of "lawfare" adjoined to reports of warfare. Surely, the US Air Force—employing, as it does, some 1,300 lawyers—can allocate the personnel required to fill what is currently a dangerous vacuum in the media briefings.

- As pointed out by Professor Heintschel von Heinegg, the armed forces cannot afford the interminable delays occurring prior to the publication of the final conclusions of "in-house" armed forces fact-finding reviews of lethal incidents in which something has gone wrong. The high command must understand that, in the context of "lawfare," such investigations must be drastically condensed in time: they may even deserve priority over some military operations. The critical exigencies of "lawfare" demand putting an end to the present state of affairs in which charges of wrongdoing are immediately splashed all over the front pages of the world press—without any authoritative response—whereas results of the in-house inquiries, once released (frequently, many weeks later), are buried at the bottom of a back page. By then, irrespective of the outcome, the public is convinced that the charges have been vindicated.

- New procedures must be found for fact-finding reviews of this nature. I do not believe that human rights NGOs should take over the investigations. On the other hand, when all is said and done, the incontrovertible reality is that the public has become (rightly or wrongly) skeptical about the credibility of in-house probes. The time has come to consider the possibility of leavening the fact-finding process with the addition of some impartial observers to the board of inquiry.

B. The Nature of the Armed Conflict

Diverse views were voiced at the conference as regards the nature of the armed conflict in Iraq. As far as I am concerned, from a US standpoint this has been—and still is—an international armed conflict. The United States (and its allies) went to war against the Baathist Iraq of Saddam Hussein (as to the sequence of events in the Gulf War, see *infra* J). This was an inter-State war when it started, and it remains an inter-State war until it is finished. It is true that Saddam's government has been overthrown and a new Iraqi government has been installed in Baghdad. The US (and allied) forces have been acting in full cooperation with that new government, which has been recognized by the Security Council and by the international community at large. The United States–Iraq Agreement on the Withdrawal of United States Forces from Iraq and the Organization of Their Activities during Their Temporary Presence in Iraq, signed in 2008, only attests to that continued cooperation. Yet, remnants of the Saddamist forces (minus Saddam himself)—strengthened by jihadist foreigners—are still fighting in Iraq, and they have yet to be rooted out. As long as US troops persist in waging combat operations against them, the hostilities constitute an international armed conflict. The belligerent occupation of parts of Iraq by US troops formally ended in 2004 (see *infra* G), but the war has gone on. I was glad to glean from various presentations at the conference that, in practice, the US military authorities in Iraq continue to apply the law of international armed conflict. This is as it should be. The war in Iraq is not over until it is over.

This is the US outlook on Iraq. Evidently, the position is different insofar as internal Iraqi affairs are concerned. Side by side with the international armed conflict still raging between the US (and allied) forces and the remaining Saddamists, Iraq is plagued by a non-international armed conflict, in which the Baghdad government is equally trying to eliminate the last vestiges of the *ancien régime*. That is a non-international armed conflict: since the fighting is protracted temporally and widespread spatially, it is impossible to consider the ongoing violence as merely a "below the threshold" internal disturbance.

If I interpret correctly the presentation by Professor Turns, I think that he agrees that we encounter in Iraq two parallel armed conflicts: one international and the other non-international. There is nothing exceptional about the phenomenon of the simultaneous prosecution of an international and a non-international armed conflict within the borders of the same country.[2] This possibility was expressly acknowledged by the International Court of Justice in its *Nicaragua* judgment of 1986.[3] Iraq is just a paradigmatic recent example of two-pronged armed conflicts, which are waged concurrently.

Legally speaking, the parallel armed conflicts must be analyzed discretely. In many respects, the contemporary rules of LOAC in both international and non-international armed conflicts have virtually blended.[4] However, there is a crucial divergence with respect to a number of pivotal subjects, primarily where post-capture treatment of personnel is concerned: the privileged status of prisoners of war is strictly confined to international armed conflicts.[5] The issue came to the fore in the personal case of Saddam Hussein. When captured, the United States treated him—rightly—as a prisoner of war. Of course, Saddam could have been prosecuted by an American military tribunal for war crimes (i.e., grave breaches of LOAC). But the United States chose not to proceed with the case. Instead, Saddam was handed over to the Iraqi government, and—once subject to Iraqi jurisdiction—he no longer benefited from the advantages of prisoner of war status. The end of the story is well known.

C. Precision-Guided Munitions

The wide availability and accuracy of precision-guided munitions (PGMs)—especially in air warfare (and particularly when employed in combination with unmanned aerial vehicles (UAVs))—was extolled by many participants in this conference. There is no doubt about the radically increased capability to conduct surgical attacks that minimize collateral damage. Yet, several caveats have been corroborated by the proceedings.

The first point to bear in mind is that accuracy in delivering a weapon to a target is contingent not only on the availability of PGMs but also—perhaps, preeminently—on a good reading of the target area and meticulous preplanning. The trouble is that there are numerous instances in which air attacks (especially, albeit not exclusively, when launched in close support of ground troops) are not linked to any in-depth preplanning. Absent the element of advance preparation, the accuracy of a precision-guided munition cannot by itself be a sufficient guarantee of avoiding mistaken identity of targets.

In the final analysis, accuracy in attack is predicated on good intelligence (this is where reconnaissance by UAVs may be a vital component in the equation). The key to a successful attack may lie less in the availability of PGMs and more in the collation and evaluation of reliable data. If an attack is launched on the basis of outdated or otherwise flawed information, the PGM may strike the target "on the nose," and nevertheless the results can be devastating to civilians. For a vivid illustration, suffice it to remind ourselves of the unfortunate episode of the Baghdad bunker in 1991, in which hundreds of Iraqi civilians lost their lives by mistake since they had sought shelter from air raids in the wrong place.[6]

It must be added that the post-event gauging of the legality of any attack must be predicated not on hindsight but on foresight. In other words, what really counts is not what we clearly see after the event, but what is glimpsed through the "fog of war" by the commander in real time. Decisions on the battlefield are often warped by an honest but mistaken belief in the existence of a constellation of facts which is not borne out by reality. It is therefore useful to recall that Article 32(1) of the 1998 Rome Statute of the ICC (International Criminal Court) recognizes mistake of fact as an admissible defense, thereby excluding criminal responsibility for war crimes.[7]

D. Proportionality

The principle of proportionality is the key to the effective protection of civilians and civilian objects from collateral damage in attack. The trouble is that, while everybody pays lip service to the principle in the abstract, its specific dimensions are not always understood by the media, by NGOs or by the general public. Obviously, proportionality is a relative term: it presupposes a comparison between A and B. What are these A and B in the context of LOAC? It is frequently suggested by the media that the proper comparison to be drawn is between the number of human losses sustained—and the amount of property destroyed—by both sides. Nothing is farther from the legal truth. The proportionality that really counts for the purposes of weighing collateral damage is (A) the expectation of excessive incidental loss of civilian life, injury to civilians, damage to civilian objects or a combination thereof, compared to (B) the anticipation of the concrete and direct military advantage to be gained (see Article 51(5)(b) of Additional Protocol I of 1977).[8]

It is necessary to stress several points. The first is that proportionality has nothing to do with injury to combatants or damage to military objectives. LOAC does not require any proportionality between combatants' losses on the two warring sides: the losses inflicted on enemy combatants and damage to military objectives may be immeasurably greater than the counterpart casualties and destruction suffered at the enemy's hand. Indeed, nothing precludes a belligerent party capable of doing so from pursuing a "zero casualties policy" where its own combatants are concerned, while inflicting horrific losses on the enemy's armed forces. Proportionality is strictly limited to collateral damage to civilians and civilian objects.

Even where collateral damage to civilians and civilian objects is concerned, proportionality is by no means determined by purely crunching numbers of casualties and destruction on both sides. The quintessence of proportionality is that the expectation of collateral damage to civilians and civilian objects must not be "excessive." Some NGOs appear to confuse "excessive" with "any." The ICRC (International Committee of the Red Cross) commentary on Additional Protocol I seems to mix up the term "excessive" with "extensive."[9] Both are misreadings of the text.[10] Even "extensive" civilian casualties may be acceptable, if they are not "excessive" in light of the concrete and direct military advantage anticipated. The bombardment of a vital military objective (like a naval shipyard or an industrial plant producing military aircraft) where there are hundreds or even thousands of civilian employees need not be aborted merely because of the palpable hazards to those civilians.[11]

The whole assessment of what injury or damage is excessive in the circumstances entails a mental process of pondering dissimilar considerations lacking a common denominator—namely, civilian losses and military advantage—and is not an exact science.[12] In the words of the Elements of Crime of the Rome Statute of the ICC, this is a "value judgement."[13]

From the text of Article 51(5)(b) of Additional Protocol I one can clearly deduce that the appraisal of proportionality is not about results: it is about the initial expectation (of injury to civilians or damage to civilian objects) and anticipation (of the military advantage). In other words, what counts is what is foreseeable before the event.

The concrete and direct military advantage must be perceived in a contextual fashion. According to Article 8(2)(b)(iv) of the Rome Statute, what counts is the "overall" military advantage anticipated.[14] By introducing the term "overall," the Statute clearly permits looking at the larger operational picture, as distinct from focusing on the particular point under attack. The attacker may argue, e.g., that an air raid of no perceptible military advantage in itself is justified by misleading the enemy to shift its strategic gaze to the wrong sector of the front (the extensive air raids in the Pas-de-Calais on the eve of the Allied landings in Normandy on D-Day in World War II are an emblematic illustration).[15]

Preplanning, albeit of major significance, is not conclusive: the scene of a military encounter frequently changes rapidly. In training, it is required to underscore the importance of situational awareness to the risks of excessive collateral damage.

If an aviator or a platoon commander on the ground finds out that reality does not match the pre-attack briefing, he has to abort the attack.

E. Direct Participation in Hostilities

Civilian protection from attack is vouchsafed, in conformity with Article 51(3) of Additional Protocol I, "unless and for such time as they take a direct part in hostilities."[16] Direct participation in hostilities has proved to be a matter of critical importance in both Iraq and Afghanistan where the enemy flagrantly disregards the cardinal principle of distinction between combatants and civilians. The need to define activities coming within the ambit of direct participation in hostilities is perhaps the "hottest" topic in LOAC today. It has become even hotter after the ICRC published (in June 2009) an "Interpretive Guidance" on the subject,[17] formulated after thorough consultation with a fairly large group of experts but in disharmony with the views of most of the Western members.

In the Newport conference of 2007 I addressed the specific (and complex) hypothetical scenario of a civilian driving a munitions truck to supply the armed forces.[18] There is a host of new settings of direct participation in hostilities coming to light all the time. This year we heard about civilians who have to move around Iraq for strictly civilian purposes, but—in order to get from one place to another—have no choice other than joining a military convoy for their protection and en route they are handed over weapons to be used against attack, thus becoming gunmen. No doubt, in case of an actual exchange of fire with the enemy, such civilians will be viewed as directly participating in hostilities.

The most controversial issue in the context of direct participation in hostilities is that of the "revolving door" syndrome, i.e., the case of persons who repetitively take up arms against the enemy and then reassume the posture of innocent civilians. The ICRC maintains that civilian immunity from attack is restored each time that the person ends his engagement in a hostile act and that no prediction as to his future conduct is allowed.[19] I and others profoundly disagree. In fact, the proposition is irreconcilable with the universal rejection of the concept of "a soldier by night and peaceful citizen by day," even by the ICRC commentary on the Additional Protocol.[20]

I do not want to go at length into the complex details of the "revolving door" problem or other related issues, since I have a proposal to the organizers of the Newport conferences. My proposal is to devote next year's session to a systematic examination of the whole topic of direct participation in hostilities.

F. Private Military Contractors

This is a subject that has gained priority on the international legal agenda because of Iraq and the large numbers of private military contractors (PMCs) involved there (according to some estimates, the number of PMCs in Iraq equals that of the US troops deployed). Intensive consultations by inter-governmental experts produced in 2008 *The Montreux Document on pertinent international legal obligations and good practices for States related to operations of private military and security companies during armed conflicts.*[21] According to this document, PMCs retain their civilian standing as long as they are not incorporated into the armed forces and do not directly participate in hostilities.[22]

PMCs include engineers, technicians, instructors, construction workers, providers of food services and weapon specialists (tasked with training, maintenance and repairs).[23] However, if PMCs are hired by the military to actually operate weapons systems or otherwise take part in the hostilities, they lose their civilian protection.[24] Even PMCs who retain their civilian status run a tangible risk of being the victims of collateral damage (for instance, should the enemy attack a military base in which they are employed).[25] PMCs are particularly vulnerable to attack if they put on military uniforms while in service.

G. Belligerent Occupation

Many of the presentations at the conference (for instance, those by Brigadier General Tate and Colonel Pregent) were linked to the dilemmas of occupation in Iraq, whether under the guise of a belligerent occupation regime or in the context of a post-occupation regime. The underlying questions are when belligerent occupation begins, what occupation is all about while it lasts and when it ends.

As far as the beginning of belligerent occupation is concerned, Professor Benvenisti rightly pointed out that it is necessary to distinguish between the invasion and occupation stages. But in my opinion it is advisable to note the possibility of a hiatus between the two stages.[26] This came to light in Iraq at the time of the looting of the National Museum in Baghdad in April 2003. The Iraqi troops in the area had already been defeated and driven away. The US combat troops advanced through the area in pursuit of the enemy, but—being on a combat mission—had to proceed to other destinations. The rear echelons had not yet established effective control in Baghdad; the result was chaos enabling the Iraqi looters to act freely.[27] What is the lesson learned? General Rogers has suggested that MPs should in the future be assigned to accompany combat troops.[28] But is this practical? One thing is regrettably clear: you cannot prepare for everything.

The legal foundation of the law of belligerent occupation can be traced back to Hague Regulation 43 of 1907, which reads (in its common non-binding English translation):

> The authority of the legitimate power having in fact passed into the hands of the occupant, the latter shall take all the measures in his power to restore, and ensure, as far as possible, public order and safety, while respecting, unless absolutely prevented, the laws in force in the country.[29]

The international law of belligerent occupation thus makes it plain that it is incumbent on the occupying power(s) to ensure, as far as possible, security to the population. Indeed, I submit that—if in real estate the three predominant considerations are location, location, location—in belligerent occupation the three preponderant considerations are security, security, security.

I found it almost amusing to hear in this conference that the US occupation authorities were deeply concerned about the revision of the Iraqi copyright law. I can well understand that the existence of an outdated copyright law may become an issue after a prolonged belligerent occupation. After all, the local law cannot be frozen for many years (let alone decades), and over a stretch of time the reasons for law reform become compelling. Yet, when the belligerent occupation lasts in theory from April 2003 through June 2004, how did copyright even come into the minds of the authorities of the occupying power(s)? They should have worried about security, security, security, and then perhaps Iraq would have been a better place to live in today.

As for the end of belligerent occupation, I bow to the binding decision of the Security Council in Resolution 1546 (2004), which—acting under Chapter VII of the Charter of the UN—established that the occupation of Iraq was terminated by the end of June 2004.[30] I do so because I strongly believe that, by virtue of the combined effect of Articles 25 and 103 of the Charter,[31] the Security Council is vested with the power to override all norms of international law (with the possible exception of peremptory norms constituting *jus cogens*),[32] including those of LOAC. De jure, the end of belligerent occupation in Iraq in June 2004—as decreed by the Security Council—was therefore unassailable. De facto, however, the end of belligerent occupation of Iraq in 2004 was more notional than real.[33] In realistic terms, the belligerent occupation should have been looked upon as continuing in some parts of Iraq to this day. Only now when US combat troops are finally evacuating the main Iraqi urban areas is the belligerent occupation of certain parts of Iraq perhaps coming to a close. Like war, an occupation is not over until it is over.

The de jure termination of the belligerent occupation in Iraq in June 2004, of course, made it possible for the legislation adopted there to become "transformative"[34] without being in breach of international law. But de facto, one may well ask if the effective control of substantial parts of Iraq by US (and allied) troops has been really affected by the Security Council resolution defining the end of belligerent occupation. Who actually has looked after the security and the welfare of the population? The Iraqi government in Baghdad? There is an anecdote told in Iraq about an inhabitant of an area controlled by Romanian troops (no offense to the Romanians intended) coming to a local police station complaining that a Swiss soldier has just stolen from him a precious Romanian-made watch. The sergeant at the desk asked the Iraqi if he was drunk. "Surely," said the sergeant, "you mean that a Romanian soldier stole from you a precious Swiss-made watch." "You said that," answered the Iraqi, "not I." Well, just as it is pure fiction that there are Swiss soldiers in Iraq, it is pure fiction that between 2004 and 2009 all Iraqis have been under the effective control of the Baghdad government.

H. "Stability Operations"

Captain Stephens quoted a manual on stability operations, telling us that these have become "a core Army mission." Assuming that stability operations (or, as they were called by some other participants in the conference, "nation-building") are not merely a euphemism for counterterrorism combat missions, I am worried. Undertaking such a transformative mission transforms not only the occupied country: it is bound to transform also the armed forces of the occupying power(s). Soldiers are supposed to be soldiers, not policemen or experts in political, social and economic affairs. The core mission of an army is to carry out combat missions, in order to defeat the enemy and win the war. This is what officers and other personnel are—and ought to be—trained for.

Stability as such, in any event, is overrated. Saddam's regime was stable. What is sought is stability under a democratic government based on the rule of law. However, while assistance in the building of a new democratic and stable Iraq is a worthy cause, I think that it should be rendered by those qualified to do so. For every task in life there are qualified professionals. When the need arises, we rely on a doctor, a lawyer or a plumber to do what is required. Even in American football there are separate teams for "defense" and for "offense," each requiring different skills. By the same token, you cannot expect the same folks in the military to specialize both in combat and in "nation-building." It is far better for the Army to concentrate on what it does best—combat—and to recruit civilian professionals to do what they do best.

I do not deny that the civilian professionals that I am addressing have to discharge their duties under the overall supervision of the armed forces. Indeed, it is a basic premise of belligerent occupation that the government of an occupied territory must be military, and any civil administration must function as a subdivision of the military government.[35] Yet, even a military government is entitled to—and in appropriate cases should—employ civilian professionals with the proper credentials, in order to fulfill specific tasks that in my view do not constitute part of the core mission of any army.

I. Human Rights Law

At the conference, we heard (principally, from Ms. Modirzadeh) about the issue of the relationship between human rights law (HRL) and LOAC. Let me add, however, that it is often forgotten that most human rights are subject to derogation in wartime. As a good illustration, take internment (a topic that we heard about from Captain Bill). Under HRL, in principle, "a policy of preventive internment, that is the arrest and detention of those who are considered dangerous without any intention of bringing them to trial" is inconsistent with the basic human rights instruments.[36] Yet, the same European Court of Human Rights—which is the authority for this proposition, underlying its very first judgment, in the *Lawless* case of 1961—also pronounced that the norm is subject to derogation in time of war or other public emergency,[37] as per Article 15 of the 1950 European Convention on Human Rights and Fundamental Freedoms (ECHR).[38] Derogation of most human rights is also possible under Article 4 of the 1966 International Covenant on Civil and Political Rights (ICCPR).[39]

Unlike HRL, derogation from LOAC rights—although possible in some extreme instances[40]—is limited to specific persons or situations and no others. Certainly, wartime per se does not justify derogation from LOAC: after all, by its very nature LOAC is designed for application in wartime. The upshot is that LOAC may provide a better solution to a given problem than HRL. Thus, where internment under belligerent occupation is concerned, we have Article 78 of Geneva Convention IV of 1949: this provision explicitly permits preventive internment for imperative reasons of security, but this is subject to a procedure including the right of appeal as well as a "periodical review, if possible every six months, by a competent body" (to be set up by the occupying power).[41]

It ensues that in wartime, as far as internment goes, LOAC has a humanitarian edge over HRL. It is true that in peacetime, HRL attains a higher level of humanitarianism—let's even say one hundred—but, if derogated in wartime, the level of protection can drop to zero. LOAC may not aspire as high as HRL, but it never drops so low: it delivers a constant fifty. I find the half loaf most reassuring in the face of a possibility of getting no loaf at all.

Admittedly, some human rights are non-derogable: freedom from torture is a leading example (see the aforementioned provisions of the ECHR and ICCPR). Yet, most non-derogable human rights coincide with rights established directly by LOAC, independently of HRL. Thus, torture in international armed conflicts is expressly forbidden by all four Geneva Conventions,[42] as well as Additional Protocol I.[43] An ICTY (International Criminal Tribunal for the former Yugoslavia) Trial Chamber held in the *Furundzija* case, in 1998, that the LOAC prohibition of torture constitutes a peremptory norm of customary international law (*jus cogens*).[44]

The International Court of Justice held, in the advisory opinion on *Nuclear Weapons*, that—in the conduct of hostilities—the test of an (unlawful) arbitrary deprivation of life is determined by the *lex specialis* of LOAC.[45] The *lex specialis* construct of LOAC has been reaffirmed by the Court in its 2004 advisory opinion on the *Wall*.[46] The full connotations of the *lex specialis* status of LOAC can best be appreciated in the context of the fundamental right to life, addressed by the Court in the *Nuclear Weapons* advisory opinion. In allowing lethal attacks against enemy combatants, LOAC runs counter to the basic tenets of human rights law concerning extrajudicial deprivation of life.[47] Nevertheless, in the event of an international armed conflict, the LOAC norms—as *lex specialis*—prevail over the *lex generalis* of human rights.

This does not mean that relations between LOAC and HRL law are characterized by constant friction. In reality, there are only a few examples of collision between them.[48] Still, there is no denying the incompatible approaches of LOAC and HRL to some central issues, and it must be observed that the discrepancies are not limited to the treatment of combatants. Thus, in the words of Theodor Meron: "Unlike human rights law, the law of war allows, or at least tolerates, the killing and wounding of innocent human beings not directly participating in hostilities, such as civilian victims of lawful collateral damage."[49]

J. Jus ad Bellum

Lieutenant Commander Wall addressed the issue of *jus ad bellum* in Iraq. This, as everybody knows, is a controversial topic. I have addressed the subject myself in a previous Newport conference,[50] and do not wish to repeat my arguments. Let me just say, very succinctly, that—for my part—the key to unlocking the conundrum of Iraq lies in understanding that (a) the Gulf War that started with the invasion of Kuwait in 1990 is still going on, (b) the period between 1991 and 2003 was largely one of ceasefire (punctuated by sporadic hostilities between Iraq and the coalition led by the United States), (c) Iraq (as authoritatively determined by the Security Council[51]) was in material breach of its ceasefire obligations (especially insofar as the destruction of weapons of mass destruction (WMD) was concerned), and (d) the fighting of 2003 and thereafter should be viewed merely as the resumption of general hostilities by the coalition in response to that material breach.[52]

The fact that no WMD were actually found in Iraq does not affect the legal analysis. Iraq had clearly amassed WMD at earlier times—in material breach of the ceasefire—and all intelligence services worldwide were convinced that it continued to do so. Even those who were opposed to the coalition's military action in 2003 did not deny that basic fact and merely wished to postpone the clash of arms (some commentators now argue that Saddam himself deliberately misled the world to believe that he possessed WMD for some convoluted reasons that escape me). Well, in wartime, smoke and mirrors can become all too real. In the sphere of the *jus ad bellum*—no less than in that of the *jus in bello*—what ultimately counts is reasonable evaluations of the facts as they appear at the time of action, rather than post-event hindsight knowledge.

K. Conclusion

Although the worst appears to be over in Iraq, the "nation-building" there is still in many respects a work in progress. The United States finds itself still on a learning curve. Winston Churchill famously said that Americans always come to the right decision—after they have tried everything else. In Iraq it seems that everything else has already been tried. Let us hope that Americans will arrive at a right decision soon.

Notes

1. Carol J. Williams, *Legal experts want more from Obama on Guantanamo*, LATIMES.COM, Apr. 21, 2009, http://articles.latimes.com/2009/apr/21/world/fg-obama-gitmo-law21.
2. *See* YORAM DINSTEIN, THE CONDUCT OF HOSTILITIES UNDER THE LAW OF INTERNATIONAL ARMED CONFLICT 14–15 (2004).
3. Military and Paramilitary Activities (Nicar. v. U.S.), 1986 I.C.J. 14, 114 (June 27).
4. *See San Remo Manual on the Law of Non-International Armed Conflict* (Michael Schmitt, Charles Garraway & Yoram Dinstein eds., 2006), 36 ISRAEL YEARBOOK ON HUMAN RIGHTS 2006 (Special Supplement).
5. *See id.* at 40–41.
6. *See* DINSTEIN, *supra* note 2, at 117–18.
7. Statute of the International Criminal Court, July 17, 1998, 2187 U.N.T.S. 90, *reprinted in* THE LAWS OF ARMED CONFLICTS: A COLLECTION OF CONVENTIONS, RESOLUTIONS AND

OTHER DOCUMENTS 1314, 1329 (Dietrich Schindler & Jiri Toman eds., 4th ed. 2004) [hereinafter Rome Statute].

8. Protocol Additional to the Geneva Conventions of 12 August 1949, and Relating to the Protection of Victims of International Armed Conflicts, June 8, 1977, 1125 U.N.T.S. 3, *reprinted in* THE LAWS OF ARMED CONFLICTS, *supra* note 7, at 711, 736 [hereinafter Additional Protocol I].

9. *See* Claude Pilloud & Jean Pictet, *Article 51 – Protection of the civilian population*, *in* COMMENTARY ON THE ADDITIONAL PROTOCOLS OF 8 JUNE 1977 TO THE GENEVA CONVENTIONS OF 12 AUGUST 1949, at 613, 626 (Yves Sandoz, Christophe Swinarski & Bruno Zimmermann eds., 1987).

10. *See* Christopher Greenwood, *Current Issues in the Law of Armed Conflict: Weapons, Targets and International Criminal Liability*, 1 SINGAPORE JOURNAL OF INTERNATIONAL AND COMPARATIVE LAW 441, 461–62 (1997).

11. *See* W. Hayes Parks, *The Protection of Civilians from Air Warfare*, 27 ISRAEL YEARBOOK ON HUMAN RIGHTS 65, 110 (1997).

12. *See* William J. Fenrick, *The Rule of Proportionality and Protocol I in Conventional Warfare*, 98 MILITARY LAW REVIEW 91, 102 (1982).

13. *See* KNUT DÖRMANN, ELEMENTS OF WAR CRIMES UNDER THE ROME STATUTE OF THE INTERNATIONAL CRIMINAL COURT: SOURCES AND COMMENTARY 161 n.37 (2003).

14. Rome Statute, *supra* note 7, at 1318.

15. *See* MICHAEL BOTHE, KARL JOSEF PARTSCH & WALDEMAR A. SOLF, NEW RULES FOR VICTIMS OF ARMED CONFLICTS: COMMENTARY ON THE TWO 1977 PROTOCOLS ADDITIONAL TO THE GENEVA CONVENTIONS OF 1949, at 318, 325 (1982).

16. Additional Protocol I, *supra* note 8, at 736.

17. NILS MELZER, INTERPRETIVE GUIDANCE ON THE NOTION OF DIRECT PARTICIPATION IN HOSTILITIES UNDER INTERNATIONAL HUMANITARIAN LAW (2009), *available at* http://www.icrc.org/Web/eng/siteeng0.nsf/htmlall/review-872-p991/$File/irrc-872-reports-documents.pdf.

18. *See* Yoram Dinstein, *Distinction and Loss of Civilian Protection in International Armed Conflicts*, *in* INTERNATIONAL LAW AND MILITARY OPERATIONS 183, 191–92 (Michael D. Carsten ed., 2008) (Vol. 84, US Naval War College International Law Studies).

19. INTERPRETIVE GUIDANCE, *supra* note 17, at 70–71.

20. *See* Jean de Preux, *Article 43 – armed forces*, *in* COMMENTARY ON THE ADDITIONAL PROTOCOLS, *supra* note 9, at 505, 515.

21. DIRECTORATE OF INTERNATIONAL LAW, INTERNATIONAL COMMITTEE OF THE RED CROSS, MONTREUX DOCUMENT ON PERTINENT INTERNATIONAL LEGAL OBLIGATIONS AND GOOD PRACTICES FOR STATES RELATED TO OPERATIONS OF PRIVATE MILITARY AND SECURITY COMPANIES DURING ARMED CONFLICTS (2008), *available at* http://www.icrc.org/web/eng/siteeng0.nsf/htmlall/montreux-document-170908/$FILE/ICRC_002_0996.pdf. The text is reproduced in 13 JOURNAL OF CONFLICT AND SECURITY LAW 451 (2009).

22. *See* Part 1, paras. 24–26, of the Montreux Document. *Id.* at 458.

23. *See* Jeffrey F. Addicott, *Contractors on the "Battlefield": Providing Adequate Protection, Anti-Terrorism Training, and Personnel Recovery for Civilian Contractors Accompanying the Military in Combat and Contingency Operations*, 28 HOUSTON JOURNAL OF INTERNATIONAL LAW 323, 333–34 (2005–6).

24. *See* Avril McDonald, *Ghosts in the Machine: Some Legal Issues Concerning US Military Contractors in Iraq*, *in* INTERNATIONAL LAW AND ARMED CONFLICT: EXPLORING THE FAULTLINES, ESSAYS IN HONOUR OF YORAM DINSTEIN 357, 382–86 (Michael N. Schmitt & Jelena Pejic eds., 2007).

25. *See* Lisa L. Turner and Lynn G. Norton, *Civilians at the Tip of the Spear*, 51 AIR FORCE LAW REVIEW 1, 26 (2001).

26. *See* YORAM DINSTEIN, THE INTERNATIONAL LAW OF BELLIGERENT OCCUPATION 41–42, 208–9 (2009).

27. *See* John C. Johnson, *Under New Management: The Obligation to Protect Cultural Property during Military Occupation*, 190/191 MILITARY LAW REVIEW 111, 149–52 (2007).

28. A.P.V. ROGERS, LAW ON THE BATTLEFIELD 159 (2d ed. 2004).

29. Regulations Respecting the Laws and Customs of War on Land, Annex to Hague Convention, No. IV Respecting the Laws and Customs of War on Land, Oct. 18, 1907, 36 Stat. 2227, *reprinted in* THE LAWS OF ARMED CONFLICTS, *supra* note 7, at 55, 66, 78.

30. S.C. Res. 1546, U.N. Doc. S/RES/1546 (June 8, 2004), *reprinted in* 43 INTERNATIONAL LEGAL MATERIALS 1459, 1460 (2004).

31. U.N. Charter, *reprinted in* 9 INTERNATIONAL LEGISLATION 327, 339, 361 (Manley O. Hudson ed., 1950).

32. *See* YORAM DINSTEIN, WAR, AGGRESSION AND SELF-DEFENCE 322–25 (4th ed. 2005).

33. Adam Roberts, *Transformative Military Occupation: Applying the Laws of War and Human Rights*, in INTERNATIONAL LAW AND ARMED CONFLICT, *supra* note 24, at 439, 488.

34. *See id.* at 486–87.

35. *See* DINSTEIN, *supra* note 26, at 56.

36. A.H. ROBERTSON AND J.G. MERRILLS, HUMAN RIGHTS IN EUROPE 66 (3d ed. 1994).

37. Lawless v. Ireland (No. 3) (Eur. Ct. H.R.), 3 JUDGMENTS AND DECISIONS OF THE EUROPEAN COURT OF HUMAN RIGHTS 27, 54–62 (1961).

38. Convention for the Protection of Human Rights and Fundamental Freedoms, Nov. 4, 1950, 213 U.N.T.S. 222, *reprinted in* THE RAOUL WALLENBERG COMPILATION OF HUMAN RIGHTS INSTRUMENTS 81, 85–86 (Göran Melander & Gudmundur Alfredsson eds., 1997).

39. International Covenant on Civil and Political Rights, Dec. 16, 1966, 999 U.N.T.S. 171, *reprinted in* THE RAOUL WALLENBERG COMPILATION, *supra* note 38, at 43, 44–45.

40. *See* Convention Relative to the Protection of Civilian Persons in Time of War art. 5, Aug. 12, 1949, 6 U.S.T. 3516, 75 U.N.T.S. 287, *reprinted in* THE LAWS OF ARMED CONFLICTS, *supra* note 7, at 575, 581–82 [hereinafter Geneva Convention IV]; Additional Protocol I, *supra* note 8, art. 54(5) at 738.

41. Geneva Convention IV, *supra* note 40, at 603.

42. Convention for the Amelioration of the Condition of the Wounded and Sick in Armed Forces in the Field art. 12 (2nd para.), Aug. 12, 1949, 6 U.S.T. 3114, 75 U.N.T.S. 31, *reprinted in* THE LAWS OF ARMED CONFLICTS, *supra* note 7, at 459, 465; Convention for the Amelioration of the Condition of Wounded, Sick and Shipwrecked Members of Armed Forces at Sea art. 12 (2nd para.), Aug. 12, 1949, 6 U.S.T. 3217, 75 U.N.T.S. 85, *reprinted in* THE LAWS OF ARMED CONFLICTS, *supra* note 7, at 485, 491; Convention Relative to the Treatment of Prisoners of War art. 17 (4th para.), Aug. 12, 1949, 6 U.S.T. 3316, 75 U.N.T.S. 135, *reprinted in* THE LAWS OF ARMED CONFLICTS, *supra* note 7, at 507, 518; Geneva Convention IV, *supra* note 40, art. 32 at 590.

43. Additional Protocol I, *supra* note 8, art. 75(2)(a)(ii) at 748.

44. Prosecutor v. Furundzija, Case No. IT-95-17/1-T, Judgement (Dec. 10, 1998), *reprinted in* 121 INTERNATIONAL LAW REPORTS 213, 254–57, 260–61 (Elihu Lauterpacht, Christopher Greenwood & Andrew Oppenheimer eds., 2002).

45. Legality of the Threat or Use of Nuclear Weapons, Advisory Opinion, 1996 I.C.J. 226, 240 (July 8).

46. Legal Consequences of the Construction of a Wall in the Occupied Palestinian Territory, Advisory Opinion, 2004 I.C.J. 136, 178 (July 9), *reprinted in* 43 INTERNATIONAL LEGAL MATERIALS 1009, 1038–39 (2004).

47. *See* Cordula Droege, *The Interplay between International Humanitarian Law and International Human Rights Law in Situations of Armed Conflict*, 40 ISRAEL LAW REVIEW 310, 344–46 (2007).

48. *See* Jean-Marie Henckaerts, *Concurrent Application of International Humanitarian Law and Human Rights Law: A Victim Perspective*, *in* INTERNATIONAL HUMANITARIAN LAW AND HUMAN RIGHTS LAW: TOWARDS A NEW MERGER IN INTERNATIONAL LAW 237, 262 (Roberta Arnold and Noëlle Quénivet eds., 2008).

49. Theodor Meron, *The Humanization of Humanitarian Law*, 94 AMERICAN JOURNAL OF INTERNATIONAL LAW 239, 240 (2000).

50. *See* Yoram Dinstein, *The Gulf War: 1990–2004 (and Still Counting)*, *in* INTERNATIONAL LAW CHALLENGES: HOMELAND SECURITY AND COMBATING TERRORISM 337 (Thomas McK. Sparks & Glenn M. Sulmasy eds., 2006) (Vol. 81, US Naval War College International Law Studies).

51. *See* S.C. Res. 1441, S/RES/1441 (Nov. 8, 2002), *reprinted in* 42 INTERNATIONAL LEGAL MATERIALS 250, 251 (2002).

52. For more detail, see DINSTEIN, *supra* note 32, at 294–300.

APPENDIX

CONTRIBUTORS

Contributors

Editor's Note: In order to most accurately portray the events of the conference, the biographical data in this appendix reflect the positions in which the authors were serving at the time of the conference, as set forth in the conference brochures and materials.

Professor Eyal Benvenisti is the Anny and Paul Yanowicz Professor of Human Rights, Tel Aviv University Faculty of Law. Previously he was the Hersch Lauterpacht Professor of International Law at the Hebrew University of Jerusalem Faculty of Law. He holds LL.B. (1984) and LL.M. (1988) degrees from Hebrew University of Jerusalem, and a J.S.D. (1990) from Yale Law School. Professor Benvenisti has served as the Director of the Cegla Center for Interdisciplinary Research of the Law (2002–5) and Director of the Minerva Center for Human Rights at the Hebrew University (2000–2). He serves on the editorial boards of the *American Journal of International Law* and *International Law in Domestic Courts*. He is the founding Co-editor of *Theoretical Inquiries in Law* and served as the Editor in Chief from 2003 to 2006. Professor Benvenisti is a Humboldt Fellow at the Humboldt University and the University of Munich and a Visiting Fellow at the Max Planck Institute for International Law at Heidelberg (Germany). His areas of teaching and research include international law, constitutional law and administrative law. His publications include *Sharing Transboundary Resources: International Law and Optimal Resource Use* (Cambridge University Press, 2002) and *The International Law of Occupation* (Princeton University Press, 1993; second edition with Oxford University Press, 2010).

Captain Brian J. Bill, JAGC, US Navy, graduated from the University of Dayton in 1980 with a B.S. in criminal justice, Rutgers School of Law–Newark in 1988 with a J.D., and the University of Virginia in 1995 with an LL.M. in international law. He began his career in the Navy in 1982, initially as a naval flight officer in the E-2C Hawkeye, flying from *USS Coral Sea (CV-43)*. Following completion of law school, he became a judge advocate in 1988. His assignments include Chief of International and Operational Law, US Special Operations Command; Professor of International and Operational Law at The Judge Advocate General's School, US Army; Executive Assistant and Special Counsel to the General Counsel of the Navy; and Professor of International Law and Associate Dean of the College of International Security Studies, George C. Marshall European Center for Security Studies. In May

2007 he volunteered to deploy to Iraq as an individual augmentee, and served as the Legal Advisor to Task Force 134, Detainee Operations, in Baghdad, Iraq, until June 2008. He returned to The Judge Advocate General's Legal Center and School immediately following his deployment, where he is now a Special Assistant and Professor in International and Operational Law.

Commodore Neil Brown, Royal Navy, has been the Royal Navy's Director of Naval Legal Services since September 2007. He is a former staff senior adviser for the development of the Armed Forces Act 2006 that created a single, harmonized discipline system governing all members of the UK armed forces. Before that he was the senior military legal adviser to the UK's Chief of Joint Operations, responsible for advice on operations in Iraq and Afghanistan, the Democratic Republic of the Congo and the response to a tsunami. In 2003 was the senior legal adviser to the UK's National Contingent Commander for Operation Telic (operations against Iraq), co-located with US Central Command Forward and the Australian National Command Headquarters. Commodore Brown has completed a wide range of logistics and legal appointments at sea, deploying to the Persian/Arabian Gulf in destroyers and again as Logistics Commander of the aircraft carrier *HMS Illustrious*. He was a member of the UK delegation on the Proliferation Security Initiative and later to the Major Maritime Powers Conference. He has trained military lawyers and commanders in many countries and presented widely at the US Naval War College, the British Institute of International and Comparative Law, the Royal Institute for International Affairs (Chatham House), the Royal United Services Institute, Wilton Park, the International Law Association and the International Society for Military Law and the Law of War (UK branches), and the Aspen Institute.

Mr. Laurent Colassis is Deputy Head of the Legal Division of the International Committee of the Red Cross (ICRC). Mr. Colassis obtained his legal education at the University of Lausanne (Switzerland). He joined the ICRC in 1997 and served as an ICRC delegate in Afghanistan, field coordinator, Head of Sub-delegation in Rwanda and Deputy Head of Delegation in Congo-Brazzaville. In 2000, Mr. Colassis began working at the ICRC Legal Division in Geneva. From 2000 to 2004 he served as legal advisor to operations covering the Middle East, and northern, central and southern Africa. Prior to his current position, Mr. Colassis served from 2004 to 2008 as head of the unit of legal advisors.

Professor Yoram Dinstein is Professor Emeritus of International Law at Tel Aviv University (Israel). He is a former President of the University, as well as former Rector and former Dean of the Faculty of Law. Professor Dinstein served two appointments as the Charles H. Stockton Professor of International Law at the Naval War College. He was also a Humboldt Fellow at the Max Planck Institute for International Law at Heidelberg (Germany), a Meltzer Visiting Professor of International Law at New York University and a Visiting Professor of Law at the University of Toronto. Professor Dinstein is a Member of the Institute of International Law and Vice President of Israel's national branch of the International Law Association and of the Israel United Nations Association. He was also a member of the Executive Council of the American Society of International Law. At present, he is a member of the Council of the San Remo International Institute of Humanitarian Law. He has written extensively on subjects relating to international law, human rights and the law of armed conflict. He is the founder and Editor of the *Israel Yearbook on Human Rights*. He is the author of *War, Aggression and Self-Defence*, now in its fourth edition, and *The Conduct of Hostilities under the Law of International Armed Conflict*. Professor Dinstein's latest book is *The International Law of Belligerent Occupation* (2009).

Major General Charles J. Dunlap Jr., US Air Force, is Deputy Judge Advocate General, Headquarters US Air Force, Washington, DC. General Dunlap assists The Judge Advocate General in the professional oversight of more than 4,400 active, Air National Guard and reserve judge advocates, civilian attorneys, enlisted paralegals and civilians assigned worldwide. General Dunlap was commissioned through the ROTC program at St. Joseph's University, Philadelphia, Pennsylvania, in May 1972, and was admitted to the bar of the Supreme Court of the Commonwealth of Pennsylvania in 1975. The general has served in the United Kingdom and Korea, and deployed for various operations in the Middle East and Africa, including short stints in support of Operations Enduring Freedom and Iraqi Freedom. He has led military delegations to Uruguay, the Czech Republic, South Africa, Colombia and Iraq. General Dunlap speaks widely on legal and national security issues, and his articles have appeared in a variety of publications ranging from the *Washington Post* to the *Stanford Law Review*.

Judge Raid Juhi al-Saedi served from 2004 to 2006 as Chief Investigative Judge of the Iraqi High Tribunal (IHT). During that time, he supervised all cases before the Tribunal and indicted Saddam Hussein and seven others for crimes against humanity perpetrated against the citizens of Ad-Dujayl. Juhi also indicted Saddam Hussein and Ali Hassan al-Majid al-Tikriti ("Chemical Ali") for genocide arising out of the massacre of over 100,000 Kurds from 1987–88. During the trial of Saddam Hussein, Juhi continued to serve as Chief Investigative Judge and the court's spokesperson, handled all press queries and frequently appeared before

Western and Arabic media. Juhi also negotiated the IHT's rules of evidence and procedure which were ultimately adopted and used in all proceedings. Previously, Juhi investigated and indicted radical Shiite cleric Moqtada al-Sadr for the murder of cleric Abdul Majid Al-Khoei, which occurred in 2003 outside one of Shiite Islam's holiest sites, the Shrine of Imam Ali in Najaf, Iraq. Juhi is a graduate of Iraq's Judicial Institute and served as a family court judge and criminal investigative judge under Saddam Hussein. He was a Senior Fellow at the United States Institute of Peace in 2008. Judge Juhi is the Cornell University Law School Clarke Middle East Fellow.

Ms. Naz K. Modirzadeh is a Senior Associate and Head of Policy at the Harvard Program on Humanitarian Policy and Conflict Research, where she oversees the international humanitarian law and Middle East portfolios. Ms. Modirzadeh has led HPCR trainings and workshops for humanitarian professionals around the world, including in the occupied Palestinian territories, Afghanistan, Jordan and throughout Europe. Ms. Modirzadeh previously worked for Human Rights Watch, and later served as Assistant Professor and Director of the International Human Rights Law graduate program at the American University in Cairo. She has carried out field research in the Middle East and Afghanistan, focusing on the intersections among Islamic law, international human rights and humanitarian law, and speaks regularly in academic and professional circles on these topics. Ms. Modirzadeh received her B.A. from the University of California, Berkeley and her J.D. from Harvard Law School. Her publications include "Taking Islamic Law Seriously: INGOs and the Battle for Muslim Hearts and Minds," in the *Harvard Human Rights Journal.* Recent lectures and events include "Who's Afraid of Shari'a? A Conversation about 'War, Law and Humanitarian Intervention' with Naz Modirzadeh and Mahmood Mamdani."

Professor John F. Murphy is professor of law at Villanova University School of Law. In addition to teaching, Professor Murphy's career includes a year in India on a Ford Foundation Fellowship; private practice in New York City and Washington, DC; and service in the Office of the Assistant Legal Adviser for United Nations Affairs, US Department of State. He was previously on the law faculty at the University of Kansas and has been a visiting professor at Cornell University and Georgetown University. From 1980–1981 Professor Murphy was the Charles H. Stockton Professor of International Law at the Naval War College. He is the author of numerous articles, comments and reviews on international law and relations, as well as the author or editor of various books or monographs. Most recently, he has authored *The United States and the Rule of Law in International Affairs* (Cambridge University

Press, 2004). His casebook (with Alan C. Swan), *The Regulation of International Business and Economic Relations* (2d ed. Lexis Publishing, 1999), was awarded a certificate of merit by the American Society of International Law in 1992. Professor Murphy has served as a consultant to the US Departments of State and Justice, the ABA Standing Committee on Law and National Security, and the United Nations Crime Bureau and has testified before Congress on several occasions. He is currently the American Bar Association's Alternate Observer at the US Mission to the United Nations.

Major General Michael L. Oates, US Army, is Commanding General, 10th Mountain Division (Light) and Fort Drum, NY. General Oates is from San Antonio, Texas. He was commissioned in the infantry upon graduation from the United States Military Academy in 1979. General Oates' duty assignments include rifle platoon leader, company executive officer and battalion maintenance officer in 2d Battalion, 7th Cavalry, 1st Cavalry Division, Fort Hood, Texas, from 1979 to 1982. From 1983 to 1986, he served as company commander and battalion S3 Air in 2d Battalion, 187th Infantry (Airborne), 193d Separate Infantry Brigade, Republic of Panama; and aide de camp to the Commanding General, US Army South. He served as an infantry assignment officer at Personnel Command from 1987 to 1989. After graduation from Command and General Staff College, General Oates served with 2d Battalion, 187th Infantry (Air Assault), and 3d Brigade, 101st Airborne Division (Air Assault), Fort Campbell, KY, from 1990 to 1993 as Battalion S-3 and Brigade S-3 and S-4. From 1993 to 1995 he served in J3, Joint Chiefs of Staff (JCS). He commanded 1st Battalion, 32d Infantry, 10th Mountain Division (Light), Fort Drum, NY, from 1995 to 1997. After graduation from the Naval War College, Newport, RI, in 1998, he assumed command of 1st Brigade, 101st Airborne Division (Air Assault), Fort Campbell, KY, until 2000. He subsequently served as Division Chief of Staff from 2000 to 2002. From 2002 to 2004 General Oates served as Executive Officer to Honorable Tom White, Secretary of the Army; and as Chief of Staff to the Chief Operations Officer, Coalition Provisional Authority, Baghdad, Iraq. From 2004 to 2007, he served as Deputy Commanding General (Operations), 101st Airborne Division (Air Assault), Fort Campbell, KY. From 2007 to the present, General Oates serves as Commanding General, 10th Mountain Division (Light) and Fort Drum, NY. From June 2008 to May 2009, 10th Mountain Division deployed in support of Operation Iraqi Freedom with General Oates initially serving as Commanding General, Multi-National Division–Center, later redesignated as Multi-National Division–South. General Oates holds a master's degree in national security and strategic studies from the Naval War College.

Professor Raul "Pete" Pedrozo was assigned to the Naval War College in May 2009 as associate professor of international law, pending his retirement from the US Navy as a captain in the Judge Advocate General's Corps. Prior to graduating from Eastern Kentucky University, he served in the US Army in the infantry for eight years. He graduated from the Ohio State University College of Law. He has an LL.M. in international and comparative law from Georgetown University Law Center, where he received the Thomas J. Bradbury Award for the highest academic average in his graduating class. As a judge advocate, Professor Pedrozo served in the following assignments: Naval Legal Service Office, Guam; Assistant Force Judge Advocate, US Naval Air Forces Atlantic Fleet; Staff Judge Advocate, Commander Carrier Group TWO/CTF 60 (embarked *USS Coral Sea*); Staff Judge Advocate, US Naval Station Panama Canal/Commander, US Naval Forces Southern Command; Naval Justice School staff; Law of the Sea Branch Head, Navy JAG International and Operational Law Division; Special Assistant to the Under Secretary of Defense for Policy; Assistant Judge Advocate General, Navy JAG International and Operational Law Division; Force Judge Advocate, Commander, Naval Special Warfare Command; and Staff Judge Advocate, US Pacific Command. He was also Staff Judge Advocate for Task Force SEMPER FI (Operation Just Cause) and Legal Advisor to the US contingent to the UN Protection Force in the former Yugoslavia.

Ms. Alexandra Perina is an attorney-adviser in the Office of the Legal Adviser at the US Department of State. Her current portfolio includes political-military matters related to Iraq and Afghanistan, and she was part of the US negotiating team for the US-Iraq security agreement in 2008. Prior to joining the State Department, she worked as a litigator at Debevoise & Plimpton LLP in New York. Ms. Perina graduated from Haverford College and received a law degree from New York University School of Law, where she served on the Editorial Board of the *Journal of International Law and Politics* and received a Foreign Language and Area Studies fellowship. Ms. Perina also serves on the Board of Governors of the Washington Foreign Law Society and on the American Advisory Board of Humanity in Action, Inc., a non-profit foundation.

Colonel Richard Pregent, US Army, was the Director of the Interagency Rule of Law Coordinating Center and the Law and Order Task Force in Iraq. He has served fourteen years overseas with deployments to Honduras (1983), Rwanda (1994), Kosovo (2001–2) and Iraq (two). During his first tour in Iraq he served as the Deputy General Counsel for the Coalition Provisional Authority. He returned to Iraq in May 2008. He has served as the senior legal advisor for several NATO commands in Italy and the Balkans, as well as the US Army's Criminal Investigation

Command and the Intelligence and Security Command. He received a bachelor of arts degree from Williams College in 1976; a J.D. in 1979 from Albany Law School at Union University, New York; and an LL.M. at the US Army Judge Advocate General's School in 1990. He is the author of "Presidential Authority to Displace Customary International Law," *Military Law Review*, 1990. He was commissioned in the US Army Judge Advocate General's Corps in 1981. In July 2009 Colonel Pregent assumed the duties as Chief of the International and Operational Law Division of the Army's Office of The Judge Advocate General.

Captain Dale Stephens, CSM, Royal Australian Navy, commenced his S.J.D. degree studies at Harvard Law School in February 2009. His doctoral dissertation is titled "The Role of Law in Military Decision Making." In 1989 Captain Stephens obtained his law degree from Adelaide University, South Australia, and joined the Royal Australian Navy that same year. He has occupied numerous staff officer appointments throughout his career, including Fleet Legal Officer, Director of Operational and International Law, Director of the Military Law Centre and Director of Naval Legal Services. In 1999 he deployed to East Timor as legal advisor to the naval component element of International Force East Timor Headquarters. He subsequently deployed to East Timor again in 2000/2001 as the Chief Legal Officer of the United Nations Transitional Administration in East Timor Peacekeeping Force Headquarters. In 2003 he was awarded a Conspicuous Service Medal (CSM) for his service as Fleet Legal Officer during Operation Falconer, which related to Australia's contribution to the war in Iraq. In 2005/2006 Captain Stephens undertook a deployment to Iraq as the principal legal advisor to the Australian National Force Commander and was responsible for providing advice in relation to Australian Defence Force operations in both Iraq and Afghanistan. He completed a second tour of Iraq in December 2008 as Chief, International Law in the MNF-I Staff Judge Advocate Office. In 2004, Captain Stephens completed a master of laws degree at Harvard Law School and taught at the US Naval War College in 2004–5. He is a member of the Editorial Board of the *Australian Yearbook of International Law* and has published widely in Australian and international law journals on matters relating to operational law.

Brigadier General Clyde J. Tate II, US Army, is the Commander of the US Army Legal Services Agency and the Chief Judge of the Army Court of Criminal Appeals. General Tate's recent assignments include Commander and Commandant of The Judge Advocate General's Legal Center and School; Staff Judge Advocate, Multi-National Corps–Iraq; Staff Judge Advocate for III Armored Corps and Fort Hood, Texas; Legal Counsel, Army Office of the Chief of Legislative Liaison; Chief of the

Personnel, Plans, and Training Office in the Office of the Judge Advocate General; and Staff Judge Advocate, 82d Airborne Division. Brigadier General Tate possesses undergraduate and law degrees from the University of Kansas and holds an LL.M. in military law from The Judge Advocate General's School and a master's degree in National Security Strategy from the National War College.

Professor David Turns is Senior Lecturer in International Laws of Armed Conflict at the Defence Academy of the United Kingdom (Cranfield University). Prior to assuming his current position, he was a lecturer in law at the University of Liverpool (1994–2007). Since 1997 he has been on the Visiting Faculty of the International Institute of Humanitarian Law (San Remo, Italy). At the XIVth Congress of the International Society for Military Law and the Law of War (ISMLLW) in 1997, he was the National Rapporteur for the United Kingdom. Since 2008 he has served as the President of the UK National Group of the ISMLLW and as a member of the Society's Board of Directors. In 2002 he was a visiting professor at the Institute for International Law and International Relations, University of Vienna, Austria. Since 2004 he has designed and developed a new training course for military and defense ministry legal advisers from Central and Eastern Europe in collaboration with the Austrian Federal Ministry of Defence and the International Committee of the Red Cross. Professor Turns specializes in public international law, with particular emphasis on international humanitarian law and international criminal law. He has published on several public international law topics in a variety of journals in the United Kingdom and other countries, including leading journals in Australia, Austria, China, Germany, Israel and the United States.

Professor George K. Walker is a professor of law at the Wake Forest University School of Law, where he teaches international law, national security law, admiralty and civil litigation subjects. He was the US Naval War College Charles H. Stockton Professor of Law, 1992–93, and published *The Tanker War 1980–88*, Volume 74 in the College "Blue Book" series. After graduating from the University of Alabama, he had three years' commissioned service in destroyers of the US Atlantic Fleet, qualifying as officer of the deck and chief engineer. After commanding six Navy Reserve units, he retired as a line captain in 1989. After graduating from the Vanderbilt Law School, he clerked with a US district judge and was a trial lawyer with Hunton & Williams in Richmond, Virginia, joining the Wake Forest law faculty in 1972. He holds master's degrees in diplomatic history from Duke and in law from the University of Virginia. He has authored or edited over ten books and has researched fifty law review articles. Besides Navy Reserve duty, he has been a speaker at Navy JAG programs and has drafted statutes and rules for alternative dispute resolution, including the Model Family Law Arbitration Act. Currently he chairs the Law of the Sea Committee of the American Branch, International Law Association (ILA), and is a US appointee for the ILA law of the sea baselines committee.

Andru E. Wall is a visiting researcher at Harvard University and the former Senior Legal Advisor for Special Operations Command Central/Combined Forces Special Operations Component Command, where he advised commanders on the law of armed conflict, intelligence law and unconventional warfare. He served in over forty countries, including Iraq and Afghanistan. He has written extensively on international law and has taught at the US Naval War College and Roger Williams University School of Law. He is an elected member of the International Institute of Humanitarian Law in San Remo, Italy.

Colonel Marc Warren, US Army (Ret.), is the FAA's Deputy Chief Counsel for Operations. He assists the Chief Counsel in overseeing all aspects of the FAA's legal activities with special focus on nationwide aviation safety enforcement, airports and environmental law, personnel and labor law, and Regional and Center Counsel office activities. A native of Florida, Colonel Warren received both a B.A. (1978) and a J.D. (1981) from the University of Florida; an LL.M. (1993) from the Judge Advocate General's School, US Army (TJAGSA), Charlottesville, Virginia; and a master of strategic studies degree (2002) from the US Army War College, Carlisle Barracks, Pennsylvania. He is a member of the bars of Florida, the Court of Appeals for the Armed Forces and the US Supreme Court, and coholder, with the late Colonel Waldemar A. Solf, of the Solf-Warren Honorary Chair in International and Operational Law, TJAGSA. He was the American Bar Association Outstanding Young Army Lawyer, received the Florida Bar Association Clayton B. Burton Award of Excellence and is in the University of Florida Hall of Fame. Prior to his FAA appointment, Colonel Warren served in the U.S. Army Judge Advocate General's Corps. He served as the Special Assistant to the Judge Advocate General and as the Staff Judge Advocate (senior attorney) for the Combined Joint Task Force 7/Multi-National Forces in Iraq, V Corps in Iraq and Germany, and the 101st Airborne Division (Air Assault). He was the Legal Advisor for the worldwide activities of the Joint Special Operations Command and Regimental Judge Advocate for the 11th Armored Cavalry Regiment, and served in numerous other assignments as a judge advocate in the United States, Germany, Grenada, Bosnia, Kuwait and Iraq, including as an instructor in the International and Operational Law Department of TJAGSA. He was the Editor of the *Operational Law Handbook* and has published articles in the *Army Lawyer, Military Law Review* and various other military and legal professional publications.

Index

A

B

C

J

K

L

M

P

R

S

T

U

W

www.ingramcontent.com/pod-product-compliance
Ingram Content Group UK Ltd.
Pitfield, Milton Keynes, MK11 3LW, UK
UKHW051029041026
15470UKWH00016B/1818